INNOVATION IN TEACHER EDUCATION

INNOVATION IN TEACHER EDUCATION ;

A study of the directions, processes and problems of innovation in teacher preparation with special reference to the Australian context and to the role of co-operating schools

Edited by C. TURNEY

SYDNEY UNIVERSITY PRESS

SYDNEY UNIVERSITY PRESS
Press Building, University of Sydney

UNITED KINGDOM, EUROPE, MIDDLE EAST, AFRICA, CARIBBEAN
Prentice/Hall International, International Book Distributors Ltd
Hemel Hempstead, England

NORTH AND SOUTH AMERICA
International Scholarly Book Services, Inc.
Forest Grove, Oregon

National Library of Australia Cataloguing-in-Publication data

Innovation in teacher education.

Index.
Bibliography.
ISBN 0 424 00032 6.

1. Teachers, Training of—Addresses, essays,
lectures. I. Turney, Clifford, ed.

370.7108

First published 1977
© Sydney University Press 1977

This book is funded by money from
THE ELEANOR SOPHIA WOOD BEQUEST

Printed in Australia by Macarthur Press (Books) Pty Limited, Parramatta

CONTENTS

ACKNOWLEDGEMENTS

The projects upon which this book is based were made possible by funding from the Australian Government. A generous grant from the Commission on Advanced Education facilitated the co-operation of an inter-institution team in the general investigation of innovation in teacher education with special reference to the Australian context. An equally generous grant from the Australian Advisory Committee on Research and Development in Education enabled another small group of investigators to undertake the more sharply focused study of the changing role of co-operating schools in teacher education.

The authors wish to thank a number of people—the many busy teacher educators for their valuable participation in the surveys; the teacher educators, teachers and students connected with the case study activity for their substantial contributions and their hospitality when the investigators visited their institutions; the research assistants in various phases of the two projects, Clelia Winton, Penny Hawse, Paulene Heiler and Kerry Hudson, each of whom helped greatly in gathering and organizing material for this book; and Kerry Beaumont and Dympna Casey who skilfully handled the considerable amount of typing involved in the projects.

ABBREVIATIONS

CAE	College of Advanced Education
CBTE	Competency-based teacher education
IAE	Institute of Advanced Education
PBTE	Performance-based teacher education
SCV	State College of Victoria
TC	Teachers College

PREFACE

This book has emerged from two projects sponsored by agencies of the Australian Government. One project was broadly concerned with new developments in teacher education programmes, the other with the special part played by co-operating schools in teacher preparation.

The study of innovation in Australian teacher education began as a project supported by the Commission on Advanced Education in 1974. In part, the study grew from the success of the previous narrower study of microteaching which had culminated in a report published by Sydney University Press.[1] The innovations project, undertaken by a team comprising C. Turney, D. Jecks, D. Thew and R. Traill, sought to investigate significant innovative approaches to teacher education both overseas and in Australia. The resultant report aimed to provide teacher educators with (i) a background knowledge of current general trends and developments in teacher education; (ii) an understanding of the theory, possibilities and problems of important new approaches to aspects of teacher preparation, especially in Australia; (iii) detailed case studies of the most promising Australian innovations; and (iv) useful guidelines for action by teacher educators already involved in, or contemplating innovation in certain areas of teacher education.

Eight months after the commencement of the innovations project, the Australian Advisory Committee on Research and Development in Education funded a related project concerned with the new roles of special co-operating schools in teacher education. This investigation, pursued by C. Turney, J. Dunn, P. Renshaw and G. Williams, aimed to (i) historically review the changing activity of special co-operating schools in teacher preparation overseas; (ii) provide detailed accounts of a number of contemporary on- and off-campus co-operating school arrangements in North America; (iii) survey the functions of co-operating schools in Australian teacher education programmes; (iv) make case studies of selected Australian co-operating school arrangements; and (v) offer suggestions for the introduction and operation of laboratory-type schools in the Australian context.

Fundamentally both the above projects sought to achieve the same thing: to take stock of contemporary teacher-education developments, both locally and abroad, in such a way as to provide a useful stimulus for reflection, discussion and action among Australian teacher educators. While there is currently a great interest in innovation in teacher education, especially in the new colleges of advanced education, there seems to be a serious want of information, not only about what is being achieved overseas but also elsewhere in Australia. More particularly, as many teacher education programmes are beginning to recognize

[1] C. Turney, J. C. Clift, M. J. Dunkin and R. D. Traill, *Microteaching; Research, Theory and Practice*, Sydney 1973.

the potential value of having close links with one or a number of schools in proximity to their campuses, the sharing of experience on such innovative plans would seem instructive and timely.

Thus the decision was made to combine into this book the reports on the two projects, having as they did, similar purposes and methodologies. This was seen as the easiest and most effective way of disseminating the results of our work. Moreover, to facilitate the exchange of ideas the book includes an appendix listing the innovators who co-operated with the projects. Readers expecting to find in this book a closely coherent, deeply reflective work on teacher education will be disappointed. The book is rather conceived as an ordered but abundant smorgasbord of ideas, plans and practices which people involved in teacher education might find both informative and stimulating.

University of Sydney
August 1976   *Cliff Turney*

CONTRIBUTING AUTHORS

J. G. DUNN
Senior Lecturer in Education,
Salisbury College of Advanced Education

D. A. JECKS
Principal,
Churchlands College of Advanced Education

P. RENSHAW
Tutor in Education,
University of Sydney

D. M. THEW
Principal Lecturer in Education,
Alexander Mackie College of Advanced Education

R. D. TRAILL
Fellow,
Canberra College of Advanced Education

C. TURNEY
Professor of Education,
University of Sydney

G. WILLIAMS
Assistant Lecturer in Education,
University of Sydney

The quality of a nation depends upon the quality of its citizens. The quality of its citizens depends—not exclusively, but in critical measure—upon the quality of their education. The quality of their education depends more than upon any factor, upon the quality of their teachers....The quality of the teachers depends largely upon the quality of their own education, both that portion which precedes and which comes after their entrance into the profession. It follows that the purpose and effectiveness of teacher education must be matters of profound social concern.

Commission on Teacher Education, *Teachers For Our Times*, American Council on Teacher Education, Washington 1944, p. 2.

INTRODUCTION

For the greater part of the twentieth century teacher education, or teacher training as some people still rather disparagingly call it, has been in the doldrums. It has been regarded by many as a comparatively unglamorous educational task lacking the challenges and delights of teaching children on the one hand, and the prestige and intellectual demand of tertiary scholastic pursuits on the other. Paradoxically however, few have disputed its fundamental importance to the entire field of education and to the society it serves. All proposals to improve the quality of schooling have inevitably returned, albeit reluctantly, to the question of preparing teachers to carry out the improvements. While this has been often contemplated, in practice many attempts to improve the work of schools have been unsuccessful because of inadequate pre-service and in-service teacher preparation. Just as most people would have acknowledged the significance of teacher training, they probably would also have recognized the complexity of the task. The preparation of large numbers of young persons to be effective teachers of children and the continuation of this work to ensure that, as teachers, they maintain a high level of effectiveness, involve a multitude of problems with often elusive solutions.

Although there has been a slowly growing realization of both the central importance and complicated nature of teacher preparation, it is only really over the past fifteen years that the quality of teacher training has been critically and widely scrutinized and important positive steps taken to improve it. Amid this activity two notions have become generally accepted. The first is that preparing teachers involves very much more than a 'training' in techniques and procedures and that adequate preparation is commensurate in both quality and extent to that required for other professions. The general adoption of the term 'teacher education' indicates the marked shift from the limited concept of training to that of the development of individuals with the sensitivities, understandings and skills necessary for working creatively with children. A second important notion which has emerged is that 'change is central to all thinking about teacher education' (Cohen *et al.*, 1973, p. 1). 'Change' has two important major implications for teacher education. Teacher education must change in response to changes in the nature and purposes of schooling. Besides reflecting such changes teacher education must also promote changes in schools through the new attitudes, ideas and approaches it introduces to teachers. Teacher education must reflect and stimulate change.

Thus in recent years change has become a growing feature of teacher education. As Ryan (1975) has put it, 'practitioners are *doing* teacher education in new ways. Scholars are conceptualizing the process of teacher education in new ways. Researchers are applying new tools of inquiry to teacher education' (p. ix). In institutions of teacher education, many of them only recently established, new programmes, new components, new methodologies and new technologies

1

are being introduced. Naturally, however, the inertia and conservatism of the past is dying hard in some places, and one suspects that some of the reported changes are more apparent than real. Nevertheless the changes are many and many of them are genuine. Against this background the literature on the theory, research and practice of teacher education has expanded dramatically. As a result of this new thinking, teacher education is rapidly developing its own new language. The literature abounds with such new terminology as 'protocol materials', 'simulation laboratories', 'situational teaching', 'competency-based modules', 'microteaching', 'mini-course', 'performance-based certification', and 'field-centred programmes'. Perhaps one of the most frequently employed words, both in the literature on teacher education and on schooling in general, is 'innovation'. This is where the present work comes in. As part of the expanding literature on teacher education, this book focuses not on theory or research as others have recently done, but on innovation. It examines the changes that are going on in teacher preparation particularly in Australia, and tries to tease out and explain those innovations which seem to hold most promise for the future. Since the book's concern is essentially with 'innovation' in teacher education, the meaning the authors attach to the term should be clarified.

In our use of the term innovation we chose, after exploring several alternatives, the following definition: 'a deliberate and novel attempt to improve practice in relation to certain desired objectives'.[1] By 'deliberate' is meant that some planning, no matter how little, has preceded and accompanied the implementation of the innovation. The inclusion of the word 'novel' is not meant to refer to something objectively new but to something perceived as new by the individual or group concerned. The word 'attempt' signifies something that is being tried, has been tried or is yet to be tried: that is, the innovation may have been successfully or unsuccessfully introduced; it may still to be operationalized; or it may be in the process of implementation. Besides being a 'deliberate and novel attempt' innovation was seen as improving practice; as producing something better for somebody or some group. 'Practice' is broadly interpreted as any aspect of the on-going educational enterprise, ranging from major organizational concerns to say specific modes of teaching. Finally, innovation is shaped by objectives, may be implicit but hopefully stated, which are seen as worthwhile by the individual or group. Such objectives could be existing ones, or they could be revised or completely new. The important thing is that they are present. Thus in this book we are concerned with innovation as purposeful and planned change designed to improve education in some way.

In the design of the survey instrument and case-study methodology, the *process* of innovation was considered in order to provide a conceptual framework for our investigations. It was decided to follow the 'Planning-Research-Development-and-Diffusion' model of the innovation process recently used by the Centre for Educational Research and Innovation (CERI, 1973, pp. 54–5). This model reflects the steps which seem most commonly accepted as part of the process of innovation, namely, (i) problem identification and definition; (ii) innovation planning; (iii) innovation programming and development; (iv) experimentation; (v) evaluation and revision; (vi) dissemination and production; and (vii) implementation.

---

[1] Adapted from the similar definition in Centre for Educational Research and Innovation (CERI), *Case Studies of Educational Innovation: IV. Strategies for Innovation in Education*, OECD, 1973, p. 36.

We realized that few innovations would pass through all these steps or even follow this sequence. For example, it was known that many innovations did not originate with a problem, a weakness or a breakdown in the functioning of a teacher education programme. Some were clearly 'bandwagon' innovations inspired by what others were doing. Similarly we were aware that experimentation, evaluation and revision were steps ignored or poorly treated in a number of innovations. Nevertheless it seemed worthwhile to direct our investigations towards the overall possible process of innovation. We were particularly interested in six aspects: specification of objectives; sources of innovation; planning and implementation strategies and problems; personnel and resources in the operation; modes of evaluation; and revision, expansion and dissemination.

As our investigations proceeded we also became interested in typology of innovation. Existing systems for categorizing educational innovations, although helpful, did not provide adequately for the variety of innovative practices reported in our survey returns. Finally, a six-unit system was decided upon and subsequently proved useful in analyses of the lines of innovation. The main categories are:

1. *Organizational and administrative innovations* within an institution and its programmes.
2. *Total programme innovations* involving the introduction of a comprehensive course of teacher education.
3. *Curriculum specific innovations* concerned with the aims, organization and content of a single programme component.
4. *Technological innovations* featuring the use of media, materials and plant.
5. *Evaluative innovations* connected with student selection, assessment and graduation policies, as well as with course and programme appraisal.
6. *Methodological innovations* concerned with improved approaches to teaching and learning.

In the area of methodological innovations our special concern has been with the changing role of schools in the preparation of teachers and indeed in the process of innovation itself. Here attention has been directed mainly at special co-operating arrangements between teacher education programmes and schools which seek to improve both the theoretical and experiential learning of students. A number of these arrangements, however, go beyond pre-service education to the provision of continuing education for teachers and the promotion of collaborative research and curriculum development activity. Many teacher educators justifiably regard the special co-operative involvement of schools in teacher education as a very important and promising innovatory trend, one deserving much further deliberation and inquiry.

Given the great significance of teacher education in contemporary society, it is vital that efforts to improve and upgrade it are unrelenting. Despite current financial constraints, other circumstances seem favourable to such endeavour. With the growing oversupply of teachers, institutions involved in educating teachers may well shift their concern from numbers to quality. As important as innovation in teacher education is however, if it is not purposefully planned and carefully evaluated but is merely a fad or frill, it is perhaps better that it not be carried out at all.

This book is written by people actively engaged in teacher education for people actively engaged in teacher education, as well as for the growing community of scholars and researchers interested in the area. By delineating innovative trends, discussing ideas and examining the process of innovation, maybe it will promote some few improvements itself.

1 INNOVATIVE TRENDS IN TEACHER EDUCATION ABROAD[1]

The great volume and variety of innovations in teacher education reported in the literature over recent years, especially in the United States, are impressive and, one must admit, a little bewildering. They almost defy analysis. All levels and facets of teacher education seem to have been touched by innovative activity. The innovations span both the initial and the continuing education of teachers and deal with the many diverse elements in the teacher education process— organization and administration, recruitment and certification, design of totally new programmes, renovation and articulation of specific programme components, strategies of teaching and learning, and so on. This chapter attempts to review some of the literature on these innovations. No claim is made for the comprehensiveness of the descriptions. In many ways they are far from comprehensive. The account concentrates on what appear to be the main innovative trends, the converging lines of change which seem to be emerging. Attention has been particularly directed towards programme innovations judged to be of interest to practising teacher educators. Further, the review has been limited by the literature that could be collected in Australia, and thus a large amount of important material has not been read. It is acknowledged too that many things we have said could now be out-of-date, so rapid are changes going on, and that some of our reporting, being second- or even third-hand, might not represent with complete accuracy what is in fact being done in the various locations.

The review of the literature is organized into a number of main sections:

Minor Innovatory Trends. This section examines several selected important but, in terms of the literature, relatively minor lines of change in teacher education programmes not covered in the subsequent major themes. It briefly describes trends in offering programme options and in integrating programmes.

Competency-based Teacher Education. This highly systematic approach to teacher education is perhaps the dominant idea in the field of teacher education in the United States. However, elements of the competency-based movement have not been without influence in other countries.

Humanistic Teacher Education. Seen by some of its proponents as almost the antithesis of the competency-based idea, this approach emphasizes the 'humaniz-

[1] Authors mainly responsible for the various sections of this chapter are: C. Turney, Minor Innovatory Trends, Competency-based Teacher Education, and New Methods, Materials and Technology; D. Thew, Humanistic Teacher Education and Renovating Practice Teaching; and D. Jecks, Renewal of In-Service Education.

5

ing' of the teacher education experience, which often means that the prospective teacher is expected to learn about himself as an individual before he can interact effectively with learners.

Renovation of Practice Teaching. As the importance of practical experience in teacher preparation has been generally recognized, there have been numerous attempts to investigate its many problems and improve its effectiveness.

Field-based Teacher Education. The close co-operation between schools and teacher education institutions in both the provision of in-school experiences and other components of teacher preparation is a growing area of innovation. Most of the work is carried on at school sites with tertiary and school staff co-operatively involved. While several of these co-operating ventures will be mentioned in the 'Renovation of Practice Teaching' section, a much fuller treatment will be found in Chapter 4.

New Methods, Materials and Technology. Largely in an endeavour to exemplify the kind of teaching being advocated and to improve student learning, many teacher education programmes have departed sharply from traditional lecture methods. There are numerous variations on the themes of individualized and small group instruction. A number of such changes have been stimulated by advances in software and technology, leading to the emergence of such techniques as simulation and microteaching.

Renewal of In-Service Education. Although there has long been general agreement on the fact that no matter how effective pre-service teacher education may be, there will be a need to provide for the continuing professional education of teachers throughout their careers, only in the last decade have there been concerted attempts to improve and extend this endeavour. Among the most interesting innovations in this area has been the development of induction programmes for beginning teachers and the establishment of teachers' centres. Since in-service education is little touched on in the study of innovation in Australian teacher education, the review of overseas developments will also make reference to the Australian context.

MINOR INNOVATORY TRENDS

Programme Options

Although the offering of elective courses within teacher education programmes has been a common practice for many years, the provision of options between a number of complete programmes is of recent origin. It is an apparently growing trend in the United States for an individual institution to offer multiple programmes in any one field of teacher preparation. For example, students interested in becoming elementary school teachers at such an institution might elect to pursue say 'an off-campus or an on-campus program; can choose a series of courses geared toward urban education or stay in a mainstream of courses aimed at the general population of students; can select a program with a particular philosophical bent, such as behavior modification or open education, etc.' (Atkin and Raths, 1974, p. 17).

While many American institutions offer a small number of alternative teacher education programmes, institutions prominent in offering a wide array of programmes are the University of Massachusetts, Indiana University and the

University of California at Los Angeles. At the University of Massachusetts, the Dean of the School of Education, Dwight Allen, believed that teacher education programmes should, as far as possible, reflect the views and experience of staff and doctoral students. It was admitted that 'no one knows the best way to prepare any person for any teaching role', and use was made of the fact that 'many people are excited about and committed to ideas of preparing prospective teachers in particular ways' (Clark and Kingsbury, 1973, p. 479). For these, and for the additional four reasons listed below, a multiple-programme approach was adopted:

1. Students could have much greater choice in the 'how, where, and for what' of their preparation. With this might come greater commitment.

2. Programs would be smaller, increasing the potential for personalizing and individualizing, and decreasing alienation and anonymity, in spite of the institution's large size.

3. Faculty and doctoral student commitment of time, energy, thought, and care would increase in direct proportion to the degree to which they could design, control admissions to, and operate programs on their own terms.

4. It would be vastly easier to start new programs or to terminate existing programs. (Clark and Kingsbury, 1973, p. 479).

The range of alternative programmes at Massachusetts is supervised by a 'Teacher Preparation Program Council' (TPPC). This body, comprising ten faculty members appointed by the Dean, has, among other things, responsibility for screening proposals for new programmes from interested teams of staff and doctoral students and for considering the termination of unsuccessful programmes. Programmes submitted to the TPPC are appraised on the basis of the following specially devised guidelines:

1. The proposed program or component should have an explicit and thoughtful rationale. The rationale should include:
a. An explanation of the goals of the proposed program in terms of teachers, learners, schools and the wider society schools serve. (An explicit goal of combating racism must be included here.)
b. An explanation of how the various components of the proposed programs are designed to reach the goals and how they relate to one another.
c. A reasoned explanation of the learning theory explicit in the program.
d. An explicit statement of the terms in which the success of the program is to be assessed.

2. A major component of any program should be in the clinical area and should involve working with other learners of other ages. We do not intend that these other learners necessarily be children nor do we intend that the clinical component be necessarily designed in conformity with current student teaching or internship practices.

3. A major component of the program must be designed to help students develop both the capacity and inclination for reflective analysis. By this we mean essentially the ability to learn from one's experience. It implies learning of a second order—an ability to reflect not only upon one's own behaviour but about the assumptions upon which one's behaviour is based. (Atkin and Raths, 1974, p. 18)

The creativity of programme planners was stimulated by the removal of two main constraints. First, all existing School of Education requirements for teacher education students were abolished. Second, the state education commissioner agreed to accept the recommendation of the TPPC that graduates from the various programmes had satisfied certification requirements. It seems that faculty soon became genuinely excited about developing their own programmes. Within two years more than twenty alternative programmes were being offered, graduating nearly a thousand students annually. These programmes included, for example, the following three: (i) *Urban Teacher Education Program*—Students had one-semester internships in inter-racial settings, lived in a neighbourhood close to school sites, developed relationships with pupils in and out of school, and participated in community activities. This was followed by on-campus 'evaluation' seminars designed to identify the student's strengths and weaknesses and to provide intensive training in the needed knowledge and skills. (ii) *Off-Campus Teacher Education Program*—Designed to provide opportunities for student teaching in a variety of types of schools, it enabled students to teach in distinctive schools in various states, in Canada, Europe, and New Mexico. University staff visited students on site and worked with them on their return to campus. This programme had an important role in 'deprovincializing' its prospective teachers, 90 per cent of whom lived in Massachusetts. Student costs were reported to be much the same in the off-campus semester as during a resident semester with room and board. (iii) *Open Education Program*—Dedicated to concepts of open education, this programme was pursued at the University Laboratory School, Mark's Meadow and was staffed by school faculty and two doctoral students. Students were gradually phased into full teaching responsibilities, undertook systematic studies of child development and followed coursework and seminars which reflected on their teaching experience.

As the number of programmes multiplied and the numbers of faculty involved with any one programme decreased, it became increasingly difficult for the staff in each team to provide the background and expertise necessary for teaching every aspect that students or staff thought should be available. Thus core components were designed and offered to students in all programmes as required. The 'Methods Potpourri' was an example of such components. It provided ten different six-week methods courses which students could elect to follow.

By 1973, after two years of implementation, it was reported that the 'organizational mechanisms' of the alternative-programmes approach were working satisfactorily. Students seemed 'more satisfied' with their teacher education experiences. Increased numbers of faculty and doctoral students were involved. Relationships with schools and school systems were 'more systematic and positive'. School systems were seeking more of the programmes' student teachers than could be provided (Clark and Kingsbury, 1973, p. 479). All was not perfect, however. A series of questions had emerged requiring investigation. Among these were:

—Has the commitment to simultaneous alternative programs nurtured an 'intellectual cop-out', an atmosphere which uncritically encourages an 'anything goes' syndrome?
—Can the TPPC, or any central authority, effectively play the dual roles of program nurturer and critical evaluator?
—As program directors and their staffs compare approaches, share evaluations, and make revisions, can we maintain a broad range of alternatives or is a 'creeping sameness' emerging?
—What is the balance between program proliferation and consolidation such that

economy, efficiency, and clarity of options for students are preserved without destroying smallness, program director "ownership" and control, and truly different alternatives?
—At what point does personalization become dangerous by limiting students' ranges of exposure to ideas and by allowing faculty and staffs to become isolated from the press of competing points of view?
—Given positive evaluations of many programs by their respective staffs and students, to what degree is this valuing simply a function of the time, energy and personal commitment made by the individuals involved?
—While many 'innovative' school administrators have expressed excitement about TPPC's approach, will enough prospective employers see program graduates positively so that all can get jobs? (Clark and Kingsbury, 1973, pp. 479–80).

It is interesting to note that several teacher education institutions in Canada have introduced the idea of alternative teacher education programmes. A number, for example, are offered at the University of British Columbia in the professional year of its elementary and secondary Bachelor of Education degree courses. Most of the now existing alternatives began as modifications of the then current programmes. In part, this was done deliberately to enable programmes 'to begin without the lengthy and energy-sapping process of securing the University Senate's approval of new courses and new programs' (Bentley, 1976, p. 3). Most of the programmes are school-based and involve 20–50 students, with teachers and professors working in co-operation. Some idea of the nature of the programmes may be gained from the following descriptions of three of them:

The Collaborative Program for Professional Development was conducted completely in a secondary school and three feeder elementary schools. It stressed decision-making (on goals, programs, evaluation) based on individual and group needs, continuity between what the participants individually knew *about* teaching and how they actually *taught*, and critical analysis, using videotape recordings, of teaching. A unique feature of this program was that it depended heavily on subject-matter teachers for methods courses and did not use university specialists. And it deliberately incorporated both pre-service and in-service components....

The Task-oriented Teacher Education Program was a competency-based program for Social Studies teachers, stressing critical analysis and reconstruction of teaching practice in the light of experience. As might be expected, the program stressed early and continuous school experience. It made great use of demonstration, simulation and videotape recording....

The Community Education Program was situated first in a fraternity house on campus and then in a church basement in downtown Vancouver. Its aim was to prepare students to teach either in community schools or in traditional schools but in a way which would make maximum use of community resources. One extended core course was offered and a number of SCIL (Short Course Intensive Learning) courses in subject matter and content. Community agency field work was expected of all students. The emphasis was on shared program planning (shared by students, professors, consultants, and members of the community) and 'collegial' teaching and decision making. (Bentley, 1976, pp. 4–6)

The objectives underlying the introduction of alternative programmes such as these were somewhat different to those at Massachusetts. They included:

(i) To get participative rather than authoritative innovation—that is, 'grass roots' rather than 'laid-on' change.

(ii) To provide opportunities for those faculty members who had the eagerness, energy, commitment or readiness for change—and, hopefully, to reinvigorate those who had become jaded in attitude or routine in endeavour.

(iii) To respond speedily with appropriate programs to special needs of students and the field.

(iv) To develop a number of small programs which eventually could provide stimulus or practices or procedures for changes in the regular programs. (Bentley, 1976, p. 3)

Although, as has been seen in the case of the Massachusetts developments, quite serious questions have been raised regarding the operation of such programmes, it seems that the 'alternative programme' movement will continue to grow. If it does nothing else it will tend to increase the quantity and quality of dialogue about teacher education, harness the interest and enthusiasm of staff, and provide students with an opportunity to choose a programme which seems most relevant to their needs.

Programme Integration

Although the integration of teacher education learnings has increasingly occupied the attention of educators over recent years, the details of various plans which have been devised are seldom described in the literature. Nevertheless it is possible to trace the main lines of innovation along three dimensions: the general integration of theory and practice among the teacher education components; the integration of courses within teacher education components; and the integration of teacher education with that of other professions.

Integration of theory and practice in teacher education

A long-standing problem, which has attracted considerable attention in recent years, has been the relationship between the theoretical and practical aspects of teacher education. Teacher education has frequently been criticized for exhibiting a dichotomy between theory and practice. In the general sense teacher education itself has been charged with being insufficiently related to the needs of society and its schools. Within programmes, theoretical learnings are frequently not practically applied and practical learnings are insufficiently informed by theory. Often too, theory is emphasized at the expense of practice and sometimes the reverse is the case. Many teacher educators believe that the establishment of a balanced and close relationship between theory and practice is crucial if teacher education is to have maximum meaning and relevance for students and to have a significant impact on their prospective careers.

Concern for the integration of the theoretical and practical elements of teacher education has taken many forms. First, programme designers have tried to develop comprehensive and coherent teacher education curricula which are carefully articulated with specified objectives. This has been the feature of the competency-based teacher education movement in the United States, to be discussed later. Second, efforts have been made to point up relationships between the two main sectors of teacher education, general academic studies and professional studies. As Renshaw (1973) has stated, 'There is a growing body of opinion that academic and professional studies are not dichotomous but rather complementary' (p. 229). One result has been the introduction of course structures in which academic and professional courses run concurrently from the early stage of the programme thus facilitating both incidental and planned relating of theory to practice. A second outcome has been the study of certain academic disciplines 'within a professional frame of reference' which would include an examination of the nature of the discipline; the place of the subject in education; the psychological aspects of learning the subject; the sociological dimension of teaching the subject; and subject-matter for schools and teaching method (Renshaw, 1971, p. 236). Third, probably the question which has received most attention is that of integrating the strictly educational theory and practice within the professional area of teacher education, which typically comprises studies in the foundations of education (psychology, philosophy and sociology), courses in curriculum and instruction, and experience in the practice of teaching.

The issue of relating educational theory and practice within the professional area of teacher preparation has prompted the planning and implementation of a number of schemes, examples of which follow.

Co-ordinated courses.   A fairly widespread endeavour seems to have been made to co-ordinate course learnings between the theoretical study of education, curriculum and instruction courses and/or practice teaching experiences. For example, as early as 1966 in Ontario, Canada, the Minister's Committee on the Training of Elementary School Teachers proposed that courses in curriculum and instruction should both carefully integrate previous 'methods' courses and also should generally relate to theoretical studies in education. These proposals came in response to teacher criticism of 'meaningless repetition' in methodology courses and an 'overemphasis on teaching patterns and techniques insufficiently related to the foundations of education' (p. 25). The committee went on to recommend a 'co-operative approach' to planning and teaching by staff in education and curriculum courses:

> Working closely together in the presentation of educational theory and the demonstration of teaching procedures, they could emphasize the relationship and integration of educational aims, psychological principles, courses content, and instructional procedures. (p. 25)

Many programmes have adopted such co-ordinated approaches and have complemented them with carefully developed sequences of practical experience designed to help further the integration of theory and practice and to phase the student gradually into full teaching responsibilities (see Asian Institute for Teacher Educators, Third Workshop, 1972). These experiences include: child and school studies, observation of live and recorded teaching, microteaching, and increased participation in the task of teaching. Strategies such as these will be discussed more fully in a later section of this chapter.

Situational teaching of theoretical knowledge.   In a thought-provoking book Smith *et al.* (1969) asserted that to prepare teachers adequately to apply theoretical learning in classrooms, the conventional procedure of preaching theory and then providing opportunities for students to apply it should be drastically changed. Instead, real or simulated teaching situations should be the focus and principles drawn from research and theory, in such fields as pedagogy, psychology and sociology, should be introduced as needed to explain the situations. This is the way students will need to make decisions when they are teaching: theoretical knowledge will be used to interpret on-going situations, not teaching situations used to illustrate theory.

This idea has influenced considerably the development and use of materials in teacher education which model teaching behaviours or simulate teaching exchanges, and, as will be discussed later, has done much to bring new vitality and meaning to the consideration of theoretical knowledge in teacher preparation.

Development of learning modules. Linked particularly, but not exclusively, with the competency-based teacher education movement, individualized learning modules have been developed which specify objectives, suggest learning activities and outline assessment procedures. Many of these modules require student teachers to acquire theoretical understandings and demonstrate them in operation in their teaching, thus having the effect of integrating the theory and the practice connected with a comprehensive range of teaching competencies believed to be fundamental to effective teaching. Examples of individualized learning modules are the American WILKITs. The initial WILKIT module deals with four generally desirable features of lesson planning and teaching and focuses particularly on questioning strategies. Various readings are suggested, audiovisual programmes for viewing and analysis are listed, and written and peer group exercises provided. The culmination of these learnings is participation in a microteaching clinic where their application and refinement is undertaken until appropriate levels of proficiency are reached (WILKIT 1, *The Four Cons of Teaching*, 1974).

New relationships with schools. The formation of closer, more productive relationships with schools has been a major way that teacher education programmes have endeavoured to facilitate the integration of educational theory and practice. Such relationships involve close co-operation between tertiary institution faculty and school staff and not only have the effect of improving conventional student teaching but often open-up other valuable educational opportunities for both the student, teachers and faculty. Since much will be said of co-operating relationships with schools in Chapter 4, only a few details need be presented here. Perhaps one example of some clear-headed plans will suffice.

In a recent report on integrating theory and practice emerging from a workshop organized by the Asian Institute for Teacher Educators, it was suggested that every teacher education institution collaborate closely in 'partnership' with a 'laboratory school' on the same campus and with nearby 'co-operating schools'. The 'laboratory school' was seen as 'an established demonstration and pilot centre with special staff and facilities so as to provide a reasonably good model of a teaching-learning environment' for student teachers. The main functions envisaged for such schools were:

i. to provide laboratory experiences to student teachers in order to develop skills and professional attitudes to teaching and school government and to make them effective teachers and class managers;

ii. to test and try out new techniques and new teaching materials;

iii. to provide feedback to improve theory and practice;

iv. to provide facilities to the staff of the training institution and to student teachers to try new programmes and practices;

v. to make investigations and to conduct simple action research on live educational problems so as to bring about change and improvement;

vi. to install tested results of experimentation as a model for other schools;

vii. to provide up-to-date, efficient and successful learning experiences to pupils according to their needs and potentialities using the latest methods and techniques;

viii. to conduct supervision and evaluation of student teachers in line with criteria laid down at meetings of staff with those concerned with student teaching in the training institution, and participate in the post-teaching conferences arranged for helping student teachers in their professional growth. (pp. 28–9)

Among other things, it was stressed that the laboratory school should draw its pupils from all socio-economic levels; that the staff be highly qualified and be afforded some privileges within the tertiary institution; and that 'interchange' of staff between school and institution would be 'desirable from time to time'. Further, a close relationship with other co-operating schools, used mainly for student practice teaching, would serve the following purposes:

i. provide an example of a type of school generally available in the community;

ii. give student teachers the opportunities to gain insights into the conditions of a regular school in matters of organization, administration, and facilities for teaching and learning;

iii. provide a variety of experiences for student teaching;

iv. give student teachers opportunities for testing the applicability of new ideas gained in the laboratory school in regular classroom situations, which may offer variations, both of degree and kind;

v. develop in student teachers resourcefulness and initiative when working with limited facilities, and put to test their capacity for decision-making;

vi. provide an opportunity for the teachers in the co-operating school to keep up-to-date with the new ideas and innovative practice currently advocated by the training institution. (pp. 29–30)

Within each co-operating school it was proposed that a teaching centre be established to incorporate various facilities and resources and be made the site for the student teachers, co-operating teachers, and teacher education staff to meet for guiding, planning and evaluating student teaching experiences. It was emphasized that if teachers were to have greater responsibility for supervising student teaching, they should have a clear understanding of principles advocated in the teacher education programme, and be personally and professionally well-qualified to undertake the guidance of students.

Writing recently on the problem of integrating educational theory and practice, Marklund and Gran (1974) agreed that theoretical studies in isolation from reality are undesirable. They affirmed that the student teacher needs 'to see what theoretical things look like in the context of practical teaching' and should be given opportunities to apply in teaching what he himself has learned in principle (p. 32). The writers, however, caution teacher educators that practical application must wait upon the development of theoretical understandings:

Obviously an advanced integration of studies and teaching practice is doomed to failure. The practice of details and parts before the trainee has acquired a sound general view of his subject, of the subject matter involved and of the latter as a means to the personal development of the pupils, can easily result in mechanical and rigid teaching behaviour during the practice period. Advanced integration in this sense is also a dubious proposition because the trainee's studies would acquire a short-term objective gauged exclusively according to what was useful for the moment. A constant preoccupation with 'useful' things is liable to result in a fragmentary view of the subject and in a simplification of issues. (p. 32)

Although there is merit in these thoughts, they seem to assume that theory and practice should be in consecutive blocks, the latter waiting on the former. In effect, two important possibilities are overlooked: (i) the development of the theory and practice of teaching in a continuous, parallel relationship, and (ii) the application of theory to bring understanding to the previously experienced practical teaching situations.

Integrated courses within teacher education components

The integration of various subdivisions within the theoretical and practical areas respectively has also been attempted in many teacher education programmes and has often been associated with interdisciplinary team teaching. There have been at least three main reasons for this endeavour: (i) Rationalized subject integration has been undertaken to prevent unnecessary duplication and to save staff and student time. (ii) Subjects have been interrelated so that content aspects will reinforce each other and learning will become more meaningful and interesting. (iii) Programmes have tried to exemplify the new integrated, interdisciplinary curriculum being developed in the schools.

Moves to foster the integration of subjects have included the relating of content by the study of the subjects in a certain sequence, alternately or in a parallel fashion; the separate treatment of common topics across a number of subjects; and the fused consideration of a number of themes. Perhaps one of the main areas of integration activity has been within the special 'methods' or curriculum courses. Efforts have been made to avoid overlap and conflict and to focus more on the needs of the child as a whole than on special subject needs. Although such measures have been common in the United States for some time, only recently do they appear to be attracting attention in Europe. In Britain, for example, the development of new college curricula has sometimes featured integrated courses. Eggleston (1974) reports several important innovations with integration.

Programme development at Crewe and Madeley Colleges of Education conducted in association with the University of Keele Institute of Education has resulted in an integrated curriculum studies course. This sprang, in part, from the work in schools by the Keele Integrated Studies Project and from the belief that the previous 'specialized subject-based courses were not necessarily the most appropriate means of initial teacher education' (Eggleston, 1974, pp. 90–1). The new course seeks, in particular, to introduce students 'to a general theory of curriculum that will have relevance to the full range of decisions on curriculum they will be called upon to make in their teaching careers'. In the first year of the curriculum studies course, *all* students examine the curriculum in mathematics, English, physical education, religious education, arts and crafts and music in relation to the needs of their chosen age groups. In the second and third year of the course, students elect two areas of study from the following: Life Sciences; Environmental Studies; Man in a Technological Age; Physical Education and the Use of the Environment; The Creative Arts Today; Man's Search for Meaning; Mass Media; and Studies Based on Literature. Reports on a number of former students of the course have indicated that it is bringing students 'to the point where they are able to initiate new approaches in the schools at an early stage after the completion of their initial training' (Eggleston, 1974, p. 91). Similar integrated programmes are being developed in three colleges associated with the Lancaster School of Education and are reported upon in Warwick (1974) and Eggleston (1974).

Integration of teacher education with that of other professions

In many institutions prospective teachers pursue academic studies in subjects like English or mathematics alongside students preparing for such professions as law and business. Often too students preparing to be teachers at various levels of schooling (e.g. primary and secondary) undertake common courses not only in academic subjects but also in a number of professional studies (e.g. curriculum and instruction units and even in-school experience). While one suspects that an important consideration in these developments has been to maximize the use of staff and resources, valuable educational advantages are frequently proposed in support. For example, referring to such moves in Sweden Marklund and Gran (1974) revealed:

> It is claimed that the co-ordination of teacher education with other education within the same or adjoining subject spheres would be conducive to a subsequent co-ordination of education, vocational activity and leisure activity, which in turn would help to de-institutionalize the school. (p. 33)

The writers add the warning, however, that 'integration requirements of this kind may impede the integration of theory and practice in teacher education' (p. 33).

Carrying further the theme of integrating the education for different professions, some institutions in the United States have developed programmes where the professional courses themselves provide for a variety of related professions. For example at Mankato State College, Minnesota, a programme of 'Interdisciplinary Teacher Education in Early Childhood' has been designed and recently received a Distinguished Achievement Award from the American Association of Colleges for Teacher Education. The programme centres on the 'Children's House', a spacious and exemplary demonstration and participation facility for the care-instruction of 100 children, ages three to six. Largely within this setting experiences and subjects are provided for the pre- and in-service education for early childhood education teachers, child development occupations teachers, consumer homemaking teachers, family life education teachers, and food service occupations teachers and personnel. Learning 'is heavily experiential with an environment which fosters understanding and appreciation of diverse approaches to the education and development of the child'. The diversity which characterizes the trainees is said to promote 'cross-stimulation and exchange of perspectives among students' which 'significantly extends the boundaries of learning and growing opportunities for the trainees and, it is important to note, for the staff as well' (Buck *et al.*, 1973, p. i).

Despite the efforts to promote integration along the three main dimensions sketched above, much yet remains to be done before optimum co-ordination of experiences within and between programmes is achieved. There is no doubt that this problem will continue to occupy the attention of teacher educators for some time to come.

COMPETENCY-BASED TEACHER EDUCATION

Of all the recent developments in teacher education in the United States, the one currently having the most profound influence is the competency-based approach to teacher education (CBTE), also known as performance-based teacher education (PBTE). Although the substantial literature contains a wide variety of definitions of CBTE, perhaps an adequate general description is that made by Cooper *et al.* (1973): a CBTE programme is one which 'specifies the competencies to be demonstrated by the student, makes explicit the criteria to be applied in assessing the student's competencies, and holds the student accountable for meeting those criteria' (p. 14). The competencies include those attitudes, understandings, skills and behaviours believed necessary to facilitate the intellectual, social, emotional and physical growth of children. In other words, the competencies for which the student is responsible are the judged qualities of effective teaching. In determining the student's level of achievement in the various competencies, three types of criteria are used: (i) knowledge criteria, to assess his cognitive understandings, (ii) performance criteria, to appraise his teaching behaviour, and (iii) product or consequence criteria, to evaluate the student's effectiveness by examining the learning of his pupils. More particularly, Elam (1971) believed there was 'general agreement on five essential elements' of competency-based programmes. These were:

1. Competencies (knowledge, skills, behaviors) to be demonstrated by the student are
—derived from explicit conceptions of teacher roles,
—stated so as to make possible assessment of a student's behavior in relation to specific competencies, and
—made public in advance;

2. Criteria to be employed in assessing competencies are
—based upon, and in harmony with, specified competencies,
—explicit in stating expected levels of mastery under specified conditions, and
—made public in advance;

3. Assessment of the student's competency
—uses his performance as the primary source of evidence,
—takes into account evidence of the student's knowledge relevant to planning for, analyzing, interpreting, or evaluating situations or behavior, and
—strives for objectivity;

4. The student's rate of progress through the program is determined by demonstrated competency rather than by time or course completion;

5. The instructional program is intended to facilitate the development and evaluation of the student's achievement of competencies specified. (pp. 6–7)

A number of factors seem to have combined to lead to the origin and to increase the impact of the CBTE movement. One important general factor was the public call for teacher accountability—the request that teachers be held responsible for the level of achievement of their pupils. It was realized that the large sums of money channelled into education in post-Sputnik years had not produced the results expected. Taxpayers wanted 'visible dividends on their investments in education' (Elam, 1971, p. 3). Many were disappointed in the effectiveness of teaching. Teacher education programmes were apparently not 'delivering the goods'. A result was that a number of state legislatures passed 'accountability laws' mandating performance-based certification of teachers.

Accompanying public demands for teacher accountability were professional and lay discontent with existing teacher education programmes in the United States. This was strongly expressed in the critiques of Conant (1963) and Koerner (1963) and reinforced by complaints from teachers about the uselessness of their training (Holt, 1964; Kohl, 1967).

Paralleling these influences, and partly in response to them, there were several important developments in teacher education which later coalesced into CBTE. Teacher educators were giving more attention to flexibly scheduled programmes with some form of individualized instruction and self-analysis being provided for students through new materials which were being developed. Attempts were made to analyse the complex act of teaching into specific behavioural components. Microteaching using the new technology of television and using a systems approach was developed to facilitate the students' acquisition of repertoires of specific behaviours or skills. These innovations were backed by increasing research into the elusive criteria of teacher effectiveness.

In 1967 the U.S. Office of Education, recognizing the demand for reform in teacher education, supported the development of ten model elementary teacher education programmes. Significantly, the models developed 'called for modification of traditional curricula to incorporate in some form an analysis of complex teaching strategies into specific teaching skills, explicit skills practice, and corrective feedback' (Ryan, 1975, p. 150). This emphasis on essential teaching behaviours was to be strongly taken up by the pioneers of CBTE.

During the 1970s CBTE has had a remarkable growth—a large volume of literature has been devoted to it; a number of organizations have been formed to co-ordinate and promote it; many teacher education programmes have adopted it; and a number of state legislatures have mandated its introduction. Some estimate of the impact of CBTE on programmes may be derived from the results of a survey conducted in 1972 by the American Association of Colleges for Teacher Education (AACTE). Over 1,200 institutions were approached and of the 783 respondents, 125 indicated the operation of CBTE programmes, 366 indicated the planned introduction of CBTE, and only 228 indicated no current involvement in CBTE. In a later survey Wilson and Curtis (1973) tried to ascertain the extent to which each of 50 states had mandated CBTE. They found that 10 states had made it mandatory and at least 10 other states were contemplating similar action. During its brief history CBTE has become the centre of a considerable amount of controversy. Probably no other development in teacher education has had at the one time so many staunch advocates and strong critics.

The proponents of CBTE stress that it has at least four strong and worthwhile features. They are quick to point out that most of these features incorporate important ideas which teacher educators have supported over the years in one form or another (Elam, 1971; Cooper *et al.*, 1973; Houston and Howsam, 1972; Schmieder, 1973).

1. *Precise learning objectives*. These are determined in advance, specified in behavioural terms, made explicit to the student and used as the basis for evaluating performance.

2. *Individualized instruction*. Competency-based programmes give the student opportunity to select objectives and learning activities of personal relevance to him; to pursue the activities on a self-directed, self-paced, largely independent

basis; and to obtain individual feedback concerning his progress towards the objectives. However, not all instruction takes the form of independent activity. Group and even mass instruction are sometimes very effective alternatives.

3. *Accountability*. The student knows the specified objectives and the criteria connected with their achievement, and he accepts responsibility and expects to be held accountable for their attainment.

4. *Integration of theory and practice*. Competency-based programmes are generally 'reality-oriented'. Students spend a great deal of time in simulated or real-life teaching situations interacting with children. Learning activities lead them directly to such settings for the integration and translation of theory into practice and many of the competencies students develop are evaluated in such settings.

Beyond the above four features of CBTE many other 'desirable characteristics' are claimed for it. For instance, because competency-based programmes emphasize exit requirements rather than entry requirements, they are seen as advantageous for students denied educational opportunity who might otherwise, because of entrance requirements, not be given a chance. Evaluation of student's work focuses not only on what he knows but how he performs in teaching situations and this is seen as a most effective basis for evaluation. Another worthwhile feature is said to be the assurance given to employers that student graduates have reached an adequate level of mastery in the specified competencies. In all, advocates of CBTE claim that 'both students and teachers appear to have a high degree of satisfaction with the preparation programs' (Schmieder, 1973, p. 6). Students particularly seem 'highly motivated' to pursue individualized learning activities that will help them attain stated objectives.

While such 'admirable features' of CBTE as those above have been voiced by advocates of the movement, a number of important criticisms have been levelled at it. These may be divided into two main categories, want of 'humanity' and lack of empirical basis.

1. *Want of 'humanity'*. Strong criticism of CBTE has come from humanistic educators, such as Combs (see p. 25), who view it as the mechanistic antithesis of humanistic teacher education and as being an approach deleterious to prospective teachers. In effect, many humanistic educators regard CBTE as 'inhumane' and as 'dehumanizing' the teacher education process. They seem to part ways with those who support CBTE not so much on an understanding of how the programmes operate, but largely on the issue of the metaphor employed to describe the operation (Atkin and Raths, 1974). Competency-based programmes tend to use an industrial metaphor, referring to such things as input, products, performance skills, modules, feedback and so on. Humanistic educators are repelled by such language and the concept of the educational process it suggests. They see education as the growth and development of a person through experience, the outcomes of which cannot be determined. Thus they reject both the specification of goals as an initial step in the learning process, and planning the introduction of activities and assessment related to the achievement of these goals. Humanistic teacher education emphasizes personal development rather than learning how to teach; personal attitudes, beliefs and understanding rather than teaching behaviours. In particular, the humanistic educator sees the use of the computer in some CBTE programmes as dehumanizing, and the use of the videotape recorder as threatening.

Proponents of CBTE argue that it is neither mechanistic nor dehumanizing. As Schmieder (1973) has put it:

> On the contrary a competency-based program offers the student the opportunity to be very selective in his instruction activities. The emphasis is on the goals and not the means. We would assume that even a conventional program has some goals or objectives no matter how loosely defined and hidden. A competency-based program liberates the student and individualizes the entire process.
>
> Certainly nothing is more dehumanizing than the traditional instructor-student relationship in most institutions of higher learning where the student is often at the mercy of the capricious and often hidden criteria of the instructor. (p. 25)

Most unbiased commentators do not, in fact, regard CBTE as incompatible with the humane treatment of students (Atkin and Raths, 1974). Indeed Gage and Winne (1975) assert that such aspects of CBTE as individualized instruction, the large degree of student choice of learning activities, and the purposeful development of the student's attitudes and understandings along with his acquisition of skills are not necessarily antagonistic to the views of humanistic educators. In their judgement 'benefits can be derived' from the concurrent use in teacher education of both the competency-based and humanistic orientations (p. 152).

2. *Lack of empirical basis.* Fundamentally CBTE rests on its ability to sepecify teacher competencies which promote pupil learning. Many would dispute the fact that it currently has this ability. For example, from their analysis of existing research, Heath and Nielson (1973) draw three conclusions:

> First, the research literature on the relation between teacher performance and student achievement does not offer an empirical basis for the prescription of teacher-training objectives.
>
> Second, this literature fails to provide such a basis, not because of minor flaws in the statistical analyses, but because of sterile operational definitions of both teaching and achievement, and because of fundamentally weak research designs. Last, given the well-documented strong association between student achievement and variables such as socio-economic status and race . . ., the effects of techniques of teaching on achievement (as these variables are conventionally defined) are likely to be inherently trivial. (pp. 15–16)

In replying to such criticism of inadequate knowledge about the effectiveness of various teaching competencies, one proponent of CBTE, Schmieder (1973), has written:

> Again, if this is true of competency-based programs, it is also true of the conventional ones. The advantage again falls to the former because at least we know what has been done to the students in the way of competencies. . . . We cannot guarantee at the 100 per cent level that the competencies identified in any program are the ones which can faciliate pupil growth. Having identified the specific competencies that the graduates have, we should be able to engage in a much more meaningful follow-up analysis to ascertain the relevance of the competencies. (p. 26)

More recently, Gage and Winne (1975), while admitting that causal connections between teacher behaviour and pupil learning are presently inadequate, argue for further experimental studies which would not only investigate the effects on learning of single teaching competencies but also the 'effects of *patterns* of interrelated teacher behaviour variables' (p. 157). They advocate that a major part of the cost of putting CBTE into effect be devoted to research 'needed to identify and validate teacher competencies' (p. 162). Gage and Winne were also critical of the lack of sound empirical evaluation of total CBTE programmes, of their components and of their modules. A large number of such evaluations had been completed but they were lacking in objectivity and penetration.

While the literature on the general theory and implementation of CBTE abounds, it is relatively silent on how specific programmes operate in practice. Atkin and Raths (1974) do, however, endeavour to sketch a generalized picture of CBTE in action and it is worth quoting, even if it is rather negative in tone:

> For the most part, the competency-based approach is utilized in the core of experiences most often termed 'methods courses'. Generally, those courses are dropped as the competency-based program is introduced. In their place are substituted lists of objectives that a student is to pursue according to his own time-table. Faculty members are available to help students on a one-to-one basis as they undertake the suggested activities which lead to the attainment of the objective. In one mid-western university, a large room is set aside for faculty and students to meet. Students wait patiently as though they were patients in a physician's reception room until a professor is free to discuss the work. Once a student senses that he has acquired the objective, he can then visit an examination room. This facility is usually staffed by a clerk who upon inquiry selects the appropriate examination corresponding to the objective pursued by the student. The student takes the examination to a seat in the room and privately completes the examination. The clerk then grades the paper. (Almost always, the competencies in this program are assessed by objective multiple-choice tests or fill-in-the-blank items.) The clerk then prepares a computer punch card upon which is entered the student's name, the date, the form of the examination taken, the competency that was assessed, and the student's score. Once a week the accumulated computer cards are fed into a computer. The print-out, addressed to students and professors, indicates to both which objectives have been met during the previous week and which ones are most appropriate for the attack next. If a student were clever enough, he might complete all of the objectives in one week. However, it would be very unusual for a student to finish so quickly. One program we visited had over sixty objectives with more than half of them specifically required of students. Certainly it would take more than a week for an accomplished teacher merely to take that many achievement tests. (pp. 25–6)

Microteaching is generally an important component of competency-based programmes. Most microteaching sessions focus on the student teacher's application with a small group of children of such performance competencies as explaining and questioning. Students who perform at a low level are frequently given the opportunity for re-teaching to demonstrate their improvements. In some programmes, it is not so much the student teacher's application of skills as the learning of pupils participating in the microteaching which is examined. It is rare, however, for pupil 'outcome measures' to be the sole basis of determining a student's progress. Typically in the last phase of a competency-based programme the student enters student teaching which, according to Atkin and Raths (1974), is not very different in format from the conventional practicum. The student is assigned to a co-operating teacher who appraises and guides the student's development. Many programmes endeavour to inform the teachers of the objectives towards which students have been educated.

At the heart of any CBTE programme are the instructional modules which provide the learning activities intended to facilitate the student's acquisition and demonstration of particular competencies. Fundamentally, it is the module which enables the self-paced, independent study, and the selection of alternative means of instruction, often claimed as key advantages of CBTE. In general terms, an instructional module comprises the following seven elements:

(i) A rationale that (a) describes the purpose and importance of the objectives of the module in empirical, theoretical, and/or practical terms; and (b) places the module and the objectives of the module within the context of the total programme.

(ii) Objectives that specify the competency or competencies the student is expected to demonstrate.

(iii) Prerequisites, i.e. any competencies the student should have prior to entering the module.

(iv) Pre-assessment procedures—usually diagnostic in nature—that provide the student with an opportunity to demonstrate mastery of the objectives or relevant to the objectives.

(v) Learning alternatives, which are the various instructional options available to the student and each of which is designed to contribute to his acquisition of the objectives.

(vi) Post-assessment procedures that permit the student to demonstrate achievement of the objectives.

(vii) Remedial procedures to be undertaken with students who are unable to demonstrate achievement of the objectives on the post-assessment. (Cooper *et al.*, 1973, p. 17)

Teacher educators designing elements for such modules would emphasize that the pre-assessment procedures both give the opportunity to the student to demonstrate the relevant competencies he already has, and the option to bypass the instructional learning activities related to these competencies. Also the pre-assessment and post-assessment procedures would employ testing situations as close to reality as possible. Thus performance and product criteria are often used to appraise student progress.

One of the most impressive, and controversial, byproducts of CBTE has been the endeavour by various groups to develop comprehensive catalogues of teaching competencies or skills, not just to facilitate programme planning, but to assist teaching by indicating training or protocol materials and/or general strategies that might be used in developing the competencies, as well as what competencies have yet to have materials developed on them (see Houston, 1973a and b). One such catalogue was developed at Indiana University by a federal funded project headed by R. I. Turner. It was published in December 1973 by the Multi-State Consortium on Performance-Based Education and the Leadership Training Institute for Protocol Materials, under the title, *A Catalog of Teaching Skills*. The skills included are both generalized ones relating to such areas as 'Socialization and Classroom Management' and more specialized ones relevant to say teaching social studies. Within such broad areas skills are organized in groups under teacher 'functions'. For instance, in the area of classroom management one teacher function is 'appraises student behaviour'. This is broken down into several skills and a minimum set of tasks to be acquired and demonstrated by student teachers is suggested.

FUNCTION: APPRAISES STUDENT BEHAVIOR

SKILL: DISTINGUISHES AMONG ON-TASK, OFF-TASK AND DISRUPTIVE BEHAVIORS

college classroom or learning lab

Given a film or videotape of classroom student behaviors:

—codes student behaviors as on-task or off-task

—codes student behavior as non-disruptive or disruptive

microteaching or actual classroom

—praises students only when they are on-task

—reminds students who are off-task but not disruptive by an unobtrusive remark or a touch or a facial expression

—does what is necessary to stop disruptive behavior as quickly as possible

SKILL: ACCURATELY REPORTS NATURE AND SIGNIFICANCE OF STUDENT'S BEHAVIOR

college classroom or learning lab

Given a film or videotape focusing on a particular student's behavior:

—observes and keeps running records of the student's behavior

—summarizes 10 minutes or so of such behavior into a paragraph that is balanced and does not over look significant behavior

Given a parent-teacher role-play simulation:

—praises student when appropriate

—mentions criticisms of student if necessary, while maintaining rapport and minimizing defensiveness of parents

microteaching or actual classroom

—observes, perhaps keeps running records, of individual student's behavior

—reports fairly both good and bad behavior of a student

—does not stereotype a student with insufficient evidence

Given a private parent-teacher conference:

—praises student when appropriate

—mentions criticisms of student if necessary, while maintaining rapport and minimizing defensiveness of parents

Given an occasion for written evaluation:

—upon request, substantiates any coded symbol with specific behavioral evidence

—accurately reports in detail a conflict situation and surrounding factors. (Turner, 1973, pp. 8–9)

Another searching analysis of teaching skills is the *Florida Catalog of Teacher Competencies* (1973) which emerged from a project headed by N. R. Dodl and sponsored by the Florida Department of Education. Using a complicated indexing system, the catalogue lists 1,276 competencies, noting the teaching materials available on each, and cross categorizing each one according to such things as education topic, teacher behaviour, pupil level, and content area. Sixty-five general teaching behaviours are covered by the many competencies (see Table 1.1).

Table 1.1 FLORIDA CATEGORIES OF TEACHER BEHAVIOR

10. Assessing and Evaluating Student Behavior
    11—Selecting assessment instruments
    12—Designing and developing assessment instruments
    13—Collecting and quantifying data
    14—Diagnosing student difficulties or abilities
    15—Summarizing and interpreting data
    16—Involving students in self-evaluation
    17—Diagnosing student affective characteristics

20. Planning Instruction
    21—Selecting and specifying goals, aims and objectives
    22—Selecting instructional strategies
    23—Organizing students
    24—Selecting or developing materials and activities
    25—Collaborating with others in planning
    26—Developing procedures and routines
    27—Evaluating instruction/instructional design

30. Conducting and Implementing Instruction
    31—Structuring/establishing rapport/providing atmosphere
    32—Motivating/reinforcing students; providing for feedback
    33—Conducting discussion/small group activities
    34—Individualizing instruction/conducting individual activities
    35—Presenting information/giving directions
    36—Utilizing deductive, inductive thinking or problem solving
    37—Questioning and responding
    38—Utilizing audio-visual equipment and aids (resources)

40. Performing administrative duties
    41—Supervising aides, tutors, etc.
    42—Arranging physical environment
    43—Establishing/maintaining procedures/routines
    44—Maintaining records
    45—Organizing materials

50. Communicating and interacting
    51—Conferring with parents
    52—Counselling students
    53—Representing school/school program
    54—Involving others in the school program
    55—Establishing/maintaining professional relationships

60. Developing personal skills
    61—Accepting self
    62—Evaluating self
    63—Planning for self improvement/improving self
    64—Accepting responsibility
    65—Developing subject related skills
    66—Accepting others
    67—Solving problems

70. Developing pupil self
    71—Developing pupil self concept
    72—Developing pupil social interaction skills
    73—Developing pupil learning to learn skills
    74—Developing pupil acceptance of responsibility
    75—Developing pupil attitudes and values.

(Dodl, 1973, p. 13)

The *Florida Catalog* includes suggestions for teacher educators concerning the selection of competencies, their arrangement in 'clusters' concerning high-and-low-level competencies, and the development of learning modules. For example, a programme might choose to construct learning activities on a cluster of competencies related to standardized testing. Three of these competencies might be:

1. Teacher can choose appropriate standardized tests for use in specific classroom situations.

2. Teacher can administer a variety of standardized tests, following to criterion all procedures necessary for attaining reliable results with groups tested.

3. Teacher can accurately interpret the results of standardized tests administered in specific classroom situations. (Dodl, 1973, p. 400)

The suggested content layout of the student-teacher learning module on competency 1 might then be:

Module 1—The purpose of this module is to prepare a teacher in training to choose appropriate standardized tests for use in the classroom situations.

Instructional Objectives:

1. The student will be able to recall how standardized tests differ from other tests in terms of administration, scoring, and test construction.

2. The student will be able to recognize situations in which the use of standardized tests is appropriate.

3. The student will recognize situations in which standardized testing is inappropriate or is being used improperly.

4. Student will be able to categorize tests from their descriptions as being measures of aptitude, achievement, or personality.

5. The student will be able to categorize testing situations as being appropriate for use of measures of aptitude, achievement, or personality.

6. The student will recognize the following references as sources of reviews of tests, and will recall the relative merits of each:

(a) Test manuals
(b) Buros' *Mental Measurements Yearbooks*
(c) *Educational and Psychological Measurement*
(d) *Journal of Consulting Psychology.*

Pre-Test—This module would include a diagnostic pre-test providing the learner feedback on his readiness to perform at Assessment Level A (i.e., knowledge and skill mastery). The pre-test would also provide the learner with feedback data useful in making wise choices from instructional alternatives available to him.

Instructional Alternatives—The module would include a description of the instructional resources available to the learner. e.g.,

Item 1—Video Tape EDR 401-003: A 25 minute lecture; demonstration by instructor of basic types of standardized tests and the situation for which they are most useful.

Item 2—Slide tape series EDR 401-St 021: Three fifteen minute presentations depicting general dimensions of aptitude, achievement, and personality tests.

Item 3—Read:
Lindeman, R. H., *Educational Measurement*. Glenview, Illinois: Scott Foresman, 1967, pp. 113–114.
Lindvall, C. M., *Measuring Pupil Achievement and Aptitude*. New York: Harcourt, Brace and World, pp. 136–137.

Item 4—Seminars EDR 401-S001-S003: Scheduled twice each quarter (see master schedule).

Pots-Test—The module would provide a mastery type post-test on all objectives.

Mastery level is 90% on all objectives. Achievement of mastery on all objectives constitutes competency at Level A on Competency No. 1.

Remedial Alternatives—The completed module would provide directions to the learner who needs assistance beyond the structured resources provided as regularly available instructional alternatives. (Dodl, 1973, pp. 402–3)

The specification of objectives and the selection and arrangement of competencies for inclusion in a CBTE programme should not be a haphazard process. They are ideally based on a rationale of basic assumptions concerning the role of the teacher or on some model of the teaching process. Apparently all too often, however, the planning of programmes and their materials has not consistently taken place on such a basis. As Houston has stated:

Many initiate module specifications and materials development with no explicitly stated philosophy for the program, no conceptualization of the roles the graduates will assume, and sometimes no stated objectives. With the need for a 'quick return', this short-cut often seems necessary since overall design of a program is time-consuming, often frustrating, and causes a teacher preparation staff to confront themselves with their philosophical differences. Faced with seemingly insurmountable barriers to progress, the program designer often turns to piecemeal development, hoping the pieces will eventually fit together. Each piece stands alone, isolated, often excellent in its own right, but contributing little to an integrated preparation program. (Houston, 1972, p. 70)

While it is a difficult task, total programme design is a necessary prerequisite to the selection of competencies and the development of modules.

In attempting to take a 'reasonable position' with regard to the future of CBTE, Gage and Winne (1975) strongly avoided the extreme alternatives of either returning to conventional teacher preparation or legally enforcing the universal installation of CBTE. They saw the first of these alternatives as squandering the improvements already achieved by CBTE:

Without the kinds of behavioural, pedagogical, and philosophical analysis that are the essence of PBTE, teacher education will necessarily flounder with overly global and complex variables (for example, unanalyzed student teaching, 'humanistic gestalts', and large but vague and unattainable goals) that hindered teacher education before the advent of PBTE. (p. 171)

On the other hand, they saw danger in installing CBTE through legal coercion. CBTE was not yet well enough established 'scientifically, educationally or ethically' to justify its general enforcement. Gage and Winne concluded by advocating that CBTE 'be encouraged, tried, studied, and improved' and warned that 'overly hasty installations of the approach—installations that will inevitably disappoint as they go beyond the state of the art—will only produce setbacks' (p. 172). Despite this warning, one has the uneasy feeling that it is perhaps too late, and that the CBTE bandwagon will roll on largely regardless of efforts to research and refine its operation.

HUMANISTIC TEACHER EDUCATION

A school of thought on teacher education, proposed as an alternative to the current behaviouristic impetus towards competency-based teacher education, is that exemplified by the work of Arthur Combs and his colleagues at the University of Florida, Gainesville. The programme they have developed and termed 'humanistic' stresses the importance of the 'self' of the teacher. The 'humanistic' approach is philosophically rooted in the progressive movement of the 1930s. In Combs' view, teaching is a 'helping profession' and as such the client (child or student) occupies the central position in the interaction between the helper (teacher or lecturer) and the client: 'It is the client who knows what he is feeling, what he would like to know, what his goals are and what meanings certain experiences provide for him' (Atkin and Raths, 1974, p. 31).

The Florida Childhood Education Program (CEP) sees good teaching as a highly personal matter. Its theoretical base is derived from perceptual-humanistic psychology which locates the causes of behaviour in the belief systems of the behaver. Beginning from those understandings, it follows that teacher education is not a question of learning 'how to teach' but a matter of personal discovery, of learning how to use one's self and surroundings to assist other persons to learn. The Florida programme is thus designed to help each student find his own best ways of teaching. As an innovative programme it was developed in a systematic fashion rarely seen in curriculum development: (i) It began in twelve years of basic research on the nature of the helping professions, especially on the nature of good and poor teachers (Loper and Combs, 1962; Combs and Soper, 1963; Combs, 1964; Usher, 1966; Combs *et al.*, 1969; Combs *et al.*, 1971). (ii) These research results were then combined with recent developments in perceptual-humanistic psychology (Rogers, 1959, 1962) to formulate a theory of teacher education (Combs, 1965; Combs *et al.*, 1969). (iii) This theory was given practical expression in an experimental programme designed and placed in operation side by side with a traditional one (Blume, 1971; Wass *et al.*, 1974). (iv) A programme of research was then instituted to provide information concerning the relative effectiveness of the programme (Busby *et al.*, 1970; Wass and Combs, 1973). (v) The experimental programme was adapted by the department and over a two-year period replaced the old programme. It has now been in operation some five years.

More explicitly, CEP at Florida is based on the following principles:

—People do only what they would rather do. That is, people behave according to choices they make from many alternatives they see available to them at the moment.
—Learning has two aspects: (a) acquiring new information and (b) discovering the personal meaning of that information.
—It is more appropriate for people to learn a few concepts rather than many facts.
—Learning is much more efficient if the learner first feels a need to know that which is to be learned.
—No one specific item of information and no specific skill is essential for effective teaching.
—People learn more easily and rapidly if they help make the important decisions about their learning.
—People learn and grow more quickly if they aren't afraid to make mistakes.
—Objectivity is not a valuable asset for a teacher. What is needed instead is concern for students.
—Teachers teach the way they have been taught and not the way they have been taught to teach.
—Pressure on students produces negative behaviors such as cheating, avoidance, fearfulness, etc.
—Teachers are more effective as their mental health improves thus freeing creativity, self-motivation, and concern for others. (Blume, 1971, pp. 411–15)

Students entering this programme participate in three distinctive components—field experience, the seminar, and the substantive panel. In order to awaken people to new challenges, the programme has abolished courses and regularly scheduled classes, replacing them with individual and small group study, closely linked with field work with children.

In the programme, field experience is used as the central means of developing a sense of reality and a discovery of oneself in teaching. There is a continuous often daily involvement in schools for a gradually increasing period of time and an increasingly responsible role in the classroom during each quarter. The graded levels of involvement range from that of tutor, to teacher initiate, teacher-assistant, teacher-associate, and to intensive teaching.

Regular seminars provide a home group for counselling and discussion in a supportive atmosphere with a tutor. A group of thirty students is assigned to a tutor (lecturer) for the duration of the two-year sequence of professional education. The students range from beginners to those who are about to graduate. The thirty students operate in two sub-groups for discussion, two hours per week, usually in an informal setting off-campus. The discussions focus on the personal meaning and self-development aspects derived from the student field experiences and may take the form of group problem-solving or role-playing exercises. Student involvement in these seminars is seen as the best way to help them find 'a personal meaning in experiences', acquire a 'sense of their own beliefs', and develop 'understanding of the feelings and purposes of others'. Students are said to be very motivated by such involvement largely because a 'sense of becoming' is engendered at a very personalized level.

For each group of 120 students there is a 'substantive panel' of 'lecturers' in methods, curriculum and foundation courses. Panel members do not conduct conventional classes; instead they prepare and distribute a list of learning activities which students are to complete. Some of these activities are required of all students, but many are optional, and further, students are encouraged to propose their own substitute activities if they wish. Students pursue the activities when they need them to assist their field experiences. During the progress of the learning activities, panel members act on a consultative basis. Students themselves also plan 'community sessions' where large groups of students are introduced to such things as controversial issues in education and new methods, and are provided with the opportunity of hearing guest speakers.

The programme is also characterized by systematic and continuous evaluation procedures. Self-evaluation of progress and achievements by students is a strong feature of this approach to develop maturity as a professional and as a participant in the teacher education process. However, a mid-point evaluation is undertaken by the seminar leader in consultation with the student and the substantive panel members. A similar evaluation process is undertaken prior to graduation. If the student's work is judged to be less than adequate, he is asked to repeat the assignment until quality results are produced.

A study by Busby *et al.* (1970) comparing students from the new Childhood Education Program and from the original traditional lecture course showed that students in the humanistic programme were significantly more adaptable, secure and sensitive as persons and as teachers. Professional understandings of why, as well as what, the student believes and knows about teaching were also found to be greater. A follow-up study of students in the Florida programme some one or two years later (Wass and Combs, 1973) supported the differences attained behaviourally and perceptually as related to the humanistic approach in teaching.

The work of Combs and others in the sphere of humanistic teacher education has given impetus to other educators. For example, Patterson (1973) claims that teacher education must be more concerned with the development of persons with humanistic beliefs about people and attitudes toward them. It must make it possible for the student to develop an adequate self-concept and it must foster the development of self-actualizing teachers. Teachers cannot be told how to teach humanistically: they can be taught how only by experiencing humanistic teacher education. The pre-practice teaching experiences which are a graded sequence of experiences culminating in practice teaching are ways of assisting students to be concerned with pupils and self-exploration. The practice teaching must also change from its traditional format. It should be similar to the supervised practicum in counselling or psychotherapy and should receive as much attention and support. At present not only are students in practice teaching lacking in a consistent theory of instruction from their teacher education programmes, but also, more basically, they have no theory of human behaviour in or out of the classroom. Patterson further proposes that a continuous seminar or an encounter-group experience is desirable, for through such experiences students come to see themselves as adequate and able, worthy, wanted, and acceptable when they are treated that way in a supportive and facilitating situation. In this way teacher education can work with individuals in developing humanistic or self-actualizing persons.

A plea for humanizing teacher education is also made by Iannone and Carline (1971). To them the 'human' teacher must be an adequate person who is able to facilitate the learning of others. Teacher education must help students dis-cover for themselves their human potential in order that they may realize it in the schools. The programme Iannone and Carline report at West Virginia University is based on learning experience modules that area related to sensitizing the prospective teacher to human and personality development by techniques of group processes and counselling, and human encounter with the community, youngsters and peers. There are four modules: (i) Participation as a continuous activity in an encounter group composed of both elementary and secondary student teachers at varying stages of the programme. Interpersonal skills of sensitivity and communication are fostered in this situation and it is hoped to promote personal and teacher growth through expression of values and feelings. (ii) 'Human encounter' with self, community and youngsters in which students are assigned to a community agency, health or welfare group to work with social workers, counsellors and to share their experiences. Later students may tutor one pupil having difficulties in basic subjects. (iii) Experience with basic teaching skills in which there is an analytical study of teaching and related concepts. The student works with a small group of pupils of different abilities for at least three days a week to co-operatively plan, implement and evaluate group tasks. (iv) Involvement in real teaching during which the student is an associate of a qualified teacher and shares his classroom teaching responsibilities. The programme aims to give the student teacher an opportunity to relate theory to practice, and to search for greater personal understanding of himself and of the learning processes of children.

A group approach to in-service training in which humanistic teacher education concepts are used is reported by Dinkmeyer (1971). The new approach combines access to both affective and cognitive domains, and is labelled the 'C-group' because so many of the components begin with C. For example, they include collaboration, consultation, clarification, confidential discussion, confrontation, communication, concern and commitment. For teachers, who meet in groups of six, there is personal involvement and an opportunity to test new ideas, to see how they fit with one's personality, and to exchange with colleagues the results of new approaches. Using each of the components in successive meetings with a leader trained in group counselling and psychodynamics of behaviour, sensitivity is facilitated so that a helping relationship is established. This scheme was used in a pilot programme at Northeastern College in Chicago and feedback indicated that the C-group method can be a powerful tool in facilitating teacher development.

Other proposals to improve teacher education by emphasizing human relations skills and self-discovery are evident in the preparation of 'human service educators' at Vermont (Durcharme and Nash, 1975). This programme is founded on the belief that the need in the future is for a range of personnel in the 'helping profession'—teacher, counsellor, group organizer, facilitator, social worker—and that helping and human relationships are of crucial importance in our way of life. Buchanan (1971) uses exercises in relaxation, eye contact and tactile contact to develop affective techniques for teaching and 'opening oneself' to pupils. This programme has reportedly changed some students into secure and caring teachers with affective competency in acceptance and appreciation of others.

Halamandaris and Loughton (1972) speak about empathy-competence as a much needed balance to skill-competence in teaching. They claim that personality characteristics of student teachers, such as empathy, openness, maturity and the potential ability to relate to children, peers and/or parents, have been neglected in traditional teacher education programmes. The teacher must be first and foremost the possessor of empathy-competence. Empathy-competence is defined as the ability of the teacher to genuinely consider, as a first priority, the rights, feelings and achievements of the individual pupil and parents in all teaching and community activities. Teacher education programmes must be designed to initiate, support and evaluate the potential empathy-competence of student teachers. To evaluate empathy-competence it is suggested that the student, after completing his internship, should work in a teaching and learning centre in close contact with pupils, a supervisor and peers for an extended period. Supervising staff, the faculty tutor and the student himself should then evaluate his empathy-competence.

The emphasis on competence in the affective domain is also suggested by Cohen and Hersh (1972) who propose a synthesis of behaviourism and humanism for teacher education. This would imply the development of 'behavioural humanism' for teachers in order to focus on pupils. Questions concerning goals, rationale, instructional procedures, and assessment are focal points around which behavioural humanism can be created. A synthesis of concepts concerning objectives in behavioural terms, clarification of behaviour in terms facilitating honest confrontation and discussion of issues, group solidarity and experience, flexible strategies and value clarification are suggested as not incompatible behavioural humanistic components for meeting the needs of student teachers.

Personal experience, greater individualization of instruction and field experience are advocated as essential elements of 'humane teacher education'

(Taylor *et al.*, 1971), and these are integrated in a unique approach reported by Petersen *et al.* (1975). A student-centred, self-directed, school- and community-oriented approach to teacher education is outlined. Its main features include: (i) continuous human relations training; (ii) a focus on self-awareness and the student's commitment to teaching; (iii) student contracting for course work with evaluation based on self-assessment; (iv) student individualizing of the programme in terms of courses and school and community activities; (v) use of student 'facilitators' as classroom assistants; and (vi) regular school experience. Considerable success is reported with this evolving programme at Indiana. It is concluded by Peterson and his team that the programme provides a broad base on which to build a quality teacher education programme because it changes students, relates theory to practice, presents a humane approach, provides early validation of career choice and it incorporates intensive self-direction and self-selection into or out of teaching.

Another example of a humanistic competency-based programme is that described by Battaglini *et al.* (1975) related to science teaching. Elementary science teachers undertake a unified science programme of three sequences. The programme involves individualized and small group work for the completion of a range of learning modules which emphasize process rather than content and of laboratory and outdoor field work based on inquiry. The programme is thus self-paced and performance-based. The modules also include some teaching of children which may be videotaped. A feature of the student's self-discovery in teaching science is the 'personalized' teacher-student relationships which are provided for in the regular counselling with a staff member during evaluation discussions on the modules completed. An effort is made by the staff to build the student's confidence and to facilitate their self-discovery in teaching science in a supportive non-assessment setting. These staff-student encounters are considered to be the main strength of the programme in helping students in turn to establish good relationships with children in their teaching. Feedback from the students and the schools in which they teach has been encouraging and indicates success in terms of both attitudes towards children and teaching and the fostering of inquiry approaches in the teaching of science.

A Personalized Teacher Education Program (PTE) is a feature of the University of Texas approach (Fuller, 1974). In the programme, the student is at the centre of her own education both in her own view and in the view of her 'lecturers'. The teacher educator and student develop a deepening personal relationship through a variety of planned encounters with one another. Both student and teacher educator are engaged in a process of gathering information which the student wants and needs, of becoming aware of the importance of that information, of forming a fruitful relationship, of making choices and of implementing those choices. The programme initially tries to meet the students' first concerns—concerns about self and the teaching task. Counselling sessions are scheduled in which students share feelings and build a team spirit to reduce apprehensions. The processes of instruction are individually tailored to students' needs and take place through reading, discussion and a variety of other resources and practical experiences.

Personalized instruction is also the theme of an educational psychology programme at Northwestern University (Menges and McGaghie, 1974). Personalized instruction in the form of mastery learning techniques is used to teach the principles of operant psychology. Students choose a wide variety of behaviours, such as interpersonal behaviours or communication, and apply these principles in their own self-modification projects. The method provides a humanistically acceptable way of teaching and applying behavioural psychology. It provides pre-service teachers with an opportunity to experience behaviour modification 'from the inside' and this sensitizes them to its use with children in their classrooms. Instructors prepare mastery materials and act as consultants and facilitators on student projects. Research is being conducted on the self-modification projects in relation to the personality and ability characteristics of the student teachers.

With respect to the personality characteristics of student teachers, the ability to provide warm positive relationships with children was the subject of a study by Bown and Richek (1969). The study demonstrated that the prospective teacher who is introverted perceives her world less positively than a colleague who is extroverted. Negative percepters may render the introvert to be less likely to form warm positive relationships with children. It is suggested that introverted elementary teachers may be more suited to assignment to certain teaching roles than for others; for example with older children rather than the younger children. Further investigation is proceeding with this idea by Richek.

Giving student teachers a strong personal control over their environment and their learning is a central belief of the Project Change scheme, operating for master's level teacher education students at the State University College, Cortland, New York (Lickona, 1973). It is reasoned that teachers too should be active learners, pooling their resources, experimenting and creating, making choices and taking a good deal of responsibility for their own learning. If teachers feel that they can make an impact on their environment, that they have within themselves the resources for success, then change and modification of behaviour for new teaching approaches can be achieved. The programme structure, however, must create the conditions under which teachers develop a different view of themselves and their profession. The programme must facilitate learning and support students in every way. At Cortland this is achieved by having the student teachers themselves direct and select modules for knowledge and behavioural competencies emphasizing child-oriented teaching and change projects in the schools. There is the expectation that the students will share the responsibility for developing a good teacher education programme. The result is honest feedback, a flow of concrete suggestions for improvement and an atmosphere of equality and mutual respect and support. An evaluation of the project's 'person-centred approach' to performance-based teacher education has shown the achievement of a greater degree of openness in the classroom teaching style of the teachers compared to that of teachers in the traditional programme at the college.

The humanistic approach to the preparation of teachers is gathering momentum in many spheres. One common belief seems to be that student teachers need to experience for themselves the kind of teaching that it is hoped they in turn will implement; that is, teaching which basically has a strong personal concern for the individual. Facilitative interpersonal relationships between teacher and pupils are needed in new styles of teaching which emphasize small group teaching, individualized instruction and open education. To create such relationships teachers need to be autonomous, sensitive, thinking and compassionate persons. Only a facilitative supportive relationship frees the student teacher to develop this way. A climate of trust, recognition and acceptance must be created and this is the major condition of humanistic education. The emphasis on experience to ascertain the need to know about teaching and the development of competencies in interpersonal relationships are commendable features of the teacher education programmes outlined. In such instances they should do much to blend theory and practice for relating to children and to promote an inquiry process of learning which fosters the individual's development as an active thinking person. In all, such new programmes seek to meet the need to prepare teachers who can cope with more informal teaching styles, who can change and adapt to future changes in education, and who can focus on the child as a first priority.

RENOVATION OF PRACTICE TEACHING

Even the strongest critics of current teacher education programmes have generally conceded that student teaching is a desirable, if faulty, part of such programmes. Furthermore, surveys have indicated that most teachers perceive teaching practice as that part of their preparation that was of most value (Cope, 1971; Lomax, 1973). A look at the research and innovation literature, however, raises many questions concerning definitions of terms, the underlying theory and the establishing of objectives for teaching practice. Above all, the question of effectiveness is a major issue largely unanswered.

A Need for Definition

Emerging concepts of teaching practice seem to range over a wide variety of experiences, some old, others new. There is a need for clearer definitions in the area which may sharpen both the underlying theory and the establishing of more definite objectives for such components. The use of the word *practicum* as a generic term to encompass many subsidiary components is suggested in view of the differing interpretations of such terms as clinical experience, student teaching, in-school experience, teaching rounds, field experience and micro-teaching. As suggested by Thew (1976), the practicum refers to that body of professional experiences during which the student applies, tests and reconstructs the theory which he is evolving, and during which he further develops his own competence as a teacher. The possible elements of the practicum may be classified as follows:

1. *Teaching Practice*

a. *Block Teaching Practice* which provides an opportunity for the student to assume a major responsibility for the full range of teaching duties in a real situation, under the guidance of qualified personnel from the teacher education institution and from the co-operating school. It is based on learning experiences included in all other professional studies but is not a substitute for them. The block teaching practice usually refers to a period of teaching and related activities in a school which involve placement for two or more weeks.

b. *Internship* is an extended period of placement in the school with complete responsibility for the teaching of pupils but with a limited or lesser work load than that for a full qualified teacher. The internship requires also continuing regular contact and liaison with the training institution for the satisfactory completion of final attainments for a teaching qualification.

c. *Continuous Teaching Practice* provides an opportunity for the student to engage in regular teaching tasks for a period of half day, one day, or two days per week such as in schemes of school attachment or day-release involvement in schools.

2. *Skills Acquisition*
This may be achieved by experiences which are programmed specifically to modify and improve teaching behaviours. Such experiences may include microteaching, simulations, competency-based modules, interaction analysis, situational teaching and the like, and may take place in the teacher education institution or in a school.

3. *Field Experiences*
These are scheduled activities involving students in contact with children, teachers and other adults in a variety of instructional tasks. They may include:

a. observations—child study, demonstrations, excursions.
b. helping—as teaching aides, welfare aides.
c. tutoring children, adults (e.g. literacy projects).
d. community projects—leisure centres, play centres, latch-key clubs.
e. exchange experiences (interstate; rural/urban; international). (Thew, 1976)

Flaws of the practicum

The rationale for such a range of practicum experiences as outlined above generally is that prospective teachers need frequent contacts with school environments and other community situations so that their theoretical understanding and teaching competence grow hand in hand. It is assumed also that school personnel share with the staff of colleges and universities a common purpose and interest in teacher education and that a working partnership recognizing a shared frame of reference is essential in developing the professional responsibilities of student teachers. Yet evidence often points to a contrary situation existing between colleges and the schools. Eggleston (1974), in commenting on the situation in the United Kingdom, described the profession's view of it as follows:

> Allegedly the student arrives in the school full of college-inspired faith in the individual goodness, and creativity of children with fanciful lesson plans suggested by lecturers who have not taught for many years, devoid of knowledge of how to control the turbulent and restive oversized classes and supervised by an unknown tutor. . . . In such circumstances the student is in a double bind. Not only is his faith in the credibility of the college shattered by the school staff, he is also overwhelmed by their enthusiasm to help him to 'really get to know the job'. Teaching practice becomes an undercover initiation into an alternative style of teaching unrelated to the work of the college. Problems may indeed arise when the college assessment takes place but the school staff are loyal to their student and conspire with him to put on the sort of show that can be relied upon to satisfy the college. (p. 97)

Also, commenting on the English pattern, Logan (1971) claims that teaching practice is seen as a distinct and separate compartment of teacher education activity in which the objective is to survive the rigours of work on a day-to-day basis. Teaching practice gives many students the view that it is their own personal qualities which are central to their success as a teacher and that the course is only marginally helping to develop these qualities. The whole course in a college of education is in itself seen as an initial and encapsulated pre-employment experience, the real skills of teaching are to be learnt 'on the job'.

It has been argued also that a great deal of dissatisfaction exists concerning the organization and evaluation of practical experience in pre-service training (Lewis, 1975) and that in spite of a detailed criticism of weaknesses of conventional approaches, block teaching practice is still the most common practical experience of students in training. As a learning situation, teaching practice often fails to meet even the most rudimentary set of objectives. Nevertheless students paradoxically demonstrate a high degree of satisfaction with such experience (Cope, 1971).

In general, the major defects of many teacher education programmes, as seen by those who have been or are being trained, are the lack of concentration on practical preparation for the future job, coupled with the enormous emphasis on academic studies which are seen to have little relevance to immediate classroom concerns. Even when teaching practice is emphasized, many factors mar its effectiveness. It is clear from Cope's studies (1971) that the major factors preventing school experience from being an effective learning situation for students are institutional. She cites the major flaws which characterize the organization of teaching practice as: (i) lack of functional liaison between school and college staff; (ii) complex and only partially acknowledged role and human relationship problems; and (iii) considerable uncertainty as to the purpose and effectiveness of supervisory visits. The factors which inhibit the learning potential of school experience are well within the control of those involved. If classroom experience is to become a useful learning experience to complement and extend the learning which has taken place in the abstract world of the institution, then it is the situation in which this takes place that must be remedied. Functional school-college co-operation must be developed, and at the institutional level criteria for introducing or maintaining' courses must take into account their direct relationships to classroom performance. The problems of teaching then must be the prime focus of interest.

The concentration in courses and in the practicum could well be upon the investigation of the range of ideas, approaches, methods and materials which might be considered appropriate to specific pupils' learning, rather than the simplistic, often irrelevant, approach of conventional courses and teaching practice where either college schemes are produced without reference to the classrooms in which they will be implemented, or where students merely take over the teacher's standard pattern of working (Lewis, 1975). The practice teaching situation should become one of shared learning and personal interaction, rather than an assessment of the acquisition of prescribed behaviour patterns. In this way what is learned will be the result of co-operative analysis of the events in a particular classroom and the needs of a specific group of children. Provided such programmes of experiences are related to essential areas of the curriculum (e.g. reading and maths) in order to give concentration of emphasis and to minimize diffuseness of outlook, there is every reason to suppose that school-based experience can form an essential and highly valuable central component of initial training courses. These experiences, supplemented by in-college skill-based approaches like microteaching, and detailed exploration and discussion of curriculum material and teaching strategies, should combine to ensure that if teaching practice does take place, students will be able to acquire a range of practical skills on the performances of which they can be effectively evaluated.

Borg (1975) maintains that student teaching seems to have failed in most traditional programmes for three main reasons: First, the student teacher typically does not focus on specific teaching skills, but rather is thrust into the classroom and attempts to develop some procedure which would get him through the day. Secondly, the student has no effective model to emulate. Although many supervising teachers are competent they have usually learned whatever skills they have by trial and error and are often unaware of the specific nature of the skills they have developed. The student teacher typically sees a mixture of good and bad teaching procedures modelled by the supervising teacher and receives little or no guidance as to what is happening or why. Thirdly, the student teacher receives little specific feedback on his performance that he can translate into specific changes in his teaching behaviour. The college supervisor has usually been the source of feedback, and this rarely focuses on specific skills that the student teacher can apply in the classroom. A number of studies have demonstrated that typical supervisory feedback has little or no effect upon the behaviour of the student teacher. Indeed, one study by Tuckman and Oliver (1968) actually found supervisory feedback to have a negative effect on student teacher performance.

Objectives of the Practicum

At the moment school practice fulfils diffuse purposes and provides for wide but undifferentiated learning experiences. The result is that students have difficulty in realizing and coming to terms with their school-practice role. Cope (1971) indicates that students attach much importance to the opportunities practice provides for their personal adjustment to the demands of the teaching role. The adequate performance of the teacher's role requires, however, not only opportunity to practise it in realistic situations; it requires the acquisition by the students of specific skills and techniques, the willingness to subject behaviours to critical appraisal, and the capacity to analyse a task and adopt the most appropriate procedures. This kind of learning might be accelerated by providing different kinds of practice experience, conducted through different approaches and at a different pace. Such activities might include all elements of the practicum as outlined, but it seems essential that each element is systematically planned and carefully supervised and yields meaningful feedback to the student. The need for carefully graded and structured activities is implied (Thew, 1976).

Views on the objectives of the practicum are varied and often vague. In some programmes they are non-existent. Cope (1971) and McFarlane (1973) suggest the following:

(i) The enhancement of the self-concept so that the student may make an easier adjustment to the new role.

(ii) The provision of a basis for the realization of real needs in teaching which will become a basis for later learning.

(iii) The development of commitment to teaching and attitudes of open-mindedness and flexibility.

(iv) The opportunity to apply prior theoretical learning in real situations.

(v) The opportunity to develop skills in interpersonal relations, teaching and class conduct.

Barnett (1975) maintains that practice should extend beyond a training for survival; it should offer student teachers the opportunity to exercise their creativity as well as their adaptability. To prepare lessons for the 'what is' without experience in the 'what ought to be' would be a misuse of the responsibilities of teacher preparation. A plan in which teacher education students can become involved in on-going attempts to restructure children's learning environments is needed to provide students with the opportunity to bridge the gap between what is and what ought to be.

In analysis of the planning of student teachers' practical experiences, Smith and Sagan (1975) propose that a structured format for experiences could do much to eliminate redundancies and improve the quality of experiential teacher education. They believe that becoming a teacher involves sequentially the processes of role orientation, role conceptualization, role learning and commitment, role assumption and role evaluation in which the student needs continuously to build concepts and generalizations and to test them out through analysis of teaching in real and simulated situations. Progression through these processes provides students with a logical unfolding of professional development with appropriate graduated levels of practical experience at each stage of the teacher education programme. Continuous and graduated experiences gradually initiate the student into role assumption and finally evaluation. This longitudinal progression, it is claimed, would ensure the education of the teacher who can truly relate to the needs of the children and school.

Similar sequences of practical experiences may be devised by using the elements of the practicum outlined earlier. Each element has specific objects and could be combined into a developmental approach. Teaching practice specifically seeks to provide direct substantial participation in a full range of teaching duties in the real school and classroom environment. Skills acquisition is concerned with more specific learning of particular behaviours in order to adopt an analytical approach to teaching so that the student may modify and improve teaching performance. Simulated, modelled and real situations may play a part in such acquisitions. The objective of various field experiences is basically to develop awareness of concepts and needs and to provide familiarization with many instructional tasks, settings and issues. These elements, used in appropriate combinations, could produce a graded and sequential range of activities to provide more specific practical components for role-development in teacher education programmes.

General Effectiveness of the Practicum

Students seem to find school practice a highly valued learning experience. From a sample of 322 students in England, 95 per cent felt that they learned a great deal or a reasonable amount from it, and only 5 per cent felt they learned little or nothing. No doubt a deal of the learning is negative, as on three specific questions 32 per cent of the sample felt that the class teacher contributed very little or nothing to their learning; 34 per cent of students felt they learned little or nothing from the visits of general supervisors; and 42 per cent felt they learned little or nothing from the visits of education lecturers (Cope, 1971).

A number of studies carried out during the 1960s attempted through observations at the beginning and end of student teaching practice to determine some of the changes that took place in the student teacher as a result of that experience. With very few exceptions, these studies present a depressing picture of the typical effects of student teaching. For example, a number of studies, including those of Jacobs (1967), Osmon (1959), Gewinner (1968) and Muuss (1969), found that student teachers actually became significantly more authoritarian as a result of student teaching even though most programmes attempted to achieve the opposite result. Walberg *et al.* (1958) found that student teachers became more control-oriented and less pupil-centred as they progressed through their student teaching experience. Matthews (1969) carried out a longitudinal study of 52 student teachers and found that by the end of student teaching they had become more restrictive of pupil behaviour, they spent more time stating facts, they showed less acceptance of pupil ideas and that the length of pupil responses in their classrooms became progressively shorter. Hoy (1968) observed that during practice teaching students became more 'custodial' when confronted with the realities of teaching problems. An interesting study by Burge (1967) looked at the effects of traditional student teaching experience on the classroom behaviour of students as measured by the Flanders Interaction Analysis System. The student teachers were *not* instructed to try to teach in the desired style represented by Flanders' system. The consequence was that they showed no change during their student teaching on any of Flanders' dimensions.

The effects of practice teaching on students' educational views has been investigated. In studies undertaken at Kansas State University (Weinstock and Peccolo, 1970), 156 students preparing to teach elementary level and secondary school subjects were compared on how consistently they held to their ideas about education before and after student teaching. Students were classified on a Logical Consistency Scale and compared on the basis of their philosophical position in education—humanistic, scientific, vocational. The students as a group were shown to retain theoretical aspects of educational points of view where they were of a more practical nature. Students of either a humanistic or scientific academic point of view retained their set of accepted views about desirable teaching practices to a higher degree than did students of a vocational point of view. Students preparing to teach in the elementary school were superior to those preparing to teach in the secondary school in retaining their views about desirable teaching practices and were more logical in their ideas about education. The researchers suggest the relationship between logical consistency of ideas about education and the maintenance of desirable attitudes towards teaching should be of particular concern in the preparation of secondary student teachers. With respect to changes in students' views, Hussell and Smithers (1974) noted that students became more tough-minded and increased in dogmatism during college experience and practice teaching.

Research has also revealed a degree of personal shock encountered by students during their teaching practice. Iannaccone (1963) analysed the daily logs of 25 students written during student teaching and found that 24 of the 25 students initially expressed shock and horror at the 'incorrect' methods employed by their co-operating teachers, but that, when faced with the task themselves, they too began to use formerly unacceptable methods. Their logs tended to justify their actions on the basis of the fact that 'it works'. Their original expressed concern for individuals was also replaced by a concern for 'getting the class through the lesson'. Petrusich (1969) reported that some student teachers suffer tremendous 'ego-shattering' experiences in practice teaching. Other reports of psychological discomfort and anxiety have been made by Sorenson and Halpert (1968). Cope's study (1971) indicates that the students' concern during practice teaching is with the adjustment of their personality to the demands of the new role of student teacher, but nevertheless 71 per cent reported that they enjoyed practice teaching because of relationships with pupils and school staff. Their frustrations stemmed from acceptance of authority of other teachers, their student versus teacher status and the shortness of the practice period.

Despite the apparent trauma, students derive satisfaction from practice teaching. In a study by Poole and Gaudry (1974), students perceived the most satisfying aspect of practice to be their experience of encouraging and satisfying pupil response and of overcoming difficulties with discipline. Relationships with the supervising teacher or support from the school staff and university staff were seen as less important factors of satisfaction. However, those who felt they had learnt a lot from teaching practice tended to be those who had been given close supervision and good facilities in the school, in addition to getting a good response from the pupils.

Opinions vary on how practice teaching may be improved. As a result of a survey of experienced teachers on ways of improving student practice teaching, Johnson (1967) makes a strong recommendation for more and larger periods of contact with children, the combining of methods courses with student teaching, the provision of observations of 'master teachers' both before and after student teaching, and the inclusion of a wide variety of teaching situations at different grade levels. Other ideas frequently recommended were team teaching, laboratory experiences to screen out students unsuited to teaching, more experience with resources and teaching materials and less emphasis on a teaching grade for student teaching. Deiseach (1974) proposes an elaborately graded involvement of students with children to phase them into full practice teaching and to provide for a more individualized approach which he calls 'custom-tailoring', to meet the students' specific needs. There is a substantial amount of evidence that specifying objectives and planning the student teaching experiences accordingly are required. Many methods for 'phasing in' students to the class-room are currently being developed.

Range of Practicum Experiences

The reaction to new demands for change in current procedures of student teaching has resulted in the development of various experiences to initiate the aspiring teacher into the classroom, and to attempt to solve the problems of relevance, competency and substantive content. The problem is not in the amount of theoretical training but rather how to facilitate the operational use of these concepts. One answer to the problem may be in professional field experiences where concepts, generalizations and theories emphasized in pro-fessional courses are evaluated with respect to their relevance and usefulness in the real situation (Smith and Sagan, 1975). A well-balanced programme should be able to blend the theoretical and experiential to make theoretical knowledge more functional for prospective teachers. At the same time, however, a new school-college relationship in the preparation of teachers is required— one which shares a common orientation to the rationale and a depth of involve-ment in providing graduated experiences articulated with the professional programme.

Many sequences of practical experiences have been suggested as appropriate. For example, the Asian Institute for Teacher Educators (1972) in a report of a sub-regional workshop on experiences for integrating theory and practice in teacher education, suggested a classification for direct and indirect experiences. Direct experiences included child study, school study, community study, leadership experiences in school and community, observation of classroom teaching, and student teaching experiences in laboratory and co-operating schools. In particular, it was recommended that

> Student teachers should be introduced to teaching practice through carefully graded steps and under guidance. They should proceed from:
> (1) individual teaching, through small groups to entire class units;
> (2) from brief periods of teaching experiences to progressively larger ones; and
> (3) from simulation techniques to real life situations. (p. 9)

The report also advocated team teaching experiences, extended periods of full responsibility, and internships. Among the indirect experiences recommended were simulated teaching situations, microteaching to improve specific skills, preparing instructional materials, and planning various teaching strategies. The clearly stated objectives for each of the experiences recommended is a particularly valuable contribution to understanding the whole range of practicum possibilities. A somewhat similar classification of experience is outlined by Lee (1972) as either school-based techniques and college-based techniques. An additional concept suggested is the use of a resident class at the college for four to six weeks for both observation and controlled teaching exercises by the students. This activity he observed in operation at Queen's University, Kingston, Canada.

The argument for a variety of practical experiences is also supported by the findings of Cope (1971). Out of a sample of 158 students in 1968 and 159 students in 1969, 80 per cent and 84 per cent, respectively, indicated they wanted more than one type of practical activity. Varied and flexible practice arrangements to meet varied student needs is advocated but such variations demand (i) a clear specification of objectives to indicate specific learning goals, and (ii) some designation of the kinds of supervisory behaviours required.

A pattern of differentiated field experiences is a major component of the teacher education programme at the University of Florida, Gainesville (Blume, 1971; Wass *et al.*, 1974). Field experience is a continuous part of the programme, with students actively involved in responsible roles in schools in each quarter. The levels of involvement and expectation of students include:

(i) *Tutor*, who helps children on a one-to-one basis, becomes familiar with classroom procedures, and explores relationships with children.

(ii) *Teacher-initiate*, who helps the teacher with supervision of small groups, helps individuals, and assists with routine tasks.

(iii) *Teacher-assistant*, who in addition to previous tasks is expected to help evaluate the work of children and to plan and implement lessons with small groups.

(iv) *Teacher-associate*, who plans and implements a series of lessons for a full class.

(v) '*Teacher*', who, during the final stage of 'intensive teaching', undertakes the full role of the teacher in all its aspects for a block period of five weeks.

The idea of involving students in schools as early in their programme as possible is being pursued in a number of institutions. The Indian Teacher Education Program at the University of Saskatchewan engages students in five weeks practice teaching in each of the five semesters of the programme (Barnett and Aldous, 1973). A similar programme at the University of British Columbia involves students in practice teaching and on-site educational background courses of one or two weeks during the first two years of the programme (Dean's Committee on a Native Teacher Training Program, 1974). The Winnipeg Center Project, a teacher education programme designed to provide for low-income and inner-city groups, also places students in practice teaching situations in each year of the programme (Deines, 1973). Such early experiences with schools and children enable student teachers to see a more meaningful relation-ship between their coursework and actual teaching situations, and to make informed decisions about teaching as a career. It also enables school personnel and tertiary staff faculty to better assess the potential abilities of student teachers over a longer period of time (Barnett, 1975).

Early practical experience for student teachers by working as a teacher's aide is increasingly being tried. In an evaluation of such a scheme at Dalhousie University, Halifax, 66 per cent of students rated the experience as excellent, good or of some value and 82 per cent of the teachers indicated that they would like the scheme to continue (Engel, 1975). In this project an attempt was made to match the teachers' requests with the students' requests with respect to particular type of aide ranging from clerical duties to instructional support on a contract basis. Harp (1974) reports the success of an aide project to help students in their first year to gain confidence in working with children and to develop an instructional programme related to study periods and playground activities. As compared to a control group, the students showed a significantly greater development in maturity and a change in concern from self-survival towards that of pupil-centred teaching. At Grand Valley State College, Michigan, (De Long, 1971) an observation, teacher-aide, student teaching sequence is followed. The teacher-aide programme of ten weeks is presented on a pass or fail basis and no student continues into student teaching without a written endorsement from the school administration and college instructor involved. As an aide, the student may assist in a wide range of school activities from outdoor education projects and field trips to assisting teachers at the grade level in which they wish to teach. The students endorse the programme for the variety of experiences which provide opportunity to explore personally many facets of the school. The student can also discover the classroom environment in which he feels he can most effectively function and the prolonged contact with the schools tends to make teacher education and methods courses more meaningful.

Quite a number of programmes have an internship as an important practical experience. One example, the Portland Urban Teacher Education Project (Parker and Withycombe, 1973), is a twelve-month, field-based intern programme to prepare teachers to be successful in inner-city schools and to meet the needs of student teachers. On the basis that the students' background is incongruent with the school with respect to race, culture, wealth and attitude, the programme aims to help individuals cope with disparities. Group seminars which aim to provide open communication and support to the student in his teaching while coping with sources of conflict, are a feature of this intern pro-gramme. Another internship specifically aimed to help prepare teachers for the inner-city elementary schools is that at Wayne State University (Stewart and Hart, 1972). The one year internship is at four-fifths of the beginning teacher's salary and interns are contracted for one year to the school system.

The internship is supervised by an experienced teacher-consultant released full-time for this purpose. The school system has retained 85 per cent of the interns from this programme.

Pre-student teaching laboratory experience is another feature of differentiated practical work. The experiences are generally designed to prepare the student for practice teaching. They are often linked closely with methods courses and studies in education or psychology, are undertaken in a co-operating school, take into account students' individual needs, and are supervised by school and/or tertiary staff. The experiences typically include such activities as studying children individually and in groups, examining and developing curriculum materials, studying and constructing learning units, helping children with specific learning tasks, exploring community resources, and participating in staff meetings and meetings with parents. Many of these experiences have become learning activities embodied in the modules used for competency-based teacher education.

In the area of pre-student teaching laboratory experiences, Price (1972) of Michigan State University reports the use of a 'clinical-cluster' programme in which the teacher from the host school, the university lecturer and ten to twelve students all make up a cluster with the teacher and lecturer acting as clinical consultants. Each student has an individualized programme of laboratory experience carefully planned in sequence to meet his needs. The students share their common concerns and assist each other. Such experiences are claimed to be broader, more interesting, flexible and highly individualized in meeting the strengths and weaknesses of the student. Mayfield (1973) made an evaluation of a sequence of pre-teaching field experiences and of extended laboratory experience programmes for students majoring in elementary or secondary education. The findings revealed that students valued highly the preliminary laboratory experiences and that students developed positive attitudes and greater commitment to teaching from their experiences with children. A study by Copeland (1973), however, casts some doubts on the assumption that laboratory training designed to foster certain teaching skills will result in an increased use of the skills in the classroom after the close of the training. Nevertheless, studies by Huber and Ward (1969), Belt (1969) and Goodkind (1968) have all reported that students gained considerably in confidence from their participation in laboratory skills training.

One outcome of laboratory experiences in teaching has been the production of materials which simulate teaching incidents, provide for role-playing techniques, and develop case studies for intensive discussion (Keach, 1966; Cruickshank, 1967; Kersh, 1965; Twelker, 1968; and Shaftel and Shaftel, 1967). More will be said of simulation in a subsequent section.

Work experience in the community is another form of student practical involvement. Blomgren and Juergenson (1972) report the success of placing student teachers (pursuing studies in such areas as home economics, agriculture, industrial education and business) in relevant work stations for college credit. Through the programme the teachers gained insight into the problems encountered by their pupils when they leave school and enter the job world. Campus meetings, pre and post self-evaluation, and the submission of a weekly report plus other assignments enabled the students to critically examine their own programmes in relation to job training and opportunities. The programme was supervised by a course co-ordinator who both served as liaison officer for the university and provided support for the students. Koontz and Maddox (1972) report the placement of student teachers at 'Job Corps Centers'. Such centres offer career training programmes for jobs available in particular locations. Most training programmes are fairly individualized and self-paced for the applicants who may be trained in auto-mechanics, forestry work, electronics, and so on. Evaluations have shown that student teachers gain in confidence and awareness of instructional problems.

One note of warning concerning the administrative pitfalls of experiential learning off-campus is given by Hogle (1974) who identifies five issues to be resolved: (i) faculty attitudes and participation; (ii) cost and funding; (iii) administrative procedures; (iv) transport facilities; and (v) community co-operation. He agrees with Eberly (1969) and Cullinan (1969) that an effective off-campus learning programme requires one or more full-time persons to administer it. As a consequence the 'Center for Experiential Education' at Indiana University has a full-time co-ordinator who provides greater unity and continuity to the various components of the field-based programmes. The centre is involved in maintaining open and friendly communications with schools and agencies, co-ordinating the evaluation of particular programmes, providing adequate supervision, arranging transport, planning programme development, and seeking ways of meeting the needs of staff and students and of school and community personnel.

In all, there seems to be much valuable learning to be derived from a wide range of practical experiences in teacher education. The contribution to students' confidence and growing commitment to teaching are significant products of these activities.

College-School Relationships and the Practicum

The need for close, meaningful, co-operative relationships between teacher education institutions and schools is generally recognized as indispensable for the development of effective practical experiences for students. Some institutions have looked to the special laboratory school as providing a close working relationship, but generally relationships with a large number of co-operating schools is a problem which besets many institutions for most of the time. Begging for places for student teaching practice periods is often an unfavourable basis for a working relationship. The Plowden Report (1967) examined the problems of school-college relationships in the United Kingdom and stated that the evidence presented to their investigation revealed that half the school principals considered that students were adequately prepared by colleges; over one-third disagreed. Some criticisms were made that the students receive too little help and that some college lecturers are considered to lack up-to-date knowledge and experience of primary work. 'Our main conclusion from these criticisms', the report read, 'is that colleges and schools need to be brought into closer contact and to understand one another better' (p. 344). The conflict of values and approaches to teaching which frequently exists between the colleges and the schools has adversely affected practice teaching. In some instances hostility and mistrust add to the dichotomy of theory versus practice. Visiting supervisors who have continuing commitments to college courses have little opportunity for good functional liaison between school and college staffs which Lewis (1975) sees as essential. Studies by Cope (1971) report discussions with class teachers and head teachers which reveal that while contacts with the colleges were socially pleasant, they did not constitute genuine working partnerships. For example, teachers mentioned that they knew nothing of the students' courses prior to school practice and principals remarked that they had no real liaison with the college. It seems that teachers did not have a clear understanding of what the college expected of them during practice, and 65 per cent of supervisors and 75 per cent of students agreed that this was the case. Teachers had little sense of responsibility for the students' work and only 14 per cent expressed satisfaction from guiding and helping a student. Cope concluded that, while colleges remained aloof from schools and used, as supervisors, academic personnel not qualified or experienced in supervision of students at particular school levels, there is a situation of tension and suspicion where communication is garbled and confused and energy dissipated.

The attitude of the schools to teacher education is frequently poor. A survey by Griffiths and Moore (1967) of twenty school principals revealed that 'the majority of schools regard teacher training as peripheral to their main tasks, they are not structured in such a way as to contribute systematically to the process, nor are the teachers trained in the specialist role of supervisors' (pp. 38–9). The investigation indicated also that no school had ever had a staff meeting on practice teaching and that the principals were lukewarm on the issue of liaison, claiming that although co-operation might be good on an individual level, it broke down at a higher level. The principals were critical of supervision by college staff considering it to be inadequate. Criteria for judgements of students were not explicit. The majority of the principals also considered that college courses produced 'unrealistic teaching' but they admitted no detailed knowledge of the theoretical content of these courses. Although school practice was regarded as essential there was little agreement as to the factors which bring about student improvement.

To help overcome some of the problems in achieving a college-school partnership in teacher education, the Asian Institute for Teacher Educators report (1972) proposed the setting up of teaching centres as a shared facility in co-operating schools. Each centre would provide a site for meetings between school and college staff and the student teachers in pre-teaching and post-teaching conferences, for evolving criteria for evaluating student teaching, and for giving the student teachers help and guidance; the teaching centre could also facilitate research and experimentation. In addition to conference rooms and offices, each centre would have a library and other professional resources.

The role of the co-operating teacher in the practicum needs greater attention. Lawther (1968) noted in his survey of 250 students that they wanted not only more effective performance evaluation and feedback from supervising teachers but they also wanted a professional relationship to be established with the teacher which would include a generous amount of trust, support, understanding and consideration. Trimmer (1961) revealed that student teachers desire their co-operating teacher to (i) permit them freedom to plan and execute what is going to take place in the classroom, (ii) hold regular discussions with the student teacher, (iii) make suggestions about methods and materials, (iv) know his subject matter thoroughly, and (v) be helpful, co-operative and provide constructive criticism. Garner (1971) also reported a study to identify the role and expectations of co-operating teachers. The investigation revealed that the most desired personal qualities of co-operating teachers are those concerned with 'democratic human relations'—the ability to establish a good interpersonal relationship with students based on friendliness, encouragement, concern, interest and helpful suggestions. Garner stressed that an effective co-operating teacher must be alert to the student's emotional needs for security, recognition and understanding, and that an effective learning environment for the student teacher will not exist when the co-operating teacher exhibits poor human relations.

A study by Beckett (1968) was conducted to determine the degree of consensus among co-operating teachers concerning their role. They perceived their role to be that of helping the student to apply himself to his teaching, and facilitating through suggestion, observation and critique the student's productive participation in a variety of activities. Vasberg (1970) surveyed the problems of 430 co-operating teachers in secondary schools and located the following main areas of concern: orienting student teachers to the school, helping them to understand adolescents, and planning and the evaluating of student teachers' work. In particular, the teachers identified the major professional problems as being helping the student teacher (i) earn the respect and confidence of the pupils; (ii) provide for individual differences; (iii) motivate the pupils; (iv) diagnose pupil difficulties; (v) involve all the pupils; and (vi) carry out long-range planning.

What does seem lacking in these perceptions of the role of the co-operating teacher is the opportunity for him to contribute directly in teacher education courses. In one innovative practice programme, a small group, consisting of a teacher, lecturer and four students, was given the opportunity of planning and carrying out their own pattern of working over a full academic year. Results indicated that students, teachers and lecturers could work co-operatively together for each other's advantage (Lewis, 1974). The teachers felt that their professional knowledge was being put to good use for the first time in connection with training. They felt that being directly involved rather than passive recipients of college decisions enabled them to become active partners in the training enterprise. Lecturers and students also reported value in the extensive practical involvement which linked theory with practice in a specific practice situation. The net result of the evaluation was to suggest that similar patterns of co-operative-autonomous working would be a valuable addition to courses.

In order to achieve a close special relationship with schools, some colleges have developed what are known as portal schools. Such schools volunteer, or are selected on the understanding that the co-operation will be extensive, intensive and continuous. These schools are often located in depressed low-income areas and the belief is that, if training is effectively conducted in difficult schools, then the students will be equipped for all other teaching situations. Portal schools expect to have large numbers of students and their lecturers about continuously because the basic overriding principle is that the education of both college students and school pupils will benefit. Teachers and lecturers co-operate in supervising teaching and in methods classes at the school. The portal school encourages realism in teacher education and brings together tertiary staff and teachers, thus facilitating in-service as well as pre-service education (Evans, 1975).

The Temple University Experimental Program for Inner-City Teachers is an example of the portal school concept. In this programme, methods courses are taught to undergraduates in selected elementary schools in Philadelphia. The teachers receive in-service instruction as credits towards a master's degree through their participation in the programme. University instructors work closely with teachers in providing course instruction that relates to and follows up students' classroom activity in which the undergraduates participate. Materials from university and school are shared in conducting the programme. Other portal schools are in operation at Florida State University, Atlanta University, University of Toledo and University of Georgia (Portal Schools, 1972).

On a narrower front, Knight and Wayne (1970) reported a co-operative programme between schools and a university in which both students and teachers were engaged jointly in a specific school-based experience and seminars related to the development of pupils' critical thinking and to the most appropriate teaching strategies to achieve this. Both students and teachers reacted very favourably to the joint venture. The teachers found the partnership with the university very worthwhile and the students valued the realism of the programme in the schools. The programme enabled ideas to be shared in devising valuable programmes for both student teachers and the pupils. The co-operating teachers seemed to be convinced of the need for a continuing partnership.

To establish a working partnership between teacher education institutions and schools, a considerable effort must be made to achieve effective liaison and communication of objectives so that all participants have a shared frame of reference to the task and to their role in it. Other activities which contribute to building and maintaining a co-operative relationship include the development of in-service opportunities for teachers which complement the in-school activities of the students; joint curriculum planning committees; and collaborative research and development. It seems clear from the evidence that a true partnership is needed, and, when it is achieved, there is mutual benefit for students, pupils, teachers and lecturers. Much more will be said of co-operating relationships with schools in Chapter 4.

Supervision of the Practicum

Perhaps the greatest shortcoming of teaching practice lies in the supervision of the student's work with a class. Just when the new student teacher is faced with a class and a curriculum to be implemented, the institution often abandons him precisely at the time he is in need of help. College lecturers in England have expressed their disquiet at the limited time spent with students compared with the length of time spent travelling from school to school. Principals also have regretted the brevity and infrequency of supervisory visits (Cope, 1971). Because of the expansion of student numbers and the need to utilize schools at considerable distances from the colleges, school practice supervision is becoming increasingly expensive both in financial terms and in terms of energy expended.

The factors which militate against the efficacy of supervision are complex. In many cases they can be attributed to the irreconcilable demands on supervisors' time and the organizational arrangements which dictate that often lecturers will be supervising unknown students in unknown schools. In a minority of cases they can be attributed to a particular supervisor's lack of relevant experience. These problems inevitably restrict the extent of the supervisor's contribution within present practice arrangements and, in addition, add to the fundamental problem of dichotomy between the college and school (Cope, 1971).

The system of supervision widely used in England in relation to block teaching practice is expensive in terms of money, time and energy and is relatively ineffective in terms of giving the right kind of help students need and at the time they need it (Tibble, 1971). The person the student is in daily contact with in a somewhat 'apprenticeship situation' is the class or subject teacher in the school. But no matter how much help the student in fact gets from the teacher, it must be noted that the teacher is not officially responsible for the student; at best it is a divided responsibility. However, the teacher may withhold help for fear of interfering. More seriously, the teacher may feel resentment that someone so fleeting and remote as the college lecturer should be thought better able to help than he, the person on the spot and responsible for the children in question (Tibble, 1971). The system under which the college supervisor often operates thus does not provide the conditions necessary for giving the students the most effective support and assistance in the acquiring of practical skills. There is a need for more thoroughly defined objectives, narrowly defined tasks, and the opportunity for critical analysis of the task performance. The basis for this to come about is a working partnership of all the participants (tertiary staff, teachers and students) who share a consistent frame of reference for analysis of the situation. The present lack of clear-cut roles for supervisor and teacher and confusion and lack of congruence concerning the activities to be performed does little to promote the students' professional learning. Negative attitudes and doubts about the effectiveness and worth of supervision are fostered.

Studies have revealed a number of interesting and rather disturbing aspects of the supervision of student practice teaching. McKean and Mills (1964) see the supervisor as a facilitator, helping each school, each teacher and each student teacher to develop the goals and methods appropriate to the particular educational climate within that school. Yet a study by Miller (1973) showed that, on the one hand, the co-operating teacher was the most important individual of all the supervising personnel in the evaluation of the student teacher's development, and, on the other, that the co-operating school itself played a significant role in the student's preparation. A study by Elliot (1964) into the 'openness' of student teachers and their supervisors in student teaching concluded that significant negative changes occurred in the openness of the student teachers during the practice. These changes in the openness were significantly related to the openness of their supervisory teachers but not to the openness of their college supervisors. Yee (1968) found that co-operating teachers influenced their student teachers' attitudes largely in the direction of their own attitudes. He discerned little evidence of the student teachers influencing the attitudes of their supervising teachers. In a study of the relationships between the student teacher, co-operating teacher and the college supervisor, Yee (1969) found that over a semester coalitions were formed between the college supervisor and co-operating teacher but relationships between the student teacher and supervisor became more negative. Underhill (1969) found that student teachers tended to change in empathy level towards their co-operating teacher; but if a student teacher who had a low empathy score was placed with a co-operating teacher with a high empathy score, the student teacher tended to become even less empathic. A study by Seperson and Joyce (1973) showed that co-operating teachers substantially influence the behaviour of the student teachers and that the influence was felt during the very early weeks of student teaching rather than being the result of the slow and cumulative impact. The co-operating teacher was a powerful influence for good or ill, especially in terms of the extent to which the setting (use of groups, open education) is influential on the teaching styles of student teachers.

In order to counter some of these problems related to co-operating teachers, Kahn (1971) reported a teaching practice scheme in which student teachers were placed with beginning teachers who had themselves just finished their final teaching practice. The programme sought to provide mutual support for both student teachers and the beginning teachers who were designated as co-operating teachers. The findings revealed that student teachers benefited. They reported that they were more at ease, that there was no generation gap, and that they learnt from one another's strengths and weaknesses. Because the new teachers were more flexible they were also more receptive to, and willing to experiment with, new ideas. When student teachers made mistakes the beginning teachers did not moralize. It was concluded that the assignment of student teachers to beginning teachers offers some promise provided that the beginning co-operating teachers were not encountering overwhelming disciplinary problems and provided that adequate college supervisory support was also made available.

Many institutions have turned their attention to encouraging their co-operating teachers to enrol in a practical course or workshop for preparing supervisors of students teachers. Some of the more creative attempts to prepare supervisory teachers are the use of microteaching (Aubertine, 1967), residency or internship in supervision (Ogletree *et al.*, 1962; Ezen and Lambert, 1966), the integration of supervisory theory with laboratory practice (Erickson, 1969; Du Vall and Yutzey, 1971), and released-time workshops on specific topics (Nelson, 1972). Some specific materials also have been produced to train supervisors. Hale and Spanjer (1972), for example, have developed a training format for 'The Systematic and Objective Analysis of Instruction' and within this there is a programme which concentrates on interpersonal communication for improving the supervising teacher's skill in relating to, and communicating with, the student teacher. This particular programme includes skill components such as paraphrasing, behaviour description, non-verbal communication, and feedback. Another training programme which emphasizes the student teacher/co-operating teacher relationship is 'Enriching Student Teaching Relationships' (Clothier and Kingsley, 1973). Included in this programme are such considerations as expectations for the student teaching experience, behaviours which enhance the supervisor-student teacher relationship, analysis of problem situations, and a supervisory cycle of planning, teaching and assessment. The training sequence combines role play, case studies, paper and pencil exercises, interviews and rating forms. Tom (1975) claims that the main tasks in training supervisors is to develop a coherent set of skills for supervision. He suggests a skill cluster based on the 'analysis of teaching, human relations and conferencing'. Once skills have been isolated, sets of training materials of high quality should be developed and applied.

The task of conducting the supervisory conference with the student teacher has been examined by a number of researchers. Cornett (1966) conducted survey research on supervision and concluded that the individual conference was the most effective technique in supervising student teachers in secondary schools. A poor conference with the supervisor was one of the most frequent criticisms by students in a survey conducted by Milanovich (1966). The main points of criticism were that the number of conferences were too few, that they were short, shallow and that the work of the student teachers was not evaluated thoroughly or honestly enough. Hilliard and Durrance (1968) proposed a set of guidelines for effective conferences which included such points as constructive analysis of performance emphasizing strengths; problem-centred analyses; and encouraging the students' self-analysis and self-direction. Chambers (1969) suggests that the individual conference needs to proceed through four phases: (i) a statement of the teaching problem the supervisor identified; (ii) analysis of the solution attempted by the student teacher; (iii) analysis of the thinking and identification of knowledge brought to bear on the problem; and (iv) proposed alternative solutions to similar problems when encountered in the future. In this way theory is fully related to the practices adopted or explored by the student. Browning (1968) surveyed co-operating teachers in Kansas and found that lack of opportunity during the school day for planning and for conferences with student teachers seemed to be the factors making for the most dissatisfaction with the student teaching programme.

A form of supervision which has been developed at Harvard since 1956 is that termed 'clinical supervision'. This has been explained in detail by Goldhammer (1969). Clinical supervision is a more rigorous way of fostering student learning because it is explicit and coherent in its focus on the evidence of pupil and teacher behaviour. The assumption is that teaching behaviour should be a conscious, rational action subject to understanding. The supervisor's task is to assist the teacher to achieve this understanding. Goldhammer suggests five essential stages: (i) pre-observation conference in which objectives, content, approaches and methods of evaluation are explicitly spelled out and overall plans for the practice are vetted; (ii) observation or videotaping of the lesson is then taken as a full record of verbal interaction; (iii) the lesson is considered separately by the student and supervisor; (iv) supervisory conference in which a selection of points about teacher and pupil behaviour is discussed and alternative strategies are explored; and (v) post-conference analysis in which the supervisor or a group of supervisors appraise the preceding discussion. It is important that supervisors combine such a procedure with sensitivity to the individual student and his unique learning requirements. Eaker (1974) describes an adaptation of Goldhammer's clinical supervision procedure. Stage one includes explaining and clarifying the rationale, assumptions and procedures of the supervision in a pre-observational conference during which student and supervisor agree on what will be observed. In stage two, observation occurs as objectively as possible in order to focus on certain behaviours only. Stage three is the post-observation conference during which there is an analysis of what occurred in terms of behaviours which supported objectives or impeded them or which had no effect on the attainment of the objectives. The crucial part of the clinical process is then the planning of strategies which will change or strengthen certain patterns of behaviour. An important goal of this supervisory process is to help the student teacher to become more independent and to develop self-analysis. Clinical supervision changes the role from that of evaluator to that of a consultant with more direct participation in the student's professional development (Harwood and Miller, 1972). The use of videotaping in the supervising process is especially advocated by Young (1969). It provides a common, objective record which the student teacher and supervisor can analyse together and select aspects for improvement.

Materials developed by the Northwest Regional Educational Laboratory (Hale and Spanjer, 1972) convert the concept of clinical supervision into a training format entitled 'Systematic and Objective Analysis of Instruction'.

The training activities include: taking verbatim transcripts, analyzing the transcripts for patterns of teaching behaviour, relating patterns to teacher goals, deciding which patterns to change, and planning and conducting a conference. The programme involves the trainee supervisor in simulated exercises and in actual teaching situations and in interpersonal relations training.

Several recent articles emphasize the idea of 'humanistic supervision'. Abrell (1974) claims that all persons in the so called 'supervisory alliance' will experience growth and fulfilment through humanistic supervision. The humanistic supervisor is a helper, facilitator and learner. Such a supervisor is receptive, asks rather than tells, tries to constructively use the aspirations, needs and talents of the student teacher, and co-operatively works with him in sharing information and planning solutions to problems. Buttery and Michalak (1975) believe that student teachers should no longer be subjected to a supervising process, but should rather co-operate with supervisors in the study of educational problems. A teaching clinic centred on specific problems was designed to involve a group of student teachers and supervisors working together to assist each group member to improve his teaching skills.

A promising version of supervision developed in Britain is the appointment of professional tutors or school-based tutors who are teachers designated to work with student teachers and also to work with probationary teachers in their first year. In some instances, professional tutors also have a role in facilitating the continuing education of teacher colleagues (Knowlson, 1973). Leicester University has operated a system of teacher-tutors in varying forms over a decade. The teacher-tutors work closely with members of school staff, are consulted on relevant matters and are paid for their services. In some instances the supervision is not based on direct observation of teaching but on asking for a detailed account by the student of what happened and helping the student to make a self-assessment (Caspari and Eggleston, 1965; Clark, 1967). This method would seem to have advantages in that it reduces conflict; the student is encouraged in observation and recall; he is involved in evaluation; and he is more likely to explore improvements when he perceives a co-operative process can be helpful (Tibble, 1971). The teacher-tutor can offer day-to-day advice to the student that relates his college work with his teaching in the school in a way that a visiting college supervisor can seldom do. Arrangements of this kind have also been established at Bristol an Keele Universities. In all of the many varied forms of teacher-tutor arrangements, two essential functions are involved: (i) the administrative function of ensuring that the student finds his place in the school and is made aware of the requirements and the resources and facilities available to him; and (ii) the more personal, pastoral function of analyzing and overcoming professional and personal problems (Eggleston, 1974). While tutor-teacher schemes are promising Silberman (1971) is cautious about giving entire responsibility of student teaching to the school system. Rather than improving matters, the schools might make the situation worse. They would tend merely to reproduce the kinds of teachers they already have.

The general success of supervision seems to be contingent on many factors—the choice of supervisor, his preparation, the procedures of supervision and the types of relationships established with student teachers; yet in all of this, the kind of feedback the student receives is probably crucial.

Feedback and Evaluation

Two important questions related to the pacticum are, how should student teachers receive feedback on their progress in practicum experience? and how should students' work be evaluated?

Silberman (1971) claims that students receive incredibly little feedback on their performance, for supervision tends to be 'sporadic and prefunctory'. More importantly, supervisors and teachers usually have only a vague conception of education from which to criticize and evaluate student teaching. Medley (1971) claims that the supervisor's main function is to provide the student teacher with accurate and comprehensive information about his teaching and that another useful source of feedback is from the pupils themselves. Surprisingly, perhaps, Tuckman and Oliver (1968) found that feedback from pupils led to improved teaching behaviour, whereas feedback from the student teacher's supervisor produced no additional effort when combined with pupil feedback, and actually had a negative effect when used alone. Stanton (1971, 1972) has devised and tested an instrument, the Diagnostic Rating of Teacher Performance Scale, to effectively tap pupil reactions. When used with pupils, student teachers, class-room teachers and college supervisors, some interesting results were obtained. Although pupils and the student teachers agreed rather well on relative strengths and weaknesses, supervising teachers provided very different opinions. College supervisors, in turn, differed quite markedly from classroom teachers in their indication of strengths and weaknesses in the student teacher's performance, but tended to agree more closely with the trainees' own self-evaluation and that of the pupils. Thus the frame of reference one person creates is likely to vary from that created by another. Hence communication can become difficult and this is an important reason why feedback is often quite ineffective.

Usually, the supervisor has to verbally recreate the teaching he has observed so that he can criticize what has occurred, and this re-creation is in terms of his own frame of reference. This predisposes him to see particular aspects as important and these may be at variance with the viewpoint of the student teacher. There is considerable support for the proposition also that teachers inaccurately perceive much of what occurs in their classrooms (Lett, 1970; Ehman, 1970; Lantz, 1970; McDonald, 1971; and Morgan, 1972). Recollections of what has occurred tend to vary yet there is often absolute reliance upon the ability of supervisors and student teachers to conceptualize the teaching-learning process in the same way. A study by Coulter (1974) made a comparison between supervisors' and student teachers' perceptions with those of an independent trained observer on twelve dimensions of classroom behaviour as described by Emmer (1970). On three-quarters of the dimensions, more than one-quarter of the supervisors and the student teachers disagreed with the trained observer and in one-quarter of the cases supervisors and students disagreed with each other. The major areas of disagreement between supervisors and students were on pupil-centred classroom behaviour. The data suggest that supervisors and students have no shared frame of reference within which communication may take place.

More concrete methods of recording and interpreting what goes on during the lesson to provide feedback have been investigated. Rowlands (1968) in a pilot study used a walkie-talkie unit to permit the supervisor to speak quietly and privately to the student while the lesson was in progress. Appropriate responses were reinforced immediately and inappropriate responses were mentioned advising the student to change his behaviour. Considerable modification of behaviour was achieved with the student teachers. A study by Medley (1971) with supervision and kinescope recording of lessons concluded that neither supervisors nor the recordings had any effect on student behaviour. However, MacGraw (1966) found that feedback based on 35mm time-lapse photography could be effective in changing the behaviour of student teachers in contrast to another group which did not receive such feedback. Providing objective indicators to student teachers has also been investigated. Ishler (1967), using Withall's Social and Emotional Climate Index, tested the effects of feedback versus no feedback in two comparable groups of student teachers. Those who received feedback become significantly more learner-centred than did the student teachers in the group who received no feedback. Heinrich and McKeegan (1969) used colour coded cards for the supervisor to provide immediate feedback each time the student teacher showed a desirable or undesirable kind of teaching behaviour. The control group received verbal feedback from the supervisor after the lesson. The immediate and specific feedback system proved effective in achieving a greater reduction in inappropriate teaching behaviours. The use of videotape is another attempt to create a common frame of reference. Winn (1974) reported a study at Sherbrooke University, Quebec, in which student teachers were videotaped during student teaching as part of the supervisory process. It was concluded that the videotape adds little to the feedback that is already available from the supervisor, even though students appreciated the use of the videotape. The use of supervisor-student contracting involving agreement on objectives of a lesson is reported by McNeil (1971). 'Supervision by objectives' is a process by which a supervisor and a student teacher agree in advance on what they will accept as evidence that the student teacher has or has not been successful in changing the skills, competencies or attitudes of his pupils. The agreement is drawn up and may then be used for guiding the observation of the lesson and the feedback on the lesson.

Blumberg and Cusick (1970) analysed the verbal interaction which took place between the student teacher and the supervisor in the post-observation conference. Their findings revealed that the interaction was mostly a 'telling' affair with the bulk of the supervisor's behaviour being the giving of information. A fair amount of energy on the part of the supervisor was given to inducing a positive social-emotional climate. Low emphasis was given to asking student teachers for ideas about action or problem-solving. It was concluded that student teachers do not seem to be engaged with the supervisor on matters critical to the problems they face in the classroom and they did not appear to collaborate. The interactions analysed could be described as the kind of interaction neither party wants to have and from which both parties would like to disengage as soon as possible. The interpersonal insights and skills possessed by many supervisors were inadequate as far as the demands of the helping relationship are concerned. Clearly the selection and training of supervisors to provide effective feedback are issues which need to be seriously considered.

However conscientiously the supervisor tries to provide helpful feedback, the question of evaluation and assessment of the student's teaching performance often creeps in to add a further constraint on the effectiveness of feedback. Cope (1971) observed that some students refrain from approaching college supervisors with real problems, not only because it may affect the grade they receive, but also because they wish to preserve their self-esteem. Supervisors and teachers have problems not only in grading students but, more fundamentally, in evaluating them as part of the process of assisting their learning. Both student teachers and teachers saw assessment as important, while ironically supervisors saw themselves as guides. Teachers consequently gave strong support to students even by 'staging shows' to convince the supervisor of the student's ability to teach. When evaluations are made such subjective impressions are often influential (McFarlane, 1973).

The use of multi-item evaluation codes requiring a ranking of one to five is seen by some institutions to help the supervisor to be more objective in his assessment and to analyze components of the teaching process. However, these methods are questioned by Detwiler (1971) on the basis that the multiplicity of items used detracts from and hinders the supervisory process because value judgements are called for. As an alternative, he suggests that five broad categories for evaluation be used: content, methods, rapport, management, and environment, so that the supervisor may concentrate on the whole teaching performance and the important aspects in the teaching process.

In a survey of co-operating teachers Jordan (1967) reported that one of the greatest problems for the co-operating teacher is that of student evaluation. Britts (1969) proposed a co-operating teacher's scale listing such areas as (i) involvement in the learning process; (ii) motivational techniques; (iii) presenting subject matter; (iv) classroom control; (v) individualization; (vi) knowledge of subject; (vii) depth of preparation; and (viii) personal qualities. Such headings are fairly typical of those listed on report forms, detailing the evaluation and eventually assessed grade for the student teacher. Very often, however, the comments made are so generalized as to be of little use for the student's re-direction of effort.

Given the uncertainties and vagueness of feedback and evaluation practices, it is little wonder that many students develop the view that their own personal qualities are central to their success as a teacher (Calthrop and Owens, 1971), and that what the college has presented in courses or in teaching practice for that matter, has little relevance to the real world of full-time teaching.

Generally the literature reviewed has revealed some of the vexing problems associated with teaching practice. To begin, some consistency in the terminology used for the components of the 'practicum' in teacher education is needed to help clarify specific objectives for what is attempted. Systematic research into the range of practicum experiences and the establishing of objectives in terms of changed student knowledge, skills and attitudes has been regrettably neglected. Much of what is current practice is by tradition, especially block teaching practice, without consideration of the real needs of students or of establishing a carefully structured learning experience in the schools. Students somehow survive, and surprisingly claim that teaching practice of all the components of their programme was the greatest in value to them. This view raises serious questions about the nature of courses, their relevance, and the applicability of theoretical concepts to the practical classroom situation.

A wide range of innovative experiences is being implemented in many institutions, but often these lack specific purposes, are not well co-ordinated, and are inadequately related to educational concepts being advocated. The dichotomy of college and school and the vague bases of co-operation are further issues of great concern. There can be no professional development of teachers without a truly working partnership with the professional practitioners who will eventually accept the beginning teacher as a welcome colleague. Tied in with this issue is the problem of the supervision of student teaching. There are no clearly defined and agreed dimensions for the observation of teaching. There is limited preparation of supervisors and there are only somewhat rudimentary attempts to analyze the actual process of supervision. Further, without adequate and specific feedback to the student, given in a systematic and supportive manner, there can be no really effective re-direction of behaviour to achieve improved classroom performance. The evaluation and assessment expectation of supervisors is another factor which mars their relationships with students and, to some extent, teachers, and inhibits the supervisory process.

Clearly much needs to be done. The following suggestions are based on the experience of this reviewer and other reviewers such as Andrews (1967), Cope (1971) and Lomax (1973). Systematic investigations need to explore such issues as

(i) what is the potential contribution of teaching practice to the objectives of teacher education;

(ii) how can various components of the practicum improve the student's understanding of the theoretical courses;

(iii) how can simulated learning be used to reinforce teaching practice;

(iv how can the quality of laboratory and skills acquisition experiences be improved;

(v) what is the role of the supervisor and how can the effectiveness of supervision be improved;

(vi) how can teaching practice be adequately organized and financed;

(viii) how most effectively can pre-service education and the practicum interact with in-service education; and

(viii) how can new and fruitful co-operating relationships be formed with schools.

In summary, then, the present developments do not indicate firm trends but rather a series of promising approaches to persistent problems. Few institutions can boast of either a modern well-designed total programme of practicum elements integrated with theoretical knowledge, or of a true partnership with schools for the mutual benefit of all parties. Some good beginnings have been made, but much remains to be done before the full value of the practicum, in terms of students' professional growth, is realized.

NEW METHODS, MATERIALS AND TECHNOLOGY

The most pervasive and clearly recognizable changes in teacher education in the past decade or so have been in the methods and techniques, materials and equipment employed to improve the process of educating teachers. Foremost among these changes has been a strong swing to small group and individualized teaching strategies, to team teaching by tertiary staff and by teachers and student teachers, to the use of microteaching and simulation techniques and associated modelling and protocol materials, and generally to the extensive employment of educational media and technology of all kinds, especially television.

Small Group and Individualized Teaching

In order to improve teaching and learning within teacher education programmes and to exemplify changed methodologies in the schools, teacher educators have moved strongly away from the formal large-group lecture approach. This is not to say that the lecture has been abandoned; it has not, for many realize it has a justifiable place. But certainly small group methods and, to a lesser extent, individualized learning, seem to be important general trends in teacher education (Hilliard, 1971).

There has been a limited amount of research which tends to support the use of small group methods in teacher education. McLeish (1968) reported that tertiary students were critical of the lecture method and preferred, in the ratio of two to one, the informal, participatory tutorial and seminar approach. Studies by Husband (1951), Eglash (1954) and Ruja (1954) compared lecture and discussion methods largely on the basis of subject-matter mastery, and found no significant differences in achievement between the treatments. It must be added that most of these discussion groups had more than thirty-five students. In studies which considered more complex outcomes the results are somewhat different. For example, Hirschman (1952) compared the presentation of material by dictation with presenting written materials followed by discussion, using a measure of concept learning. The reading-discussion treatment proved to be significantly superior. Barnard (1942), comparing the lecture-demonstration method with problem-solving discussion, found that whereas students in lecture-demonstration groups were superior on a test of specific information, the discussion students were superior on measures of problem-solving and scientific attitude. Elliott (1950) found that students in psychology discussion groups displayed greater interest in electing to pursue further psychology courses than did students in large lecture groups. Casey and Weaver (1956) located no differences in knowledge of content but superiority in attitudes (as measured by the Minnesota Teacher Attitudes Inventory) for students in small group discussions as compared to lectures. Although Beach (1970) found that students in a conventional lecture course achieved slightly better than the small group participants, the latter showed a significant improvement in critical thinking and testified of a greater increase in interest. Generally, these studies suggest that the transmission of information is best achieved through formal exposition while such things as concepts, thinking skills, and positive attitudes are best developed in the discussion setting.

Interestingly, the Department of Education and Science in Britain has funded a major project to explore, develop and appraise the use of syndicated learning groups in courses on sociology in a number of colleges of education. The term 'syndicate' is used to describe a small group of about six students, sometimes self-selected, within a college section. The syndicate groups work on assigned questions or problems and are supplied with reading lists and other relevant materials. As a result of its research and deliberation each group prepares a report which will become the basis of discussion by the whole section. This approach, and variations of it, are seen as a method which might 'enhance motivation and involvement on the part of the students so that they may develop a more independent attitude and critical judgment towards the subject matter they are studying' (Eggleston, 1974, p. 96).

A number of recent reports on teacher education have emphasized the need for the wider adoption of informal small-group approaches. For example, a report on elementary education in Ontario (1966) recommended that

General procedures followed in the professional program should not be stereotyped nor formal. They should exemplify the methods which it is hoped the student will incorporate into has own teaching. . . . Specific goals should determine the selection of methods, the main criterion being that the method selected should stimulate the students to develop intellectual curiosity and help them to gain critical insight into the topic or problem being studied. Student teachers who have planned their own programs, organized committees, and guided discussions are most likely to encourage their pupils later on to develop a sense of responsibility and display initiative for similar action. (p. 26)

Similarly, a report of the Asian Institute for Teacher Educators (1972) proposed that teaching techniques should promote student-student and student-lecturer interchange and foster their close co-operation. In addition, techniques should encourage the 'spirit of enquiry, research and self-study' (p. 25).

The provision for student teachers to undertake some form of independent study has long been common in teacher education programmes. It may, for example, take the form of a child study or an investigation of a particular educational issue (Hilliard, 1971). Alternatively, as is popular in the United States, a contract system may be followed. For instance, in the Temple University teachers corps programme, the student is asked to consider a practical educational problem that he would like to study systematically and to plan briefly how he will approach the study. Subsequently, in private conference with the instructor the study plan is refined and when both student and instructor are satisfied with it, it is transcribed in contract form and both sign it (Sorber, 1969). Most recently, students have been enabled, through the provision of self-instructional materials, to learn independently and at their own rate in both theoretical and practical aspects of their course (Clark *et al.*, 1974). As has been seen in a previous section, individualized student progress has become a feature of the influential competency-based teacher education movement.

Team Teaching

In many teacher education programmes it has become an increasingly common practice for staff in the same or different programme areas to collaborate in planning, teaching and evaluating a particular course (Hilliard, 1971). Of course, team teaching in teacher education is by no means new. Troy State Teachers College in the United States, for example, organized its staff into inter-disciplinary teaching teams as early as 1941 (Sterns, 1972). Team teaching by teacher education staff can take many forms. For instance, a psychologist, English specialist and a skilled practitioner might co-operate in offering a course on teaching reading; or, sociologists, psychologists, or experts in special education, school principals and several teachers might develop a course on problems of inner-urban education. The actual teaching of such courses might be shared in various ways—different topics might be handled by different team members, or certain topics might involve the conjoint participation of some or all team members. Such arrangements as these are seen to hold at least three important advantages: (i) they use both the special and combined talents of staff; (ii) they facilitate inter-disciplinary teaching which breaks artificial subject barriers and tends to make learning more meaningful; and (iii) they provide students with a working example of team teaching so prevalent in schools in which they will have to teach.

During the 1970s there have been numerous plans to bring students and classroom teachers together in off-campus teams, such experience being regarded as important in the professional education of both groups. Especially common in the United States is for students to be teamed with teachers for practical work in schools. For instance, the Wisconsin State University in co-operation with the La Crosse Public Schools has developed a microteaching team programme involving teams of three students and one teacher (Altman, 1969). At Marshall University student teaching features student involvement in both curriculum planning and teaching in 'team structures' within the schools. Such plans are believed, among other things, to enable students to appreciate advantages and difficulties of team teaching, to develop skills in team planning and management, to learn how to relate productively with fellow professionals and para-professionals, to experience both a variety of instructional settings (e.g. individual and small group) and a variety of roles (e.g. planning, evaluating, teaching and supporting), and to receive substantial feedback from the team on their teaching performance (Sterns, 1972).

Simulation

As mentioned in an earlier section, conventional teacher education programmes tend to examine in their on-campus courses theoretical issues concerning classroom teaching-learning processes and leave students to experience the practical application of such theory in off-campus teaching practice. Unfortunately, as Hughes and Traill (1975) point out

> Integration of the two experiences was often not achieved and as a result student teachers were left with a confused notion of the theoretical basis of what motivates so much of the interaction which occurred in their classrooms. This situation also often thrusts student teachers into classroom situations where they were confronted with issues with which they were not able to cope. This was often a result of their lack of any previous experience in decision-making situations which were in any way identifiable with those raised in the classroom. (p. 113)

In an endeavour to alleviate this problem a large and increasing number of teacher education programmes have introduced into their on-campus courses simulated experiences which anticipate those which students are likely to encounter in their own teaching. Besides such concern to improve the conventional relationship between on-campus theory and off-campus teaching practice, the use of simulation in teacher education has been promoted by at least two other factors. One has been the development and use of educational technology which has permitted a more controlled and systematic study of teaching and learning. Another has been the growing recognition mentioned earlier, 'that theory can be taught best in the context of reality from which the theory is generated' (Cruickshank, 1971, p. 187).

'Simulation' has been accorded many interpretations. Several broad definitions which would probably be acceptable to most experts in the field are the following: 'Simulation is an operating representation of central features of reality' (Guetzkow, 1963); and 'Simulation is a means for letting learners experience things that otherwise might remain beyond their imagination, a means to practise skills safely and without embarrassment, and perhaps even discover insights into problems . . .' (Twelker, 1970). As far as its application in teacher education is concerned, simulation seems to exhibit a number of characteristics foreshadowed in the above general definitions. Essentially it involves student teachers (or experienced teachers) in situations representing selected aspects of the real world of the classroom and school. Most frequently these reproduced situations portray problems of various kinds which encourage the participant to reflect on causes and solutions and to decide upon and even act upon the strategies seen to be most adequate to overcome the problems. According to one of the leading advocates of the use of simulation in teacher education, Professor Donald Cruickshank (1971, 1972a), the method holds a number of important advantages. These include:

(i) Simulation establishes a setting wherein theory and practice can be joined as participants apply theoretical learning to life-like situations.

(ii) Simulation involves participants intellectually and emotionally as they become engaged in and react to situations.

(iii) Simulations are relevant since they re-create the real world and focus students' attention on it.

(iv) Simulation is controlled and permits participants to experience selected and simplified elements of reality rather than trying to understand it all.

(v) Simulation is relatively safe. It enables participants to engage in potentially dangerous or threatening situations without physical or psychological harm to themselves, the pupils or parents.

(vi) Simulations broaden the teacher education horizon by making it possible to create for students on-campus various educational settings and experiences often missed in student teaching.

Simulation, as currently used in teacher education, takes numerous forms and employs various techniques. In some programmes it is introduced in only a minor, incidental way in a few courses; in other programmes it forms a major component in its own right and it is carefully related to other course components. Sometimes simulation is confined to one technique such as role playing; at other times it embraces a comprehensive range of techniques. A surprising amount of simulation activity seems to be based on local staff-developed materials, but increasing use is being made of commercially produced multi-media packages. Perhaps a description of the approach adopted in one of the most widely-used commercial packages will best illustrate the range of simulation possibilities in teacher education.

In the United States, Cruickshank *et al.* (1967) have developed the *Teaching Problems Laboratory* and, more recently, Cruickshank (1969) has produced the *Inner City Simulation Laboratory*. Both packages have been made commercially available through Science Research Associates. The former, especially, seems to have had a fairly extensive impact on teacher education both in America and overseas (Tansey, 1971; Hughes and Traill, 1975). By 1971 in the United States alone, it was being used by over three hundred universities and public school districts in either pre-service or in-service teacher education. The *Teaching Problems Laboratory* is designed to provide student teachers with experience in making decisions about a variety of incidents occurring in a lifelike classroom environment. Each student participant assumes the role of Pat Taylor, a first year teacher of the fifth-grade class at the Longacre Elementary School in the township of Madison. The teacher is introduced to the community, the school district and the school by means of gramophone record and filmstrip. The teacher also receives faculty and curriculum handbooks and pupil progress cards for the thirty-odd children in the class. Pat Taylor then encounters thirty-one critical teaching incidents, considered to be the most troublesome problems for first-year teachers. These relate to such aspects as pupil behaviour, relationships with parents, teaching method, classroom management, curriculum planning and evaluation of learning. A number of techniques are used to simulate the various incidents—colour films, role playing by students and written accounts. In requiring students to make decisions about the incidents, no single correct answers are suggested by the designers. Rather the written responses from students form the basis for discussion.

As useful as such multi-media packages as the one described above are, they are often quite expensive to purchase, sometimes retailing for in excess of $1,000. This has been one factor that has prompted the development of less sophisticated local materials by a number of institutions and encouraged the publication of a variety of cheap paperbacks which simulate incidents and situations through written descriptions, transcripts of interaction, case studies of children and 'in-basket' items such as letters, records, and newspaper cuttings. Examples of this approach are books prepared by Bishop and Whitfield (1972), Hunter (1972), and Telfer and Rees (1975).

Unfortunately there has not been much research on the effectiveness of simulation when employed in the teacher education context. The studies that have been undertaken have yielded only limited data. For example, an investigation by Cruickshank and Broadbent (1969) set out to examine the effectiveness of simulation in presenting teaching problems, and to determine whether exposure to simulated teaching problems effected student teachers' subsequent behaviour. The simulated 'critical teaching problems', based on reports from teachers, were centred upon a hypothetical fifth-grade classroom and reproduced using videotape, role plays and written incidents. The results of the study led the researchers to conclude that

> the simulation training when tested under the most stringent conditions was an unqualified success as a teaching device that motivates and involves students and that, although simulation was only partially successful in changing student teachers' behavior, it was at least as effective as an equal amount of student teaching. Changes in the materials, placement (of the simulation) in the program and in the role of the instructor promise to increase the overall effectiveness of this set of simulation materials in future trials. (p. 110)

Although the use of simulation needs to be validated by many more research studies such as this, it seems that the generally favourable impression that teacher educators and their students have of simulation will continue to encourage its extended use in teacher education. In the United States, in particular, these favourable impressions have been officially bolstered by the stance taken by the National Council for Accreditation of Teacher Education. Its new standards recognize simulation as an alternative practical training method: 'Each advanced program in education includes direct and/or simulated experiences ... which relate specifically to the school position for which the candidate is prepared' (quoted in Cruickshank, 1971, p. 188).

Microteaching

Of all the methodological innovations in teacher education over the last decade that of microteaching has been one of the most widespread in its impact. The concept of microteaching is simple and, in view of its achievements, powerful. It is teaching in miniature—teaching scaled-down in terms of class size, time, task, and skill. It is contrived, but nevertheless real teaching. Typically it involves a sequence of four main phases. First, a *model performance* of a teaching skill is presented. Often this model is a short videotaped recording of an experienced teacher demonstrating a clearly defined specific teaching skill. This is then discussed and analyzed by student teachers with a view to establishing the skill's underlying psychological and pedagogical principles and to discriminating its main components. Second, there is the *teach-record* stage where students prepare and teach an episode of five to fifteen minutes with a small group of three to ten pupils. The emphasis of the episode is on the particular skill. Often this is videotaped. Third, there is *play-back critique* where the student's performance is replayed to give him immediate feedback in relation to the skill concerned, and to facilitate evaluative discussion with his supervisors and perhaps fellow students. Fourth comes the *reteach* session. Following the feedback the student reteaches, if necessary, the episode to another pupil group embodying the suggestions for improving his use of the skill. This phase is sometimes followed by further feedback-critique.

Microteaching was first introduced at Stanford University in the United States in 1963. Faced with the problem of preparing graduates from liberal arts colleges to assume teaching responsibilities as interns after several months' initial training, a group of faculty members, of whom Bush, Allen and McDonald were prominent, sought a more potent measure than the traditional approach of lectures supplemented by student practice and observation in schools. The solution, microteaching, met a number of important criteria. First, a real teaching situation was required so that, from the beginning, students could practise and refine teaching skills and experiment with their own ideas and those suggested in the course. Second, the most suitable teaching situation would have 'low risk' for the student teacher and pupils. Students would not be presented with complexities and difficulties that they could not be expected to surmount initially, and pupils would not be subjected to sometimes very poor teaching. Third, the practice context should embody some well-established principles of learning: for example, 'numerous distributed practice sessions would seem more valuable than fewer, more extended sessions; immediate supervisory feedback would be far more valuable than delayed feedback; immediate opportunity to rectify errors and weakness would be preferable to extended periods of living with the weakness; low anxiety from a low threat situation should be more conducive to learning than a highly threatening situation' (Allen and Clark, 1967, p. 76). Fourth, the practice scheme should be economic in terms of time and resources. Microteaching was seen to provide more effective, concentrated use of students' time in practising a variety of skills and in freeing students to spend more time in preparatory work. Further, the best use of staff supervisory talents could be made.

Portable video equipment became available at Stanford in 1963. At first it was used to show instances of teaching as a substitute for the traditional observational training. Soon it became evident that this equipment had considerable advantages in supplying students with feedback, as well as in demonstrating teaching behaviour. Microteaching captured both of these advantages of television recording. The student taught a small group of pupils for about five to ten minutes, the lesson being videotaped for later analysis and discussion. Initially the teaching behaviours that were studied and practised were very general, such as 'clarity of presentation'. However, it became apparent that these behaviours were too broad and that more specific skills needed to be investigated. One of the first was reinforcement. Students were given details of the skill and told why it was considered important. Later, audiovisual models of skills were presented to students and modelling rapidly became part of the microteaching procedure (Berliner, 1969).

Since these beginnings microteaching has had rather an exciting history. The technique has been considerably refined and has been extensively applied in a variety of educational settings. Though used mainly in pre-service teacher education programmes, it has been employed successfully in improving the competence of experienced teachers, in refining the skills of supervisors and counsellors, and in research on the teaching-learning process. From the United States microteaching has spread to many countries throughout the world— Canada, England, Scotland, Ireland, Sweden, Israel, and Malaysia, to mention a few. In the United States by 1969 more than half the teacher education institutions were using microteaching (Ward, 1970). By 1973 the position was much the same in Australia (Turney *et al.*, 1973). Research on various aspects of the micro-teaching process, especially in the United States, has multiplied dramatically and by 1972 the results of over a hundred studies had been reported, with many more in progress.

It is not intended in this discussion to embark on a review of these numerous research studies. Such reviews are available in other specialist publications. Probably it is sufficient to report here that investigations of the effectiveness of microteaching in changing student behaviour tend to support quite strongly its use in teacher education: 'Not only does it seem to facilitate significantly the acquisition of teaching skills and the development of favourable attitudes towards teaching, but it does so in relatively short time' (Turney *et al.*, 1973, p. 7).

Microteaching is being employed in a variety of ways in teacher education programmes. For example, a survey of the implementation of microteaching in secondary teacher education of the United States (Ward, 1970) indicated that 72 per cent of responding programmes had incorporated it in the general methods course, 43 per cent in the subjects methods course, and 18 per cent in student teaching. About two-thirds of the programmes involved less than 150 students most of whom were provided with six or fewer microteaching encounters. Most of the programmes were conducted on-campus in education and audiovisual departments using college 'peer' students as pupils, while some programmes carried out microteaching in their laboratory schools or in public schools, using children in the microclass. Although some programmes followed the complete teach-reteach sequence, many had attenuated it. The majority of programmes involved both the student, college supervisor and microclass pupils in the critique-feedback sessions. There seemed to be a general lack of knowledge or uncertainty about the teaching skills being introduced through microteaching programmes. Less than a third of the programmes had a written rationale and videotaped or filmed model for the specific teaching behaviours being treated.

One interesting example of the numerous microteaching programmes in the United States is that developed at Illionois State University where it is viewed as 'a basic component of elementary education prior to, and in preparation for, student teaching' (Short and Rozum, 1972). An important feature of this programme was that it was initiated, planned and implemented largely by the staff of the Metcalf Laboratory School in close collaboration with university faculty. The planners not only saw microteaching as a valuable means of promoting student learning of basic teaching skills; for them, it provided 'increased opportunities for meaningful communication and co-operation among and between college students, Metcalf faculty, and instructors of college courses', and enabled 'the laboratory school to assume an increasingly viable role in the research and development of pre-student teaching experiences' (Short and Rozum, 1972, p. 4). Other features of the programme were: (i) it required no special funding and was carried on within the resources of the annual Metcalf budget; (ii) student microteaching experiences were supervised by thirteen members of the school staff and eighty-six college students pursuing the Middle Grade Curriculum course participated; (iii) the 'teaching packets'[2] on each skill for the students' use were prepared by the school staff (one packet dealt with orientation to the programme, one with lesson planning, and three others described the skills of set, pacing and closure); (iv) all microteaching sessions took place at the school and its microteaching 'stations' were in operation from nine until three o'clock daily from Monday through Friday, involving pupils, aged from six to fourteen years, drawn from fifteen of the twenty-two regular classrooms; (v) the college faculty who taught the curriculum courses co-operated with the school staff by monitoring the progress of students through weekly reports from the school supervisors, by participating in RAP sessions ('recapitulation and projection' conferences where the student and supervisor assessed the work completed and planned for the development of the next teaching skill), by introducing in their college classes theory and activities relevant to the on going microteaching programme, and by becoming involved in the overall assessment of the programme; and (vi) the microteaching programme lasted for five weeks, the first week devoted mainly to a 'pre-test' taping of a fifteen minute lesson taught by each student to establish a 'base profile of teaching skill' prior to the microteaching experiences, and the final week a post-test taping to determine change in the students' 'overall teaching performance'.

Although the use of microteaching is not nearly as widespread in Europe as it is in the United States, an increasing number of institutions are introducing it. One of the first centres in Britain to incorporate microteaching into the teacher education programme was the University of Stirling, Scotland. Under the direction of Perrott and Duthie the programme required students over a period of twelve weeks to conceptualize and practise five identified teaching skills as a prelude to practice teaching in schools (Eggleston, 1974). This microteaching programme was an integral part of courses in education. Before practising each skill with small groups of children, students were given four lectures introducing them to the particular skill. These provided relevant psychological theory, videotaped illustrations, an analysis of the skill's components, and practice in the use of observation instruments which students subsequently employed in analysing their microteaching. From the experience of the first few years, it became clear that the lecture courses were an inappropriate means of underpinning the programme. Commenting on this finding Duthie (1973a) wrote:

---

[2] Each packet included a definition of the skill, justification for the skill, procedures for achieving the skill, a demonstration videotape, a performance scale to be used in evaluating the student, and a sample lesson plan illustrating the skill.

This is particularly true for practice in the use of analytical instruments in which students have to develop a skill through constant viewing and re-viewing of a tape; but it is also true in the case of theoretical aspects of the course. Students vary in their degrees of conceptualization of the teaching process. Some students work initially at a fairly concrete level; others prefer to work from the abstract to concrete. What we require is an *individualised audio-visual self-instructional programme* which will enable students to work at their own pace and at their own conceptual level, to repeat parts of the course which they have failed to understand on the first occasion or which they have missed through illness, and to follow up in detail, with audio-visual support, those parts of the course which they find most interesting. (p. 1)

To facilitate this approach plans were made to develop and evaluate materials, to construct a resources centre embodying a specialized twenty-carrel unit in which students could study audiovisual materials, and to render semi-automatic a suite of microteaching and viewing rooms (Duthie, 1973b and see Figure 1.1).

Microteaching is fast becoming an established teacher education procedure. However, as Allen and Eve (1968) point out, the phenomenal growth of microteaching 'should not obscure the fact that the technique is still in its infancy'. The ultimate potential of the innovation depends largely on the energy and ingenuity of teacher educators and researchers in 'developing and testing new ways of applying microteaching principles and techniques to the problems of education' (pp. 210–11).

Modelling and Protocol Materials

The introduction of microteaching has highlighted the need for good quality examples of particular aspects of teaching. It is essential that students have a clear understanding of a teaching skill before they attempt to apply it in microteaching. They must know definitely what they should do and why. This can be accomplished in two main ways, used either separately or in combination: (i) by the use of oral or written explanations and instructions; and (ii) by providing live or recorded demonstrations of the special teaching behaviour. In current microteaching programmes these approaches have been embodied in the 'modelling' phase of the procedure.

Experience and research have indicated that a vital element in microteaching is the presentation and analysis of sharply focused 'models' of teaching behaviour generally recorded on videotape or film (Turney *et al.*, 1973). The development of such materials has become a concern in many teacher education institutions and has been strongly influenced by several commercial packages. Understandably the first group to become involved in this activity was Allen and his associates at Stanford University. Their materials include manuals and films which model three groups of teaching skills—increasing student participation, questioning and lesson presentation skills. These programmes, published by the General Learning Corporation in 1969, were designed for use in pre-service teacher education microteaching.

Probably the widest-known and most carefully developed and tested modelling materials are the *Minicourses* developed by a team led initially by Borg at the Far West Laboratory for Educational Research and Development, now located at San Francisco. The minicourses, published in the early 1970s by Macmillan Educational Services, built on the work at Stanford, and were conceived essentially as a self-instructional microteaching system for in-service use by teachers with their own pupils. The handbooks and films were designed to

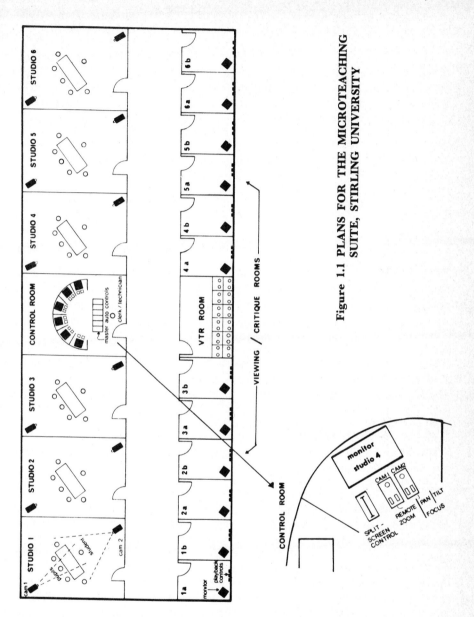

Figure 1.1 PLANS FOR THE MICROTEACHING SUITE, STIRLING UNIVERSITY

facilitate the teacher's acquisition of a range of behaviours, believed to be associated with effective teaching, by taking him through each of the phases of microteaching—instruction and modelling, teach, evaluate and re-teach. The minicourses treat teaching behaviours related to such areas as effective questioning, developing children's oral language, tutoring in mathematics, organizing independent learning, and classroom management through positive reinforcement. Since their introduction the mini-courses have been extensively used in both pre-service and in-service teacher education programmes and have been adapted for use in several European countries, especially notable in this respect being the work at the University of Lancaster (Perrott, 1974).

Not unrelated to the development of modelling materials for use in micro-teaching has been a growing interest in the United States in the development of so-called 'protocol' materials. As mentioned earlier, in 1969 the American Association of Colleges for Teacher Education published *Teachers for the Real World* which had an important impact on thinking about teacher preparation. In it Smith and his associates advocated the systematic development and use of protocol materials. Such materials were viewed as 'recordings of behaviour in educationally relevant situations that could be used to help teachers (or teacher trainees) relate basic theoretical knowledge of pedagogy to the teaching process', thus bridging the gap between educational theory and practice (Borg and Stone, 1974). In 1970 the Bureau of Educational Personnel Development of the Office of Education stimulated the development of protocol materials by funding a number of universities to pursue this work. A variety of materials has been subsequently developed. Most of these take the form of multi-media instructional packages in which 'educationally relevant concepts have been illustrated on motion picture film, videotape, or slides and have been supported by printed guides which provide concept descriptions, classroom examples, simulations, and other materials designed to help the learner relate theoretical concepts to actual teaching' (Borg and Stone, 1974, p. 2). For example, protocols on the language arts have been developed at Ohio State University, on curriculum by the Educational Development Center, on teaching by the Utah State University (see Cruickshank, 1972b). Of these, Borg's work at Utah has been perhaps most impressive. During 1971–2 his team developed six self-instructional modules, each concerned with an important concept related to teacher language (namely, extension, encouragement, clarity, emphasis, feedback and organization). These materials have been favourably received by students and have been effective in promoting understanding of and skill in applying the basic teacher-language concepts (Borg and Stowitschek, 1972; Borg and Stone, 1974). More recently, Borg has found that application of these concepts in teaching has been positively related to desired pupil gains.

Although the United States has led the way in the development of materials to facilitate student-teacher learning, other countries are beginning to take up the challenge. In Britain, for example, the Science Teacher Education Project (STEP) has developed a series of curriculum units designed to prepare teachers to implement more effectively new school science curriculum. Curriculum units suggesting student experiences and approaches to be taken by the college tutor, have been prepared on such topics as aims and objectives, conceptual thinking in science, methods and techniques, resources, curriculum design, and under-standing and communication. Some of the important features of the STEP units have been described by Eggleston (1974): (i) they are concerned not with science content but with methods of teaching and their theoretical under-pinnings; (ii) they involve students in a variety of activities and materials, including such things as small group discussion, analysis of taped or filmed teaching, role playing, team planning and teaching, systematic observations, and teaching small groups; (iii) they specify objectives in terms of teacher qualities to be enhanced; and (iv) they are reasonably short in duration of implementation—usually not more than two hours.

Media and Technology

Over the last twenty years considerable advances have been made in educational technology. Various technologies to improve learning have been both refined in quality and extended in range. These run from the simplest of teaching aids to video recording systems and comprehensive resource centres. The changes in technology impinge on teacher education in two ways: On the one hand they have influenced the school situation where students are to teach and, on the other hand, they have directly affected the techniques of teaching within the teacher education institution itself. Thus educational technology is changing both the objectives and course content of teacher education programmes and the processes by which the objectives are to be attained. This section focuses mainly on general methodological changes rather than on the new courses on media that have been introduced.

Already there is a great volume of literature on the use of media and technology in teacher education. However, several recent documents and deliberations (from the United States and England respectively) will serve to illustrate the strong impact that developments in educational technology are having on teacher education processes. In 1971 the American Association for Educational Communications and Technology published *Basic Guidelines for Media and Technology in Teacher Education.* These were designed to assist the staff and administration of colleges and universities more realistically to incorporate media and technology in their programmes by amplifying the new Standards for the Accreditation of Teacher Education prepared by the American Association of Colleges for Teacher Education. Each guideline relates to the relevant standard and is followed by a number of questions to help institutions in re-developing teacher education programmes, especially those which are about to receive accreditation visits. The guidelines concern both the incorporation of media studies and media-based methodologies and touch most components of teacher education. Several extracts from the document will indicate its nature and comprehensiveness.

One of the guidelines for the General Studies Component is set out as follows:

Guideline: *The General Studies Component should provide the teacher education program with a general foundation for the literate use of the modern media of communications—linguistic as well as nonlinguistic.*

1.2.1 Are all modern media studied as a part of the communication tools needed by the student—books, newspapers, magazines, photographs, motion pictures, television, radio, and recordings?

1.2.2 Do students have an opportunity to learn in the areas of general studies through the quality application of a variety of media and technology as a part of the various teaching methods used?

1.2.3 Are newer media packages obtained as documentaries of significant social and political issues in the General Studies Component?

1.2.4 Are both linguistic and nonlinguistic media used as primary documentation for scholarly pursuits—e.g., in the areas of history, sociology and the sciences? (p. 3)

Again, this time in the Professional Studies Component, the following is one of a number of guidelines:

1.3.3.3 Guideline: *Newer media and technology can particularly serve the clinical needs of the Professional Studies Component of modern teacher education programs.*

1.3.3.3a What provision is made for a wide variety of instructional technologies appropriate to various learning problems and teaching styles and applied to different modes of learning as a part of the individual student's clinical experiences?

1.3.3.3b In what ways are modern media used to provide prospective teachers with simulated teaching situations?

1.3.3.3c How are media used to evaluate the effectiveness of the clinical experience aspect of the Professional Studies Component?

1.3.3.3d Are mediated clinical teaching situations used with all prospective teachers?

1.3.3.3e How are students helped to use technological resources in preparing for and carrying out clinical experiences? (p. 4)

Similarly, the Practicum Component has its guidelines. One reads

Guideline: *Direct, substantial participation in teaching should include realistic opportunities to use modern media and technology, under personnel qualified to help develop quality application of such materials.*

1.3.4a Does the institution select collaborating schools for internships that have the necessary services to provide the wide variety of media generally available to teachers?

1.3.4b Is supervision of the practicum carried on by personnel who also understand the role and use of modern media in the classroom?

1.3.4c Does the institution make contribution to offset any shortcomings that cooperating schools may have in their ability to service the internship teacher with the kinds of media, equipment and technology needed?

1.3.4d Is it possible for every prospective teacher to have an opportunity to assume full responsibility for including media in the classes he is teaching? (p. 5)

There is also a series of guidelines concerning a 'Materials and Instructional Media Center' to maintain media and provide help to both staff and students. A selection of questions drawn from the various guidelines are these

Are a wide variety of instructional media and technology packages available (i.e., films, filmstrips, realia, audio and videotapes, transparencies, programmed instruction materials, and closed-circuit television segments) which are indicative of the wide array that teachers can use in their classrooms once they are in the field?

Can faculty and staff obtain equipment, materials and other services needed to produce instructional materials—e.g., making their own slides, developing their own audio and/or videotape recordings, and preparing their own computer-facilitated instructional tasks?

Are professional and instructional media personnel who operate in the center available to the faculty for developing and redeveloping the learning experiences needed for the Professional Studies Component?

Are instructional communications and technology personnel who service the education faculty members professionally competent in teacher education and in the use of media for such programs?

Does the budget of the institution allow (in the media center's budget or otherwise) funds for adequately redeveloping courses to properly use newer media and technology without undue strain on the normal departmental budgets?

Are learning spaces used for the program planned in such a way as to anticipate the use of a variety of modes and materials, including the acceptance of electronic equipment and distribution systems presently needed by newer media and technology? (pp. 7–8)

In teacher education institutions in England important advances in the use of media are being promoted by the National Council for Educational Technology. In 1971 this body established a study team to examine the need of colleges of education for learning materials of all kinds. After visiting a third of the colleges it became clear to the team that the main problems in the area of educational technology facing the colleges were:

—The lack of an information service about available materials;
—The lack of machinery for designing, producing and testing the learning materials;
—The lack of machinery for enabling the decision-making bodies in the colleges to test the materials and the approach for themselves;
—The lack of any consultancy service to which colleges could turn for advice in this field, whether in the design of materials, the defining of objectives, the evaluation of courses or the design of resource centres. (Eggleston, 1974, p. 95)

Impressed by these problems, the National Council has been successful in launching a development project with the following aims:

(i) To help the colleges to make the fullest and most effective use of the study materials in the various media already available from within the college system itself and from other sources, including the broadcasters and commercial suppliers;

(ii) To help the colleges to develop their individual and cooperative production of evaluated study materials in accordance with their felt needs, using existing facilities;

(iii) To help the colleges to express their requirements for study materials to the broadcasters and commercial suppliers and to improve the existing feedback paths for comment and evaluation;

(iv) To help college academic staff to develop their understanding of the principles and techniques of educational technology;

(v) To help colleges to develop their procedures for the organisation and management of study materials and associated resources. (Eggleston, 1974, p. 95)

The activities of the project are centred in a number of colleges of education throughout England.

Of all the new media, television has had the greatest impact on teacher education. All its technologies are now quite common in teacher education institutions (e.g., studio recording and editing facilities, closed-circuit systems, outside broadcast vans, light portable recording equipment, and remote-control recording facilities). Besides facilitating the development of such techniques as microteaching and simulation, television has been used to provide students with 'live' or recorded observations of children and teaching (Johnson *et al.*, 1969); to provide videotaped feedback on students' practice teaching performance (Winn, 1974); to provide models of specific teaching behaviours (Turney *et al.*, 1973); to devise self-instructional courses on teaching (Borg *et al.*, 1970); to evaluate student recognition of teaching skills (Garten and Hudson, 1974); to provide in-service experiences for teachers (Foxall and Evans, 1973; Thomas and Jones, 1974); to mediate special training programmes for supervising teachers (Tom, 1975); to construct protocol materials illustrating particular concepts of education (Cruickshank, 1972b); and to enable the 'remote supervision' of students in schools through recordings of teaching sent to the training institution (Reed, 1976).

In sharp contrast to the wide use of television in the teacher education process, the other powerful piece of technology of the present, the computer, seems to have had limited impact. The use of computers in assisting instruction, especially in secondary schools, has led to the introduction of pre-service and in-service courses on the employment of computers in the teaching of various school subjects (*Computers and the Schools*, 1972). However, the literature on the applications of the computer in the general methodology of teacher education is slight indeed. One important application has been the use of the computer to provide student teachers with an immediate flow of information on aspects of teacher-pupil interaction as their classroom teaching proceeds. At Indiana University, Semmel and his associates have developed, with encouraging results, a Computer-Assisted Teacher Training System (CATTS). This system is conceptualized as 'a closed loop cybernetic system' which, among other things, permits the 'continuous and instantaneous observation, coding analysis, and feedback of relevant training information to the trainee *while he is teaching*—with feedback delivered through some meaningful auditory or visual source within the teaching environment' (Semmel, 1972, p. 563). At the Pennsylvania State University Cartwright has led a team in developing an in-service teacher education course titled 'Computer Assisted Renewal Education (CARE): Introduction to the Education of Exceptional Children'. The programme is designed to assist teachers in 'identifying the problems of handicapped children'. To implement the programme with teachers in their rural home communities, an expandable van was built and fitted with a computer and fifteen teacher stations, each equipped with a cathode-ray tube to display information and diagrams, a typewriter keyboard and a light-sensitive pen for teacher responses, a rear screen image projector addressable by the computer, and headsets to relay prerecorded messages. The teachers interact with the instructional programme at these stations and the computer also generates a final examination (Hall *et al.*, 1974). Using this facility approximately 1,000 teachers have been able to complete the programme each year.

RENEWAL OF IN-SERVICE EDUCATION

Increasing attention is being given to the in-service education of teachers both in Australia, Europe, North America and elsewhere. In this section some of the factors which will influence this area up to the end of the century are discussed. While no attempt is made to outline or to suggest a specific range of in-service activities, an attempt is made to describe briefly some of the main overseas developments with the aim of highlighting some of the issues to be faced in Australia.

Australian Trends

Prior to 1950 very little provision was made for the in-service education of teachers in Australia. It is fair to say that the view which prevailed strongly was that pre-service training, limited though it was in many cases, was an adequate base to be a teacher. While many teachers added to their formal qualifications through their own efforts, this was viewed as a matter for each teacher. Employing authorities gave very little support as it was expected that teachers would take these courses in their own time and at their own expense. There were a few short in-service courses conducted by the various State Education Departments but teacher participation was extremely limited considering the total number of teachers in service.

Between 1950 and 1975 the situation changed. Employing authorities began to accept responsibility to give financial assistance to teachers who were studying to improve their formal qualifications, and study leave (usually without pay) was granted more frequently. During these twenty-five years the employing authorities had considerable difficulty in staffing the schools as it was a period of rapid increase in enrolments and of teacher shortages. The primary administrative focus was on providing both classrooms and teachers. In spite of staffing difficulties the State Education Departments established and strengthened their own in-service education sections and encouraged teachers to undertake further formal study. By 1975 the employing authorities had accepted in-service education as one of their basic responsibilities and were increasingly concerned about the quality of the teaching service.

Australian tertiary institutions have increased the opportunities for in-service education. It has long been usual for teachers to study for additional qualifications following their pre-service teacher education course. For many years the universities provided most of the opportunities which were available to teachers. More recently, the colleges of advanced education have also provided opportunities and their role is expanding. The Cohen Committee's Report, *Teacher Education 1973–1975*, approved funding for the colleges of advanced education to conduct six-month and twelve-month courses for practising teachers, and noted the particular need to upgrade two-year trained teachers to three-year trained status. The committee considered that short courses of half-a-day and of up to one or two weeks were the joint financial responsibility of the employer and of the employee. These views have had significant impact on planning by the colleges since the report was released in March 1973 (Australian Commission on Advanced Education, 1973). Since 1974, Conversion Courses have been offered to two-year trained teachers to enable them to gain the three-year Diploma of Teaching. And throughout Australia thousands of teachers have enrolled. The Diploma of Teaching is the basic qualification which provides a means for teachers to go on with studies either in a Graduate Diploma course or in a Bachelor of Education course.

Also the colleges have acted to have various in-service courses assessed and registered with the Australian Council on Awards in Advanced Education. The first category comprises Graduate Diplomas in specialist fields such as reading, music education, aboriginal education, and remedial education. These Graduate Diplomas provide an opportunity for intensive and in-depth study of a specific area such as reading over a two-year period if the course is taken part-time. The usual pattern is a number of specialized units, and a total requirement of some 360 course hours. The second category is the Bachelor of Education degree. Generally this is an in-service degree, available only to experienced teachers and pursued after attaining the pre-service Diploma of Teaching. The total requirement is some 450 course hours, and the degree differs from the Graduate Diploma in that it provides for broader study of general units in education and in educational psychology and in content areas such as English, mathematics, science, social science, art, drama, music, and physical education, and so on. The degree course also takes a minimum of two years to complete, if studied part-time.

The position of in-service education in Australia has changed rapidly during the past decade and particularly during the past five years. The employing authorities have made increased provision, the teachers' organizations have adopted policies supporting, and demanding, such provision, and the teachers themselves have become increasingly aware that in-service education is a necessary base for their work as teachers. An excellent example of teacher demand was evidenced immediately after 1964 when the decision was taken to introduce 'new mathematics' courses. Thousands of teachers were provided with background mathematics courses related both to content and to methodology in an effort which had had no parallel in Australian education up to that time.

In the next twenty-five years there will probably be a continuing trend in the following directions in Australia: (i) Employing authorities will increase and strengthen their in-service activities, particularly in the area of curriculum development. (ii) Teachers' organizations increasingly will press for all teachers to be given the opportunity to achieve degree status through in-service courses. (iii) The release of teachers on full pay for further education will become a right. (iv) Employing authorities will attempt to build up the number of teachers employed to such a level that a proportion may be released at any time for various types of in-service education, conducted by tertiary institutions, state authorities, and teachers themselves. (v) Greater attention will be given to the induction of newly graduated teachers, especially to those in the first year of teaching. The predicted slow-down in enrolment increases and the slight surplus which has developed in the number of teachers available may provide opportunities for greater attention to be given to the continuing education of teachers. This will be the first opportunity during the lifetime of most Australian teachers where the additional teachers are available so that some teachers may be released for longer periods to engage in one of the many forms of in-service education.

The Need for In-Service Education

There seems to be general acceptance in most nations, among both the public and the teachers themselves, that no period of pre-service teacher education is an adequate base for a lifetime of teaching. Many would agree with Hyer and McClure that 'Governments have an *obligation* to provide for the retraining necessary for teachers adequately to plan and implement new instructional practices' (OECD, 1974, p. 63). Twenty-five years ago there was little, if any, discussion of professional obsolescence among teachers; by 1975 this had changed considerably. For example, in the United States Cogan recently stated:

> The established professions require the practitioner to continue his education throughout his entire professional life. The rationale for this requirement derives from the need to help the doctor, lawyer, or engineer to gain the new knowledge and competencies he must master if he is to avoid lapsing into rapid professional obsolescence. (Ryan, 1975, p. 213)

Further, in England Eggleston stated:

> But, even more important, the concept of in-service training as a process of restocking teachers with new working capital became markedly evident. Indeed, a number of experts made it clear that they now saw the development of in-service rather than initial training as being of more fundamental importance in the creation and development of new teacher roles. (OECD, 1974, p. 12)

The public have become critical of the quality of education in many countries. There has been questioning of the capacity of teachers to cope, and whether or not standards are falling. At the same time there has been direct criticism of the amount of money being spent on education. In 1965 a member of New South Wales Parliament queried whether the Education Department was being voted funds to the detriment of revenue producing departments, and said 'if we do not take a balanced view of this matter we could reach the situation of having an educated people yet insufficient water and food' (cited in Jecks, 1974, p. 130). The quality of teachers and of education will come under increasing scrutiny.

Teachers have become increasingly aware of the need for continuing education. More and more it has become one of the demands that their professional organizations make on governments. The stage seems set for significant developments in the continuing education of teachers between 1976 and 2000. And, as in-service education becomes a right more than a privilege, there is no doubt that teachers will demand that it be both of high quality and broad in its range (Watkins, 1973).

The need for in-service education has been well and briefly stated by Lord James. In essence he argues that it is necessary because of changes in knowledge, changes in techniques of teaching, changes in society, changes in teachers themselves, and changes in schools (Watkins, 1973). Few would dispute his view. But there are those, like Haberman, who can speak with tongue in cheek regarding 'the over abundance of needs attributed to teachers':

> Teachers should: know more subject matter, go through sensitivity training; learn verbal and non verbal teaching strategies; diagnose, prescribe, and evaluate learning; consume and conduct research; learn to work in teams; create, select, and evaluate media and materials; teach aides, students and interns; function as change agents. (Ryan, 1975, p. 215)

Although all teachers do not demonstrate all these needs, demands on teachers are heavy and their needs must be met. In these circumstances, and if in-service education is broadly defined 'as any structured educational experience undergone by a teacher in service' (Watkins, 1973, p. 41), there is need in Australia for significant development in the range of in-service opportunities available to teachers.

These in-service opportunities would fulfil various objectives. In the Australian context, for instance, Neal and Mossenson have listed the following general objectives for in-service education:

(i) To enable teachers to master the new knowledge and skills involved in the introduction of new curricula and techniques;

(ii) to create opportunities for stimulation and 'refresher' activities for teachers; to encourage thinking about the problems of education; to exchange ideas and disseminate ideas; to gain new enthusiasm from shared reinforcement and forward thinking;

(iii) to provide facilities for deeper study into the background knowledge associated with subject content and with educational theory;

(iv) to assist teachers to acquire proficiency in the performance of new tasks whether in specialist fields or in administration; and,

(v) to provide professional activities wherein teachers can debate theories, examine ideas, solve problems, and contribute to the development of educational policy throughout a system. (Richardson and Bowen, 1976, p. 167)

Release and Support of Teachers

In various countries there is a distinct trend towards a situation where teachers have the right to be released on full pay for in-service education. In 1973 Lord James, in discussing the James Report stated:

> What we did affirm is the need for the teacher to have a *right* to a more substantial period of in-service education. Our suggestion is for one term in seven years which we hope will improve to five years. (Watkins, 1973, p. 13)

In Australia, David Verco, when he was Director General of Education in New South Wales in 1970, stated that he hoped that the time would come in Australia when teachers could be released on a similar basis. Reports of the Organisation for Economic Co-operation and Development have repeatedly pointed to the right of release teachers have. Ferry (1974) noted that in France since 1972, following negotiations with trade unions, the principle had been adopted that during the course of their careers primary teachers were to be entitled to full-time training equivalent to one school year and that both six-week courses and thirteen-week courses were being conducted. Marklund and Gran (1974) reported that since 1964 all Swedish teachers have been required to spend five days in in-service education each year and that in Scandinavia it is proposed to follow the pattern of one term of in-service education for each teacher for every seven years of service.

Practice in North America varies widely. For example, some teachers are supported for extended graduate courses in tertiary institutions, while in Texas, school system annual budgets provide extra salary to enable each teacher to have ten days of in-service education each year (Mullins, 1972).

In Australia it is probable that teachers' organizations will seek to negotiate for the release of Australian teachers as a right. And it is quite probable that senior educational administrators will support this development. The problem the professionals will face is to obtain the necessary funds. This decision may be political rather than educational. However, the present full supply of teachers is the best chance yet in this century for such release to occur. It is to be hoped that the opportunity is neither neglected nor missed.

If teachers are to be released for in-service education on the basis suggested in the James Report, it will be necessary to have additional staff up to some five per cent of the total teaching service. Lord James has stated the necessity for this quite forcibly:

> If in-service education is to become a reality on any significant scale, one preliminary and essential condition must be recognised: what we consider the normal staffing ratio for schools must take adequate account of it. (Watkins, 1973, p. 17)

And, also in the United Kingdom, the National Union of Teachers has not been slow to point out the problems faced, with Britton stating:

> I suspect a little cynically that provision of in-service training along the lines of the James Report will not be made unless there is a measure of compulsion on the part of the teacher, for such compulsion implies a compulsion on the part of the Local Education Authority to make the necessary provision. (Watkins, 1973, p. 26)

In the future quite substantial planning and budget provision will be necessary to release a significant number of teachers during school time. Cogan has described the problem thus:

Part of this difficulty derives from the fact that most in-service education requires the teacher to put in a great deal of non-reimbursed time after school. The in-service programme comes out of the teacher's hide, and few of them willingly work overtime for nothing. (Ryan, 1975, p. 217)

In Australia a significant number of teachers have undertaken tertiary study in their own time, and in addition many short in-service courses have been conducted both during school vacations and during school time. In the latter case, courses have usually lasted one or two days only. During the next twenty-five years a key issue which must be faced is whether teachers will be released during school time for significantly longer periods of in-service education. If the French pattern of six-week courses and of thirteen-week courses becomes common, the schools will need to be staffed on the basis of some 105 per cent of the teachers now employed. While the attainment of this level of staffing will take time, a worthwhile start needs to be made now.

An Administrative Structure for In-Service Education

Some of the issues involved in implementing the James Report in the United Kingdom have already been discussed. Hewett has urged the need for an organizational structure to avoid profusion and duplication in the various agencies providing courses in an in-service jungle. Hewett argued for an administrative structure which would facilitate a responsible and genuine partnership among the employers, the teachers, the training institutions and the central government as those who had legitimate interests in the in-service education of teacher. He suggested a body which had the power to organize and to rationalize provision, and warned against the continuing education of teachers as discontinuous and fragmented experiences (Watkins, 1973).

In Australia the formal establishment of an administrative structure to bring together all those who have legitimate interests in the in-service education of teachers is an essential first step which needs to be taken. If this is long delayed an uncoordinated, and possibly competing, pattern of provision may become established. This is a matter for each state minister of education to consider so that there is co-ordination and rationalization at state level. In addition, there is a case for the Australian Education Council to consider a federal structure to facilitate and to promote in-service education so that contact and co-operation are encouraged and developed across state boundaries.

The Views of Teachers

In devising any programme of in-service education it is important to seek and to know the views of teachers. In Australia there is a notable lack of such information. Indeed, it is an area where a number of relatively simple survey research projects would be of value. In such research, studies already carried out in North America and in the United Kingdom could give a worthwhile lead to the type of information to be collected and analysed.

In North America there have been numerous surveys of teachers' views on in-service education. Only one study is noted here and it relates to general questions. Brimm and Tollett (1974) conducted a state-wide research study in Tennessee and usable returns were received from 646 teachers, or 65 per cent of the sample. Teacher opinions were obtained on an inventory of 34 statements regarding in-service education programmes. The five statements with which teachers most strongly agreed were:

The teacher should have the opportunity to select the kind of in-service activities which he feels will strengthen his professional competence.

In-service programs should include special orientation activities for the new classroom teacher.

The real test of an in-service program is whether it helps the teacher to cope with his professional tasks more successfully.

In-service programs must include activities which allow for the different interests which exist among individual teachers.

Teachers need to be involved in the developing of purposes, activities, and methods of evaluation for in-service programs.

The five statements with which teachers most strongly disagreed were:

Most in-service programs are virtually useless.

The objectives of in-service programs in my system are always specific.

Orientation activities for the new classroom teacher in our system are adequate.

There is adequate follow-up to determine the effects of in-service activities in my system.

I wish more of our in-service programs were scheduled as three hour sessions at night. (Brimm and Tollett, 1974, p. 522)

In the United Kingdom, Cane and Townsend have conducted surveys related to the demand for continuing professional training among teachers (O'Hare, 1971). In general the teachers preferred the bulk of their in-service training to take place close to their own home or school and some 75 per cent of teachers indicated willingness to attend vacation courses for one week at convenient centres. Some 80 per cent of the teachers who responded to the questionnaire indicated their need for in-service training. Priority areas for most teachers came under the headings of: teaching methods; aids and materials; and the development of new teaching schemes and programmes. In discussing these same surveys in 1973 Cane listed primary mathematics, the teaching of reading, art and craft and junior education as the five most popular topics in order of requests by primary teachers. For secondary teachers the five most popular topics were comprehensive education, use of audiovisual aids, school organization and management, careers guidance, and the counselling of pupils (Watkins, 1973).

Developments in Britain and North America

In this part a selection of new developments in in-service education in Britain and North America is reviewed. It is believed that most of these developments have some relevance to the Australian context.

Teachers' Centres in the United Kingdom

British teachers' centres have commanded world-wide attention. Much of their development has occurred since 1967, and Walton has described them as 'an attempt to involve the teachers ... at grassroots level in curriculum development' (Walton, 1972, p. 15). An excellent overview of teachers' centres up to 1972 is given by Poliakoff in presenting an ERIC report. She described these centres as being concerned to provide resources for teachers in curriculum and instructional materials, and as a major means both of providing information for teachers and in stimulating them to be active in curriculum innovation (Poliakoff, 1972). In discussing British teachers' centres, Rust of the University of California, summed up thus:

> Of crucial importance to the continued development of Teachers' Centres was the enduring notion that national bodies were in no position to impose their ideas upon teachers. The Schools Council continued to maintain that the essence of curriculum review and development is new thinking by teachers themselves, as well as their appraisal of the thinking of others. Teachers should have regular opportunities to meet together. They should look upon the initiation of thought, as well as the trial and assessment of new ideas and procedures, as an integral part of their professional service to society. (Rust, 1973, p. 187)

The Institute of Education at the University of Exeter, for example, established some years ago, a Regional Resources Centre to serve schools in the institute's area. This regional centre became associated with some eighteen teachers' centres spread throughout Devon. A regional committee for in-service education was established which included representatives as follows: nine from the employing authorities, five from the colleges of education, six from the teachers' associations, two from the University of Exeter, and two from the Department of Education and Science. The primary focus was on curriculum development and the membership of the committee shows the broad representation of those directly concerned with the schools (University of Exeter, 1972; Walton, 1974). In fact direct teacher participation is one of the key advantages which is usually claimed for these centres.

O'Hare noted that an increasing number of colleges of education in England were offering their facilities and resources to teachers' centre groups and that college tutors were showing a growing interest in identifying with teachers' centres (O'Hare, 1971). Certainly there is no sense in duplicating facilities. In 1974 Eggleston described the teachers' centres as 'probably one of the major innovations in professional education to have taken place in England and Wales in recent years' and went on to highlight the good sense of colleges of education providing professional centres for teachers (OECD, 1974, p. 104).

The Bachelor of Education Degree in the United Kingdom

In 1973 Hewett noted the important role which tertiary institutions could play in providing in-service education. He expressed the opinion that 'it would be unfortunate if local authorities through their own inspectorate, advisory services and teachers' centres became the major provider of in-service activity', and went on to point out the potential contribution colleges could make in teaching an in-service Bachelor of Education degree (Watkins, 1973, p. 44). Mattock has also pointed out the important role the universities might play in in-service education (Watkins, 1973).

The collaboration between colleges and universities to provide a Bachelor of Education degree has been a significant development in the United Kingdom since 1945. The work of the colleges in offering a professional degree has done much to upgrade the colleges themselves and the teachers they train. The trend towards providing all teachers with a four-year Bachelor of Education degree is one which will interest those involved in the in-service education of teachers in Australia. The collaboration which has occurred between British colleges and the universities has been based on the continuing independence of both institutions, and a recognition that all teachers should have the opportunity to study for an appropriate professional degree (OECD, 1974).

Lee (1975) has noted that surveys conducted in the United Kingdom in the late sixties showed that 75 per cent of all teachers from primary schools wanted courses on teaching methods, aids and materials, that some 25–30 per cent of teachers wanted to take a Bachelor of Education degree, and that 25 per cent more wanted to take a higher degree. In providing opportunities for teachers to study for a degree, it is obvious that the Open University is already filling a need and that the colleges also have an important role to play:

> It is inevitable that the colleges of education will be the main centres for the in-service Bachelor of Education degree course. They alone have the facilities, outlook and locations required. The pressure will be severe in centres of concentrated urban development. (Tibble, 1971, p. 147)

The role of colleges and universities in North America

In the United States there is a well-established pattern of colleges and universities providing a very wide range of in-service courses both for individual teachers and for school systems. While the employing authorities conduct their own in-service activities, tertiary institutions are called upon to make a very significant contribution. In contrast to Australia and to the United Kingdom the four-year pre-service degree for all teachers is firmly established both in the United States and in Canada. Present indications are that in Australia there will be no early move to offer four years of pre-service education for all teachers, and that many Australian teachers will complete the fourth year of a bachelor's degree in-service. In both the United States and Canada the universities have tailored graduate degrees for practitioners who work in school systems, especially in such fields as guidance, counselling, science education, educational administration, reading, and educational psychology. However no detailed discussion of graduate qualifications available in North America is intended here. Rather, the aim is to give five examples of how colleges and universities are involved directly, very often in the actual school situation, in the in-service education of teachers.

1. *The Western Ontario Field Centre.* The Ontario Institute for Studies in Education established its first field centres in 1969. The Western Ontario Centre has a field staff of three, is located in an elementary school in London, and serves an area with a population of about 500,000. The main objective of the centre is to relate the work of the institute to the school systems and other educational bodies of the region. This is done in two ways: (i) 'by communication of Institute research findings and educational innovations of the region', and (ii) 'by using the resources of the Institute to meet regional needs' (Stinson, 1972, p. 269). The centre conducts workshops on topics such as Understanding the Reading Process and on Moving Towards Continuous Progress. This example shows how an internationally renowned centre for graduate studies is directly concerned with work in the field.

2. *Political Science Institutes at Denver.* East (1972) describes how the Graduate School of International Studies at the University of Denver provided an in-service programme for secondary teachers which took two general forms. The

first of these was an extended in-service institute which met periodically during the year and for which graduate credit was offered by the university. Each participant was required to develop some sort of classroom oriented materials in the general area of international affairs. The second related to regional institutes which usually lasted for three days and in which the objective was to provide each participant with ideas, materials and even units which were ready for the classroom.

3. *Science Programmes at Ohio State.* Since the 1950s the National Science Foundation has supported hundreds of teacher retraining programmes in the form of summer institutes, in-service institutes, and co-operative college-school programmes. Usually these courses have been conducted by colleges and universities on behalf of the Foundation. Mayer, Disinger and White (1975) of Ohio State University discuss the evaluation of one such programme which had the objectives of improving teachers' understanding of earth science principles and concepts, and of assisting teachers in the use of investigatory techniques in teaching earth science courses. They concluded that the programme was effective in changing teacher behaviour toward more enquiry orientated approaches, concurrent with increasing the teacher's information base and understanding of relevant concepts.

4. *School District and State College Courses.* Mason and Rohde (1972) report a programme of courses which were developed for teachers in White Bear Lake School District and which could be taken either for school district credit or for college credit. South West Minnesota State College and several other colleges co-operated. A sample of the courses is given below.

1966–7
Creativity in Education

1967–8
Developing Instructional
  Objectives
Developing Individualized
  Instruction
Interaction Analysis

1968–9
Strategy for Change
Team Building Series
Advanced Instructional
  Objectives

1969–70
Human Relations
Developing Teacher Self-Assessment
Individualized Instruction—
  Theory and Practice
Educational Games and Simulation
Nongrading
Bookreporting

5. *An Experimental In-Service Teacher Education Programme for Distressed Elementary Schools.* In 1974 the Stanford Centre for Research and Development in Teaching published a report related to an attempt to apply social-psychological research to classroom interaction for the purpose of improving achievement motivation and achievement behaviour. An elementary school with an enrolment of 750 children, of whom 98 per cent were black, was chosen because both teachers and children had low group morale, pessimistic attitudes towards school experiences, and personal dissatisfaction and unhappiness at school. The project staff believed that if the teachers could become more satisfied with their teaching

experiences and more positively reinforcing to individuals, pupils, pupil attitudes and behaviour would become more positive. In structuring an in-service pro- gramme the fundamental purpose was to provide a support system for change. The report describes in detail how the task was undertaken. At the end of the school year teachers were asked for their opinions concerning the programme. The response was mixed and the project staff concluded that in general the goals of changing teacher and pupil attitudes and behaviour, as objectively measured, had not been met. This project is an example of how a research and development centre of a leading university became engaged in trying to improve a particular school situation (Whitmore *et al.*, 1974).

Social districts and in-service education in North America

Teachers teaching teachers. Not all major in-service activities are headed up by college or university academic staff. The Florida Department of Education estimated that it would take fifteen years of sponsoring weekly workshops to reach Florida's some 88,000 public school teachers to give in-service courses in environmental education. Consequently a scheme was developed to teach teachers to teach other teachers so that a multiplier effect was achieved. The master plan is set out below:

Phase 1 One state meeting was held which was attended by 130 persons most of whom were to act as school district contacts for environmental educa- tion. Seven regions were established by designating some of Florida's universities as regional environmental education centres.

Phase 2 Seven regional workshops were held and these were attended by a total of 600 persons. At these workshops planning was extended to take the programme to the school district level.

Phase 3 Thirty-five district workshops were held and these were attended by a total of some 3,500 persons. Emphasis was placed on curriculum development and teaching-learning materials were developed.

Phase 4 Three hundred and fifty local school workshops were held and these were attended by a total of some 35,000 teachers. In this way the environmental education programme was introduced over a relatively short time span to a great number of teachers. (Tillis and Lattart, 1974).

Open education—an in-service model. Muskopf and Moss (1972) report a four week workshop in which thirty-two teachers participated. The basic purpose was to assist as many teachers as possible to internalize open education, to feel it deeply, so as to know what it is to learn in a free and supportive environment. To try to achieve this aim the teachers were placed in a simulated classroom setting filled with stimulating and manipulative materials. In addition, a demonstration class of some twenty children was attached to the workshop. Muskopf and Moss describe six basic dimensions of the in-service model:

(i) Teachers needed an extended period to become immersed in the learning process.

(ii) The purpose of the initial stage of in-service work was to give teachers an emotional experience with open education.

(iii) Teachers needed to be helped to become proficient and comfortable in undertaking the many activities involved.

(iv) Outside specialists were little used and every attempt was made to draw skills from within the group.

(v) The concept of voluntarism was rigidly adhered to.

(vi) A demonstration class of children in an open classroom was part of the in-service programme.

Muskopf and Moss concluded that programmes of this type help to overcome the superficiality which characterizes some in-service work and give teachers the chance to become personally involved in a long-term programme of self-growth.

The above examples have been drawn from a great range of similar courses in the United States and Canada. The basic purpose has been to illustrate the direct 'grassroots' involvement of colleges and universities and to indicate the considerable effort that is made to plan and implement viable programmes. In this, much more use is made of in-service consultants and of summer schools than is the case in Australia. Similarly training packages of various types are used in an attempt to place good resource materials in the hands of teachers (Baum and Chastian, 1972; Merwin, 1974; OECD, 1974).

Future Developments in In-Service Education in Australia

In light of the discussion so far, four of the five propositions set out at the beginning of the chapter relating to the next quarter century are now considered further. The fifth proposition, relating to the induction of newly graduated teachers, is discussed in some detail in the concluding part of this section.

Employing Authorities

The Cohen Report stated clearly that short in-service courses were the financial responsibility of the employer and of the employee. The employing authorities will fund most of these courses and will either conduct courses using their own personnel or will contract with others, such as the tertiary institutions, to provide courses for their employees. Indeed in a well planned and co-ordinated pattern of in-service education it may be expected that from now on greater use will be made of outside contracts than has been the case in the past. Just as pre-service education is no longer largely monopolized and directly provided by the employing authorities, it may be expected that short in-service courses will also cease to be so exclusively monopolized by the employers. A balance needs to be made so that both employers and employees have a greater range of contacts with courses and with persons who are not part of their own relatively closed system.

But the employing authorities will not only be concerned with short in-service courses. Part of the increase and strengthening of their in-service activities will relate to longer courses and to formal qualifications. Their concern for the quality of their employees will result in increasing support for their employees to take longer courses and to add to their qualifications. In this, the colleges of advanced education and the universities will have an important role. Further, the employing authorities will increase and strengthen in-service education relating to curriculum development using both internal and external resources, facilities, study materials and personnel. There is a strong case for the Australian tertiary institutions to become more directly involved in the concerns of practising teachers, particularly in the field of curriculum development. These institutions have the potential to make a significant contribution which could benefit both the schools and the tertiary institutions.

Teachers' Organizations

It was only in the early 'seventies that three years of pre-service education for all Australian teachers was finally achieved following many years of pressure from the teachers' organizations. Therefore, in 1976, it is not surprising that the teachers' organizations have not yet campaigned as vigorously to achieve the aim of a graduate profession with degree status for all teachers. Even so, this policy has been adopted and it will soon be pursued as the next broad objective as far as teachers' formal qualifications are concerned.

In the past the universities have provided an important avenue for teachers to gain degree status. This will continue, excepting that the universities increasingly will concentrate on graduate level studies. By 1980 the colleges of advanced education will have their in-service Bachelor of Education degrees well established and many teachers will gain degree status by this means. Some colleges have already commenced these Bachelor of Education courses.

Release for in-service education

The extent of development of in-service education in Australia will depend on whether an increased number of teachers can be released for full-time study. While there will be administrative and industrial support within the profession for such release, the final decision will be a political one. Examples have been given of the strong trend towards teachers having a right to such release in some European countries. There is little doubt that this is the fundamental issue to be faced in Australia in the immediate future. Are Australian teachers to have this right?

Staffing ratios and in-service education

In Australia it has been only very recently that there have been enough teachers adequately to staff the schools. Now, for the first time in some forty years, there is a slight surplus and there are signs that this surplus will continue. This represents a significant opportunity to improve staffing ratios in schools to a level where the release of teachers for in-service activity is practicable. For the first time in the memory of almost every practising teacher there is the possibility of establishing a logistic base which could result in the release of teachers. Whether this opportunity is taken, whether this base is established, and whether Australian teachers will have a right to release for in-service education tend to be political decisions. The professional advice given will be that a significant move should be made.

In-service education in the year 2000 will relate directly to these decisions. It is to be hoped that overseas developments and directions are both noted and followed in all four areas.

Induction of Newly-Graduated Teachers

In spite of efforts made to assist young teachers by inspectors, by headmasters and by other teachers, the first year of teaching in the Australian context historically has tended to be largely a matter of 'sink or swim'. While the beginning teacher is usually keen to have a class of his own and to feel at last that he is a teacher, there are many problems to be faced. And often these are faced in isolation, for teachers have tended to work on their own and to have particular responsibility for an isolated teaching situation. Until recently there has been either a shortage, or a bare sufficiency, of teachers in most Australian states and in this situation every teacher, no matter how inexperienced, has been needed to staff the classrooms.

Of course, the problems of beginning teachers have been recognized, and the teachers' organizations have urged that beginning teachers should be placed in classes and in schools where there was a reasonable chance of success and where experienced counsellors were available to assist them. Employing authorities also have tried to do as much as possible to facilitate the entry of beginning teachers into teaching. Even so, there are many who would feel that in terms of the need, the provision made has not been nearly enough. Indeed, it is reasonable to compare the situation in Australia with that in the United Kingdom where in 1967 Plowden concluded that it was doubtful if the majority of young teachers are given the conditions and guidance in their first posts which will reinforce their training and lead to rising standards in the profession as a whole; and, the James Committee was to note later that nothing depressed them more than 'the gross inadequacy of the present arrangements for the probationary year' (James, 1972, p. 21). In Australia it is to be hoped that the present adequate supply of teachers will result in a thorough examination of the induction of beginning teachers and some real progress in dealing with this general problem.

While many beginning teachers are eager to be seen as fully qualified, 'in reality a teacher just entering the profession is at *best* prepared only to *begin* learning how to teach' (Evans, 1976, p. 28), and it seems reasonable to argue that the probationary year should be 'a process of advanced induction into a full time professional role with parallels to the internship programme of hospitals' (OECD, 1974, p. 32). While the major focus of the discussion in this part will be on the first year of teaching there is no wish to exaggerate the needs of the first year teacher, nor to deny that some form of induction support is necessary over several years.

Release of teachers for induction courses

Obviously any programme of induction for beginning teachers must receive adequate financial support. In the United Kingdom the Liverpool Education Committee has reported fully on its scheme for the induction of newly graduated teachers. The report is significant in that it highlights the practical problems and issues and what actually happens in practice when an attempt is made to release a large number of beginning teachers for induction purposes.

First there is the matter of cost. In September 1974 the average salary cost of a probationer in Liverpool was £1,974. In the Liverpool induction scheme an additional amount of 25 per cent of the salary costs of beginning teachers was available to support the scheme. In addition, up to £120 for each probationer could be claimed from a Department of Education and Science research grant. The Liverpool Education Committee set out in detail its planned budget for some 700 probationers for the year beginning 1st April, 1975. The total cost was £524, 352 with income shown as £491, 433. The balance of £32, 919 was a charge against rates (Liverpool Education Committee, Report No. 1, 1975).

These figures show clearly that an induction programme is not cheap.

In the Liverpool scheme beginning teachers were released for not less than one-fifth of their time to engage in induction activities. This amounts to approximately thirty days' release each year and this release was spread on a sessional basis week by week as this permitted a greater degree of continuity of contact between the beginning teacher and his own pupils. Also, it made timetabling easier within the school and replacement staff could be more easily recruited. Because the beginning teacher was available to teach for only four-fifths' time each week a formula was adopted where each beginning teacher was rated as 0.7 of a teacher and where three beginning teachers were equated as two teachers when schools were staffed (Liverpool Education Committee, Report No. 4, 1975).

In implementing the induction scheme the policy was established that the beginning teacher should spend the greater part of his time in his own school:

> The Advisory Committee was strongly of the opinion that for the first term the newly qualified teacher should not be withdrawn from school to pursue an induction programme at the professional centre but should be allowed this term to 'settle in', to 'feel his feet', to savour the feel of being a teacher. (Liverpool Education Committee, Report No. 4, 1975, p. 39)

In spite of the funding which was available for this induction scheme, real difficulties were met as far as the release of beginning teachers was concerned. Because of problems in finding replacement teachers it was estimated that 34 per cent of beginning teachers might reasonably have been withdrawn (Liverpool Education Committee, Report No. 6, 1975). However, it seems that in most cases the schools chose to release their beginning teachers for induction. As this was the major problem faced, the solution suggested was that all schools should be staffed in such a way that sufficient teachers were available to allow for release for in-service courses, for illness, for secondment, and so on. 'Obviously a scheme cannot continue in this manner, reliant upon the goodwill of teaching staff for its continuance, without incurring some resentment and replacement teachers must be found' (University of Liverpool, 1975, p. 3). Experience gained in the Liverpool scheme is recent and the data contained in the various reports make good reading; it contrasts with generalized discussion and exhortation concerning induction.

In Australia each state Education Department would face a significant financial outlay if an induction scheme along the lines of the Liverpool scheme were introduced. For example, in addition to finding expert instructors to handle induction activities, for every 1,000 beginning teachers there would be the need to find 300 additional teachers if the staffing formula of 0.7 used in the Liverpool scheme were adopted.

Teacher-tutors

Paragraph 3.50 of the James Report stated in part that:

> It is important that no school should be without a teacher-tutor: it is equally important that he should be properly prepared for his work. It would not be enough simply to affix lables to a number of teachers already in the schools however effective and conscientious they might be. (James, 1972, p. 37)

Subsequently teacher-tutors became an important element in the Liverpool scheme since much of the induction programme was carried on within each beginning teacher's own school. James severely criticized the informal help beginning teachers were given by headmasters and by other teachers. In establishing a system of teacher-tutors the aim was to select experienced and competent practising teachers. Bolam and Baker (1975), in discussing teacher-tutors, noted that 'tutors are being encouraged to adopt a training and pastoral, rather than simply a pastoral role in helping probationers' (Bolam and Baker, 1975, p. 10).

Report No. 2 of the Liverpool Education Committee includes a good discussion of teacher-tutors and shows that of some 369 who were appointed, slightly less than half were either deputy headmasters or headmasters. In doing so, Report No. 2 raised the question as to whether the appointment of deputy headmasters and headmasters was consonant with the James Report. The general issue arises as to who should be appointed as teacher-tutors.

The Liverpool Education Committee outlines the role of the teacher-tutor thus:

> The responsibilities of the teacher-tutor will not reduce in any way the ultimate responsibility of the head teacher for the control and conduct of the school. The head teacher will retain responsibility for reporting on the competence of the new teacher during the probationary year although he may wish to discuss the progress of the new teacher with the teacher-tutor.
>
> 1. General oversight of all the practical experience of professional work that new teachers undergo in the first year of their appointment.
>
> 2. Assistance to the new teacher prior to taking up his first teaching post (arranging preliminary visits, supplying schemes of work, etc.)
>
> 3. Assisting the new teacher with professional and/or personal problems that may arise during the probationary year.
>
> 4. Assisting the new teacher to make optimum use of the facilities in the school and the surrounding area.
>
> 5. Assisting the new teacher, either directly or through specialist colleagues, to develop effective teaching techniques in the classroom.
>
> 6. Facilitating contact between the new teacher and the professional centre. Advising the new teacher on the suitability of courses available at the professional centre and in appropriate cases contributing to the work of the professional centre. (Liverpool Education Committee, Report No. 2, 1975, pp. 10–11)

The clear intention is that teacher-tutors work closely with beginning teachers and provide an essential support role within the school to facilitate the induction of the newly graduated teacher.

Content of induction courses

Most beginning teachers both require, and want, specific advice on an individual basis. While this is not to say that value does not derive from group activities, it does indicate that a great deal of specific and individual advice is necessary. It is well to remember that the beginning teacher is clearly concerned about his own survival in the teaching situation and with the consolidation of the teaching skills he has started to develop. It is a primary objective that the beginning teacher should gain self-confidence, and usually the beginning teacher himself has quite definite ideas about the assistance he needs. In seeking this advice the beginning teacher will 'usually seek support and technical assistance from more experienced teachers' (Evans, 1976, p. 9). While due attention should be given to the expressed needs of beginning teachers, it is well to remember that their perspective may be limited and self-centred and the employing authority should seek to broaden their horizons and to focus on the needs of children as well as on their needs as beginning teachers. Evans is of the opinion that 'as the pinch of beginning teaching eases, another transition begins to occur. . . . Perhaps for the first time, a teacher's primary concern is for the quality of learning and the general welfare of pupils' (Evans, 1976, p. 10).

The general objective of the Liverpool scheme is 'to offer practical and individualised help to probationers and that the main focus should be upon the problems and opportunities facing them in their own classrooms' (Liverpool Education Committee, Report No. 5, 1975, p. 43). It seems that beginning primary teachers are much concerned with discipline problems and with attempting to work to a syllabus. It is self-evident that beginning teachers are much concerned with specific matters of detail where they lack both knowledge and experience and the Liverpool Committee has set out in good detail the type of course which it feels is most appropriate. This centres around giving information concerning the employing authority, the profession, their own school, and around problems of working in the school community, problems in particular subject areas, teaching methods and classroom management. Of course, these topics form part of pre-service education. However, for many young teachers they take on urgent and real meaning once they are in the classroom situation. The Liverpool Committee summed up thus:

> The evidence collected so far would indicate the need for a programme to cover the following four broad areas:
>
> 1. Familiarisation with the school. (Policies, objectives, organisation, resources, methods, curriculum, etc.)
>
> 2. Re-inforcement of teaching techniques and material relevant to the newly qualified teacher's immediate needs in the classroom.
>
> 3. Information regarding the general pattern of education provision in Liverpool linked with a deeper consideration of educational methods in the light of the actual teaching experience of the newly qualified teacher.
>
> 4. Personal problems of the newly qualified teacher. Meeting other newly qualified teachers. Time for planning and consolidation. (Liverpool Education Committee, Report No. 5, 1975, p. 46)

Teacher induction pilot schemes—an evaluation

Late in 1975 an evaluation report was presented which reviewed official pilot schemes both in Liverpool (as already discussed in some detail) and in Northumberland. Bolam and Baker (1975) reported favourably on both pilot schemes and said that they provided 'a basically sound model towards which other authorities may build' (p. 1). They reported that the Liverpool scheme had involved 758 beginning teachers and the Northumberland scheme 210. Both schemes gave the beginning teachers teaching loads which had been reduced to 75 per cent of a full load, and Bolam and Baker reported that many beginning teachers 'would have left their schools had it not been for the lightened teacher load' (p. 4). The use of teacher-tutors proved valuable: 'In both authorities school-based activities were highly valued because of their immediate relevance to the individual problems of probationers' (p. 5). Activities outside the school were not highly valued, but Bolam and Baker recommended these be retained with 'the right balance between the two' (p. 5). There were, however, problems related to the role of the tutor-teacher. Many tended to concentrate on the pastoral role and most were unsure of how to conduct their training role.

> The extent to which they did adopt a training role probably depended on their own personal inclinations, the views of their probationers (many of whom regard extra training as a threat to their status as a fully qualified professional) and the climate of opinion in their schools. (Bolam and Baker, 1975, pp. 5–6)

As a result of experience gained in the pilot schemes, both authorities have accepted that an active training role is necessary and will follow this up, but it is expected that some tutor-teachers will remain ambivalent. It is clear that 'many tutors want some form of continuing support or in-service training as they actually carry out their new roles' (Bolam and Baker, 1975, p. 9).

Bolam and Baker concluded that 'the most valuable single feature of the two official schemes was, by general agreement, the reduced teaching load for probationers' (p. 9). There was also agreement that the schemes eased the probationers' entry into the profession. In addition there have been better relationships between the schools, centres and colleges. Finally in any induction scheme staffing is a key issue—who are to assist the beginning teachers and in what ways? This is a matter which, Bolam and Baker believed, required further consideration.

Induction of newly graduated teachers in Australia

At the beginning of this section the proposition was stated that in the next decades greater attention would be given to the induction of newly graduated teachers, especially those in the first year of teaching. Already moves have been made in this direction and some of these have been reported in this book. Two particular issues stand out as far as Australia is concerned. First, there is the need to reduce the teaching load for beginning teachers. In the United Kingdom three beginning teachers have been equated as two teachers when staffing schools, and the adoption of a similar policy in Australia would seem an essential base for the successful development of an induction scheme. This is an objective which should be established and met as soon as possible. Second, there is the need to provide appropriate support for beginning teachers both within their own schools and outside the schools. In at least one Australian state consideration has already been given to placing more professional staff in the schools to assist teachers. The role and mode of operation of these staff are critical variables in any induction scheme, and difficulties encountered in the United Kingdom have already been discussed. Before induction schemes are developed in Australia it is essential to define clearly and in detail the means by which professional guidance will be available for beginning teachers.

The foregoing review of the literature on innovative trends in teacher education abroad provides a backdrop for the consideration of new developments in Australian teacher education programmes. All the trends that have been discussed will be discerned as operating with varying degrees of impact in the Australian setting—some are already well developed, but others are only just manifesting themselves. This is not to say that Australian teacher educators are lagging behind overseas innovators. In many specific instances their work is imaginative and in the vanguard.

2 SURVEY OF INNOVATION IN AUSTRALIAN TEACHER EDUCATION PROGRAMMES

Nowadays the words 'innovation' and 'innovative' seem frequently on the lips of Australian teacher educators. They are being employed to describe almost anything in a programme perceived by an individual as being new or different. Consequently the terms cover activities of greatly varying worth; activities characterized by varying degrees of purposefulness, planning, appraisal and wider applicability; activities varying considerably in size, complexity and originality. It almost seems it is fashionable to be an innovator.

Struck by these impressions, the investigators expected to find a fair number of so-called 'innovations' in Australian teacher education. At the same time it was thought that many of these innovations could not be properly classified as such, in the sense that the term is being employed in this book; namely, a planned, novel attempt to improve practice in relation to certain desired objectives. It was believed also that much of the innovatory activity would be so slight in purpose and scope as to be of little significance to other people. In many ways these expectations proved wrong. We were soon to discover a great variety of truly innovatory activity, much of which is carefully devised, refreshingly new and having important implications for teacher preparation. The current impression is that many worthwhile and interesting changes, major and minor, are being introduced in Australian teacher education programmes. It is really quite an exciting picture, especially in the colleges of advanced education. The new autonomy, new buildings and plant, new staff, and new challenges associated with these institutions have brought with them a certain vitality—a strong inclination to re-think objectives, devise improved courses and implement more effective methods. But the colleges have not a monopoly on innovation. Even in the schools of education in the older universities new approaches are being explored.

However the picture, on closer analysis, is perhaps not as bright as it seems. There is substantial scope for the improvement and support of the innovation process. Problems are not always carefully identified and defined. Objectives are not clearly specified and pursued. Planning strategies are sometimes clumsy. Implementation, evaluation and revision procedures are often ineffective. Provision for dissemination both within and outside the institutions is generally poor. Financial and moral support for the innovators and their schemes are frequently minimal.

The following account of the processes and problems, categories and content of innovatory activity in Australian teacher education institutions is based on a survey carried out during May-August 1975. The survey was undertaken with seven main objectives:

1. To establish what innovations have been recently introduced, and by whom, in each of the teacher-education programmes.
2. To find out the source, purposes, features and effectiveness of the innovations as perceived by the innovators.
3. To discover the differing planning and implementation strategies adopted in connection with innovations.
4. To disclose the evaluation and dissemination procedures employed.
5. To find out the special financial, personnel and material resources connected with the innovations.
6. To isolate the main problems encountered in implementing innovations.
7. To locate plans for the refinement and expansion of innovations and for pursuing fresh lines of innovation.

The investigation was directed at the complete range of teacher education programmes—those carried on in universities, colleges of advanced education, government and non-government establishments. The concern was mainly with pre-service education activities, though in-service provisions in these institutions were not necessarily excluded. Preliminary letters were sent to principals, directors or heads of programmes asking for brief descriptions of innovative activity and the names of the innovators. In this letter the definition of an 'innovation' was deliberately very loose with the object of casting a wide net to collect as many activities as possible. The response was excellent. Of the 77 institutions approached, 70 replied, representing a 91 per cent response. These replies cited a total of 703 different innovations—a figure which at once surprised, delighted and rather over-awed the investigators.

Next a detailed questionnaire was distributed to all the nominated innovators. With the knowledge that tertiary institutions had recently been rather inundated with questionnaires from official and private sources, the investigators decided to visit as many of the institutions as possible (especially those with numerous innovations), explain the project to staff, briefly discuss innovations, and invite co-operation in completing the questionnaire. Forty-nine institutions were visited in this way, the remainder were sent the questionnaire through the post. This personal approach seems to have paid dividends. The response to the questionnaire was good, bearing in mind its length and the surfeit of such instruments that many of the teacher educators had already completed in the preceding months (see Table 2.1). Little wonder that some people failed to

**Table 2.1 GENERAL RESPONSE TO INITIAL
LETTER AND QUESTIONNAIRE**

Institutions originally contacted	77	
Replies received	70	
No. of innovations originally cited	703	
No. of questionnaires returned		348
No. of responses, materials only		31
Total responses		379

respond and that others returned the document after several reminders. Unfortunately, too, some respondents completed the questionnaire hurriedly, omitting items and making little comment in the open-ended items. Of the 703 innovators who received questionnaires, 348 completed it and 31 returned only materials describing their work because of lack of time or judged irrelevance of many of the questionnaire items. Thus the response rate for the questionnaire itself was about 50 per cent and for the questionnaire *and* the descriptive materials, 54 per cent.

The subsequent analysis of the survey's statistical data and of its descriptions of innovation took four tedious months. The results are discussed under two main headings—Process and Problems of Innovation, and Categories and Content of Innovation.

PROCESS AND PROBLEMS OF INNOVATION

Sources of Innovation

The reported sources of the innovations in Australian teacher education programms were analyzed in two parts—(i) the person or persons within or even outside an institution who played the key role in initiating the idea of the new plan, and (ii) the origin of the ideas introduced by the initiating person(s). Tables 2.2 and 2.3 indicate the responses received on these two sources of innovation.

Individual course co-ordinators appear to have played an important part in initiating changes in teacher education programmes. Some 52 per cent of ideas

Table 2.2 SOURCES OF INNOVATION
Person(s) who initiated idea

	No. responses	*% responses*
Programme or course co-ordinators	180	52
Staff discussion	87	25
Senior staff	35	10
Institution/school staff discussion	26	7
Institution/government department staff discussion	14	4
Others	6	2

Table 2.3 SOURCES OF INNOVATION
Origin of innovatory idea

	No. responses	*% responses*
Problems and needs within institution	151	44
Observations overseas	57	16
Overseas publications	42	12
Observations in Australia	41	12
Australian publications	34	10
Conferences in Australia	15	4
Others	8	2

for innovation were derived from this source. When senior staff (10 per cent) are added to this group the picture emerges of the majority of ideas for innovation being introduced by people either in or close to the hierarchy of authority. This picture is, however, offset by the fact that 25 per cent of ideas for innovation emerged from discussions among staff at all levels, and another 8 per cent from institution and school staff interaction, as well as 4 per cent from staff and government-department personnel discussion. One is nevertheless left with the feeling that greater encouragement, opportunity and support might be given for junior members of staff to play a part in initiating ideas for innovatory activities. The part that school staff played in conceiving innovations should not go un-noticed, since they can provide an important fund of information on the needs of the teaching profession.

The main trigger of innovatory ideas seems to have been the perception of problems or the realization of a need to improve aspects of the teacher education programme. In 44 per cent of cases innovatory ideas were developed in direct response to a distinctive problem or need. In the other sources of innovation, it seems that the ideas, gleaned elsewhere, first pointed to the desirability for change. These other sources of inspiration for new ways were fairly strong in influence, especially observations abroad and overseas educational publications (together, 28 per cent of responses). The tendency to borrow ideas from other countries has long been a feature of Australian education. Interestingly, however, observations within Australia, local educational publications and national professional conferences appear to be playing an increasingly important part in disseminating new ideas concerning teacher education (together, 26 per cent of responses). These three broad local sources clearly need to be strengthened and expanded, just as much as the study of overseas developments.

Planning Innovation

While the main sources of innovative ideas seems to have been individual co-ordinating and senior staff, Table 2.4 records that the translating of these ideas into plans of action typically involved groups of people. In only 22 per cent of innovations was the planning carried out exclusively by one or two people. The most common strategy was for plans to be formulated through group discussion (33 per cent of responses). Almost as common a procedure was for one person to take responsibility for planning but to consult other individuals in the process (31 per cent of responses). As indicated in Table 2.4, 57 per cent of staff-planning groups involved 2 to 5 people, with 10 per cent of planning groups comprising 10 or more members.

The range of personnel involved in planning activities is an important feature of planning strategies. It seems that numerous institutions are endeavouring to involve in planning as many representatives of the groups to be engaged in the plan's implementation as is feasible. Especially interesting were the involvement of large groups of students (33 per cent of responses) and of teachers (28 per cent of responses). The bringing in of consultants and of personnel from state depart-ments of education seem to be quite recent elements of planning strategies.

If wide involvement and group-decision making are seen as worthwhile features of planning strategies, Australian teacher education programmes appear to be on the right track in their innovatory concerns. Of course, as Table 2.5 suggests, there is ample scope for the extension of these two aspects.

Table 2.4 PLANNING INNOVATION
      General strategies

	No. responses	*% responses*
Planning by discussion of a group of people	116	33
Planning by one person who consulted others	109	31
Planning by one person	61	18
Planning by one person who consulted others and by discussion of a group of people	36	10
Planning by two people	14	4
Planning by two individuals who consulted others	12	4

Estimates of the general period of innovatory planning and of the number of hours per week spent in planning (Tables 2.6 and 2.7) indicate the limited time spent in formulating plans. A period of less than three months spanned the planning sessions of 32 per cent of reported innovations, and 3 to 6 months planning went into 33 per cent. As far as the number of hours per week devoted to planning is concerned, 36 per cent of planning occupied only 1 to 2 hours and 20 per cent 3 to 4 hours. Although it is difficult to interpret these estimates, since the amount of planning required is often dependent on the size and complexity of the innovation, one gets the impression that the amount of time available for planning is generally minimal and sometimes sub-minimal. In the majority of cases it seems that innovators had planning sessions only when their busy teaching schedules permitted. Few apparently had been given reduced teaching loads to facilitate concentrated and sustained planning sessions. It is probable that because of the limited number of hours available for planning each week 14 per cent of innovatory planning dragged on for more than a year.

Another interesting aspect of planning for innovation is revealed in Table 2.8. Only a very small percentage (5) of reported innovations was planned as carefully designed and specially funded research projects presumably with specified objectives, evaluation procedures and budget items. It is evident from a perusal of the lines of innovation being attempted that many could well have been conceived as research projects possibly deserving funding. There are probably several main reasons for this situation—one would be the want of research expertise among college staff and the dearth of expert advice on developing research proposals; another would be the relatively small amount of funds available from outside bodies or allocated within institution budgets for the promotion of research and development. There is a basic need for staff training in research techniques and for the employment of research leaders or advisers. The need for substantially expanded funds is equally great but contingent upon the availability of people with the skill and knowledge to plan and conduct research.

Introducing Innovation

It is interesting to note from Table 2.9 that 14 per cent of respondents regarded as innovatory and novel plans which had been implemented before 1973. The

Table 2.5 PLANNING INNOVATION
Numbers and categories of people involved

No. of people	Academic staff	Non-academic staff	Students	Teachers	Outside consultants	State dept personnel	Children	Parents
					No. of institutions involving categories			
1 only	61	39	8	20	9	28	—	2
2–5	201	15	28	29	29	19	7	3
6–9	53	2	11	15	1	—	2	—
10 and more	33	—	69	32	—	—	1	5
Total responses	348	56	116	96	39	47	10	1
% responses	100	16	33	28	11	14	3	

Table 2.6 PLANNING INNOVATION
Estimates of period of planning

Period	No. responses	% responses
Less than 3 months	110	32
3–6 months	117	33
7–12 months	68	20
1–2 years	44	12
3 or more years	6	2
No response	3	1

Table 2.7 PLANNING INNOVATION
Estimates of hours per week spent in planning

No. hours per week	No. responses	% responses
1–2 hours	127	36
3–4 hours	66	20
5–6 hours	64	18
7–16 hours	44	13
17 hours or more	10	3
No response	37	10

Table 2.8 PLANNING INNOVATION
Innovations planned as specially funded research projects

	No. responses	% responses
No. innovations planned as funded research projects	18	5
No. innovations not planned as funded research projects	330	95

Table 2.9 INTRODUCING INNOVATION
Year of introduction

	No. responses	% responses
Pre-1969	2	1
1970–2	45	13
1973–5	289	83
Post–1975	12	3

great majority of the innovations reported, however, were comparatively recent in origin—83 per cent having been introduced during 1973–5. A further 3 per cent of reported innovations, though on the drawing-boards, were not to be introduced until after 1975. The apparent burst of activity during 1973–5 in part reflects the concept that people have of innovation, 'something new, recently introduced'. It also clearly indicates the flush of innovatory activity as

Table 2.10 INTRODUCING INNOVATION
Mode of introduction

Mode of introduction	No. responses	% responses
As a limited pilot study	30	9
On a small-scale basis	158	45
On a full-scale basis	133	38
Limited pilot study then small-scale only	5	1
Limited pilot study then full-scale	3	1
Limited pilot study, then small-scale, then full-scale	3	1
Small-scale then full-scale	7	2
Innovation planned, not yet introduced	7	2
No response	2	1

colleges gained new autonomy, sought course accreditation, recruited new staff and, in some cases, moved into new buildings and acquired updated facilities.

The strategies employed for introducing innovations are set out in Table 2.10. Most reported innovations (45 per cent) were introduced on only a small-scale basis and have remained as such. The main reasons for this seems to be that only a small number of staff are typically committed to each project and that funds and facilities for extending innovations are generally very limited. On the other hand, 38 per cent of reported innovations were introduced directly on a full-scale basis. Very few of these developments seem to have been carefully appraised through a limited pilot study, and revised before more extended implementation. It appears that much more thought needs to be given to appropriate strategies for introducing changes in teacher preparation to ensure the ultimate success of the new venture and to prevent the waste of time and money.

As indicated by Table 2.11, only 16 per cent of innovations were provided with special funds for their introduction. Surprisingly, perhaps, state departments of education seem to have been quite heavily involved in such funding for 17 innovations, while the institutions themselves found money for the introduction of a further 15 projects. The Australian Government through its research and development committee, its Schools Commission, and special funds for in-service education provided monies for most of the remainder of supported innovations. The fact that only two other sources of finance were reported underlines the limited range of possible funding agencies for those interested in introducing change in teacher education. Perhaps it also indicates a reluctance among teacher educators to activity seek funds from both government and non-government bodies. If teacher education is, as many believe, the pivot of any education system, its improvement through research, development and innovatory activity should become a top priority.

An attempt was made to discover relationships between the number of innovations introduced and the age and size of institutions, the traditional supposition being that the older and larger the establishment the more conservative it is in outlook. No significant patterns were, however, discernible. The older and larger institutions seemed to be just as innovative as the smaller and younger ones. One suspects that the number of innovations in any one institution was largely related to the climate established by the leader of the teacher

Table 2.11 INTRODUCING INNOVATION
Special funding for initiation

Source of Funding	less than $1,000	$1,000– 5,000	$6,000– 10,000	Amount of funds $11,000– 20,000	$21,000– 30,000	more than $30,000	Totals
State dept of education	2	7	—	2	—	6	17
Institution	5	4	2	—	—	4	15
Australian Advisory Committee on Research and Development in Education	—	4	3	1	1	1	10
Australian Government	—	5	1	1	—	3	10
Other	—	1	1	—	—	—	2
Grand total							54

education programme, or of a department within it, and to the interest and talent of individual staff members.

Operating Innovation

Although reported innovations spread across all the various levels of teacher education, Table 2.12 reveals that the majority clustered in the primary education area (54 per cent), a trend probably not unassociated with the new approaches currently challenging the elementary school itself. This contrasted rather sharply with 28 per cent of innovations in the secondary education area and only 11 per cent in the area of early-childhood education. Certainly it appears there is much more scope for new approaches to the preparation of teachers at these two levels. In the institutions surveyed the provision of in-service education was seen as a growing concern but merely accounted for 5 per cent of innovatory activity. One might well expect tertiary institutions, educational authorities and teachers' groups to co-operate more extensively and creatively in the in-service area in forthcoming years.

Within each year of the main levels of teacher preparation there was no apparent concentration of innovatory activity in any one particular year, first, second, third or fourth. Innovations were spread evenly through all course years.

The innovations reported touched most course components found in teacher education programmes (Table 2.13). The general component of educational studies embraced 15 per cent of innovations with the related fields of history, geography and social science accounting for 14 per cent. The component of teaching practice (including such activities as microteaching and systematic observations) is one of growing concern and included 12 per cent of innovations. It is interesting to note that a number of innovations (14 per cent in all) cut across subject boundaries to be applied to either a group or all course subjects.

The number of staff directly involved in the running of innovations varied considerably (Table 2.14). Some 28 per cent of innovations were conducted by only one member of academic staff and 26 per cent by 2 to 3 academic staff. At the other extreme, 18 per cent of innovations were staffed by more than 10 academics. Only one non-academic staff member, typically providing some form of technical assistance, was attached to 18 per cent of projects. One teacher worked in 6 per cent of innovations and there were more than 10 teachers on the staff of 21 per cent of reported innovations. A few innovations involved people from outside the programme in their implementation. For instance,

Table 2.12 OPERATING INNOVATION
Level of teacher education to which innovation applies

Level	No. responses	% responses
Primary education	188	54
Secondary education	98	28
Early childhood education	40	11
In-service education	16	5
Other	6	2

Table 2.13 OPERATING INNOVATION
Programme subjects to which innovation
is applied

Subject area	No. responses	% responses
Educational studies	52	15
History/geography/social science	50	14
Teaching practice	43	12
English/drama	37	11
Science	36	10
All subjects	30	8
A group of subjects	20	6
Mathematics	20	6
Music	17	5
Physical education	16	5
Art and craft	15	4
Languages	9	3
Economics	3	1

Table 2.14 OPERATING INNOVATION
Staff directly involved on the operation

Number	Types		
	Academic	Non-academic	Teachers
1 only	96	61	20
2–3	89	30	15
4–5	46	10	7
6–7	22	4	5
8–9	14	0	3
More than 10	61	5	72
No response	20		

Table 2.15 OPERATING INNOVATION
Other persons directly involved
in operation

Persons	No. of responses
Parents and children	24
Consultants	14
Personnel from state dept of education	8

9 per cent involved parents and children, 4 per cent consultants with appropriate expertise, and 2 per cent personnel from the State Department of Education (Table 2.15). No innovations apparently involved inter-institution teams tackling common problems and none deliberately recruited the services of members of the community—possibilities that could well be explored in future innovatory activity.

Table 2.16 OPERATING INNOVATION
Main basis for staff involvement in innovation

Bases	No. responses	% responses
Voluntary, on the basis of interest	166	48
Assigned because of interest	111	32
Specially appointed	35	10
Assigned regardless of interest	32	9
Invited	4	1

Table 2.17 OPERATING INNOVATION
On-going co-ordination

Source of co-ordination	No. responses	% responses
An individual	94	27
One person in consultation with others	118	34
A small group	65	19
All staff involved	60	17
Combination of above	5	1
No response	6	2

Table 2.18 OPERATING INNOVATION
Students involved in operation

Numbers of students	No. responses	% responses
1–19	53	15
20–39	45	13
40–59	43	12
60–79	32	9
80–99	22	7
100–199	57	17
200–399	52	15
More than 400	29	8
Uncertain	15	4

The main bases for the involvement of institution staff in innovatory activity are set out in Table 2.16. In 48 per cent of innovations staff became voluntarily involved because of interest and in 32 per cent staff were assigned for apparent interest in a particular innovation. Only 9 per cent of responses reported that staff were assigned regardless of interest, while in 10 per cent of innovations staff were specially recruited for participation.

The responsibility for co-ordinating the operation of innovation rested with one person in 16 per cent of cases, often acting in consultation with others (Table 2.17). In 19 per cent of innovations co-ordination was undertaken by a committee and on 17 per cent all staff involved assumed this responsibility.

The number of students involved in innovations also varied widely (Table 2.18). There was a slight tendency for groups to polarize either below 60 or

Table 2.19 OPERATING INNOVATION
Degree of student participation

	No. responses	*% responses*
All eligible students participate	203	58
A selection of students participate	125	36
No response	20	6

Table 2.20 OPERATING INNOVATION
Bases for selecting students to participate

Bases	*No. responses*	*% responses*
Elective	89	26
Lecturer's decision	16	5
Random sample	10	3
Student experience	10	3
No response	223	63

between 100–400 in size. In 58 per cent of innovations all eligible students participated, while in 36 per cent only a selected group became involved (Table 2.19). The main basis for student entry in these latter cases seemed to be student choice in the light of their interests or needs (Table 2.20). The numbers of hours per week that students were involved in the operation ranged widely between 1 to 2 hours through to more than 20 hours. In 30 per cent of responses, however, students spent less than 3 hours a week in the work.

In the 54 reported innovations which were provided with special funding for their operation, it seems from Table 2.21 that salaries or allowances for specially appointed academic staff and the purchase of audiovisual equipment were the two major items of expenditure. It is perhaps also interesting to note that 7 innovations required special accommodation and 20 incurred travel expenditure. Although not specially funded, a further 20 responses reported that special accommodation largely in the form of 'room conversion' was necessary. Six responses reported the provision of special accommodation outside the institution.

The need for timetable adjustments to facilitate the operation of innovations was reported by 30 per cent of projects. Most of these adjustments involved the provision of blocks of time to permit flexible use of time, the integration of subjects, or off-campus activities. Twelve innovations involved after-hours scheduling to enable their full operation.

The majority of reported innovations involved a combination of basic teaching approaches (Table 2.22). Although the conventional lecture approach is still fairly strong, there seem to be three important methodological trends. First, small-group teaching in the form of workshops and seminars is a dominant method. Second, independent study by students is frequently encouraged. Third, the concern for the practice of teaching and linking it with theoretical considerations is evident. The introduction of practical work (involving such things as simulation, microteaching, helping individual children, and developing curriculum materials) is common to many innovations; so too are observations and practice teaching in schools.

Table 2.21 OPERATING INNOVATION
Running costs of specially funded innovations

Item	less than $1,000	$1,000–5,000	$6,000–10,000	$11,000–20,000	$21,000–30,000	more than $30,000
			No. responses			
Personnel						
Academic	2	3	1	4	2	4
Non-academic	—	3	2	—	—	1
Administrative	—	—	—	—	1	—
Teachers	1	3	1	2	1	—
Others	2	1	1	—	—	—
Equipment						
Audiovisual	7	7	6	1	2	—
Software	3	4	—	—	—	—
Other	7	2	1	—	—	—
Accommodation	2	3	2	—	—	—
Travel	14	6	3	—	—	—
Other	6	5	2	—	—	—

Table 2.22 OPERATING INNOVATION
Basic teaching approaches involved

Teaching approach	*No. responses*
Practical work	206
Workshops	190
Independent study	172
Lectures	165
Seminars	158
In-school observation	148
Teaching practice in schools	139
Field work	39
Individual student-staff discussion	15
Student self-evaluation	13
Others	12
Not applicable	24
No response	9

Problems of Implementing Innovation

It was reported by 61 per cent of respondents that the implementation of their innovations encountered problems. In most cases any one of these innovations faced more than one problem. An analysis of the main difficulties appears in Table 2.23. The difficulties are quite evenly spread. The most frequent problem was suspicion, sometimes bordering on resentment, mainly from senior staff of the institution. Some of these staff, it was reported, appeared to feel threatened by the innovation. Many innovators, as a result, seemed to be rather unpopular people within some colleges. Such negative attitudes to innovation and innovators were no doubt related to the further problem of poor co-operation from staff members outside the innovation.

Staffing was another common problem. Part of this lay in providing staff with time to participate, and another part in involving those staff with the desired interest and expertise.

Table 2.23 PROBLEMS OF INNOVATION
Difficulties of implementation

Difficulty	*No. responses*
Suspicion of approach	70
Staffing	57
Scheduling time	56
Lack of co-operation	50
Finance	43
Equipment	36
Insufficient time to assess and plan	34
Unsuitable accommodation	32
Poor communication	32
Recognition of course content	14
Others	9
Not applicable	137

Table 2.24 PROBLEMS OF INNOVATION
Degree of opposition

Opposition	No. responses	% responses
Very strong opposition	3	1
Strong opposition	20	6
Moderate opposition	34	10
Some little opposition	81	23
No opposition	200	57
No response	10	3

Table 2.25 PROBLEMS OF INNOVATION
Sources of opposition

Source	No. responses
Fellow staff in department or faculty	75
Students	27
Institution administration	25
Teachers	20
Staff of another department or faculty	19
State department of education	10
Other institutions	6

The scheduling of time to permit the full implementation of the innovation was also quite frequently cited as a difficulty. Connected with this was the problem of simply finding time to assess the progress of the innovation and refine plans. The want of funds for additional staff, equipment, and software together with accommodation difficulties were also quite common. Interestingly, poor communication between both staff working on the innovation and between them and the other staff of the institution was regarded as a difficulty which sometimes led to opposition, misunderstanding and decline in involvement and enthusiasm. Difficulty in having the new course content recognized in the institution was also encountered in a small number of cases.

Some degree of opposition was faced by 40 per cent of the reported innovations (Table 2.24), such opposition being moderately strong in 16 per cent of cases. Table 2.25 reveals the main source of opposition to be from staff of the very department or faculty in which innovation is being implemented. The sources of opposition were then evenly spread among all other parties seemingly affected by or associated with the innovation's implementation. Both tertiary students and school teachers came into this category for some innovations. The potential range of sources of opposition underline the need for careful communication and interpretation of the aims and nature of a new development to all concerned both before and during its implementation.

Evaluating Innovation

Most innovators (79 per cent) believed their innovations to be moderately to most effective (Table 2.26). None saw their work as ineffective, although a few

Table 2.26 EVALUATING INNOVATION
Innovator's estimate of effectiveness

Degree of effectiveness	No. responses	% responses
Most effective	150	43
Moderately effective	126	36
Somewhat effective	21	6
Not effective	0	0
Too early to tell	41	12
No response	10	3

Table 2.27 EVALUATING INNOVATION
Innovator's judgement of how the staff
involved in the innovation regard it

Nature of regard	No. responses	% responses
Most favourable	208	60
Moderately favourable	90	26
Somewhat favourable	18	5
Not favourable	1	0
Undecided	14	4
No response	17	5

Table 2.28 EVALUATING INNOVATION
Evaluation attempted

	No. responses	% responses
Some form of evaluation attempted	201	58
No form of evaluation attempted	141	40
No response	6	2

apparently had reserved judgement. The majority of respondents (60 per cent) also thought that the staff involved in the innovation regarded it most favourably (Table 2.27). While such definite estimates of effectiveness and staff attitude may be well-based, they also seemingly indicate the operation of the so-called 'Hawthorne effect'—an enthusiasm for innovation largely because of its newness but not necessarily its soundness. Not that such an effect is a bad thing. Indeed enthusiasm for a teacher-education task is to be admired and encouraged. It needs, however, to be consistently accompanied by careful and critical evaluation.

Thus it was of some disappointment to find that only 58 per cent of respondents were attempting some form of evaluation of their innovations (Table 2.28). The most common means of gathering information on an innovation's effectiveness was through questionnaires (directed mainly to staff and students involved) and through informal staff discussion (Table 2.29). Obtaining feedback from

Table 2.29 EVALUATING INNOVATION
Means of evaluation

Mode of evaluation	No. responses*
Questionnaire	81
Staff discussion	74
Discussion with students	32
Observation and/or analysis of students' work	31
Special measures of change in student behaviour leading to a statistical analysis	18
Combined staff and student discussion	17
Individual interviews with staff and/or students	10
Written reports from staff and/or students	9
No response	147

* Some respondents cited several modes of evaluation

Table 2.30 EVALUATING INNOVATION
Reasons for no evaluation

Reasons	No. responses	% responses
Innovation unsuitable for evaluation	51	15
Insufficient time	17	5
No finance	11	3
Too many students and staff involved	11	3
Innovation not yet introduced	7	2
No response	50	14
Not applicable	201	58

students through questionnaires, discussion, interviews and reports seems to be a commendable feature of evaluation approaches. Only a few evaluation approaches apprently involved the collection of 'hard data' through the use of standardized tests (in such cases as teacher attitudes, anxiety and dogmatism), the use of special observational analysis systems, and of specially devised tests of student achievement. The emphasis on gathering 'soft data' is perhaps not to be criticized since many of the objectives of innovation seem amenable only to this kind of evaluation. What is to be criticized, and strongly so, is that 40 per cent of innovations, be they large or small, were being implemented with no attempt to appraise their effectiveness and to adjust or reject them in the light of such appraisal. Looked at in this light, many innovations could well be regarded simply as fads of their originators.

The reasons given by innovators for not attempting to evaluate their work are far from convincing (Table 2.30). Fifty-eight per cent of respondents believed their innovation was simply not suited to any form of evaluation, and 11 per cent gave insufficient time and money and too many staff and students as reasons for no evaluation. Surely, any innovation having definable objectives, no matter what financial and other logistical limitations, can be subject to some form of useful appraisal.

Another surprising and rather disturbing aspect of reported evaluation

Table 2.31 EVALUATING INNOVATION
What results indicate

Results indicate	No. responses	% responses
Innovation satisfactory in present form	152	44
Innovation needs improvement	29	8
Innovation not worthwhile	0	0
Evaluation unfinished	20	6
No response	147	42

approaches is that 44 per cent of respondents stated that the evaluation had indicated that the innovation was satisfactory in its present form (Table 2.31). Only 8 per cent reported need for improvement and none believed the work was not worthwhile. It seems that very few people are using evaluation continuously with the operation of their innovation to promote its formative improvement. One senses an air of complacency among innovators towards the effectiveness of their innovatory endeavours. In most cases evaluation is being undertaken entirely by the people who planned and implemented the innovation (mainly the co-ordinator, a few staff and sometimes students). Only four innovations were subjected to an outside research group or independent evaluator.

Overall, the evaluation of innovations seems to be one of the most neglected and poorly handled aspects of Australian teacher education practice. Much more thought and care needs to be given to specifying objectives and to the means of assessing how well new plans are achieving them. Many teacher educators seem either unmindful of the need to evaluate, suspicious of the evaluation process, or uninformed on evaluation procedures.

Disseminating Information on Innovation

The dissemination of information on innovatory activities is clearly inadequate (Table 2.32). Less than half the innovations had the results of evaluation communicated to other members of staff within the institution itself. The effort to communicate results to students is promising but that of communicating to other institutions is quite dismal. The results of many innovations, it seems, never go beyond the parent institution.

Despite this situation, 60 per cent of respondents indicated that other insti-

Table 2.32 DISSEMINATING INNOVATION
Communication of results of evaluation

Recipients of results	No. responses*
Members of staff not involved in innovation	151
Students	96
Initial planning committee	79
Other teacher education institutions	28
Relevant journals, newsletters and newspapers	28
No communication	27
No response	147

*Some respondents had communicated results to a number of bodies.

Table 2.33 DISSEMINATING INNOVATION
Interest from other institutions

	No. responses	*% responses*
Interest shown by staff of other institutions	209	60
No interest shown by staff of others institutions	138	40
No response	1	0

Table 2.34 DISSEMINATING INNOVATION
How interest of other institutions is mainly displayed

Interest by	*No. responses*	*% responses*
Initiating informal verbal communication	85	25
Written request for information	64	18
Paying visits for observation and discussion	28	8
Direct participation in work of the innovation	17	5
Attending expositions at conferences	15	4
No response	139	40

Table 2.35 DISSEMINATING INNOVATION
Publications describing innovation

	No. responses	*% responses*
Publications made available	46	13
No publications made available	298	86
No response	4	1

tutions had shown some interest in their project (Table 2.33). It seems knowledge of their work was spread through the few published accounts, 'on the grape vine', or by reports at conferences. This interest of people from other institutions was shown by the initiation of conversation about innovation in 25 per cent of cases and by written requests for information in another 18 per cent (Table 2.34). Only 13 per cent of innovations reported publications being available describing their operation (Table 2.35).

Much needs to be done to improve the dissemination of information about new developments in Australian teacher education programmes. For some reason existing journals are not fulfilling this role. Perhaps there is a reluctance among teacher educators both to write up and publish accounts of their work. Institutions themselves might produce more frequent bulletins on new approaches. Conferences should provide more opportunity for reporting and interchange on innovatory activities. Opportunities for visits to observe and discuss new developments in other institution should be more extensively provided and inter- and intra-institution meetings of teacher education staff with common interests might be arranged. There could even be a consolidated annual report from a central body listing and describing the research and innovative work in teacher education programmes, thus providing the basis of the exchange of ideas between staff. Anything that is done in the above regard can only improve the communication situation.

Future Plans for Innovation

Many of the innovations reported in the survey seem to have been accepted into programmes and were to be continued at least into 1976 (Table 2.36). Responses revealed that it was planned to continue 53 per cent of innovations on their present scale, while 40 per cent were to be expanded in operation. Only 4 per cent of innovations were to be reduced in scale or abandoned. These plans are perhaps a little disconcerting when one recalls that many innovations have not been thoroughly or even minimally evaluated. This worry is eased a little, however, since 36 per cent of innovations were to be revised and refined in the light of experience and the results of evaluation. It was interesting also to note, especially in view of poor apparatus for communication, that 66 per cent of responses indicated that their innovation had clear implications for practices in other institutions.

Only 51 per cent of respondents indicated the future lines of innovation that they or others might well introduce into Australian teacher education programmes. Although some of the proposals were fairly specific, in general the innovatory trends were evenly projected as being:

i. School-based teacher education facilitating an intimate relationship between theoretical and practical considerations;
ii. In-service teacher education, especially concerned with such matters as the induction of the beginning teacher; as full-time or part-time post-diploma courses leading to a bachelor's degree; and as the training of practice teaching supervisors;
iii. Competency-based teacher education characterized by self-directed student learning and the careful analysis of the teacher's role into specific understandings, tasks and skills;
iv. Humanistic teacher education concerned with the needs and interests, the personal and interpersonal development of student teachers, and featuring more flexibility and choice within programmes;

Table 2.36 FUTURE OF INNOVATION
Plans for present innovation

Plans to—	No. responses	% responses
Continue operation on present scale	186	53
Extend the operation	139	40
Reduce the operation	6	2
Abandon the operation	7	2
Undecided	4	1
No response	6	2

v. Teacher education-community relationships involving more contact with, and service to, children and adult members, especially in the areas of special education and the education of minority groups;

vi. The development of more valid and reliable means of determining student entrance to teacher education, and of assessment of student progress during preparation;

vii. The formation of relationships with one or a number of schools for laboratory-type professional experiences, exchange of staff, and co-operative research and development activities;

viii. Many-sided endeavours by teacher educators to 'practise what they preach' leading to more 'open learning' situations, more integrated courses and interdisciplinary teaching, more flexible pursuits, and greater and more varied student involvement;

ix. Increased understanding of the use of media in teacher preparation through the establishment of well-equipped and serviced resource centres, and through such techniques as microteaching, simulation, modelling and multi-media learning packages;

x. The opening of channels of communication between Australian teacher educators through increased opportunities for visitation and observation, discussion and exchange, and collaborative research and planning;

xi. The design of teacher education programmes more accurately and strongly attuned to analyses of the changing needs of children, of school systems, and of contemporary society.

It is probably not unusual that many of the above eleven innovatory concerns are remarkably consistent with those being expressed by teacher educators abroad. The thing that is surprising, and rather disappointing, is that almost half of the respondents to the questionnaire seemed either unable or disinclined to nominate likely promising improvements to teacher education. If such a large proportion of 'innovators' failed to produce such suggestions, then one wonders seriously about both the probable dearth of innovatory ideas and low commitment to improving teacher education among the vast majority of seemingly 'non-innovative' teacher educators.

CATEGORIES AND CONTENT OF INNOVATION

Categorizing Responses

In order to divide the questionnaires and other related materials between the investigators for the analysis of the lines and content of innovatory activity, a system for categorizing the 379 returns was devised. This grew to some extent from the four categories developed by the Centre for Educational Research and Innovation in the report *Case Studies of Educational Innovation. IV. Strategies for Innovation in Education* (OECD, 1973). Its categories were (i) objectives and functions, (ii) organization and administration, (iii) roles and role relationships, and (iv) curriculum. For the purposes of the present study a six-unit system of classification has been developed after much reflection upon the contents of questionnaire responses.

Category 1. Organizational and administrative:
Innovations mainly concerned with the organization and administration of the institution and its teacher education programmes. Such innovations might

involve staffing arrangements, control, decision-making, and communication (e.g. flexible timetabling [Mt. Lawley CAE], panel of education associates [Tasmanian CAE, Mt. Nelson]).

Category 2. Total programme:
Innovations concerned with the introduction of a comprehensive programme or trial of a scaled-down version. Such innovation might involve formulating objectives and organizing principles and developing the content and methodologies of the courses (e.g. four-year undergraduate programme in environmental studies [SCV Rusden], courses for provisionally registered teachers [Kelvin Grove CAE]).

Category 3. Curriculum Specific:
Innovations concerned with the aims, organization and content of a single curriculum component, course or unit of a programme (e.g. oral communication of literature course [Kelvin Grove CAE], interpersonal skills development units [Canberra CAE]).

Category 4. Technological:
Innovations, sometimes linked with specific courses, featuring the use of media or special plant and materials (e.g. audiovisual programme in sign language [SCV Burwood], basic statistics and computers [Claremont TC]).

Category 5. Evaluative:
Innovations concerned with student selection and assessment procedures, diagnosis and remediation of student weaknesses, graduation requirements, course and programme appraisal (e.g. analysis of entry and exit profiles [SCV Ballarat], study of the role of teachers in technical education as a basis for appraisal of programmes [SCV Hawthorn]).

Category 6. Methodological:
Innovations concerned with improved approaches to, and modes of teaching and learning. Because of its complexity this category was broken down into ten sub-divisions :

6.i   *Microteaching* (e.g. microteaching models for science students [Macquarie University]).

6.ii   *Particular curriculum approaches* (e.g. encounter group methods in drama [Mackie CAE]).

6.iii   *Special co-operating school arrangements* (e.g. on-campus laboratory secondary school [Salisbury CAE]).

6.iv   *Practice teaching* (e.g. small group teaching approaches [University of Sydney]).

6.v   *Inter-disciplinary approaches* (e.g. integrated social science [SCV Rusden]).

6.vi   *Self-instructional and programmed learning* (e.g. programmed instruction in recreation [Claremont TC]).

6.vii   *Practically-oriented studies of ethnic and minority groups* (e.g. course on insight into aboriginality [North Brisbane CAE]).

6.viii *Developing specific skills* (e.g. specific tasks for prospective teacher librarians [Macquarie University]).

6.ix   *Offering services in special or remedial education* (e.g. the Communication and Clinical Resources Centre [Mount Gravatt CAE]).

6.x   *Providing methodological exemplars* (e.g. Integrated, Open Space Programme [Mackie CAE]).

Table 2.37 INNOVATION CATEGORIES
Analysts and response numbers

Analyst		Category		*No.* innovations	*%* innovations
Jecks	1.	Organizational and administrative innovation		18	5
Thew	2.	Total programme innovation		30	8
Traill	3.	Curriculum-specific innovation		57	15
Traill	4.	Technological innovation		29	8
Jecks	5.	Evaluation innovation		40	10
	6.	Methodological innovation		205	54
Traill	6.i	Microteaching	11		
Thew	6.ii	Particular curriculum approaches	49		
Turney	6.iii	Special co-operating school arrangements	7		
Turney/Thew	6.iv	Practice teaching	39		
Traill	6.v	Inter-disciplinary approaches	16		
Traill	6.vi	Self-instructional and programmed learning	11		
Turney	6.vii	Practically-oriented studies of ethnic and minority groups	19		
Turney	6.viii	Developing specific skills	7		
Turney	6.ix	Offering services in special or remedial education	19		
Turney/Jecks	6.x	Providing methodological exemplars	27		
		Total		379	

On the basis of these categories the innovations' survey returns were classified. Since a number of innovations overlapped several categories they were initially classified according to what was judged to be their main feature. Each of the investigators wrote the discussion of the lines of innovation in the categories allocated to him. There was some exchange of questionnaires among the team because it was felt that a few innovations could well be cited in more than one category. Table 2.37 indicates the investigators responsible for the category analysis, and the number of innovations in each category.

It is clear from Table 2.37 that the major innovatory concern of Australian teacher educators is the introduction of improved means of teaching and learning (54 per cent of total response). While much of this endeavour appears to be directed towards the teaching of specific courses of professional study there is clearly an increasing concern for the nature and quality of the practical experience. In view of the high cost and questionable effectiveness of the practicum, this last trend is especially timely. It is interesting to note that microteaching, believed so innovative some four years ago, is now apparently generally accepted and regarded as a new development in only a small number of institutions. An interesting spin-off from microteaching's stress on specific skills has been the attempt to analyse the teacher's task within certain curriculum areas into skills. In the endeavour to up-grade the practical experience of students and to relate it more closely to theoretical aspects of courses, a number of institutions have formed close co-operating relationships with several on- or off-campus schools. Besides using the community's schools, some institutions are beginning to offer services to schools and the community: a few teacher education programmes are using the expertise of their staff, the interest and developing skill of their students and the resources of the institution to provide schools or on-campus clinics with diagnostic, therapeutic and remedial services for mentally handicapped children and pupils with specific learning difficulties. To improve the course learning of student teachers and to practise what is being preached, a number of institutions are endeavouring to provide for such things as individualized instruction and inter-disciplinary teaching. Some institutions have carried this trend further and have consciously sought to provide courses exemplifying the major features of open education and special approaches to school curriculum areas.

While the strong trend in innovations towards directly improving teaching and learning is to be commended, it is rather disappointing that new developments in the categories of organization and administration and of evaluation are not more numerous and varied. Perhaps many teacher educators see such changes as either beyond their influence or too difficult to introduce. Perhaps too, administrators are disinclined to encourage subordinate staff to meddle in areas traditionally regarded as largely their special responsibility.

The following discussion of the main lines of innovation in Australian teacher education programmes is organized around the categories developed. Four things must be stressed at the outset: First, the general scope of the analyses has been determined by the responses to the questionnaire. Other teacher educators could, of course, be pursuing similar or other lines of innovation, but their work was not discussed simply because the investigators did not know of it. Second, the detailed commentaries on the innovations are based almost exclusively on the questionnaire data and other materials supplied by the innovators. In some cases the information provided was scant and at times vague. Thus, while we have endeavoured to follow the innovators' descriptions as closely as possible, there are occasions when we have had to interpret rather liberally how certain innovations operate. If any of these interpretations have turned out to be, in fact, misinterpretations, we apologize. Where our own descriptions are unavoidably brief or cryptic we hope the interested reader will endeavour to secure further details from the innovator. Third, some innovations receive mention in more than one section of the analysis, not because they are necessarily regarded as more important or meritorious than others, but simply because their operation straddles the several categories concerned. Four, limitations of space and time have prevented reference to each of the 379 innovations reported. We have tried to mention as many as possible. To have cited as examples of categories and sub-categories of innovation all the reported innovations would generally have meant needless belabouring of the discussion.

1. Organizational and Administrative Innovation

In Australia, teacher education programmes are offered both in universities and in colleges of advanced education. While the older and more established universities may not conduct large teacher education programmes, some of the newer universities are extensively engaged in this field. In the college of advanced education sector, teacher education is the largest of all the advanced education programmes.

On the whole, organizational and administrative change related to teacher education has been less in the universities than in the colleges of advanced education. Largely this is an outcome of the Federal funding of the advanced education sector, in that from July 1973, the Federal Government assumed full responsibility for the recurrent and capital funding of some forty teachers colleges, most of which had previously been part of the various state education departments. This change freed the former teachers colleges from the administrative control of each state education department and from the system of each state's public service funding and control. This system had resulted in a pattern where the state teachers colleges were staffed by academic staff who had first established their efficiency and seniority as state education department teachers, and who, when they applied for positions in the state education department's teachers colleges had the right of appeal if not appointed or promoted. Critics of this system claimed that teachers college staff did not gain their appointments on merit alone but that public service seniority was also a factor.

Some critics of the teachers colleges claimed that they resembled the state education department's high schools in their organization and administration more than they resembled other tertiary institutions. With teachers college students paid by, and bonded to, the state education department, some critics also claimed that academic progress was as much influenced by the state education department's policies and requirements as much as it was by tertiary level academic considerations. In short, the teachers colleges were seen to be more part of the attitude, policies and general ethos of the public service and of the state education departments than they were part of the tertiary system.

For the college of advanced education sector, the complete break with the state education departments after July 1973 was a change of great significance. Some of the outcomes were:

(i)   a new system of tertiary government and administration;
(ii)   representation in the councils which controlled and administered tertiary administration in each state;
(iii)   open advertisement of academic staff vacancies with appointments made in line with usual tertiary institution practice;
(iv)   tertiary level salaries and conditions for academic staff, including greater opportunities for study leave;
(v)   greater control in selection and admission of students;
(vi)   greater internal control in formulating academic policies; and
(vii)   the opportunity to diversify the academic programme beyond teacher education.

Organizational and administrative innovation tends to centre on the deployment and utilization of resources. These resources include money, manpower, buildings and supplies and equipment. It is against this background that administrative policies are formulated and organizational patterns implemented. In practice, there is considerable freedom in each institution to arrange and utilize resources differently, although once policies and patterns are set, these tend to be ongoing and may resist change. There are some obvious constraints. These include:

(i)   academic manpower and academic staff hours available to the programme;
(ii) non-academic manpower and non-academic staff hours available to the programme;
(iii) the availability of teaching spaces of different types;
(iv) specialist facilities, such as libraries;
(v)   the number of timetabled weekly student hours in the programme;
(vi) the structure of the course itself;
(vii) teaching methods used; and,
(viii) the amalgamation of all factors into a timetable.

Particular organizational and administrative innovations may relate to such matters as admission and selection procedures, the structuring of course electives, the establishment of curriculum centres, organizing practice teaching, advising students, special staffing, and so on. However, in the final analysis, all of these matters come back to the deployment and utilization of resources. In this, the administrative officers of any institution may establish a climate in which innovation is possible.

In view of the very significant changes which have occurred in teacher education programmes in both universities and colleges during the past twenty years, the response to our survey in the areas of administrative and organizational innovation was surprisingly small. Some of these responses are discussed in the following sections.

Selection and admission procedures

The question of how to select students for admission to tertiary institutions has been a vexed one. Certainly, administrators in these institutions have expressed doubts that the methods followed ensured that the 'right' students were admitted. Where teacher education courses are concerned, school principals and others have argued that admission on matriculation level marks alone is not an adequate base and that some other measure, such as interviewing to determine suitability for teaching, should also be used. The examples which follow show some of the different procedures which particular institutions have tried.

At Torrens College, Watson introduced an approach to admissions where criteria other than examinations and written tests were used. Teachers rated applicants' academic ability and gave an opinion on their suitability for teaching. On this basis some applicants were chosen for interview and considered for direct entry. Other applicants were admitted on the traditional basis of examinations. Hughes and Traill, at Canberra College of Advanced Education, tried an 'early-offers' scheme where students with a Higher School Certificate aggregate teachers' estimate of at least 450 marks were offered the opportunity to enrol prior to the Higher School Certificate results becoming available. They claimed that the scheme attracted committed students and about 50 per cent of those who were made early offers accepted these and enrolled. Traill also reported a scheme where mature age students, who did not have the normal entry qualifications, were given a chance to enter the teacher education course of Canberra CAE on the basis of interviews and other measures. At the Nursery School

Teachers College (Lewis) a selection procedure is used whereby an attempt is made to weed out applicants of unstable personality, who were cognitively rigid, and who had difficulty in relating to young children. This required that each applicant be interviewed. The procedure placed lesser reliance on Higher School Certificate results and other measures, such as I.Q. tests. The basic aim was to try to select applicants who would work successfully with young children. From Mackie CAE, Tyndal and Symonds described a scheme for selecting applicants who wished to train as art teachers. Schools were asked to provide a confidential report on each applicant's ability and aptitude in art, and each applicant was interviewed. This approach resulted in less emphasis being given to Higher School Certificate aggregate marks.

Course structures and requirements

Often, degrees or diplomas are organized rather rigidly, with little opportunity for alternative patterns. Further, sometimes there is a different pattern of studies required for secondary student teachers, primary student teachers and kinder-garten student teachers. Generally, students have very limited freedom in which to operate when planning their courses. The examples given below show some of the more flexible patterns being developed.

Grundy and Simpson, at Flinders University, outlined an alternative diploma of education course, which was at the planning stage. This programme incorporated flexible practice teaching arrangements and aimed to provide also for the non-teaching interests of students. Salisbury College (Paul) has pioneered a common diploma pattern, where students taking the Early Childhood Education course, or the Primary course, or the Secondary course, followed a common pattern of studies in structuring their diploma programme. Mackie College (Thew) introduced an integrated and co-ordinated programme of teacher development which aimed to provide more flexibility in course components and to provide for individual student interests and competencies. Students were given personal responsibility for selecting and planning their courses. Individual-ized programming and timetabling by students was possible.

Varying school experience patterns

Increasing consideration is being given to organizing school experience patterns for student teachers, and sometimes there is a sharp difference of opinion as to the most appropriate pattern. This matter is discussed more fully later in this chapter and the single example given below is intended to show one pattern which has been attempted. A second matter which has concerned some teacher educators has been that the beginning teacher cuts loose from the institution on graduation and thereafter receives little, if any, assistance from it at a time when he probably needs it most.

At Mackie College (Thew) a pattern of practice teaching has been commenced in which student teachers attend schools to undertake practice teaching for one day, or for one half-day, each week, thus achieving a pattern of continuity with a class, the teacher and the school. This required the college to re-arrange its timetable, and some readjustment of lecture content and lecture loads was also necessary. An internship scheme has been introduced at Flinders University (Teasdale) whereby the institution's staff work with the employing authority to provide a planned support, including emotional and social support, for beginning teachers. This scheme ideally requires reduced work loads for first-year teachers.

Organizing course units

A fuller discussion of some of the more flexible approaches lecturers have tried in planning and presenting their courses is provided in subsequent sections. Some lecturers have organized particular units to try to meet the interests and needs of students and several examples are given below.

At Claremont College (de la Hunty) an elective course in mathematics designed for students with no mathematics background has been established. A problem with tertiary level courses in areas such as mathematics is that the nonspecialist tends to be frightened off. This example shows how an attempt has been made to attract the non-specialist. Phillips, at Macquarie University, has implemented a scheme of offering optional units in a history course so that students had a wide variety of choices and were able to plan their individual courses within a flexible unit grouping. Each unit was of six weeks' duration and students were required to complete four of these. The scheme involved academic staff in more hours of direct commitment and timetabling problems occurred. At Rusden College (Byrt) a course was offered where the normal timetable was completely revised to provide a wide range of elective offerings in an education course so that students were able to follow particular interests in depth. While some academic staff did not agree with the wide choice students were given, students preferred the approach to the usual course.

Tutorial advising and tutorial teaching

Most teacher education institutions have faced the problem of personalizing both the advice available to students and the instruction they receive. Each of the following examples illustrate arrangements which have been tried.

Thew, at Mackie CAE, reported a scheme where academic staff were responsible for a small group of students and interviewed these students each fortnight. There was a problem in finding suitable and willing academic staff to help students in the advisory role, but previously no system of supportive guidance had existed. A scheme of tutorial teaching, introduced at the Nursery School Teachers College (Simons), has the aim of personalizing instruction. While the scheme placed heavy pressure on room usage, made timetabling difficult, and involved academic staff for more contact hours, the scheme operated in every course in the college and was generally supported both by staff and by students.

Associate staff

A perennial problem in teacher education programmes is the need to ensure that methodology courses are taught by lecturers who are directly in touch with current school practice. Where permanent lecturers are appointed to teach methodology courses, the usual criticism is that the lecturer grows increasingly remote from the current school situation. Two of the following examples show attempts to overcome this problem. Another problem is that often teachers in the schools consider the school experience programme, as operated by the institution, as not fully relevant. Sometimes there is direct criticism by the teacher of the institution's programme. The final example below shows how one college has attempted to overcome this problem.

At Ballarat College (Coman) associate staff, who were proven practitioners, are employed to teach methodology courses. These appointees replaced full-time seconded staff from the Education Department, because it was felt that some method lecturers had lost credibility with students. As the associate staff were practising teachers it was necessary to timetable the course they conducted between 4 p.m. and 7 p.m. each day. An additional benefit was that the associate staff helped improve school-college relationships. Salisbury College (Homer) has appointed method lecturers ('lecturer-teachers') who spend part of their time working in schools and teachers ('teacher-tutors') who participate in method courses and the supervision of practice and microteaching. In this way method courses were fresh and relevant and relationships with schools were facilitated. Yaxley, at the Mt. Nelson Campus of the Tasmanian CAE, described a plan under which schools nominated associates who meet regularly with college staff to discuss the school experience programme. The basic purpose was to means improve college-teacher relationships and to provide a means for open discussion and the flow of ideas between the college and the schools.

Curriculum resource centres

At Canberra CAE (Burkhardt) an impressive curriculum resources centre has been developed to provide curriculum materials for some 1,000 student teachers and for in-service teachers. Unless administrative policy supports the establishment of such centres, it is difficult to conceive how the necessary range of resources for teaching and learning will be available.

2. Total Programme Innovation

A wide range of substantially new, comprehensive programmes has been reported. The variety of programmes provides many stimulating concepts for meeting the needs of student teachers, teachers and schools. It is these new ideas which are important in the following analysis.

In the last decade teacher education institutions have been taking a more critical look at the structure and components of their courses. This move has been stimulated considerably by the requirement that colleges of advanced education submit detailed course proposals for assessment by a panel of expert educationists in order to determine accreditation of the course and national recognition of the award for the programme. Along with a general sharpening of focus on objectives and components and their justification, there is currently a trend towards the establishment of bachelor's degrees for teachers. Somewhat allied to this upgrading is a further reconsideration of the one-year end-on diploma in education which for so long has been the source of criticism from students, teachers and lecturers alike. Numerous alternative approaches to the diploma year are being explored. In both these types of programmes there are a number of interesting innovations which may be mentioned.

Diploma of Education programme

In the Diploma of Education programme for 460 students at Monash University (Theobold), a greater degree of student involvement in the planning of the programme is achieved by a diploma of education committee composed of students and staff so that the programme has some minor modifications continually in operation. The programme provides two days per week for teaching practice and a concurrent core of units and electives. The elective offerings are substantial with approximately ninety courses available. Additional features include microteaching sessions and practice teaching blocks of two or three weeks in terms II and III followed by post-practice camps. Remedial microteaching is also available.

At Flinders University (Grundy) there is an experimental or alternate diploma course for a small group of students only, which aims to provide the maximum possible degree of flexibility. Students direct their own studies to areas of special interest and arrange their courses in patterns which they find effective. The programme concentrates on student planning, exploration of educational issues and research. The programme functions through a series of meetings for orientation, group and tutorial purposes. School experience and academic work contracts are also required. The emphasis is on developing a sense of personal adequacy in teaching.

With a similar theme of freedom for the student the Dip.Ed. programme for 500 students at SCV Melbourne (Hindley) has recognized that a large measure of freedom and opportunity for initiative are vital in the preparation of teachers for their professional responsibilities. The students and staff have elected to operate in nine teams with each team determining its alternative activities. Generally students in each team are of mixed course background with respect to teaching subjects for secondary teaching or primary teaching. As a result of the team arrangements there are six identifiable styles for the programme:

Team 1—*Subject-based Programme* which uses a traditional model based on particular subject methods and the usual lecture-discussion, seminar format of programme.

Teams 2 to 5 follow a *Core-elective Programme* which provides a variety of elective opportunities. The core consists of educational foundation studies and electives are selected in modules of eight hours. Some eighty elective courses are listed.

Team 6—*Elective Programme* has a concurrent arrangement for college and school experiences. Students spend 2 days per week in the schools and in Term III carry out a contract programme in the school. Three elective education courses are also included.

Team 7—*School-based Programme* involves 2 days per week teaching practice, 1 day per week in seminars and courses at a school in conjunction with the school staff and the remaining 2 days are at college for meetings and for elective courses.

Team 8—*D.E.E. (Dip.Ed. Experiment) Programme* emphasizes decision-making and the development of an adequate self-concept. Students contract for educational work each week. A tutorial leader guides the students work in schools and their progress on the contract work.

Team 9—*Community-based Programme* has students located in schools and the community for a large part of time. The programme aims to bridge the gap between students, school, community and college. Students spend 2 to 4 days in the field with Friday set aside for planning and workshops and method activities. The community component has included i) the operation of a shop-front service in the evenings and weekends for local pupils, ii) Creative Holiday Club activities, and iii) an Adult Literacy teaching programme.

Across all nine programmes students must fulfil school experience requirements, choose some electives and complete either method work or a multi-method course. Variety seems to be the thing in this most interesting Dip.Ed. programme, with students electing a programme which interests them.

As a further example, the Flinders University (Teasdale) Diploma in Education for graduates who wish to teach at the primary school level is a two-year course. There is one year full-time study for 36 course units, followed by a one-year teaching internship of 6 units in an Adelaide school. During the second year the student assumes full-time teaching responsibilities but is given leave to attend short conferences and regular seminars to complete a further 12 units of study. The Diploma totals 54 units of credit and is not awarded until the student has demonstrated his competence as a classroom teacher after one year of teaching. The programme corresponds to Years III and IV of the B.Ed. degree course at Flinders. The internship period of students has created some salary problems concerning their employment status and these problems are as yet unresolved.

At the Western Australian Secondary Teachers College (Vlahov), the NEDAP (Nedlands Action Project) is a pilot study involving fourth-year secondary students in concentrated work in schools. Integrated subject method tutorials are held in the schools with both college and school staff. The schools share in the preparation of teachers in four core subjects, English, mathematics, social studies and science. Each student and his tutor teacher negotiate a mutually acceptable timetable of tutorials and teaching experience. The programme aims to integrate theory and practice and to provided more meaningful teaching practice and school experience.

Bachelor of Education programmes

A B.Ed. concurrent course of four years has recently been introduced as an alternative to a degree and the end-on Dip.Ed. programme at Tasmania University (Selby-Smith). The programme allows students to commence education studies at a much earlier stage in the degree.

At Churchlands CAE (Jecks) a B.Ed. has been approved for Primary and Early Childhood Education students. In essence it is an extension of the Diploma in Teaching to a degree after a fourth year. It is anticipated that the majority of students would return to complete the fourth year after one year of teaching but it is possible for Churchlands diploma candidates to proceed directly to the degree. Students from other institutions may be required to undertake bridging courses before admission to the fourth year. The programme is derived from a philosophy emphasizing flexibility, openness and the application of theory to practice. Objectives related to attitudes and interests, knowledge and understanding and skills and techniques are comprehensive, well balanced and clearly outlined. In the B.Ed. fourth-year students undertake elective courses in each of the three strands, Education Studies, Curriculum and Instruction Studies and General Studies.

Following a somewhat similar concept, Kelvin Grove CAE (Hardingham) has proposed to extend the Diploma in Teaching to a B.Ed. degree after a minimum of one year's teaching experience. The programme aims to give an opportunity for a more mature examination in the light of teaching experience, of such areas as curriculum development, sociology, philosophy and psychology as a building-on to the pre-service Diploma in Teaching. The fourth-year programme includes Education Foundations and Curriculum Studies, with Independent Study as a major component.

Both Gippsland Institute of Advanced Education (Lawry) and the SCV Melbourne (Biddington) also have proposals for a B.Ed. which provides a degree for all teachers. The Gippsland programme includes a Diploma in Teaching award plus one year of teaching and a B.Ed. year. The Melbourne programme plans to delay specialization till the fourth year of the degree but a Diploma in Teaching may be possible after three years.

At Flinders University (Paddick) a Bachelor of Education in Physical Education is available. Year I of the programme is common to that of all other graduate courses and there is physical education specialization from Year II. There is no orientation specific to teaching until Year IV, where there is an internship of one term and methodology units in physical education.

Graduate Diploma programmes

The Graduate Diploma is regarded as an advanced qualification for qualified teachers with work experience. An interesting variety of such diploma programmes has been introduced in all states.

For example, at Salisbury CAE (Paul) a Graduate Diploma in Teaching provides the opportunity for an extension of the teacher's work beyond the first diploma. Advanced studies and in-depth investigations may be undertaken in professional and general studies mainly through individual study contracts to cater for the student's special interests. The course is one year full-time (or equivalent part-time study) and its components include a major investigation, one selected subject course at an advanced level, a professional experience project and one other optional course study.

A Graduate Diploma in School Administration is offered at Mt. Gravatt CAE (Tronc) as a one-year part-time programme to prepare potential school administrators and to upgrade the administrative skills of practising administrators. Considerable use is made of simulation techniques in workshop sessions and the emphasis of the programme is predominantly practical and applied. The central focus is also upon the school rather than the educational system. Flinders University (Briggs) also has a Graduate Diploma in Educational Administration. This is a one year full-time programme as a post-graduate qualification. Students must have had at least two years' work experience. The course comprises some thirty-six units of credit and includes some elective units.

Other graduate diplomas reported in the survey seem to be more specialized qualifications. For example, Claremont TC (Gibbs) offers a Graduate Diploma in Drama in Education. This programme provides an in-depth study of the whole area of drama in education and aims at a specialist development of the teacher. It also aims to improve the teacher's understanding of children, play and their own resources. The course includes the teaching of retarded and maladjusted children through drama. There are core and elective studies but 50 per cent of the course comprises practical work in schools and institutions.

At Mt. Lawley CAE (True) a Graduate Diploma in Music Education aims to train resource teachers of music for primary schools. Teachers need an initial three-year diploma in teaching. It is a one-year full-time or part-time equivalent course and is presently conducted after school from 4 p.m. to 9 p.m.

A Diploma in Educational Technology is provided at SCV Toorak (Miller) to train experienced teachers as media specialists for all levels of schooling. Candidates need to have a minimum of four years teaching experience. It is a one-year full-time or equivalent part-time programme which includes educational psychology, curriculum studies, educational administration and library studies components in addition to specialized work in resources, audiovisual techniques, graphic design, educational television, photography and cinematography. An interesting feature is provision for school placement two or three days per week in terms II and III.

A proposed Graduate Diploma in Outdoor Education at Kelvin Grove CAE (McIntyre and Feeney) seeks to prepare students to provide the leadership, organization and co-ordination necessary to conduct outdoor activities embracing a wide variety of disciplines (science, ecology, environmental science, geography, music, art, drama and social psychology). Field experiences are planned for both recreational and academic interests in the community.

At Kuring-gai CAE (Trask) a Graduate Diploma in Teacher Librarianship has recently been introduced. It is a three semester full-time programme in education studies and library information studies. Field work and practice are strong features of the programme. The programme aims to emphasize the librarian's role as a member of the school's education team with special expertise in the information needs, resources and methods required for service to pupils and staff. The teacher librarian is both a materials specialist and a mediator in the teaching learning process. Proposals have also been submitted for a four-year degree in teacher librarianship.

Specialist programmes

Some specialist programmes provide insights into perceived needs in schools and the special preparation of student teachers to meet these needs. For example, the Tasmanian CAE northern campus at Launceston has a four-year programme (Croft) specializing in English, speech and drama teaching in secondary schools. The E.S.D. course focuses both on practical and academic studies and includes in-depth study of literature, language arts, and associated arts including theatre arts and crafts, music, art and movement. Curriculum studies, activities workshops and education studies are linked with practice in secondary schools and add to a comprehensive 'specialist' preparation.

The SCV Rusden (Stocks and Duke) offers a four-year programme in environmental studies which leads to a Higher Diploma of Teaching (Secondary). This programme aims to produce environmentally literate persons and competent teachers of environmental-studies-based courses. Scientific study in biology, geography and physical science are combined with professional studies. Individual research projects in the field are conducted at Yarralock and Sheltons Land rural centres.

A modern languages teacher education programme for primary level students is offered at Mt. Lawley CAE (Malcolm). Students elect the language major in Years II and III. Special practice teaching in language is organized in schools. Indonesian, French or Italian may be elected and this is supported by linguistics, method studies, cultural and literary studies and education. The college perceives a growing need for primary teachers qualified to teach languages and hopes to extend the programme to offer a Graduate Diploma in Modern Languages eventually.

Claremont TC (McKercher) has a two-year tertiary course for health education. Studies are provided in communications, public health practices and environmental studies. The award given is an Associate Diploma in Health Education.

Many specialist programmes are concerned with the needs of children with handicaps. Special education courses have been introduced by many institutions. At Flinders University (Cooper), for example, a Bachelor of Special Education has been introduced. Post-graduate students and teachers with a diploma in teaching and some teaching experience may enrol in a two year full-time course which generally is completed as a one year full-time study or two years' part-time study to enable students to gain more practical experience. The programme tries to give a broad generalist emphasis in special education to meet the needs of teaching children who will be in the 'mainstream' of schooling. Education studies relate to exceptional children, learning difficulties, and diagnostic and remedial programmes. Elective courses may be related to a specific handicap problem. Research methods, reading, practicum and special projects are other features of the degree components.

A one year full-time pre-service Diploma in Special Education after two years in the Diploma in Teaching is offered at Newcastle CAE (Bennett). An in-service programme after two years' teaching is also offered as a one year full-time Diploma in Special Education. These programmes prepare teachers for work with intellectually handicapped children, or those with physical and sensory defects, mild emotional and behaviour disorders, or those with learning disabilities. A special Education Clinic and Teaching Centre has been built on the campus as a new college-community facility for the programme. The course is a multi-disciplinary one involving education, English, maths, art, physical education, craft and music. These areas are integrated to focus studies on three units—Understanding the Child; The Child in the Society; and The Child in the School.

At SCV Burwood (Duerdoth) a special orientation programme of two to three weeks is arranged for all applicants for a Graduate Diploma in Special Education. The scheme aims to provide a meaningful introduction to, and insight into the problems of deaf children by having students observe in schools and be introduced to the philosophy and terminology of a particular handicap before studies commence on a wide range of handicaps requiring specialized teaching approaches.

3. Innovations in Specific Curriculum Areas

Increasing emphasis is being given by teacher educators to ways in which curriculum studies programmes need to be amended to keep in step with changes in society and in the school system. New offerings are being considered to reflect changes in the way society is meeting present-day problems (e.g. the increased emphasis on the preservation of the environment has created an interest in offering curriculum courses which focus on environmental studies). Changing emphases in schools are also bringing an influence to bear on what is being offered in existing curriculum courses (e.g. an emphasis on music as a creative art is leading to many changes to the music curriculum courses offered in teacher education programmes). The survey revealed a widespread interest in Australian teacher education programmes in developing innovative approaches to the curriculum studies areas.

The introduction of the teaching of *mathematics* to student teachers has been a concern of teacher educators for a long time and this current survey revealed that it is still a problem which commands considerable attention. One area of concern has been to develop self-instructional programmes which will not only give student teachers ideas for the teaching of mathematics but will at the same time develop a degree of self-competence in this subject area. The work of Schleiger at the SCV at Coburg, and Billington and Perry at Mitchell CAE are indicative of such approaches. Attention is also given in several approaches to the long-standing problem of trying to get student teachers who are not academically strong in mathematics to develop more positive attitudes to the teaching of this subject area in primary schools. An example of this approach is given by Hassall at Mercy College. A unit entitled 'Mathematics as part of our culture' is offered an elective in the second- and third-year programmes. The approach used is to emphasize non-operational aspects of mathematics and 'enable students to discover maths by studying patterns in areas apart from the customary technical or specialist maths fields'. Hassall reports a heartening change in the attitudes to mathematics held by students who complete this unit. Many programmes give emphasis to introducing new ideas for classroom teaching to students. Particularly interesting work in this area is being undertaken by Jones at Kelvin Grove CAE. A laboratory setting is used to provide learning experiences in both mathematics content and curricula for primary schools. A mathematical model approach provides teaching strategies which interrelate problem solving and mathematical skills. This is facilitated by the use of a mathematics laboratory equipped with games, puzzles, mathematical materials and support audiovisual equipment. This innovation represents an Australian adaptation of the Mathematics Methods Program at Indiana University. In collaboration with Hall, Jones is also developing a course to give student teachers experience in the construction of mathematical materials from easily accessible and non-expensive sources. In this course students are also provided with training in identifying children's error patterns in mathematics and in constructing diagnostic kits to use when helping children to remedy such error patterns. This programme should also prove of considerable interest to other teacher educators.

Another curriculum area which has concerned teacher educators has been *science*, and, as in the case of mathematics, considerable attention has been focused on the non-specialist teacher who will teach science in the primary school. Several programmes indicated that efforts are directed towards achieving more positive attitudes to science in these students. An example of such an approach is found at Kuring-gai CAE (Dawes, Kennedy *et al.*). All students in the primary and early childhood courses follow a one semester unit entitled 'Processes of Science'. A major objective of the course is to promote student enthusiasm about investigations in science. Emphasis is placed on experimental work at the student's own level that can be later adopted for use in primary classrooms. The scientific content emerges as a means of achieving this classroom related work, rather than being the major focus of the unit. Several science education programmes reported that efforts were being made to have secondary science specialists see their subject in a wider perspective. Ryan at the SCV Melbourne, outlined a course which was aimed to get students specializing in chemistry education to regard their specialist area in the context of the less complex terms appropriate for secondary school studies. At the SCV at Rusden, Clift tackled the problem of biology specialists who had no background in physics and chemistry. A course was developed which was environmentally oriented but based on the physical sciences. At Mt. Gravatt CAE Cullen and Roberts have developed a course to get secondary science specialists to view science in a wider context than that of the particular subject content of a discipline. Science lecturers teamed with the social studies staff to present an interdisciplinary study of science through looking at the social, philosophical and religious implications of scientific developments.

The survey revealed that several teacher educators are undertaking innovative work in the area of *environmental curriculum studies*. At the Claremont TC McMillan has developed an Environmental Biology course for primary student teachers which aims 'to create an interest and understanding of the environment' and 'to identify problems that can arise when the environment is altered'. An indication of the success of McMillan's course is reflected by the fact that the efforts of the students have led to four habitats being now classified as 'reserves'. Marsh at Kelvin Grove CAE offers a course for secondary students who are not specializing in science. This course considers a number of the issues raised by environmental studies for teachers who would not in their normal course have contact with such issues. Crowther at Townsville CAE has introduced a course on Environmental Studies which aims to give primary students 'further awareness of the environment and the effect of it on man, and of man on it' while at the same time developing the students' 'skills in scientific investigation and observation and the spirit of inquiry, so that they may be transferred into schools and the teaching situation and also into community life'. An interesting feature of this course is the involvement of students in an empirical study and the consequent development of simple field study skills which can be taught in classrooms at a later date.

In the general field of *English* curriculum studies, many programmes outlined courses which were aimed to assist students in the more creative approaches to this area. At the Institute of Early Childhood Development a course in Creative Writing and Writing for Children has been developed by Rogers which gives students opportunities to write imaginatively through participating in writing workshops. Students are encouraged to write for children and through this are led 'to utilize and synthesize their knowledge of children and of literature'. The area of children's drama is a feature of several interesting courses. Roberts at Nepean CAE runs a drama course for primary students which leads to the presentation of a children's play in an outdoor multi-scene garden setting in which children follow the student teacher actors as they move from scene to scene. Students during the course read a number of children's stories which they adapt for acting. Students in the course also visit schools where they introduce the characters and the story to the children before the later presentation of their play. At Claremont TC Gibbs has developed a course in Children's Theatre in which tutorial assistance is given by professional theatre players. The students plan, direct and present theatre presentations to their fellow students and also work with children in producing plays. Both of these examples are illustrative of innovatory approaches in getting student teachers away from the text-book study approach to children's drama to a more involved, creative experience in learning the skills of teaching in this area. The study of the role of the film as a means of communication is the focus of a course developed by Bruce at Kelvin Grove CAE. The course aims to give student teachers a perspective of the Australian film and its relationship with literature, and young film makers and their films are used as a main resource for discussion. Many programmes continue to seek ways of introducing student teachers to the problems of language development. Typical of such interesting courses is that given at Claremont TC by Gallagher. Based on the scientific study of language development, the course is developed through an emphasis on the cultural backgrounds of children and establishing teaching strategies which take into account children's use of language.

Another curriculum area which was frequently mentioned in survey responses was the area of *music*. A problem which has long been of concern to teacher educators in this area has been how to help the student teachers with no previously acquired musical skills to develop these in the relatively restricted time available in a pre-service programme. This has always been of more particular concern to those involved in early childhood programmes and Bridges at Sydney Nursery School TC has developed a course which tackles this problem. The course includes experiences in piano playing in group tutorial situations, improvisation and playing 'by ear' preceding note reading, music through movement, and creative activities using elementary music materials similar to those used with children. The Kodaly method is used in several programmes to develop musicianship. Mahon at the Mitchell CAE uses the Kodaly approach not only to help the students' musical ability but also to provide students with a means of helping children to read, write and create music. At the Mt. Gravatt CAE McKinley is using the Kodaly method not only for music teaching purposes but also to develop an interrelationship with language development. Efforts to present music as a creative art are a feature of a course being conducted by Cooke at the Sydney Kindergarten TC. Through using materials such as the Carl Orff melodic percussion instruments, students are encouraged to explore the nature of musical sound and to be involved in their own creative music making. A most extensive range of innovative approaches to the music curriculum area can be found at the SCV at Frankston. Here a whole range of courses are being developed to explore methods of aural discrimination. Bilsborough is running a course on aural discrimination through movement and music, and Jones has courses on listening experiences and group teaching of the guitar and of the piano. In addition, Jones is also working with students on a most interesting approach to the teaching of the piano to young children.

In the area of *physical education* most innovative approaches reported in the survey involved the development of self-paced skill development courses. Typical of such courses is that offered by McKercher at Claremont TC. The course involves students working through a programmed list of activities which have associated self-testing instruments also available. Attention to the primary school teacher who will be a semi-specialist rather than a specialist or non-specialist physical education teacher is given by Whittingham at Torrens CAE. This innovative approach seeks to place in primary schools general classroom teachers who will be able to act as team leaders in developing physical education programmes in schools.

In *art* most developments involved making students aware of the wide range of activities which may operate in this area. Kendall at the Canberra CAE has planned a Creative Arts course where students are involved in a range of activities which cover many arts fields. This interesting approach stresses the inter-relationship of the arts and the development of a language for the creative arts which is of a concrete nature and therefore readily understood by children. Different approaches to the use of particular materials has been the focus of several courses.

At the Wollongong Institute of Education, Bell has worked with students on the use of plastics with primary school children. A course in creative stitchery at Claremont TC (Madigan, Calcutt *et al.*) shows student teachers how children can be involved in a range of creative experiences through possessing stitchery skills. Barnacoat and Polglase at Kuring-gai CAE involve students in a Ceramics and Man course which explores the many activities associated with working with ceramic materials. An extensive range of courses in this curriculum area was reported in the survey response from Alexander Mackie CAE. Of particular interest was a course involving art students in gaining practical experiences in schools other than 'normal' (e.g. in a psychiatric hospital school).

A few programmes reported innovative approaches in *social science* curriculum areas. At Newcastle CAE Gill developed a course aimed at assisting student teachings in developing teaching resources and strategies appropriate to recent primary school social science curriculum units. At the Mt. Gravatt CAE a team co-ordinated by Russell has developed the Multiphase Programme in Social Studies Curriculum for Teacher Education. Students are involved in a series of self-instructional activities to develop the skills used by teachers in this subject area.

Several survey responses outlined curriculum studies courses which introduced a variety of areas into programmes which are not normally included in the traditional range of curriculum offerings. Typical of these was one interesting course offered by Holland at Kuring-gai CAE. This involves a study of the *mass media* as a means of communication and in helping students to devise activities which could be used with children in classrooms. Dent and Kiek outlined a course in Educational Media at Adelaide CAE which provides a series of self-tutorial exercises aimed to help students develop competencies in using educational media and in teaching about the media in schools. Several survey responses discussed fascinating courses in *computer studies*. De la Hunty at Claremont TC has an excellent course established which not only gives student teachers skills in this area but also identifies activities which are appropriate for primary and secondary pupils. A course especially designed for primary school student teachers is offered at Townsville CAE by King. This course does not place emphasis on the programming aspect of computer studies but is rather a study of the implications and applications of computers. A very useful course in *Driver Education* has been developed by Reed at the SCV at Bendigo—this would provide students with a very good model course which they could introduce into a secondary school curriculum. In the area of *religious education* Smith's course on Religion and Society at the Newcastle CAE should prove of interest to other educators. Wells is concerned that children's insights into *geometry* are neglected and at the Goulburn CAE involves students in a course on Shadow Geometry. *French* in the primary school is under discussion in several parts of Australia and a course to train student teachers to be primary school French teachers has been developed at the Claremont TC by Coroneos. Helping student teachers move into *open plan schools* is of concern to many programmes and teacher educators will look with interest at the work of Mannison at Kelvin Grove CAE. A course entitled 'Environmental Psychology' allows students to examine the influence of various forms of classroom environment. However, the course also looks at the wider concept of open education and explores with students the implications of this philosophy as it is put into practice.

The above review clearly indicates that Australian teacher educators are giving considerable attention to curriculum studies programmes. Many new initiatives are apparent to either re-structure the existing or to introduce new areas. Dissemination of what is happening in the various institutions is evidently a barrier to many further advances as the survey responses clearly indicated that many people were quite unaware of developments occurring within their curriculum field in other Australian teacher education programmes.

4. Technological Innovation

Teacher education, like many other aspects of education, has been much influenced by the recent advances made in technology. Availability of technological equipment has enabled teacher educators to offer a wide range of experiences for their students—an involvement which extends from the use of a single item of equipment (e.g. a cassette tape recorder) to the provision of an environment which has been totally created through the use of a variety of technological resources.

Use of a particular item

The survey revealed a widespread usage in Australian teacher education programmes of an extensive range of technological equipment. The examples of particular usages of a single item of equipment are far too numerous to review in total and therefore this analysis has been confined to some instances of usage which are illustrative of ways in which programmes are using single items in an interesting manner.

Photography is a process which has been available for use by teacher educators for quite a time, but Endersby at the SCV at Bendigo has explored ways in which photography may assist in meeting a recurring problem for a particular group of teacher educators. Endersby has developed activities relating to the use of photographs in art education courses to overcome 'students' initial reluctance to draw'. Similarly, audiotapes have been available for some time, but again their use in meeting recurring problems is being explored by several programmes. McGowan at Claremont TC is using audiotapes as a means of developing the skills of oral presentations in social science classes. Films continue to be used in developing the effectiveness of programmes, and Bruce at Kelvin Grove CAE is exploring their use in helping students to develop the skills of critical analysis.

Of the more recently produced technological items, videotaping apparatus has made the most widespread impact on teacher education programmes responding to the survey. The use of videotape equipment has enabled a closer analysis to be made by students of the processes involved in teaching and learning. Newton, Stroobant and Harrison have used videotapes at the Sydney KTC to provide student teachers with studies depicting child development and using Australian pre-school children in a natural setting. Elms at Townsville College of Advanced Education has made videotapes of children involved in learn-to-swim campaigns to provide physical education students with data on children that was not accessible to on-campus courses prior to the availability of videotaping equipment. A similar approach has been used by Julian and Gibbs at Claremont TC to present examples of modern techniques in primary school drama to on-campus classes. In all three examples, the teacher educators concerned have indicated that the use of videotaping equipment has helped in a significant manner to overcome the gap which previously existed between the theoretical and practical components of a teacher education programme. A slightly different use of videotaped materials by Fitzgerald and Thompson at the SCV at Coburg has meant that another aspect of a teacher education programme might be changed by the use of technological aids. Videotapes are being used in this instance to provide an alternative means of determining student assessments. Introduction of video-cassette VTR models into the Australian market will also undoubtedly lead to interesting changes in existing patterns of teacher education. At the SCV Melbourne, Mitchell and Goode are developing video-cassette materials as a major source of storage and retrieval of information for that institution's programmes. In many of the usages of videotaped materials described previously, concern has frequently been expressed about the problems involved in actually recording the material in off-campus situations. Intensive attention to this problem has been given by Shave at the Goulburn CAE. An outside ETV van has been built which enables high quality videotapes to be made of classroom situations.

Another technological item to have had a recent impact on teacher education programmes is the computer. Several institutions reported that they were looking to computer facilities as a major source of innovatory procedures for their programmes. McKay at Armidale CAE has examined ways in which the computer might be used as a means of supplying feedback information to student teachers. The computer has been used to provide a rapid feedback of interaction analysis patterns from data collected by using the Flanders' system of interaction analysis. Student teachers have also been provided with a quick means of gaining information on their pupils by the use of the computer. As a preliminary stage to the use of a computer, Flanagan at the Newcastle CAE has used programmable calculators to develop teaching units. Ashley at the Western Australian Secondary TC has used tonal memory trainers as a means of programming instructional sequences for secondary music student teachers.

Simulated environments

Technological advances have created many opportunities for teacher educators to develop simulated situations in on-campus facilities which represent approximation to the real-life school classroom situation. A considerable amount of innovatory work is occurring in Australia in efforts to produce simulated environments, particularly with situations which represent an Australian setting in contrast to situations which use materials more identifiable with overseas environments.

On major source of interest in this development is the focus on situations where students practise teaching skills on each other, have such experiences recorded, and then play back the teaching episode for analysis and discussion. The major reason for such an approach to be possible is the advances made in videotaping equipment and most questionnaires returned by institutions indicated some usage of this facility. Considerable attention to the type of facilities needed for this activity has been given at the Canberra CAE (Hughes *et al.*) where for several years different types of equipment and organizational models have been investigated. This work has resulted in the development of studios which contain durable flexible facilities. Neal of the WAIT has used video and audio facilities to help students develop individualized teaching styles as they practise teaching strategies in micro-curriculum situations. Many programmes are using videotaping facilities to get student teachers to practise sets of teaching skills presented to them as models (e.g. use of the Sydney Micro Skills series [Turney *et al.*]). Examples of such programmes using facilities in this way are University of Sydney, Canberra CAE, Newcastle CAE and Salisbury CAE.

Several programmes have developed means of using several items of technological equipment to present a simulated classroom or school experience. At Mt. Gravatt CAE Tronc has used a wide range of equipment to produce simulated activities involving students in decision-making experiences as material is presented to them through videotape, printed and audio sources. A similar use of equipment has been made by Gallagher and Marland at Townsville CAE to produce an environment in which student teachers can make decisions in quite a similar situation to that which they would face in a school.

An interesting use of many technological items to devise a learning environment is that planned for art education students by Thomas at Mt. Lawley CAE. A 'kinesthetic-synergetic environment' has been provided by fitting a studio with special light, sound and projection equipment. Students experience a range of creative activities in this environment.

This brief discussion reveals a range of approaches to the use of technology in teacher education. Equipment which has been available for many years continues to be used in innovatory ways; of the more recently developed equipment, videotaping facilities have been extensively used to open up many new approaches in teacher education. At this survey revealed, the use of computer facilities is very much at an exploratory stage. It would seem that this technological development could have much to offer in the future for teacher education programmes.

5. Assessment and Evaluation Innovation

Most tertiary students have reasonably well established opinions about marking and grading both of assignments and of courses. Similarly tertiary academic staff have their opinions, with some regretting that any assessment at all is necessary as it overshadows the teacher-student relationship and influences negatively too many of the affective aspects of the learning-teaching situation. And some students openly reflect the associated problems in their almost exclusive focus on the grade to be received at the end of the course. Critics of grading often complain that it emphasizes and fosters competition among students and has the potential too often to sour the teacher-student relationship.

There is another viewpoint that at the tertiary level a key concern is academic excellence and that grading is perfectly natural. Sure, there is an element of competition, but this has the positive effect of sorting out honours students from pass students, and of separating the conscientious student who meets course requirements fully from the pedestrian student who intends to try to judge, and to make, the minimum effort which hopefully will result in a marginal pass.

While the positions stated are rather stereotyped, they do reflect several of the recurring factors which come up frequently in the debate about both assignment and course assessment. Certainly, there has been a swing away from the dominant final examination in many tertiary courses. And in the first two sections which follow examples are given related to assessment and to marking.

The final three sections which follow relate to the evaluation of practice teaching, to longitudinal studies of students both in college and post-college and to the evaluations of a college teaching procedure. The examples given show various evaluation procedures which are aimed at trying to improve current policies and practices. Too often, policies and practices once established and ongoing are not thoroughly evaluated except when some breakdown occurs or seems about to occur.

Assessing tertiary courses

The following eight examples show some of the ways in which teacher educators have tried to swing away from the traditional pattern of assessment in which the final examination tended to be the dominant factor. The continuous assessment pattern is becoming well established at the tertiary level in Australia, even though there is some student complaint that the load of such is heavier than the major final examination pattern. Certainly there has been a real attempt in the schools in the last few decades to lessen the dominance of examinations and the use of 'norms' in assessment, and to focus more on learning and on individual differences. And it is fitting that tertiary students, who are to be teachers, experience in their own tertiary courses the same emphasis.

From Salisbury CAE, Schultz reported how students were given a choice in assessment procedures which ranged from three assignments during the semester coupled with no final examination to two lesser assignments during semester coupled with a final examination which carried 60 per cent of the marks. There was a distinct student preference for the procedure mentioned first above. Obviously the lecturer's marking load increased during semester as a direct result of this student preference. Schultz claimed that an increase in student motivation was noted by staff and that the approach appeared to benefit most those students who were potential failures. Similarly, Haselhurst and Hooker, at Claremont TC, have introduced a flexible approach to assessment in the light of lecturers' and of students' preferences. This involved the spreading of assessment over the duration of the course and the reduction of the final examination to 30 to 40 per cent of overall assessment. They claimed their scheme derived from their observation of unsatisfactory student study techniques, poor performance and low level of interest of students in a purely lecture, essay, examination approach to courses. Kelvin Grove CAE (Adie) employs a form of assessment in a psychology course which puts emphasis on continuous assessment and involvement through the course. Students record their own learnings and evaluations in a 'Journal of Personal Learnings' and each journal is evaluated on the basis of its scope, the accuracy of use of psychological concepts, and the degree of effort and creativity shown. This approach requires students to apply the content of the course to their own lives and experience.

Brown and Putt, at Townsville CAE have experimented with open-book assessment which aimed to take the emphasis off recall and associated stereotyping of answers, and to give students the opportunity to make judgements in conditions similar to those of teacher-decision-making in the school. The approach was tried in a mathematics curriculum studies course.

Peer assessment is being employed in a number of institutions. For example, Claremont TC (McKercher) has employed an approach to the assessment of student teachers in teaching situations by their own peers. All students concerned were taking a major option in Physical Education and McKercher reported that student assessment correlated highly with staff assessment of teaching effectiveness.

Independent problem solving is a feature of an assessment procedure introduced at Mitchell CAE. Taylor reported a scheme which incorporated some 150 folders containing reading and material relevant to small schools teaching and some 50 problem cards which required student teachers to tackle specific problems they would face in small schools, and in which assessment was based on a print system built up according to the value of assignments and folders. Taylor claimed that the approach threw responsibility for progress onto students and that each student knew when he had reached a pass, credit or distinction level.

The desirability of non-competitiveness in assessment has concerned a number of teacher educators and has resulted in some interesting schemes. For example, McConnochie, at Flinders University, has pioneered a system of non-competitive grading in which students were able to contract with the lecturer for work loads and for grades. Students who participated in seminars received a 'C' pass, those who in addition completed one assignment received a 'B' pass, and those who in addition completed a second assignment received an 'A' pass. He noted that there was some opposition from other lecturers, who criticized the approach as lowering academic standards, as a soft option, and as stealing students from other courses.

Variety of assessment procedures is the essence of many innovations. An unusual approach to this is evidenced at Newcastle CAE, where Wilson has developed a system of teaching and evaluating an Education II course in which a different assessment approach was taken in each of three terms. One aim was to provide a fairer basis for assessment by using a variety of methods. He claimed that this approach resulted in a more meaningful course for students and to more student research and direct involvement.

Marking

Few students, at any level, experience what they view as satisfactory marking procedures. Too often exercises are worked and are submitted for marking and thereafter there is too much delay in reporting back to students, and even then feedback is minimal. Sometimes there is heavy emphasis on marking and highlighting errors. Sometimes the only feedback is a bare grade without meaningful comment. The first example shows a marking system where the exercise was returned within a set time and where individual consultation was possible. The second example relates to the testing of three marking procedures at primary school level.

At Kuring-gai CAE, Holland has introduced an approach to assessing an English course which aims to minimize anxiety about assessment. During the semester, each exercise was marked by a different tutor and was returned to students within ten days of submission. This was coupled with close tutorial contact and individual consultation, which were intended to help develop student confidence. A few teacher educators have explored with students the effectiveness of various marking procedures in schools. One instance of this comes from Newcastle CAE, where Haywood is conducting an experiment to evaluate the effects of three different marking procedures on the creative writing of primary school children. He noted that, while marking out all errors was a widely used method, pupil and teacher efficiency may be improved by other methods of marking. At the time of writing the experiment was still in progress.

Practice teaching

The efficiency and effectiveness both of the broad pattern of practice teaching and of the actual assessment of the student teacher in the teaching situation have long concerned teacher educators. In fact, both of these aspects may be discussed critically more often than are other aspects of tertiary level assessment. The three examples which follow show only some of these concerns since practice teaching is a major section later in this chapter.

Many institutions are experimenting with general and specific rating scales and check lists. For example, at the Australian College of Physical Education, Butt uses a fifteen-item multiple choice check list to assess student teachers' practice teaching. He noted the advantage of the ease of completion of the check list by supervising staff and that the source of this approach was from a course at the University of Oregon.

A few investigations into the practice teaching policies and their effects on students were reported. At Kuring-gai CAE, Browne is seeking to discover what factors significantly influence students' practice teaching performance. The project commenced in 1972, is still continuing, and has the objective of attempting to determine what modifications may need to be made to practice teaching organization. In a much larger study, Browne of the Darling Downs Institute is collecting survey data relating to practice teaching policies and practices, with the purpose of foreshadowing desirable future directions.

Following-up newly graduated teachers

The four examples which follow show some of the ways longitudinal studies are carried out and ex-students are followed-up in the teaching situation to evaluate or critically review various aspects of the teacher education programme. From Salisbury CAE, Otto and Paul have completed a pilot study to investigate the effectiveness of the college's teacher education programme. At the end of their first year of teaching, some fifty college graduates were invited to comment on their college training. The respondents gave a low ranking to college academic courses and ranked block practice teaching experiences as the most valuable part of the college programme. These findings follow the pattern of similar studies. Young, at Sturt CAE, is pursuing a study which examines the effectiveness of practice teaching. The plan is to study all exit students and to continue a longitudinal study of these teachers with the aim of establishing guidelines for pre-service courses. Fitzgerald, at SCV Ballarat reported a study to provide data as a basis for assessment of the predictive validity of selection procedures and variables. This entailed following through entry college students into their first years of teaching after graduation. Selection procedures are a matter of concern in most institutions and research in this field is welcome. Finally, at SCV Burwood, Power described a study in which an attempt was made to empiricize bases for student selection by correlation with on-course and post-course measures. He noted that previous selection had been by non-validated 'rule of thumb' methods and that the aim was to improve this and to make interview procedures more reliable and valid.

Evaluation of teaching procedures

Too often teaching procedures are planned and implemented, but insufficient attention is given to evaluation. Often there is a 'general feel' for the procedure and this is the only level of evaluation. The example which follows shows an approach to the evaluation of a tertiary teaching procedure. Considerably more work needs to be undertaken in carefully appraising tertiary teaching methods. Miles, at Newcastle CAE, reported the evaluation of an open teaching procedure. The objective was to assess the differences between an experimental and a control group on three 'styles' (locus of control, acquiescence, and introversion/extroversion) and on the Minnesota Teacher Attitudes Inventory, before and after nine months of 'treatment'. A special group of 'research' students administered and scored the tests.

6. Methodological Innovation

6.i Microteaching

One of the major innovations in teacher education of the past few years has been the introduction of microteaching. This involves student teachers in a scaled-down teaching experience in which they practise one particular skill with a small class group (usually about six members) over a limited time span. Detailed research analysis has been made of the process and most innovatory practices revolve around such issues as—the protocol material used to model the teaching skill; the composition of the class group; the means of recording the teaching experience; methods followed in feedback sessions; and various forms of follow-up activities for a microteaching experience. An extensive study was made of such innovatory practices in 1973 by a research team headed by Turney following the establishment of a grant by the A.A.C.R.D.E. to enable an Australian study to be made of microteaching. In the report to the A.A.C.R.D.E. and the later text containing a discussion of the report, *Micro-teaching: Research, Theory and Practice*, the research team indicated that thirty-five programmes were offering microteaching courses, and nine more indicated their intention to introduce such programmes. The research team devoted quite a deal of their attention to outlining innovatory practices present in these Australian microteaching courses and the reader of this review is referred to that source for a detailed discussion of some of the innovations in microteaching. For the purposes of this current survey, some of the major emphases of a few of the reported microteaching courses have been outlined.

A major source of many of the innovatory practices in microteaching in Australia is the work of Turney at the University of Sydney. In particular, this is reflected in the development of an excellent range of protocol materials to be used for the presentation of teaching skills. Under Turney's leadership, a research and development team has developed the *Sydney Micro Skills* series which are now used in many Australian programmes. The team developed the series after analysing research on teaching skills and discussing the needs of teacher education programmes with a number of Australian educators. The materials consist of half-hour videotaped or filmed programmes which demonstrate the components of specified teaching skills and their application in teaching episodes plus printed Handbooks prepared for both lecturer and student use.

Several other institutions have been involved in developing protocol materials which can be used to model teaching skills suited to the particular purposes of their own programmes. At Macquarie University, Butts has been developing models of science teaching skills which are relevant to science teachers but not as relevant to teachers in other subject areas. Haywood at Newcastle CAE has developed protocol materials to show the skills of the teacher involved in teaching English as a Foreign Language. McKercher at Claremont TC is developing skill models for the teaching of health and physical education. These are but three examples of many, where protocol materials to suit the needs of a particular type of teacher education programme are being developed.

Several programmes continue to seek ways in which microteaching might create a changed emphasis in their courses. Fullerton at Newcastle CAE is using microteaching as a means of helping student teachers 'to be introduced to schools, teaching and professional responsibilities in a gradual and systematic fashion'. Tyney and Drew at Salisbury CAE list among their objectives for microteaching that the programme will identify students in need of remedial assistance. Morgan *et al.* at Sydney Kindergarten TC see their microteaching programme as providing 'more individualized and specific teaching experiences for students'. Several programmes for in-service education have looked to microteaching as a means of generating new experiences for participants. An interesting example is that developed at the Goulburn CAE by McNeill. Teachers with at least seven years teaching experience attended a five-day residential course in which microteaching was used to get the teachers to investigate recent work on teaching effectiveness.

Microteaching represents a source of much innovative thinking in Australian teacher education. In addition to the programmes discussed above, approaches developed at several other institutions have helped to create many new experiences for student teachers. In some programmes, as will be discussed later, microteaching has been a factor stimulating teacher educators to analyse teaching into specific skills and to seek various ways of developing these competencies in student teachers.

6.ii Particular Curriculum Approaches

Many current innovations in teacher education have been directed at devising differing and alternative methods for the preparation of student teachers and to help them meet their needs in teaching. This development has four major divisions. In various *curriculum areas* new methods have been developed to give students greater involvement with the spirit and content of areas to be taught. In other instances emphasis has been given to providing insights into more general *teaching issues* and circumstances. Another recent development has been a growing emphasis on understanding *human relations*. The knowledge, skills and attitudes required of teachers in humanistic education have been presented in a variety of ways. Somewhat allied to this concern for others, various forms of *community experiences* have been initiated to help student teachers develop a greater awareness of environmental factors and of the people with whom they must interact. These four divisions are discussed below with selected detailed examples.

Methods in curriculum areas

In the study of the teaching of the English curriculum, Kelvin Grove CAE (Young) has adopted a workshop approach which encourages students to plan their own learning experience, work co-operatively and evaluate materials and strategies for teaching. Students in this course are active learners engaged in relating theory to practice by directing their own learning. A course providing improvisation and sensitivity experience through drama at Alexander Mackie CAE (Fone) aims to develop self-knowledge and understandings of human relations in order to apply these insights in drama and in the classroom situation. Encounter group methods in drama are adopted to help students explore their capabilities and to gain self-confidence. At Nepean CAE (Roberts) an English communication workshop entitled 'Teaching Presence in Language' has been developed as a practical experience with the assumptions of Stanislasky's role theory. The workshop emphasizes, through speaking and listening, mental concentration, physical relaxation, eye contact and communication of emotions in order to develop a 'teaching presence' in students.

In the creative arts area, Canberra CAE (Kendall) has applied the concepts of 'organic teaching' designed to develop imagery in children, to a workshop for students in which all the creative arts (art, music, drama, movement, language) contribute. This assists final-year students in the Early Childhood programme to develop their self-expression, self-realization and creative activities and to use this approach in their teaching. The SCV Melbourne (Scott) has developed an Outdoor Education Centre in a rural setting at Noojee which is within a state forest. The purpose of the centre is to provide studies in recreation and camping and to cater for field work in a wide range of educational experiences related to science, art, craft, and social science. A further aim of the centre is to offer students an opportunity for personal development and group involvement in both social and educational activities. At Kuring-gai CAE (Keith) a new elective Environmental Science course has been introduced after a pilot study with a Pollution Studies course. The new course provides for in-depth work with a scientific bias for investigation and research in the field. In physical education the teaching of games' skills at Claremont TC (McKercher) has a new development in that core skills for both male and female games are presented as 'unisex instruction' with student peer-group tutoring. Finally, in Education studies at SCV Bendigo (Cannon) an elective course for third-year primary students is based on contemporary education issues, most of which are controversial. There is student-centred learning through the evaluation and analysis of the relevance of students' own views on problems in education. The seminars are frequently conducted off-campus in an informal setting.

Methods for general teaching issues

In the approaches to general teaching issues for students or teachers the three innovations mentioned here were chosen for detailed case study. Fuller accounts of these innovations are thus presented in a later chapter. A Teaching Problems seminar for final-year students has been instituted at Newcastle CAE (Rees) based on materials specially prepared by Telfer and Rees (now published in a book).[1] The course provides simulated data on community, school and classroom situations relevant for a critical incident discussions with risk-free decision-making being encouraged. The course aims to make the student aware of roles and expectations existing in the real school and community situation. At SCV Rusden (Gill) an evening in-service workshop-seminar is provided for teachers in their first year of teaching. The course aims to provide support for the teacher and concentrates on such issues as curriculum planning and resources, classroom

[1] R. Telfer and J. Rees, *Teacher Tactics*, Syme, Sydney 1975.

management and the organizational aspects of teaching. In a similar scheme Finalyson of Macquarie University has pioneered an 'Adjusting to Teaching' in-service course for secondary teachers in their first year out. The course aims to support the teacher through discussion and role playing of issues related to school problems, classroom management skills, understanding child behaviour, and the examination of new methods and curriculum materials.

Approaches to human relations

Many different approaches have been adopted by innovators in the area of human relations. A decade ago such courses would not have appeared in teacher education schedules but with an upsurge of interest in interpersonal behaviour, humanistic education and informal, more open teaching, the acceptance of the value of such courses is seen as a significant contribution to meeting the needs of student teachers in their preparation for teaching.

At Canberra CAE (Kendall) an Interpersonal Skill training programme is provided. It includes empathy training and value clarification. The course teaches a process of analysis and a theory of children's needs as related to inter-actional skills in the classroom. A course in the Psychology of Interpersonal Behaviour is offered as an elective to final year students at Townsville CAE (Bamford). This course includes a study of personality linked with regular sensitivity training sessions and introduces the student to human relations experiences to promote group interaction and self-awareness. A Human Relations course is conducted at Nepean CAE (Smith) with small groups and extensive use of films, kits and simulation games. There are discussion groups and an opportunity for community field work on stress situations and social issues. At Kuring-gai CAE (Gledhill and Smith) a programme for secondary science teachers seeks to foster meaningful group experiences. Small group experiences are arranged under the guidance of trained facilitators from the Health Commission. As a joint project it is aimed to assist students to act as agents of change for good mental health in schools, to communicate, to develop self-awareness and to understand group processes. The project involves some practice in teaching and is also used to assist science teachers in their first year of teaching. An unstructured and informal learning situation embracing all subjects may be elected as an alternative teacher education experience by first- and second-year students at Newcastle CAE (Crago). The Open Group in primary education seeks to enable students to gain personal meaning, to enhance their self-concept and to demonstrate that teaching is a helping relationship. Individual and small group work proceeds on the basis of personal instruction and needs and this is supported by weekly discussions and work in schools. As part of a project in personal development at Claremont TC (McKercher) students and staff are encouraged to combine into mutual interest groups. In all there are nineteen such optional groups involving first year primary students and the activities offered range from chess, wine tasting to karate and photography. At the SCV Institute for Early Childhood Education (Foote) a course on 'Interpersonal Relations: Principles and Practices' focuses on the parent-teacher relationships and arranges for students to work with parents in local programmes and asso-ciated field work. The course aims to help students understand the role of parents in education.

Community experiences

Experience in working in the community is considered by many institutions a valuable introduction to an understanding of the context in which teaching takes place. An example of this concern is the Learning Network scheme at SCV Toorak (Ryan, Johnson and Noble) which invites students to contract their time to work with a variety of community groups. There is optional participation by both students and staff but it is an advantage for both the college and the community. Students mainly help with children in children's homes, the Austistic Children's Association, Children's Hospital, latch-key clubs, youth clubs and the like. At Torrens CAE (Resek) the Alberton Project is an integrated activity with the work of the Department of Community Welfare. Students help in disadvantaged areas mainly with mothers and children. It is a co-ordinated programme of assistance under the supervision of a social worker and a welfare representative. Discussion groups of three students and eight mothers provide a basis for understanding problems and for giving the help most appropriate. The Utilization of Community Resources is a course promoted at SCV Coburg (Griffin) for first-year primary students as an elective. Educational resources outside the classroom are studied and their contribution to curriculum considered. Field trips to open access areas, museums, art galleries, display centres, etc., are assessed as suitable resources for specific teaching objectives. At Mt. Gravatt (Cronk) second-year commerce students are placed for a work experience of two weeks in community commercial businesses. Such experience in say accounting or bookkeeping enables students to evaluate their college experience against the reality of the business world.

6.iii Special Co-operating School Arrangements

A small but growing number of teacher educators has realized the potential of the school context for school and institution co-operation in improving both teacher education and the education of children. A few teacher education programmes have developed new relationships with one or a number of local schools for achieving old and new objectives. As much more will be said of this movement in Chapter 4 of this book, several instances will be sufficient here.

Salisbury CAE has an on-campus laboratory secondary school (Dunn *et al.*) and an off-campus laboratory primary school (Tyney *et al.*). These schools provide settings which facilitate such activities as student observations, micro-teaching and remedial practice teaching, and investigations of teaching and curriculum. A feature of the scheme is cross-institution staff appointments. The college has appointed seven lecturer-teachers and the South Australian Department of Education has appointed five teacher-tutors to the laboratory schools. The lecturer-teachers spend half-time in college and half in schools. They conduct specific curriculum courses in co-operation with teacher-tutors, teach in the school, and advise the school on course planning. The teacher-tutors are released from some of their teaching duties to participate in curriculum courses, work with lecturers and students in planning, demonstrating and teaching lessons in connection with these courses, provide counselling and assistance to students having special teaching difficulties, and supervise microteaching.

The University of Sydney (Turney *et al.*) is also developing a special relationship with North Sydney Demonstration School. The future functions of the school, as conceived by a joint planning committee of representatives of school, parents and university, are as follows:

Student practice teaching. Besides providing conventional practice teaching opportunities, an important focus will be the implementation and evaluation of innovative approaches to in-school experience. For example, pilot schemes could be introduced in such areas as gradualistic induction to teaching, counselling and supporting students encountering major problems with teaching, competency-based practice, and school-based teacher education.

Microteaching. The development and refinement of microteaching techniques will be a continuing function. This work will range from the development of videotaped modelling materials to piloting new modes of practice and feedback.

Systematic observations. New approaches to observation and demonstration will be trialled. This work will involve close collaboration between school and university staff in both planning, executing and evaluating the programmes.

Research and development on teaching, learning, and curriculum. Working jointly, and sometimes independently, school and university staff will be concerned with generating new ideas and approaches to teaching and learning and with evaluating new ideas and approaches. An important aspect of this work will be co-operative curriculum development, especially with regard to construction and evaluation of curriculum resources. Where appropriate, both students and parents might become involved in this innovatory activity.

Co-operative staffing and shared resources. Where feasible and appropriate, school staff will participate with university staff in seminars/workshops on teaching and curriculum. Similarly, university staff might become co-operatively involved in teaching within the school. Such arrangements will promote the exchange of ideas and integration of theory and practice. When required, university staff will provide advisory and support services to various aspects of the school's work.

Also the material resources of school and university department will be shared, where necessary, for the advancement of the co-operative enterprise and other educational concerns.

In-service education activities. School and university staff will collaborate in providing in-service courses for teachers from other schools. Here again, approaches will be innovative and will be appraised accordingly. The in-service activity will seek both to promote educational improvement and disseminate ideas and practices emerging from the co-operative programme.

Communication and dissemination. A vital activity within the co-operative programme will be communication, and both formal and informal channels need to be clearly established. Communication will be of two kinds: (i) horizontal, whereby ideas and information are transmitted between school and university staff, and (ii) vertical, whereby information flows to parents, the community, administrative authorities and, importantly, to other teachers and schools. This last concern will probably involve such devices as a liaison officer, visitation days, newsletters, and conferences.

Exploration of school-university co-operation. In pursuing the foregoing functions, models of inter-institution co-operation for the improvement of teacher education and the advancement of education in general will be progressively investigated and developed.

Co-operation with nearby schools can take many forms. An interesting move in the endeavour to relate theory and practice and to bring reality and relevance to courses based in the tertiary institution is the bringing of school pupils and also school teachers to the campus. Though this kind of operation is often fraught with transport, teacher-release and timetabling difficulties, a number of institutions are employing it. For example, Murray Park CAE (Golding) has 'campus classes' of pupils. About fifty children aged five, six and seven and their two teachers from the neighbourhood school spend about 50 per cent of time at the college. Student teachers (some 300 of them) in methodology and curriculum studies are provided with opportunities, formal and informal, to observe and participate in teaching and learning activities in a less threatening situation than is often found in practice teaching. The classes also provide college staff with opportunity to work with the classes in demonstration work and curriculum development. Teachers and children use the college library and audiovisual resources and seem to enjoy and value the experience. At Adelaide CAE (Ey) two hundred children are transported to the campus to provide observation and practice teaching opportunities for students pursuing primary and secondary physical education courses. At the SCV Institute of Early Childhood Development (Dougan) four groups of six toddlers (aged fourteen months to three years) attend the campus for one and a half hours, morning and afternoon on up to two days a week. Mothers accompany the toddler groups and join in the programme with an experienced fully-trained kindergarten teacher. Since groups work in special rooms with one-way-vision screens students can unobtrusively observe (i) the development and learning of young children, (ii) parent-relationships, and (iii) how toddler groups might operate. Students are also familiarized with appropriate material and equipment to facilitate learning. In all, about 570 students use the facility for both co-ordinated and incidental observations.

Similarly concerned with the idea of relating theory and practice through school co-operation, a number of institutions have introduced teacher-tutor schemes similar to that at Salisbury CAE. At Murray Park CAE (Golding) fourteen classroom teachers are employed as tutors to work in the curriculum studies and in-school experience programmes. These people co-operate with college staff in the development and teaching of the courses. Visits to schools for observation, demonstration, and practical involvement flow directly from the tutor's work. This tutor-teacher scheme has brought into the curriculum studies course young and enthusiastic teachers with plenty of practical ideas. Liaison with schools is also facilitated. Some difficulties were found in selecting teachers, in having them adopt a workshop-seminar approach, and in timetabling to avoid teachers' school commitments.

6.iv Practice Teaching

Student practice teaching in schools (in some states known as the practicum or teaching rounds) has become an increasingly high-valued focal point of teacher preparation. For years practice teaching was a low-valued activity in Australian institutions. There were few real links between the work at college and what students did in schools. College staff supervising practice were often as unhelpful as they were unsympathetic. Many class teachers regarded students as intruders and time-wasters. Students generally found the practice period threatening, divorced from the principles preached in the training institution, poorly supervised, artificial in the kind of contact it provided with children, and dominated by a competitively sought teaching mark.

During the last decade there has been growing awareness that many past practicum policies are misguided or inadequate. It is recognized that educational principles alone are not enough—that practice is important—and that the integration of both is critical. The realization is abroad that if beginning teachers fail to find satisfactory ways of translating theory into practice, the chances are they will fall back into the established ways of the education system—to follow worn paths which, for many older teachers, have unfortunately become ruts.

Evidence of the new concern among teacher educators for improving the practicum is provided by the number of innovations reported in the area. In order to provide a framework for the consideration of these diverse practicum innovations we have raised what are considered twenty basic questions about contemporary in-school experience (see Table 2.38). The issues asterisked in the list seem to be attracting very little new thought and action. Only those issues for which details of innovations were available are discussed in the following sections.

Objectives of the practicum (Question 1, Table 2.38)

It seems rather astonishing that very few Australian teacher education institutions have constructed, made known, and consistently applied a comprehensive, meaningful and realistically attainable range of objectives specific to student teaching practice. Much more deliberation needs to be given to the knowledge, skills and attitudes that might well be developed in students through the practicum.

Table 2.38 TWENTY BASIC PRACTICUM ISSUES

---

*1. What should be the objectives of the practicum in terms of changed student knowledge, skills and attitudes?

---

*2. What should be the nature, scope and sequence of student experiences in the practicum to achieve the objectives?

---

*3. How should the experiences of the practicum be integrated with the other components of a teacher education programme?

---

*4. How should student experiences and tasks in practicum be initiated and structured?

---

*5. What should be expected of students involved in various experiences and tasks?

---

6. How should individual and group needs and concerns of students be catered for in the practicium?

---

7. How should student teachers receive feedback on their progress in practicum experiences?

---

*8. By whom and how should practicum be supervised?

9. How should supervisors be prepared to effectively pursue their work?

*10. What should be the respective roles of college and school staff in planning, organizing, supervising, evaluating and following-up the practicum?

11. How should students be prepared at the college for the practicum?

12. How should students be phased into the practicum in the school?

13. What are the most effective supplementary, support or alternative procedures to the in-school practicum?

14. How should the practicum be organized in terms of location, timing, and sequence of experiences?

15. On what bases should students be allocated to schools, classes, teachers, supervisors, and groups or peers?

*16. How should the students' work in the practicum be evaluated?

17. How should students' learning in the practicum be followed up?

*18. How should the effectiveness of practicum itself be evaluated?

19. What relationships should be developed between college and co-operating schools for the promotion of teacher education and the improvement of education?

20. How should students be phased out of the student-teacher-practicum role into that of beginning teacher with full professional responsibilities?

There are, however, a number of interesting moves in the seemingly right direction. For example, in the In-School Experience Programme (ISEP) at Milperra CAE, Koder *et al.* have developed a series of specific objectives in terms of knowledge, skills and attitudes to be acquired by students in each of six semesters. The programme begins with specific teaching skills in semesters 1 and 2, moves to general teaching strategies in semesters 3 and 4, and concentrates on curriculum and organizational issues in semesters 5 and 6. The pages of the ISEP Handbook setting out the objectives and format of semesters 1 and 2 are probably worth quoting in full:

Semesters 1/2 : Skill Development
3.1 *General Aim*
The aim of ISEP is to promote effective pupil learning by providing student teachers with the opportunity to acquire appropriate knowledge supporting basic skills of teaching and to facilitate the development of these skills through controlled practice, observation and evaluation.

3.2 *Specific objectives*

    3.21 *Knowledge*

        The student will be expected to demonstrate:

        (i)   a thorough understanding of the theoretical foundations of the basic skills presented in ISEP;

        (ii) effective development and construction of specific behavioural objectives and evaluative procedures appropriate to the constraints present in the controlled teaching environments;

        (iii) an ability to plan lessons integrating skill and content;

        (iv) an integration of the knowledge and behavioural components of ISEP with particular reference to the appropriate components of courses in the Principles of Teaching, Teacher Presence and Academic areas.

    3.22 *Skills*

        The student will be expected:

        (i)   to teach in peer teaching sessions and demonstrate a growing proficiency in the application of basic skills to teaching;

        (ii) to accurately and objectively observe, classify and record various teaching behaviours exhibited by himself, his peers and professional teachers;

        (iii) to demonstrate a growing ability in the insightful evaluation of teacher effectiveness in terms of presage (personal qualities), process (skills and strategies) and product (pupil achievement) criteria.

    3.23 *Attitudes*

        The student will be expected to demonstrate a professional attitude to teaching through the display of:

        (i)   co-operation;

        (ii)   interest and enthusiasm;

        (iii) thorough preparation;

        (iv) punctuality;

        (v)   attentiveness;

        (vi) appropriate appearance;

        (vii) open-mindedness and a readiness to assimilate knowledge and advice;

        (viii) sensitivity to the needs of pupils and peers;

        (ix) appropriate ethical behaviour.

3.3 *Evaluation*

    Student achievement in ISEP will be evaluated in each semester, in terms of the following criteria:

    (i)   Written tests based on the knowledge component;

    (ii)   Student products based on lesson preparation and observation data;

    (iii) Self and peer appraisals based on prepared data sheets;

    (iv) Ratings of the effective application of principles and skills in the classroom as determined by supervisors, teachers and lecturers;

    (v)   Ratings of the attitudinal component based on involvement in and commitment to ISEP as determined by supervisors, teachers and lecturers.

In the last few years teacher educators have given increasing attention to defining the broad and distinctive aims of their total programmes from which more specific practicum objectives could flow. In fact, some programmes have already followed through into the practicum some of their dominant aims. For instance, at the Sydney Nursery School Teachers College (Fountain *et al.*) the aim of promoting knowledge and skill in co-operative curriculum development is held to be important. Consequently, in the practicum several students drawn from various years of the course ('cross-age grouping') are allocated to pre-school classes, and a feature of their work is involvement in jointly developing interest or learning centres comprising curriculum materials of various kinds to focus and facilitate children's learning. Similarly, the Sydney University's Dip.Ed. programme (Hatton *et al.*) is identified with the idea of innovative teaching and, accordingly, students are encouraged to carry out small-scale action research projects on problems of teaching and learning identified during in-school experience.

Microteaching has led to the clearer specification of basic teaching behaviours thought worthwhile for students to develop. In many cases these are being pursued into practice teaching through the use of feedback instruments listing such behaviours and by acquainting supervisors with the skills. This is perhaps most highly developed at Newcastle CAE where Fullerton *et al.* have designed an elaborate set of workbooks to facilitate specific skill acquisition and the transfer of the skills to macro-class teaching.

Not unassociated with microteaching is the growing interest in competency-based teacher education. This has two main aspects: (i) the analysis of teaching into a range of competencies (knowledge and behaviours) which are believed necessary for student teachers to attain, and (ii) the construction of learning modules to facilitate and evaluate student progress in the development of the specified competencies. These modules permit individualization, are applicable to all components of the programme, integrate theoretical and practical considerations, and have implications for what students should try to achieve in classrooms. Currently at Macquarie University, Levis *et al.* are planning to develop and evaluate competency-based approaches in the institution's teacher education programme (see case study).

Evaluation of the practicum (Question 18)

Just as there appears to be a general lack of concern for the objectives of the practicum, there is little systematic attempt to evaluate the effectiveness of it. Of course, any attempt to evaluate the practicum must wait on the specification of objectives and establishment of criteria for appraising their attainment. When one considers the substantial cost of conducting the practicum in terms of supervision fees and staff time, it is almost scandalous that we do not yet know if it is achieving worthwhile objectives.

As far as can be ascertained, only one institution, Sturt CAE (Young), is attempting to evaluate the short-term and long-term effects (as perceived by students) of in-school experience.

Integration of theory and practice (Question 3)

The question of attempting to relate the experiences of the practicum with other components of the teacher education programme is occupying the attention of a number of institutions, and a variety of approaches is being devised. Several examples will suffice here. In the Diploma in Education programme at Sydney University Turney *et al.* try to integrate the theory and the practice of teaching through a core course, 'Background to Teaching'. Conducted in small student-groups by all curriculum and education staff, the course runs concurrently with practice teaching and tries to bring research and theory (drawn from the various educational disciplines) to the analysis of modelled or simulated teaching situations and of problems drawn directly from students' in-school experience. Running parallel to these seminars is a staff seminar-workshop in which staff discuss, develop and refine learning modules or units on various aspects of the teacher's work. Each module has a common format setting out its objectives, basic research and theory, practical implications, media resources and readings. Though the 'Background to Teaching' course is flexible in its specific structure so it can focus on issues and problems arising from practice teaching, its general pattern moves in 'expanding environments' (from say teaching and learning in classrooms, to staff curriculum development, to broad school-community and system questions).

One of the most exciting recent approaches to integrating theory and practice is the so-called field-based or school-based teacher education programme. Currently there is a growing number of pilot studies in Australia which typically provide for a small number of students and sometimes are limited to one curriculum area or a part of a total programme. For example, there are school-based programmes at SCV Hawthorn (Smith *et al.*), SCV Melbourne (Hindley), Western Australian Secondary Teachers College (Vlahov), University of Queensland (Smith *et al.*) and the University of Melbourne (Dow).

These school-based endeavours subscribe with varying degrees of adherence to some or all of the following five characteristics: (i) the programme, or the majority of it, is pursued by a group of students in school locations, (ii) practice teaching is conducted concurrently with other course components, (iii) there is a close and continuous relationship between practice teaching and work in education and/or curriculum courses, (iv) both school and college staff (and indeed students where possible) are co-operatively involved in planning, organizing, conducting, supervising and evaluating both the theoretical *and* practical components of the professional programme, (v) college, school staff and students are co-operatively involved in teaching children, in action research and curriculum development to improve the quality of teaching, and even in activities related to the community.

The reaction, so far, of persons involved in these programmes seems to have been very favourable: students comment on the reality, relevance and stimulation of such courses; college staff speak of their increased professional credibility in the eyes of students and of the salutary challenge of translating ideas into practice; school staff remark on their increased professional knowledge and skill, on a lift in morale, and on a keener awareness of their own and students' professional needs.

As promising as the school-based movement is, it needs both careful evaluation in terms of its objectives, and cost-effectiveness studies of its implementation. More will be said about major school-based innovations in Chapters 3 and 4 of this book.

One group of small school-based activities relates to the teaching of particular curriculum areas. For example, at Mackie CAE (Anderson) there is a school-based workshop on science teaching in the second and third years of the primary programme. The course seeks, among other things, to increase the practical relevance of primary science by providing students with direct opportunity to design, develop and test primary science materials in the school situation and to apply and practise new approaches to science teaching. The course involves fifty students, two teachers, and two college staff for at least two hours a week in workshops and in teaching small primary groups. At SCV Melbourne (Poynter), school-based units in social science education have been introduced for up to sixty third- and fourth-year primary students who expressed a preference to pursue this approach. The workshops involve two college staff and ten teachers with students working at least three hours a week in school locations. The course has three main objectives: (i) to reduce the theory-practice dichotomy in social science education by linking curriculum studies to the reality of schools; (ii) to involve college lecturers and school staff in a co-operative enterprise within teacher education; and (iii) to provide richer and more meaningful experiences for trainee teachers. Students, working in pairs, design and trial with a group of twelve children units of the social science curriculum in consultation with college and school staff.

Organizing the practicum—timing, locating and sequencing of
experiences (Question 14)

As suggested earlier, quite a number of institutions have adopted carefully co-ordinated teacher-preparation programmes which include teaching practice as an integral aspect. In general, such programmes attempt to integrate theory and practice by utilizing a variety of elements which link the students' experiences and focus on actual teaching. Some examples of programmes with co-ordinated elements follow.

The Diploma in Education programme for secondary teaching at Sydney University (Hatton *et al.*) requires students teach two days per week during part of terms one and two and then have a three-week block practice before the end of second term. Some students then may undertake remedial work, including microteaching, on two days per week in term three. Other co-ordinated elements include Foundational Studies in Education, Curriculum Studies, Background to Teaching courses, which run concurrently with practice so that issues and problems related to instruction, management, discipline and role conflicts may be examined in a context of theory into practice. In the teaching practice pro-gramme at the Nursery School Teachers College (Simons) the integration of theory and practice is achieved by having continuous practice of one or two days per week linked closely with on-going course work. Additional components include field-work tasks, and the setting up and operation of 'interest and core learning centres' in classrooms. At Milperra CAE (Crawley and Koder) in a Diploma in Teaching programme for primary teachers there is a combination of micro- and macro-teaching programmes to develop skills, strategies, curriculum and organization issues and these are keyed into blocks of practice teaching. This programme has been mentioned previously as the In-School Experience Programme (ISEP). Finally, in a secondary programme at Rusden (Atkinson) there is a concurrent provision of two days per week for professional and educa-tional studies involving work in schools for students in the third and fourth years of the programme.

Other institutions have organized practice teaching to provide for greater professional support for students or to set out graded expectations in the deve-lopment of teaching tasks. For example, at North Brisbane CAE (Streets) a new approach to practice teaching has changed the role of the lecturer from being an assessor to that of adviser to students. Through a college-school committee and team co-ordinators, regional groupings of schools are each associated with a team of curriculum lecturers representing a spread of subject specialties. This team works with students advising on their planning and the use of college resources for their teaching. It is interesting to note also that the assessment of teaching performance of first-year students in the responsibility of the school principal and his staff. Mitchell CAE (Taylor) has arranged a graded pattern of practice experiences to cope with the institution's problems of the geographic isolation of their school placements in the far-western area of New South Wales. Stage I students undertake community-aid projects, stage II students engage in local field work, while stage III and IV students have block practice periods of nine and seven weeks alternating with methods workshops. At Sturt CAE (Palmer) the field-experience programme provides for a gradual introduction to schools and practical work in curriculum areas. Students begin as teacher aides and work through a graded set of expectations and tasks to qualify in the two units of practical experience required. At the SCV Institute of Early Childhood Development (Martin) field work and practice teaching are graded and complement one another throughout the four-year course. Some field work relates to a longitudinal study of young children and involves students in direct experiences with children in the home. This child study is then related to practical work in nurseries and pre-school centres.

Various forms of supplementary, support and alternative practical procedures are also being organized to provide a more realistic involvement of student teachers in schools and in the community. Some quite unique aspects of field experiences in terms of location, timing and the sequence of experiences are also being developed. One example of a special kind of field experience related to practice teaching comes from Mackie CAE (Thew) where there is a three semester programme of 'school attachment' for second and third year students. In semester 4, half-day per week in schools is devoted to a 'teaching workshop' in a particular curriculum subject. In semester 5 one day per week in schools is spent in a teaching workshop concerned with two curriculum subjects. In semester 6 which follows six weeks of block practice teaching the student continues on with the same teacher and class on one day per week as a teaching assistant. Several insitutions, Xavier Teachers College (Larkin), Armidale CAE (Newman and Cole) and the Nursery School TC (Fountain) have students in schools regularly for half day per week for both observations and teaching sessions.

Other types of field work, often involving teachers, are sometimes offered to students to broaden their personal and professional experience. For example, Newcastle CAE (Telfer) provides a country community practice teaching experience of four weeks for a small group of final-year students as a simulation of a country school appointment. The students live on the properties in the small communities and involve themselves at weekends in community projects. Also at Newcastle CAE (Newling) a scheme of one week of teaching in a different community (Griffith) has been tried with a diverse group of students in order to assist them to cope in a new situation. Mitchell CAE (Taylor) has a community-aid programme to link the students with the community and its children through involvement in non-teaching activities with voluntary agencies. At the Nursery School TC (Fountain) Year II students undertake one term of field work in some community project for children. The Australian College of Physical Education (Butts) places all final-year students for a four week residential block practice in country or interstate boarding schools. For final-year students studying aboriginal education Graylands TC (Ibbotson) arranges a thirteen week internship in aboriginal communities in the north-western area of Western Australia. A number of interstate exchange practice teaching sessions for two or three weeks have been arranged by Claremont TC (Marsh) to give students an understanding of Australian school systems and to enrich their teaching experiences.

To cater for group and individual student concerns and needs, some institutions have devised specific field tasks to be undertaken with children in the classroom. These tasks provide both experience and practice in developing particular concepts of teaching. One advantage of these experiences is that they are frequently supported by continuous feedback to the student. For instance, in studies related to child development, both at Wollongong Institute of Education (Winser) and the Nursery School Teachers College (Huntsman), a sequence of practical field experiences for the observation and study of children is arranged to provide an integration of theoretical and practical studies in understanding human development. Similar integrated child development field studies are provided by SCV Frankston (Walker). More generally, Riverina CAE (Pinson) provides a practice teaching clinic in nearby schools to introduce students to teaching strategies in a controlled sequence through teaching small groups of children. In the area of communication skills several institutions have provided concentrated practical work with children. In the Diploma in Education at Sydney University (Rothery and Arnold) practice with small groups for language development skills is provided for two days per week. At SCV Rusden (Gill), also with Diploma in Education students, there is practice for two days per week on strategies associated with teaching English, and at Hawthorn (Enshaw) practical work in schools on one day per week is arranged to develop teaching techniques for drama work in the classroom. In curriculum studies in mathematics, Newcastle CAE (Coulton and Murray) provides additional macro- and microteaching work for secondary mathematics student teachers which focuses on concept development. Similarly at Wollongong Institute of Education (Aylward) secondary mathematics students have regular additional teaching and videotaped analysis on specific aspects of mathematics teaching. A final example of special teaching tasks is at SCV Bendigo (Courtis) in art education where practical work in schools is used to emphasize sequential teaching and the planning necessary for small group work.

The roles and preparation of practicum supervisors (Question 9)

Given that students' work in the practicum should be supervised, few teacher educators seem to be seriously considering the varied roles of the supervisor and ways of preparing personnel to effectively play these roles. Some institutions (e.g. Sturt CAE) attempt to state clearly in a handbook the differing supervisory tasks of college and school staff; other institutions have regular meetings with supervisors (e.g. Macquarie University's master teacher programme); a few institutions (e.g. B.Ed. programme at Sydney University) have attempted to involve supervisors in aspects of the programme having particular relevance to the practicum. Only one institution, James Cook University, is carefully examining the effectiveness of specially preparing supervisors. There, Hawkins is investigating the effects of training supervisors in specific teaching skills on the practice teaching performance of students.

Much more thought needs to be given to selecting and preparing supervisors. Teacher training institutions are relying heavily on co-operating teachers in schools to undertake the bulk of supervisory work. In view of the influence that these teachers can have on the work of student teachers the importance of carefully choosing and training supervising teachers is underlined. In many practicums a major effort of teacher supervisors seems to be the introduction of the student to the established and perhaps ill-advised ways of the education system. Many questions need to be investigated. For instance, what background should supervisors have in terms of professional knowledge and experiences? Should they be identified with the objectives of the practicum?—if so, how is this to be achieved? Should they be able to model and advise on teaching behaviours?—if so, how can they develop such competencies? Should they be sensitive student counsellors?—Should they be involved in teaching and/or attending courses in the programme? and so on.

Preparing and introducing students to the practicum (Questions 11 and 12)

The ways in which students can be effectively prepared on-campus and then phased into teaching responsibilities within the practicum itself are receiving increasing attention. Probably the most important recent movement for preparing students on-campus for the practicum (either before it and/or concurrently with it) has been the consideration, in theoretical and practical terms, of recorded and simulated school experiences. The movement has two main divisions: (i) *Modelling.* Quite a number of institutions have introduced a course in their programmes concerned with the theoretical analysis of models of specific teaching behaviours (mediated through audiovisual programmes and handbooks). The analysis of the modelled behaviours is generally followed initially by their application by students in microteaching, then in macroteaching in ordinary classrooms. The most influential project in this area is the Teaching Skills Development Project of Sydney University (Turney *et al.*) which since 1972 has been developing courses on specific teaching skills. These courses have been widely applied, adapted and supplemented in many programmes (see case study). (ii) *Simulation.* Various forms of teaching simulation are also being commonly employed, and a number of institutions are developing distinctively Australian materials. For example, at Newcastle CAE, Telfer and Rees have recently developed a very useful book called *Teacher Tactics* which comprises case-study material and an array of described critical incidents concerning education in the mythical schools of Illoura. These incidents are grouped into those concerned with teacher-pupil relationships, teacher-teacher and teacher-administrator relationships, and teacher-community relationships. Similarly, at Townsville CAE, Gallagher and Marland have developed an excellent range of paper mediated simulations connected with the so-called Vale School. On a narrower front, at Sydney University the Inner-City Education Project (Turney *et al.*) is developing a multi-media collection of simulations for an Inner-City Simulation Laboratory. This developmental activity is based on research into the problems and concerns of children, teachers and parents of inner-urban schools. At Canberra CAE, Hughes and Traill have developed a major simulation programme touching each year of their courses. It involves about 50 staff and 1,000 students. The wealth of materials used comprise both commercially produced kits, modified and unmodified, and original resources developed by groups within the institution.

The idea of phasing students into full-scale teaching responsibilities, the so-called 'gradualistic approach', is also receiving the attention of a few institutions. The idea is, of course, by no means new. It was the feature of what were termed 'participation programs' in the United States during the 1930s. In Sydney University's one-year postgraduate Diploma in Education programme (Rothery *et al.*), the first term of continuous practice is given over to students working initially with individual pupils, then with small groups, with campus course-work especially relevant to these contexts. Students move into full-class and multi-group teaching in second term according to their readiness. Similarly, in the first-year course at Nepean CAE (Roberts) there is a progressive build-up in pupil group size in practice teaching. Pupils are carefully selected for the initial small groups and student teachers concentrate at first on teaching basic areas of English and mathematics. In the field-experience programme at Sturt CAE (Palmer) there is a progressive build-up of time and expectation. First-year students work for several weeks as a teacher aide, have informal teaching and observation experiences, and carry out in-school practical activities required by curriculum studies. In second year students spend three weeks in schools and are required to demonstrate the beginnings of competence in planning, organizing, providing, supervising and evaluating learning experiences of children in both small and large groups. In third year students spend nine weeks in schools and are required to display increased competency in handling learning experiences over both short and extended periods, the capacity to work with other teachers, and the possession of a suitable and sufficient store of resource materials.

Following-up students' practicum learning (Question 17)

It seems educational common-sense that not only should student involvement in the practicum be carefully prepared and concurrently supported, but it should also be systematically followed-up. This idea has been basic to a number of Australian developments. For example, post-practice remedial microteaching, tailored to the needs of individual students, has been successfully introduced in a number of institutions, particularly in the Diploma in Education programmes of the University of Sydney (Hatton and Owens). Further remedial classroom practice and counselling in specially selected school contexts (sometimes with small class groups), supervised by skilled and sensitive staff, is employed in a few programmes (e.g. the B.Ed. programme, University of Sydney, Cairns *et al.*) This practice focuses on clear, mutually agreed areas of student deficiency and highlights individual student support. Sturt CAE (Gunning) has developed an 'Issues in Teaching' course which is directly based on student-perceived concerns and problems arising from practice teaching. In third year, after a nine-week period of block practice, students communicate their needs in curriculum method and content and in teaching. This information provides the basis for construction of a four-week course which involves student groups in planning projects, and attending lectures and workshops given by resource people, and in student initiated seminars (see case study).

Inducting the beginning teacher (Question 20)

This is a topic of great significance. What happens to the beginning teacher during the first months of his full-time appointment is likely to influence strongly his future career. Beset with problems and pressures in classroom and school, it is then that novice teachers need assistance, support and guidance probably more than at any other time.

There are several interesting developments in this regard. The fourth year of the Flinders University B.Ed. primary programme features an internship which endeavours to bridge the gap between student teaching and teacherdom (Teasdale *et al.*). Students are appointed on a full-time, full-salaried basis to Adelaide schools and during the year receive supervision and guidance from (i) senior school staff, (ii) visiting university lecturers, and (iii) teaching advisers. The latter are skilled teachers of deputy-headmaster status seconded from the Department of Education. Each adviser is allocated a group of fourteen interns and spends an average of half-a-day a fortnight per term per intern (with a concentration on term 1). Interns also pursue two courses during the year: (i) in the first half-year they undertake a course 'Problems of Educational Practice', which tries to relate educational theory to problems students are encountering in their internship experience. This involves them in three, two-hour after-school seminars, in a one-day conference, and in a two-and-a-half day conference. In addition, they prepare three assignments which explore problems of teaching and learning; (ii) in the second half-year interns pursue one elected curriculum course which makes an in-depth study of a primary curriculum area. Their course loading is only slightly lighter than that of the previous half-year (see case study). In the Western Metropolitan Directorate of Education in New South Wales Findlayson has pioneered an in-school support, in-service education programme for beginning teachers. The programme has two components: (i) workshops-seminars in individual schools, and (ii) residential, three-day courses each for forty teachers. The programme cuts across curriculum areas and focuses on teaching skills and the development of understanding of children and their learning, of teachers and society (see case study).

6.v Inter-Disciplinary Approaches

Teacher educators have often expressed concern that the organizational pattern of their institution has meant that a student enters a programme which is sectionalized into subject departments. This often results in such divisions as a gap between the studies of the theoretical and practical aspects of teaching. Some attention is being given in Australian teacher education programmes to looking at ways in which such gaps might be closed. The survey revealed several innovative plans in this area.

Many programmes while wishing to view teacher education in an integrated manner, find that existing organizational patterns are very difficult to change. However, Hughes at Canberra CAE was able to plan an inter-disciplinary approach at the commencement of a new teacher education programme. The initial staff represented the planning team for the programme and additions to the staff over the years have been introduced to an established inter-disciplinary programme. Hughes indicates that the major objectives of the Canberra three- and four-year undergraduate inter-disciplinary programme have been to 'illuminate the nature of educational problems'; to 'give means for solving educational problems'; and to 'involve specialists in a joint effort'.

Several institutions have attempted to introduce inter-disciplinary programmes in a complete teacher education course through renovation of graduate one-year programmes. An example of an innovatory attempt to present an integrated Diploma in Education course is the Integrated Studies Programme at the SCV at Hawthorn (Crawley *et al.*). The planning team for this innovation aimed to present 'some students with an alternative to the subject-centred course by offering a more integrated course of teacher-training' and to provide a 'greater opportunity to exchange ideas with students who will become teachers in different areas of expertise in the school, and to experiment with team teaching and integrated studies'. Students work in a variety of group situations—cross-method, special method, large group meetings and electives—as well as completing an in-depth study and a school experience programme.

Other institutions have looked at ways to phase-in integrated studies for a particular semester or year of a three- or four-year programme. At Churchlands CAE, a team of staff members co-ordinated by Liddelow has developed an integrated first-year programme for the undergraduate course. This programme integrates Educational Studies, Curriculum and Instruction and Teaching Experience which are usually offered as separate areas in such a programme. Also at Churchlands, Braubach has introduced an integrated Education Studies and Educational Psychology course into the third year of the undergraduate programme. Students were offered a number of 'mini' courses which were grouped as either Curriculum Studies, Practical Classroom Issues and Problems, or Independent Study Projects. The courses were inter-disciplinary in content and involved staff members from several of the college's departments. At Kuring-gai CAE (McFarlane *et al.*) an integrated course has been introduced into the first-year programme so that 'demonstrations, method lectures and practice teaching' are offered as a combined course introducing students to teaching.

Several interesting innovations are occurring where teacher educators are looking at ways to integrate specialized subject areas. At Mt. Gravatt CAE, Hart has introduced a programme in special education for in-service teachers which integrates studies for specialists working in several branches of special education. Hart describes a main feature of this programme to be the achievement of 'the closest integration between specialists working in the areas relating to psychological and cognitive foundations of teaching the exceptional child and specialists working in areas relating to practical experience'.

A most interesting innovative approach has been developed by Kendall at Canberra CAE to offer an inter-disciplinary study in the creative arts. Intending primary and early childhood teachers experience studies aimed to help them teach creative art themes in primary schools not through a study of separate areas such as music, art, movement, etc., but through studies and involvement in perceptual experiences in creative arts themes (e.g. through participating in auditory discrimination experiences). Several developments at the Queensland Conservatorium of Music also highlight innovatory steps to offer different experiences in the arts. Lane has been looking at ways to draw together for music specialists their experiences in practical performance, theoretical studies and historical studies. A course is offered to final year music students which integrates these aspects through relating studied techniques to contemporary and self-created music and materials. Gilfedder has developed an inter-disciplinary approach to a History of Music course at the Conservatorium through offering a 'Total Culture of the Age' course which shows students how many other disciplines have contributed to the history of music and the arts.

Environmental and social studies are other subject areas where inter-disciplinary programmes are being developed. At the SCV at Rusden (MacKenzie *et al.*) a five-week programme for fourth-year students specializing in teaching different social science areas brings the specialists into an integrated studies approach. Scott at the SCV Melbourne, has developed an Environmental Science course in which students are involved in inter-disciplinary problem solving practices in looking at a number of environmental issues and problems. Gunstone at Monash University is involved with other science staff in presenting an Environmental Education experience to Diploma of Education science students. This involves subject specialists in considering science areas other than their own specialist field through looking at learning units of interest to secondary children. This is principally achieved through experience gained in educational camps. At the SCV Rusden, Duke has developed an Environmental Studies course which gives students experiences of the inter-disciplinary nature of issues which involve the environment. At Goulburn CAE, Laws and Kruger have developed a team taught, integrated natural science/social science course to show student teachers the links between the natural sciences and the social sciences, and also to reveal common approaches to problem solving. As a result of the course, it is claimed that student teachers themselves have become better able to develop thematic curricula.

It is apparent from the survey responses that quite a considerable degree of attention is being given by Australian teacher educators to ways in which integrated study approaches might be introduced. However, it is also apparent that many would-be innovators have encountered very real organizational and management problems when attempting to introduce programmes which cut across existing structures in institutions. Most of the practices reported in this aspect of the survey highlighted the need for further investigation of the problems encountered by educators in introducing such innovations into established programmes.

6. vi Programmed Learning and Self-Instructional Programmes

Efforts to individualize the learning process have been a feature in most areas of educational endeavour during recent years. Teacher education has been no exception to this and programmed-learning units, self-instructional programmes and competency-based teacher education have been some of the means by which individualization has been introduced into Australian programmes. Several of the innovatory practices revealed by the survey are reviewed as examples of such efforts.

At the SCV at Coburg, Schleiger has focused attention on developing individualized mathematics programmes for intending primary school teachers. Schleiger lists the objectives of this programme as to 'give students a necessary background in mathematics', 'change the student teachers' attitude favourably towards mathematics', 'equip teachers with the survival kit for successful primary maths teaching', 'teach mathematics for useful recreation' and 'relate mathematics to the environment and everyday life'. Extensive trialling and evaluation of the learning units which have been produced have meant that a series of sound, individualized programmes are available. The work has also been publicized through the publication of a number of booklets which describe, in detail, the various programmes. The team at Coburg who have been associated with Schleiger in this work are now developing programmes in science as well as adding to the units already available in the area of mathematics. Another team which has developed individualized mathematics units is located at Mitchell CAE. Billington and Perry state the objectives of their work to be 'providing for individual differences in students', 'allowing students to use discovery techniques' and 'motivating students towards mathematics'. In their programme, Billington and Perry have explored ways in which they may not only provide their student teachers with a self-instructional programme but at the same time provide their students with a mathematics programme that can be taken into primary school classrooms.

Butts at Macquarie University has developed a series of self-instructional modules to assist student teachers to become competent in operating the items of science equipment which they will have available in schools. So far, over two dozen modules have been developed and each student is required to work through six modules in a half-year session. At Adelaide CAE, Dent has developed a self-tutorial system on educational media for the use of third-year students. The units upon which the independent learning is based are supplemented by small group activities where team work is essential (e.g. in film making).

At the Claremont TC, McKercher has developed programmed instruction units within a Recreation course where the students are involved in individualized skill development. Students are provided with a workbook which sets out instructions, practices, observation tasks, practical tasks and self-testing exercises. Students work through the tasks at their own rate but meet with their tutor in small group sessions on four occasions for tutor demonstrations and counselling. McKercher has developed a similar programme for his physical education students who are involved in a Biomechanics course.

At the SCV Burwood, Jeanes has examined ways in which student teachers who are specializing in working with children who have impaired hearing might develop skills of manual communication. Jeanes has developed programmes which provide materials enabling students to practise 'reading back' manual communication while at the same time progressing at their own rate as they master the material. Videotapes have been developed to present the learning material and these provide a 'movement' dimension to manual communication learning where previously dictionaries and photographs were used to provide only a static representation of a movement.

A programme of self-paced learning has been developed by Clark at the SCV at Melbourne. Students in the second year Physics course follow an ordered sequence of units, each of which has clearly stated behavioural objectives and a range of associated resource materials. When the students feel they have mastered the unit they take one of a number of tests set for the unit—if they are successful they progress to the next unit, but if unsuccessful they re-study the unit and, when ready, sit for a different test in the series provided for that unit.

At Murdoch University a variety of self-instructional modules (SIM) has been developed by Marsh. These modules provide a wide range of electives dealing with teaching-learning situations. Each contains a theoretical segment plus an observational/teaching segment to be undertaken in classrooms.

The above programmes indicate that some work is being undertaken in Australia on self-learning in teacher education with a major emphasis apparently given to developing units of work associated with a particular subject discipline— most frequently in the science or mathematics areas. It will be interesting to observe how Australian teacher educators will develop innovative modifications in response to the examples set by competency-based teacher education programmes which have become popular in North America in recent years. This would appear to present an exciting challenge to educators, a challenge which already has begun to be explored by several programmes (see Chapter 3).

6. vii Practically-Oriented Studies on Minority and Ethnic Groups

As Australian society and its schools have become increasingly aware of the educational problems and challenges of minority and ethnic groups, teacher education programmes have themselves been responsive to such problems. In many institutions courses of various kinds and practical experiences have been introduced to provide prospective teachers with an understanding of these groups and a preparedness to teach children belonging to them. A number of programmes provide special courses in Aboriginal education. Within the Diploma in Education (secondary) and the Bachelor of Education (primary) programmes at Flinders University (McConnochie) a course is offered for students who intend to teach in remote Aboriginal schools. The course has three main features: (i) an emphasis on Aboriginal language and traditional culture; (ii) extensive fieldwork in isolated areas; and (iii) the development of curriculum and simulation materials. Similarly at Graylands Teachers College (Ibbotson) there is an Aboriginal Studies elective in the second and third years of the primary programme. In addition to campus seminars and workshops, in third year students undertake a thirteen-week 'internship' in a school with a high percentage of Aboriginal pupils. During the 'internship' students also become involved in numerous community activities peculiar to locations with large Aboriginal populations. On a much larger scale, at Mount Lawley CAE (Sherwood) a major course of six hours a week on Aboriginal Studies is provided in second and third years of the Diploma in Teaching programme. The course is complemented by a one-week field trip and two periods of practice teaching in predominantly Aboriginal schools. The course itself integrates studies in anthropology, linguistics and education. The college also conducts a Graduate Diploma in Aboriginal Education. This Diploma is currently being pursued externally by a hundred teachers seeking specialized training in teaching Aboriginal children. Several institutions offer Aboriginal studies without necessarily linking them directly with teaching children. For instance at North Brisbane CAE (Cook) there is an elective course on Aborigines which features student home visits with Aboriginal families, and similarly at SCV Bendigo, there is an Aboriginal Studies course which involves face-to-face contact with Aboriginal adults.

A variety of courses is being offered on Australian migrant groups. For example, there is a Migrant Studies elective course for secondary students at SCV Rusden (Overberg) designed to bring students into direct contact with people of other cultures and to equip students with the technical expertise to teach in schools where the student population is multi-lingual. Claremont Teachers College (Eastwood) has introduced an elective course for primary students on Linguistics and Teaching English as a Foreign Language which is linked with practice teaching on child and adult migrant classes. At SCV Toorak (Henry and Ridsdale), there are an elective pre-service primary course and an in-service course on the Migrant Child in the Classroom. The course integrates the study of sociology and linguistics and involves practical work with migrant language problems in normal classrooms. Migrant Studies is a compulsory unit for all students in the primary programme at Mercy College

(Fisher and Cigler) and is designed to prepare them for their role in multi-cultural classrooms. At the Institute for Early Childhood Development (Boreham and Volk) the course Migrant Education is a twenty-hour compulsory unit for all third year students. The course involves three areas: (i) examination of attitudes to minority groups; (ii) teaching and curriculum for migrant children; and (iii) visits to schools and a case study of a migrant family.

It is interesting to note that at least one institution, SCV Toorak (Edwards), has realized the potential value in schools with a large migrant population of skilled teachers who are themselves migrants. Courses are offered at two levels: (i) a first-year course in intensive English for migrant student teachers; and (ii) a retraining programme for suitably qualified migrant teachers which features both an intensive English course and an Australian Studies course to acquaint them with Australian history and culture.

As Australians have shown an increasing interest in South East Asia and as this interest has been reflected in school curricula, teacher education programmes have begun to introduce courses related to it. At Kuring-gai CAE (Driscoll and Blewitt) for example, Asian Studies is an elective course in the general studies programme. The course draws on the disciplines of history, geography, sociology and anthropology, attempts to develop generalizations concerning the relationship between social and political systems, and examines three Asian societies as case studies. As a strand of the Social Science programme at Mount Lawley CAE (Coroneos) students may elect to pursue the course Introductory Indonesian which aims to give them some acquaintance with the Indonesian language, a background in Indonesian culture and literature, and skill in the methodology of teaching Indonesian at the primary level. At SCV Bendigo (Silverback) students may elect to take a Language Studies course on Pitjantjatara and Bahasa Indonesian languages, and a compulsory unit of music at the same college (Reed) is an interesting course entitled, Ethnomusi-cology—a study of life and culture in Indonesia. The course is conducted by an inter-disciplinary team from the music, art and social science departments. Students learn to play and sing Indonesian music integrated with realistic studies of Indonesian life and culture, including cooking! At the North Brisbane CAE (Carvor) an elective course within the Health and Physical Education programme concerns Ethnic Dance studied against the cultures of various ethnic groups. At least one institution has introduced overseas field work in connection with Asian studies. For example, at the Tasmanian CAE, Mt. Nelson (McKay), students pursuing courses in South East Asian History and curriculum work in social studies visit Malaysia and Singapore to investigate tradition and change of culture in multi-racial, underdeveloped countries. Students are billeted in private homes and receive lectures from staff of institutions in places visited. This field work is subsidized by a combined grant of $5,000 from the college and the Tasmanian Department of Education.

6. viii Development of Specific Skills

Accompanying the increasing research interest in analysing the general teaching act into specific behaviours, and the development of the microteaching technique to help teachers acquire them, there has been endeavour to isolate and communicate basic skills and understandings related to particular subject areas. For example, at Macquarie University Walsh has designed a number of student-learning modules on science concepts and skills relevant to primary teaching; at Kuring-gai CAE Edmonds and Ticehurst have constructed a course of specific laboratory techniques for secondary science teaching; and at Macquarie University, Hall and Sim have developed a course based on their analysis of the specific tasks of teacher librarians.

6.ix Offering Services in Special or Remedial Education

A number of teacher education programmes have used the expertise of their staff, the interest and developing skill of their students and the resources of the institution to provide schools or campus clinics with diagnostic, therapeutic and remedial services for mentally handicapped children and pupils with specific learning difficulties. The activities have much to commend them. The community and professional regard for the institution cannot but be enhanced, and students are given real experience in community service and in counselling and teaching children with very specific needs. Probably the most highly developed work in this area is the Communication Centre and Clinical Resources at Mt. Gravatt CAE (Hart). The centre investigates language problems of both typical and a typical children and seeks to help children with communication difficulties. Related to these activities are educational clinics (conducted by staff in psychology and special education) for mentally handicapped, deaf, visually handicapped and orthopaedically handicapped children. These clinics are both a public resource and a teaching resource providing both lecturer and student with practical contact with children's problems. Similarly, but on a much smaller scale, at SCV Burwood (Cameron), there is a Learning Difficulties Clinic providing a public service and linked with a course undertaken by primary students.

Other institutions have introduced schemes whereby students and lecturers work with children in schools in locating and helping children with particular needs. For example at Wollongong IAE (McLellan) students in a special education elective participate in individualized remedial reading activities in neighbouring disadvantaged schools. Similarly at the Catholic Teachers College (Martin) a group of students are involved in remedial reading instruction in local schools using 'precision teaching' techniques. At Mercy College (Finkel and Jackson) students in a combined psychology and physical education elective are involved in identifying early primary children with weaknesses in perceptual or perceptual-motor skills, and at Kuring-gai CAE (Turnbull and Mist) students are involved in a study of children's motor performance to provide them with an understanding of stages of physical and motor development, and the differences between children which necessitate more individualized teaching.

6.x Providing Methodological Exemplars

The dichotomy between educational theory and practice has increasingly concerned teacher educators. In recent years there has not only been an endeavour to develop a close relationship between professional studies and practical teaching experiences, but also a deliberate effort by some teacher educators to 'practise what they preach'. The design and methodology of a growing number of programmes has begun to exemplify the very principles and practices which are being advocated to student teachers for use in classrooms. All too often student teachers are prone to teach as they themselves were taught at school, and the break in the modelling pattern provided by the new methodology of teacher education should, it can be reasonably argued, have a salutary influence. There are many examples of this movement, and a selection will be sufficient to indicate its nature. At North Brisbane CAE (Fogarty) a course on Modern Developments in Primary Education is organized and taught following many of the methods being explored in the course. The course has a number of features: (i) team planning and teaching by three college staff; (ii) use of a combination of whole group lecturers, small group seminar-workshops, simulation and gaming, field experiences, and independent study; (iii) involvement of students in developing the course; and (iv) providing for individual interests of students. Another interesting example is an Integrated, Open Space Programme at Alexander Mackie CAE (Conners and Barry). Conducted by lecturers in the fields of education, health education, mathematics, psychology of reading and of teaching methods, the programme aims to: (i) give the student experience of working in a flexible environment; (ii) allow the student to individualize his studies by pursuing areas of interest in-depth or by working in areas where individual deficiencies exist; (iii) give the student the opportunity to participate in course organization and experience the responsibility for self-directed learning; and (iv) provide students with the opportunity to develop educational research skills. The programme endeavours to incorporate many characteristics of open education, some of the organizational features of the scheme being—*Free scheduling of time:* Two full days a week were devoted to the programme during which time each student was responsible for planning his own use of time since there were few compulsory lectures. Students could also use other 'free time'. *Provision of resources:* A double lecture room was converted to a central work area and organized like an open space classroom with mathematics, reading, health education and teaching-method centres set up each week. The college Resources Centre was also set aside for half a day weekly so students could view films and make aids. *Co-ordinated and individualized curriculum organization:* Where possible, the subject areas integrated their courses, and students proceeded largely through the courses on a contract or task system completing a required number of units or tasks. Student reaction to the programme was very favourable, especially to the freedom to plan their own time, to work at their own pace, and to choose studies suited to their own needs. They believed it raised their standards of work and was a more effective and efficient means of teacher education than conventional approaches.

Most instances of teacher educators endeavouring to involve students in experiences which exemplify advocated approaches are to be found in specific subject or curriculum studies areas. In the field of science, for example, a team at Nepean CAE (Trist) has developed a field studies course to provide primary student teachers with practical experience in the methods and approaches recommended for use with pupils. At Mercy College, Scott uses toys in the first-year course for primary students to illustrate principles of physics. This course not only models approaches to be applied with children; it also has proved most informative and enjoyable for students. Examples such as these can be multiplied across all curriculum areas.

The foregoing analysis of the categories and content of innovation in Australian teacher education programmes has revealed a remarkable number and variety of activities, even though the discussion has been necessarily selective (a full list of reported innovations appears in Appendix 2). Although individual innovations vary considerably in originality, size and value, as a group they represent an impressive forward movement. They touch upon all areas regarded in world-wide teacher education circles as important 'growing edges' in the preparation of professionals. This does not mean Australian innovators in teacher education should feel complacent. The majority of their colleagues are apparently doing little to improve programmes. There are a number of quite fundamental areas that are in need of much further exploration and development. The process of innovation itself requires more attention and care devoted to each of its phases, especially evaluation.

Of the general areas of teacher education which have been touched upon by present innovatory activity but are promising enough to warrant much more, the following six seem to be the most important: (i) the analysis of the existing and projected roles of the teacher into requisite skills and understandings and the development of courses, techniques and materials to promote their acquisition by students; (ii) the development of programmes which recognize the individual personal and professional needs and interests of students, and employ course structures and methodologies to facilitate student learning; (iii) the modelling in all aspects of teacher education of the teaching and learning strategies and technologies that are being advocated for use in schools; (iv) the realistic and purposeful integration of educational theory and research with the various practical and field experiences in which students engage, particularly practice teaching; (v) an examination of the most appropriate ways of facilitating the students' smooth transition to full teaching responsibility and of providing them, as teachers, with motivation and opportunity to continue and deepen their professional education; and (vi) on the wider front, a penetrating consideration of the short- and long-term goals of teacher education in terms of continuity and change in education and society, and of complete programmes designed to serve these goals.

In the chapter that follows a sample of the reported innovations is brought into sharper focus so that the purposes, features, problems and effectiveness of their operation can be more clearly discerned.

3 CASE STUDIES OF INNOVATION IN AUSTRALIAN TEACHER EDUCATION

During October-December 1975 case studies were made of twenty-two innovations selected from the range revealed by the survey of Australian teacher education programmes. Innovations were selected on the basis that they seemed to satisfy at least three of the following criteria devised by the investigators: (i) the close relevance of the innovation to current Australian teacher education concerns; (ii) the worth of the innovation as a viable new approach to a continuing or emergent problem; (iii) the significance of the innovation in terms of its size and complexity within the teacher education institution; (iv) the ways in which the innovation provided an apt example of a new approach within an important area of teacher education; and (v) the generalizability of the innovation to other institutions.

The case study methodology adopted had two main parts. First, persons responsible for the respective innovations were invited to compile a 1,500 word statement describing their work. As far as possible the statement was to be in continuous prose dealing with a number of points raised under five main headings: (i) background and context; (ii) aims and principles of operation; (iii) the plan and its implementation; (iv) problems and effectiveness, and (v) recommendations. Second, each statement was to be supplemented by a 500 word commentary prepared by one of the project team. Data for the commentary were collected by structured interviews with representatives of various groups involved in the innovation; by observation, where feasible, of the innovation in operation and of associated facilities and equipment; and by analysis of printed material connected with the innovation. This two-strand methodology sought to tap and organize the first-hand knowledge of the innovator himself and to give him an opportunity to be involved in the dissemination of his work. It also recognized the need to provide more objective and reflective comments on the innovation by persons outside it.

Of the twenty-two case studies completed, all, except one, involved visits for interviews and observations by project investigators. The one omission from this procedure (Gill's at SCV Rusden) was caused by the innovator's absence overseas when the case studies were being conducted. The case studies appear under the name(s) of person(s) who wrote the statement. The initials concluding the accompanying commentary refer to the project member who compiled it. The case studies are organized loosely into the following nine groups, according to what seems to be their central concern: (i) *individualized student learning* (innovations concerned with devising, implementing and/or evaluating schemes for independent, individualized, self-paced learning); (ii) *inter-disciplinary and co-ordinated courses* (innovations aimed at promoting course integration and team teaching); (iii) *interpersonal relations approaches* (innovations which highlight techniques to develop understanding of, and skill in human relations); (iv) *practice of teaching* (innovations which attempt to prepare, organize, guide and/or follow-up students' in-school experience in a way that relates theory and practice); (v) *resources development* (innovations connected with the development of teacher education materials and technology and/or their storage and dissemination); (vi) *laboratory school schemes* (innovations which make special use in teacher preparation of one or several co-operating schools either on-campus or nearby); (vii) *school-based preparation* (innovations which pursue all or part of a teacher education programme in school locations and with the close collaboration of school staff); (viii) *teacher induction* (innovations which seek to provide support and guidance and to further the professional learning of the beginning teacher); and (ix) *special in-service programmes* (innovations at graduate diploma level which provide additional and often specialized professional education for experienced teachers).

INDIVIDUALIZED STUDENT LEARNING

SELF-INSTRUCTIONAL MODULES PROGRAMME

Faculty of Education
Murdoch University

Dr C. Marsh
Senior Lecturer in Education

Background and Context

Pre-service teachers embark upon teacher education programmes with a variety of talents and skills. Yet despite this, educators start them off with the same courses at the same rate. In reality, pre-service teachers have already developed varying levels of expertise in interpersonal, organizational and communication skills. It is unwise, if not folly, for teacher educators to provide a range of courses that *all* students must undertake to complete the requirements of the teacher education programme.

It was a combination of these factors that led to the development of a series of *Self-Instructional Modules* (SIM) for Murdoch University pre-service teachers towards the end of 1974. It was evident that some students needed guidance in personal skills related to such personality attributes as self-concept and ego. It was felt that the development of these personal skills could be effectively carried out by students working on individual packages at their own pace. Other aspects of teacher education programmes, especially planning of lessons, routine organizational activities and classroom management, also seemed admirably suited for inclusion in SIM packages.

Aims and Principles of Operation

It was intended that the SIMs would be carefully sequenced. Key concepts and generalizations were reinforced at various stages throughout each SIM package. It was considered essential that each SIM should contain both *theoretical* commentaries, papers and outlooks, together with *practical* follow-ups using observational questionnaires and small group and large group teaching situations. The practical teaching arrangements for Murdoch students facilitated the theoretical/practical components of the SIMs, as tutor-supervisors were available to assist students during their concurrent day-a-week school experiences.

After a period of experimentation with a number of different approaches, goals, and materials, an agreed format was reached. For the February intensive course for Diploma in Education students in 1975, seven SIMs were developed, from which students chose two for particular study based upon the following goals: each SIM was to provide

(i) relevant materials for pre-service teachers who had varying levels of skill and competence;

(ii) sequenced, self-instructional materials that could be studied both on campus and in the schools; and

(iii) activities and materials that could form the basis for further discussion with tutor-supervisors and with co-operating teachers.

SIMs cover both personal and procedural topics, as indicated by the following titles: grouping, classroom management, discipline, self-awareness, lesson presentation, individualization of instruction, and classroom evaluation.

The Plan and Its Implementation

Activities in each SIM normally involved students in reading several short articles, or chapters, viewing a videotape or slide/tape presentation, and undertaking observations, surveys, questionnaires and lessons in the school context.

As an example, the following page is the cover sheet for the SIM on *Lesson Presentation*:

This Self-Instructional Module represents the first experience in actual techniques of teaching. As such, it is quite elementary and aims to do nothing more than examine the basics. It is on the foundations developed here that your efficiency and confidence as a teacher will grow, and which will provide the springboard for your further enquiry into specific teaching techniques.

Learning Experiences

1. *Read* the monograph on 'Four Focus Points in Teaching'. The system used in this monograph constitutes a fundamental approach to teaching which can be applied to instruction of typical classroom groups or individuals. The system is of particular value because it provides a basic frame of reference for self-evaluation of your teaching performance.

2. *View* the videotape 'Variability'. It illustrates a series of actual classroom situations and fundamental teacher roles, stressing the importance of variability in approach.

3. *Read* Chapter 4, 'The Skill of Variability', *Sydney Micro Skills*, Series 1 Handbook. An accompaniment to the above videotape, it elaborates on some of the techniques observed, as well as providing some of the research background and findings on variability.

4. *Complete* 'Lesson Critique Form', one form at primary level, and one at secondary level. This is a minimum requirement. Greater benefit will be acquired, if a separate form is completed for each different teacher observed.

5. *Report* on two lessons which you have observed. These reports should be based on the materials contained in the 'Four Focus Points in Teaching'. For preference, the lessons should be quite diverse in character. Remember to preserve the anonymity of the teacher concerned. It will most certainly assist you in making your report if you discuss the lessons with the teachers concerned.

Further Reading/Experiences

The following are suggested additional reading, viewing or activities which will build on the basic framework established. They are not compulsory, but will prove most useful to your development.

(a) *View* videotapes 'Reinforcement' and 'Basic Questioning'. These explore particular basic teaching skills and are similar to the tape on Variability.

(b) *Read* Chapter 2, 'The Skill of Reinforcement', Chapter 3, 'The Skill of Basic Questioning' in *Sydney Micro Skills*, Series 1 Handbook.

(c) *Have* pupils complete from one or more of your practice classes a 'Pupil Comment Sheet' on your performance. Sheets are available for both primary and secondary level. The questions to be answered are based on the video 'Variability' and student responses will provide you with a valuable insight as to your performance.

Problems and Effectiveness

Feedback information from students at the end of their four-week intensive course enabled the existing SIMs to be revised and expanded before the introductory courses were offered to other students during their first and second semesters.

At this stage, no formal evaluation of the SIMs has been attempted. Verbal and written comments received from participating students have been encouraging, but this by itself is insufficient. A comprehensive evaluation of all School of Education courses is planned for 1976–7 and it is envisaged that more appropriate evaluation data will then be available. However, as a vehicle for introducing pre-service teachers to specific teaching/curriculum topics, it does appear to have potential.

The major problem faced has been the amount of time and effort needed to develop each SIM. Further, there is a need to develop a wide range of SIM topics and this development must be based on a number of able persons who are willing to plan and to produce modules of high quality. The production of SIMs is a key factor both in establishing and in expanding the scheme.

Another aspect is that some SIMs are not wholly self-instructional, in that certain topics require the contribution of resource persons. However, this is not a general problem and it may well be that some topics cannot be treated wholly as a self-instructional unit.

Some problems have also been experienced in providing sufficient accommodation for students to use SIM materials, especially as the scheme has expanded.

Recommendations

It is intended to continue and to expand the scheme. In doing this it is intended to try to vary the presentation of the SIMs in which the main focus to date has been on typewritten notes. In future it is hoped to develop particular SIMs as video and/or audio tapes and to provide for more use both of charts and of slides.

If another institution were considering developing a SIM scheme it is recommended that sufficient time is allowed to plan and to prepare the materials. Unless there are enough creative people to develop well prepared, stimulating and provocative materials any scheme of this type will flounder. And in developing particular modules, it is important first to have an over-all concept of the total scheme so that implementation is well planned and is not haphazard.

Commentary

The individualization of instruction at any level will depend in the final analysis on the learning-teaching resources available. While much has been spoken and written about the bright new world educational technology seems to promise in dealing more effectively with individual differences and individual needs in the learning-teaching process, the truth is that sufficient and relevant software is rarely available. While some of this software may be produced commercially, it seems certain that much of it must be produced by academic staff directly involved in particular situations. And, it is evident that the production of good quality materials requires skilled persons who have the time to plan and to develop these resources. An apparent weakness in this general area has been, and is, a shortage of software production personnel. There is no shortage of hardware, and its relative cost has decreased significantly in recent years.

The software problem is well illustrated in the SIM scheme. The first materials were hurriedly produced to enable the scheme to start, and a number of academic staff contributed time and skill to get the scheme going. Since then more modules have been produced, but the range of topics needed still is wider than those currently available. And to increase this range, creative and skilled persons will have to make significant contributions. A desirable approach would be:

(i) The planning of a comprehensive set of units or modules which fitted a master plan of a learning-teaching scheme.

(ii) The availability of a team of creative persons who had the time and the resources to produce the full set of units or modules, varying the presentation of each according to its topic and to the full range of available hardware.

(iii) The field testing of the full range of materials resulting in any modifications which may be shown to be necessary.

(iv) The use of the materials as a full and relevant package, including the participation of personnel who engaged in the first three steps set out above.

Rarely do academic staff in Australian tertiary institutions have the opportunity to follow this approach. Almost always software is needed urgently and there is a lack of time and a shortage of production resources.

The SIM scheme was planned to provide both flexibility of choice for student teachers, and materials for discussion with classroom teachers, with tutor-supervisors in the schools and with university lecturers. In addition, the scheme represented an attempt to put theoretical ideas, such as grouping, into practice. As already noted, the main problems were the practical ones of enough time to develop the SIMs, the need for a wide range of units and the availability of creative persons to develop particular units. There is little doubt that the opportunities student teachers had for discussion each week with tutor supervisors in the schools facilitated student teacher use of the modules.

In view of the problems of developing software such as the SIM materials in Australia, there is a need for co-operation among the tertiary institutions to develop self-instructional materials which are available across institutional boundaries. And this would require a continuing register of developments across Australia so that interested parties had simple access to current information through some form of clearing house.

[D. J.]

THE CONSTRUCTION AND EVALUATION OF A SERIES OF COMPETENCY-BASED MODULES FOR PRE-SERVICE AND IN-SERVICE TEACHER EDUCATION

School of Education
Macquarie University

Dr D. Levis, H. Thompson, L. Crabtree and G. White

Background and Context

In the United States in recent years considerable interest has been shown in competency-based teacher education (CBTE). A survey conducted in the United States (Cook, 1973), showed that out of the 783 teacher training institutions which responded, 125 had fully developed competency-based programmes and a further 366 were in the developmental stage and planned to establish competency-based programmes.

At Macquarie University a number of curriculum areas within the Teacher Education Programme have begun to experiment with competency-based instructional modules. Also, discussions with teacher educators at the South Pacific Association for Teacher Education Conference held at Macquarie University in 1975 revealed a high level of interest in the CBTE approach.

Recently the CBTE movement has come under strong attack for its lack of a research base (Heath and Nielson, 1974). A search of the professional literature failed to find evidence to support either the CBTE approach or the validity of the component teaching competencies upon which it is based. For this reason an experimental evaluation programme has been mounted.

The Plan and Its Implementation

The experiment will have two phases. Phase I will be concerned with:

(i)   a thorough review of the professional literature on competency-based instruction and related issues;
(ii)   the design and trialling of five competency-based modules;
(iii) the development and validation of evaluative instruments; and
(iv)   the planning and trialling of experimental procedures to be used in phase II of the study.

Phase II will be a large-scale empirical study involving 72 pre-service and 40 in-service teachers. Phase I will be completed in 1975 and phase II in 1976. However, it is not expected that reporting will take place before the end of 1977.

The pre-service section of phase II will be conducted using trainees enrolled in the course, Curriculum and Instruction in the Secondary School. This is an introductory course for trainees within the Macquarie TEP and it is offered in the third year of a four-year B.A. Diploma in Education programme. The in-service segment will be conducted with teachers participating in a series of in-service skill development courses offered by the Centre for the Advancement of Teaching at Macquarie University.

The specific questions asked in this research project are:

(i)   Are the modules effective in bringing about behavioural changes in pre-service trainees and in-service teachers which are significantly greater than those measured in control groups following a parallel tutorial pro-gramme involving group discussion and videotape modelling of selected teaching skills?

(ii) Assuming that the behavioural changes are significant, are the changes sustained when measured six weeks after the completion of the modules?

(iii) Are the competencies developed by the modules and evaluated initially in a microteaching setting, transferable to the regular classroom?

(iv) Does the acquisition and use of the selected competencies lead to pupil growth in the classroom?

(v) Are the modules equally effective for pre-service trainees and in-service teachers in terms of:
  a. initial acquisition;
  b. retention;
  c. transfer to the regular classroom; and
  d. pupil growth.

(vi) Is the competency-based approach equally effective for all learners? What are the effects of such factors as differences in personality or preferred learning styles?

(vii) In relation to performance competencies, to what extent is task description a viable alternative to the symbolic and perceptual modelling embodied in the training modules?

Given that many teaching performance competencies, such as explaining, questioning etc., are acquired in the course of natural social interaction, a clear task description may be sufficient to elicit the desired responses.

The sample

A. *Pre-service trainees*

The sample will consist of 72 Social Science trainees drawn from a total of 380 enrolled in the course, Curriculum and Instruction in the Secondary School, at Macquarie University.

At enrolment time groups of 24 will be assigned to each of the time periods:

Tuesday	9.00 a.m.–11.00 a.m.
Wednesday	11.00 a.m.– 1.00 p.m.
Thursday	2.00 p.m.– 4.00 p.m.

Within each group of 24, the trainees will be assigned at random so that two sub-groups, one control and one experimental, will be formed from each time period.

Tuesday   Wednesday   Thursday

9.0–11.0 | n = 12 | Control
          | n = 12 | Experimental

                    11.0–1.0 | n = 12 | Cont.
                              | n = 12 | Exp.

                                        2.0–4.0 | n = 12 | Cont.
                                                 | n = 12 | Exp.

B. *In-service teachers*

The sample will consist of 40 teachers who enrol in a series of in-service courses to be conducted in association with the Centre for the Advancement of Teaching

at Macquarie University. The courses will be offered as a series, over five consecutive weeks. The 40 teachers will be randomly allocated to control and experimental groups.

A model for the development of competency-based modules

In their book *Models of Teaching*, Joyce and Weil (1972) identify a wide range of
models which have been designed to create environments for learning. They
group these models into four different 'families' of approaches to teaching:

1. Social interaction models.
2. Information processing models.
3. Personal source models.
4. Behaviour modification models.

If one accepts the view that the teaching style developed by a teacher is a
unique personal decision and that the teacher may wish to adapt different
styles to different situations, it would seem important that a programme of
teacher education should provide the prospective teacher with a knowledge of,
and an ability to call upon, a variety of teaching styles.

In the long run, and assuming that the evaluation of the initial five modules
shows satisfactory results, it is intended that training modules will be developed
progressively within each of the four categories listed above. As an initial step,
Series A, which includes the first five modules used in this experiment, is based on
an information processing model.

Within the information processing category, Joyce and Weil identify a number
of models:

the Taba model;
the Bruner model;
the Suchman model;
the Ausubel model;
the Piagetian model, and
the Gagne model.

Because of its clarity of development and the manner in which the model relates
learning theory, teaching strategies, and learning outcomes, the Gagne model
has been selected as the basis for Series A (see Figure M.1).

According to Gagne (1974, p. 15) the model represents 'the essential features
of the most modern learning theories'. In Figure M.1, Gagne's model has been
modified slightly to show a range of teacher input variables. In addition, an
attempt has been made to locate each of the selected competency-based modules
within the model.

It should be noted that the five modules selected are not intended to cover all
aspects of the information processing model. Future modules are likely to
include such aspects as questioning, non-verbal communication, and evaluation.

The specific modules chosen for development within the project are:

Module I *Selecting an information processing model for teaching.* This module
outlines the various models of teaching, describes the information
processing model with particular reference to Gagne, and acts
as a general introduction to the series.

Module II *Defining instruction objectives.* This module is concerned with determining the outcomes of instruction and the selection of performance
objectives.

Figure M.1 AN INFORMATION PROCESSING MODEL OF TEACHING

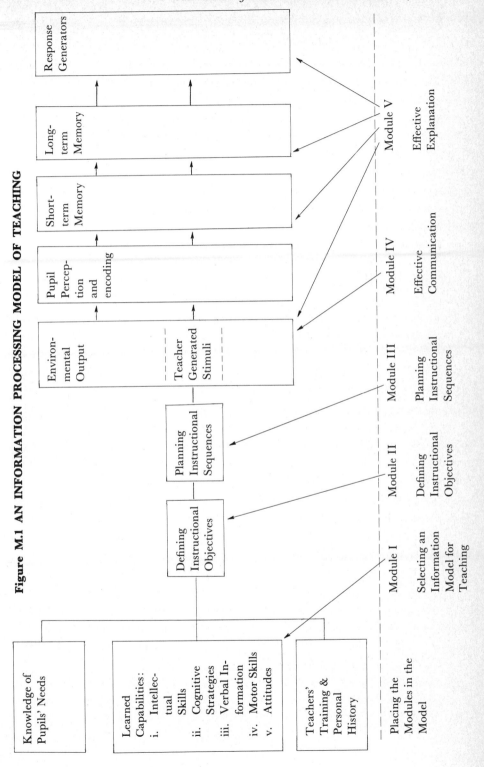

Module III *Designing instructional sequences.* The emphasis in this module is on showing how instructional objectives can be achieved through the use of appropriate learning sequences.

Module IV *Effective communication.* The teachers' instructional strategies will be unsuccessful unless information can be effectively communicated to the learner. This module concentrates on the verbal aspects of communication.

Module V *Effective explanation.* The effectiveness of a teacher's explanation will influence not only pupils' perceptions but also memory storage and availability for retrieval. This module deals with a range of techniques to promote concept development.

Experimental procedures

A. Contextual problems

A major problem facing this research project is the basic conflict which exists between the need for experimental controls and the individual freedom inherent within the competency-based approach to teacher education. For example, CBTE students are usually allowed to progress at their own rate and to omit modules in which they can demonstrate satisfactory levels of competency.

Generally, the aim will be to provide as much flexibility as possible without losing experimental control. The specific limits to individual freedom will include:

(i) All subjects will be required to take the pre-tests. Generally, a choice is given and only those who feel they are able to demonstrate the competency at the required level take the pre-test.

(ii) An upper time limit will be imposed for the completion of each module. The subjects of the experiment will be required to take their post-tests at the specified time, even if they feel that they have not reached criterion levels. However, sufficient time will be given for the average student to reach the required standard.

(iii) All subjects will take the modules sequentially. However, a subject who shows that he has reached criterion level on a pre-test will be allowed to omit the module concerned.

B. Evaluation procedures

The modules will be evaluated at two levels. Firstly, in terms of their effects on the subjects' teaching behaviour and secondly, in terms of their effects on pupil growth in the classroom.

However, not all modules will be evaluated directly in the classroom. This is because Modules I, II and III are of a planning nature, whereas Modules IV and V are more concerned with the actual process of teaching. The first three modules, therefore, will be measured initially in terms of teacher growth in the areas of knowledge and planning ability. However, it is anticipated that these modules will have a cumulative effect upon the teachers' classroom activities and this will be evident when control and experimental groups are compared in classroom pre-test prior to the completion of Module IV. The planned evaluative procedures are shown in Figure M.2.

Before commencing a detailed description of each stage it should be noted that the treatments for pre-service trainees and in-service teachers will be identical, with the following exceptions:

(i) During stages 2 to 5 the pre-service trainees will work with micro-classes composed of 6–8 school pupils. However, the in-service teachers will work with micro-classes composed of 6–8 fellow participants. The use of peer classes in the in-service courses is convenient in that it would be difficult to have access to school pupils at the time when in-service courses are usually provided. In addition, the microteaching studies, recently completed (Levis, 1975) indicated that the acquisition of teaching skills by participants using peer classes was not inhibited when compared to groups using school pupils, as long as the procedure is not prolonged.

(ii) For the pre-service trainees, stages 4, 5 and 6 will involve measures of pupil growth. However, for the in-service teachers this will be confined to stage 6 as it is not considered appropriate to use pupil growth measures with peer classes.

Figure M.2   MODULE EVALUATION

Stage 1 Organization and Familiarization	1. Organization of control and experimental groups. 2. Familiarity with equipment and controlled settings. 3. Personality and attitude tests.
Stage 2 Pre-test	The aim well be to obtain a measure of each teacher's ability to implement, in a 10-minute lesson, a given set of instructional objectives.
Stage 3 Completion of Modules I, II and III	There will be a post-test at the end of each module.
Stage 4 Completion of Modules IV and V	1. Pre-test for each module. 2. Post-test for each module. 3. Measure of pupil growth.
Stage 5 Retention Measures	1. Measure of competency retention by the teacher. 2. Pupil growth measure.
Stage 6 Measure of Transfer	1. Measure of the transfer of the competency to the regular classroom. 2. Pupil growth measure.

Stage 1: Organization and Familiarization

The aim of this stage of the experiment is to introduce the participants to the experimental programme. They will be given experience in the controlled settings in which they will work and familiarization with the recording equipment and procedures to be used. During this period a number of personality and attitude tests will be administered.

Stage 2: The Pre-test

The aim here will be to gather base-line data on such aspects as:

(i)   The ability to write behavioural objectives.
(ii) The ability to plan instructional sequences.
(iii) Competence in verbal communication.
(iv) Competence in a range of explaining skills.

Each participant will be required to teach a ten-minute lesson to a class of 6–8 pupils. Lesson guides will be issued giving the precise aims of each lesson. Lessons will be videotaped for later analysis.
Note: In each stage all lessons will be videotaped and in each case a lesson guide will be provided to unify lesson content.

Stage 3: Completion of Modules I, II and III

Modules I, II and III are concerned with knowledge competencies and as such they will not be evaluated in the classroom. However, post-tests appropriate to the objectives of each module will be administered.

Stage 4: Completion of Modules IV and V

Before commencing Modules IV and V all participants will complete a pre-test. Since these modules involve both knowledge and performance competencies two types of tests will be given:

(i) a written test, and
(ii) a ten-minute lesson with a class of 6–8 pupils.

In regard to each pre-test lesson the control group of 36 will be evenly divided into three sub-groups of 12 in order to measure the effects of varying degrees of task description.
Within this context, task description will be defined as the provision of written information regarding the criterion variables which are to be evaluated.
There will be three levels of task description:

Group A (n = 12) will be given no information about the criterion variables. Each participant will, however, receive a lesson guide stating the aims of the lesson.

Group B (n = 12) will be given minimal task information. Each participant will receive a list in which the criterion variables are named, plus the lesson guide.

Group C (n = 12) will be given maximum task information. Each will receive written material naming and fully describing each of the criterion variables. Lesson guides will also be supplied.

The experimental group will not be exposed to varying degrees of task description. Following the pre-test they will proceed directly through the modules.

At the completion of Modules IV and V post-tests will be applied. These will involve written tests of knowledge competencies and microteaching lessons to measure performance competencies. After each lesson a pupil growth measure will be taken.

Stage 5: A Measure of Retention

Approximately six weeks after the completion of Module V all participants will be required to teach another ten-minute lesson. The aim will be to measure the retention of the competencies after a six-week interval. A pupil growth measure will be applied. Shortly after this lesson participants will complete an inventory aimed at assessing attitudes towards the competency-based experience.

Stage 6: A Measure of Transfer to the Regular Classroom

In 1977 those teacher trainees who participate in the experiment during 1976, will undertake a school experience programme, teaching in a regular classroom as part of their final year of training. Early in the year a stratified random sample of 36 trainees (18 from control and 18 from experimental) will be requested to teach a ten-minute lesson in a regular classroom. Each trainee from the experimental group will be asked to concentrate on the performance competencies exemplified in Modules IV and V. In the week prior to the lesson these trainees will be asked to revise Modules IV and V to ensure that the test will measure transfer rather than retention.

The in-service teachers will be asked to arrange a ten-minute lesson with a regular class within each teacher's school. Pupils will be selected at random from the pool comprising each form.

In the case of both pre-service trainees and in-service teachers a pupil growth measure will be applied.

Measurement

A number of specific measuring devices will be applied:

(i) Instruments to measure the performance of pre-service trainees and in-service teachers in regard to each of the competency-based modules. There will be two types of instruments:
  (a) written objective tests to measure knowledge objectives;
  (b) observation instruments to measure classroom performance where this is the desired objective.
(ii) Instruments to measure pupil growth in terms of intellectual skills—with special emphasis on concept development.
(iii) Instruments to measure an array of personality variables. The IPAT (16 PF) is being considered for this purpose.
(iv) Instruments to measure the attitudes of participants to the training programme.

TIME SCHEDULE
1976 Semester I

	Pre-service	In-service
Week 1	Organization and familiarization	
2	Pre-test	Advertise in-service course
3	Complete Module I	
4	Complete Module II	
5	Complete Moudle III	
6	Pre-test Module IV	Contact participants and arrange familiarization visit
7	Complete Module IV	
8	Complete Module IV	In-service familiarization visit
9	Post-test Module IV	
10	Pre-test Module V	In-service pre-test
11	Complete Module V	
12	Complete Module V	
13	Post-test Module V	

1976 Semester II

Week 1		
2		Complete Module I
3	Retention test	Complete Module II
4		Complete Module III
5		Complete Module IV
6		Complete Module V
7		
8		
9		

10		
11		
12		Retention test
13		Transfer test

1977

	Pre-service	In-service
Week 1		
2		
3		
4		
5	Transfer test	
6		
7		

The research team

The planning and control of the experiment will be conducted by a team of three researchers under the general supervision of Dr D. S. Levis. The team is Harry Thompson (Leader), Lew Crabtree, and Graham White. Although the team leader will be responsible for the planning and the co-ordination of the entire experiment the two remaining researchers will be allocated areas of substantial responsibility. Specifically, Lew Crabtree will be responsible for—planning, conducting and reporting that part of the experiment concerned with the effects of variation in task description. In addition he will design, trial and edit Module IV concerned with effective communication. Graham White will be concerned with planning, conducting and reporting the aspects of the experiment concerned with the relationships between the selected competencies and pupil growth. In addition he will design, trial and edit Module III concerned with designing instructional sequences.

REFERENCES

Gagne, R. M., *Essentials of Learning for Instruction*, Dryden Press, Hinsdale, Illinois 1974.

Heath, R. W. and M. S. Nielson, 'The Research Base for Performance-based Teacher Education', *Review of Educational Research*, 1974, 44, 4.

Joyce, B. R. and M. Weil, *Models of Teaching*, Prentice-Hall, Englewood Cliffs, N. J. 1972.

Levis, D. S., 'Effects of Practice and Feedback Variations on Questioning Skills and Attitudes', unpublished doctoral thesis, Macquarie University, 1974.

Commentary

The nature and extent of the competency-based teacher education movement as it has developed in the United States has been outlined in the initial chapter of this book. Considering the power of its influence in that country, it is perhaps surprising that the movement has been so slow in finding protagonists in Australia. Costs and facilities, conservatism and suspicion of American educational 'band-wagons' have doubtless been some of the general inhibiting factors. This is not to say that Australian teacher educators are not interested in the movement. Many are. Moreover, numerous programmes have already adopted some of the methodologies amalgamated in the competency-based movement (e.g. the development of specific performance teaching skills through microteaching and the employment of self-instructional materials). Of the Australian teacher education programmes, the one at Macquarie University perhaps has shown greatest interest in the competency-based approach. A number of people working in curriculum areas seem to be attracted by it and education staff, after experience in microteaching, have a growing interest in adopting it (an interest which, they urge, does not necessarily commit them to a competency-based teacher education programme!) Given this background and detachment of mind, it is perhaps fitting then that Macquarie University staff undertake this country's first major investigation of the competency-based approach.

Funded by a small initial pilot-study grant from the University in 1975, the project received a grant of $24,249 in 1976 from the Australian Advisory Committee on Research and Development in Education. The research plan is elaborate and the questions it seeks to answer are important ones. The overall research design is impressive. If anything, the project is rather over-ambitious. Among other things, it seeks to (i) develop quite sophisticated student learning modules, (ii) evaluate these modules in terms of student-teacher learning and its transfer to classroom teaching, (iii) analyse personality factors associated with the effectiveness of competency-based approaches, and (iv) validate, in terms of pupil learning, the competencies developed in the programme. Any one of these four aspects is potentially a major project in itself.

The project faces some problems. The four researchers have 'full-time' commitments in the teacher education programme and involvement in both the development *and* research will be an extra burden. Substantial open space is ideally required for the varied individualized and small group activities involved in the competency-based approach, but the available space will be apparently limited. The students work will have to proceed largely within the time constraints of the existing teacher education programme. Care also will need to be taken that the 'Hawthorne effect' does not be-meddle the work of the experimental groups.

This is an interesting project. Its results should yield valuable information for Australian teacher educators contemplating some excursion into competency-based teacher education.

[C. T.]

INTER-DISCIPLINARY AND CO-ORDINATED COURSES

CO-ORDINATED METHODS PROGRAMME (CMP)

Churchlands College of Advanced Education

D. K. O'DWYER

Assistant Vice-Principal, Professional School

Background and Context

The foundation staff appointed to the new Churchlands Primary Teachers College in 1973 were presented with the opportunity to plan a programme of teacher education with greater freedom than had generally been the case up to that time. The challenge to overcome criticisms commonly suggested as contributing to the poor image of the State Education Department teachers colleges was taken up. One aspect of the new developments to emerge from this situation was the Co-ordinated Methods Programme. Replacing the traditional general methods and demonstration lesson courses, the CMP was planned as a central element of the core course in professional studies for first-year students. With a basic aim of providing communication and co-ordinated planning among the departments of education and educational psychology, teaching practice and sections of subject departments which deal with teaching methods and learning strategies in the various school subjects, the programme was intended to involve the majority of staff and to facilitate the application of theory in practice.

Under the leadership of Mr John Liddelow, Vice-Principal, a co-ordinating committee was established early in 1973 and planning and implementation of the programme proceeded together throughout the year. With only first-year students admitted in 1973 and relatively few staff at this stage, virtually all personnel were involved and by the commencement of 1974 a stable programme format had been established. The co-ordinating committee has continued to plan and co-ordinate activities since the inception of the CMP, allowing progressive review and adjustment to occur. Mr Liddelow has been replaced as chairman of the committee by the Assistant Vice-Principal, Professional School, an appointment made for the commencement of 1974. No special financial provision was necessary initially as the programme simply sought to utilize staff in a new way.

The Plan and Its Implementation

The CMP format established during 1973 and continued with minor variations until 1976, was organized around three units: Planning (Term 1); Teaching and Learning Activities (Term 2); and Evaluation (Term 3).

There were twelve topics overall, each topic being treated for a period of two weeks. In the first week the theoretical background to a topic (usually drawn from education or educational psychology) was presented by a team of lecturers in a lead lecture followed by a workshop period. In the second week the application of the theoretical principles to classroom practice was presented in demonstrations which were followed by discussion periods in which the demonstrating teacher, college supervisor and student teachers participated. In each week two hours were allocated for these activities. Also during the fortnight lecturers in the subject departments illustrated in their own courses the relevance and applications of these principles and practices to their special subject areas. Where possible subject lecturers and demonstrating teachers attended lead lectures. No direct evaluation of students on the programme was made. The effects of the programme were considered to be reflected in student attitudes and teaching skills assessed on teaching practice.

Problems and Effectiveness

Toward the end of 1974, the second year of operation, a survey of all current first-year students was conducted by the co-ordinating committee to appraise student reaction to all aspects of the programme including its relevance to teaching practice. At the same time the views of demonstrating teachers were sought. A general conclusion which could be drawn from these surveys, the results of which were distributed to all staff, was one of general support for the purpose and content, with qualified support from students with regard to implementation. The qualifications registered by students pointed to a variability in the quality and effectiveness of procedures, particularly workshops, demonstrations/discussions, and the subject-department-follow-up of topics.

The action undertaken through the co-ordinating committee in 1975 in response to the results of these surveys attempted to improve communications to staff, increase the effectiveness of workshop and demonstrations (in the latter instance by greater use of college staff to demonstrate using in some instances video-replay facilities), review the relationship between programme sequence and teaching practice expectations, encourage varied utilization of the time allotted and investigate staff attitudes and commitments to the programme. In addition, an eighteen-hour microteaching course run over six weeks was introduced to the CMP. School pupils were brought to the college and each student saw at least one video-replay of his efforts. On other occasions audio-replay was available. Some minor changes to topics presented in the main programme were made as a consequence of this new element.

The results of the staff survey, conducted in August 1975, provided general support for the findings from the student questionnaire. Quite evident also was the existence of polarized positions among some staff, either in strong opposition or highly favouring the programme, and of a general ineffectiveness of communication about the programme to all staff.

Analyses of the situation in the light of the response to the three surveys conducted appears to indicate a basic problem stemming from the adoption of the principle of all staff being involved. As an ideal this principle has merit, but as the college has grown in size and increasing diversification of staff has led to the stage where some staff are not involved at all, or used only intermittently. The consequences appear to negate the effectiveness of communications, the commitment of some staff and thus the implementation of the programme. It has been evident too that there are those who see the programme as too teacher-centred and providing a reinforcement for the situation in schools encountered on teaching practice. They feel that college efforts to produce teachers for the 'new education' are negated by such effects occurring in the first year. At the opposite end of the spectrum are the contenders for the students' need to be able to handle the expectations of schools both during training and in their initial years of teaching, and in most schools a teacher-centred approach still predominates.

Whither 1976?—hopefully with the first 'h' still intact. Based on the distributed results of surveys a great deal of soul searching, discussion, staff submission and meeting have taken and are taking place in an attempt to find an effective balance. In late 1975 the final weeks of the programme were modified to meet individual student needs sought in a survey after their final teaching practice for the year. The original Plan-Teach-Evaluate cycle of presentation over three terms has been changed for 1976, aided and abetted by the adoption of a semester organization and a more gradual introduction to classroom teaching. The programme now opens with a focus on children and their learning. Workshop/demonstration staff will continue throughout a semester with the same group of students, and accompany them on field experiences including teaching practice periods. It is hoped in this way to affect the schools and their expectations of student teachers. A greater proportion of teaching models presented in the programme will use college staff as demonstrating teachers. The co-ordinating committee remains representative of all departments but its members under the reorganization are those who are actually implementing the programme.

The CMP has been incorporated together with microteaching and media studies in new units, 'Foundations of Teaching Practice' 101 and 102, and each unit will be separately assessed, students receiving a grade for each unit. The CMP is still allotted two hours per week throughout the thirty teaching weeks of the year. The microteaching component has been increased to thirty hours in the first ten weeks of a semester with the new media studies being conducted for ten hours over the remaining five weeks of the same semester.

Basic problems remain in co-ordinating with other areas of professional education. The CMP runs *throughout* the year, for all students; other subject areas are confined to their respective semester. Microteaching and media studies are, due to logistic problems, in different semesters for each half of the student body.

Recommendations

This year will be a crucial one for the Co-ordinated Methods Programme. The changes that have been introduced are to be appraised to ascertain to what extent they meet the needs revealed in the surveys conducted. It is clear that to mount such a programme successfully a realistic appreciation of the staff time necessary for its implementation is realized. The conception of the CMP remains worthwhile; its implementation requires committed staff representing the full range of professional studies.

Commentary

A weakness of many traditional teacher education programmes has been the way in which the various 'methods' or curriculum studies courses handle the consideration of special methodologies of teaching. Often there was needless repetition, not only between 'methods' courses but also between them and the 'general methods' or education strands. Sometimes there were even glaring contradictions between the procedures advocated. Methodologies were also given uneven treatment. Certain methods courses provided thorough-going consideration; some gave only passing mention; while others chose, probably through ignorance or inexperience, to ignore teaching procedures and approaches and to concentrate on content. Another common weakness of teacher preparation has been the discontinuities between the principles and practices of teaching propounded, what students observed in demonstration lessons, and what students were expected to do or did in practice teaching. Clearly the need exists for co-ordination between the main components of teacher preparation— between general education-psychology courses, special curriculum studies and the practical elements. Numerous teacher education programmes are attempting to achieve a measure of co-ordination, but few have attempted it so extensively and with such success as the Co-ordinated Methods Programme at Churchlands CAE.

Co-ordinated by a committee representing all the college's departments, the CMP pursues the theoretical and practical study of topics organized within three units—planning, teaching and evaluation units. The pursuit of these units involves students in six more or less articulated experiences designed to link theory with practice and to relate general pedagogical considerations with particular curriculum studies: (i) *The weekly one-hour-a-week 'lead lecture' on a topic* providing students and staff with a basic overview; (ii) *A one-hour-a-week small group workshop* which considers the practical implications of the lead lecture; (iii) *Follow-up of the topic in curriculum studies* by relating ideas to particular content; (iv) *School-based demonstrations* (followed by discussion) illustrating the application of the ideas in classrooms; (v) *Microteaching* (where appropriate) in skills related to the programme; (vi) *Practice teaching* during which students attempt to implement CMP learnings.

A feature of the programme is a necessarily elaborate system of communication. This beguns with departmental representation on the planning and co-ordinating committee. Staff are encouraged to attend lead lectures and all receive copies of the programme, of lecture notes, of demonstration, microteaching and practice teaching arrangements. These are progressively filed in a special folder. The college's practice teaching staff try to communicate CMP expectations and ideas to both demonstration and practice schools.

The implementation of CMP has had increasing difficulties as the college's student and staff numbers have grown quite sharply. The main difficulties seem to be: (i) *Staffing*. Staff who conduct the small-group workshops are from subject departments. Most already have full teaching loads beyond this work. Some apparently do not feel committed to the programme while others do not seem to have the background to carry out the work effectively. A number of staff also disagree with concepts of teaching being propounded in the programme. To spread subject-staff involvement in the programme, the leaders of workshop groups are often changed, thus breaking continuity of staff-student contact; (ii) *Scheduling*. Specific curriculum courses do not run continuously throughout the year and this makes the follow-through of CMP ideas very difficult; (iii) *School liaison*. The communication of CMP ideas to schools is difficult and requires close liaison with teachers in both demonstration and practice schools. The co-ordinating committee is fully aware of these problems and is planning to take steps overcome them in 1976.

Despite these problems the programme has been very successful. Student reaction has been generally favourable but tends to vary according to the work-shop and curriculum leader commitment to, and knowledge of the programme. The students interviewed all believed that the programme helped in 'drawing theoretical and practical threads together' and that work in the various college courses tended 'to zero-in on the CMP topics in approximately the same week or two', both of which aspects the students thought were very worthwhile.

[C. T.]

INTER-DISCIPLINARY COURSES IN AN UNDERGRADUATE TEACHER EDUCATION PROGRAMME
Canberra College of Advanced Education

P. Hughes
Head, School of Teacher Education

Background and Context

The plans for the undergraduate courses in the School of Teacher Education, Canberra College of Advanced Education, took their initial form during 1970. The head of school, Phillip Hughes, was appointed to the CAE at the beginning of that year with the responsibility of drawing up courses, appointing staff and commencing the programmes in March 1971. Significant base material was available. The Education Committee of the College's Council had written to all teacher education institutions and to a very large number of individuals in Australia, seeking suggestions for the focuses and structure of courses. In addition, at the request of Council, the head of school travelled in Canada, U.S.A. and U.K. to assess recent developments in teacher education. There was, in addition, the details of very considerable discussions held in Canberra and made available by the Council.

In one sense, there was less inhibition on the nature of the courses to be deve-loped than in other institutions. There was no single predominant employing authority whose requirements would form part of the course rationale. On the contrary, intending students were preparing for a number of state departments, for private schools, for Papua New Guinea and for the Northern Territory. It was not thus possible to predict the particular educational and social milieu of the initial teaching. This made it seem more crucial to enable the student to develop a strong theoretical rationale which could serve as the basis for effective operation in a variety of settings.

Aims and Principles of Operation

As a starting point to the course plan, a number of aims were specified. These were as follows:

(i)   To make students sensitive to the needs and characteristics of children, as individuals and in groups;

(ii)   to make students aware of the social implications of education, and aware also of the contributions to be made to these problems and issues by various disciplines;

(iii) to develop an awareness in the student of his own concepts and values with respect to teaching, and of his own modes of performance in communication and in the encouragement of learning;

(iv)   to convey sufficient knowledge and skills, and to develop appropriate attitudes for the student to operate effectively in his early teaching career;

(v)   to develop a desire for continued study and development which will assist growth as a teacher throughout a career;

(vi)   to develop mastery in and enjoyment of at least one area of knowledge; and

(vii) to develop a flexibility to enable the student to work constructively in a given set of conditions and still seek better solutions.

The Plan and Its Implementation

The aims outlined above implied that particular contributory disciplines would be the basis of the studies; philosophy, psychology, sociology and history. These disciplines would not initially be the subject of formal study but would be used in two interrelated areas:

Education: a study of the general context of education in society and its relation to schooling.

Curriculum: a study of the ways in which schools select and organize learning experiences, devise and design materials, develop and evaluate teaching and learning programmes.

The inter-disciplinary character of these studies was to come essentially from the operation of a team, committed to work towards agreed objectives with an agreed rationale, and whose members would contribute specialized knowledge, skills and experience towards the agreed ends. The team approach was an initial feature of the planning and it remains a key feature of the operations. A more detailed treatment of the rationale is given in the publication, Melbourne Studies in Education 1974, S. Murray-Smith (ed.), *New Directions in Teacher Education III*, Melbourne University Press, 1974, pp. 118–30.

The initial appointments were of ten staff members and these constituted the first planning team, both for graduate and undergraduate courses. The number of teams is now six. The initial funding was the total resources available to the programme, involving academic staff of ten, twenty and thirty respectively in the years 1971, 1972 and 1973.

Problems and Effectiveness

A major issue in the development of inter-disciplinary courses has been and will continue to be, the operational meaning given to the concept. The commitment at Canberra might have been better termed 'pluri-disciplinary' rather than inter-disciplinary since the intention was and is to show the operation of several disciplines in educational problems rather than to develop a unitary approach of some sort of composite discipline. It was the viewpoint here that psychology and sociology, for example, give distinct and different insights into particular issues. This does imply that those working in the various teams will have sufficient mastery of a particular discipline to be able to determine its relevance to particular situations and sufficient commitment to the teaching process to be strongly motivated to finding workable solutions. Individuals with these particular dual strengths are not common.

There is a natural tendency in those with strong disciplinary bases to seek to give institutional form, as in subject-departments. This possibility has arisen and been considered in various ways but the decision so far has been firmly against it. It is felt that the increased flexibility of the team approach and its common focus on teaching problems represent advantages worth maintaining. It does mean, however, that there is a continuing debate on the roles and emphases of the various disciplines, with each of them claiming, and perhaps feeling, that their unique contribution is being undervalued.

There is a continuing emphasis on evaluation and the course development consequent on it. This had depended on various sources: (i) students and graduates; (ii) staff; (iii) teachers in schools; and (iv) outside teacher educators. Each of these sources has been involved in continuing evaluation, which is gradually developing form and structure. As one example, each unit is now to begin using student evaluation forms with one common section and one developed uniquely for the unit. It has been interesting and helpful to note that the assessments made by students during the courses are not necessarily re-iterated after graduation. This implies a need for some caution in responding to student assessment.

It would for this reason, and others, be premature to speak of evaluation as a final process. Our graduates from the undergraduate courses will have been in schools now for two-and-a-half years. It is clear, however, that the major response is positive. There is a frequently expressed feeling by students that the emphasis on theory is too high but in course discussions this has not proved to lead to major changes, particularly since many graduates on return visits for assessment seminars strongly support such elements.

Recommendations

Regular staff discussion on our approach, using the various evaluation sources, has re-affirmed our continuing commitment to it. The courses have recently been re-accredited for a further five years and the basis of the new forms was one of continuing development rather than massive change. The emphasis over the next few years will be, accepting the inter-disciplinary approach as given, to work more systematically and comprehensively to give operational effect to it. Towards this end a number of 'vertical' course committees has been instituted to review the flow and articulation of concepts, knowledge, skills and attitudes developed in the various units.

It is difficult to say just what the implications *should* be for other institutions. Departmental boundaries acquire a sanctity which can lead to permanency. It can also lead to rigidity. The Canberra attempt is essentially an attempt to operate through a focus on objectives, rather than on subjects or content. This type of approach, although in many possibly different forms, might well be tried by others.

Commentary

The issue of whether a school or faculty of teacher education should offer courses through a series of divisions within that school or faculty based on the various supportive disciplines, or whether such courses should be presented as a series of inter-disciplinary studies, has long been a topic of interest to teacher educators. Even when the debate comes down on the side of inter-disciplinary studies, however, the problems of initiating such an approach will often present many challenges. It will therefore be of interest for teacher educators to study the approach adopted by Hughes at the Canberra CAE in developing a school of teacher education which fundamentally offers to its students a series of inter-disciplinary studies.

One advantage that Hughes had in adopting this approach was, clearly, that the innovation took place at the establishment of a new programme. There were none of the 'territorial' claims of subject departments, divisions of studies, etc. to be overcome. The first appointments to the school were thus able to be selected on the basis of suitability to work in teams which would develop inter-disciplinary courses. New appointments made in subsequent years were similarly able to be identified by suitability to work in such a situation. In addition, prospective staff were able to be informed of the way in which courses were organized prior to their acceptance of an appointment. In this way, new staff additions were committed to working in an inter-disciplinary framework.

As stated previously, the theme of advantages or otherwise of an inter-disciplinary based programme of teacher education continues to arouse controversial debates in educational circles. It is certainly not an issue which the research team proposes to take up in the context of this report. However, in so far as the Canberra approach was meeting its stated aims and objectives, dis-cussions with students indicated that they certainly felt that the inter-disciplinary approach was successful. The students regarded their courses as being problem-centred and practically-based but at the same time they claimed they were being made aware of the theoretical bases of educational decisions.

The major disadvantage observed in the operation of this innovation appeared to be the considerable amount of time staff spent in planning-team meetings in order to ensure that the inter-disciplinary approach was being followed. It was obviously difficult for all staff members to work in teams with the same degree of ease and it was evident that in some teams quite a lot of time was spent in pro-viding mutual support to such staff members.

Although not present in the Canberra CAE example, a disadvantage of this approach which would have to be faced by others in established programmes wishing to introduce inter-disciplinary studies is the problem of replacing existing subject- or discipline-based divisions. In such cases, the commitment to work in inter-disciplinary teams would be much harder to achieve. This does raise some questions on whether this innovation could be transferred to other institu-tions. Apart from organizational restructuring, the changes which would have to take place in the attitudes of the staff concerned could well present a very difficult barrier for the would-be innovator to overcome. It was also apparent from the Canberra case study that a range of supportive facilities and resources had been provided to back up the inter-disciplinary studies approach. An example of this was evident in the provision made for simulated classroom activities to take place. Other institutions might find that a change to an inter-disciplinary programme might also involve a commitment to providing a range of additional facilities.

The Canberra CAE case study therefore presents quite a few challenges for the teacher educator who would wish to introduce a similar inter-disciplinary-based programme. The advantages and disadvantages would need to be clearly assessed before such a commitment was made. However, it might well be that the impact of the Canberra approach on the effectiveness of a teacher education programme could justify an acceptance of such challenges

[R. T.]

INTERPERSONAL RELATIONS APPROACHES

INTERPERSONAL RELATIONS AND PROFESSIONAL COMMUNICATION COURSE

Kelvin Grove College of Advanced Education

Dr R. Adie

Senior Lecturer in Psychology

Background and Context

This course forms part of the total one semester in-service course for those teachers who are to be prepared to be 'Resource Teachers' in secondary schools. The total programme was commenced in early 1975 and is being continued. Normally, the intake for the course would be 15–25 participants, all of whom would undertake the particular course which is the focus of this case study.

Most of the participants in the programmes so far have been between 30 and 50 years of age, with two or three on either side of that. There have been roughly equal numbers of men and women. The course has been principally developed by Ron Adie, although the Resource Teacher Course was established by a wider team included amongst whom were Mr Barrie O'Connor, Mr Enzo Belligoi and others from the Kelvin Grove College together with staff from the State Education Department and schools.

Essentially, in organizing the course, the planning team was very aware that educators as a whole and resource teachers in particular, are in constant communication with colleagues and students and need effective skills to maximize the value of that communication. They need to establish valuable trust relationships with teachers and with students especially, since they would be seeking improvements in student performance, changes in teacher behaviour and sometimes in the patterns of classroom and school organization and practice. A knowledge of some of the dynamics of effective change process would be a high priority.

It was out of this kind of background that the course arose. Adie had worked previously in the Presbyterian Church's Christian Education Department in Queensland, where he had conducted a wide range of human relations courses, and had considerable experience in sensitivity training. He thus set out to use that experience to provide a course to help meet these needs for resource teachers.

Aims and Principles of Operation

The aims of this course are:

(i) To develop the teachers' awareness and understanding of human relationships with particular reference to ways in which their own behaviour

184

influences, and is influenced by, the behaviour of others with whom they interact.

(ii) To develop professional interpersonal communication skills, including interviewing and informal counselling skills.

(iii) To provide information, models and strategies related to personal and social change action and some analyses of the consequences of those actions.

(iv) To develop skills for consultative and sharing roles applied in relationships with colleagues in other disciplines and members of the community.

The Plan and Its Implementation

The course is conducted over forty-eight hours, four hours a week in two, two-hour blocks. The approach is to employ a workshop style predominantly, using a wide variety of group procedures and participative methods including, for example, structured exercises, simulation, audiovisual methods and actual practice sessions involving particular inter-personal skills. Adie elected not to use T-groups because they did not then have acceptance among staff and were too threatening to the students within this environment. But he does place considerable stress on the dynamics of the group itself assisting the students to increasing awareness of: (i) the way the group is developing through the semester; (ii) their own influence on the group and the group on them; and (iii) changes in relationships within the group as the group dynamics alter during the semester.

Regular evaluation of the group life and of the tutor's relationship with the group is undertaken and is a focal point for assessment of leadership, leadership styles, communication, decision-making and intimacy issues.

Particular exercises are chosen to be used on three bases: (i) their relevance to the conceptual issues basic to the course; (ii) their relevance to the group at that particular stage in its development; and (iii) their appropriateness for individual members of the group, especially to those who are having specific personal difficulties in some area (e.g. with conflict, self-disclosure, trust-building).

The tutor's concern is to model a warm, open and authentic set of relationships with the group on an adult-basis mainly, but to be free to use a wide variety of roles with them—both flexibly and responsibly, and to attempt not to ask anything of the group that he is not willing to accept as his own standards. In interaction with the group, he openly attempts to move the group towards Jack Gibb's norms for effective group life, viz. diagnostic norm, feedback norm, 'provisional try' norm, 'here and now' norm, objectivity norm, participative norm, threat reduction norm, self-disclosure norm, participant observer norm, and the norm of ongoing evaluation of group life.

Input is definitely included in the course in at least the following ways: short prepared handouts; lectures (a few); 'short bursts'; group methods such as forum, panel, 'Pandora's Box'; film and filmstrip; and student resource. A combination of inductive and deductive methods is used.

Some of the concepts central to the course are: (i) an overview of interpersonal relationships; (ii) communications and communication skills (verbal and non-verbal); (iii) inclusion, affection, trust; (iv) power, authority, influence, leadership; (v) emotionality, defensive responses; (vi) competition and co-operation; (vii) social and personal change; (viii) conflict and its constructive resolution; confrontation; (ix) intimacy, acceptance, affiliation; and (x) self-concept and its influence on behaviour.

One major focus—about two-thirds of the way through the course in order to provide a 'gestalt'—is on transactional analysis as an aid in understanding interpersonal relations.

The course is founded as part of the total Resource Teachers Course and so far has been backed up well by finance for resource equipment.

Problems and Effectiveness

In each of the two courses conducted so far, some of the early exercises have proved to be fairly threatening to these mature-age teachers even though chosen as less confronting ones. Support has been given in those instances until more trust and evidence of the values of the exercises have been forthcoming and with almost every participant, the semester has ended with these teachers very accepting of the approach on the whole.

At the start of the innovation, there was certainly some doubt on the part of fellow staff members of the efficacy, and even of the legitimacy, of the approach, but these have now been dispelled, allowing a somewhat wider freedom of choice of activities.

The depth of learning for the group depends to some extent on the growth of individual members. Since the standard followed with the group is not to force individual members to live by standards of interaction they do not themselves accept, the stage of development reached by the group will depend to some extent on the attitudes of individual members, e.g. in relation to the amount of self-disclosure and/or feedback allowed in the group. This can be limiting, but has not been excessive so far. It is believed the reduction of external force is a good standard to maintain.

Evaluation is undertaken (i) informally through the semester as a whole, and (ii) formally through sub-groups and written assessment at the end of the semester.

Feedback certainly does indicate a high degree of affirmation of the value of the course for the students, both for their personal and professional lives. Normally they consider the course to be needing more time. The transactional analysis segment is highly valued. Results have been disseminated to other staff members but not so far to other educational institutions.

Recommendations

The course is certainly to be continued. In future courses, some changes will be made; for example:

1. In the first week of the course, a two-day workshop will be held for the group together with all staff participating in the total Resource Teachers Course. The facilitation for the workshop will not be one of the staff working with the group. The hope for the workshop is that it will help knit both staff and students early into a developing working group through a series of communication and 'team building' exercises.

2. More stress on the group's own development will be made than in the past, and students will be encouraged to introduce more of their own powers of independent thinking and resource into the course by being requested to choose an element within the course, research it and to work with the tutor in its presentation at an appropriate point in the course.

3. The assessment of the course for grading purposes has so far been by means of a 'Journal of Learnings' compiled progressively through the course. This has not produced evidence of sufficient reading undertaken by students and in future, will be supplemented by the critical evaluation of say eight to ten books of high relevance to the course.

Implications for other institutions: It is the innovator's belief that courses similar to this are of high relevance for other teacher education institutions in both in-service and pre-service courses. However, he contends strongly that staffs of those institutions undertaking these courses should have adequate preparation themselves in sensitivity training, and where such training has not already been possible, opportunities be made available for them to receive such training. In any case, fairly structured experiential programmes with some elements of T-groups incorporated seem to be more acceptable to students and administrators in teacher education at this stage rather than the relatively unstructured T-group. (The research evidence* does seem to indicate that in sensitivity training the degree of risk to participants relates closely to the style of the facilitator trainer).

Adie hopes that similar courses will find a place in more tertiary educational institutions and overall for more students in order to enhance the student's effective working in relationship with others.

REFERENCES

Some of the references associated with this course are:
James, M. and D. Jongeward, *Born to Win*, Addison Wesley, Reading, Mass. 1971.
Johnson, D. W., *Reaching Out—Interpersonal Effectiveness and Self-Actualization*, Prentice-Hall, Englewood Cliffs 1972.
Jourard, S. M., *Self-Disclosure*, Wiley, New York 1971.
Jung, C. *et al.*, *Interpersonal Communications Materials Kit*, North-West Regional Educational Laboratory, Portland, Oregon 1973.
Keltner, J. W., *Interpersonal Speech Communication*, Wadsworth, Belmont, Cal. 1970.
Schaller, L., *The Change Agent*, Abingdon, New York 1972.
Scheflen, A. and A., *Body Language and the Social Order*, Prentice-Hall, Englewood Cliffs 1972.
Shaw, M. E., *The Psychology of Small Group Behaviour*, McGraw Hill, New York 1971.

Commentary

Most institutions which offer teacher education programmes will currently provide some experiences for their students in the area of interpersonal relations. However, it is also quite evident that most of these institutions are still seeking ways in which appropriate courses in this often highly sensitive area of teacher education might be further developed. The course designed by Adie at Kelvin Grove CAE will provide many valuable insights for teacher educators, not only for its information on course content and activities but also for the advice contained in the innovator's description of the course. This is especially useful coming as it does from an educator with many years of experience in conducting courses with teachers in this area.

An interesting aspect of the course described by Adie is that the student population was composed of mature-age students most of whom had had several

* See R. T. Golembriewski, *Sensitivity Training and the Laboratory Approach*, Peacock, Illinois 1970.

years of teaching experience. The need to offer a range of carefully selected experiences has been stressed by Adie, particularly as so many of the experiences often included in interpersonal relationships courses may so often present threatening situations to such students. Adie has identified the role of the tutor as a key factor in handling not only the easing of students through difficult times within the group experience but also in the general supervision of courses of this nature. Many teacher educators will welcome Adie's stand that the courses should only be taught by staff who have had an 'adequate preparation themselves in sensitivity training'. It is to be hoped that more sessions at conferences and seminars for teacher educators will be made available for such training.

Student reaction to this course was generally positive and it is interesting to note that those who were out in schools after completing the full-time section of their programme, indicated that more work in interpersonal relationships would prove useful to them in their school situations. Adie has stressed the need for the tutor to be constantly aware of group reactions to the experiences provided throughout the course, and his strategies to gauge these reactions will be useful models for others to consider.

One of the problems identified in the Kelvin Grove experience which will also be familiar to those who have participated in the development of interpersonal relationships courses, is that of gaining the acceptance of colleagues for this type of course being offered to students. It would seem from this case study that the breaking down of resistance by colleagues is an exercise where the planner must himself display all the skills in interpersonal relationships which he will cover in his course! It does seem necessary that colleagues are kept informed of the details of such courses and that the general rationale for the inclusion of the various activities are satisfactorily explained to others who are involved in the total programme for the group of students.

The Kelvin Grove model should therefore prove of considerable interest to teacher educators. The innovator has devised a wide range of activities, readings, and general information sheets on this type of course and an inspection of this resource material and discussion with Ron Adie would provide a sound basis for planning a similar type of course in another teacher education programme.

[R. T.]

PRACTICE OF TEACHING

TEACHING PROBLEMS: POSSIBLE SOLUTIONS
TO SIMULATED SITUATIONS

Newcastle College of Advanced Education

J. Rees and R. Telfer
Lecturers in Education

Background and Context

This course and the subsequent book* were developed in response to student and teacher request for assistance with common problems associated with the practical component in teacher education and with early years of teaching. The expressed need was for a means of relating theory to teaching practice, and to bring an awareness of the expectations of others and of the wide range of possible responses to critical incidents in the educational context.

The course is provided for two hours per week as an elective for final year students. It commenced in 1974, attracting 40 per cent of the students. In 1975 the percentage grew to 45, and in 1976, 50 per cent of the students elected to participate. This course is one of eight electives coupled with a course in sociology of education to form a compulsory Education III course for all students undertaking the three-year Diploma in Teaching course. The Teaching Problems groups are of about twenty-five in number, usually homogeneous in terms of primary, secondary and infants school level in orientation.

The authors initiated the concept of such a course in 1973 with one having primary school teaching experience and the other having taught in secondary schools in New South Wales. It was decided to provide students with an eclectic review of theory found to have been relevant to teaching, and then to detail problem situations which were reported by practising teachers and student teachers.

The first step was to make such a collection of incidents from as many sources as possible. The staff of the college contributed significantly. Practising teachers assisted by detailing problems especially associated with recent developments such as the use of parent aides in the classroom.

The problems were discussed, evaluated and categorized so that four groups resulted: Teacher-Pupil Relations; Teacher-Teacher Relations; Teacher-Administrator Relations; and Teacher-Community Relations. This was the framework upon which the course was developed.

* Telfer, R. and J. Rees, *Teacher Tactics*, Symes, Sydney 1975.

Aims and Principles of Operation

The course has five main aims:

(i) To integrate and consolidate aspects of previous study in education and teaching experience.

(ii) To provide a meaningful link between educational theory and teaching practice.

(iii) To enable participants to learn of the expectations of others, which may be encountered in the school situation.

(iv) To lead the student to discover the extent to which his own educational philosophies and practices are shared by his colleagues.

(v) To provide the student with a controlled, stress-free setting in which to test reactions and discover their probable consequences.

The Plan and Its Implementation

To reduce some of the variables involved in the critical incidents a simulated teaching situation was evolved. This included a set of record cards, a class roll, a staff list, school policy and layout, community map, colour slides, sociometric data, and a calendar of the school year. This information with the incidents were presented in book form in 1975.

After each incident, some suggested responses are provided together with space for the student teacher to add notes or others' views. Some of the suggested responses are deliberately inappropriate to provoke discussion.

The team of lecturers involved in the course vary presentations to suit perceived student needs. In general, each student presents responses to allocated incidents justifying the approach suggested to the rest of the group. Interposed with these discussions are visits to schools, and discussions with or lectures from such people as an inspector of schools, teachers, administrators, teachers' union representative, child welfare officer, counsellors, innovators, teachers' centre representatives, etc.

One member of the team was elected co-ordinator. His role is to call and conduct team meetings (about two per term) and to co-ordinate student assessment and exercises to ensure uniformity in demands from lecturers. This is especially valuable in terms of informing lecturers of guest speakers and resource people who will be available. The electives take place in four possible time slots, with students available at all four times, but scheduled for only one. This enables guest speakers to address all groups if appropriate, at the one time. This is rarely the case. It is more common for two or three groups to combine to hear a speaker (such as a secondary subject master discussing classroom control).

Payment of guest lecturers and for demonstrations in schools are made through the Education Department budget. Such allocations have to be predicted and requested the previous year.

Problems and Effectiveness

The first step was to have the course approved. The faculty meeting accepted the proposition that the elective replace an existing approved course offered by one of the initiators. If the course was additional to those existing, the result may have been different due to a college-wide restriction on increasing the number of elective courses.

A problem in this course is to maintain continuity of staffing. Complications are study leave, priorities in allocations, clashes with other courses (such as Education I or II) and the vital aspects of appropriate experience and attitude.

An evaluation sheet has been distributed to all involved students, and a lecture team meeting has been used to discuss these evaluations.

Student reactions, when asked to give possible reasons for the course's apparent effectiveness, included the following:

(i) The course's practical nature; e.g. the students were almost unanimous in their appreciation of the balance between theory and practice in the course.
(ii) The flexibility in the course programme; e.g. if a certain 'problem area' evolved from seminar or lecture discussion, then lecturers, visitors, excursions, films etc. could be organized to cover that area.
(iii) The informality of the lecture approach; e.g. students appreciated the fact that the lecturer was not dominant in discussions.
(iv) The opportunity for frankness in verbal interchange provided in both lectures and seminars.

Recommendations

1. The course lends itself more to final year students than beginning students. Final year students seem more school-oriented, and tend to have more realistic expectations of the teaching profession. They also have had more practice teaching experience. This tends to be a distinct asset when discussing critical incidents and formulating realistic approaches to teaching problems.

2. It is essential that the staff be enthusiastic about the course. A prerequisite should be that they have had recent teaching experience in the field and that they have been recognized as efficient and progressive in their outlook (e.g. promotions position would be ideal). If academic staff are co-opted for the course rather than chosen according to the above criteria the course could tend to develop a theoretical and somewhat unrealistic bias. (A bias which is completely against the stated aims and objectives of the course).

3. It is suggested that some large lecture room be incorporated into the course schedule. On occasions when a visiting speaker (e.g. district inspector) has been invited to address the groups it is essential, for maximum effect, that groups of similar interest (e.g. primary) combine. On normal lecture days groups of no more than twenty are recommended. Discussions tend to be more effective in the smaller groups.

4. It would be a decided asset to schedule the course so that 'in-school' hours predominate. This allows for maximum school/college contact both for allowing teachers with differing areas of experience to visit the college and for the students to visit the schools while they are in operation.

Before initiating the course it is advisable to canvass the schools of the district to determine the reaction of schools to having students visit and also to enlist the co-operation of teachers in various categories of experience (e.g. probationers, masters, principals, small schools, etc.).

Commentary

Telfer and Rees have devised an interesting adaption of the critical incident approach for understanding teaching. Problems for beginning teachers have been categorized for discussion against a background of the New South Wales school system. Appropriate simulated data on pupils, classrooms, school and the community in their book *Teacher Tactics* add realism to the particular incidents. Thus the main advantage of the method is its realism for final year students and the opportunity for discussion of school circumstances in a stress-free situation. The participants are able to freely explore the ramifications of their decision making.

Such discussion involves the sharing and exchanging of ideas so that the student teacher has an expanding repertoire of responses to call on to meet a particular challenge. In addition the theoretical basis for such a response is evident. Students come to test their own philosophy of education and approach to teaching.

The format of the course is flexible to meet the needs of the particular group of primary or secondary student teachers. Key speakers are invited at appropriate stages to explore the school situation more directly. For example, school inspectors, counsellors or welfare workers may address the students and often there are follow-up excursions which further add to the realism of the experience.

Students are particularly enthusiastic about the course and regard it a most relevant experience for their needs in teaching. However, for implementation, the size of the discussion group is an important factor as is the choice of seminar leader. In many cases the discussions generate a high degree of personal involvement demanding indirect leadership of the group. Not all staff have had extensive experience in schools or with an intensive group discussion. As the course has increased in popularity with the students, more staff have been co-opted rather than being volunteers for group leaders. Continuity of staff involved has also been a problem with the expansion of demand for the course.

The integration and consolidation of ideas about teaching has been the main objective adequately fulfilled by the programme. With the publication of the book *Teacher Tactics* many other institutions even in other states have shown great interest in using it as a resource to develop a similar discussion-type critical analysis of Australian teaching issues. Already this course and the resource materials published so far have made an important contribution to the particular problems of awareness with regard to theory into practice and relevance in teacher education.

[D. T.]

PROGRAMME OF TEACHER DEVELOPMENT
Alexander Mackie College of Advanced Education

Dr Dawn Thew
Principal Lecturer in Education

Background and Context

This project is a compulsory component of the three-year Diploma in Teaching in the Primary Education Programme. It was developed as an integrated professional studies strand emphasizing practical teaching performance and experience.

The programme is a cumulative six-semester study of teaching consisting of three semesters of *situational teaching* (including microteaching) followed by three semesters of *school attachment* as a regular weekly involvement in schools. It commenced in 1974.

The author initiated the programme as an essential part of a reorganized Diploma in Teaching as planned by the Primary Education Programme committee in 1973. The programme extended the concepts of a teaching course and school demonstrations which were already in existence as course components, and introduced both microteaching for skills development and the continuous school attachment scheme.

Aims and Principles of Operation

The programme has five main objectives:

(i) To initiate, integrate and consolidate an analytical approach to the study and practice of teaching.
(ii) To help students to develop their capacity for self-analysis in the process of teaching.
(iii) To assist students to gain and practise the fundamental skills of classroom teaching.
(iv) To provide specific curriculum guidance in a school-based teaching workshop.
(v) To provide extended and regular involvement with in-school experiences.

The Plan and Its Implementation

To provide students with a progressive development of skills, techniques, procedures and strategies, the situational teaching course is divided into three parts: (i) basic skills of teaching (Semester 1); (ii) operational skills in the classroom (Semester 2); and advanced skills of teaching (Semester 3).

Each part consists of two lecture hours per week for a semester and focuses on a simulated theoretical consideration of teaching situations. Four microteaching practice sessions in nearby co-operating schools are provided in each semester. The skills practised range from introductory set, reinforcement, basic questioning, stimulus variation, higher order questioning to discovery procedures, small group teaching, individualized instruction, teaching outdoors, and an open education simulation experience.

The situational teaching courses are supported by teaching lectures examining principles, objectives, theories and methods for teaching and by regular school observations.

During semesters four, five and six the students are attached to schools on a regular basis. In Semester 4 this is for a half-day per week 'teaching workshop' in a curriculum area chosen as a depth subject. In Semester 5 there is a full-day teaching workshop elected in two curriculum areas. Teacher/lecturer/student planning sessions support these activities. The final semester is a full day attachment as a 'teaching assistant' on the same class following on from a six-weeks period of practice teaching.

A team of lecturers, drawn from all subject departments, is involved in the microteaching, demonstrations and school attachment components. Three or four Education lecturers present the theoretical lectures and modelling procedures of the situational teaching and the lectures of the teaching course.

Approximately 120 students are involved in each semester stage of the Teacher Development Programme. Other activities include inviting guest speakers, excursions and visits, media studies in the use of audiovisual equipment, and annual three-day residential conferences to expand the students' concepts of education through varied and active participation in learning situations related to a scheme.

Budgeting for all activities as part of the recurrent expenditure for the operation of the Primary Programme is undertaken by the Director of the Primary Education Programme. Portable video equipment was purchased in 1974 to facilitate the microteaching sessions in the schools.

Problems and Effectiveness

A problem of the course is to maintain the continuity of staffing and to obtain staff for the situational teaching who are well versed in microteaching and competent in the use of audiovisual equipment. The time factor and poor school facilities for the microteaching practical sessions have also been a continuing problem.

The innovation has proved generally successful, as indicated by a survey of students in 1974 and 1975. However, particular aspects of organization with large numbers of students have been a source of frustration for both students and staff. The school attachment components have had fewer problems of organization and students particularly value this time in schools.

Recommendations

Although the situational teaching courses in Semesters 1 and 3 have been the most successful, the Semester 2 course needs to be modified and to follow a different format as after practice teaching, the microteaching cycle seems to have less impact.

It is essential that the staff be enthusiastic about the practical sessions and have the competence to offer more specific skill-oriented feedback to students. Further, it would be a distinct advantage to have audiovisual technician assistance to support the lecturers in the field.

In all, the concepts embodied in the total Teacher Development Programme seem readily transferable to other teacher education programmes interested in developing in students important professional skills.

Commentary

The development of a range of observable, clearly defined, specific teaching behaviours or skills seen as important in effective teaching, is a growing concern of many teacher education programmes. The Teacher Development Programme at Mackie CAE illustrates how one institution has co-ordinated various course components to facilitate this skill development.

The skill development is initiated in a situational teaching course; so-called because simulated teaching situations (generally on videotape) are analyzed through the application of theoretical knowledge drawn mainly from the psychology of teaching and learning. This is carried out in large-group lectures because of limited staff expertise, space and equipment. Ideally perhaps, this could be most effectively carried out in a small-group seminar setting. Nevertheless, there seemed to be no negative attitudes among students or staff towards the situational teaching scheme.

The teaching skills introduced are next applied by students, first in microteaching and later in practice teaching. Most of the difficulties of the programme seem to cluster in the microteaching area. While students and staff are unanimous about its value, they pointed to the following aspects in need of improvement: (i) videotaped replays of microteaching lessons alone are insufficient feedback, and lecturer and peer comments are also desired; (ii) school personnel often organize poorly the microteaching sessions; (iii) videorecording equipment is frequently badly serviced and breaks down; (iv) the introduction of the opportunities to informally re-view and re-teach micro-lessons would be appreciated; (v) the length of the micro-lesson should be gradually increased beyond six minutes, especially after students have had practice teaching when such a time span seems particularly unreal; and (vi) microteaching involvement seems time consuming in off-campus locations since students devote some two hours (9–11 a.m.) travelling and settling in, only to give one six-minute lesson.

One of the major factors in the successful introduction of a co-ordinated course of teaching development is the availability of sufficient numbers of interested, expert staff. Typically, such courses rely heavily on the work of a committed few and the rather reluctant co-operation of a majority. To operate such a course effectively all involved should be able to participate productively in the introduction of the skills and in following them through in supervisory situations in both microteaching and practice teaching. One of the common problems is that of involving methods staff in the scheme. The staff at Mackie CAE were mindful of such staffing difficulties. They commented on the need to recruit appropriate staff and to provide staff training sessions for others. They also believed that the programme would be promoted among staff by both a detailed statement of its aims, principles, structure and content and a carefully conducted evaluation of its effectiveness.

[C. T.]

CONTINUOUS PRACTICE TEACHING PROGRAMME
Armidale College of Advanced Education

Dr W. Newman
Director, Educational Services

Background and Context

The Continuous Practice Teaching Programme at Armidale CAE had its origin late in 1971 when, as Co-ordinator of Practice Teaching for the college, the author presented a proposal to the staff suggesting that first-year students be provided with regular weekly practice teaching sessions rather than blocks of full-time teaching.

The proposal was prompted by two considerations. In the first instance, it was felt that students should be eased into the teaching situation. One of the problems which had been concerning us was that many schools who accepted our first-year students for periods of block practice were dissatisfied because the students were too inexperienced and inadequately prepared to face a whole class situation for an extended period. The second consideration was a purely practical one. The college was finding it increasingly difficult to find enough block practice places for all its students and to release lecturers for supervision duties in a very large practice area.

Following the initial presentation of the proposal in 1971 and its acceptance in principle by the college staff, the author was instructed to begin negotiations with the schools. The original idea was that only the Armidale Demonstration School would be involved because of its specialized function and its proximity to the college. The demonstration school was approached and after considerable discussion with all teachers, the continuous practice scheme was accepted and it was agreed that the scheme could be introduced in 1973. The proposal was then put to the District Inspector of Schools for his comment. While he supported the scheme fully, he felt that all primary schools in Armidale should be involved. It was consequently decided that introduction of the scheme should be delayed until the beginning of 1974.

During 1973, negotiations with all schools in Armidale continued. At the same time, two members of staff began working on the instructional aspect of the scheme. Mr Bruce Cole accepted responsibility for the development of a workbook which the students would use to direct their weekly activities in the schools. He worked in close co-operation with Mr Ted Kearns whose task it was to co-ordinate the practical aspects of the scheme with the lecture and seminar programme in education offered to the students.

Aims and Principles of Operation

The scheme of continuous practice teaching which was evolved has two main objectives:

(i)   To introduce students gradually to the responsibilities, tasks and skills of classroom teaching *before* full-time block teaching practice.
(ii) To help students make *direct links* between theoretical learnings in lectures and tutorials and what they observe and attempt in classrooms.

The two major principles underpinning these objectives are:

(i)   Students are best eased into the teaching-learning situation by (a) working initially with individual children, then with a small group and finally with complete classes, (b) teaching small lesson segments before attempting larger ones, and (c) progressively developing basic teaching skills. The rate of progression through these phases will differ from student to student.
(ii) To optimize integration with theoretical courses, practice teaching should run continuously parallel to them and be supplemented by tutorials, by structured in-school observations and teaching tasks, and by follow-through into the classroom setting by the lecturers initiating the ideas.

The Plan and Its Implementation

The innovative feature of the programme was that the practical experiences of the students in the schools were strongly integrated into the education courses offered at the college. The intake of first-year students in 1974 was divided into groups of 16. Each group was assigned to a lecturer who acted as academic counsellor, education tutor, and practical supervisor in the schools. Each group of 16 students was further divided into groups of four and assigned to particular classes. This meant that each teacher taking part in the scheme had four students and each lecturer taking part had responsibility for assisting 16 students and working with four teachers. Each term, each student is issued with a 'Log Book' communicating arrangements, principles, observational and teaching tasks.

First-year courses at the college were timetabled so that Wednesday mornings were kept free. Students were transported to schools by bus to spend three hours with their teachers. These visits formed part of a standard weekly pattern of work as follows:

(i)   Group lectures at college on some aspect of the teaching process.
(ii)   Tutorial discussions for each group of 16 on the content and implications of the lecture.
(iii) Visits to schools to observe or implement the points covered in the lecture and tutorial and to pursue activities set out in the 'Log Book of Professional Experiences'.
(iv)   Follow-up discussion at the college for each group of 16.

Problems and Effectiveness

Teachers involved in the programme were asked to provide a report on each student at the end of each school term and they were paid according to standard state-wide Public Service Board rates. At the end of each term, the groups of students were rotated so that they experienced a different class situation. In the course of the year, students had experience on infants and primary classes.

In the first year of operation, 1974, students made visits to schools in all three terms. General opinion from students, teachers and lecturers was that the programme was too lengthy. The first and second terms were described as 'interesting' and 'worthwhile' but third term was seen as being not as useful as the others. Many students commented that they felt they had had an effective introduction to teaching by the end of the second term and that they would have preferred to have a couple of weeks of block practice to try out the ideas they had acquired. Many teachers reported a drop in student enthusiasm and application during the third term. Many lecturers felt that the programme had served its introductory purpose by the end of second term and that its continuation into third term in future years should perhaps be re-examined.

A general criticism of the scheme in its first year of operation was that the schedule of skill development activities included in the programme was too rigid. Teachers found it difficult to emphasize particular skills and students tended to think of particular skills in isolation from others.

As a result of reaction to the programme in its initial implementation, a number of changes were made for 1975. The time spent by students in schools was reduced from three terms to two terms. The third term of continuous practice was replaced by a period of two weeks of block practice. Students commented favourably on the change. A typical comment was that the first two terms of continuous practice served as a worthwhile introduction to teaching but that block practice was more rewarding.

Another change made in 1975 was a revision of the skill development activities of the programme. The same skills were included but they were not sequenced as they had been in the previous year. Teachers involved found this revision more manageable and there were fewer instances of students viewing the teaching process as a series of isolated skills.

In general terms the programme has served the purposes for which it was designed, that is, to provide students with a phased introduction to teaching and to prepare them more adequately for their first block teaching experience. While no formal evaluation of the programme has been attempted, it is felt that the programme has also helped to link college courses in education more effectively with practical classroom situations.

By its nature, however, the programme has some disadvantages. The most significant is that the practical experience it provides tends to be disjointed and without continuity. With a week between each school visit, students and the pupils they contact, find it difficult to develop rapport. It should be mentioned, however, that there have been a significant number of cases where students, in their own time, have made extra visits to their classes and have developed excellent class associations.

Another disadvantage is that by visiting schools at the same time on the same day of each week, students do not gain an adequate understanding of school management and routine.

Despite these disadvantages, the scheme has been successful and well worth the effort it has demanded. Part-time visits to schools, by their nature, are different from full-time practice sessions. Each has its particular contribution to make in the preparation of teachers and general opinion in the college and in the schools is that the balance which has been struck is effective.

Commentary

All groups involved in the continuous practice programme agreed on the importance of its two main advantages:

(i) It enables students to be phased into teaching responsibilities early in their teacher education course. The gradual build-up in experience through observation of children and teachers, through individual and small-group teaching and the like was judged to be a realistic but comparatively non-threatening introduction to professional skills and tasks. Students seemed less anxious, more relaxed and steadily gained in confidence.

(ii) Basic to the programme are the on-going guidance, support and feedback provided for the students. These take various forms. College tutors, involved on campus with a particular group of students, follow through the in-school work of the group helping members to relate theoretical learnings to the practical situation. Supervising class teachers help and guide students individually and as a group. The small group of four or five students attached to a class often develops a mutually supportive climate while still offering constructive peer criticism. The log book of professional experiences provides a structure for child studies, observational work, self-evaluation and teaching skill development. Videotape and audiotape recordings are employed to provide feedback in the application of teaching skills with small groups. In all, it was felt that the continuous practice in the first two terms gave reality and relevance to the college courses and prepared students to undertake full-class teaching responsibilities in the third term block practice.

More generally, it had brought the schools and college into much closer collaboration. As one teacher put it, 'dialogue had been established and the way is open to increased co-operation'.

The programme has a number of problems. Too many student teachers per class and insufficient time per week were complaints of some teachers and students. It was suggested that the student group attached to each class be limited to four and that the weekly commitment be extended to at least three hours (some teachers suggested a whole day). Only then would teachers have adequate time to provide demonstrations, advise individual students and hold profitable feedback and planning discussions with their group. There were mixed opinions about the log book. All agreed on its value, but some suggested it be much more explicit in its requirements, while others believed it should be very generalized (i.e. not too directive for either student or teacher) so that individual teachers and their students could develop approaches adapted to particular needs and to the situation. Some teachers felt they should be involved in discussions on the development of the log. Most teachers thought they could help students more with the suggested activities if they had more time with students and if they knew more about what was going on in the college courses. College staff agreed that there was a need for greater school involvement in planning, implementing and evaluating the practice programme. Another problem perceived by lecturers, teachers and students was that, in first term especially, students gained little theoretical background to teaching and curriculum and tended to copy the style and practices of the class teacher. While this was seen as inevitable and even desirable when the classroom teacher provided a worthy model, it was felt that some students had initially developed rather unsound teaching patterns as a result. This possible problem underlined the need to carefully select, brief and even train the teacher supervisors. Some teachers expressed the need for greater support and guidance in their supervisory work from college tutors. In relation to the on-campus courses on education running parallel to practice, several college tutors admitted that they sometimes found it difficult to follow through ideas presented in education lectures. Their attendance at these lectures sometimes clashed with other timetable commitments and in many cases it constituted an extra load on an already full schedule.

The Armidale Continuous Practice Programme is a good example of how one institution has endeavoured successfully to improve upon conventional block practice teaching arrangements.

[C. T.]

FIELD EXPERIENCE WORKSHOP

Sturt College of Advanced Education

P. GUNNING
Senior Lecturer in Education

Background and Context

In the third year of study for the Sturt CAE Diploma of Teaching, students are required to do a nine-week block of practice teaching followed by a four-week intensive workshop based on this experience. The aim of this four-week workshop is to provide people with opportunities to consider their teaching and as a result, design and implement appropriate responses in anticipation of their full-time teaching responsibilities.

This four-week workshop was first offered in the Sturt Diploma in July-August 1974. The planning for the unit commenced in January 1974. One member of the education staff was appointed as co-ordinator of the course, with the responsibility to devise an organizational structure and philosophy for perusal and ratification at a staff seminar in mid February. This was done and the proposal was accepted with no fundamental modification. All subsequent planning and organization was handled by this staff member who frequently consulted with colleagues as to progress, and in the months immediately preceding the course organized consultation sessions with those members of staff who were to be most immediately concerned.

Aims and Principles of Operation

The prior situation with this workshop was an intensive and rather demanding experience in the schools at a time not far short of the first appointment of the student as a teacher. Students were likely to be highly motivated or at least conscious of where they needed to enrich their preparation.

The planning for this workshop was based on this assumption. Given this, it was essential to structure a situation which could capitalize on this motivation without in any way producing an environment which prescribed certain experiences and thus reduced the capacity of the individual to make decisions relevant to his or her own needs. A complexity was the ideas of the college staff about appropriate student action following this extensive exposure to the classroom. The validity of these ideas was recognized, but it was felt to be a tenuous exercise to operate on them to the extent that they became prescriptions. The compromise was to retain the ideas, aided by student feedback during the practice teaching, but to steer clear of prescription. To do this, it was necessary to provide within the structure of the workshop a 'core' of experiences which, it was assumed, most students could benefit from, but to give them an open choice with regard to what they would do with these experiences.

Thus there were a number of components which can be represented as follows:

The student	*The teacher educator*
—fresh from nine weeks of practice teaching; first appointment to school within four months	—with considerable experience in what may be necessary in terms of skills and knowledge for people in this situation

—highly motivated to be better prepared for the task, particularly in light of the nine weeks' field experience

—possessing experience concerning personal difficulties and successes in teaching, and thus in a situation where identification of problems was possible.

—not in possession of accurate measuring instruments to determine specifically if these ideas were appropriate to all people

—aware of the need to be careful about prescribing experiences but still professionally responsible to students.

The reconciliation of these varying components was achieved by the decision to establish a communications network with the dual purpose of providing appropriate experiences and choice according to need.

Thus a three-component *learning network* was established as the organizational centre of the workshop. This network strongly resembled Illich's ideal learning environment.

The network

More specifically, the network took the following form:

(i) Resources Convenient and easily accessible arrangements of curriculum materials, books, magazines, aids, etc. related to the work of the classroom teacher were provided for the students.

(ii) Peers Students were encouraged to exchange experiences and information, get together on common tasks, experiment and develop materials. This was facilitated by providing notice boards, rooms and booking facilities.

(iii) Models A context was established in which students had access to people who could give advice, demonstrations and assistance in modifying and establishing approaches to teaching. The 'models' were practising advisory teachers, teachers, administrators and other specialists from the South Australian Department of Education, as well as lecturers and tutors from within the college.

All people participated on the basis of open invitation and the offer of their services to the network. The college met incidental and travel expenses for people from the department.

Student responsibilities—contracting and assessment

For the first two days of the workshop, students and lecturers worked together in groups of 15, identifying problems and issues which needed to be dealt with. Students, by this time, had a comprehensive programme which listed all the necessary details on the consultant sessions offered in the 'models' network and thus were able to select sessions appropriate to their needs. Booking sheets were provided for consultant sessions to determine demand and also control numbers where necessary.

At the end of the first two days students submitted a contract in which they indicated the major themes of what they intended to do and the use they planned to make of the network. At the completion of the unit students wrote a self-evaluation in which they reflected on their original aims in terms of what they had done to fulfil them, the outcomes, and their personal assessment of the value of the experience.

The workshop reflected a position on assessment which placed the student as central to the procedure with the lecturer as a consultant and adviser who could, if troubled by what he saw in the contract or report on the same, intervene.

Thus, the major responsibility in the areas of planning, identification of objectives, reflection and evaluation of outcomes, rested with the student. Carl Rogers' views on relevancy and meaningful learning were not far in the background in the establishment of these procedures.

Overview

It is possible to view this workshop as an 'open' educational experience. Three themes were implicit in its design and operation. They were structure, trust and responsibility.

These themes were reflected in the workshop as follows:

Structure	—provision of a communications network.
	clear statement of general purposes and procedures designed to facilitate these.
	assistance from college staff in student planning and implementation of programmes.
Trust	—students were trusted to do what they stated they would do.
	apart from initial planning sessions and weekly follow-through on these, no formal check was taken on attendance.
	students had the major responsibility for evaluating their work and the design of the workshop conveyed quite clearly that there were no tangible ways of objectively determining otherwise.
Responsibility	—students had to take the initiative in the planning and implementation of their work.

Problems and Effectiveness

In the two years that this workshop has been offered, there have been no fundamental problems. Questionnaires have been administered both times and student response has been most positive. This is not to say that there have been no difficulties, in fact the second year of the programme revealed a number of weaknesses in terms of organization and spread of the consultants, particularly in the secondary area. However, it is gratifying to note that the basic concept of the course has met with near total approval from all those involved. Students particularly like the opportunities the course offers them to concentrate on practical issues as well as the trust placed in them as professionals.

Recommendations

It would seem that in professional training there are many opportunities for institutions to tap the resources of the schools and associated services. There are also many opportunities for student determined use of these resources and planning of their learning experiences.

This innovation has shown that people can take responsibility for important aspects of their learning and that the structure is a most viable way of marshalling resources from within the total professional community.

Commentary

All too frequently in teacher education programmes there is little real endeavour to integrate campus studies with the students' practice teaching experience. Also, while there may be an increasing concern to prepare students for practice teaching in some programmes, the attempts to follow-up students' practice-teaching needs and problems are rare or piecemeal. The field experience workshop developed by Gunning seeks to provide such integration and, at the same time, permit students to pursue activities likely to meet their teaching needs.

The design of the workshop programme rests on several powerful principles. Basically, it gives the students a *large measure of responsibility* for their own learning. Their opinions are sought in pre-planning the programmes; they then select sessions and work with peers and resources according to their needs; they evaluate the outcomes. Nevertheless it is by no means a *laissez-faire* programme. Staff develop the general structure and timetable, choose consultants, approve student contracts, and meet groups regularly for planning and follow-through sessions. The *motivation of students is high*, not simply because of the need-oriented choices the course provides, but because of a sense of urgency felt by participants. They have just completed their final practice period. Appointment to schools looms a few short months away. Now apparently is the time to overcome practical problems, to eliminate teaching weaknesses, to plug gaps in professional knowledge.

The general reaction of students to the workshops has been very favourable. Most comment on the reality and relevance of the activities and many see the course as the most valuable one in their teacher preparation. They did, however, make a number of worthwhile suggestions for its improvement and expansion. Some students felt lethargic and tired at the beginning of the course because no break was provided between it and nine weeks of sustained practice teaching. They suggested a day be provided to relax and talk in friendship groups, to let off steam, before the start of the workshops. It was also suggested that after the completion of the workshops that students come together to share products (materials, devices, catalogues etc.) of the four-week programme. Other students suggested that they be alerted to the follow-up workshops before practice teaching (not towards its end) so they could reflect upon their needs and what should be included in the course. Some students felt the four weeks of workshops was not adequate enough time to meet their needs and suggested that the course be extended. A few students believed that workshops of similar design should be conducted concurrently with practice teaching on one day a week through third year and even in second year. Only then would their needs be located early and sufficient time be provided to fulfil them. One must remark that these last comments have much to recommend them, even though the workshops might lose that 'sense of urgency' (mentioned above) of an end-on course.

The running of the course in its present form has a number of problems. The identification of student problems and needs is often difficult. Staff make a list of suggestions (based on previous experience), and request students to comment on these and to suggest others during practice teaching. Communication with students in scattered schools is difficult. Common problems are chosen for consultant sessions, but the unique and perhaps substantial needs of some individuals are unavoidably neglected. The selection of consultants to cover the various workshop topics sometimes presents difficulty since a combination of relevant expertise and fresh practical outlook is considered a necessary qualification. Scheduling the various sessions is often difficult. Some sessions are overbooked and need repeating. The timetable limits the choices of some students with certain combinations of needs.

But despite these difficulties, the course works, and works well. It is a purposeful, real and progressive programme which could well be adapted in other institutions.

[C. T.]

RESOURCES DEVELOPMENT

TEACHING SKILLS DEVELOPMENT PROJECT (TSDP)

Department of Education
University of Sydney

PROFESSOR C. TURNEY

Background and Context

Since the beginning of 1972 the *Teaching Skills Development Project* (TSDP) in the Department of Education of the University of Sydney has been engaged in the production of videotape-based courses on specific teaching skills for use in both pre-service and in-service teacher-education programmes for primary and secondary teachers. These courses have been named *Sydney Micro Skills*.

Funded by a grant from the Australian Advisory Committee on Research and Development in Education, the TSDP team has carried out its work with the co-operation of three main organizations: the Sydney University Television Service has produced the audiovisual programmes, the New South Wales Department of Education has facilitated access to schools and the co-operation of teachers, and the Sydney University Press publishes the printed materials and markets all the courses. The courses are made available on a *non-profit basis* under copyright held by the University of Sydney.

After a long and rather fruitless search for a single overall criterion of teacher effectiveness, in the early 1960s a number of educationists in the United States began to look for an alternative approach. The answer was to take the same path that the more mature sciences had already followed: 'If variables at one level of phenomena do not exhibit lawfulness, break them down' (Gage, 1968, p. 602). A search was commenced for the so-called 'micro-criteria' of teacher effectiveness—the effectiveness of small, specifically defined aspects of the teaching act (Gage, 1962). This new line of endeavour soon coalesced with the concept of microteaching which was then being developed. If research could analyze teaching into fairly precise, manageable units in the form of skills then microteaching seemed an admirable means of developing the skills in teachers (as well as being in itself an important tool for research on teaching). Over the last decade researchers and teacher educators have gradually realized the exciting promise of these two movements, and though research and development have only really just begun, already they have yielded valuable scientific bases for teaching about teaching. The *Sydney Micro Skills* courses emerge from this general background and it is hoped that they will make some small contribution to it.

Aims and Principles of Operation

The courses have the general purpose of developing in teachers a practical and penetrating understanding of a limited number of teaching skills which, in the light of research and experience, seem to be significant in changing pupil behaviour. More particularly, the courses aim at facilitating the acquisition of the skills through observation, practice and evaluation. Though the courses have been constructed with a view to their application in the various phases of microteaching and in whole-class settings during practice teaching, they could have a range of other uses in teacher-education programmes. For example, at one end of the scale, they might be used simply to support and illustrate lecture or seminar courses on teaching, or at the other end, they might be employed to help remedy individual student-teacher weaknesses identified during practice teaching.

The courses are not intended to be an inflexible system rigidly adhered to by their users. Hopefully they provide teacher educators and student teachers with a resource of ideas, materials and activities. Some of these might be discarded and others refined and supplemented to meet the requirements of the programmes or the needs of the student teacher. Nor are the skills themselves to be rigidly applied. Teachers should be encouraged to experiment with them, to adapt them to their own personal style, to the children they teach, and the purposes and context of their teaching.

The Plan and Its Implementation

The priority skills

The selection of teaching skills to receive priority in course development was based on two main considerations: (i) an assessment of the needs of Australian teacher-education programmes, and (ii) the checking of these needs against an overview of research and theory on teaching.

During July to September 1972 a survey was conducted of the practices, needs and problems of Australian teacher-education programmes implementing microteaching (Turney *et al.*, 1973).

Among many other things, respondents from all of the thirty programmes purporting to be conducting microteaching expressed the need for high-quality, essentially Australian videotaped or filmed models on teaching skills, supplemented by a variety of printed instructional materials. When asked to list the skills upon which Australian models should initially be developed, the respondents indicated that there were clearly nine skills or clusters of skills which should receive priority. In rank order these were:

Questioning
Classroom management and discipline
Variability/varying the stimulus
Reinforcement
Explaining/exposition
Set induction/introductory procedures
Small group teaching
Developing thinking
Individualizing teaching.

Questioning was cited by approximately 90 per cent of respondents, and individualizing teaching by about 56 per cent. Next after individualizing teaching was closure or conclusion, cited by 30 per cent of respondents. Many other skills or behaviours were mentioned, among them being skills related to discussion, demonstrating, valuing, diagnosis and remediation, verbal flexibility, non-verbal cueing, using pupils' ideas, making structuring comments, and facilitating role playing.

The importance of the above nine priority skills areas was next checked against an overview of research, theory and development. The evidence seemed to support the contention that each area was significant in pupil learning in modern classrooms. The kind of data gathered on each skill is illustrated in the reviews in each Handbook. However, a word of caution. Though the research and theory related to each of the *Sydney Micro Skills* are compelling, especially when supplemented by experience of teacher educators, the final validity of the skills has yet to be proven.

Course series and sequence

Focusing mainly on the priority skill areas, the courses were progressively developed in groups or series of two or three. The grouping and sequencing of the courses have been somewhat arbitrarily made according to the skills' related-ness, complexity and degree of teacher dominance. The courses begin with relatively simple rather teacher-directed skills such as basic questioning, and lead on to more complicated child-oriented skills such as those related to small group teaching and discovery learning. The general sequence of courses is as follows:

Series 1—deals with the teaching skills of reinforcement, basic questioning, and variability.
Series 2—deals with explaining, introductory procedures and closure, and advanced questioning.
Series 3—includes discipline and classroom management skills.
Series 4—treats small group and individualized teaching skills.
Series 5—deals with skills related to developing pupils' thinking through discovery learning and creativity.

Course design

The survey data from Australian teacher-education institutions indicated the strong need for courses embracing two kinds of materials: (i) videotaped and filmed teaching episodes modelling the teaching skills, and (ii) printed materials including such aspects as a review of research and theory related to each skill and a statement of principles and practical suggestions for its implementation. Following the decision to produce materials to cover these two areas, the next major task was the determination of the design of the audiovisual part of the courses. Here an attempt was made to fashion the programmes on evidence derived from research on modelling in teacher education.

Each *Sydney Micro Skills* course has two complementary parts: (i) an *audiovisual programme* on film or videotape mediating models of the skill, and (ii) a *handbook* containing printed support materials (see Figure S.1).

Each of these parts has several main sections. The audiovisual programme contains first, illustrations of the components of the skill and a graphic summary;

Figure S.1 COURSE FORMAT

AUDIOVISUAL PROGRAMME	HANDBOOK
Model Components	Review of Research and Theory
	Rationale for Applying Skill in Classroom
Model Episode	Activities for Developing the Skill

and second, a complete teaching episode highlighting the use of these components. Each of these sections is of about fifteen minutes duration and emphasizes positive instances, visual cueing, and minimal basic commentary. The audiovisual programmes are available using either primary or secondary school pupils.

The handbook material on each skill has three sections: first, a review of the classroom and laboratory research and the theory related to the skill, with a teasing out of its implications for teaching; second, a section dealing with the rationale for applying the skill in the classroom and including a statement of the objectives of employing the skill, a discussion of principles underlying its use and an analysis of the skill's component practices; and third, a section containing student involvement activities and devices to help them acquire the particular teaching skill. These include (i) recognition exercises on the skill model and its transcript; (ii) application exercises using a peer-group class; (iii) suggestions for implementing and evaluating the use of the skill in microteaching (including skill observation records, simple coding systems, and pupil response sheets); and (iv) suggestions for implementing the skill during practice teaching. Finally there is a select bibliography of further basic reading.

Process of course development

Following the preceding ideas on course design each of the *Sydney Micro Skills* courses currently passes through a six-stage process of research and development:

1. *Data gathering* This initial step includes a review of the literature (both research and theory) related to the skill, and the preparation of a report which will provide a theoretical and empirical basis for the course.

2. *Planning* This step concerns the translation of the evidence, consolidated in stage 1, into objectives, principles and component practices for implementing the skill in the classroom. It includes the identification and definition of specific skill components to be used in the course, a statement of objectives and principles, and determination of course organization.

3. *Developing preliminary course materials* This includes preparation of videotaped teaching episodes and making the initial draft of the handbook. The teaching episodes are collected in school locations and follow a four-step procedure of development: (i) teacher briefing, (ii) videotaped rehearsal, (iii) feedback and refinement, and (iv) final videotaping. This work is carried out in conjunction

with the Sydney University Television Service and the New South Wales Department of Education.

4. *Developing prototype courses* The main task in this stage is the production of videotaped programmes. This involves (i) the study and analysis of material collected and a selection of specific episodes, (ii) the preparation of scripts and graphics, (iii) the audiorecording of commentary, and (iv) the studio editing of the tapes. A second draft of the handbook is made to correlate with special aspects of the audiovisual programme. Activities are devised to assist student teachers in the recognition and application of the skill.

5. *Field testing and prototype course revision* Both the audiovisual and printed parts of the course are introduced to student teachers and teacher educators by members of the project team. Data are collected mainly by questionnaire and interview. The course is revised in the light of this feedback.

6. *Course dissemination and distribution* This final step includes reporting on the courses to professional meetings and in journals, and issuing notices to institutions. It also includes collaboration with the Sydney University Press which is publishing the handbooks and assuming responsibility for the distribution of the courses, and with Sydney University Television Service which is managing the transposition of the audiovisual programmes to specified videotape standards or 16mm film.

The *Sydney Micro Skills* courses are in no way conceived as the be-all and end-all of teacher preparation. If teachers are to learn to play such roles as scholar, innovator, administrator, curriculum planner, and child psychologist in school contexts, then teacher education programmes obviously need to go far beyond the teaching behaviours treated in these courses. Nevertheless, the development of a repertoire of basic teaching skills and competencies which have sound empirical and theoretical foundations, undeniably forms a vital task of teacher education.

Problems and Effectiveness

Since the first public airing of Series 1 in 1972, the courses have experienced a range of reactions—strong support from some, mild disapproval from others; suspicious trial by some, immediate implementation by others. Now it seems that such polarized positions have given away to generally favourable and widespread acceptance. In that initiating year, four main groups of teacher educators reacted negatively to our work: (i) those who regarded teaching as an art which, if subjected to analysis, would be destroyed; (ii) those who regarded teaching as a science to be subjected to rigorous research, who claimed that it would be some decades before anything could be validly said about it; (iii) those proponents of open education who believed our skills were irrelevant to open settings and were even counter-productive to pupil learning; and (iv) those curriculum specialists who saw the intrusion of our courses into their domains as rather impudent and perhaps threatening.

Gradually, in the hands of people who believed in our work, the courses have largely surmounted these sources of opposition. Indeed, the acceptance which Series 1 and 2 have won has been much more extensive and approving than we had ever hoped. These courses have been purchased by over 75 per cent of Australian teacher-education institutions. So far this has involved the dissemination of over 500 individual audiovisual programmes and more than 11,000 handbooks.

The *Sydney Micro Skills* are being used in a variety of settings and in a variety of ways. They have been employed in pre- and in-service education of primary and secondary school teachers, in military education, in training practice teaching supervisors, in the education of tertiary teachers, in research projects, and in parent education. In such settings they have been used to illustrate lectures, as stimulus materials in seminars, in group preparation for microteaching and for whole-class teaching, in self-instructional courses on teaching, and in classrooms of individual teachers. Some institutions use the courses with no adaptation; some supplement them with their own materials; others modify them liberally; and others use them as the basis for developing new local materials.

We are naturally delighted with the success of the products of the Teaching Skills Development Project. But it has not been easy. Our greatest problem has been pressure of work. All members of the research team are full-time academics. We have had, however, the help of one harassed research assistant, and the co-operation of a small group of equally busy television personnel and teachers. The research team's lack of time has combined with the want of expertise in some areas of teaching to require the co-option of several consultants to share the responsibility for the development of certain courses. Money, or want of it, also has been a problem. Although the funding for the TSDP has been quite generous by Australian standards, compared with similar (and perhaps less successful) research and development projects overseas, our annual budget has been extremely small. This has meant constant worries about seeking the cheapest 'best' way to carry out our work.

Finally, we realize there will ultimately be a need to refine, extend, up-date and even discontinue some aspects of all the courses we are constructing. This will be necessitated by the emergence of new research evidence on teaching, by the results of careful evaluation of our courses, and simply by changes in styles of teaching. Eventual obsolescence is a problem to be faced by all innovative approaches. Certainly we have not said the first or the last word about teaching competencies and their mediation, but at least we have said and done something—something which evidently is fulfilling a real need in Australian teacher-education programmes.

REFERENCES

Gage, N. L., 'Paradigms for Research on Teaching' in Gage, N. L. (ed.), *Handbook of Research on Teaching*, Rand McNally, Chicago 1963, 94–141.

Gage, N. L., 'An Analytical Approach to Research on Instructional Methods', *Phi Delta Kappan*, June 1968, 49 (10), 601–6.

Turney, C., J. C. Clift, M. J. Dunkin and R. D. Traill, *Microteaching: Research, Theory and Practice*, Sydney University Press, 1973.

Commentary

The Teaching Skills Development Project is one of the first important research and development projects in Australian teacher education. The work of the project has at least four features largely new to the Australian educational scene: (i) *Translating research and theory into practice*. A central concern of the research team has been to base their analysis of teaching skills on existing research and theory—a concern too often neglected in the field of education. (ii) *Mobilizing collaborative effort.* The production and dissemination of high-quality, reasonably priced products have been facilitated by the close co-operation of a number of agencies both outside and within the university. (iii) *Basing project orientations on an analysis of client need.* Both the design and content of the courses have been strongly influenced by the survey of the needs of Australian teacher educators. This fact accounts for much of the success of the project in terms of courses purchased. (iv) *Field-testing and revision of prototype courses.* The products of the project have been revised in the light of feedback from potential users to improve the materials' relevance, style and effectiveness.

Although the courses developed by the project were initially greeted by strong and somewhat unreasoned opposition from some teacher educators, they have now won wide acceptance. Part of this acceptance has been due to the courses' flexible format. The courses were not conceived as a tightly structured system but rather a resource to be adapted by teacher educators to their own needs and those of their students.

One of the problems of the development of educational materials is their ultimate obsolescence. In a few years there will be the need to revise and update the courses with the emergence of new research evidence, new modes of teaching, and new techniques for mediating audiovisual and printed materials.

It is to be hoped that the TSDP will not be suddenly disbanded with the completion of its schedule courses. The expertise acquired by team members, the areas of co-operation built up, and the interest engendered among teacher educators underline the good sense of the project continuing its work. There is a whole range of teaching behaviours and responsibilities to be explored, and there are some areas of teacher education (especially tertiary teaching) in great need of materials similar to the *Sydney Micro Skills* courses.

[D. T.]

THE AUSTRALIAN SCIENCE TEACHER EDUCATION PROJECT

Canberra College of Advanced Education

D. Driscoll

and

Monash University

Professor P. Fensham

Background and Context

The Australian Science Teacher Education Project (ASTEP) is based on two institutions (Canberra College of Advanced Education and Monash University) although a number of other teacher education institutions have been involved in the project at the developmental, field-testing or evaluation stages.

ASTEP is an Australian adaptation and extension of a United Kingdom version of a similar name which began late in 1969 with financial support from the Nuffield Foundation. STEP attempted to pool the collective wisdom and experience of those working in the field of science teacher education as a basis for producing a number of units of work suitable for use in colleges of education and university departments of education. One of the co-ordinators (Driscoll) visited the University of Leicester in 1969–70 where he was associated with one of the two STEP co-ordinators, and was involved in the production of one of the STEP units. His experience there led him to want to see the STEP materials adopted and extended to meet Australian needs. During 1971 he sounded out a number of other science teacher educators, in particular Peter Fensham, and as a result late in 1971 approached the Myer Foundation for support for a pilot study involving the use in Australia of STEP trial material. The perceived usefulness of such material prompted the innovators to bring together a planning group representing universities, teachers colleges and CAEs, and involving people from several states. In 1972 the STEP material was field-tested in all Australian states with a view to identifying: (i) those STEP units which were appropriate as they were for the Australian scene; (ii) those STEP units which needed some significant modification before they would become useful— translation into 'Strine', changing English examples to Australian ones, and the like; and (iii) areas of interest to science teacher educators where STEP materials did not meet needs and where additional units could usefully be developed.

In early 1973 some fifteen working parties were established in five states, and in 1973 and 1974 some fifty additional units, suitable for use with intending teachers of science, were produced. In 1974 and 1975 these were field-tested, evaluated and re-written, and the final materials will be produced in early 1976.

About two-thirds of all relevant teacher education institutions, and over half of those involved in science teacher education in Australia have been involved in the project in one form or another.

Apart from the two overall co-ordinators already mentioned (Driscoll and Fensham), the main personnel are two regional co-ordinators (Mr J. R. Northfield, Monash University, and Mrs J. Gledhill, Kuring-gai College of Advanced Education), an evaluation co-ordinator (Associate Professor L. D. Mackay, Monash University) and a Services and Resources Co-ordinator (Mrs J. E. Driscoll).

The project was intended to meet several needs in the education of intending teachers of science in Australian schools. Firstly, there has been in many countries a recent change in the approach to teaching science. The emphasis is now less on the didactic teaching of an established body of facts, concepts and principles, and more on the viewing of science as a way of looking at a situation or of approaching a problem, and a wide variety of excellent materials have been developed to serve this end. The effectiveness of these new curricula has however been less than it might because of the tendency of teachers to teach the new materials in the traditional ways. There is a belated but general recognition of the need to educate the incoming generation of teachers (and to re-educate those already teaching) in the spirit of the new courses. The recognition of this need in the United Kingdom led to the establishment of STEP, but only some ten years after the Nuffield science materials began to be produced there. There seemed a need to reduce this time lag in Australia.

A second *raison d'être* for the project was the lack of communication that existed between those involved in the education of science teachers in Australia, or even within a particular state. It was hoped that the project would provide a means of markedly increasing this dialogue through the establishment of a number of working groups and intensive working parties who would work together in both the developmental and trialling stages.

Aims and Principles of Operation

The main aims of the project were to provide a range of options (in the form of curriculum materials) to science teacher educators at the primary and secondary level which would lead to a greater ability of science teachers to cope with the changing approach to the teaching of science in schools, and with the greater degree of curriculum autonomy and responsibility which individual schools and teachers are being required to assume. Additionally, as indicated above, the project was intended to establish something of a communications network amongst science teacher educators in Australia in order to fill the existing communications gap.

The Plan and Its Implementation

The intention of ASTEP was not to produce a course complete in itself, but to develop a varied collection of units of work from which an individual tutor could select those most appropriate to his course. Generally speaking, it was felt that the units should avoid a lecture-type presentation of material, but adopt a workshop approach in which students, in groups of varying size, would address themselves to a variety of tasks—role-playing in a simulated classroom situation, analyzing a transcript of pupils' discussion of a particular experiment, organizing the concepts in a particular area into a reasonable teaching sequence, and so forth.

To this end, the planning group established some fifteen working groups in all states except Western Australia and in 1973 each group produced 2–3 units in areas of interest to them and/or in which they had particular experience or expertise. These units were printed in trial form and field-tested in 1974 in a large number of teacher education institutions. The units in this first 'wave' were analysed from the point of view of content, approach followed, and the extent to which certain perceived needs were being met by the unit concerned. (These student needs were derived by Dr L. D. Mackay from his evaluation work with STEP in a sabbatical year at the University of Leicester.)

As a result of this analysis and of the feedback comments of those who field-tested the 'Wave I' units, a number of 'gap' areas were identified. Additional units were developed from late 1973 to early 1975 to fill these gaps, the development being undertaken by most of the 1973 working groups and by two intensive two-day working parties in late 1973. These Wave II units were field-tested and evaluated in 1974 and the first half of 1975. In the light of the trials of the material, the units were re-written during 1975 and the final material (print, videotape, audiotape and slides) will be published in early 1976. The print material will be available at no cost to participants in the project and to relevant institutions in Australia, and the non-print material will be available at cost.

The pilot stage of the project was funded by a small grant ($1,500) from the Myer Foundation; the development, trial and evaluation section was supported by AACRDE to the extent of $20,000 for the period 1 January 1973 to 31 December 1974, and it is anticipated that a supplementary amount of some $4,200 will be granted to cover the cost of publication.

Problems and Effectiveness

The problems encountered stemmed from two sources, viz., the 'shoestring' nature of the budget, and the dispersion of those involved. More specifically, the project would have benefited from having expertise readily available in the graphics, design and photography areas, from having the funds to run more than two intensive working parties (which were potentially, and to an extent actually, very fruitful), and from being able to follow up the ideas and suggestions thrown up at the working parties.

The effectiveness of the materials produced was evaluated by the giving of a questionnaire to the following groups of people:

(a) Tutors who had actually used the material.
(b) Tutors who 'armchair' evaluated the material.
(c) Students with whom the material had been used.
(d) Teachers who had just begun teaching who 'armchair' evaluated it from a pre-service and in-service use viewpoint.
(e) Experienced teachers.
(f) Experts in particular subject areas or areas of educational theory.

The evaluation feedback is currently being analysed by Professor Mackay.

The following papers concerning the ASTEP Project have been written:

Driscoll, D. R., 'How Shall We Teach the Future Science Teachers?', N.A.T.E. Workshop Paper, Canberra, October 1972.

Fensham, P. J., J. R. Northfield, and D. R. Driscoll, 'ASTEP: A Model for Developing Curriculum Materials in Teacher Education', *The South Pacific Journal of Teacher Education*, 1974, 2 (3), 5–11.

Mackay, L. D. and J. R. Northfield, 'The Use of a Formative Evaluation Model for ASTEP', *Research in Science Education*, 1974, 4, 65–76.

Mackay, L. D. and J. R. Northfield, 'Validity of Perceived Need Satisfaction as a Curriculum Evaluation Criterion', *Research 1975*.

Northfield, J. R., 'The Australian Science Teacher Education Project', paper presented at the SPATE Conference, Macquarie University, July 1975.

In addition, three newsletters have been circulated to all participants and other interested parties.

Recommendations

Some of these have been implied by earlier comments. These concern the need for a more realistic budget which could lead to a more efficient use of time of the professional participants. The project will formally terminate in 1976. However, since the view of the project is one which provides an increased number of options to the science teacher educator rather than to produce a complete course, it is in a very real sense open-ended. To the extent that it does not turn out this way in practice, the project will have failed in a very important respect.

Although the materials were designed with the needs of intending science teachers in mind, much of it is not science-specific, and could be either used as it is or readily adapted for other teachers. Quite a number of the units, especially those concerned with the development of curriculum skills, could also be used with little or no modification at the in-service level. This has, in fact, occurred in two states.

Commentary

In recent years there have been many examples of efforts to introduce curriculum materials produced in overseas countries into various levels of the Australian educational system. The Australian Science Teacher Education Project as described in this case study represents a most interesting and carefully devised approach to the introduction of such overseas curriculum materials.

A feature of the project has been the procedures developed by the co-ordinators to ensure that the materials were subjected to a thorough review and, if appropriate, revision before they were accepted for widespread usage in Australian programmes. The review and adaptation stages have been approached through a 'grassroots' model—the involvement of a large number of science educators (who would later use the materials) in the initial trialling and later reviewing to produce the adapted versions of the materials. This has led to several advantageous aspects of the ASTEP approach. The target population (i.e. science teacher educators) were brought into an active participatory role from the early stage when overseas materials were being considered for use in an Australian situation. This provided an opportunity for the science educators to have a close contact with the ideas underlying the new materials as well as being in a situation where they could use the materials in an exploratory manner and suggest adaptations to suit local requirements. This approach is a welcome contrast to the widespread approach so often used whereby the users' first contact with the materials is when it is presented in a finally packaged form ready for use in a teaching programme. The innovators have also commented on the value of their approach as a means of assisting science teacher educators in their professional development. It certainly represents a contrast to the type of involvement such educators might have experienced had the new curriculum materials been presented to them in conferences or seminar situations where the professional development was far more passive than that present in the ASTEP approach.

Another advantage of this project has been the way in which it has provided a channel for communication between teacher educators who are involved in a particular curriculum field. The establishment of working parties in the five states involved meant that considerable discussion has taken place within the various states by people who may have had little previous opportunity to be involved in lengthy discussions about their curriculum area with colleagues from other institutions. The fact that such discussions and allied activity have led to the production of some fifty units of work would in itself justify such communication taking place. This is also noteworthy when one considers the distances which separated many of the working groups as this could, in fact, represent a disadvantage in the curriculum development model adopted by the ASTEP innovation.

The ASTEP innovation does, therefore, illustrate one of the major problems which innovators face if they are introducing a new curriculum project across several of the Australian states. The dissemination of information becomes a very demanding part of the budget in such a task and this item alone could often push budget estimates so high that funding authorities may be concerned about accepting sponsorship for the project. If the highly commendable 'grassroots' approach as used by the ASTEP project is adopted, an Australia-wide innovation will require strong financial support. The co-ordinators' report on the project has referred to their concern that the on-going success of ASTEP might be affected because of the project's 'shoestring' budget and they make some interesting comments on estimated costs for similar projects.

Interviews with participants in the project have clearly indicated to the research team that the innovators have been most successful in getting science teacher educators to feel involved with the development of ASTEP materials. Typical of the comments made to the team was the following statement, 'Before ASTEP we ran around in circles ... ASTEP has sent us in the right direction'. It is also interesting to note that the co-ordinators built into the model means of gaining feedback from participants. Teachers, students, 'armchair' evaluators and specialists from outside the science curriculum area were some of the sources used for such information. Interesting work on student need satisfaction is being undertaken by Mackay and the information he makes available on the evaluation of the ASTEP materials should prove of interest to all involved in teacher education.

The ASTEP project is recommended to teacher educators as an example of how an Australian-wide curriculum innovation might be approached. It is particularly useful as a model to involve the user in the development of the curriculum materials and in its approach of making subsequent evaluations of how effective such materials have been when introduced into teaching programmes.

[R. T.]

CURRICULUM RESOURCES CENTRE (CRC)

School of Teacher Education
Canberra CAE

G. BURKHARDT AND SYLVIA RICHARDSON

Background and Context

The Curriculum Resources Centre in the School of Teacher Education of the Canberra College of Advanced Education was established in 1972 before the school moved into its own building. Planning for the new building included the design for the Curriculum Resources Centre and the centre moved into its permanent location when the building was opened at the beginning of the 1974 academic year. The Curriculum Resources Centre occupies the ground floor of the building and affords ready access to adjacent tutorial and workshop areas (Figure C.1).

The Centre comprises a multi-media collection of teaching materials and teaching aids, materials workshops, as well as display and workshop facilities.

The CRC is used by the 1,200 students now enrolled in education courses. In addition to this number, some seven hundred teachers in Canberra schools are associated with those students in teaching practice, which association carries an entitlement to use the facilities of the centre.

The primary function of the centre is to provide a support role to the study of curriculum, and the materials and services which the centre offers are designed

Figure C.1 FLOOR PLAN OF CURRICULUM RESOURCES CENTRE (and adjacent facilities)

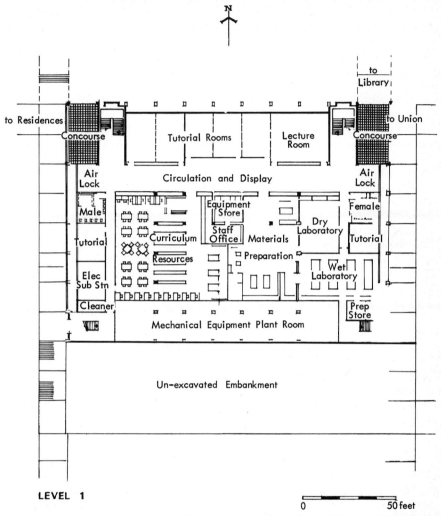

LEVEL 1

0   50 feet

with that end in view. This factor plus the intensive use of the centre by education students tends to pre-empt both facilities and services.

However, within the main context of its role the centre provides a number of ancillary services, some of which may be of interest to the community at large. Because of the extensive range of materials held, the centre is able to accommodate visiting groups of people, in particular those concerned with the purchase of materials for schools, who are interested to preview significant teaching kits, for example, with the object of evaluating them in terms of their own requirements. The centre holds an up-to-date and comprehensive range of educational catalogues and brochures which, taken in conjunction with the resources held, enables it to provide a considerable body of information on what educational materials are available.

The gallery which runs the full length of the building and is easily accessible, is capable of housing graphic and three-dimensional displays of interest to educators and, at times to the community in general. In the latter instance notice is given in *The Canberra Times* and visitors are welcome without prior notice or formality.

Aims and Principles of Operation

The special status of the CRC, with the ever-growing diversity of functions which continue to develop from that status, demands flexible organization free from the strictures and limitations which obtain in established systems. In addition, the highly specialized nature of the centre's holdings and facilities demands, for logistical reasons, that the diversity within that specialization be manifest. Organization, therefore, is flexible, fulfilling needs already implicit in the establishment of such a centre itself, whilst responding to needs which emerge in the day-to-day running of the centre. Consideration was given to curriculum workshop needs on the one hand, and on the other hand to the individual client both in his capacity as student and prospective teacher. Meanwhile, display function was to be integral to the collection. The system, therefore, disperses materials through a range of subject categories which correspond to school curriculum pre-requisites, provides for the inclusion of categories which have special significance for certain groups of teachers, as, for example, pre-school teachers and those preparing to teach in the Northern Territory, and keeps in contiguity on the shelves materials relating to a special subject area irrespective of their medium. Meanwhile, within this integrated multi-media collection spaces are used to display, in rotation, a number of significant materials. A subject index has been compiled which in turn considers the needs of the client, and which represents a compromise between a hierarchical system and specific entry system, based on a thesaurus devised to direct the user either to a tool of his trade, such as an abacus, or to educational theory and issues such as 'vertical grouping', 'compensatory education', and 'simulations'. Whereas level-ability codings are used in sequential learning materials, the use of such codings in general is avoided as they impose arbitrary restrictions, limiting range of choice.

The inter-filing of media on the shelves allows the student to be aware of alternatives. The complex shelf arrangement is counter-balanced at the circulation desk, however, where items borrowed separate into two categories— 'print' and 'non-print', the distinction being reinforced by two distinct types of borrowing slip each of which has two duplicates. The method of filing the duplicates enables immediate retrieval of all the information necessary to the smooth running of the loans function, and provides statistics which picture borrowing patterns and trends, in both print and non-print categories, giving important feedback on the use of the centre.

This organization, while supporting the on-going functions of the centre, is so devised that it can be transmuted into computer operational terms without interruption or modification. It is planned that the computer-link will fulfil a twofold purpose, to store information and to handle daily transactions at the circulation desk. Here the dichotomy of print and non-print categories flows on. For information storage, data are established which clearly define the item in question, distinguishing on the one hand the various forms of print material, and on the other hand the many forms and technical specifications of audio and visual materials as well as of three-dimensional learning devices such as mathematical equipment. The storage system assumes the possibility of new forms of learning materials. The store of information which will eventually build up will extend the subject index function in providing other channels of retrieval such as those of format and medium.

The statistics for borrowings indicate the high number of daily out-goings and imply a comparable number of daily returns. While computer assistance does not fully usurp the function of the desk attendant, it will enable that person to play a more effective part in the running of the centre.

The Plan and Its Implementation

The centre is fulfilling the following main functions:

(i) *Teaching:* It provides facilities for curriculum courses in pre-school, primary and secondary specializations available to both staff and students. In this way it fulfils an *information function* in respect of materials relevant to curriculum courses.

(ii) *Research and References:* The centre acts as a reference and borrowing centre for students and teachers preparing for curriculum studies workshops and school practice and for those staff with teaching interests in the various curriculum areas. In this way the centre fulfils a *storage and loans* function complementary to the college library. Although the college library plays a major role in the stocking and lending of some types of curricular materials, students and staff in teacher education will always require ready access to special materials and equipment such as test materials, maps, charts, kits, tapes, photographic materials, etc. not normally available in the college library.

(iii) *Materials Preparation:* The centre provides facilities for students to prepare materials for teaching practice, e.g. transparencies for overhead projection, picture displays, filmstrips, duplicated materials, slides, models. etc. The centre provides a *workshop function* with facilities for
—duplicating—lettering devices etc.;
—photocopying;
—filmstrip and slide projection;
—caneite and cork display areas;
—simple equipment for model construction with wood, metal, plastics, fabrics, etc.;
—school science and social science lab./prac. activities;
—dark room and photographic facilities for making filmstrips, enlarging, etc.;
—audio-taping and recording facilities—videotaping facilities;
—typing facilities—large lettering types for signs, displays and posters;
—facilities for making a variety of overhead projection transparencies;
—facilities for making 8mm films; and
—facilities for map-tracing and chart-making.

(iv) *A Display Function:* Facilities are available in the centre for display of curriculum materials as requested by lecturers either in the form of short exhibitions, or for specific teaching purposes, e.g. displays of photographs, teaching kits, models, charts, etc. Arrangements can be made through CRC staff for special publishers' display of books and equipment.

The public exhibition gallery is available for use by teacher education tutorial groups, groups from other schools of the college and community groups who wish to display material of various types. The gallery is large enough for two exhibitions simultaneously. Heavy bookings by groups have restricted each display to about two weeks. At least two months notice of a display or exhibition is required when booking the exhibition area.

(v) *Tutorial Support Function:* Tutors who wish to organize their tutorial group activities in the centre, using kits, facilities and equipment in the materials preparation area, are offered assistance in the setting-up and arrangement of curriculum materials and items from stacks and shelves. Trolleys can be made available (given advance notice) to enable tutors to take materials to nearby rooms where their workshop sessions are held. Special equipment and items can be held on restricted loan, or for use only in the centre, on the request of tutors who require their students to work with specialized materials in the centre.

The Curriculum Resources Centre is wholly funded and staffed through the budget of the School of Teacher Education. Six staff are employed in the centre; a senior curriculum officer, one curriculum officer, two curriculum assistants, one clerical assistant and one technical assistant. Excluding salaries for staff, recurrent expenditure for materials and equipment averages about $25,000 per year.

Problems and Effectiveness

The effectiveness of the centre is illustrated by the major innovative features which have been identified as highlights of its operation.

The innovative features claimed for the CRC encompass a combination of functions designed to serve the various needs of curriculum tutorial workshop classes, independent study and research needs of students and lecturers, and service functions in audiovisual and photographic facilities for students in their practical teaching programmes in schools. A public exhibition gallery is incorporated within the physical and administrative control of the centre.

A computer link project has been designed to provide a unique system of print and non-print materials classification for the control of indexing, cataloguing and borrowing, using a computer terminal linked with the College Computer Centre. This system for meeting the programme needs of information storage and retrieval is sufficiently flexible to enable control of a diverse range of items from non-print multi-media packages and kits, to films, diagrams, maps, charts, cassettes, records and books.

The system of administration for the centre through a Curriculum Resources Committee of the School of Teacher Education provides for representation from lecturers from respective curriculum areas, student representatives, representatives from librarianship courses in the School of Liberal Studies, College Instructional Media Centre, together with senior curriculum centre staff. On-going management of the centre is the responsibility of the senior curriculum officer, while decisions affecting financial policies and purchasing priorities are taken by the committee as a whole.

The development of relationships with community organizations and local schools is effected through the facilities of the public gallery which is part of the centre and exhibitions are arranged by the curriculum centre staff. Community organizations and other schools of the college use the gallery for display of their materials, items, etc. from time to time.

In so far as students are made aware of alternatives in teaching styles through the wide range of materials held, and in that, in this context, they enter into discussion with the personnel of the centre, the CRC plays in important consultative role. This role is extended by the use of audiovisual carrels as a testing ground, and by the use of the materials workshop where students learn to produce a variety of teaching aids using both simple bench operations as well as sophisticated audiovisual techniques.

This consultative function within its integral status in the School of Teacher Education determines that the CRC plays the role not only of support service but the dynamic role of enabling the student to translate into practical terms the inferences he has drawn from theoretical studies. This is well illustrated in the use of the Science Curriculum Laboratory where materials may be deployed in a teaching situation. With this dynamic role in mind, the centre is organized to present, in the form of facilities and materials, a range of educational experiences which, whilst not representing a totality, reflects the educational world in microcosm.

The principal problem encountered by the centre has been that as the range of materials held in stock increases and as the usage of the centre's facilities becomes more intense, availability of additional space is of concern. This is particularly connected with having sufficient room in the centre for workshop groups to move there for group activities.

Recommendations

The innovators considered that a more open-plan design for a CRC than the one in Canberra might deserve consideration by those planning to add a CRC to their available facilities. Apart from this suggestion, the innovators felt that the operation of the centre as described would prove a worthwhile model for teacher educators wishing to provide a similar range of services in a teacher education programme.

Commentary

The growth in available curriculum resources in recent years has meant that classroom teachers need a heightened, critical awareness of such resources. In addition, teachers now find that they have increasing supplies of technological equipment readily available to them and a need exists for those entering the teaching service to have had experiences in using a range of such equipment. Demands are therefore made on teacher education programmes to provide the pre-service teacher with a range of contacts with curriculum and technological resources during the pre-service years.

The CRC described above offers a wide range of experiences for student teachers. An extensive selection of commercially produced materials enables students to develop the critical skills so necessary when confronted with the task of selecting a particular project package from the many made available by the various publishing companies. At the same time, students are provided with facilities which would enable them to adapt such materials for their particular classroom teaching purposes or in fact to produce their own curriculum packages. The 'materials preparation' areas are seen as one of the real strengths of the

Canberra centre. Students who use such facilities should be well versed in the production skills needed to produce a range of curriculum resources for their own classrooms.

Teacher educators should find that the plan of the Canberra centre provides interesting guidelines. The provision of facilities which cater for many different kinds of activities, all of which interrelate in some way, will appeal to planners who are looking for flexible usage of a centre. The suggestion that a more open plan design may have added to this flexibility, should also be considered. It is also interesting to note that community usage has been envisaged—by attracting teachers to come to the teacher education institution to use the curriculum resources, and by attracting the general public through the availability of an extensive display area and exhibition gallery.

Intensive use of borrowing services, and constant revisions to the range of materials held by the centre has led to an investigation of how computer facilities might be called upon to make the operation of the centre more efficient. Institutions in similar circumstances would find it useful to explore this development further with the Canberra centre.

One other feature of the way in which this CRC functions is worthy of comment. Great care has been taken to develop the centre as an integral part of the various programmes run by the School of Teacher Education. This is not only reflected in the physical lay-out of the centre and its proximity to teaching spaces, but also in the organization and administration of the centre, and in the day-to-day relationships which exist between the school's teaching activities and usage of the CRC's facilities. It is interesting to note the composition of the committee which establishes the main administrative procedures for the centre, and the way in which this provides constant feedback on how staff and students view the centre's activities.

One question which this centre, and other facilities providing a similar range of services must inevitably face, is that which concerns the costs involved in offering such a resource to its students, Replacement of out-of-date and/or damaged stock, provision of materials for preparation areas, and the constant need to add resources which reflect new curriculum developments, are but a few of the sources of financial commitment which such a centre faces. Teacher educators contemplating the provision of such a facility need to be aware of the on-going nature of this problem and it should perhaps assume a more prominent role in the planning of such facilities.

In summary, the Canberra model for a curriculum resources centre is commended to teacher educators as well worthy of their closer inspection if they are concerned with providing student teachers with a wide range of experiences in curriculum studies and the resources available for classroom teachers.

[R. T.]

LABORATORY SCHOOL SCHEMES

LABORATORY SCHOOL ON CAMPUS

Salisbury East High School and Salisbury College of Advanced Education

J. G. DUNN
Senior Lecturer in Education

R. J. PEARMAN
Campus School Liaison Deputy Principal

Background and Context

The projected siting of a new teachers college on land adjacent to a secondary school offered a unique challenge for the development of a teacher education programme which would achieve successful integration of theory and practice. The Director of the college, R. S. Coggins, while in the United States in 1963–4, had visited a number of tertiary institutions which had associated schools, and had become aware of many of the intrinsic difficulties which have subsequently led to the phasing out of many on-campus schools in that country. The Secondary Division of the South Australian Education Department from the outset had laid down certain conditions under which a close relationship between the college and the school could develop. The administration and staffing of the school was to remain the responsibility of the Education Department. Both the Director and the South Australian Education Department agreed that it would not become a special school with over-elaborate facilities, a selective student intake and a highly selected staff.

Believing that one of the most effective ways of initiating and maintaining the close interrelationship between the college and the school would be through a joint appointment of certain staff to both institutions, the Director of the college proposed the introduction of the position, 'lecturer-teacher'. The lecturer-teacher would be responsible for curriculum courses at the college and would also teach a number of classes at the school. Half of his time would be spent at the school and the remainder at the college. The payment of the salary of the lecturer-teacher would be a shared responsibility of the Secondary Division of the Education Department and the Division of Teacher Education and Services, which then administered the college. While agreeing to accept college staff as regular teachers at the school, for short or extended periods, the Secondary Division of the Education Department did not, however, accept the concept of a

223

Figure SE.1 SALISBURY EDUCATION COMPLEX

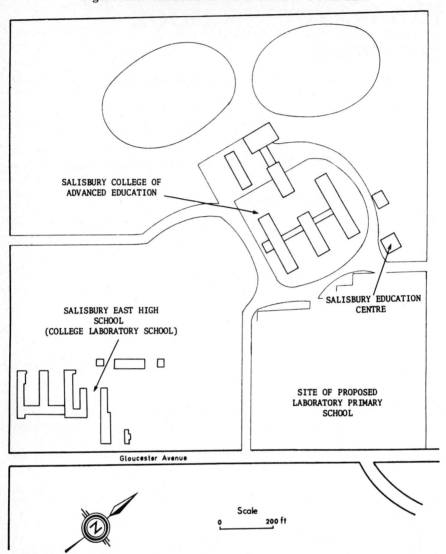

SALISBURY COLLEGE OF
ADVANCED EDUCATION

SALISBURY EDUCATION
CENTRE

SALISBURY EAST HIGH
SCHOOL
(COLLEGE LABORATORY SCHOOL)

SITE OF PROPOSED
LABORATORY PRIMARY
SCHOOL

Gloucester Avenue

Scale

0   200 ft

formal half-time appointment and contribution towards the salary of a lecturer-teacher.

Notwithstanding this difficulty, the decision was made by the college to proceed with the appointment of lecturer-teachers to the college staff. The full salary, by necessity, would be paid by the Division of Teacher Education and Services as part of the college salary bill. A concession granted to the college, because these staff members would be working half-time at the school, was the increase in staff establishment by one-half for each lecturer-teacher appointed. In 1970, the year in which the college moved to the Salisbury East site (Figure SE.1), the first two lecturer-teachers were appointed and commenced college duties, which included regular teaching at the campus school. Further lecturer-teachers, covering a range of subject fields, were appointed in subsequent years. These appointments were supernumerary in the school staffing pattern.

A further staffing innovation of note is that of the 'teacher-tutor'. This position on the laboratory-school staff was instituted as a result of an initiative taken by the Secondary Division of the South Australian Education Department in 1974. The integration of college curriculum studies courses with classroom activities had grown to such an extent and had proved so successful that there was an obvious need for some school staff to be given responsibilities more particularly related to college courses and students. It was initially proposed that the teacher-tutor position would be openly advertised and that teachers throughout the state would be given the opportunity to apply for it. This procedure was not, however, followed. Instead, the school was allocated an additional deputy principal with school-college liaison responsibilities and the total staff entitlement of the school was increased by two teachers. Final selection of teacher-tutors was made from present staff who had expressed interest in extending their involvement with the college programme. The relevant college curriculum-studies lecturers were invited to take part in discussions leading to the choice of the teachers who were subsequently invited to become teacher-tutors.

Aims and Principles of Operation

The aims of the campus school in its relationship with the college include the following:

(i)   to provide opportunities for the integration of theory and practice in professional courses;
(ii) to provide special teaching opportunities (including microteaching) for students;
(iii) to facilitate the involvement of college staff in classroom teaching (including opportunities to teach co-operatively with school staff and college students);
(iv) to provide opportunities for educational research by college staff in conjunction with school staff and sometimes with graduate diploma students;
(v)   to enable close supervision of remedial teaching undertaken by college students who have experienced difficulties during teaching practice.

The role of the lecturer-teachers and teacher-tutors are identified with the aims of the campus school as outlined above. The lecturer-teacher through his close contact with school children sets out to support the curriculum studies course with classroom illustrations involving college students in observation and participation. The following aspects of the teacher-tutor role are complementary to those of the lecturer-teachers:

(i)   to apply in the classroom concepts introduced during lecture/tutorials;
(ii) to participate in tutorial discussions with college students;
(iii) to assist college students in the preparation of student teaching assignments to be carried out either at the laboratory school as part of curriculum studies courses or at other schools during the block practice teaching periods;
(iv) to act in a consultative capacity during block teaching practice (including visits to the schools);
(v)   to provide remedial assistance in post-practice teaching situations;

(vi) to facilitate access to classrooms for research projects;

(vii) to draw upon and co-ordinate college and school resources in the in-service training of teachers.

Underlying the planning and implementation of the innovations associated with the on-campus laboratory school has been a recognition of, and respect for the autonomy of each institution and the acceptance of the fact that each necessarily has a different prime responsibility.

The Plan and Its Implementation

The statement of aims in the preceding section relating to the roles of the campus school, lecturer-teachers and teacher-tutors suggests the main features of the laboratory school-college interrelationship. These activities have not been imposed, but may be seen as natural developments taking place over a considerable period of time and only as a result of discussion and mutual agreement between the college and the school.

The first two lecturer-teachers (appointed in 1970) who were given the responsibility of initiating a close relationship between the college and the school were assisted considerably by their familiarity with the South Australian Education Department. Both had been senior teachers in the department, had taught in large city schools, and had worked on education department curriculum committees. The understanding was that they would 'feel their way', using their own school classes in association with the college curriculum courses in their subject fields.

During the first year of the interrelationship of the college and school the involvement of college students with school pupils extended to include other teachers and other lecturers. The range of activities involving staff from both institutions widened considerably to encompass team teaching, experimental teaching, guest lessons and lectures, and small-group activities (including microteaching).

The increased number of lecturer-teachers (to six in 1975) and the appointment of teacher-tutors in 1974 have provided greater opportunities for college students to identify with the school. The activities of the teacher-tutor have been outlined above. One aspect of their position which has been found beneficial is their reduced teaching load which enables them to have adequate time for meaningful interaction with college students.

The relationship between the college and the school is not one that can or should be taken for granted. Meetings involving liaison staff, principals of the institutions, college students, and, from time to time, officials of the Education Department, facilitate continuous assessment and review and lead to the taking of new initiatives and the modification of existing ones.

The nature of the special staffing has been commented upon. Secondary to this, but of some importance, is the question of material resources. When the college moved to the Salisbury site the school and the college, although in separate divisions, were both under the control of the Education Department. This fact facilitated the incorporation of special classrooms into the additional wing that was added to the school in 1969. These include two observation classrooms with associated viewing rooms, a science laboratory with an accompanying viewing room and a seminar room for college students. The college has provided additional facilities in these rooms. Currently, remote-control television cameras are being fitted to one of the classrooms to enable videotaping of lesson segments for discussion, 'modelling', microteaching, and remedial teaching. These latter developments have occurred since the removal of the college from the administration of the Education Department and its establishment as an autonomous college of advanced education.

Many benefits additional to those associated with college courses have resulted from the close relationship between the college and the school. The in-service education of teachers, both at the campus school and elsewhere has been facilitated. (The college and the school have jointly sponsored in-service courses for local teachers). A library of protocol materials which is being built up is drawn upon not only for college pre-service courses, but also for teacher development and induction programmes and to meet other in-service needs. The proximity of the college to the school has enabled the school to make frequent use of many of its facilities.

Problems and Effectiveness

For reasons which have been mentioned earlier there were few problems encountered in establishing the 'laboratory' function of Salisbury East High School. Facilitating factors were the complete co-operation of the principal of the school, the regular involvement of curriculum studies lecturers (lecturer-teachers) in the school programme, and the willingness of all concerned to progress slowly and consider possible effects of any proposed innovation on both institutions. It should be remembered also, that initial discussions with the Education Department had established the boundaries within which developments could occur.

The objectives of the programme have been stated above. As mentioned, the kinds of activities and experiences that were planned have become a reality. College students are able to include school experience as a regular and integral part of their course.

A problem which was more acute before the 'teacher-tutor' position was implemented was that of finding sufficient staff in the school who were willing and able to work closely with college students throughout the year. Because of the opportunities provided by an on-campus school for an on-going close involvement of college students with teachers and pupils, a case could be put for a higher than normal proportion of highly qualified and highly effective staff in such a school. This problem has not yet been fully resolved.

An initial difficulty in establishing an interrelated programme has been the yearly and day-to-day timetables of the college and school. Changes have recently been made to the college calendar which have led to a longer period during which students and staff have the opportunity to work in the school.

As mentioned earlier, the programme is reviewed at regular periods. During these meetings feedback is obtained from all groups concerned. The programme was commented upon very favourably in the report prepared by the accreditation panel which recently examined and approved the new awards (Diploma in Teaching and Bachelor of Education) submitted by the college. A recommendation was made, however, that the school should be encouraged to present reports to the Academic Committee of the college.

Descriptions of college-laboratory school activities are published in the college paper, 'Intercom', which is distributed to all college and laboratory school staff and copies of which are sent to all schools with which the college is associated.

Recommendations

The 'lecturer-teacher' position, discussed earlier, is one which has proved most successful. Regrettably, college staffing constraints and revised bases for funding will probably prevent the curriculum studies lecturers from spending as much time in the classroom as has been the case in the past. (In future the college staffing allocation will not allow lecturer-teachers to be equated to half a staff member.) However, the college is committed to the view that methods and curriculum studies lecturers need frequent classroom experiences and this policy will be maintained.

The success of the 'teacher-tutor' position whereby certain teachers are given reduced teaching loads and are more directly involved in college courses suggests that this should be further developed. It would be desirable for these positions to be openly advertised and, to ensure continuity of personnel, that they be at senior level.

The question of quality of staffing in a laboratory school was raised earlier. Because of the greater frequency of contact with college students it would seem desirable that all teachers be given the opportunity to elect to teach at the school in full knowledge of the wider range of demands that may be made upon them. On the other hand, the creation of a completely abnormal staff position could be disastrous.

The advantages that this college has experienced through ready and natural access to classrooms, teachers and pupils suggest that in decisions concerning the siting of future tertiary institutions and schools the proximity of college and school could well be considered a high priority. The evidence to date suggests that a shared campus can provide unusual opportunities both for teacher education and for the school—but these opportunities develop only through the closest possible co-operation between the educational authorities concerned.

REFERENCES

The following articles are not specifically referred to but are relevant to the above outline:

Coggins, R. S., 'Teacher Education in a Changing Society', *New Horizons in Education*, Spring 1971, 46, 7–13.

Coggins, R. S., 'The Salisbury Teachers College Teacher Education Programme', Paper delivered at South Pacific Association for Teacher Education, Canberra 1972.

Coggins, R. S., 'Some problems associated with education of teachers for secondary schools in a rapidly changing society', Paper delivered at World Congress of Comparative Education Societies, Geneva, Switzerland 1974.

Intercom, Schools-College Paper, numerous issues.

Commentary

Few Australian teacher education programmes have yet fully realized the great benefits that can stem from the development of close relationships with one or several schools situated either on campus or nearby. The arrangement at Salisbury CAE provides a striking instance of many of the values which such a scheme can have for both the college and the school.

Avoiding much of the atypicality in facilities, staff and pupils which were associated with the demise of a number of laboratory schools in the United States, the Salisbury High School in its relationship with the college is clearly fulfilling most of the stated objectives, except perhaps little has been achieved in co-operative college-school research and development activity. However, other ventures have emerged, such as school-college co-operation in providing in-service education for other teachers.

The introduction and development of the arrangement has been facilitated by a number of factors, not least of which has been the goodwill existing between the college administration and the Department of Education and subsequently between college and school staff. In this latter regard the sensitivity and commitment of both the college and school liaison officers have paid dividends, especially in the area of communication. A feature of the scheme has been the two sets of joint appointments, 'lecturer-teachers' and 'teacher-tutors'. The teaming of these people for the professional education of students and for the education of school pupils is an admirable arrangement. One is also impressed by the easy and informal access that lecturers and students have to teachers and children whether to teach, observe or simply chat. Open and direct access rather than strict scheduling of arrangements has become the keynote of the operation. Students visit the school in large or small groups and individually either as planned by the lecturer or by the teacher.

The scheme is not, however, without its problems. For example, the complicated semester, daily and period timetabling of the school and college respectively have sometimes made co-operative activities difficult. The desire to retain the school as an 'ordinary' institution has meant there have been some problems of staff quality and continuity. Nor has the scheme escaped criticism. Teachers would like to see the provision of more accommodation, the development of open teaching areas and a resources centre. Several teachers seem a little uneasy about the burden the scheme puts on them. Some students believe the teaching in the school is rather conservative, and a few complain of the four-minute walk between institutions! Only rarely does a parent express concern that his child is a 'guinea pig' in the scheme.

Despite such isolated criticisms, most people concerned with the campus school speak highly of the arrangement and commend it for a wide variety of reasons. For instance, lecturers speak of the reality and relevance it provides for their courses. Teachers talk of it as providing rich inservice experiences for them and an enrichment for their pupils. Students comment on value of the help and practical wisdom gained from contact with school's teachers. A recent external accreditation panel had this to say:

> The interchange of lecturer-teachers ... and teacher-tutors ... provides for close articulation between college and the school to integrate the practical experience with the theoretical training. The existence of the laboratory high school on the campus, the excellent relationships between this and other co-operative schools ... provide a unique opportunity for the practical training of students at Salisbury.

Since the work of teacher education increasingly acknowledges the great potential of close links with schools, teachers and pupils, the scheme pioneered at Salisbury should provide numerous useful examples of how such links might be forged.

[C. T.]

SCHOOL-BASED PREPARATION

THE NEDLANDS ACTION PROJECT (NEDAP)

The Western Australian Secondary Teachers College

L. VLAHOV
Senior Lecturer in Education

Background and Context

In response to recommendations made in the Karmel Report, May 1973, the Western Australian Secondary Teachers College saw the opportunity to bring about changes in its teacher education programme, especially in the one-year Diploma in Education, through an innovations project funded from monies recommended for allocation for such purposes by the Karmel Committee. In September 1973 a proposal was prepared by Mrs Lawanna Blount, lecturer in education in which a one-year diploma course was outlined with the view to improving the existing one-year Diploma in Education course. A special committee was formed (L. Vlahov (chairman), L. Blount, T. Draber, A. Peacock, S. Richards, I. Whitford, and J. Williamson) and it drew up a detailed proposal in December 1973.

During August 1974, the proposal was considered by the college's Research and Planning Committee which decided that the project was not feasible in its present form. Mr L. Vlahov undertook to revise the project and the revised project was approved by the Academic Council of the college in November 1974.

During November 1974, the Western Australian Education Department was asked by the college whether two nearby high schools could be used in the pilot project and the official reply granting permission was received by the college in February 1975. The project commenced in March 1975.

Aims and Principles of Operation

On the basis of the premise that in order to train more competent, confident and effective teachers to teach pupils in a rapidly changing society, teacher education institutions and schools must develop closer, co-operative links and reconsider their approaches to the teaching-learning process, the following goals were originally established for the Nedlands Action Project (NEDAP):

Societal goals

To develop a teacher education programme which prepares teachers more adequately for their future role.

To test the hypothesis:

230

'Student teachers (Experimental Group) who undertake a one-year integrated theory and practice teacher training programme will demonstrate a higher level of teaching skills (teacher effectiveness)
than
student teachers (Control Group) who undertake the present one-year non-integrated teacher training programme at W.A.S.T.C.'

To obtain the co-operation of the school staff, college staff, student teachers, school pupils and community members in conducting the experimental integrated theory and practice teacher programme.

System goals

To develop and maintain close liaison between the W.A.S.T.C., the Project Schools and the Western Australian Education Department.

To develop a one-year secondary integrated theory and practice teacher training programme for graduate Diploma of Education students of the W.A.S.T.C.

To develop and conduct a comprehensive programme of evaluation to test the above hypothesis over a minimum period of three years.

To provide open forum discussion sessions in the Project Schools and at the W.A.S.T.C. where educational issues can be discussed.

Institutional goals

A. W.A.S.T.C.

That the W.A.S.T.C. conduct a pilot research project for an experimental group of graduate students within its present Diploma of Education programme in a one-year integrated theory and practice teacher training programme.

To develop a close liaison between the various departments within the W.A.S.T.C.

To redistribute the course work load for the Experimental Group so that an increased teaching load in the Project Schools could be accommodated in the second semester.

To initiate and develop a research role at W.A.S.T.C. in co-ordination with the Project Schools.

B. Project Schools

To involve all staff participants within the Project Schools in pre-service and in-service education as a continuing process.

To make provision for student teachers to participate in a gradually increasing teaching role which is closely related to the integrated course work.

Some of the above goals were modified during implementation of the project because of the difficulty of maintaining control over the great number of variables that were likely to influence the results. The change in emphasis resulted in the project being primarily an innovation programme which could be implemented and tested.

The underlying principles upon which the implementation of the project rested were co-operation and integration. A close liaison between the participating institutions was essential to facilitate the integration necessary for the programme.

Plan and Implementation

In order to establish the close liaison between the participating institutions needed for an integrated programme, the following became the main features of the plan:

Integrated tutorial sessions in the Schools

There were three types of integrated tutorial sessions:

(i) *Specialist Method Tutorials*—these were to replace similar tutorials normally conducted in the college. The tutorials were to be conducted during subject meeting times in the school where the participants would include a college lecturer, the two student teachers from the college, the tutor teacher and other school staff teaching in particular subject areas.

(ii) *Basic Issues in Education Tutorials*—again replaced the tutorial normally conducted at college. The participants were to include a college lecturer in education, the tutor teachers, the eight student teachers and the principal of the school.

(iii) *Measurement and Evaluation in Education Tutorials*—again these were to replace the tutorials normally conducted in the college. The participants were the same as for the Basic Issues tutorials.

The above arrangement was possible because the college courses consisted of a lecture followed by a tutorial each week. Thus the lectures were conducted at the college while the tutorials were held in the schools with the school staff participating.

Tutor teachers

For student teachers to experience a meaningful teaching practice, a system of 'tutor teachers' (four in each school) was implemented. Each tutor teacher was assigned two student teachers and it was the responsibility of the tutor teachers

(i)   to see that each student had a gradually increasing teaching practice over the two semesters;

(ii) to provide opportunities for the students to be involved in school activities other than teaching;

(iii) to assist the students so that their teaching performance could be improved; and

(iv) to participate in the integrated tutorial sessions.

Gradually increasing teaching practice

This feature of the project replaced the normal block practices and it was necessary for students to reduce their work load at college in the second semester to accommodate an increasing teaching practice load.

Integration of theory and practice

The integrated tutorial sessions in the school in which the practising teachers participated, provided the opportunity for theories to be put into practice.

In addition, the gradually increasing teaching practice provided the student teachers with the opportunity to try out some of their own ideas and develop their own teaching technique.

Research in education

The extra time spent in the schools enabled students and college staff to engage in some mini-research projects. One such project resulted in a useful Reading Kit being developed for 'non-readers'.

In-service education for school staff

The close liaison between the project schools and the college and participation of the school staff in the integrated tutorial sessions provided the school staff with a form of in-service. They were being acquainted with recent developments in their respective subject areas as outlined by the college lecturers.

The approval of the project by the participating institutions was the first step in the implementation of the project. Subsequently, the project administrator held briefing sessions firstly with the principals of the two project schools and then with the staff of the project schools. The tutor teachers were determined by the principal in consultation with the project administrator. The number of school personnel involved was five from each school—the principal and four tutor teachers.

The college lecturers required to participate were approached individually by the project administrator and a total of thirteen college staff were involved.

The number of students required for the pilot project was sixteen and these formed the Experimental Group, A further sixteen students were required for the Control Group. Both groups were selected from a total population of 81 students—all graduates enrolled for the Diploma in Education. In order to arrive at a sample of people eligible to participate in the project it was necessary to eliminate all part-timers, all those students who did not own a car, all those who lived outside a fifteen mile radius (to avoid excessive travelling) and all those whose major teaching area was not in mathematics, science, English, or social studies. Those eligible to participate were stratified into groups (mathematics 8, social studies 8, English 8, science 11). A stratified random sample of four, based on teaching practice experience, became the experimental group while the next stratified random sample of four became the control group. Students were allocated, where possible, to the school of their choice.

The only funds required for the project were the payments to the tutor teachers and the principals of the project schools. A total of $5,000 was set aside for this purpose from the central college research budget. Most tutor teachers were happy with the allowance, but one tutor teacher was prepared to perform the task for no extra allowance. The funds needed for stationery used and the hire of secretarial assistance were not specifically allocated and came out of general recurrent funds of the college. Students only received their normal travelling allowance reimbursements from the Education Department.

Problems and Effectiveness

Because approval of the project was not obtained until after the commencement of the school year the implementation of the project was delayed and this in turn necessitated changes being made to the original aims of the project.

The time commitment by tutor teachers in the school was reduced to about one-quarter to one-third of what was originally planned because of the difficulty of making changes to timetables. This reduced the degree of integration possible.

Timetabling for the integrated specialist method sessions and the Education and Psychology tutorials was made difficult by the delayed implementation so that time constraints became a critical issue and affected the willingness of people to co-operate.

The lack of co-operation on the part of some school staff and some college staff was a limiting factor.

The lack of precise directions to tutor teachers and student teachers about the form of the relationship between them led to uncertainty about their respective roles.

In one of the project schools, there was considerable antagonism to the project from one of the subject groups and it appeared that most of their anxiety was caused by inadequate information on the project and a fear they would be involved in much more work for insufficient compensation.

Because of the above limitations it was necessary to modify the research and experimental aspect of the project and instead develop the exercise as an innovations project. This was necessary because of the demands by the schools for a greater degree of flexibility in the implementation of the project.

A preliminary evaluation of the project was made at the end of the first semester in 1975 by means of a questionnaire administered to all the participants. The questions asked were aimed at obtaining statements of fact and statements of opinions and perceptions about the project in general as well as about specific aspects of the project. In addition, the respondents were asked to make suggestions for the improvement of the programme.

The results of the questionnaire were disseminated to all who participated in the project in the form of an interim report. The effectiveness of the innovation may in part be gauged by the findings presented in the report. The conclusion drawn from the results obtained indicated that almost all of the goals outlined earlier were being achieved and as such the innovation had been a success. Specifically the results showed that the predominant attitude towards the innovation was a positive one with all participants benefiting from the experience to varying degrees. Eighty-seven per cent of the participants agreed that students would be more adequately trained under the NEDAP programme than under a non-integrated programme. This gives some idea of the effectiveness of the programme in the first semester. In addition, 85 per cent of the students considered their NEDAP practice was much more realistic and rewarding than previous practices. The other fifteen per cent indicated that it was not as good as previous practices.

Recommendations

In view of the results contained in the interim report, the Academic Council of the college endorsed the continuation and expansion of the innovation in 1976 subject to certain modifications being made to the programme. One of the major problems to emerge from the programme was the need for a considerable amount of travelling necessitated by the integrated approach. Many of the difficulties experienced stemmed from the relatively late implementation of the programme and the impossibility of making timetable changes causing the finalized timetables of the students and college staff to result in an inefficient utilization of time. It is anticipated that these problems will be overcome in 1976 by earlier implementation and the earlier adjustment of the timetables at college and in the schools. An increase in the number of student teachers per school will result in more viable tutorial groups in the schools—especially in the integrated specialist method tutorials. It is hoped that the expansion of the programme in 1976 will involve some private schools as well as the government schools.

The development of a school-based integrated teacher training programme if adopted as an alternative is likely to lead to a greater involvement of school staff in the pre-service training of teachers. The NEDAP innovation however, is unlikely to replace entirely the conventional college oriented programme for mainly logistic and financial reasons. The innovation does provide a flexible framework within which future developments could be accommodated. The current trend towards open area education in the high schools and the associated concepts of differentiated staffing and individualized instruction are likely to be incorporated in future developments within the NEDAP programme.

That NEDAP programme appears to be a viable school-based teacher training programme indicates the need for further investigation and experimentation to develop alternative teacher training programmes. To this end NEDAP is likely to provide the opportunities for the college to develop more personalized teacher education programmes that more adequately cater for the individual needs of students.

Commentary

In Australia there has been a long established practice that secondary teachers spend three years gaining a university degree in Arts or in Science, and then spend a fourth, and professional, year at a university or at a college where they gain their professional teacher education in a diploma of education course. Often these diploma of education students have been loud in their criticism of this course, and a review of the student press of particular institutions often clearly shows this. Consequently various institutions have tried, and currently are trying, schemes to help overcome some of this criticism.

Some of the criticism has been poorly based. The new university graduate in history, or in mathematics, or in some foreign language, or in one of the sciences, has successfully specialized in the study of an area where he or she had particular talent and where the study of its subject matter satisfied his or her own special and individual interests. Sometimes the new graduate is convinced that his or her subject discipline is more difficult, or more relevant, or more worthwhile, than other subject disciplines, many of which are clearly inferior. And some new graduates are impatient to begin teaching in schools convinced that their subject base is adequate, that subject matter is the essence both of teaching and of education, and that for them the professional year is a waste of time concerned as it is with educational ideas and practices which distract from their subject discipline. Such a view is not without a strong element of 'subject-matter arrogance'.

On the other hand, some of the criticism has been well based, and the Nedlands Action Project is an example of an attempt to remedy one of the apparent weaknesses of diploma of education courses.

Some diploma of education students have viewed school experience as helpful and institutional lectures and tutorials largely as a waste of time on the grounds that these were 'talk sessions' separated from schools and controlled by lecturers who were out of touch with the reality of school experience.

The major thrust and strength of the Nedlands Action Project is its attempts to integrate theory and practice in the school situation. Specialist method tutorials conducted in the school with both the lecturer and the tutor teacher present as resource persons seem more likely to be seen by student teachers as real and as relevant. And the grouping of lecturers, student teachers, tutor teachers and the school principal for other tutorials seems also more likely to centre in the real world of the school.

The Nedlands Action Project staff had logistic problems both with human and with physical resources. Obviously any scheme must relate to the realities of such factors as the school's timetable and the tertiary institution's timetable, and the perceived load by all of the people involved, if it is to have any chance of acceptance and of success. The case study has shown how problems can arise with tutor teachers, and their reaction is natural enough.

Schemes such as the Nedlands Action Project, which are perhaps limited in their application, and in which particular focus on all participants must occur, may result in a Hawthorne effect. Even so, this is not a factor which should be used to discount the value of the scheme, because it can only be through a wide range of attempts to tackle some of the traditional criticism of the diploma of education course that improvement will come. Certainly the concept of the integration of theory and practice is a primary talking point in teacher education in Australia, and action to achieve this integration is both appropriate and welcome.

[D. J.]

THE SCHOOL-BASED COURSE (SBC)

Faculty of Education
University of Queensland

Dr R. Smith, Professor G. Evans,
R. Cowie, and Marjory Carss

Background and Context

The School-Based Course (SBC) was conceived in late 1974 in response to a critique of the existing Diploma in Education course by staff of a Brisbane high school and a proposal for an 'alternative' course by Richard Smith. In brief, the SBC was to be an attempt to introduce student teachers to the practice of teaching in a way which circumvented the perceived artificiality and briefness of existing theoretical courses and practice.

Planning of the SBC began with two meetings of the high school and members of the SBC team. Smith's proposal was discussed and agreement to implement the SBC was reached. An important factor in the acceptance of the proposal by the school staff was the relationship established with the Toowong school staff in 1974 by Russ Cowie, a university staff member. During the 1975 Diploma in Education orientation week the SBC was explained to the students and a call made for volunteers. Eighty-six students wished to participate and from these, twenty-eight were randomly selected so that subject areas and classes available at the school were accommodated. In the period November 1974- January 1975 a course statement and outline was prepared by University staff.

The team of University staff with main responsibility for the SBC included Richard Smith (Sociology), Glen Evans (Psychology/Curriculum theory), Russ Cowie (History Curriculum studies) and Marjory Carss (Mathematics Curriculum studies).

Aims and Principles of Operation

The rationale and objectives of the SBC are best illustrated by reference to the course outline.

Rationale for the course

(i)   Through an on-going involvement at a particular school (Toowong High School), you will receive greater opportunities to relate theory to practice and ideals to reality.

(ii)   Seminars and discussion groups held at the school instead of on the campus are likely to be more fruitful because of the three-way communication between student teachers, practising teachers and university staff.

(iii) The individual needs of student teachers may be better catered for through a long-term involvement with two supervising teachers in addition to your curriculum lecturers and your personal tutor.

(iv)   Through your willing participation in this programme you may contribute to a review of what is most suitable and feasible in pre-service teacher education.

Aims and Objectives

Aims: To prepare teachers for Australian secondary schools with specialist abilities in at least two subject areas.

Objectives: By the end of the course students should

(i)   Demonstrate an ability to teach typical classes at each grade level in their chosen disciplines.

(ii)   Have a knowledge of the formal structure and organization of a typical high school at both subject department and school levels.

(iii) Demonstrate a knowledge of children and of curriculum principles appropriate for the various grade levels.

(iv)   Demonstrate through discussion and action a wide knowledge of educational problems/issues/theories.

(v)   Demonstrate a knowledge of curriculum innovations.

The Plan and Its Implementation

The main features of the SBC are as follows: Firstly, there was the attempt to provide for students a continuous involvement with the everyday-life of a typical high school. The theoretical assumption is that students need to develop the perspective of 'teacher' before they can realistically make sense of theoretical perspectives. Secondly, there was the use of school experiences as case material for foundational studies (Educational Psychology, Cultural Foundations of Education, Evaluation in Education and Curriculum Studies). Thirdly, there was an emphasis on the supervisory role of the classroom teacher responsible for inducting the student into the classroom. Fourthly, the attempt was made in weeks 1–6 of Semester 2 to add a theoretical perspective to the commonsense knowledge gained in Semester 1. This deliberate attempt to critically analyse school experiences was made in intensive seminars.

The plan was initiated by placing the students into the school during the first teaching week of the First Semester. Students were allocated to curriculum areas beforehand, and after a brief meeting with the school staff were placed with supervising teachers by subject masters. Students were responsible for arranging their teaching and observation periods so that clashes with the on-campus programme (e.g. curriculum studies) were avoided. The special SBC seminars and personal tutorial groups were pre-timetabled on the master Dip.Ed. timetable so that it was possible to avoid intrusions into student teaching time and to facilitate in-school sessions when school staff could attend (i.e. 3.00 pm-5.00 pm).

No special funding was required for the SBC. However, the programme demanded a staff commitment to students in the ratio of 1:17. This figure is conservative because of special demands by students on curriculum lecturers not included here.

Problems and Effectiveness

Few difficulties were encountered in introducing the innovation. The organizational complexities of providing spaces for SBC seminars/tutorials in the Dip.Ed. timetable and allocating students to classes in the school were minimal. However, a number of difficulties become apparent as the programme progressed. They range from inconsequential to what might be termed serious weaknesses. The major difficulties appear to be school/campus articulation, the on-campus programme, assessment of the students, and the exclusiveness of the SBC student body. Each difficulty is discussed in turn.

While the school is in close proximity to the university, students experienced difficulty in travelling between the two locations. A lot of time was wasted finding parking space at the university and consequently SBC students found themselves arriving late for on-campus lectures, etc. In some cases, students elected not to attend at all and serious gaps appeared in their work programme, particularly in curriculum studies.

In addition, the contact between university staff and the school was limited due to the pressure of other teaching, research and administrative commitments.

The SBC on-campus programme and the school programme were poorly articulated. That is, students missed lectures because of the pressure of school commitments and travel difficulties. Further lectures in the foundation areas, outside the SBC, which depended on tutorial assistance apart from lectures, become almost meaningless to some of the SBC students. Evaluation in Education, in particular, suffered badly in this respect. An attempt, therefore had to be made to make the study of the foundation areas self-sufficient within the SBC in the Second Semester.

The SBC seminars (4 hours per week) involving both in-school and on-campus sessions and based on school problems as perceived by students, tended to lack cohesion and relevance to the students in First Semester. Such seminars were multi-disciplinary in approach but, in retrospect, were too theoretical too early. The comment of one student that the seminars would have been 'spot on' in Second Semester would seem to be appropriate.

Administratively, the SBC students' academic results for Semester 1 were difficult to compile. Students had not in fact 'done' the courses prescribed by course convenors although they had read and discussed much of the course work material. The three multi-disciplinary assignments set for the SBC students had to become the basis for assessment in the foundational areas of Cultural Foundations of Education and Educational Psychology. The last of these assignments was moderated by the teaching team to provide results in those two areas while Evaluation in Education results were held over into Semester 2. In general, the grades received by SBC students for assignment 3 compared more than favourably with those received by mainstream Diploma in Education students for the two courses.

The SBC student group were seen by other Dip.Ed. students, university staff and by themselves as a separate group. The cohesiveness of the SBC group in a monolithic Dip.Ed. course (student $N = 380$) has many advantages and these were evident. But a major disadvantage which became apparent to university staff in Semester 2 was that the SBC students assumed an attitude of superiority to other Dip. Ed. students because of the amount of school experience they had accumulated. In the view of some university staff, the SBC students gave the impression that they had little further to learn.

The major problems of the SBC might best be located in the relationship between an alternative structure and a pre-existing set of rules and courses that are inappropriate for the new structure. By tying the SBC to central elements of the mainstream course (i.e. curriculum studies and general lectures) serious tensions between competing ideologies and different student commitments were made virtually inevitable. The importance of conceptualizing the frames for new and existing courses is therefore seen to be critical.

An assessment of the effectiveness of the SBC must take into account the perspectives of students, the school staff and university staff. It can be stated with certainty that students consider the SBC to have been a success, but university and school staff have reservations about the teaching ability of at least a quarter of the SBC students in respect to the problems outlined previously. The SBC students have evaluated the course from their point of view and the other two groups have completed a questionnaire, but the data has not yet been analysed.

The department is to introduce a new Diploma in Education programme in 1977. Current discussion indicates that elements of the SBC will be taken into account in that planning exercise. In the meantime, the SBC will continue in 1976 together with an extension of the scheme to another Brisbane high school. Clearly, the present SBC is defective on a number of counts but at the same time is positively perceived by students. This latter point is important because student criticisms of the mainstream course continue to be made on the grounds of workload, unrelatedness to schools, relatively little in-school experience, and so on.

Recommendations

What is perhaps emerging from the SBC exercise is that pre-service preparation needs to be varied so that different student, staff and school needs and wants can be accommodated. The present pattern of a monolithic 'set-course' Dip.Ed.

programme seems not to satisfy such needs and wants. Consequently each teacher education institution has the task of creating alternative tracks for students, within the frames that are thought to be appropriate. While the SBC model remains vague, much has been learned and the 1976 version of the course will be better articulated.

Commentary

The research team found a considerable degree of interest across the many teacher education programmes in Australia in the question of how best could the traditional forms of the twelve-month graduate Diploma in Education course be varied. Of particular concern was the issue of whether a school-based programme was viable. One programme which is of interest is that described in this case study at the University of Queensland, especially as the innovative team has been able to provide a clear analysis of the advantages and disadvantages of the procedures they followed.

Clearly one of the major advantages of a school-based programme would need to be that students gain a much closer awareness of school and classroom situations. Discussions with students, teachers and the university faculty indicated that the SBC students gained a greater awareness of school situations than would have been expected in a traditional programme. Nevertheless it was quite apparent that being based in schools for a major part of the time was not in itself a determining of whether students would be effective in their teaching experiences. The university faculty and the teachers in the schools thought that one quarter of the SBC students had not made the progress in developing teacher abilities that would be considered desirable! (However, it might well be that many of these students may not have been successful in the year's teaching in any type of diploma programme). Discussions with the students who were in the SBC programme certainly showed that they understood the sociological issues of their schools. It was considered likely that when they went into schools for their first full-time appointments in the following year, they would be better equipped than the average first-year appointee to cope with staff relationships, school organization, classroom discipline and so on.

The major disadvantages of the school-based programme are principally linked with the fact that the SBC was an alternative programme offered within the normal Diploma in Education course. It therefore raised organizational problems since the SBC students had to return to campus for several of the subjects not covered by the in-school experiences. This did in fact detract from the in-school experience in a very real way as several of the teachers and the students commented on how often a valuable school experience had to be broken off through the student needing to return to campus. This often led to 'divided loyalty' situations with students providing anecdotes of how throughout the year they were out of favour with members of the campus teaching staff or the school teaching staff, dependent on whether they decided to leave school and attend the on-campus class or whether they stayed at school and missed the on-campus commitment. Discussions with the university staff also revealed that several who were not part of the smaller team responsible for the SBC group of students but still taught the students as part of the normal Diploma in Education programme, were not in favour of the school-based approach. Both student and teacher groups were obviously aware of the fact that some of the university staff were not generally supportive of the school-based approach and a degree of unease between the various groups was evident because of this.

The SBC innovation at the University of Queensland should provide a useful series of guidelines for teacher educators planning to introduce a school-based programme into a diploma in education course. It demonstrates how very difficult this can be if the school-based programme is merely an alternative part of an overall programme. It was quite evident that the success of the school-based programme depended very heavily on a high degree of commitment of all involved—students, school staffs and faculty members. In fact it might well be a question for planners to seriously consider whether a school-based programme should go ahead if such a commitment is lacking! Stress should also be placed on the importance of having all university staff and school staff members who will be involved in the programme during the year involved in the initial planning and development stages of the programme. Without such an initial and on-going involvement the underlying assumptions and basic objectives and principles of the programme may not be grasped. Without this, the necessary commitment to a school-based programme may not be achieved.

[R. T.]

'COURSE B': SCHOOL-BASED TEACHER EDUCATION

Faculty of Education
University of Melbourne

GWYNETH M. DOW
Reader in Education

Background and Context

'Course B', which started in 1973, is a total post-graduate diploma in education programme rather than a traditional course with some innovatory amendments. It was planned to relate theory and practice by providing continuous teaching practice and connecting university study to the problems of teaching. Students are in school for at least two days a week—Wednesdays and Thursdays. On Mondays and Tuesdays there is intensive work in methods seminars. Students study two methods. On Friday mornings we provide an inter-disciplinary programme entitled 'Curriculum Studies' (which we interpret broadly), as part of which the students are expected to do a depth study (a piece of mini-research of their own choice) approved and supervised by a member of staff. All academic work is related to the students' teaching experiences.

Aims and Principles of Operation

The main aim of the innovation is to provide, as well as possible in a year's post-graduate programme, capable, imaginative teachers who can enter into the life of schools with experience in working with children, and some understanding of curriculum planning, educational innovation, organization, and theory. A long-range aim is to establish a close working relationship between schools and university so that each will enrich the other.

The underlying principles are as follows:

—closely tying in the introduction to educational studies with teaching experiences will encourage students to *ask* their own questions, to spot problems for themselves, whereas much of the emphasis in education is on answering others' questions;

—developing specialization and academic rigour from the students' academic strengths (their undergraduate 'disciplines') will stimulate them to reflect upon the nature and teachability of secondary school subjects and their relatedness to allied subjects, whereas their unfamiliarity with educational thought and literature makes the education 'disciplines' a poor starting point and often leads to superficiality if not boredom. 'Subject-mindedness' can be converted to 'curriculum-mindedness' through methods work (and methods staff should play a central role in Dip.Ed.), which is supported by inter-disciplinary studies in education;

—recognizing that, since learning to be a teacher is essentially a personal, usually threatening, experience, it is best faced in action rather than remotely in lecture theatre or seminar room, and the discovery of an appropriate teaching style is fostered by feedback from children and sensitive support from supervisors;

—encouraging student self-assessment, collaborative course planning, learning and teaching—at both university and school—will increase students' self-awareness and independence, and will encourage them to acquire an informed attitude on pupil participation and autonomy in secondary schools; and

—providing 'models' of good practice—'practising what we preach'—will lead students to a critical appraisal of their role in the school, to co-operative teaching, and to collaborative innovation.

The Plan and Its Implementation

At the end of 1970, planning of the project began with a group of colleagues. In 1972 a handful of students were attached to one school for two days a week throughout the year. The enthusiasm of the students, and the school's explicit preference for continuous teaching, as distinct from three block-practice rounds, strengthened our resolve that school practice should be the 'linchpin' of a one-year, post-graduate Diploma of Education.

The other trial run was accidental. The room the writer was allotted for seminars in 1971 was a passage with a table and chairs in it, and no ventilation except when students or staff walked through on their way to the adjoining seminar room, or when the window was opened and wind blew out the lethal gas jet warming the passage. After about three introductory seminars it was decided to break into individual or group projects, and to meet periodically in groups small enough to fit into the writer's little study. The work submitted at the end of the year was so superior to what one was accustomed to that the writer resolved to adopt a similar approach to the academic component of a trial course—hence the depth study (see above).

During 1972 Bernard Newsome received a temporary position with the writer to help plan an alternative course, and at the end of 1972 the writer received assistance from the university's New Developments Fund and the Australian

Advisory Committee on Research and Development in Education to run the pilot scheme. This made it possible to continue Bernard Newsome's appointment and to add Rod Fawns, both on limited tenure. Both were experts in methods (English and science respectively), and had been dedicated, innovative secondary teachers. Thus we were able to implement our principles of emphasis on methods and curriculum.

We already had a close association with Sydney Road and Swinburne Community Schools and Trinity Grammar, which were happy to collaborate with the trial course. The writer's proposals had always been supported by the then Director of Secondary Education, Mr A. E. Schruhm, who provided some assistance to the Course.

We began in 1973 with twenty-three students, selected from volunteers in an attempt to have equal numbers of men and women, of pass and honours graduates, and to be able to balance our numbers in teaching methods. In 1974 we enrolled fifty students, and in 1975 fifty-three. We now have students in eleven schools,* chosen for their interest to work with us on course innovations. It is necessary for us to work in schools that are flexible.

Problems and Effectiveness

(i) *Students*

Students welcome an education year based on teaching experiences. At best, some students affirm that it is the most educative and liberating year spent at university. Most find the challenge of becoming teachers traumatic, and some sense that their very personalities are under public scrutiny. To avoid this without being *laissez-faire* requires tact. Much group learning and many group enterprises flourish, but a few students prefer to be solitary and can feel unjustifiably guilty. Some want more emphasis on school practice; some want more time for reflection and theoretical enquiry at university; some are happy with the balance; all are under great pressure.

A commonly expressed doubt about the Course is that students' connection with one school may handicap them if they are posted to a different kind of school. Follow-up studies give little support to this fear but rather show that our students are adaptable, enterprising and well prepared to take educational responsibilities beyond the classroom, such as in curriculum development. On balance, we believe that an intimate connection with one school has more advantages than disadvantages provided that we keep inter-school seminar groups and provide some other school experiences for those who feel they need it.

Most students thrive on the openness of the Course whereas it makes others anxious. In particular, their opportunity to negotiate alternative programmes, if existing ones are found wanting, presents difficulties to students (because it may be painful to staff). They almost never avail themselves of it; but it does lead to constant review and change.

Perhaps the most radical achievement is the elimination of competitive assessment (except for a small minority who ask to be assessed for honours) and the success of self- and participatory-assessment. This is achieved without sacrificing academic rigour, and elicits (with few exceptions) more authentic

---

* The additional schools in 1975 were Bentleigh, Flemington, Footscray, Mount Waverley, University High School, Swinburne Annexe, Williamstown Technical School, and Kingswood College.

and better quality work than the writer was used to in a traditional course, though less quantity is expected. All written and practical work is the subject of discussion and evaluation; much of it is shared with other students. Thus evaluation is intended to be educative rather than classificatory, and this is an important experience for students who are about to become examiners or assessors of hundreds of pupils.

(ii) *School supervision*

Schools, themselves, mostly appreciate the continuous teaching practice; it is their wish that students be based in one school for the year. Their representatives are on an important policy-making and advisory body, but our link with them, especially since our numbers increased, is less satisfactory than we would wish, and we lack the time to remedy this effectively. The addition of new schools and the turnover of staff in old ones are our major worries. New staff are mystified about the Course itself and their appropriate roles. If we give too many guidelines it is restrictive and prescriptive, if we give too few it is unsettling. Written documents to schools are often not read, and informal contacts, which are by far the most satisfactory solution, require more staff than we have.

The traditional notion of student supervisor in a block-teaching round is unsuitable in our situation. It can be bewildering to a teacher to have to write his reports jointly with the student. How much should the supervisor guide, accompany, criticize the student when she will be there for the whole year and the lesson is not a 'once-up' occasion? How can team-teaching be encouraged in a school where it is not customary? What is the most advantageous and proper role of the university lecturer in visiting a school? How does one give continuity in teaching to a student who is there on Wednesdays and Thursdays but her particular class also has lessons on Mondays and Fridays? How can students attend the Monday morning staff meeting? There is no formula that will suit all schools, all teachers and all students. But some schools have already found individual and ingenious solutions, and many find that by second term the student has a great deal to contribute—often in ways that full-time staff are too busy to offer.

For the student, the opportunity to observe, to meet children informally and first off in small groups for special projects, and generally to be eased into classroom teaching has obvious advantages, as has the feedback from classes when a lesson fails or written work shows one's ineffective teaching, yet the next class must be taken. Rod Fawns, who is making a special contribution to school practice, is at present working on the thesis that, with constructive supervision, the student discovers what concept of teaching she wants to adopt, and moves from an overwhelming sense that what she can do is circumscribed and determined by the kind of school she is in to an understanding of her personal attributes and their possible contribution to the given situation. Analysis of the interplay of self and system is possible with continuous teaching practice.

(iii) *Staffing*

All the problems suggested so far, and many more than are mentioned, are capable of solution if we can solve our staffing problem when external funding runs out this year. It takes a new member of the team at least six months to become accustomed to our way of doing things, and piecemeal help in staffing has limited value. Hence the loss of staff is particularly damaging. Of the nine members of staff attached to us at one time or another, only four will remain—and all of them very much part-time. The transitional period of finding replacements if we can, will strain our energies perhaps beyond what is manageable, since we already have a poorer staff-student ratio than the rest of Dip.Ed.

The Course involves staff in complex teaching activities, such as in formal groups of 4–60 students, informal groups of all sizes, community groups (for example, providing participatory drama for children in 'high-rise' areas, giving help to Turkish families, etc.) team-teaching with fellow staff or students, both in schools and at the university, usually in interdisciplinary groups. The staff must learn to spot and seize on students' concerns that require academic enquiry and to create teaching/learning situations inside and outside schools. This produces a new view of expertise in teaching, but increases administrative responsibilities.

The ideal staffing for a totally reorganized course such as ours is a core of about three or four dedicated people who can draw on the expertise of their ex-students, of the schools collaborating with the programme, and of community projects with which they are associated. Thus resources are created, but the administrative demands are heavy. The cessation of outside support for the core of staff can kill such an innovation unless the institution in which it occurs is sympathetic and actively willing to back it.

The close contact maintained between university staff and schools may not prove viable, yet we believe it essential for our counselling of students, and it is an indispensable trigger to our academic work. To lose it may well be to destroy the identity of the Course.

The experiment is being independently evaluated by the university's Centre for the Study of Higher Education which has produced one interim report and will shortly finish a major report. Both will be available on request.

Recommendations

There is little space to enumerate specific recommendations; but there are two features of the Course that we are anxious to develop.

Exit students have, each year, requested us to run in-service courses, which we have done (two or three times a year) despite our staffing shortage. There are great benefits in running workshops and curriculum sessions in which Dip.Ed. students work with first-year teachers, and we should like to see this service expanded.

We have no wish to expand the Course: we would wish, rather, to strengthen our link with schools and perhaps to engage jointly in some 'action research'. We are beginning to move in this direction.

Commentary

The Diploma in Education alternative programme known as 'Course B' is an ambitious project to develop a school-based one-year programme for graduates. For the student the project aims to develop reflective thinking about one's teaching and to exploit opportunities in teaching as they arise. The flexibility built into the course enables the phasing in of students into schools on two days per week with continual contact with teaching. Initially, it is contact with teaching done by others and then eventually with their own teaching. The programme encourages students to evolve a self-management ethos and a sense of a variety of ways in which a student learns to teach. Effective reflection on teaching is seen as arising from a student's own continuous efforts at teaching.

It is expected that students will begin teaching within their supervising teachers' classes following existing organization of subject matter and presentation. The demand to take increasing responsibility for their own teaching is expressed in the latter part of the year when the students undertake the preparation and management of a series of lessons with pupils. Students come to see themselves as teachers with a visibly accepted place in the school. A close working relationship between students and supervisors who are jointly engaged in investigating ways of teaching and of becoming colleagues, does much to increase the clarity and the refinement of the tasks involved.

The students elect the school-based programme and work fairly intimately with three lecturers and a teacher who is a supervisor. Eleven schools are used. Students are asked to keep a daily diary of their reflections and discoveries about themselves in teaching. Such diaries clearly exhibit a growth pattern in their teaching attitudes and competence. Students admit to high anxiety at the beginning of their involvement in schools but with increasing familiarity with the classroom this seems to be replaced by a growing awareness and enthusiasm for teaching.

There are administrative difficulties for the three lecturers trying to organize alternative experiences to broaden students' participation. Dedication and interest on the part of both university staff and school staff is needed. In fact, changes in staff in either schools or university have created some difficulties. It takes time to know what the course is all about and to perceive alternative opportunities to expand reflective thinking about teaching since traditional academic work is greatly reduced and more emphasis is given to students' group activities.

The programme has been evaluated systematically by an independent team. Indications from both participating students and ex-students confirm that the development of openness to experience and relevance for teaching are on-going strengths of the project, providing as it does for concentration on methods in relationship to school experiences, supportive groups in schools and participation in curriculum planning.

[D. T.]

SCHOOL-BASED TEACHER EDUCATION PROGRAMMES
State College of Victoria
Hawthorn

B. Phipps and the team of lecturers involved

Background and Context

As a means of bridging the gap between theory and practice and of making teacher education more relevant, a field study of school-based teacher education was commenced in 1975. The college had operated a form of internship for temporary teachers already employed by the Victorian Education Department (Technical Division) on a part-time basis. In response to a growing body of literature about school-based projects which provide for credibility and accessibility as important influences on student teachers, a pilot programme involving nine projects was introduced. Initial success has led to the introduction of twelve school-based projects in 1976, under the co-ordination of Brian Phipps.

Aims and Principles of Operation

Methods lecturers conduct projects of two types:

Type A. The lecturer conducting the programme provides support for all trainee teachers in a school. Seven projects are of this type.

Type B. Trainee teachers travel to a centrally located school instead of the college for their special methods lectures (maths or science, etc.). Five projects are of this type.

All students at Hawthorn complete a one-year programme for the Diploma in Education. Students teach in technical, community or secondary schools. A full range of method courses exists. One or two days per week and sometimes three days per week (for technical subjects) are school-based.

The basic objectives of the projects include

(i)   the general improvement of the quality of the in-school experience and the relevance of college courses to this experience;

(ii)   the provision of in-school support for students from the college lecturers during the teaching practice programmes;

(iii)   the development of co-operation between an autonomous tertiary institution and the schools;

(iv)   the development of stronger links between the theoretical and practical elements of the teacher education programme;

(v)   the increased credibility and influence of the college and its staff through their work in schools;

(vi)   the promotion of interaction and mutual support between students of various subject areas;

(vii)   the provision of opportunities for student-teachers to experiment with a variety of teaching styles within a diversity of classroom contexts;

(viii) the attempt to focus attention on the specific problems of particular schools (e.g. migrants, lack of resources) rather than develop generalized answers in college;

(ix)   the provision of opportunities for student-teachers to take a more active role in the design, implementation, and evaluation of the special method segment of their courses;

(x)   the attempt to support beginning teachers through the coping stage to a position of self-confidence and basic competence;

(xi)   to assist the socialization of the beginning teacher into the teaching profession.

The Plan and Its Implementation

The projects in twelve schools include students studying special methods in mathematics, science, art, commerce, fitting and machining, sheetmetal work, woodwork, home economics, humanities, social science, and drama. Some 150 students are currently involved. Most students concentrate their work with Form I.

The school-based activities in the various projects include—lecturers/seminars on teaching and curriculum directly related to work in classrooms; systematic observations of pupils and a variety of teachers; gradual and guided involvement in teaching in varying contexts and employing various skills and strategies; participation in the co-operative development of curriculum units; helping pupils with learning difficulties; and engagement in out-of-class school activities. In all this work emphasis is placed on the student as the *member of a team of professional workers*, including the lecturer. The lecturer performs many functions. For example, besides conducting methods courses, he gives lessons, demonstrates techniques and strategies, leads preparatory and follow-up discussions of students' teaching and provides individual help and support for the students.

An individual evaluator is attached to each of the school-based programmes. The evaluators are drawn generally from the education foundations staff. Each evaluator is asked to (i) conduct a preliminary discussion with the lecturer to whom he or she was allocated; (ii) undertake one or two visits to the school to observe the particular scheme in action and to talk to staff and student teachers; (iii) administer questionnaires to trainees and supervisors involved in the programme; and (iv) submit a written report of his findings. Standardized questionnaires were devised for trainees involved in the programmes, for control groups and for school supervisors directly or indirectly involved in such programmes.

Problems and Effectiveness

Evidence submitted by the evaluators indicates so far that the new approach assists beginning teachers to cope more adequately with the early survival concerns in their classrooms. Student teachers indicate that they are able to become more closely involved with a small number of pupils and because the lecturer is on the spot with student teachers, problems can be discussed as they arise. From the school's point of view there are benefits because it can result in more attention being given to weaker pupils. From the lecturers' point of view it helps keep them in touch with the realities of the school. Lecturers also consider that the school-based programmes assist the trainee to deal effectively with his anxieties and frustrations through provision of the supportive environment necessary for effective learning.

Some difficulties encountered are the co-ordination of both school and college timetables to allow both full access and follow-up of work. In some instances there was a lack of appreciation by some of the schools involved of the real nature of the school-based programme. In Type A projects it was often difficult to arrange for all the trainees to meet at the appointed time in a particular school. Some lecturers are involved with work in the school-based project as an addition to their normal full-time college commitments and this has caused some strains.

Recommendations

The college intends to expand the school-based programmes because it believes that (i) they can achieve better teaching results for students than a traditional teaching round, and (ii) they have a lasting influence on the attitudes and teaching behaviour of their students by providing the most appropriate environment for reality.

Regular committee meetings of the teams and their evaluators are needed to examine common problems and to co-ordinate school-college involvement.

Commentary

The school-based teacher education programme is an extensive project to re-direct special method work from the college and into the school where on-the-spot involvement may be experienced by both students and lecturers. The variety of method subjects which are now school-based is encouraging and the systematic evaluation of each project is a commendable procedure indicating the thoughtfulness of the planning and organization of the initial pilot study.

Generally the lecturers concerned agree that students have responded well to the school-based work. They are considered to be more open to ideas and more realistic in their attitudes. Students are also more critical of their teaching but they are more tolerant of things that go on around them in both the schools and the college. The students in a wide range of projects have indicated that they find the school-based work more helpful for their teaching than method lectures at college and particularly appreciate the helpfulness and support of the supervising teachers in the schools. Teaching was followed-up by immediate discussion either with their supervisor or the lecturer and this was regarded as a considerable advantage.

Students also note their involvement with pupils over an extended period as contributing to their establishing better interpersonal relationships and resolving any conflicts which may arise. Better curriculum planning and development is also a demonstrable achievement of the projects especially in providing good opportunities for integration of methods across subject divisions in the secondary schools. Students in different method subjects have discovered similar problems and their discussions have also involved the teachers in the schools helping to break down barriers between subjects.

The main problem for the student seems to be disruption to the continuity of his work both at college and at the school, especially with regard to timetabling. The problem for some of the lecturers has been an additional teaching load because of their interest in the school-based work. Full recognition of the project as a viable college commitment was raised by all parties and this indicates the success of this elaborate pilot programme.

The team of lecturers involved strongly believe that future teacher-education courses should be more school-based with potential for in-service opportunities for the teachers who participate. Curriculum resource materials have been an outcome of the many projects and there are some plans for the publication of these for teacher and student use.

[D. T.]

TEACHER INDUCTION

ADJUSTING TO TEACHING COURSES FOR PROBATIONER SECONDARY TEACHERS

School of Education
Macquarie University

G. H. FINLAYSON
Lecturer in Education

Background and Context

These courses grew out of the perceived need for support for teachers in their early years of teaching. Throughout 1974, the writer was acting deputy principal in a high school west of Sydney. The school, in common with all of the schools in this area, had a large staff with up to 60 per cent of teachers being in their first or second year of service.

The difficulties, uncertainties and lack of confidence felt and expressed by first-year probationers at the school at the beginning of 1974 concerned the writer so he commenced and maintained a support programme for that year. It took the form of information and problem-solving sessions, planning sessions, visits to other schools, and talks by experienced teachers and professionals from outside the school.

During 1974 the Area In-service Education Committee advertised for suggestions for in-service courses and the writer expressed a great need for probationer support programmes. The committee requested further ideas and he submitted a possible programme for an eight week course. The committee requested that he design and conduct a three-day conference for deputy principals in the area with a view to promoting in-school support for probationers on a wider front. This conference stimulated wide interest and involvement.

The deputy principals conference was followed by the first pilot three-day residential course for first-year secondary probationers drawn from forty high schools in the area. This course incorporated many of the ideas the writer had used with probationers in his own school. The success and effectiveness of the course was such that the In-service Committee provided for ten such courses to be held in 1975 to assist and provide support for all of the four hundred probationers teaching in the area.

The author designed and conducted the initial courses. At this time, he accepted a teaching post at Macquarie University. With this development, a high school principal was appointed organizer and head of the courses. The writer continued as a conductor of sessions throughout 1975 but with an inhibited capacity to adapt, develop and evolve the courses.

250

Aims and Principles of Operation

The design of the course has the underlying assumption (McLuhan) 'that the media and not the message, is the message'. Consequently, most of the sessions are flexible, experimental, work and planning oriented and involve discussion, role play and simulation. The courses are cross-discipline, providing experience in those skills and knowledges common to teaching regardless of subject taught. The overall aim is to assist probationers to adjust to the complex and multiple situations, relationships, concepts and skills involved in teaching.

The Plan and Its Implementation

Thirty to forty probationer teachers attend each course. A staff of four attended throughout; the convenor/materials organizer, the conductor of the programme, an audiovisual assistant and a teaching situations assistant. Visiting speakers were also a feature of each course. Funding was through Federal Government grants.

Lengthy problem discussion sessions are incorporated in each course. In them, probationers present their problems to the group which attempts to offer suggestions and advice. The value of these sessions rests, not just in the help received but in the general realization that the problems are common and not unique to individual probationers. The recurring problems put forward in these sessions are: class and pupil management, too many classes, insufficient time to organize and prepare, insensitive timetables that require probationers to teach many classes of low ability, being expected to teach subjects and classes for which they are not trained, relationships with staff and hierarchy, inadequate knowledge of school procedures and routines, poor communications systems, and indifferent subject masters.

One session is held on the school and the community. Small groups discuss school-society relationships, the impact of media, migrant backgrounds, teacher vs. pupil values, contrasting views of compensatory education, etc. Verbal reports are presented followed by further total group discussion.

Other sessions, which are practical and experience-oriented, are organized around the topics of group teaching procedures, the inquiry method and its application, evaluation and assessment, teaching and learning, the teacher's role and style, awareness and sensitivity, language, meaning and communication, relevance in education, child management and behaviour, teacher-staff relationships, and discipline.

Problems and Effectiveness

The success of the courses has been such that they are being continued throughout 1976. 'Adjusting to Teaching' is considered successful to the extent that probationer teachers gain understanding of themselves, other teachers, children and teaching. The probationers indicate that the courses are stimulating, of value and meet their most pressing needs. The writer sees the value of the 'Adjusting to Teaching' courses in the provision of continuing training, the introduction of new methods, the extension of experience and the development of professional attitudes.

The effectiveness of the courses has been evaluated by teachers, by officer-observers of the Department of Education, and by professional educators from the tertiary field. As well, all probationers, at the end of each course, complete written evaluations and these are available for inspection. The comments speak for themselves.

The nature and style of the course have influenced significantly in-service education. Observers from other regional areas of education in the state have commenced similar courses and draw upon our ideas and speakers. Primary in-service has commenced courses for probationers. In the schools, consideration and support for the probationer teacher is promoted and is seen to have increased. Teacher educators have indicated their interest in the programme and seek further information.

Recommendations

The need for expanded induction programmes for probationer teachers both in the schools and as residential courses remains imperative. The STEP Project, currently in progress at Macquarie University, already confirms the decline in attitudes and ideals experienced by teachers in their first years of teaching. The project findings reinforce the writer's original subjective assessment. The 'Adjusting to Teaching' course is the required improvement programme and is already operating.

There exists, however, some problems of disfunction created by the super-imposition of departmental heads over the writer as designer-conductor. The dual, even multiple controls inhibit, in the writer's view, a satisfactory development and evolution of the courses.

In rapidly growing areas where large contingents of young and inexperienced teachers are appointed, the need for such courses is great. The author has proposed that advising teams be assigned to various areas solely to work with young teachers, to assist them in initiating, carrying out and evaluating teaching programmes and management strategies. This has received no response.

It is recommended further that, rather than being merely one of many facets of in-service-probationer-teacher support be an entity in itself. The question of induction, support and follow-up of young, novice teachers is crucial to retention and the formation of humane, beneficial and professional teacher attitudes and practices. An organized 'Young Teachers' Support Corps' could operate effectively on a state or even nation-wide basis as the need is felt throughout the country.

In addition, teacher education is felt to be and is, in fact, a terminal process. In their organization, administration and staffing, colleges and universities are not adequately equipped to provide the necessary post-training follow-up and support that is required by struggling teachers. It is believed that a corps, such as the one described, would, by working in conjunction with schools and colleges, create the necessary smooth transition of the novice teacher into professional self-sufficiency as well as stimulating educational quality and innovation.

Commentary

Of all the transitional phases on the educational ladder, the ultimate one, from student to teacher, is potentially the most difficult. Few other beginning professionals are suddenly confronted with such a range of new relationships, with pupils, colleagues, parents and authorities. Few are initially given such heavy responsibilities as the care and instruction of a group of children. . . . And so the complexities could be multiplied. Truly, the concerns and difficulties of the beginning teacher are often extensive and complicated. It is at this time in his professional career, perhaps more than any other, that he requires advice, support and help.

In the last few years there has been a growing concern overseas for the beginning teacher. In England especially, a number of pilot induction schemes have been introduced. In Australia there are stirrings. Our study of innovation has revealed a small number of isolated attempts to tackle the problem. This year the Australian Advisory Committee on Research and Development in Education has commissioned a survey of teacher induction procedures to be undertaken by R. P. Tisher, A. R. Crane and W. Minns. The work of Finlayson, commencing as it did in 1974, represents one of our pioneer ventures in the area of teacher induction. The main thrust of his work occurred in 1975.

The programmes with which Finlayson has been associated have six main features (i) *They are residential.* The young secondary school teachers come together in a Leura motel for some three-and-a-half days. (ii) *They are cross-disciplinary.* The forty teachers in residence are drawn from various subject disciplines and pursue studies largely cutting across subject boundaries. (iii) *They have intellectual demand.* While sharing of problems and experience goes on, teachers are provided with basic reference works and they grapple with quite fundamental issues. (iv) *They involve the participants.* Small-group seminars and workshops, planning groups, role playing, simulation and microteaching are employed. (v) *They use resource people.* Experienced or specialist visitors attend the courses and contribute to sessions. (vi) *They are based on teacher need.* The courses have evolved from the innovator's experience with beginning teacher needs and have flexible components which permit teachers to introduce their unique problems and concerns.

These residential courses seem to have much to commend them. The immediate feedback from teachers involved clearly testifies the value of the courses in promoting self-understanding, and their understanding of colleagues, children and the teaching process. They found the course stimulating and oriented to their most pressing needs. Interestingly, all participants expressed an interest in further courses of this kind. Many wanted a further programme in several months' time. Several others suggested the provision of continuing in-school support. These last points are interesting. The short-term impact of the three-day programme seems great, but is this sufficient? Would it not be desirable to supplement it by in-school activities and perhaps additional out-of-school courses? One has the feeling that Finlayson's 'Adjusting to Teaching' programme is just scratching the surface as far as the needs of beginning teachers are concerned. Certainly, however, it is a step in the right direction. There is a great want in Australia for a thoroughgoing investigation of the needs of the beginning teacher and for the careful evaluation of pilot programmes employing different strategies to meet these needs.

[C. T.]

SEMINARS FOR NEWLY-GRADUATED TEACHERS

Western Australian Education Department

P. A. DESCHAMP
Teachers College Liaison Officer, and

E. S. STYLES
Superintendent of Teacher Education

Background and Context

These seminars were planned to explore the needs of newly-graduated teachers and to try out various means of meeting these needs. This planning occurred early in 1975 and the seminars were held one-half-day each fortnight between May and August 1975. The seminars were a response to the general absence in Western Australia of any induction for newly-graduated teachers. As the seminars were planned and conducted by the employing authority its introduction was fairly easily achieved.

Aims and Principles of Operation

Planning for the seminars was based on the following premises:

(i) There are problems encountered by newly-graduated teachers that are common to the group and which can be minimized as problems by planned group discussion and with appropriate inputs.

(ii) Peer group influence is likely to contribute positively to solving mutual problems.

(iii) Newly-graduated teachers are likely to integrate with the school system more successfully if they are supported in their first period of teaching.

At the planning stage, the following objectives were set for the proposed courses:

(i) To provide a situation in which newly-graduated teachers can discuss their teaching experiences so as to identify strengths and weaknesses in their training and means of increasing the effectiveness of their teaching.

(ii) To enable such teachers to explore problems they have in common.

(iii) To encourage such teachers to be concerned with, and to accept some responsibility for, their own professional development.

(iv) To provide a situation in which the teachers could receive specific inputs that they themselves identified as significant to them.

The Plan and Its Implementation

Newly-graduated teachers in both government and non-government schools in the North-West Metropolitan and Lower Great Southern schools districts were invited to participate. The pilot study was restricted to four groups of about fifteen. This consisted of one primary and one secondary group at each of the two centres. Applicants were accepted so as to have a reasonable balance between male and female, government and non-government teachers. In selecting the applicants an effort was made to involve as many schools as possible. Final numbers were Metropolitan primary 14, Metropolitan secondary 13, Country primary 11, and Country secondary 9.

The format of one morning seminar per fortnight throughout second term was chosen in preference to a solid block of days so that there was time for group feeling to develop. Further, the format enabled flexibility in programming so that later seminars could be modified in the light of earlier results. The format also permitted testing ideas in the classroom between seminars and reporting the results. Each seminar was chaired by a different chairman selected from both education personnel and the community at large. This arrangement was intended to minimize the influence that chairmen could have on the groups. As far as was practical, the topics for the programme were left to the wishes of each seminar group. The plan was conceptualized as involving part discussion, part input suggestions by experienced education personnel, and part workshop activities.

The pilot study was funded by the Schools Commission. Expenses mainly related to relief teachers where they were necessary, and to travel costs for country teachers and visiting speakers at the Albany centre. There was also some postage and stationery cost.

To encourage a diversity of ideas, and to facilitate preparation, a list of topic suggestions was presented to a sample of primary and secondary education personnel including superintendents, principals, experienced teachers and newly-graduated teachers, requesting their priority ratings and further suggestions. On the basis of the data compiled from these returns a draft programme for the seminars was prepared.

The programme for the first seminar allowed time for a discussion of the aims of the project and then an analysis of the draft programme. Suggestions for additions and amendments were called for and discussed. At the first seminar, the programme for the next two seminars was finalized. Some changes in starting and finishing times were made to suit particular groups.

Each seminar programme was organized so as to have inputs from guest speakers and group discussion times. At the conclusion of each seminar, each participant, including the chairman was issued with a reaction sheet and asked to complete it before leaving. The reaction sheet called for comments under two or three broad headings and requested suggestions for the seminars to follow. The information on the reaction sheets was collated and used to influence the planning of the remaining seminars. Participants were sent preliminary material along with the final programme prior to each seminar.

Problems and Effectiveness

Participants often went to some trouble to convey their opinions and suggestions. The comments from all four groups were, with few exceptions, surprisingly similar.

On matters of programme revision the groups were ready to comment and to offer suggestions. The result was that the draft programme quickly became obsolete. Each group developed its own programme. A comparison of any of the final programmes with the draft programme showed that only the first two seminars were held in the original pattern.

A major factor in the programme was the strong desire for more discussion time. One group arranged to commence half-an-hour earlier so as to take an extended morning tea for informal group discussion.

At the final seminar, time was allocated for discussion of the course. Each teacher was asked to complete a fairly lengthy reaction sheet while the discussion proceeded.

All of the 41 teachers who attended the final seminar considered that the programme was an experience that they would recommended to other newly-graduated teachers. When asked to list the aspects of the course that appealed to them some responses came through strongly. These were:

(i)   That they participated in preparing the programme and could change it to suit their wishes. (13)
(ii) That they had an opportunity to attempt to solve common problems that they recognized as important. (13)
(iii) That they could contribute and share ideas rather than just be an audience. (13)

There was some negative feedback also. The most common criticism was the lack of heating in the rooms (11). Further, there was a feeling that they would have preferred even more discussion time and less listening time (9). They suggested that a more flexible timetable would have allowed them to continue with topics when they were proving particularly interesting even if this meant deferring other topics to another seminar (8).

When asked how they would organize a course for newly-graduated teachers most thought either half a day or a whole day per fortnight was preferable (18). There was some support for weekly half days (9) and weekend or holiday periods (5). Almost unanimously (38) they suggested that primary and secondary groups should be separate for the bulk of the programme.

Most advocated a group size of between 10 and 15 (28), and seven suggested groups of less than ten. There were 21 who advocated having more seminars in the course than the six they had. Seven of the participants suggested more than twelve seminars, 14 suggested between seven and twelve seminars, 13 suggested between five and seven seminars, and two suggested less than two seminars. Most of those who were in favour of more than twelve seminars suggested fortnightly or monthly meetings throughout the whole of the first year of teaching.

The teachers were asked what they considered should be the principal focus of such a programme. Most suggested that it should be the perceived problems of the group (29). Some suggested that it should be available aids and equipment (11), and others thought it should be about bonds, transfers, and other departmental information (8). There was also some interest in details about advisory teachers and other forms of assistance (5).

All groups were supplied with a list of the topics they had had in their programmes. They were asked to list those they would include if they directed such a programme. The results were:

Problem children and discipline generally	23
Motivation in classroom teaching	17
Methods of programming (all primary)	14
Attitudes of parents and employers	12
Sharing ideas	12
Record keeping	11
Available equipment	10
Techniques of evaluation	6
Integrated programming	6
Income tax deductions for teachers	6
Career prospects	5
Guided self-analysis	4

Finally they were asked when they thought help could most profitably be given to newly-graduated teachers. The most common suggestion was a programme before schools commence, once appointments are known (11). The teachers were in favour of student teachers being issued with syllabuses and other material at least upon appointment if not when training (6). Some teachers felt that it would be profitable for newly-graduated teachers to be given more definite guidelines by principals and senior masters (6).

The following conclusions were drawn:

(i) The peer group situation enabled a relaxed atmosphere and ready acceptance of the programme. Participants were ready to talk about their problems and many had similar problems.

(ii) The rolling design of the seminars was useful because it enabled the results to be monitored. Topics that were not well received were curtailed, topics that were considered important were developed, and suggestions from the group were incorporated. It was also conducive to the development of group identity. This type of structure, however, did involve twice the travelling that three one-day courses would have involved. The participants suggested that one-day seminars would have meant that they would have had the lunch hour for informal discussion.

(iii) There were some signs of rejection of anything that reminded the participants of their training programme. Group discussion was much more readily accepted than were lecture situations. The topic of guided self-analysis, which the questionnaire results had suggested would be appreciated, was not well received by any group. Although a few individuals expressed interest, each group clearly requested its curtailment. The predominant reason given was that they had covered it in college.

(iv) Since the discussion periods proved successful and many requested increased discussion time, more topics involving just discussion were introduced. These included group discussions where each participant brought something to talk about, discussions with parents and employers, and discussions of mutual problems. The discussion periods were all well received.

(v) One session that involved a newly-graduated teacher as a speaker was particularly well received. She gave a commentary on slides of her classroom which had been arranged as a mock zoo in order to facilitate using an integrated programme. The participants expressed surprise to find that the speaker was only in her second year of teaching. The seminar programme could profitably have contained more topics of this type.

(vi) Most tape recorded sessions were not well received. Although a variety of techniques were tried, it seemed that the absence of a speaker to question lessened interest to the point where each group thought that the information could be better conveyed by some other method. This conclusion increases the difficulty of holding courses in isolated areas where guest speakers are difficult to arrange.

(vii) The flexibility of the timetable pleased the participants but this factor made co-ordinating the four programmes quite complex. Had there been more than four groups, arranging the programme centrally would have been possible only with reduced flexibility.

(viii) The change in chairmen proved to have both advantages and disadvantages. The groups were free to develop their identity without the dominance of a permanent leader. The flexibility made it possible for a wide range of people to be involved. This included both parents and employers. The negative aspects of this procedure were the extra organization that it required and the effect of a poor chairman in the seminar programme. The participants criticized some chairmen for adhering too rigidly to the programme rather than allowing interest to be followed.

(ix) Holding the seminars at teachers centres had the anticipated spin-off that over the period the teachers became familiar with, and began to use, the services of the centres. The staffs of the centres were particularly helpful and made it possible for a seminar to be held without a representative of the teacher education branch necessarily being present.

Recommendations

In view of the experience gained from these seminars, the following recommendations are made:

(i) Beginning teachers require special provision and care. There are common problems among these teachers who are receptive to in-service assistance.

(ii) This in-service provision should relate directly to problems which the beginning teachers themselves perceive.

(iii) The in-service programme should consist mainly of group discussion sessions and of workshops. These could involve discussion with an experienced teacher or discussion of a topic by the beginning teachers themselves with a chairman as a resource person.

(iv) Beginning teachers should be grouped in interest groups, and grouping by grades (primary) and by subjects (secondary) should be encouraged.

Commentary

In Australia the newly-graduated teacher has been expected to assume full responsibility as a teacher from the time he arrives at his first school. Until very recently the reason for this was simply teacher supply in that all available teachers were needed to man the schools. And during this phase any suggestion that beginning teachers should have a reduced range of responsibilities would have been dismissed as impractical. Now that there is a more ample supply of teachers it would seem to be quite practical to give beginning teachers a reduced load and to free them to participate in induction activities. Whether this occurs may depend quite as much on political and administrative attitudes and considerations as on the fact that there are enough teachers to achieve this end.

Certainly there is a case to improve the induction of newly-graduated teachers. Past policy and practice has been very much a matter of 'sink and swim' notwithstanding the interest and efforts both of school principals and of inspectors.

After graduation the tertiary institutions have done little to assist with induction. The responsibility has rested almost wholly with the employer, usually with each of the state education departments. There are several fairly obvious reasons. First, as already noted, all teachers were needed to man the schools and any release for induction activities was impractical. Second, the employer had considerable power to deny the tertiary institutions enough access to their recent graduates. Third, the tertiary institutions have been neither funded nor staffed to undertake any large scale follow-up of their newly-graduated teachers.

At the present time, it seems appropriate to reassess the whole question of induction, and any such reassessment should include the teachers, the employers, and the tertiary institutions. In any such review it would seem first necessary to distinguish between induction and the acquisition of additional academic qualifications. There is case for both, but induction should stand in its own right as a series of activities designed to assist the beginning teacher to enter the school system and to take full responsibility as a teacher.

As the employer must have a keen and direct interest to facilitate and to maximize the contribution of these beginning teachers as soon as possible for the benefit of the school system, the employer has the primary interest in, and responsibility for, induction. While the employer has a key role to play in induction, it would seem foolish to disregard the contribution which the tertiary institutions could make. If greater emphasis is placed on the induction of newly-graduated teachers in Australia, several of the possible patterns are set out below:

(i)   Induction is carried out largely, or wholly, by the employer.
(ii) Induction is carried out largely, or wholly, by the tertiary institutions in a situation where they are adequately funded for this purpose.
(iii) Induction is carried out on a sharing basis both by the employer and by the tertiary institutions, with adequate funding of the latter.

The first pattern certainly is the most likely to be adopted if past policy and practice continue. However, consideration of the second and third patterns seems most appropriate in the present circumstances where each state education department has recently ceased to be massively and directly engaged in teacher education, and where the tertiary institutions are examining their role in the continuing education of teachers. There would be a distinct loss if the pattern which emerged in the future resulted in the tertiary institutions being wholly engaged in courses for additional formal qualification and not having their academic staff involved also in areas such as induction and short courses unrelated to formal qualifications.

The case study related to seminars for newly-graduated teachers shows how the Western Australian Education Department conducted a pilot study to assess how beginning teachers might be helped to assimilate into the school system. Control of the themes of the seminars rested largely with the beginning teachers themselves and there is good evidence that they were well able to define what they wanted and that they were keen to discuss their problems. As the seminars were conducted by the employer, the release of teachers was relatively simple to achieve, but even with a strong element of employer control there were some minor difficulties. And, there were heavy demands on some of the resource persons. The seminars were labour intensive and costly, and in future consideration may be given to holding similar seminars out of school hours. This seems regrettable as teacher release has become a practical possibility considering the current level of teacher supply.

Some readers may criticize the scheme in that only six half-day seminars were held and that these were held between May and August. Some may consider that more appropriate induction schemes are possible. Even so, it should be remembered that the case study is based on a pilot project which provides a valuable preliminary survey of an area which had been long neglected. It is to be hoped that employers especially, and the teachers themselves and the tertiary institutions generally, show real interest in induction from now on. There is need for a catalyst, and the case study shows how a beginning was made and points to a current weakness in present policy and practice where beginning teachers are too often too much neglected.

If there is to be a policy of reduced load and of release for beginning teachers the present adequacy of teacher supply is the foundation on which such a policy can be based. It will be interesting over the next five years or so to see whether employers take the opportunity to plan and to implement such a policy and whether the teachers' organizations demand this policy. It is the first real chance in the past fifty years.

[D. J.]

THE FIRST YEAR OF TEACHING: AN IN-SERVICE COURSE FOR TEACHERS

State College of Victoria
Rusden

MARGARET GILL
Lecturer in Curriculum and Teaching

Background and Context

This pilot course was planned and organized within the Curriculum and Teaching Department of Rusden State College. It arose from a shared belief, common amongst those involved in initial teacher training courses, that the first year of teaching offers particular problems which cannot be solved in advance, and for which most schools fail to make adequate provision. There is an inevitable gap between school experience as the trainee teacher finds it, and the actuality of the first appointment to a school. An inconclusive debate often continues between schools and teacher training institutions: schools tend to say 'Why don't you make Dip.Ed. more relevant? Why don't you teach students how to cope?' Teacher training institutions reply 'Why do you give new teachers so little support? And frequently the most difficult classes?' It was decided to take positive steps in this debate by organizing an in-service course designed to offer support to teachers in their first year of teaching, and based on the underlying assumption that the training of a teacher is a continuing process, which does not finish when he completes his initial training.

Aims and Principles of Operation

The course was organized and run by two lecturers in the Curriculum and Teaching Department—Margaret Gill and Shirley Collins. The arrangements for Karmel funding, and the administrative and organizational details were arranged by Ted Byrt, director of in-service courses within the college. The course was planned as a ten-week unit, to run for one evening a week during term I, 1975. The programme was not defined in advance: it was designed to meet the immediate and specific needs of the teachers enrolling. It was, however, anticipated that it might include: (i) institutional aspects of the teacher's role—relationship to school, administration, staff, teachers' associations, teachers' rights, pupils' rights; and (ii) specific teaching problems—classroom management and control, curriculum theory and innovation, planning, resources, evaluation, workshops in particular subjects.

The course was open to any post-primary teacher in his first year, within a fifty-mile radius of Rusden State College, and limited to twenty participants. It was approved as an in-service course by the Victorian Education Department, listed in the *Education Gazette*, and all eligible schools were circularized at the beginning of the year.

Thirteen teachers enrolled for the course and attendance remained high (ten attended for 70 per cent or more of the course; two attended for 60 per cent or less.) The participants covered the broad spectrum of teaching subjects, ranging over art/graphics, consumer education, social studies, religion, history, science, biology, Indonesian, maths, legal studies, general studies, and English. At the first session participants were asked to explain why they had come, and what they hoped to gain. The response was varied. Three teachers had no approved secondary teacher training qualification and saw the course as a possible opportunity to achieve an instant Dip.Ed. One teacher with a tertiary Dip.Ed. qualification hoped the course would equip him to teach junior secondary classes. Apart from these seemingly inappropriate expectations, the participants all shared similar objectives for the course. These they listed in the following order of importance (determined on frequency of reference):

(i) The course should offer help in overcoming problems of discipline and classroom management.
(ii) The course should provide detailed studies in curriculum development—but at the practical level of syllabus planning, lesson planning and use of resources.
(iii) The course should offer help in answering the questions: 'How do I evaluate what I do and what the pupil does? 'How do I recognize the feedback which will tell me what kind of learning is going on?'

The Plan and Its Implementation

On this basis then, nine sessions were designed which included the following studies. Some, such as 1, 4, 5 and 6 below on a continuing basis. Others, such as 2, 3, 7 and 8 constituted one session only.

1. Classroom management and related discipline problems: Theoretical studies and practical classroom situations.
2. Detailed study of a film-making project designed for fourth form 'problem' children, including studies of films made by the children, taped discussions of the children at work, teacher's commentary on the project, discussion and analysis of curriculum implications and learning/motivation issues.
3. Curriculum innovation in maths (with guest specialist lecturer). A study of the underlying theory and its relevance for subjects other than maths.
4. Microteaching studies (using videotape) with self-evaluation and discussion, analysis of presentation and questioning techniques in a high-content subject (in this case maths).
5. Workshops in course planning held in the Educational Materials Centre of

the college library. Participants planned a five-week programme to be used in their schools later in the year. Study of resources—audiovisual materials, simulation games, new publications.

6. Workshops in which participants presented units of work already given to pupils, for group discussion.
7. Measurement and evaluation—a guest lecturer.
8. Teachers' rights and professional associations—guest lecturer.
9. Dissemination of detailed information listing support organizations such as subject associations, regional consultants, research officers and members of the board of inspectors attached to the Victorian Education Department.

Problems and Effectiveness

At the end of the course participants were asked to evaluate the course, or comment in any way they chose, on its strengths and weaknesses. These comments will be helpful for future planning. There was unanimous agreement on the value of the course for its supportive, 'morale-boosting' function. (It is interesting that this had not been listed initially as a desired outcome). All participants felt that they had benefited from meeting other teachers 'on neutral ground', discovering common problems, and gaining encouragement by re-establishing contact with 'professional thinking' as opposed to the day-to-day struggle for 'survival' and the 'cynical folk-wisdom' of the staffroom. All stressed the value of 'positive reinforcement', the chance to 'rebuild idealism'.

There was unanimous agreement on the value of the course-planning workshops held in the Education Materials Centre. The weekly nature of the programme was seen as crucial, and there was general criticism of the inadequacy of one or two-day annual conferences often organized for first-year teachers. It was felt that support had to be available on a continuing basis if it was to carry over into the school context.

The following activities were also listed as helpful: lectures on professional rights, evaluation, microteaching studies, and the opportunity to look at new curriculum developments in different subject areas. Some critical comments were offered: detailed curriculum planning needed to be carried out in greater depth, and therefore in subject areas. This proved to be impossible because of the diversity of teaching subjects of the participants, and it diminished the effectiveness of these sessions. Participants also felt there were insufficient opportunities to examine and master new resources and new audiovisual materials and techniques. Their final recommendation was that the course should have been available during the day (i.e. in school time), rather than in the evening when teachers tend to be worn out.

Recommendations

Although no major claims are made for this course, its originators felt it had been worthwhile in offering continuing support to the young teachers who participated. It is suggested that institutions such as colleges of advanced education might very well extend their role in the field of further education, by developing on-campus teachers' centres or education centres, using their considerable facilities for the benefit of all teachers within a region, and collaborating with regional directorates and advisers to discover the most effective ways to make such establishments community education centres.

Finally, it is time that effective provision was made for first-year teachers to continue their professional education. There is little value in reducing teaching loads if the time made available cannot be used effectively. The Rusden course was, in fact, little more than a 'band-aid' operation. Education departments could perhaps give more thought to the possibilities of day-release for first-year teachers, and to the best ways of meeting young teachers' professional needs once this has been achieved.

Commentary

This is a simply conceived attempt to help beginning teachers. Two college lecturers, with minimal funding, conducted a two-hour per week evening course (7–9 p.m.) for ten consecutive weeks during March through May using the college's facilities and the services of several guest lecturers. Thirteen first-year secondary school teachers representing various subject areas attended. Although the course planners anticipated some of the major course components, both the aims of the programme and the content of the sessions were determined by the group itself. Thus the course was need-oriented and involved participants from the start. After the initial planning meeting, the nine sessions followed a varied format—discussion, lecture, audiovisual presentation, microteaching, and workshop activity.

Although the course was only brief, the feedback from participants on its value was very positive and struck notes similar to those sounded by first-year teachers in other projects reported in this book. First and foremost they commended its supportive, morale-lifting function. It seems the small group sessions were flexible enough to permit a supportive kind of role to be played by the lecturers when participants described their needs and problems. All the teachers stressed that it was the support on a weekly, continuous basis that was important. Some had previously attended a short two-day conference for beginning teachers and thought that, in contrast, the continuous pattern was superior. All the teachers recommended that similar courses should be made available in school time rather than in the evening when they felt tired.

The Rusden course provides an example of how the talents of college staff and the resources of a pre-service training institution can be combined to provide for the needs of the beginning teacher. No doubt that a large measure of the success of this course was directly attributable to the expertise, enthusiasm and sensitivity of its originators. This raises questions perhaps too frequently neglected in teacher induction programmes. What roles should the leaders or advisers play, and what skills, understandings and attitudes should these people have to perform these roles satisfactorily? Certainly they are not roles that just *any* college lecturer, senior teacher, curriculum specialist, school principal or even inspector, for that matter, can easily play.

[C. T.]

BACHELOR OF EDUCATION INTERNSHIP PROGRAMME

School of Education
Flinders University

Dr G. R. Teasdale
Senior Lecturer in Education

Background and Context

Subsequent to his appointment to the foundation Chair in Education at the Flinders University of South Australia in 1967, Professor J. A. Richardson was faced with the challenging task of developing innovative teacher education courses for intending primary and secondary school teachers. Although the university was only one year old it already was gaining a reputation for its forward-looking approach, particularly in the development of flexible, inter-disciplinary degree programmes. There was consequently considerable opportunity to make a creative and worthwhile contribution in the field of teacher education. One of the few constraints was the stipulation of the state department of education that the pre-service preparation of primary school teachers generally should be limited to a maximum period of three years.

The primary teacher education programme

In developing a three-year course the basic question that emerged was: How can the programme achieve intellectual depth and rigour, and yet provide adequate practical preparation for classroom teaching? Added to this was the perennial problem of developing effective interactions (particularly from the students' viewpoint) between the theoretical and practical aspects of the course. Finally, there was some dissatisfaction with the traditional forms of student teaching experience. It was felt that teaching practice often lacks realism, imposes serious constraints on student initiative, and may force conformity to teaching styles that are incongruent with the standards and ideals of staff in the training institution (Richardson, *et al.*, 1973).

After considerable discussion between university staff and employing authorities a Bachelor of Education degree programme comprising three years of full-time study followed by a two term teaching internship was approved by the University Council. The degree was designed solely for the preparation of beginning primary school teachers, and had the following distinctive features:

(i) extensive freedom in the choice of courses, particularly in non-education areas;

(ii) the opportunity to pursue studies to second year level in any two of the academic disciplines of the university;

(iii) a total of only eight weeks of teaching observation and practice; and

(iv) appointment as a full-time teacher to a primary school in the Adelaide metropolitan area during the fourth (internship) year.

The first three years of the degree were structured in the following way: *Year One.* Students could take the first year of any degree programme in the university. Specialization by different students in such diverse areas as Spanish, earth sciences, politics or fine arts therefore was possible. *Year Two.* One-third of the year comprised studies in education, continuation of first year studies to second year level made up the remaining two-thirds. *Year Three.* The full year was devoted to studies in education, including teaching practice.

First year students attending the university in 1967 were allowed to transfer across to the B.Ed. degree, and a group of seventeen students thus entered the second year of the programme in 1968, completing their internship requirements during 1970. On average, forty-five students have completed the degree during each of the subsequent five years.

Although many minor changes have been made, the basic structure of the degree has remained the same, except for the extension of the internship programme from two terms to a full year.

Aims and Principles of Operation

From the very outset the internship programme has been viewed as an integral and essential part of the structure of the degree. The award of the degree has been dependent, in fact, upon the successful completion of both the academic and the practical requirements of the internship year.

The basic aims of the internship programme have not varied since its inception. They are:

(i)　To allow students to assume a responsible teaching position in a primary school while receiving substantial support and guidance throughout the year.

(ii)　To provide opportunities for students to relate their earlier professional and academic training to the practical teaching situation.

(iii)　To provide remedial assistance to students who encounter difficulties either in the classroom or in the broader school context.

(iv)　To ensure that students do not receive a teaching qualification (i.e. the B.Ed. degree) until they can demonstrate their competence as classroom teachers.

The Plan and Its Implementation

Some features of the programme also remained relatively unchanged. Students still are appointed as full-time teachers in the metropolitan area, with identical salaries and conditions of employment to graduates from three-year Diploma of Teaching programmes in colleges of advanced education. (On successful completion of the internship year, however, their salaries move up a double step on the incremental scale). Principals are expected to treat interns in the same way as other beginning teachers, providing similar support services and in-service activities. Interns differ, however, in terms of the very close contact that they retain with the training institution. They attend the university regularly for seminars and conferences, while support from within the school is supplemented by substantial guidance from teaching advisers.

Role of the teaching advisers

Each year since 1972 the State Department of Education has seconded well-qualified primary school teachers of principal or deputy-principal status to the university as teaching advisers. Appointments are on a half-time basis, with staffing based on a ratio of one adviser to fourteen interns. The secondments are part of the department's 'release-time scholar' scheme, and advisers are required to spend the remainder of their time working towards a further professional qualification.

The work load of the advisers is structured so that they can spend up to four days per week in schools during the first term when their assistance is most needed. Correspondingly, in third term, when the advisers' own study loads generally are at their heaviest, as little as one day per week is spent in schools. Their day-to-day programme is flexible, allowing them to spend more time with interns encountering particular difficulties and with those in less supportive schools. Some advisers prefer to work directly with the student in the classroom, often team-teaching with them in order to demonstrate a particular technique or approach. Other advisers spend less time in schools, preferring to meet students on a more informal basis after school hours. Group discussions involving interns with similar problems or those teaching at the same grade level also have proved valuable.

Essentially, the task of the adviser is

(i)   to provide individual guidance and support to interns in any area where assistance is required (e.g. programming, lesson preparation, discipline, classroom organization, etc.);

(ii) to provide a direct link between the schools and the university, especially when any difficulties or misunderstandings arise;

(iii) to facilitate effective communication between interns and the senior staff of the school;

(iv) to assist interns with written assignments, particularly those requiring the application of theory and research to everyday practice within the intern's own classroom;

(v)   in consultation with university staff, to develop strategies for helping individual interns who are encountering serious difficulties in any aspect of classroom teaching; and

(vi) to assist in the planning and organization of seminars and conferences.

To facilitate their role as mentor and confidant, the advisers do not participate in the formal evaluation of the interns' teaching competence, this task being undertaken by university staff following consultation with school principals.

University course requirements

As outlined earlier, the basic aim of the course-work is to provide opportunities for students to relate their earlier professional and academic training to classroom teaching. In seeking to improve the effectiveness with which this aim is achieved the course requirements have undergone continuous modification each year since 1970.

Originally, all teaching was carried out through fortnightly evening seminars. These did not provide sufficient scope to develop topics adequately, and in 1971 approval was given by the state department for interns to be released for five days during the year to attend conferences at the university (a one-day conference in the middle of first term; two-day conferences in the middle of terms two and three). Evening seminars continued to be held, but on a less regular basis. In general, however, the interns still felt that the courses were too theoretical, and that university staff failed to appreciate the practicalities of day-to-day teaching.

Table F.1 EXAMPLE OF A TYPICAL CONFERENCE SESSION

9.15–10.00	Talk given by university staff member
10.00–10.30	Response by a panel of teachers from the school
10.30–11.00	Break for morning tea and informal discussion
11.00–11.45	Visits to classrooms to observe particular aspects of the theme being implemented
11.45–12.30	Break into small groups to work on prepared discussion questions. Teachers, teaching advisers and lecturers join groups as resource people
12.30–12.45	Summary of major outcomes

To encourage a more dynamic encounter between theory and practice the venue for the second and third conferences was changed from the university to carefully selected primary schools. University staff continued to be involved, but in a very different way. A typical morning session of a school-based conference illustrates the nature of their participation (see Table F.1). Preparation of such a session clearly involves very close collaboration between lecturers and teachers, generally to the mutual benefit of both as well as to the advantage of conference participants.

The second and third term conferences, together with most evening seminars, are planned around two academic courses that were taught sequentially: *Applications of educational theory* examines various problem areas in the classroom (e.g. catering for individual differences) from theoretical and research perspectives. Evaluation is based upon a series of three written papers that require students: (i) to describe a particular problem that they are encountering in the classroom, and to illustrate it with a critical incident or case study; (ii) to analyse the nature of the problem within the context of relevant theoretical or empirical literature; and (iii) on the basis of this analysis, to derive practical suggestions for dealing with the problem in their own classroom. *Primary school methods* is a course that allows each intern to study in some depth one of the basic areas of the primary school curriculum. The two written assignments involve a literature review from which are derived practical guidelines for the intern's own programming and lesson planning in that subject.

Serious academic work does not begin until late in the first term. The focus of the first seminar and conference is entirely therapeutic. Interns are encouraged to express their feelings about beginning teaching using various forms of creative activity (e.g. painting, role playing, etc.), and to work through some of their frustrations and worries in small group discussions.

Problems and Effectiveness

Evaluation of the internship programme has been an on-going process. Several approaches have been adopted: (i) Questionnaires are used each year to sample student attitudes and opinions. These are followed up by informal group discussions on particular aspects of the course. (ii) Regular contact with students in their own classrooms has allowed staff to evaluate the extent to which they are applying theory and research within the context of everyday teaching. (iii) Discussions with school principals and senior administrative staff in the State Department of Education have provided useful feedback on their perceptions of the programme and its effectiveness. (iv) Towards the end of each year the teaching advisers are invited to give an assessment of the strengths and limitations of the internship. Because of their unique role in the programme their insights have been particularly valuable. (v) During the past two years a more systematic evaluation has been undertaken using a case study approach. Detailed interviews and classroom observations have been carried out at regular intervals with a small but representative sample of interns.

It is clear that the programme has become increasingly effective in achieving its aims. Nevertheless, it still has a number of limitations. The greatest restriction is that students are expected to carry a full-time teaching load during their internship year. Despite several representations to the State Department of Education since the inception of the programme, an acceptable scheme has not yet been devised whereby significant reductions can be made to the intern's work load in the schools.

Recommendations

Ideally, the Flinders' internship programme should be seen as a forerunner to the development of support schemes for *all* beginning teachers. Crane (1975) notes that four recent Australian reports strongly encourage the development of induction programmes during the first year of teaching. Most of the proposals envisage a reduced teaching load, support from special advisory teachers, and continuing contact with the training institution. In referring to the development of in-service programmes, for example, the Karmel Report (1973) states: 'Important among these are internships which enable teachers to have lighter loads in order to receive on-the-job assistance and to continue their relationships with the training authority as part of their certification' (paragraph 11. 10).

There seems little doubt that these recommendations eventually will be implemented nationally. It is hoped that the lessons learned in developing the Flinders' internship will be of some use to those responsible for introducing an overall scheme of teacher induction.

REFERENCES

Crane, A. R., 'The Occupational Socialisation of Teachers', *South Pacific Journal of Teacher Education*, 1975, 3(3), 57–64.
Richardson, J. A., G. R. Teasdale and E. M. A. McDonald, 'The Teaching Internship in a Bachelor of Education Programme', *South Pacific Journal of Teacher Education*, 1973, 1(3), 27–32.
Schools in Australia (The Karmel Report), A.G.P.S., Canberra 1973.

Commentary

The Flinders University internship programme is an exciting and bold venture. It basically seeks within the framework of an undergraduate degree course, to round-off the students' professional studies and to phase the students into full-time teaching with advisory support. The programme's detailed objectives are highly commendable, as are such special features as the employment of experienced teachers as the interns' advisers and the interns' release from teaching for attendance at full-day conferences.

As promising as this plan is, especially in the area of the induction of the beginning teacher, it has a number of quite serious difficulties, most of which its originators are fully aware of: (i) *The demands on the interns are heavy.* Complaints of the teaching, seminar and particularly the essay-requirement loads were common among interns. All connected with the programme agree that a reduced teaching commitment for interns is desirable. Some interns, however, would not like to see a corresponding reduction in salary! (ii) *The interns feel ill-prepared for full-time teaching.* They believe that the initial three years of the degree programme are too theoretical and there needs to be more practice teaching and greater attention to primary curriculum studies. This inadequacy of professional background tends to heighten the traumas of internship. (iii) *The role of the teaching advisers is confused.* The advisers believed they had insufficient preparation for their complicated role. They proposed an orientation period which would include consideration of the principles and procedures of their work and discussion with the previous year's advisers. The one-year secondment to such positions was seen as a disadvantage since it took time to build up expertise. The interns had differing views on the function of the adviser, some thought of him as an assessor. (iv) *The gap between educational theory and practice is only very tentatively bridged.* The advisers had little knowledge of the ideas being propounded in the course and some admitted that they suggest a distinctly conventional line of practice to interns and did not necessarily see their role of translating progressive ideas into practice. The interns felt little influenced by the university courses, some of which were judged to be irrelevant. Several interns admitted that they simply tended to teach as they were taught at school. (v) *The co-operation between the school staff and advisers could be improved.* The advisers reported that some senior school staff felt threatened by their presence in schools. They seemed to think the adviser was helping the intern because they were not doing their job. The interns remarked that they received little help from senior staff and believed there could be greater co-operation between these people and the adviser in helping beginning teachers.

Though the harassed interns (interviewed during the lunch hour!) were somewhat negative in their comments on their intern experience, they confessed that the programme had important values. For example: (i) They appreciated the availability of the adviser particularly in the early part of the year when they most wanted moral support and encouragement. They added, however, that the intern and adviser should agree on mutually convenient times for consultation. (ii) They valued the conferences, not so much for their formal professional content, but more for the opportunities to observe teachers in other schools and to talk with fellow interns about common problems.

The concept of internship developed at Flinders provides an interesting example of how a pre-service programme, a state education department and the schools themselves can potentially combine their interests and resources for a common cause, the induction of the beginning teacher. The scheme needs refinement. Some of its problems (particularly those related to intern employment and adviser secondment) are not easy ones to surmount. It is to be hoped that other tertiary institutions engaged in teacher education will soon devise plans to undertake some responsibility for their students' induction to teaching.

[C. T.]

SPECIAL IN-SERVICE PROGRAMMES

PREPARING RESOURCE TEACHERS FOR SECONDARY SCHOOLS: AN IN-SERVICE GRADUATE DIPLOMA COURSE

Kelvin Grove College of Advanced Education

B. O'CONNOR
Lecturer in Psychology

Background and Context

Resource teachers are being trained at Kelvin Grove College of Advanced Education to provide much needed assistance to high school students with special learning problems. Not to be confused with audiovisual resource personnel, the resource teachers take their name from the North American concept espoused by Dunn (1968) that more special education personnel should provide resource services within the regular school setting. Such a move was proposed to stem the tide of special class/school placement for students with varying degrees of learning problems.

Though difficult to find local empirical data on the incidence of students with learning problems at the secondary school level—an area requiring closer attention—it seems that problems have been accentuated in the last decade or so. In Queensland, the incorporation of the Grade 8 year into high schools, the raising of the school leaving age to 15 years, and the apparent reduction in the practice of children repeating primary grades, all suggest greater numbers of learning disabled students entering high schools who in the past would probably have entered employment after primary schooling.

Such students include the mildly mentally handicapped; children of 'low average' ability, sometimes referred to as slow learners; adolescents of average and above average ability with mild or major specific learning difficulties; the physically handicapped, many of whom have been integrated into high schools following many years in special schools; non-English speaking migrant students; the culturally different, including migrant ethnic minority and Aboriginal students; and adolescents with behavioural disorders. Students with such a broad cross-section of skills and abilities provide a formidable challenge to regular class teachers, many of whom are already burdened with the day-to-day problems of frequent class contact, large classes, and perceived inflexibility in curriculum planning and execution.

Three teaching-specialist models appeared to offer some solutions for meeting the special needs of these adolescents and their teachers in the high schools.

1. *Remedial teachers* could be trained to deal with the severe learning disability

270

cases in part-time withdrawal classes and to advise fellow teachers on corrective cases.
2. *'Special Class' teachers* could be given specific training in devising and implementing 'modified' or 'adapted' programmes of work for students unable to cope with the academic demands of the educational mainstream.
3. *Resource teachers* could be prepared with general insights in special education strategies
   —to consult with regular class teacher colleagues on students requiring special assistance;
   —to liaise closely with guidance officers on specific cases; and
   —to advise administration on desirable educational planning for such learning disabled students.

The resource teacher model was favoured as it focuses on the student in his regular classroom setting and provides important in-class supportive services for both the student and his teachers. Such a choice is in line with overseas and local primary school trends and supports the current special education philosophy stressing early intervention and specialist services within the educational mainstream. Special education writers in recent years have supported the move towards in-class support services (Andrews, 1972; Christoplos and Renz, 1969; Dunn, 1968, 1973; Lilly, 1970), discussed the training of resource teachers (Christoplos, 1973; Glass and Meckler, 1972; Shotel *et al.*, 1972; Yates, 1973), considered the roles of such teachers (Jenkins and Mayhall, 1973; Reger, 1972; Taylor *et al.*, 1972), and have begun to examine the effectiveness of such programmes (Glavin, 1973; Shotel *et al.*, 1972).

In Queensland individual high school teachers had been implementing special 'adapted' or remedial programmes for students who were not coping adequately with the demands of the regular classroom. Although dedicated and quite skilled, many were frustrated by the lack of in-service training courses which would give them the additional skills they sought.

A proposal for an in-service course to meet this need was submitted to the Queensland Department of Education late in 1973 by the Kelvin Grove College. Support for a course was forthcoming from the major teacher employers—the State Department of Education, Catholic Education, Independent Schools Association—and from the Board of Advanced Education in Queensland.

A Joint Advisory Committee was established in February 1974, with representatives invited from the three school 'systems' and the college. Meeting weekly, this committee considered guidelines for the role of the resource teacher, the implications of such a specialist for a secondary school, competencies required for the resource teacher and the implications for their training, as well as for the course content.

The Report of the Joint Advisory Committee was published in April 1974, and distributed to all secondary schools in the state in an attempt to obtain feedback from teachers. Subsequently a college submission to the Board of Advanced Education was approved and special funding, recommended in the Cohen Report (1973), was made available to launch the course in February 1975.

Aims and Principles of Operation

In particular the course aims:

(i)   to provide teachers with an understanding of contemporary issues in adolescent education;

(ii)   to provide teachers with an understanding of the psychology and education of exceptional adolescents;

(iii) to provide teachers with insights into modern developments in the field of special education and the relationship of this sphere to the educational mainstream;

(iv) to provide teachers with the theoretical understanding and practical experience to assist colleagues in diagnosing strengths and weaknesses in children's learning abilities and in providing suitable developmental and remedial programmes for secondary school students;

(v)   to prepare teachers to assist colleagues in developing student abilities in functional areas of communication in all school subjects;

(vi) to prepare such teachers with suitable interpersonal relationship skills to enable them to consult effectively with fellow teachers on matters related to their expertise; to share their knowledge and experience with other professions in the area of learning disabilities; and to interpret special programmes to parents and community groups;

(vii) to prepare such teachers with suitable skills to enable them to undertake research and to communicate the findings of research studies to colleagues.

The initial semester of the course is offered only on a full-time internal basis to ensure all teachers have an opportunity to develop necessary resource teaching skills with the advantage of closer interaction with each other, with college staff and key guest lecturers.

Later sections of the course are offered on a part-time basis to allow teachers to assume their new role concurrently with further study inputs. At this point the part-time courses are offered only externally to accommodate country teachers but later, evening internal sessions may be provided for metropolitan teachers if numbers warrant such a move.

The Plan and Its Implementation

The in-service course, leading to a post-graduate Diploma in Resource Teaching (Secondary) requires selected experienced high school teachers to undertake studies initially on a full-time basis, and subsequently part-time.

The first semester of study is taken full-time at the college for seventeen weeks with school experiences receiving high priority. Sessions are timetabled so that considerable portions of time are left available for independent reading.

Contrary to the North American concept, few of the participants have a special education background. Thus the subject 'Exceptional Adolescents' is studied to provide a breadth of insights into the special education needs of adolescents in regular and special schools. A major component of the course, 'Diagnostic and Teaching Strategies for Individualizing Instruction', aims to develop many of the core strategies for the resource teacher's new role. Observation and testing skills are put in perspective with the skills of providing suitable teaching/learning strategies. 'Communication for Exceptional Adolescents' concentrates on the contributions of linguistics to understanding learning difficulties and highlights the communication problems peculiar to each high school subject area. 'Interpersonal Relations and Professional Communication' is a subject considered vital to the success of the new resource teacher role. The ability to relate confidently and effectively with teaching colleagues whose reactions may range from hostile rejection to submissive dependency, and the ability to communicate convincingly with administrative staff on school policies and practices affecting students with special needs are skills receiving special attention.

Course participants, closely supervised by college lecturers, undertake field work in high schools where, in conjunction with class teachers, they study the needs of students in a selected class across subjects and develop a more appropriate programme for a selected student with special problems. These sessions are introduced one day per week for weeks 6–10 and then for the following fortnight full-time.

Following this initial section of the course, the resource teachers are appointed to schools where they embark on their new helping role. Their tasks may include:

(i)   assisting in screening classes and diagnosing students' learning strengths and weaknesses;
(ii) assisting in the development of programmes and materials which will help teachers individualize instruction;
(iii) working with fellow teachers in various subjects to develop relevant reading skills;
(iv) working closely with school librarians and audiovisual personnel in seeking avenues to facilitate learning by means other than difficult textbooks;
(v)   withdrawing some students with 'hard-core' learning problems for intensive teaching;
(vi) discussing with school administration policy decisions for students with special educational needs;
(vii) working closely with school guidance officers and related support agencies in assisting such students and sharing insights with parents.

This initial period is a crucial one if the resource teacher is ultimately to be successful. Skill in communicating with administration, colleagues and students lays the basis for a growing relationship. It is believed that the successful resource teacher gradually earns the confidence of those with whom he works.

Subsequent part-time study is designed to provide on-going support for the resource teachers in the field. 'Current Issues in Resource Teaching' attempts to assist the resource teacher in the formulation and implementation of his tasks which tend to be peculiar to the needs of his own schools. Similarly, 'Emerging Problems in Communication Methodology' provides on-going practical studies in the area of language skills for the exceptional adolescent. 'Contemporary Issues in Adolescent Education' challenges the resource teacher's ideas about philosophy and practice in secondary education particularly in relation to the modern understanding of adolescents. Like 'Exceptional Adolescents' in first semester, 'Modern Developments in Special Education' attempts to broaden the special education insights of resource teachers. Attention is directed to such current issues as integration-segregation, labelling, work experience programmes, problems in psycho-educational assessment, and community responsibility for the handicapped. 'Research Techniques' is aimed primarily at not only providing resource teachers with skills for action research programmes but also with insights for interpreting relevant research reports to their regular classroom colleagues.

Problems and Effectiveness

A key feature of the college programme is the stress placed on inter-disciplinary co-operation in various facets.

(i) *Interfacing experiences*

In order to clarify issues of common interest and seek ways of sharing information and professional responsibilities with other workers, the resource teachers are provided with several professional interfacing experiences in the initial semester of study.

Prior to the in-school practical sessions, the trainee resource teachers meet with school principals, guidance officers and resource teachers for sharing and consultation. Other such valuable interfaces have been conducted with trainee teacher-librarians (another in-service course at Kelvin Grove), trainee guidance officers and guidance officers in the field. It is hoped later to have similar sessions with social workers and welfare officers. Successful inter-professional relationships are seen as a cornerstone of the resource teacher's work.

(ii) *In-school supervision*

Lecturing staff maintain a close advisory relationship with the resource teachers during their practising school experiences. Assessment is made of the resource teacher's understanding of the school environment, of his ability to relate effectively with colleagues and students, of his skills in diagnosis and programme planning for a class and for a selected individual, and of his ability to relate to colleagues. Special attention is paid to the development of an alternative teaching strategy which is appropriate to a child's peculiar learning style. The close supervision allows for a more personal and effective form of advising the trainee resource teachers on facets of their practical work.

(iii) *Communication in the content areas*

The alternative teaching strategy is designed within one of the secondary school subject areas. College staff from relevant departments (e.g. maths, social studies, science, drama) offer assistance in this area. Resource teachers are not expected to have expertise in all subject areas, but should be able to assist special subject teachers with insights into those modalities and media which best suit the individual student's learning style. Greater attention is to be paid to this facet by formulating individual contracts between resource teachers and special subject lecturers so that areas of personal need can receive more specific emphasis.

(iv) *Growing co-operation between institutions*

The developing of effective and cordial co-operation is not only essential for the resource teacher and his colleagues, but also for those involved in training and employing them. The Department of Education, the Catholic Education Office, and the college co-operate closely in advertising the course and interviewing applicants. Further planning is underway for interpretation to school staffs regarding the variability of roles of the resource teacher. Such teachers cannot be imposed on schools: the school system must be able to accept them and programme more suitable educational experiences for the 'exceptional' learners.

(v) *Importance of feedback*

In 1975, two successive intakes of 14 and 11 completed the initial semester of the course, and the first group has continued with part-time study. Regular meetings of the lecturing staff and feedback from course participants have provided important learnings for later intakes. There appears to be a need for greater use of individualized learning modules within the course itself because of the differing teaching backgrounds of the participants. Additional practical experiences are also required particularly for those for whom the teaching of reading is a new skill. Questionnaires distributed prior to each course assist in planning such activities.

Probably one of the most difficult problems which has arisen is the heavy work-load experienced by resource teachers in the part-time semester of study. The three subjects offered in the first part-time semester of the course were found by some to be too demanding when added to the pressures of a new teaching role even though the course work was designed to parallel and assist the work of the resource teacher in the practical setting. Consequently several students deferred one or two of the subjects in order to concentrate on their new task.

As a result, the planned completion of the course in one full-time semester plus two part-time semesters may be difficult for some to achieve. However, the resource teachers are now encouraged to study fewer courses in the initial part-time semester unless they feel able to cope. A possible solution—a further full-time semester to complete the study—has appeal, but is not attractive to employing authorities at this time.

Recommendations

Once the course becomes fully operational—first graduates are expected late in 1976—the college hopes to develop more fully a resources centre and publish information on diagnostic and teaching procedures. No research has yet been undertaken but several projects are being planned to attempt to gauge the effectiveness of the resource teacher role. Certainly the resource teacher model should not be seen as a panacea.

In concert with this development, it may be that mandatory programmes on teaching adolescents with learning problems should be provided in pre-service and in-service courses and so reduce the need for such specialist teachers. Schools have witnessed remedial teachers in the sixties and resource teachers in the seventies. Perhaps more proficient class teachers will be seen in the eighties?

Resource teachers are not super-teachers but merely members of a team with special skills to supplement subject teacher competencies in catering for students' special needs. The success of their role will depend not only on their own merits but also on the ability of the system to utilize their services. In Queensland, both state, catholic and independent high schools are moving in this direction.

REFERENCES

Andrews, R. J., 'Integration: Teaching Children with Special Needs in the Regular Classroom' in Elkins, J. (ed.), *Developments in Teaching Children with Special Needs*, University of Queensland, 1972.

Cohen Report: *Teacher Education 1973–75*. Report of the ACAE Special Committee on Teacher Education, Australian Government Publishing Service, Canberra 1973.

Cristoplos, F., 'Keeping Exceptional Children in Regular Classes', *Exceptional Children*, 1973, 39, 567–72.

Cristoplos, F. and P. Renz, 'A Critical Examination of Special Education Programs', *Journal of Special Education*, 1969, 3, 371–7.

Dunn, L. M., 'Special Education of the Mildly Retarded—Is Much of it Justifiable?', *Exceptional Children*, 1968, 35, 5–24.

Dunn, L. M. (ed.), *Exceptional Children in the Schools*, Holt, Rinehart and Winston, New York 1973.

Glass, R. M. and R. S. Meckler, 'Preparing Elementary Teachers to Instruct Mildly Mentally Handicapped Children in Regular Classrooms: A Summer Workshop', *Exceptional Children*, 1972, 39, 152–6.

Glavin, J. P., 'Follow-up Behavioural Research in Resource Rooms', *Exceptional Children*, 1973, 40, 211–13.

Jenkins, J. R. and W. F. Mayhall, 'Describing Resource Teacher Programs', *Exceptional Children*, 1973, 40, 35–6.

Lilly, M. S., 'Special Education: A Teapot in a Tempest', *Exceptional Children*, May 1970, 43–9.

Reger, R., 'What is a Resource Room Program?', *Journal of Learning Disabilities*, 1973, 6 (10), 15–21.

Resource Teachers in Secondary Schools. *Report of the Joint Advisory Committee*, Kelvin Grove College of Advanced Education, 1974.

Shotel, J. R., R. P. Iano and J. F. McGettigan, 'Teacher Attitudes Associated with the Integration of Handicapped Children', *Exceptional Children*, 1972, 39, 677–83.

Taylor, F. D., A. A. Artuso, M. M. Soloway, H. C. Quay and R. J. Stillwell, 'A Learning Centre Plan for Special Education', *Focus on Exceptional Children*, 1972, 39, 677–83.

Yates, J. R., 'Model for Preparing Regular Classroom Teachers for Mainstreaming', *Exceptional Children*, 1973, 39, 471–2.

Commentary

Several Australian institutions which offer programmes of teacher preparation are also conducting in-service courses which aim to produce specialist teachers who can move into the school system equipped to handle problems associated with children who have learning difficulties. This case study has taken the programme at Kelvin Grove College of Advanced Education as an example of this aspect of current movements in teacher education. An innovative feature of the Kelvin Grove programme which will interest other teacher educators is the adoption of a resource teacher model as the means of placing supportive assistance to classroom teachers in schools.

The advantage of the approach developed at Kelvin Grove is that it produces a teacher specialist not only able to operate in the learning difficulties area, but who is also qualified to operate within a particular curriculum area. This is a distinct advantage when the teachers are being trained for the secondary school sphere. It ensures their more general acceptance by colleagues when developing strategies to assist children when this may involve the use of subject material from a curriculum area. However, it does mean that the resource teacher can, at the same time, approach the particular child's problem from the perspective of an across-the-curriculum viewpoint.

The course work followed by the resource teachers provides an interesting selection from the areas generally accepted as important background themes for those who work with children who have learning difficulties. Nevertheless it was noticeable that teachers who had undertaken this programme and were back in schools, indicated that they felt even more emphasis could have been given to interpersonal relationships themes. The planning team had foreseen that the resource teacher role to be successful would require teachers who were highly skilled in their ability to communicate with their colleagues. They would also need to be sensitive to all aspects of the pressures on interpersonal relationships which their activities might create in schools. The resource teachers indicated that despite this provision, they still felt additional background studies would have assisted their 'on-the-job' effectiveness.

The course commenced with a full-time involvement and continued after the first semester on a part-time basis when the resource teachers were on appointments back in schools. In theory, the continued contact with the teacher education institution appears sound but in practice the demands made by the part-time courses need to be carefully assessed. The resource teachers felt that the pressures of fulfilling the tasks identified for their position were so intense that they had difficulty coping with course work at the same time. It might well be that the type of course work offered in this part-time situation could be structured to take this into account.

It would seem very necessary that arrangements should be made between the teacher education institution and future employing authorities to ensure that the resource teachers (or whatever terminology was used to denote the kind of specialist services provided by such teachers) were used in schools for the purposes implied by their training programme. The Kelvin Grove planning group had faced this problem and had discussed with prospective employers the use of resource teachers in schools. Despite this, the students who were involved in discussions with the research team indicated that several of the first group to be in schools were finding that they were asked to undertake regular teaching duties rather than the specialist functions for which they had trained. It would seem that this is a problem which most programme planners would have to face and hopefully take steps to avoid situations where the required specialist assistance was not in fact being brought into schools.

The Kelvin Grove Resource Teachers Programme contains many examples of the issues which will occur when groups of classroom teachers return to teacher education institutions for re-training in a specialist area and then be expected to return to schools to undertake a new role. As more and more of these types of programmes become part of the Australian teacher education scene, the experiences outlined in this case study may prove a useful source of data for planning teams.

[R. T.]

4 THE ROLE OF CO-OPERATING SCHOOLS IN TEACHER EDUCATION

As mentioned in the preface to this book, a study of the role of co-operating schools in teacher education was commenced some time after the general investigation of innovation itself began. Some thought was given to integrating fully both the research and reporting of the two projects, especially as their methodologies are similar and as much of the work with co-operating schools could well be regarded as innovative. Finally, however, because of the different timing of survey and case study activities and dissimilar commitments and interests of the two teams of researchers, the two investigations were kept largely apart. Accordingly this section on co-operating schools appears as a separate section in this book. An attempt has been made, however, both to indicate relationships and avoid overlap with the study of innovation in teacher education. The investigation of the work of special co-operating schools in teacher education is in fact a sharply focused study within a wider one and conclusions from the study will be integrated with more generalized conclusions about innovation in teacher education in the final chapter of this work.

As revealed in the sections of the innovations survey analysis dealing with practice teaching, school-based activities, teachers and pupils on campus, and laboratory schools, there is a growing awareness among Australian teacher educators of the great importance of various forms of practical experience, of introducing more reality and relevance in programmes, and of intimately relating educational theory and practice. This fresh awareness has pointed to the development of a new and closer co-operative relationship between teacher education institutions and schools.

Already a number of teacher education programmes have formed, or are in the process of forming new relationships with special co-operating schools located either on- or off-campus. Many more programmes, it seems, are contemplating similar developments. This movement has been promoted by other factors than the kinds of awareness mentioned above. For instance, teacher education programmes have become increasingly dissatisfied with the work of long-established demonstration schools, especially since state departments of education have withdrawn special funding for such schools leaving the teacher education institution to find it. At the same time conventional school practice teaching, supervised increasingly and perhaps inadequately by classroom teachers, is proving both expensive and even wasteful of students' time. Are there not other arrangements with schools that can better fulfil some or all of the

278

functions of the demonstration and practice schools and perhaps have newer valuable functions as well? Prompted by like questions, some teacher education programmes have realized that a co-operating school can provide such things as (i) a setting in which unique forms of professional laboratory experience can be pursued (e.g. child study, microteaching, and participation in curriculum development), (ii) a context for research and innovation involving tertiary staff, teachers and student teachers, and (iii) a centre for various forms of in-service education and for the dissemination of new ideas, plans and materials developed in the school.

Our study of the role of co-operating schools has passed through three main phases, each of which has subsequently become a sub-section of this chapter. The investigation began with a review of past and contemporary literature concerning the involvement of schools in teacher education in Britain and the United States. Against this background, a survey was made of current co-operating school arrangements in Australian teacher education programmes. From the many arrangements reported, a range of interesting examples was selected for detailed case studies.

CO-OPERATING SCHOOL ARRANGEMENTS OVERSEAS

To provide a backdrop for the consideration of Australian ventures, the study of the role of co-operating laboratory-type schools commenced with a search of relevant overseas literature, most of it originating from the United States. The review was subsequently broken down into a number of parts and written-up by the investigators. Five main areas are discussed: (i) general background perspectives on the involvement of schools in teacher education; (ii) examples of co-operating programmes; (iii) selected functions of co-operating arrangements; (iv) current problems of co-operative ventures; and (v) future planning for special co-operating school relationships.

Background

From the time of the establishment of the first institutions specializing in the training of teachers in seventeenth-century Europe, involvement of the student teachers in schools for children linked with the institutions has been a continuing feature. These schools initially had two main functions: they provided a place where prospective teachers might observe 'approved' techniques and methods of teaching being illustrated, and where they might themselves attempt to conduct lessons under the supervision of an experienced teacher. Although such schools have gradually taken on more refined and extended functions, the themes of demonstration and practice teaching have been consistently dominant (Fristoe, 1942; Lamb, 1962).

In the last century or so, schools co-operating in teacher education have been given varied titles according to what was considered their main purpose. At least five titles have appeared: model school, training school, practice school, demonstration school, and laboratory school. Such titles did not emerge in chronological order. Sometimes, several types developed simultaneously. At times too, their work seemed to be almost identical.

The model school. These schools were seen as providing the best example of school organization and method that beginning and experienced teachers should absorb through observation and practice. They were, in fact, the model for the education system. Student classes in pedagogy mirrored the same ideas and practices exemplified in the school.

The practice school. While observation continued to be a function, these schools provided prospective teachers with the opportunity to acquire teaching methods through practice under the guidance of a master. These schools were not necessarily regarded as an ultimate example of a particular system of teaching.

The training school. Closely linked with the teacher training institutions, the training school attempted to reflect in practice the theory being advocated. In it, through observation and practice, students could experience pedagogical principles. Such experience supported and extended their study of these principles. One of the most influential American training schools was the Oswego Training School, New York (Chittenden, 1925). It initially reflected Pestalozzian principles preached at the college with which it functioned, under the same roof, as an integral part. Members of faculty worked in both places, spending a substantial amount of time in the school providing demonstrations and supervising teaching practice. Much of the teaching in the school was done by students implementing suggestions offered in theory and methods courses.

The demonstration school. These schools were founded to associate the theory and practice of Herbartian pedagogy and to demonstrate it in operation. Following Herbart's formal steps of teaching, demonstration lessons were carefully planned by specially selected teachers. Students studied the lesson plans, observed the lessons taught, and attempted to teach the same or similar lessons in practice teaching (Blair *et al.*, 1958). A vital aspect of the demonstration lesson was that it was to be integrated with the student's theoretical learning. For example, commenting on the work of the demonstration school connected with the University of Manchester, J. J. Findlay wrote in 1908: 'The demonstration lesson is selected from the regular programme of the class, to exemplify certain principles of teaching and method; it is preceded by an account in the lecture-room of the aims underlying the work and followed at a subsequent lecture hour by discussion of results. The student's part is to record the lesson and to seek an interpretation of what he witnesses' (p. 37). Like a few other demonstration schools of the time, the one at Manchester also provided an opportunity for lecturers and teachers to 'undertake research into educational problems' (p. 1). This activity, however, was in America to become mainly linked with laboratory schools.

The laboratory school. The laboratory schools, in name, grew largely out of the so-called 'scientific movement' in education towards the close of the nineteenth century. At first many of these schools were essentially experimental in character. Probably the most famous school of this category was the laboratory school founded by John Dewey at the University of Chicago in 1896. Mayhew and Edwards (1939) described its role as follows:

> Conducted under the management and supervision of the University's Department of Philosophy, Psychology and Education, it bore the same relation to the work of the department that a laboratory bears to biology, physics or chemistry. Like in any such laboratory, it had two main purposes: (1) to exhibit, test, verify, and criticize theoretical statements and principles; and (2) to add to the sum of facts and principles in its special line. (p. 3)

Other universities soon opened schools that had an experimental function. Probably the most notable of these were the Lincoln, Horace Mann, and Speyer Schools established by Teachers College Columbia, the school founded by J. L. Meriam at the University of Missouri, and the Ohio State's University School.

Although Dewey saw his school as not participating directly in training teachers, the experimental schools at Teachers College Columbia did. Besides pursuing child study and the improvement of curriculum and method, they functioned also as demonstration schools for student teachers. For example, the Horace Mann School provided opportunity for prospective teachers 'to observe good teaching under favourable conditions in order to fix ideals and to establish a practical standard of merit' (Russell, 1902, p. 3). Professors in the college supervised the curriculum of the school. Teachers were 'selected with a view to their ability to demonstrate what is deemed feasible in any grade or class' (Russell, 1902, p. 3). Opportunities for student practice teaching were limited, since the school's real object of experimentation would 'be lost if any appreciable disturbance in class work were occasioned by amateur teaching' (Russell, 1902, p. 3).

During the initial decades of the twentieth century the term 'laboratory school' became commonly applied in the United States to on- or off-campus schools associated closely with state colleges and universities in providing various professional experiences for students and in improving educational practice. They continued the classical functions of demonstration, practice and experimentation, and, in addition, accepted several new functions. It soon became 'the thing' in America for a teacher education programme to have its own designated laboratory school. Indeed, the 1926 meeting of the American Association of Teachers Colleges adopted the standard that each 'teachers college shall maintain a training school under its own control as part of its organization, as a laboratory school' (Yearbook AATC, 1926, p. 11).

During the 1930s laboratory schools played a major part in introducing 'participation' as a technique of teacher preparation. Participation had the purpose of 'gradually introducing students into the knowledge and skills demanded in the teacher's duties' (Dawson, 1937). It was conceived as a stage of training intermediate between passive observation and student teaching. Linked with campus courses the typical participation programme involved students in sharing with teachers a comprehensive range of activities—helping individual pupils, observing children, maintaining the classroom and its materials, using aids, supervising playgrounds, keeping records, checking hygiene, testing, planning the daily programme, and so on.

Also in the 1930s many colleges and universities began to use their laboratory schools to provide 'summer demonstration programmes' for undergraduate and graduate teachers. Often student teachers and tertiary staff participated in planning with teachers a progressive or comprehensive programme of work. Mornings were then spent observing the teachers implementing plans, and afternoons in seminars discussing the teaching and related theoretical issues. The programme closed with an overall evaluation of its operation (Hayes and Campbell, 1948). Sometimes, the demonstration programmes were organized to give participants first-hand contact with specific recent educational innovations (Tyler, 1940).

As the teacher education enterprise grew in size and complexity, the demands on the laboratory schools became great. As a result practice teaching increasingly became the responsibility of off-campus co-operating schools, leaving many on-campus laboratory schools to concentrate on providing a variety of other pre-service experiences for student teachers. Some laboratory schools did, however, continue to be quite heavily involved in practice teaching (Thomas, 1956). Generally the schools' research function became a comparatively minor aspect of their work. In this period of pressure and change many laboratory schools were beset by problems. By the 1950s educationists often seriously questioned the value of the laboratory schools. Was the cost of conducting them commensurate with the value of their contribution? Was the work of the school relevant to the theory of the training programme? What were the appropriate functions of these schools? Were not numbers of these schools atypical in staff and pupil population and thus not acquainting students with the real world? Had the schools really made any significant improvement to education through either training, research or innovation? When negative or uncertain answers were provided to these and other questions, a large number of laboratory schools were closed down. Currently there is still a good deal of rethinking going on as to the role of laboratory-type schools in teacher education.

In response to the criticism of campus laboratory schools and a concern for their future, during the 1950s and 1960s there were a number of investigations aiming to establish the nature, functions and problems of these institutions and to suggest ways in which they might be improved (see Blair, *et al.*, 1958; Lamb, 1961; White, 1964; Sale, 1967). An early example of such investigations was the one reported by Ashmore (1951). Through interview and questionnaire he surveyed the operation of eleven selected campus laboratory schools in four southeastern states. In the light of data collected the following were among the conclusions drawn: Most of the campus laboratory schools were not being used extensively for student teaching, but were rather concentrating on developing co-ordinated programmes of observation and participation. The great majority of schools were not engaged in research. This appeared to be 'due to lack of funds and facilities, the lack of co-operation and co-ordination between laboratory and college faculties, the overloaded conditions of the laboratory faculty, the lack of understanding, and the lack of interest' (p. 89). More generally the work of many laboratory schools was seriously hampered by the 'lack of clearly demarcated administrative responsibility and authority' (p. 91). They were given little autonomy and were too dependent on the college or department of education. Further, the majority of schools did not have 'clearly defined purposes which emanate from the laboratory faculty and which are appreciated and understood by them' (p. 91). This prevented concerted effort from school staff to accomplish desired goals. Linked with the want of autonomy and purpose was the frequent turnover of both teaching and administrative personnel which, in turn, had caused confusion in the programmes of schools. Despite all these difficulties, it is worth noting that almost all college and school staff surveyed agreed that the laboratory school should be a vital, focal point of a teacher education programme and that the essential tasks of laboratory schools were demonstration and participation *and* experimentation.

Ashmore's study was followed by others, only a few of which need to be mentioned briefly here. In 1964 White investigated the status and potential of over a hundred randomly selected college-controlled laboratory schools. Alongside their central purpose of providing a sound education for their pupils, most laboratory schools considered the provision of 'laboratory experiences' for students as a major function. Such experiences included all those planned contacts with children and teachers through observation, participation and classroom teaching which contribute to the student's understanding of individuals and their guidance in the teaching-learning process. A possible future change in laboratory schools was seen as making increased use of closed-circuit and video-recording television systems to provide students with wider opportunities for observation. In 1967 Sale analysed the functions of campus elementary schools affiliated with state colleges and universities. Among the chief findings of this study were the following:

(i)   the provision for pre-student teaching laboratory experiences was the most important function of these schools;

(ii)   the schools were attempting to perform too many functions and were failing to identify and to perform these functions at a high level of competence;

(iii)   the schools were nevertheless serving a definite need in a prospective teacher's education and should be considered as an integral part of the total teacher education programme;

(iv)   the school provided an excellent environment in which the prospective teacher may experiment with the integration of theory and practice; and

(v)   the major strengths of the schools were the quality of freedom for innovation and experimentation, and the quality of the instructional programme for pupils. (pp. 151–6).

In his recommendations, Sale underlined the need for laboratory schools and affiliated institutions to develop better mutual understandings of the school's objectives, functions and programmes, of their strengths and weaknesses, and of plans for improvement.

In another study of 115 campus elementary laboratory schools, Land (1969) obtained data on the nature and quality of the 'pre-student teaching laboratory experiences' they provided. Among other things he found that

(i)   While the schools provided adequate opportunities for students to observe and participate in the roles of the teacher in the classroom, in the school, and in the community, students did not participate sufficiently in the last two settings.

(ii)   There was little correlation between the laboratory experiences and either academic or professional college courses. The institutions generally used problems and achievements arising from the laboratory experiences as a source for related college seminars.

(iii)   In general, college lecturers did not undertake much of the responsibility and guidance of the laboratory experiences with the teacher. In half the institutions however, the evaluation of students involved both college and school staff.

(iv)   In providing laboratory experiences the schools did not consider the needs and abilities of particular students. In fact, the schools showed a disinclination to modify the nature or length of the experiences.

(v)   The schools emphasized guiding students in their experiences through pre-observation and post-observation discussion.

(vi)   The channels of communication and contacts between schools and colleges were generally inadequate.

(vii)   According to the schools' directors, the major strength of the experiences offered was the opportunity to have individual contact with pupils; and the major weakness, the provision of an insufficient number of experiences. (pp. 165–9).

Like other investigators, Land recommended greater co-ordination between college courses and the work of laboratory schools, and closer collaboration between college and school staff in planning, supervising and evaluating both the activities of students and the laboratory-experience programme as a whole.

While a number of investigations like the ones above were taking place, proponents of laboratory schools began to advocate how these schools could have new and important emphases. For example, Rogers (1952) suggested that the campus laboratory school might play a central role in connection with child development programmes in teacher education. In outlining a model programme in which student teachers observed and grew to relate to and understand children, she stressed two principles—(i) that 'theory should be used to explain the behavior of children, and children not be used merely to illustrate points of theory', and (ii) that the 'course should be of the laboratory type, with the campus school as focus. The classroom is the conference room where students learn to interpret what they see in the laboratory' (p. 233). Features of the course included co-operative planning of an integrated programme by lecturers and teachers; observing, meeting and having active dealings with children both in-school and out-of-school; campus school children visiting college classes; teachers acting as consultants in college classes; the flexibility of the programme to provide for both planned and incidental observations; and 'growth studies' of selected children over a sustained period. Thomas (1956) proposed that laboratory schools should play an important part in studying and evaluating innovative educational practices which could feed directly into teacher education programmes and into other schools. He did not believe, however, that laboratory schools having involvement in teacher preparation could satisfactorily carry out extensive basic research on teaching and learning. They should concentrate rather on being centres of innovation in which promising practices could be selectively introduced, appraised and perhaps adopted as an integral part of the ongoing programme of the school.

While American teacher educators were debating the future of the laboratory schools, colleges and universities in Britain had largely discontinued special links with demonstration schools which today have all but ceased to exist. Instead, institutions have enlisted the co-operation of a range of schools which generally agree to do little more than offer 'practice places' to students (Lomax, 1973). It seems that experience in 'ordinary schools' has been preferred to the expense and judged artificiality of observation in demonstration schools.

A similar movement has also occurred in Australia. The demonstration schools have either been closed down or have had their functions modified. Nevertheless it must be acknowledged that in this country the demonstration schools had strong and continuing involvement in teacher education at least to 1950. The 'practice' or 'demonstration' schools were highly regarded by colleges and operated in close collaboration with them. Some idea of the former nature of these schools and their relationship to training institutions may be gained from the following extract from the report of the principal of the Teachers College in Adelaide, A. J. Schulz, in 1929:

> These Practising Schools are staffed with teachers specially selected not only for their skill in teaching children, but also for their fitness to serve as guides and inspirers of student teachers. The work involves as good deal of labour and strain beyond that of an ordinary class teacher, and it is gratifying to report how whole-heartedly and efficiently the masters and mistresses of method and the demonstration assistants have carried out their highly important duties.

As a means of increasing interest and efficiency . . . combined meetings of the staffs of the College and practising schools (were regularly held) at which both specific problems and also more general problems relating to teacher training and education generally were discussed. (p. 26)

During the last three decades the role of the Australian demonstration school has declined. The reasons for this are complicated. For example, dramatic increases in student-teacher members meant that many colleges had to look beyond the demonstration school for settings for practical work, including observations. Communication between colleges and demonstration schools became poor— teachers complained of inadequate briefing and lecturers complained of inadequate translation of suggested ideas. Students were critical of the artificiality of demonstration lessons. College and school staff seemed reluctant to co-operate in improving the school's functions. Perhaps there was a tendency among some college staff to underestimate the value of observational work in schools. Some senior department officers opposed the exclusiveness of demonstration schools. Well-qualified teachers often refused to work in the schools because of the apparent pressure of the job. When colleges became autonomous and were forced to pay the demonstration teachers' special allowance, many college administrators judged that the expenditure was not worthwhile. While these and other factors have led to the demise of many demonstration schools, in some centres the teacher-education functions of the schools have been modified and extended. For instance, in 1969 the Report of the Minister of Education in South Australia, commenting on demonstration schools, revealed that consideration was 'being given to the establishment of experimental schools to work even more closely with teachers colleges' (p. 13). Two years later, the minister reported that a development in the demonstration school area had been

the establishment of laboratory schools close to the teachers colleges. Such schools provide for continuous student observation, research by college staff and students carrying out advanced work, and the interchange of teaching staff and college lecturers (1971, pp. 8–9).

During the 1970s, as will be revealed in this study, the attitudes of Australian teacher educators to school co-operation in the preparation of teachers has begun to change quite markedly. Although formal observational work still has a place, a whole range of new and quite exciting teacher education functions are being undertaken with the collaboration of selected schools. The real world of school and classroom is being seen as a focal point for teacher education programmes.

Examples of Co-operating Programmes

A survey of the relevant literature reveals a considerable diversity in planned or established co-operating programmes between institutions concerned with teacher education and schools or other educational agencies. Whereas the programmes all reflect attempts to provide a dimension of reality to teacher education courses, it would be difficult to identify elements common to them all. It is considered that a more meaningful method of illustrating the characteristics of such co-operative programmes is to present a range of representative examples. In each of the examples which follow the title draws attention to a feature considered to be of particular interest. They range from simple school-based 'methods' courses integrating theory and practice, through highly developed schemes involving tertiary institutions and school systems in the collaborative provision of both pre-service and in-service teacher education, to a remarkably successful campus laboratory school.

An Off-campus Programme

Walsh (1970) describes an attempt to provide more relevant learning experiences for students undertaking a methods course. The programme, as suggested by the title of his article, 'Let's Move the Methods Course Off Campus', is field-based. The course is structured around a series of episodes. At an inner-city school the students participate in a theoretical session in which a particular teaching strategy is introduced. The strategy is later demonstrated by a teacher who has previously met with the methods lecturer in a joint planning session. The students subsequently have the opportunity to plan and then apply the strategy themselves in a videotaped microteaching session with the pupils of the school. A later session provides opportunities for analysis, with the assistance of videotape replay.

Advantages of the programme include those of relevance and the immediacy with which teaching experiences follow theory sessions. Early introduction to the classroom develops students' understanding of the inner-city child, and further, provides opportunities for students to discover whether in fact they wish to become teachers. The videotaping of demonstration sessions enables the building up of a library of teaching episodes which students may use to assist in the planning of their own lessons.

A Methods Course-Student Teaching Co-ordinated Programme

Knight and Wayne (1970) describe an exploratory programme which was designed to overcome many of the problems traditionally associated with methods courses and student teaching experiences. The programme seeks to integrate a social studies methods course with classroom activities during the teaching practice period. A strong feature of the programme is the close co-operation between the university staff and classroom teacher. Another aspect of interest is that the programme makes little additional demands upon finance and personnel.

The essential elements of the programme comprise a Social Studies Curriculum and Methods course, student teaching experiences, and related seminars. During the student teaching period students attend two Social Studies Curriculum and Methods sessions at the university per week, each of two hours duration. In the school classroom they undertake activities related to their coursework, thus applying the theory they have currently been discussing. The co-operating teachers who supervise the students are familiar with the students' needs through their attendance at orientation and preparation sessions prior to student teaching. They also attend some sessions arranged during the student teaching period while the student teachers supervise their classes. In alternate weeks during the student teaching period, two-hour seminars are held at the school, attended by the students, teachers, co-operating teachers and the college supervisor. At these sessions problems are shared and analysed.

The project is reported to have succeeded in overcoming many of the commonly stated deficiencies associated with methods courses and student teaching. It brought lecturers, teachers, and students together in a programme which was felt to be constructive and meaningful for all participants.

A 'Teacher-Assistant' Plan

The teacher assistant programme, organized jointly by the University of Montana and the local public school system, is designed to provide teacher trainees with laboratory experiences, while at the same time meeting the needs of teachers and schools co-operating in the project.

The programme, as described by Morin (1974), forms a course unit for teacher trainees, 'Education Laboratory Experience'. A particularly interesting feature of the programme is the careful matching of students' requests for particular kinds of field experience with the needs of schools and teachers as specified on teacher assistant request froms which schools have been invited to submit.

The teacher assistants are not paid for their work in the schools but receive one college credit for each thirty hours spent in the field activity. College courses requirements are so structured that the 'Education Laboratory Experience' is taken concurrently with education subjects, providing opportunities to relate theory to the classroom. Through participation in the programme students also gain worthwhile pre-student teaching experience.

Morin's evaluation of the programme led to recommendations which included the provision of longer blocks of time for the in-school experiences, more imaginative use of the teacher assistant in the school (including more opportunities to be involved in instruction) and more adequate university supervision in the field. Some further recommendations were:

(i) the laboratory participation phase should be structured to enable more effective preparatory planning with the university student adviser,

(ii) communication with parents concerning the programme should be improved; and

(iii) provision for adequate feedback to teacher assistants, along with the making of permanent records of the experiences, should be considered.

A Co-operatively Planned and Implemented Programme

A co-operative programme involving George Peabody College and the Nashville public school system was reported by Moseley (1973). The elementary teacher preparation programme is centred upon the Cora Howe Elementary School. As the college and the Nashville public school system had worked together previously in the design of the Cora Howe Elementary School, their collaboration in the development of a school-based Foundations of Education course was a natural extension of a relationship that was already well established.

The programme, as described by Moseley, comprises three phases:

Phase 1. Students take a Foundations of Education course based at Cora Howe School. At the school the students work as teacher aides, observing teaching situations and participating in a range of activities at all levels of the school. The observations and activities are carefully planned by the teachers to meet the students' likely needs. The students meet regularly with the instructor for discussion sessions in which they are encouraged to relate their school experiences to the theory courses. During this first phase of the programme the student's activities and observations assist him to make career decisions, while at the same time the college is able to diagnose student difficulties and provide relevant assistance.

Phase 2. The college students participating in the second phase of the programme at Cora Howe School carry out teaching activities directly related to their methods courses which they are taking concurrently. An important aspect of this phase is the joint planning session when college and school staff discuss objectives, expectations of students, and appropriate classroom activities.

Phase 3. The third phase of the programme relates to the student teaching semester in which students participate with the teachers as members of teaching teams. The school faculty members work closely with the student teacher in planning sessions, analysis of teaching episodes, conferences, and in continuous evaluation. A weekly review session is organized by a college faculty member, in which students are encouraged to reflect upon and evaluate their experiences.

The George Peabody-Cora Howe programme is one in which school staff play a responsible part, not only in planning and implementation stages, but also in the evaluation of the college students. The programme is enhanced by the fact that the Peabody programme co-ordinator is at the school on a full-time basis. This enables her to be thoroughly familiar with the school, the curriculum, the staff, and available resources, and be readily accessible to the college students and Peabody instructors working within the school. The programme as outlined benefits the college students and also serves an in-service function for the school staff who participate. The close relationship between the school-based Peabody programme co-ordinator and the Cora Howe curriculum co-ordinator enables an interchange of ideas and facilitates the indirect and direct involvement of the Peabody staff in in-service work within the school.

Moseley (1973) reported that both the college and the Nashville public school system considered the programme to be a success and that plans were being made to develop a similar teacher preparation and in-service programme in further schools.

Joint Staff Responsibility for Pupils and Trainee Teachers

Shuff and Shuff (1972) propose a teacher education scheme which they believe would ensure the successful integration of theory with practice. A novel feature of the programme is that joint responsibility is to be taken by college instructors and high school teachers for the instruction of school pupils and trainee teachers.

It is envisaged that a team would comprise an equal number of master teachers (with appropriate college rank) and college instructors. There would be no differentiation in status between the staff involved in the programme. For part of the year half of a team would teach the pupils and supervise the classroom-based activities of student teachers working within the school. During this time the other half of the team would be involved with running the teacher education courses at the college. At a later period they would exchange roles.

A scheme such as this would, it is suggested, provide for a well integrated programme with benefits to the staff concerned, the student teachers, and the pupils. Certainly, team members, through their classroom teaching experience with pupils and their college coursework with trainee teachers, would be thoroughly familiar with student teachers' needs in relation to all aspects of the programme. The interrelationship of the high school classroom activities with the methods coursework would be facilitated by the joint planning of team members who hold a common interest. In order to increase opportunities for observation and analysis of class activities, Shuff and Shuff advocate the use of closed-circuit television at the school.

The funding agencies suggested by Shuff and Shuff are: university, public schools, and the state education agency. Assistance in the administration of the programme could come from professional organizations. It is a shared programme which could, they believe, lead to 'excellence in teacher education'.

Co-ordinated Use of Laboratory and Portal Schools

The elementary teacher education programme at Utah State University was modified substantially in 1972 and among the stated objectives of the new programme were the following:

> to provide a series of practicum experiences that are directly related to theories of instruction and teaching; to provide a co-operative education program for teachers utilizing the personnel and resources of the public schools and the University working together. (Taggart *et al.*, 1974, p. 1)

In order to achieve these objectives the elementary teacher educators at Utah established close links with seven schools which became known as 'portal schools'. The portal school arrangement has been incorporated into the programme in order to complement the contribution of the on-campus laboratory school in achieving the objectives noted above.

While the Utah portal schools fulfil the traditional role of schools involved in practice teaching, they have, in addition, more extensive contacts with the university or college personnel. The involvement of university staff in these schools occurs at a number of levels: (i) University staff conduct seminars for students at the portal schools on the foundational aspects of teaching. The seminars are conducted in association with the students' ongoing observation of, and involvement with, children as tutors and classroom aides during the schools' morning session. (ii) University staff are closely involved in ongoing in-service workshops with the co-operating teachers. The workshops are designed to promote the supervisory skills necessary to provide support for student teachers, and to improve the teachers' own teaching skills.

This portal school arrangement needs to be viewed in the context of the overall programme. The programme is termed SODIA which is an acronym formed from the first letter of the focus word for each level. 'S' stands for *Self*, which is normally a freshmen-level course that 'emphasizes the student understanding himself in relationship to his ability and desire to teach'. The student is involved in a variety of in-school experiences and seminars in order to provide a context for a reasonable decision about whether to continue with teacher training. 'O' stands for *Others* which is a course offered on-site at a portal school by university staff. Approximately seven hours per week are spent in seminars on foundational aspects of teaching (e.g., Educational Psychology, Human Growth and Development), while each morning is spent in the classroom working with children as tutors. 'D' stands for *Disciplines*, a course offered on-site at the Edith Bowen Teacher Education Laboratory School by a team of university staff. Students are assigned to method classes 'in Reading, Social Studies, Language, Arts, Science and Mathematics', which are offered in conjunction with practical experiences. The practical experiences are carefully prescribed in order to ensure that the students reach a degree of proficiency in teaching in all five method areas. They are involved in a teach-reteach cycle which is designed 'to help students individualize instruction'. The teach-reteach cycle is based on a competency model, where student teachers progress at their own rate as they show proficiency in the teaching methods required. Feedback is provided by the laboratory school teacher and the method lecturer from the university so that the student can concentrate specifically on the aspects of the teaching event which were deficient. The teach-reteach cycle continues until the student teacher displays the required competency. 'I' stands for *Implementation* and 'is the final step needed for basic certification as an elementary school teacher'. At this stage the students are assigned to portal schools for student teaching where they 'become part of the professional team'. The student teaching programme is monitored both by co-operating teachers and the university staff who are constantly in contact with the portal schools. The final level 'A' stands for *Associate Teaching* which is an optional elective for students 'who are interested in additional experiences in the public schools to either refine or improve upon their professional teaching methods and techniques'. These programmes are devised on an individual basis and could involve extension or remediation experiences, or specialized work in particular settings such as rural schools or team teaching arrangements (see Petrie, 1973, pp. 1–2).

As indicated above, the planners of SODIA clearly regard the task of learning the central techniques of teaching as best achieved in an intensive teach-reteach cycle with the assistance of a highly proficient model teacher. The laboratory school appears to be the most suitable venue for this learning task to be achieved. The achievement of teaching proficiency in the laboratory school leads the student to the fourth level of the programme where the skills are practised and extended by experience in a portal school. The laboratory school and portal school therefore are conceived as occupying complementary roles in the teacher education programme.

The advantages of the portal schools to the teacher education programme at Utah centre on two main areas: (i) the closer interweaving of theory and practice that the portal school arrangement facilitates, and (ii) the fuller use of existing resources, rather than providing potentially expensive new teacher education centres. The closer interweaving of theory and practice is facilitated by having teachers closely involved in the teacher education course both in directing the students' observations of children in the classroom, and guiding the students in practice teaching. It is facilitated in addition by the constant contact that university staff have with the problems of day to day teaching. The university lecturer's credibility, consequently, is increased by being seen actively on-site in the portal schools for a large part of the year. The second advantage concerns the practical problem of finance. The SODIA programme was financed from within the existing financial arrangements of the teacher education programme. The programme personnel note this is a significant factor, because it allowed planning to proceed on a solid foundation and excluded the possibility that the programme could be truncated or viewed simply as an experiment. In order to achieve the level of co-operation necessary for sharing of resources it was necessary to involve the personnel of the portal schools and associated educational administrators in the whole process of planning and evaluating the SODIA programme. The successful achievement of such co-operative planning suggests that schools and universities or colleges can beneficially consider the overlap that occurs in available resources, both in terms of personnel and materials. Where such overlap occurs it provides an impetus for a reciprocally beneficial relationship, which appears an essential element of successful co-operation.

Group Preparation and Placement of Teachers

The 'Ford Training and Placement Program', a five-year experimental pro-gramme, developed between the University of Chicago and the Chicago public schools, focuses attention upon the educational situation in which the teacher trainee will commence his teaching career.

Schwartz (1973) outlines the basic assumptions underlying the programme and related implications. 'First, each school is a unique social system characterized by institutional role sets and filled by personalities with individual needs. The implications of this assumption are to train together the persons who will be filling the roles in a specific school, and to train them as a group before they enter the school. Second, universities cannot prepare teachers for the inner-city, or any other school, without the active participation of the professionals in the field and members of the communities to be served by the school. Therefore, any effective training must be a collaborative one involving the trainer (the university), the user (the public schools), and the client (the community)' (p. 398).

The basic training unit of the programme is a 'cadre', comprising the new teachers who are to be appointed to a particular school, the principal, experienced teachers from the school, and relevant community representatives. The cadre is assisted by members of the university faculty. The cadre meets with university staff for intensive sessions prior to the commencement of the year and contin-uously during the beginning teacher's first year of teaching. (The summer session is of six weeks duration.) The cadre sessions focus upon the characteristics of the school, the curriculum, local problems, and suggestions for change. The composition of the group and the opportunities for interaction ensure the development of a productive working relationship which gives confidence to the beginning teacher, serves an in-service function for the experienced teacher, and ultimately enhances the school programme.

The problems and benefits of the programme, reported by Schwartz, were as follows:

The problems experienced by the university included

(i) the necessity to reallocate faculty resources and time, requiring a reassessment of priorities;

(ii) the need for joint decision-making with the public school administrators in areas which previously had been the sole province of the faculty; namely, staffing, budgeting, and programme content;

(iii) according parity of status to newly appointed faculty members who were to be orientated towards more practical activities than had traditionally been usual for members of faculty;

(iv) adjusting to the often challenging contributions of experienced teachers in the university courses which some teachers took as a result of being involved in the programme;

(v) unrealistic expectations of some public school personnel regarding funds and resources that could be made available by the university in areas outside the prescribed limits of the Ford funding;

(vi) the need to meet the requirements of the Chicago public schools and communities involved in the project when designing research activities associated with the programme.

Among the problems experienced by the Chicago public schools system were

(i)   reallocation of school funds to allow for the participation of school personnel in the six-week summer training programme;
(ii) scheduling rearrangements to cater for the part-time new intern teachers;
(iii) creation of special positions at the district level to administer the programme;
(iv) introducing different payroll procedures as a result of the programme;
(v)   staffing rearrangements and adjustments resulting from the placement of interns as a group within the school;
(vi) changing the established city-wide system of placement procedures for teachers to enable group placement.

The programme was seen as having a number of important benefits to the university. For instance

(i)   university programmes have become more realistic;
(ii) curricular materials and instructional techniques, more appropriate to the inner-city school child, have been developed through the interaction of university staff and public school teachers in workshop activity;
(iii) instant feedback has been obtained by university staff on ideas relating to methods and techniques presented to cadres for consideration;
(iv) a wide range of research opportunities has arisen from the association of university staff with the programme;
(v)   the Ford programme, through its research findings, has led to many developments in teacher education.

The Chicago public schools also benefited in several ways

(i)   a supply of appropriately prepared new teachers, willing and competent to work in inner-city schools;
(ii) retraining of experienced teachers through membership of the cadres, and incidental benefits to other teachers within the school;
(iii) access of teachers to recent developments in education and to research findings through close association with the university faculty;
(iv) enrichment of the school programme.

H. Schwartz, the director of the programme and author of the article summarized above, believes that it is essential that co-operative programmes such as she has described should be developed. She claims, 'If we are to reduce the dissonance between teacher training and practice, universities and public schools must develop innovative, realistic, and mutually rewarding programs and then commit tangible resources to support the efforts' (p. 400). She also urges that, in the absence of any such relationship, it is up to the tertiary institution to take the initiative.

A Mutual Programme for Pre-service and In-service Teachers, with Course Credits

A co-operating programme of particular interest both to tertiary institutions concerned with teacher education and to administrators responsible for school systems is that established by Emery University, Georgia, in association with local school authorities (Riechard, 1974). In-service teacher education and pre-service education are combined in a unique and imaginative programme.

Participants in the programme are pre-service teachers (termed 'interns') and experienced elementary teachers (referred to as 'externs'). An intern and an extern are paired to form a teaching team which operates in a local elementary school. Both the intern and the extern are enrolled in courses at the university and are working towards professional qualifications. The work in the school which is associated with the college course provides intern and extern with opportunities to gain course credits. Both the intern and extern may be undertaking a programme leading to the Master of Arts in Teaching, or, in the case of an extern who already holds a masters degree, a Diploma for Advanced Studies in Teaching. In some cases the intern and extern will be participating in the same college courses.

THE PROGRAMME SEQUENCE

During the first summer quarter on-campus courses and field experiences take place for interns and externs, during which they work together and get to know each other. Each prepares a resume of his background and interests, which in the case of the extern, includes a description of the school, class, and pupils with which he works. These details are important to the success of the programme as later (midway through the summer period) interns and externs will form pairs on the basis of background and apparent mutual compatibility. An important course undertaken by the extern during the summer quarter is that of programme planning. As part of this course he plans out his programme for the coming year, a programme which will include the intern with whom he is paired. During this period the intern is involved in fieldwork in a local elementary school where, through one-to-one and small group activities, he gains experience in relating to children.

During the fall quarter the extern teaches full-time in his classroom and attends late afternoon sessions at the college. His college programme includes a supervision course which will fit him for his supervisory role in working with the intern in his classroom. The extern assumes a major responsibility for the supervision of his team-mate, the intern. The intern spends half of each day working with the extern in the classroom. The remaining time is spent in course work at the college.

In the winter quarter both the intern and the extern are in the classroom full-time, and both attend late afternoon sessions at the college. During this period the teamwork in the classroom continues, but there is a gradual shift of teaching responsibility from the extern to the intern who in spring will assume full responsibility for teaching the class.

By the spring quarter the intern knows the class well and possesses sufficient teaching skills and abilities to be able to work largely independently of the extern. It is considered important that he be given the opportunity to assume full responsibility for planning, management and teaching of a class. The extern, being freed from the classroom for a large proportion of the time, is able to carry out more coursework during the day at the college, while his partner, the intern, does less. It should be noted that although the extern spends a relatively small amount of time in the classroom, he retains the ultimate responsibility for the class.

During the time that the intern and extern work together there are frequent discussions with other teachers, the principal, and with college faculty staff who make regular visits to the school.

During the final summer quarter when the school is in recess the intern and extern are involved in full-time coursework at the college. Whereas the programme for the sixth-year diploma extern continues into the following spring quarter, the interns and externs undertaking masters degrees fulfil their requirements ready for the August graduation.

Several advantages of this method of teacher education over conventional programme are suggested:

The extern is provided with in-service experiences which assist him to become a more effective teacher. Further, he has opportunities to develop supervisory and leadership skills and in so doing is making a positive contribution to the teaching profession. The extern, through the coursework and practical experiences, is also gaining a background which will suit him to undertake further specialized responsibilities. A particularly attractive feature of the programme as far as the personal advancement of the extern, himself, is concerned is that he is enabled to gain his degree in a shorter period of time than if his courses were confined to summer-school periods.

The close relationship between the intern and the extern, who is an experienced teacher, has obvious benefits for each. The intern gains from the team situation in which he is able to discuss plans, methods and outcomes in relation to a particular class equally well-known by his 'supervisor'. Because of the concurrent periods of coursework and classroom experience provided in the programme there are frequent opportunities for the application of theory to practice. The sustained relationship with one particular group of children is suggested as being of more benefit than the practice of more limited exposure to several classes.

A Programme Integrating School, In-service, and Teacher Preparation

> Nothing short of total reconstruction will suffice: of the courses in education, of the relationships between courses and practice, of the 'mix' of faculty conducting the program, of the school setting for practice, of inservice education of teachers, of the school year, and of all the rest.

The ideas expressed in the above statement underlie a plan for educational reform outlined by John Goodlad in the article, 'The Reconstruction of Teacher Education' (Goodlad, 1970, p. 62). He contends that a change made in one part of the educational system will be to little avail if unaccompanied by changes in other parts of the system.

Goodlad proposes that the focus of the new teacher education programme be the school. At the commencement of his teacher education course the student is to be assigned to a particular school with which the university has developed a special relationship. His role within the school, his status, and his salary change as he progresses from teacher aide to intern and then resident teacher. Other staff in the school have positions of special responsibility in relation to the teacher education programme. Goodlad refers to these staff members as apprentice 'teachers of teachers' and 'clinical members of faculty'. The apprentice teachers of teachers become affiliated with the college while retaining their basic appointment in the school. Those who show particular promise in their work with trainees may become short-term or part-time members of the university clinical faculty, working directly with members of academic faculty within the college.

THE PROGRAMME

1. *Seminars on teaching problems.* Goodlad proposes that problems confronting beginning teachers should be the focus of seminars which involve the trainees and staff from the academic and clinical faculty. The seminars provide the opportunity for theory and clinical skills to be brought to bear on matters perceived as relevant by the student in training. Goodlad stresses that the problems serve as 'departure points', rather than having a restricting influence upon the course.

2. *Modules.* As a result of feedback received from beginning teachers modules may be prepared pertinent to those teaching problems which are commonly experienced. The modules may be of various kinds and available in a range of instructional media, for individuals or groups of students. Suggested modules include 'instruction in the specification of educational objectives, evaluation, application of learning theory, use of audiovisual aids, teaching of specific aspects of various subjects, and so on' (p. 69).

3. *Critiques of teaching.* As part of the daily programme a lesson taught by a member of the school or college staff or by an intern or aide would be critically analysed by a member of the team and discussed within the group. Goodlad suggests that as teachers may initially find this experience threatening, the early critiques should be conducted on lessons given by volunteers. After a period of time, such activity will become generally accepted and the school will become 'a place of enquiry into teaching'.

Members of the academic faculty of the college are provided, in a school of the type mentioned, with an ideal opportunity to contribute towards school improvement and development through their area of special interest, whether it be the teaching of reading, curriculum, school organization or some other. It would be hoped that all staff in the school, whether beginners or those associated with the college faculty, would seek to identify problems with which all may be invited to grapple.

Goodlad suggests that for the kinds of activity mentioned above to operate successfully, the school and its principal must have a considerable measure of autonomy, rather than be too restricted by district requirements. Goodlad believes that the 'single school with its principal, teachers, students, and parents is the largest organic unit for change in [the] educational system'. The principal, as a key figure in the success of the whole enterprise, must have relevant training and thoroughly understand his potential role in the total interacting system as a facilitator of change.

Vital to the success of the programme is the availability of time for planning and the personal development of staff. On the basis of twelve months employment, with one month of holidays, two months are available for such purposes (working on a nine month year for child attendance at school). Goodlad suggests that team-teaching may provide additional time for planning, quite apart from its advantage in easing the beginning teacher gradually into teaching responsibilities.

The major value of the proposed scheme is seen to be the simultaneous three-fold development of pre-service education, in-service education and schooling within the one programme. If the involvement of the college staff is to be effective, it is felt desirable that a limited number of schools should be involved as teacher education centres in the collaborating programmes.

Some of the ideas proposed by Goodlad seem to have been incorporated in the portal schools collaboratively operated by Temple University and the Philadelphia school system.

Pre-service and In-service Teacher Education in Portal Schools

The emergence of the 'portal school' concept within the Philadelphia school system has been a gradual one. The concept appears to owe its origin to a desire to develop more effective, realistic teacher education programmes; to a desire to find effective in-service education procedures; and to a need to rationalize expenditure in both the school and university programmes. The term 'portal' is loosely used to indicate schools which have a heavy time commitment to the Temple University teacher education programmes, and in which 60 per cent of the staff have agreed to participate in the programmes (Hilsinger and Schantz, c. 1973). Advisory boards assisting the school principal function in each school. These boards share no common pattern, but are constructed to suit the particular needs of the school and its teacher education programmes. In general, however, such boards comprise parents, teachers, students, university professors, fifth and and sixth grade pupils and school district executive personnel.

Portal schools are the result of the evolution of closer collaboration between school and university authorities, which originated in discussions of ways of avoiding wasteful programme overlap in the pre- and in-service education of teachers. Apart from saving funds, avoidance of overlap was seen as a way of extending some existing, minimally staffed programmes, especially in the supervision of beginning teachers, and of making tutorials in pre-service programmes more relevant to classroom teaching.

Following extensive discussion between the school authority and the university on arrangements for collaboration, student teaching 'centres' were initially developed in schools for the 'Elementary Programme for Inner City Schools', each housing between ten and twelve students. All 'method' teaching was gradually moved from a large number of schools to the teaching centres, as subsequently, were two tutorial classes for compulsory Educational Psychology courses previously conducted in the university. Further use of the schools as student teaching centres developed from the placement there of graduate interns and teacher-aide trainees. Consequent on the presence of so many university personnel in these schools, in-service courses for teachers were also relocated there rather than on the university campus, as had previously been the case. This move was of particular significance to co-operating teachers, who were able to take a number of hours of free tuition each semester in masters degree classes, some of which were now located in the student teaching-centre schools.

The success of collaboration in these programmes formed the basis for the introduction of shared appointments, the holders of which co-ordinated and developed the teacher education programmes of both school districts and the university. Cost sharing enabled more highly qualified personnel to be attracted to these positions. Eventually, lower-level supervision personnel were also shared. These people had the dual role of supervising beginning teachers and students. Because of the relocation of student teachers in a small number of schools, time-consuming and expensive travel between schools was avoided These factors, together with increased professional status, meant that these jobs became more attractive to higher qualified personnel.

An important feature of the collaborative arrangements was that all funding for the highly significant institutional change effected was found from within existing budgetary sources. Hilsinger and Schantz argue that though external funding for research and development projects has frequently been effective in stimulating apparent change, often because projects are externally funded they result in very little modification of institutional structures. This is because senior university personnel and other key decision-makers are not closely involved with projects and are often not even aware of projects' processes and outcomes. They suggest that

> despite the guidelines calling for change, innovation, experimentation, *et cetera*, what many of the outside funded projects have accomplished is to excite and provide jobs for new and non-tenured faculty ..., allow for the testing of new ideas without the capacity to institutionally evaluate or implement them, further polarize university and school faculty, and hopefully provide more exciting education to students. (Hilsinger and Schantz, p. 2)

Briefly summarized, major advantages of the portal schools to the *school district and community* were seen to be achieved through:

—better in-service assistance to beginning teachers;
—Pre-service teacher education which was more relevant to neighbouring inner-urban school districts;
—use of students and university personnel in school programmes;
—generating opportunities for relevant research and development activities;
—the provision of six hours of free graduate instruction to co-operating teachers per year;
—more parental involvement through advisory boards and parent contact programmes;
—parent education in new curricula materials and methods; and
—better pupil achievement levels.

Conversely, advantages to *university staff and students* were seen in the provision of:

—realistic pre-service education in inner-urban schools;
—in-depth experience in a school, rather than superficial experience in several schools;
—opportunities for field-testing of curricula;
—lower supervision loads in less schools;
—promotion for university staff based on successful experience in portal schools; and
—more contact with children for both students and professors.

That wide-ranging collaboration was achieved without external funding leads Hilsinger and Schantz to suggest that 'while it is not a documented model, it is a process or concept fully capable of replication to [*sic*] any university setting which has schools near it' (Hilsinger and Schantz, p. 13).

The Campus School

It would be expected that the relationship between the traditional campus laboratory school and its parent institution would be close, for control, staffing, and finance of the school have usually been the responsibility of the college or university with which the school is associated. An orientation towards the parent institution is reflected in the ways in which the laboratory school is commonly reported to function, namely: (i) as a practice school, a place for student teaching; (ii) as a model school; (iii) as a school for student participation; (iv) as a laboratory where research and experimentation are conducted; and (v) as a leadership school in the system. These functions were identified by Bucklen from a survey of twenty-nine studies of laboratory schools published between 1945 and 1950 and have been confirmed by later studies (Shadick, 1966).

The programmes of individual institutions reflect different emphases upon the laboratory school functions mentioned above. It is generally agreed that no one school could carry out equally well each of these functions, and, as will be discussed later, some of them may well be incompatible (Shadick, 1966). The implications of the varied roles of the laboratory school will be examined in the sections relating to the problems and future of laboratory schools.

As college or university-owned laboratory schools are often financed largely from funds available to the fostering institution, the laboratory school must compete with other claimant areas within the institution for its funding. The history of laboratory schools reveals that increasing costs have had considerable effects on the kinds of programmes offered within these schools and, indeed, have led to the closure of many.

The opportunity to determine the staffing of a school would seem to place a teacher education institution in a strong position to govern the nature and quality of its total teacher education programme. Not only may this be achieved through the appointment of regular staff to the school, but by the involvement of college faculty members teaching on a full-time or part-time basis within the school.

Perhaps the most successful campus school currently operating in the United States is the University Elementary School (UES) at the University of California, Los Angeles. Under the direction of Dr John Goodlad, dean of the Graduate School of Education and with Dr Madeline Hunter as principal, the school's functions are research, development, training, demonstration and dissemination. The spirit of the school's endeavour is typified in the principal's statement that:

> Education today needs practical, effective answers to a number of critical problems. A lab. school exists to generate, investigate, field-test, and demonstrate innovative, productive solutions. It also explores and develops those educational possibilities not yet refined to the point of systematic evaluation. (Hunter, 1971, p. 1)

The UES has an enrolment of some 460 children, aged 3 through 12, selected at random from applicants representing a cross-section of socio-economic and ethnic groups. Sometimes exceptions to this random enrolment are made to increase diversity or to enrol children with particular handicaps. For example, recently ghetto children have been encouraged to attend, raising the minority population to almost a fourth.

The staff of the school includes, besides the director and principal, master teachers, teachers temporarily assigned from public school districts, and students learning to teach. Some are generalists, others specialize in a subject field. Auxiliary personnel are a social worker, nurse, guidance specialist, and consultants from medicine and psychology. The school is designed to utilize a setting combining indoor and outdoor work areas. Its plant includes seventeen classrooms, a community hall, art studio, children's library, conference rooms, film and observation room, office facilities, and a playground. Closed-circuit television provides links between classrooms and many points on the campus to facilitate observations by students.

In pursuing its research function, the UES has become a laboratory to the whole university by co-operating with some twenty departments in investigations ranging from, say the development of a foreign language course for nationwide adoption to rigorous sociological and psychological studies. As far as possible the results of the school's research are 'translated into new programs and practices, tried out in a real school setting, and modified until demonstrably effective' (Hunter, 1971, p. 3). In particular, over the last decade the school, in seeking a more effective alternative to the traditional graded organization, has become a completely non-graded school providing 'custom-tailored' instruction for its pupils who are placed in either early childhood, lower, middle and upper elementary 'phases'. Progress through these phases is not based on the child's age, number of years at school, or scores on standardized tests, but as the UES child development objectives are reasonably met (Campeau, 1972).

In addition to featuring an innovative non-graded organization, the UES has developed a strong team teaching pattern. The staff is divided into a number of teams of two to six members. Each team has a blend of experience, interest and special competencies. Members are drawn from four groups: highly skilled master teachers, junior staff members, 'transient' teachers and students. Team members are co-operatively involved in planning, teaching and evaluating the instructional objectives of their pupils. Besides facilitating flexible use of staff, teaming is seen as providing a valuable structure for staff development, especially for the student teacher.

In all, the research and development work completed in recent years, or continuing at UES is impressive. Some idea of the range of areas to which staff have contributed may be gained from the overview of the school's interests in Table 4.1.

Besides involving student teachers in its educational programme as team members, the UES also attempts to influence the university's pre-service teacher training by developing innovative approaches to teacher education. For example, in 1971–2 it identified eleven decision-making and performance skills thought directly related to pupil learning and, on that basis, developed, evaluated and refined a teacher education programme. More recently, during 1974–5, the UES developed programmes for training paraprofessionals and for retraining teachers in the field.

The provision of observational opportunities for students through a closed-circuit television system has already been mentioned. More generally, the UES makes an important contribution to both pre-service and in-service teacher education through its quite elaborate demonstration and dissemination activities. Each year, for example, the school provides observations and workshops for thousands of visiting educators. Because of the heavy demands on the school, these activities are carefully scheduled and a fee covering reservation, printed materials and lunch is charged to each visitor. Since this one school can·by no means provide for all the observational, participation, supervised teaching and internship needs of the university's teacher education programmes, these are substantially carried on in selected schools under the supervision of highly competent, experienced teachers in the greater Los Angeles area.

The ideas, approaches and programmes developed at the UES are disseminated (in addition to direct involvement in training and observation)

Table 4.1 AREAS OF INQUIRY AND DEVELOPMENT

School Organization	*Curriculum*
Independent Learning Centres*	Art*
Individual Instruction*	Drama
Mainstreaming Exceptional Learners	Early Childhood*
Non Grading*	Foreign Language*
Open Education	Health Education*
Tandem Student Teaching*	Higher Cognitive Levels*
Teacher Centered Guidance Program*	'Mankind' Concerns*
Team Teaching*	Movement*
Use of Volunteers and Aides*	Percussion-composition
Inquiry, Experimentation and Dissemination	
Building self-concept (in process)*	Physical Education and Movement
Critical attributes of thinking skills	Programs*
(in process)*	Principles of Learning*
Doctoral Dissertations and Masters	Project Linkage* (improving achievement
Theses (plus countless research projects	in inner city schools)
from 18 university departments)	Spelling—language program (in process)*
Early Childhood Education*	Staff Meetings for Inservice*
Effective Direction Giving*	Students' decision making (in process)*
Effective Practice*	Teaching Appraisal (a diagnostic
Foreign Language*	prescriptive approach)*
Independent Learning Activities*	Teaching for Independence*
Interviewing and Conferencing*	Training of Volunteers and Aides*
(Parent-teacher, administrator-teacher,	Science*
teacher-child)	Social Studies (Stock market-history,*
Observational Learning (in process)*	Culture Studies)

* Indicates publication for dissemination (articles, books, films)   (Hunter, 1974, p. 1)

through the production of training films, the publishing of information and reports, conducting university extension courses, and staff consultation activities. The printed and audiovisual materials produced by the school are of excellent quality and cover an extensive variety of topics related to teaching and learning (a catalogue of materials available and their costs may be obtained from the school's business secretary).

The impact of the UES on the work of other schools has yet to be assessed. Certainly it seems already to have been a very influential centre within the Los Angeles area. No doubt the success of the school owes a great deal to the talent and energy of its director and its principal. Other important contributing factors have been the quality of the staff and their commitment to the UES purposes, the close and vigorous collaboration with the university, the adequacy of its facilities and budget, the ability to enrol a diversified pupil population, and the freedom to perform all its functions. Hunter holds the strong belief that 'Only by experimental schools such as UES will we close the gap between knowledge generated by research and the practices in American classrooms' (Hunter, 1971, p. 3).

Selected Functions of Co-operating Arrangements

Two of the probably most talked about functions of co-operating school arrangements are (i) the pursuit of research and curriculum development, and (ii) the provision for student practice teaching. The former has traditionally been seen as a major function of the laboratory school, but it unfortunately has become rather a myth. The second has been largely taken out of the hands of laboratory schools and, for better and worse, transferred to numerous regular schools.

Research and curriculum development

Two related activities commonly espoused by laboratory schools have been inquiry into problems of teaching and learning and the translation of educational ideas into practice. In theory, at least, the laboratory schools seemed well placed to perform these functions because of their access to advice and support from the university or college faculty, their own highly competent staff, their superior facilities, and their control over pupil enrolments. In practice, however, both functions seem to have been severely limited by such factors as other demands on staff time and lack of inspiration and co-operation from the tertiary institution.

Accounts of basic research seldom appear in recent laboratory school literature. Surveys of laboratory school functions, already mentioned, have revealed the tapering off of research involvement. In one of the most recent surveys of the functions of a sample of thirty-two laboratory schools across the nation, Cappa (1972) found that 88 per cent of schools devoted less than a quarter of their time to research and experimentation. The principal factors limiting this activity were lack of finance and low staff interest, with other contributing factors being lack of co-operation from tertiary staff, want of time, supplies and equipment, and conflicting expectations.

Ironically, now that many laboratory schools have been forced to examine their past and future roles, greater participation in educational research and inquiry is being perceived as a highly desirable thing. Cappa (1972) reported that most of the schools he surveyed would like to see their role change in emphasis from student observation and participation more to research and experimentation. However, the type of research was not indicated. Thomas (1956), Principal of the Henry S. West Laboratory School (associated with the University of Miami), believed that laboratory schools can realistically carry out only unsophisticated, applied 'innovative studies'. This policy had been adopted at his school where studies to be implemented had to meet at least the following criteria:

1. The study can be carried on satisfactorily under conditions of preservice teacher observation and limited participation.
2. The study promises possible improvement in the program of the laboratory school.
3. The study is of interest to other schools in Dade County and to the University of Miami. (p. 411)

The last criterion is an interesting one and has been echoed by Mead (1950) and Fremdling (1974) who believe a laboratory school should explore issues and problems of special concern to teachers of the surrounding district and suggest ways in which these problems can be overcome.

There seems to have been a little more fruitful activity in the development and trial of curriculum approaches, materials and methods in the laboratory schools over recent years. Again, however, not much of it has been documented. In a survey of laboratory schools Palm (1941a) found that only a relatively small number participated in curriculum development at all. Only 49 per cent of schools supplied at least one staff member as consultants for state-wide curriculum development activities and the figure drops dramatically for county (12 per cent) and city (1 per cent) agencies. The relatively low level of curriculum involvement of giving advice on text book adoption (at the state level) was engaged in by 23 per cent of laboratory school staffs. The use of laboratory schools for trialling curriculum materials was also found to be at a very low level. For state agencies, for which the figures are easily the highest, 27 per cent of laboratory schools tried new courses of study; 23 per cent tried new curriculum materials; 15 per cent demonstrated the applicability of new courses of study; and 12 per cent demonstrated 'curriculum theories' (p. 645).

Palm also found that experimentation with the school's own curriculum was engaged in by only 45 per cent of laboratory schools. In many cases experimentation was on a very small scale. Larsen (1939, p. 106) reported that 'what research was done was carried on by staff members and was based upon their own initiative to see problems needing study'.

An insight into the way some laboratory schools attempted to give expression to prevailing curriculum theory for teacher education purposes is provided by the staff of the Indiana State Teachers College (Jamison *et al.*, 1940). It is an effort to interpret many of the ideals of progressive education in a highly specific way for a particular local community, rather than an attempt to develop materials generalizable over many different school environments. Having surveyed the local area to determine its socio-economic characteristics and major educational resources, the staff of the college and laboratory school developed curricula closely related to, and designed to improve, the life of the local area.

> pupils in an eighth grade Social Studies class, at that stage in adolescence in which home responsibilities and ties are among the childish things they would put away, made a study of homes as a type of group organisation which resulted in significantly improved attitudes.
> ... Classes in Home Economics have experimented with problems in meal planning and renovation of clothing. The girls are beginning to bring to school garments which can be remade.
> ... Our laboratory school is in a city located in the center of a rich coal mining area. The class decided not to go to books to find the answers to their questions, until they had learned all they could from observation and from talking with people who might know about coal. (pp. 327–31)

Some rather vague ideas on ways in which curricula assumptions might be evaluated are hinted at in this report but the overwhelming impression of this and other laboratory schools is of teacher educators working intuitively to develop a viable set of curricula for their specific situation.

The reasons for this failure of the majority of laboratory schools to contribute substantially to the curriculum field can only be surmised. The most feasible explanation is that the resources of the schools were so extended by the pre-service teacher education functions and the demands from visitors to view the best of locally relevant current practice, that very little time or energy remained for significant curriculum reform. It may also have been that the schools were not so free from outside pressure as was frequently assumed: they were, after all, responsible to parents as well as to the faculty of the tertiary institution. And as Palm (1941b, p. 632) pointed out, student teachers needed to be prepared to cope with current practice in the local school districts as well as to speculate on the form of future curricula.

There are at least two notable exceptions to the apparently low-level laboratory-school involvement in research and curriculum development. Both the University Elementary School at the University of California, Los Angeles, and the Laboratory School at the University of Hawaii have been heavily involved in these activities in recent years. It is probably significant that both schools, especially the one at Hawaii, have shed much of their involvement in teacher preparation. An account of the work of the University Elementary School at UCLA has been given in the previous section; a description of the functions of the Laboratory School at the University of Hawaii follows.

One of the most interesting contemporary laboratory schools is at the University of Hawaii. Ironically, it no longer operates directly in pre-service teacher education. It has become rather a curriculum research and development unit and, in this regard, has assumed a number of functions which could well have implications for other laboratory-type schools with continuing involvement in teacher preparation.

The laboratory school is regarded as an integral part of the Curriculum Research and Development Group (CRDG) of the College of Education in the University of Hawaii (Manoa). The state-funded CRDG was formed in 1969 under an agreement between the university and the department of education. Its main objective is:

> To enhance the quality of efficiency of educational programs for Hawaii's children and youth (preschool through grade 12) through the design, development and installation of new programs meeting top priority educational needs. (King, 1973, p. 1)

The CRDG seeks to provide a productive link between the university and the department of education by facilitating joint curriculum action. It aspires to 'utilize the best theory and practice in its endeavour'; its site on university campus and its use of the University Laboratory School 'are both of great value in this regard'.

The University Laboratory School is an old public institution embodying the former university preschool, the university elementary school, and the university high school. Largely at the recommendation of the College of Education, the laboratory school was changed from a teacher training centre to a centre for curriculum design, development and dissemination. Since this conversion the student population of the school has been altered in two main ways: the enrolment has been allowed to decrease by more than a half (from 950 to 450), and an admissions policy has been adopted which has led to the building up of a 'comprehensive student body', representative of the various sections of the state's population and thus more diverse in terms of educational need. In 1974 the staff-student ratio was 1:14.4. Annual expenditure on the school was approximately $320,000 with the cost per student (K-12) averaging $878 for the year.

The laboratory school has developed six main functions in support of the CRDG's activities. These are worth quoting in full since they convey useful suggestions as to the possible research and development functions of schools co-operating more fully in teacher education:

(i) *Analysis and Classroom Trial of Curricula Produced Elsewhere*—Laboratory School staff undertake this activity to obtain objective information about the characteristics of promising new educational programs, especially in relation to a Hawaiian student population. The activity bears a vital relation to general need assessment in the design stage of the CRDG educational program development activity.

(ii) *Exploration of Innovative Educational Ideas and Programs*—Laboratory School staff undertake the exploration of original innovative approaches in the context of their Laboratory School teaching and program planning. The activity provides a rich basis for subsequent CRDG design and development work.

(iii) *Role in Curriculum Model Development*—Prototype student and teacher materials developed to test the validity of a curricular model are utilized in a Laboratory School setting. Results can lead to a revision and further improvement of the model.

(iv) *Exploration of Curricular Implications of School Organizational Innovations*—School organizational innovations such as modular scheduling, K-12 vertical organization of faculties by subject area, and non-graded student organization are instituted to yield design information useful to CRDG developers.

(v) *Role in Early Development Stage Materials Trial and Revision*—The Laboratory School and its teaching staff typically provide the initial classroom tryouts for early versions of educational program units under development. Such small scale early trial of prototype units, with consequent revision of the materials, is extremely valuable in reducing the number of later, larger scale trial-revision cycles necessary to completed development.

(vi) *Provision of Demonstration and Longitudinal Evaluation Site*—During the installation cycle of educational program development the maintenance of the program in the Laboratory School in its full integrity is an important aid to the implementation. Such maintenance is also important in carrying on longitudinal studies of program results as Laboratory School students pass through the full range of the program. (King, 1973, pp. 5–7)

Each of these functions is said to be 'served extremely well' by the laboratory school's present arrangements. The main conditions in the school contributing to this result are regarded as being:

(i) CRDG development staff has optimal ease of access to Laboratory School activities and staff. Day-to-day, informal contact between program development staff and teacher colleagues is commonplace. Indeed the developer frequently is a teacher, doing the latter on a part-time basis. CRDG activities in the Laboratory School can thus be closely monitored with a high degree of reliability.

(ii) Laboratory School staff are hired with the clear expectation that some form of curriculum work is expected from them and that they may be expected to undertake special training from time to time in the fulfilment of this responsibility. Moreover, this expectation is of prime importance in judging the qualifications of applicants for Laboratory School teaching positions.

(iii) The principal and staff of the Laboratory School are directly responsible to the Director of CRDG. Ultimate authority for the entire curriculum, administrative arrangements, and school support activities resides with him. Thus, it is relatively easy to secure the adjustments in program, school organization and procedures needed to support high priority CRDG educational program development needs.

(iv) The Laboratory School student population is a remarkably stable one. Once admitted, students tend to pass through the entire curriculum to the twelfth grade. This factor is of great benefit to longitudinal studies of the effects of various programs.

(v) Laboratory School teachers are given reduced teaching loads in conjunction with performing the CRDG functions outlined in section "i" above. The amount of such teaching relief is commensurate with the educational program development activity being undertaken. This allows for considerable reflection, study and thoughtful planning to go into the work and greatly increases the quality of the result.

(vi) The status of the Laboratory School as a part of the University attracts and enables the utilization of a diverse array of exceptionally talented and knowledgeable specialists interested in pursuing a university career, but also concerned with frontline educational concerns. The organization reaps the advantage of artistic and scholarly expertise tempered by frequent immersions in the everyday vexations and joys of school life. Both the theoretical and practical aspects of CRDG program development are greatly benefited by this "thinking in action" aspect of CRDG activity. The diversity of specialties represented also greatly enriches the curriculum dialogue in the organization, thereby enhancing the professional development of all staff members.

(vii) Laboratory School staff utilization can be very flexible. This enables a quick response to shifting CRDG program development needs. There is a common acceptance of the practice of part-time teaching. Over a period of time personnel move in and out of heavy development program involvement with consequent fluctuations in their teaching load. A college professor with a promising educational idea in his area can to be moved in to teach one class for a year or two. A significant portion of Laboratory School teachers tend to be young, highly educated, and non-University tenured. They are fully aware that development priorities may shift over time. They tend to value the experimental atmosphere of the Laboratory School and the chance to do challenging innovative work more than the provision of long term job security.

(viii) The Laboratory School has no regular attendance area and controls its student admissions. Admission of new students to the school can be geared to special CRDG project needs. Thus, during the past few years a number of advanced instrumental music students have been brought in to enable the establishment of a full sized and well balanced instrumental ensemble group. This was done in support of development and testing of the Hawaii Music Project curriculum. (King, 1973, pp. 7–8)

Clearly many of the above factors have important implications for the successful operation of any laboratory-type school. Especially pertinent are the frequent close, informal contacts between teachers and tertiary staff; the hiring of staff with clear expectations of their involvement in the school's functions; the control over pupil admissions; and the reduced teaching loads of staff to enable them to pursue adequately the school's functions.

The laboratory school's participation in the design, development and dissemination of various CRDG projects is varied and substantial. A selection of examples will indicate the nature of the participation: (i) Among the intensive analyses and classroom trials of promising new curricula undertaken by CRDG, the laboratory school staff co-operated in work with the elementary social science courses 'Man: A Course of Study' and 'Man in Man Made World'; in an elementary school 'Science Curriculum Improvement Study'; the 'Lavatelli Early Childhood Education Program; and the 'Nimnicht New Nursery School Model'. (ii) In the exploration and trial of innovative curriculum ideas the laboratory school staff were endeavouring to upgrade the quality of elementary and secondary art teaching; to develop a model preschool programme based on experience with the Head Start Program; to develop social science units on historical and contemporary Hawaiian topics for secondary schools; and to construct a secondary mathematics programme which uses practical situations to promote the inductive grasp of mathematical principles. (iii) As part of the study of the curriculum implications of various school organization innovations the laboratory school was experimenting with such things as the use of modular scheduling to accommodate large group instruction; unscheduled periods to promote self-directed student enquiry; K-12 faculty organization by academic discipline to promote comprehensive and sequential programme planning and encourage multi-level teaching; and the organization of students into non-graded groups allowing for a measure of continuous student progress without artificial grade barriers. (iv) Developmental stage activities of the CRDG involved the school in the early trial of prototype units for the Hawaii (Secondary) English Project and the Polynesian Literature Project. (v) Installation stage activities connected with the Hawaii Music Program involved the school as an 'exemplary demonstration site' of its full implementation and as a site for longitudinal studies of its operation. The school provided similar functions for the Japanese Language Project and the Hawaii (Elementary) English Project.

Generally, it is believed that the work of the CRDG is greatly enhanced by its physical proximity to both the laboratory school and the university. The final word on this matter should be left to the Director of the CRDG, Arthur R. King:

> The lodgement of the CRDG and the University Laboratory School in the University environment provides a unique setting for the utilization of a broad array of diverse talents and knowledge specialties. Authorities in various academic disciplines are readily available to validate the knowledge bases of development projects. Cooperative ventures with College of Education personnel can be easily arranged. Persons from other academic disciplines in the University can often be induced to participate actively in design and development ventures. The possibility of making a University career while teaching at least part-time in a challenging, experimental school atmosphere is very attractive to a number of highly trained and talented artists and scholars. The diversity and quality of the resultant educational dialogue in the CRDG-Laboratory School complex contributes pervasively to all phases of the Group's educational program development activity. (King, 1973, p. 10)

Student practice teaching

LABORATORY SCHOOLS AND STUDENT TEACHING

The role of on-campus laboratory schools as the venue for student teaching has decreased significantly due to the pressure of increased numbers of teacher trainees and the criticisms which centred on the atypical nature of the experience (Ryan, 1975, pp. 11–12). Colleges and universities turned to regular schools where students were assigned to teach in the classrooms of ordinary teachers. This scheme certainly overcame the problems associated with the laboratory school, but student teaching as such remained a problematic area for teacher education courses. Research has shown that student teachers are markedly influenced by the attitudes and teaching style of their co-operating teachers, which may be at variance with the concerns of the teacher education philosophy. Price (1961), for example, found that regardless of the initial ability or outlook of the student teachers, they tended to adopt attitudes and teaching styles similar to those of their co-operating teacher. McAulay (1960) supports and extends Price's finding by showing that the influence of co-operating teachers varies according to their degree of formalized structure. It seems that co-operating teachers adopting formal teaching structures are particularly influential in changing the behaviour and attitudes of student teachers. More recent evidence from Seperson and Joyce (1973) supports the finding that co-operating teachers are influential models, but suggests that the similarity between the student teachers and co-operating teachers may be a function of the overall setting of practice teaching. Seperson and Joyce found that marked changes occurred in student teachers' behaviour and attitudes immediately after contact which suggests that the environment established by the teacher imposes severe constraints on the student teacher's freedom to explore a teaching style of his or her own.

Growth in self-direction is surely a central goal of practice teaching. Ezer and Lambert (1966) maintain in this regard 'that the mark of an effective co-operating teacher-student relationship should be the extent to which the student teacher grows as a self-directive creative teacher with ideas of his own' (p. 157). Many colleges and universities have set this as the ideal, sending students out to 'try their wings' (Nelson, 1972, p. 367), yet teachers often have accepted students as classroom helpers who could simply take over lessons normally taught by themselves (Campbell and Williamson, p. 168). Olma summarizes the dilemma by noting that co-operating teachers have been given considerable responsibility in the teacher training process but have not been provided with an opportunity to see their role in a commonly shared frame of reference (Olma, 1973, p. 88). It is interesting that most of the major criticisms of current student teaching arrangements could be solved by adopting a laboratory school venue for student practice. The modelling influence of school teachers, the type of environment established, and the fostering of a shared frame of reference all stand to be improved in a laboratory school setting. Recent innovative approaches to student teaching, however, do not suggest that laboratory schools will again become large scale venues for practice teaching.

It now appears that laboratory schools will fulfil an auxiliary role in improving the quality of student teaching. The auxiliary role may take two forms: (i) the provision of specialized student teaching opportunities, or 'laboratory experiences', and/or (ii) the provision of in-service opportunities for co-operating teachers and the training of specialized staff who fulfil key roles in student teaching (e.g., the 'clinical professor'). The provision of specialized student teaching opportunities is illustrated by the University Elementary School (UES) at UCLA. The teacher education programme is structured to allow students a choice in the particular strand that they want to follow. Those students choosing the UES-based strand are involved in an innovative non-graded team teaching approach to education (Fremdling, 1974). As pointed out earlier, this laboratory school functions specifically to generate innovative ideas, to produce new theory and to translate that theory into practice. The involvement of student teachers in this process enables them to gain competence and confidence in the translation of recent theory into practice, and thereby act as disseminators of innovative practice when they enter the public school system. The provision of in-service opportunities for co-operating teachers and the training of specialized staff was suggested by Ezer and Lambert (1966) who note that laboratory schools are particularly well placed to train more effective co-operating teachers because of their proximity to college or university personnel and student teachers, as well as the availability of teachers with specialized competencies. Ezer and Lambert suggest that these conditions could be exploited by establishing a course at the laboratory school designed specifically to increase the supervisory skills of co-operating teachers and upgrade their planning, teaching and evaluative skills. At present there is no evidence that such courses are being offered, probably because of administrative and financial considerations. Laboratory schools, however, may well become the training ground for a new professional in teacher education, who occupies a role in schools that is concerned with the in-school experiences of students as well as the in-service education of co-operating teachers. These professionals would be fewer in number than co-operating teachers, and consequently more easily accommodated within the existing commitments of laboratory schools. They are called by various names, including 'clinical professor', 'staff teacher', and 'school-based tutor', but their duties are similar. The appointment of such professionals to a laboratory school for a year would enable them to work with highly competent teachers, explore curriculum innovations, join in seminars conducted by university or college personnel, observe the teacher education programme of the university or college from the inside, and consolidate their own professional background. It seems reasonable to suggest also that laboratory school personnel themselves may provide a substantial number of these new professionals, so that the periodic restaffing of the laboratory school may be a way to provide a pool of 'clinical professors', who have both practical and theoretical strengths. In the reports of recent innovative student teaching arrangements summarized below the importance of the 'clinical professor' role is highlighted. It is significant, therefore, that although the laboratory school currently appears to have only a limited role in the upgrading of student teaching arrangements, that role may be quite crucial.

CO-OPERATIVE RELATIONSHIPS FOR STUDENT TEACHING

Student teaching arrangements are often a good index of the degree of co-operation and communication between tertiary institutions and schools. The tertiary institution is concerned that the modelling influence of the co-operating teacher is of high quality and relevant; that the student is able to experience first-hand the variety of roles required of a teacher; that the student is able to achieve competency in basic teaching skills, as well as demonstrate the ability to plan, implement and evaluate a programme of instruction. These goals cannot be achieved, however, if communication between tertiary institutions and schools is not planned for on a regular and in-depth basis. Recent attempts to achieve such communication suggests that the traditional roles of university supervisor, college lecturer, co-operating teacher and student teacher will undergo considerable change. In order to examine in detail these role changes, five accounts of innovative approaches to student teaching are presented below.

New Paltz-Haviland Co-operative Relationship. The faculty of education at State University New Paltz and the Haviland Junior High School, New York, negotiated a co-operative relationship in which responsibility for the pre-service education of teachers was shared between the university and the school. The relationship illustrates the need to build goodwill between institutions by exploring ways in which closer co-operation will be mutually beneficial. The university, for example, made available curriculum specialists, as well as guest lecturers with special expertise, for school-based seminars for teachers. The establishment of initial goodwill led to the setting-up of a joint planning committee which co-ordinates the programme. The initial involvement of student teachers at the school is planned by the committee who are able to accommodate the interests and talents of the student teachers more adequately, and place them in situations that are beneficial to the school. The New Paltz-Haviland relationship is the first of a projected programme to involve other schools in a shared teacher training centre 'where future teachers may be trained by college professors and key public school faculty members who would become, in essence, clinical professors' (Eulie and Gray, 1973, p. 416). It is clear from the report of the relationship that the faculty of education was concerned at the lack of commitment of many student teachers under existing arrangements. The hope of the faculty is that early involvement in participatory situations will enable student teachers to 'discover whether teaching is for them ... Those manifestly unfit for teaching will be counseled out ... We will have fewer student teachers but the quality will be improved' (Eulie and Gray, 1973, p. 418). Although the relationship is still at an early stage, it is possible to isolate the essential elements that are emerging: first, the upgrading of the teaching methods of the school faculty by the provision of expert advice from university personnel; second, the sharing of responsibility for pre-service teacher education with school personnel, and in particular the designation of a 'clinical professor' from within the ranks of school personnel; and third, the early and more prolonged involvement of student teachers at the school.

There is growing concern in the United States, Great Britain and Australia with the problem of educating urban children. The following three examples of co-operating relationship for student teaching resulted from dissatisfaction with existing teacher education programmes, particularly where graduates were absorbed by schools serving inner-urban populations. The relationships are examined, therefore, because they both illustrate the factors involved in co-operative relationships, and are innovative attempts to solve the problems of inner-city schools.

Temple-Philadelphia Co-operative Relationship.   Temple University, in an analysis of the low morale of inner-city teachers, shown by high absentee rates and yearly resignation rates, concluded that the central problem appeared to be a lack of support both for student teachers during practice teaching, and for graduates on their first appointment (Harwood and Miller, 1970). In order to overcome these shortcomings Temple University developed a two-year intern teaching programme for college graduates. The graduates are carefully screened before being accepted into the course in interview and questionnaire sessions, as well as by being provided an opportunity to visit the schools to which they will be assigned. Those who proceed are given an intensive six week summer programme centred on familiarizing interns with the community context of the school, and through supervised teaching experiences in summer camps, they confront the difficulties of communicating effectively with urban children. The schools chosen to become part of the programme are those with particular problems indicated by a staff turnover rate of 50 per cent. The school is assigned a clinical professor when the number of interns reaches twelve. The clinical professor supervises the teaching of the students and provides evaluative seminars during the afternoons. The topics of such seminars include 'individualization of instruction, group dynamics and learning in democratic groups, approaches to teaching basic skills, the process curriculum, and strategies to motivate the urban student' (p. 229). In addition to working with students, the clinical professor is available for consultation with teachers in the school who desire to improve their teaching skills. The dual role of clinical professors ensures that every effort is made to upgrade the level of expertise throughout the school.

The Temple-Philadelphia relationship illustrates the new role required of supervisors. The supervisor's role is incorporated within the role of the clinical professor who has responsibilities for both the in-service and pre-service education of teachers. The student teacher's role also varies considerably from existing arrangements. Their placement is done in groups in order to build a supportive environment where they 'can learn from others' successes and failures as each searches for a better way to relate to urban students, [and] find relevant topics and materials' (p. 430). The important aspect of the placement, however, is the service function that student teachers are asked to perform. They are placed in schools that are facing severe problems as shown by a high staff turnover, where they work side by side with teachers. Their presence reduces the staff-student ratio, and, when combined with the supportive help of the clinical professor, may add a freshness of approach that will improve staff morale throughout the school.

Chicago-Illinois Learning Centres.   The challenge of urban education has also caused a re-examination of teacher education programmes in the Chicago environment. Schwartz (1973), for example, notes that criticisms of urban schools was at the heart of an innovative teacher education programme at the University of Chicago. The programme was based on the establishment of a three-way partnership in the pre-service and on-going education of teachers. It was argued 'that any effective training must be a collaborative one involving the trainer (university), the user (the public schools) and the client (the community)' (Schwartz, 1973, p. 398). The programme operates on a school by school basis with intensive involvement of university personnel in the school 'to provide personal and professional support for new teachers, renew the enthusiasm and skills of the experienced teachers, solve school-wide problems, and bridge the gap between the university, the school and the community' (Schwartz, p. 398). It is significant, therefore, that the more recently created College of Education, University of Illlinois at Chicago should adopt a tripartite arrangement for teacher education. Monroe and Talmage (1970) emphasize that the programme of education of an urban university must reflect the particular needs of the urban schools. Consequently the central committee of the programme, the advisory committee, is drawn from the community, the school, and the university and has power to 'formulate policy, advise the program director, review plans, and encourage program development in keeping with the stated assumptions of the program' (Monroe and Talmage, 1970, p. 473). The teacher education programme operates through the establishment of learning centres, which are schools associated with a particular sub-culture in the city. The teacher candidate is involved at a school, in the community, and at the university. He works closely with a particular teacher in tackling a problem or issue that the working committee has identified as particularly important for the school. The teacher candidate is supported by the university supervisor, an adviser who is a recent graduate from the programme itself as well as a parent representative and a community representative. The course of action proposed by the teacher candidate is evaluated openly, feelings and attitudes are explored, and each of the members brings his perceptions to the analysis of the problem. The in-school and community experiences of student teachers occupy the whole week except for one day which is spent at the university. On that day large group and small group seminars consider the foundational aspects of teaching and attempt to tie these more theoretical questions to the student's experiences in the learning centre and the community (Monroe and Talmage, 1970, p. 474). Clearly the aim of the teacher education programmes at the University of Chicago and the University of Illionois at Chicago is to develop a new type of teacher, 'committed to the community schools and to the necessity for personal community participation' (p. 475).

Brockport-Rochester Programme. A programme involving the State University at Brockport and four Rochester elementary schools (New York) was initiated in 1968 on a similar rationale to the Temple graduate programme. The planners note in particular that 'traditional concepts of student teaching were abandoned and replaced with a systems approach to teacher education that had the potential of improving urban education generally' (Rock and Virgilio, 1971, p. 274). The 'systems approach to teacher education' in this instance meant that undergraduate students enrolled in teacher education, and graduate students beginning teacher education after completing a liberal arts degree, are assigned to one of the four schools. Each school is assigned fourteen undergraduate students plus four graduate interns whose programme is co-ordinated jointly by a clinical professor and the principal of the school. An additional teacher is assigned by the school district to work specifically with the interns. The teacher is chosen as an outstanding classroom teacher who will be capable of co-ordinating the group of interns into an effective teaching team. This group, outstanding teacher plus four interns, is given responsibility in a team teaching situation for a group of approximately one hundred children. Each intern has completed a summer session focusing on teaching techniques and foundational aspects of teaching, and receives additional seminars from the on-site clinical professor during the school year. As with the Temple graduate programme, the interns 'continue to have contact with both the college and helping teacher' during their second year of teaching (p. 276). The undergraduate teacher education students are not given the same degree of responsibility for teaching children, but still are viewed as 'assistant teachers', who work with individuals, small groups, and as their skills increase, with whole class groups. Their progress is monitored by the clinical professor and co-operating teachers.

A significant aspect of the above relationship was the high degree of responsibility that was given to the graduate interns. It should be noted, however, that the programme provided considerable support in a number of ways: the number of children per adult was comparatively low; the co-ordinating teacher was especially chosen as outstanding; and a university clinical professor was on hand daily to add support and offer advice.

Kanawha County Student Teaching Centre. The concern to improve the context of student teaching has been expressed in more large scale ways than considered so far. The Kanawha County Student Teaching Centre co-ordinates the efforts of seven colleges and universities and two large school districts. The activities of the centre are governed by an advisory committee with representation from all participants. The centre focuses its objectives on improved experiences in student teaching, upgrading the quality of supervising teachers and the encouragement of all agencies to re-evaluate their role in teacher education. The centre provides such services as 'a pre-student-teaching orientation week; joint seminars with co-operating colleges; and inter- and intra-school observation of outstanding teachers' (Maddox and Flaherty, 1971, p. 185). The achievement of such close co-operation between tertiary institutions and schools indicates the high priority that is placed on student teaching. The fact that the centre is now funded entirely from within existing financial arrangements shows that both tertiary institutions and schools are reaping substantial benefits from its operation. The benefits are not simply confined to student teaching, however, since the centre aims at creating 'an outstanding group of supervising teachers who are capable of improving the overall quality of education in West Virginia'. The centre's success has moved the county and state authorities to recognize two new staffing positions within the teaching profession. One is a 'staff teacher' whose role includes 'the teaching of demonstration lessons for analysis and the conducting of . . . seminars for student teachers, new teachers, supervising teachers'. The other is a now certification for supervising teachers who are identified as 'teacher education associates' (Maddox and Flaherty, 1971, pp. 185–7).

The innovative co-operative student teaching arrangements reviewed above emphasize three central themes:

(i) An upgrading of the role of the student teacher by providing opportunities for increased responsibility and greater participation in schools. This upgrading is accompanied by a new stress on the potential of student teachers to substantially help the schools in which they teach to reduce staff-student ratios and to individualize instruction more adequately.

(ii) The development of a new role in teacher education that may draw staff either from the tertiary institution or the school. The role, commonly termed 'clinical professor', has dual responsibilities for the pre-service and in-service education of teachers. The pre-service responsibilities include providing seminars on theoretical issues related to teaching; providing demonstration lessons; and providing advice and offering feedback on the student teachers' classroom performance. The in-service responsibilities include the provision of seminars on topics of interest and relevance to the teachers; the provision of information about available courses at university or college; the dissemination of information on curricula innovations; and the provision of advice to individual teachers on their teaching skills.

(iii) The upgrading of the role of the co-operating teacher in teacher education. The co-operating teacher, however, is asked to accept the responsibilities within a shared frame of reference, since the clinical professor is available for consultation on the role requirements of supervision and to enable teachers to keep abreast of the developments in curricula and teaching methods.

Problems Associated with Laboratory School and Co-operating School Programmes

The history of laboratory-type schools as outlined in a previous section, suggests that they have always faced difficulties of one kind or another. Whereas some problems have been peculiar to a particular setting or have arisen from responses to a prevailing educational climate, other problems are more universal and enduring. Titles of articles written during the last twenty years relating to laboratory schools reflect an atmosphere of uncertainty associated with them. For example, 'Is the Campus Laboratory School Obsolescent?', 'The Campus School: its Search for Identity', and 'Is the Laboratory School Worth Saving?'. In the present section some of the more persistent problems of laboratory schools are outlined as well as some difficulties of more recent origin.

The trend towards universities and colleges developing co-operative relationships with public schools has been noted and examples of co-operative programmes have been described. That such relationships are not developed effortlessly should be apparent in the discussion which follows. Several of the problems of laboratory and co-operating schools introduced below will be expanded further in the section devoted to the future of these schools and associated programmes.

1. *Appropriate functions of the laboratory school*

Larsen (1942) reported a study of the functions of twenty-one state teachers college campus secondary schools in which actual functions were compared with those stated to be desirable by a group comprising teacher educators and the administrators of the schools concerned. The results indicated a marked disparity between theoretical priorities and what actually occurred in practice. For example, whereas current practices demonstrated student teaching to be by far the most important function of the campus schools, this was ranked by principals of such schools as third in the list of 'desirable' functions. In order of priority, the functions that were stated as most appropriate for a campus school were as follows:

(i)   providing opportunities for observation by college classes;
(ii) providing leadership in practices of teaching, supervision and administration;
(iii) providing opportunities for student teaching; and
(iv) providing for educational experimentation.

This report highlights a common problem of the laboratory school to which attention is drawn in a number of studies (e.g., Lang, 1959; Gaskill and Carlson, 1958; Bucklen, 1952), namely, a lack of sufficiently well thought out and articulated aims which may find their expression in the practices of the school. Such an exercise in sorting out priorities would assist subsequent decision-making and enable the campus school to more effectively face-up to its major responsibilities. It would seem, however, that changes in the programmes of many laboratory schools are not made easily. McNabb's study (1973) of sixty-eight laboratory schools still functioning at that time in the United States revealed that the inability to develop relevant programmes or to change existing programmes was seen as a major problem, second only to that of funding.

The question of whether the commonly recognized functions of laboratory schools are in fact compatible is raised by Shadick (1966). The diagram used by Shadick and reproduced as Figure 4.1 demonstrates that certain generally accepted school functions may be counter-productive. Shadick's conclusions should be considered in relation to the diagram. He claims:

Figure 4.1

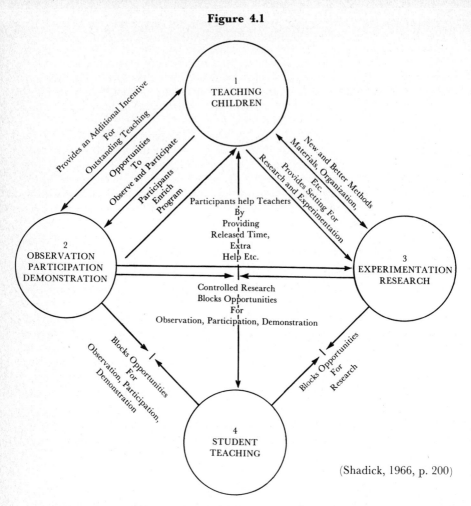

(Shadick, 1966, p. 200)

The teaching of children is improved by all of the functions assumed by laboratory schools. Student teaching leads to conflict with all other service functions; when a classroom or a school becomes primarily concerned with student teaching, it is difficult to perform the other functions. The same is true of traditional research, although to a lesser degree, perhaps because a school is seldom utilized as fully by research as by student teaching. Observation, participation, demonstration, and experimentation tend to reinforce each other (p. 204).

2. *Excessive demands upon laboratory schools*

That a campus school would be unable to meet all the demands that may be made upon it is readily understandable, and was illustrated early in the history of such schools within the field of student teaching alone (Gaskill and Carlson, 1958; Lang, 1959). Campus schools, which had generally adopted student teaching as the major activity, were clearly unable to cope with the increased number of trainees and, as a result, other schools were introduced into the student teaching programmes.

Caswell, referred to by Bryan (1961), makes a strong case for a teacher education institution taking the pressure off its laboratory school and developing further relationships:

> It seems obvious ... that no single school can possibly meet all the needs for laboratory experience on the part of a student body preparing to be teachers. On the one hand, the range of experiences needed is so wide as to require a variety of situations, and, on the other hand, the extent of activities will be so great in any curriculum which makes reasonable provision for laboratory experience as to swamp completely a single school. ... A college which is providing this desirable and, in fact, necessary range of experiences must make a whole area within its reach a laboratory. (p. 275)

Although varied experiences may be made available in other co-operating schools, there are some services that a campus school is in a unique position to offer. The overloading of a campus school, through excessive and wide-ranging demands, may limit its potential in such an area, for example, as that of research. Gaskill and Carlson (1958) suggest that other activities too often crowd out basic research from the campus laboratory school into other schools where staff are less qualified to conduct it effectively. Bryan (1961) stresses that the teacher education institution and the campus school have an obligation to initiate research projects and points towards the campus school as the most favourable location for such activities.

If the programme of the campus school is not carefully controlled, the pressures upon staff may become excessive and the quality of the school's contribution will be affected. As noted by Ohles (1962), the laboratory school teacher is involved in supervision of student teachers; preparation, conducting and evaluating demonstration lessons; pursuing experimentation; meeting with parents, visiting teachers, and with college instructors—as well as teaching his pupils (p. 62). Clearly, there is a need not only for regulation of the total demands placed upon a campus school, but a sensitive awareness of the overall contribution that any individual member of staff is at any time called upon to make.

3. Staffing

Ohles (1962) found four major problems which inhibited the integration of college and laboratory school: (i) failure on both sides to see the roles of the other; (ii) status problems; (iii) lack of contact between staffs; and (iv) teaching load and lack of time (p. 28). When the role of the laboratory school has not been clarified, misunderstandings arise between staff of the college and the school as they exercise their different expectations. Where laboratory school teachers fail to recognize the teacher education function of the school and where lecturers show insufficient consideration of the school's responsibilities to its pupils, difficulties will arise.

The need for the teacher education programme being given due consideration in the selection of laboratory school staff suggests to Bryan (1961) that college control of the campus school is highly desirable. He claims: 'Without a college-controlled campus school, the college has little or no control over the selection of the teachers in the laboratory school. Without this control the major key to shaping a program does not exist' (p. 277). As pointed out by Ohles (1962), however, control of staff recruitment does not necessarily guarantee that the institution will be able to attract the most suitable teachers. He reported that the additional responsibilities associated with the laboratory school, and the highly competitive salaries and promising opportunities in the public school, may serve to discourage potential applicants.

The laboratory school may once have been seen by teachers as a stepping-stone into the parent institution, either college or university (Ohles, 1967). This is not necessarily the situation at the present time. The question of staffing quality in the laboratory school is an important one for it has implications with respect to the effectiveness of the teacher preparation programme and the relative status of lecturers and the staff of the laboratory school.

Staffing arrangements and conditions in laboratory schools vary considerably. The majority of the laboratory schools included in the survey by McNabb (1973) had a regular full-time staff. Most of the schools, in addition, made use of some supporting staff from the related college or university. The laboratory schools associated with universities had a higher proportion of full-time staff than was the case with the laboratory schools linked with colleges. The staff of the university laboratory schools are reported by McNabb to be in a vastly superior position with respect to tenure, academic rank and fringe benefits than are the staff of college laboratory schools. Whereas all of these benefits were enjoyed by staff of the state university laboratory schools, only 50 per cent of the full-time faculty at state teachers college laboratory schools held academic rank, 17 per cent had tenure, and only 33 per cent stated that they received fringe benefits of the kind shared by faculty members of the associated institution. No part-time staff at either state university or college laboratory schools received any special considerations. The fate of the staff belonging to those laboratory schools which were closed is of interest. Where the laboratory schools had been attached to a state university, the staff generally had tenure and were absorbed within the institution. This was not the case, however, where the laboratory school had been linked with a state college. Of 46 laboratory schools associated with state colleges, 83 per cent of the original staff members were either dismissed or were employed within the local public school system.

4. *Pupils at laboratory schools*

A criticism commonly levelled at the laboratory school as a training ground for student teachers is that it is non-representative of the schools in which the student will later teach. It is to be noted that the first criterion considered in many such schools when enrolling pupils is whether the child has a parent as a member of staff of either the school or faculty (McNabb, 1973). Another query often raised is whether research carried out in these schools is relevant to other schools which are more heterogeneous in race, socio-economic considerations, and abilities. Hunter's (1970) discussion of this issue is reported in the later section on 'The Future of the Laboratory School'.

As mentioned by Hunter (1970), a research and experimental emphasis within the laboratory school may mean that at any particular time a pupil may not have undergone equivalent experiences to a child at a public school. With a carefully organized programme accompanied by systematic record-keeping, the child who completes his schooling at the laboratory school should, however, not be at any disadvantage.

Not a great deal of research has been reported on the effects of teacher preparation programmes on pupils. Some very early research findings suggested that pupils were not disadvantaged through exposure to student teachers

(Ludeman, 1929; Strebel, 1932; Deputy and Reed, 1933). Hunter's perhaps light-hearted comment concerning the need to grant 'diplomatic immunity' to the person or committee responsible for enforcing a selected pupil intake for a laboratory school may be interpreted as an indication of the popularity of such a school with parents (Hunter, 1970, p. 20).

5. *Finance*

(i) FINANCING OF LABORATORY SCHOOLS

The greater proportion of laboratory schools at public-supported teacher education institutions received at least 80 per cent of their operating revenue from the institution with which they were affiliated (McNabb, 1973). Many, at the time of the survey, were actively exploring additional sources of funding. The major problems foreseen by laboratory schools in the immediate future, as suggested by McNabb's study of sixty state college laboratory schools and eight state university laboratory schools, are as indicated in Table 4.2. The prominence of funding as a problem will be noted.

McNabb also makes reference to a survey conducted in 1969, which revealed that inadequate financial support from the associated teacher education institution and the state was the major reason given for the closing of thirty-six laboratory schools in the United States between 1964–9.

That expense, as an argument against laboratory schools, may sometimes be magnified out of due proportion, is suggested by Bryan (1961) when he points out that the real cost of such a school should be viewed only as the additional

Table 4.2

	State Universities (n = 8)		*State Colleges (formerly State Teacher Colleges) (n = 60)*	
	N	%	N	%
Lack of financial support	3	38	31	52
Lack of space			2	3
Lack of college faculty support			1	2
Inability to develop relevant programmes or change existing programmes	2	25	14	23
Inability to obtain qualified staff			4	7
Lack of support from college administration	1	13	1	2
Lack of state legislative support			2	3
Lack of public support			2	3
Upgrading morale of staff	1	13		
Change of philosophy			1	2
Obtaining a racial balance			1	2
None	1	13	1	2

(McNabb, 1973, p. 85)

expense over and above that of maintaining an equivalent public school. He further suggests that perhaps a campus school is a facility that teacher education cannot afford to be *without*. The need for a revised system of funding is of course implied. If present funding arrangements persist, however, in view of competing demands within the college or university, the future of the laboratory school would seem uncertain—unless it is clearly providing a service of a kind that cannot be readily carried out in public schools. Certainly, many institutions, for a number of reasons, are seeking to establish co-operating programmes with the public schools.

(ii) FINANCING PROGRAMMES DEVELOPED WITH CO-OPERATING SCHOOLS

Providing finance for co-operative programmes is generally recognized to be a major problem. Poliakoff (1971), however, reports on a study of several programmes involving colleges or universities and schools in which he found many imaginative arrangements serving to minimize the cost factor. The co-operative programme between Oregon State University and Corvallis School District, as operating in 1971, is an interesting example in that it did not draw upon funds outside its present budget. Some features reported by Poliakoff include:

(i) two joint appointments, one being the programme co-ordinator, financed on an equal basis by university and school, and a teacher whose salary was on a one-third university and two-thirds school basis;

(ii) a number of university staff committed for a proportion of their time to school-based work which includes conducting (jointly with teachers) student teaching seminars, team teaching, preparing schedules, assisting in the preparation of materials, and releasing teachers for work in curriculum development;

(iii) keeping costs low for teachers attending in-service courses, through the use of a fund accumulated from supervisory payments for student teaching; and

(iv) covering absences of teachers attending in-service courses through the use of student teachers, tutors, aides, and other team members in those cases where the teacher belongs to a teaching team.

After reviewing four other programmes which provide instances of what she terms a 'creative reallocation of funds', Poliakoff concludes that 'rebating tuitions; rechanneling or pooling stipends for co-operating teachers; using pre-service teachers as substitutes; sharing already available staff; and using funds budgeted for in-service teacher education, recruitment, and teacher vacancies are methods that have been tried and found successful' (p. 364).

6. *Legal problems and co-operating school relationships*

As suggested by Kachur and Lang (1975) teachers have in the past had little part in determining policy related to teacher education programmes. Teacher educators are now being forced to listen with more than bemused tolerance as teacher associations lay down conditions under which student teachers may be involved in clinical experiences within the schools.

In the formulation of many recent agreements setting out provisions under which student teaching will be permitted, the role of the university has, in fact, been minimal. As Kachur and Lang suggest, it may seem bad enough that the university is relegated to the back seat in the formulation of general policy governing clinical experiences, but when such policy has the effect of restricting the nature of the programme that can be mounted, the situation may become quite serious. Kachur and Lang direct attention to the following examples of provisions which could affect innovative programmes requiring the grouping of students for improved supervision, team teaching, differentiated staffing or open-space instruction:

> There shall be no more than one student teacher per year. (Thomaston Public Schools, Thomaston, Connecticut)

> There shall be no more than one student teacher in any one department in the High School, no more than three student teachers in the Middle School and no more than one student teacher on any grade level in the elementary school. (Mt. Pleasant Union Free School District, Mt. Pleasant, New York) (p. 203)

A further example of an increasing school influence in basic student teaching policy is the requirement in some systems that the principal and teacher concerned interview the prospective student teacher or intern before he is accepted into the school. As noted by Kachur and Lang, although formulated by the school system, some provisions may involve the university as well, if the teacher concerned were to initiate grievance procedures. The example cited is a provision of the Willow Run Public School, Michigan:

> Evaluation of a teacher's performance in the role of critic teacher, if made, shall be conducted by the building Principal, and shall be subject to [professional grievance procedures]. (p. 204)

Whereas in the past the schools have been by far the lesser partner in the planning and arranging of in-school experiences, teachers, through the activities of their associations, are now demanding that they be involved. If universities and colleges wish to maintain control of clinical experience programmes within the schools then, according to Kachur and Lang (1975), there are several options open to them:

> (i) Take the initiative in assuming a negotiation parity with school-boards and teacher associations; or

> (ii) Re-examine their current types of written agreements with public school districts to assure both their legality and inclusion of classroom teacher associations as a bargaining agent; and/or

> (iii) Re-examine their own preparation programs to determine whether, in truth, cooperative decision-making includes participation from all school personnel, from selection of candidates through certification; and/or

> (iv) Explore other types of professional services (research, consultation, curricular development, inservice training) that can be rendered to the public schools, particularly as they affect teachers, as an incentive for their continued involvement in off-campus clinical experience programs. (p. 204)

As alternatives to the above proposals, Kachur and Lang suggest that the university of college must either: (i) operate its own schools (on- or off-campus laboratory schools) or provide simulated substitute experiences; (ii) accept the public schools and teacher associations as the major determinants of policy governing in-school experiences; or (iii) abandon the responsibility for the clinical preparation of teachers.

7. *Organization of in-school experiences*

The trend towards universities and colleges developing co-operating relation-ships with schools over and above the usual student teaching arrangement is reflected by Burgess' study in 1971. Although a number of the institutions expressed some dissatisfaction with the nature of the experience, 84 per cent of the 238 questioned were able to report that they had an arrangement with the local primary or secondary schools for school experiences prior to student teaching (Morin, 1974). The problems which tended to reduce the potential benefits of these arrangements were reported to be as follows: (i) scheduling; (ii) securing co-operating teachers who would welcome an optimum experience; (iii) student transportation; (iv) public school-college communications; and (v) logistics (Morin, 1974, p. 11). Such problems as these will be recognized as those commonly experienced in co-operating programmes.

A problem closely associated with those outlined above is that of the availability of staff and time within the university or college to initiate, arrange, and follow-up in-school experience. Historically, staff status and reward within universities has been associated with theoretical pursuits rather than involvement in practical activities such as field experiences (Goodlad, 1970; Hogle, 1973). In a reference to Eberly's study of 917 United States' colleges and universities, Hogle (1974) draws attention to the finding that:

> The amount of time required to administer off-campus learning programs effectively is one obstacle to active faculty interest in field experience interludes in the usual 'publish or perish' environment. (p. 14)

The recognition of the additional demands on time made on staff involved in field experiences in the total staffing pattern of an institution is a prerequisite for the development and maintenance of a successful programme.

8. *Problems of implementation—an example*

Ruchkin (1973a) draws attention to the meaning of co-operation as usually understood in relation to co-operation between sponsoring agencies. She proposes that frequently the suggested criteria for co-operation are those of mutuality reciprocity, and parity among the agencies involved. These terms Ruchkin defines thus:

mutuality is seen as 'a situation where participants seek, give, and receive simultaneously'.

reciprocity 'exists where participants seek, give and receive alternately'.

parity 'is found where participants possess like status, number, power, resources and are evenly balanced'. (p. 659)

Whether many ventures, widely publicized for their co-operative quality, in actual practice meet the criteria of co-operation mentioned above is, Ruchkin suggests, open to question. An example is sketched to confirm this doubt.

Ruchkin reports an investigation of the project, Teacher Education Centre for Urban Schools (TECUS), which was a joint venture involving a metropolitan school system and a major university in the United States. The project commenced in 1965 and the field investigation was carried out during its fifth year of operation. Ready access was available to a variety of documentation from the commencement of the project. When the criteria usually associated with co-operative arrangements (parity, mutuality, and reciprocity) are considered, the results of the study may be thought surprising. As identified and listed by Ruchkin (1973a) the study revealed:

(i) an initially and overtly college-dominated structure with close working relationships among several levels of two institutional segments;

(ii) succeeding the phase listed above, a more distant, parallel functioning of two systems still operating in one elementary school site linked together via the co-director role;

(iii) great strain upon and related withdrawal especially by middle level administrators, that is, assistant principals, in the early close working situation;

(iv) evidence of hierarchically related cooperative consensus presentation;

(v) increasing cosmopolitanization of school segment, declining specialization of college segment, and general increase in personalization;

(vi) extraordinarily high personnel requirements;

(vii) the development of an integrative organizational myth;

(viii) relative rule-lessness coupled with an emphasis on enactment of professional roles;

(ix) variable bureaucratization related to insider and outsider leadership succession; and

(x) concentrated impact upon the program of the school serving as the cooperative site coupled with minimal, if any, influence on collegiate patterns. (p. 662)

The study is helpful in that it is suggestive of trends that may emerge over an extended period of time in an 'externally decreed' co-operative centre of two bureaucracies. It raises doubts as to whether it is realistic or desirable to expect parity between institutions in all phases of a co-operative relationship. Possible effects of institution size, and changes in the size of either of the co-operating institutions are among areas suggested by Ruchkin for future investigation of co-operating relationships.

The implications of some of the above problems facing laboratory schools and co-operating programmes will be taken up in the section which follows.

The Future of Laboratory Schools and Co-operative Programmes

The future of the laboratory school is dependent upon the ways in which the problems referred to in the previous section are faced. Showing a most perceptive awareness of the key issues involved, Madeline Hunter (1970) presents a comprehensive plan for the future in her article, 'Expanding Roles of Laboratory Schools'. In this present section it will be appropriate to make detailed reference to a number of her proposals.

The trend towards incorporating public schools into teacher education programmes has become increasingly apparent in recent years. The strong emphasis being placed upon the integration of theory and practice was illustrated in the examples of co-operative programmes. The present climate would appear to be one of experimentation in which various kinds of field-based programmes are being developed or modified to meet particular requirements. An example of an imaginative programme for the future, envisaged by Bush (1975), is outlined in this section. It represents a development of the portal school concept.

The experiences of those who have been involved in developing co-operative programmes between teacher education institutions and schools suggest that there are certain common problems which appear to be inherent in the endeavour. Hogle (1974), in reference to field experience programmes, sets out a series of recommendations which, at least in part, would seem to be useful guidelines for those responsible for planning, initiating and maintaining any co-operative programme. These are included in the convenient form in which he presented them in his article, 'Teacher Education and Experiential Learning'.

Prospects of the laboratory school

As suggested by McNabb (1973), a hint of the possible future of the laboratory school as presently conceived may well be found in the recent history of these schools. McNabb's study revealed that between 1964 and 1972 as many as 61 public-supported laboratory schools were closed, leaving only 68 laboratory schools operating at public-supported teacher education institutions in 1972. A factor contributing towards the closure of certain laboratory schools was reported to be their inability to change their functions. McNabb points out that many laboratory schools, operating at the time of his study, had the same functions as those schools which were closed down, and furthermore, the present schools expressed no intention of changing their functions in the next few years. This being so, McNabb suggests that, with increasing financial demands being made upon the parent institution, it would seem likely that many of the present laboratory schools would similarly be forced to close.

If the laboratory school is to continue to operate, it must, according to McNabb, justify its existence in terms of functions that cannot just as readily be performed in other public schools. Madeline Hunter (1970) also recognizes that the laboratory school must change its functions, believing that if this can be achieved there is reason to be optimistic concerning its future. She claims:

> For this potential to be released, however, the laboratory school must shed its role as a demonstration and training installation inducting novitiates into accepted and traditional practice. It must become a center for inquiry, an essential component of the educational design to produce new theory, to translate that theory into generalizable practice, to disseminate that knowledge and practice into the mainstream of American education, and to develop vigorous leaders. (p. 14)

In suggesting that a prime function of the laboratory school of the future should be that of 'research, experimentation and inquiry', Hunter is stating a viewpoint that will be recognized as having widespread support. Ohles (1967) believes, for example, that although making attempts in the field, the public schools are generally not capable of carrying out educational research effectively. Ohles claims that:

> As an educational laboratory under a college of education, the laboratory school can test a theory, apply expertise to every aspect of the research effort, exert adequate controls, utilize computers and other sophisticated data-handling resources, and measure failure or success with equal candor—all those things that a public school does poorly, if at all. (p. 44)

In supporting her contention that research, experimentation, and inquiry are the proper functions of the laboratory school, Hunter specifies the kinds of issues that should be investigated. These may perhaps be suggested by the following questions:

(i)   How effective are particular alternative *teacher education programmes*, which may, after development and trialling in the laboratory school be considered suitable for general application in centres concerned with the preparation of teachers?

(ii)   What part may *technology* play in education?

(iii) What *goals and objectives of education* may be factored out, made explicit, implemented and tested'?

(iv)   What *particular phases of schooling* should be singled out for concentrated study?

(v)   How does a particular *teaching methodology* reflect theory, and what are 'the discriminators that would indicate the conditions under which such a method would be effective or ineffective'?

(vi)   What *organizational schemes* may be identified as appropriate for the conduct schooling, and tested?

(viii) What are the *staffing patterns* required in schools, what are the related competencies, and what programmes are appropriate for the development of these competencies?

At a time when the laboratory school is called upon to justify its existence, it would be in its own interest to give special attention to the dissemination of research findings. Hunter suggests that if the laboratory school accepts a responsibility to influence the school system at large, then it will use a variety of media appropriate to a wide audience to get its message across.

The development of programmes appropriate for the training of potential teachers of clinical practice is seen by Hunter as a significant role of the future laboratory school. It would include the specification of relevant competencies and the determination of appropriate learning experiences such as developing the ability to interpret the curriculum and philosophy of the school to parents and other community groups, or introducing ways of improving instruction within a school.

The kinds of activity outlined above would appear to be very different from those common in many currently operating laboratory schools. Exposure to the research, experimentation and inquiry activities of the laboratory school should, in the opinion of Hunter, be an integral part of the teacher preparation programme. Through contact with the laboratory school the student's professional orientation will be enhanced as he is confronted with real educational problems submitted to critical and rigorous enquiry.

The main requirements believed by Hunter to be basic to the sound functioning of the laboratory school are the following: (i) the recognition of appropriate roles; (ii) the development of interrelationships; (iii) the appointment of appropriate staff; (iv) a heterogeneous pupil intake; and (v) provision of adequate facilities and budget. As some of these factors have been considered in relation to problems facing such schools, they will here need little further expansion.

Interrelationships.   Clearly, as suggested by Hunter, a laboratory school will only operate effectively if channels of communication are well established and kept open. Hunter refers to the need for closely developed relationships with both the school of education, other university departments, and with the wider educational community. If the laboratory school programme is to be well integrated with that of the school of education, there must be close liaison between the staff of the two institutions at all levels. Hunter suggests that:

> To achieve this liaison, conscious and explicit avenues of communication and collaborative efforts are essential so that areas of mutual concern can be identified and specialists will supplement and complement each other. A professor should find advice and assistance for his research from the staff of the laboratory school as well as experimental subjects. In turn, laboratory staff should find rigorous assistance with their clinical questions from the theoreticians. Undergraduate, graduate, doctoral, and post-doctoral students should have the availability of a laboratory school as one of the richest resources in their inquiry and education. (p. 17)

The other academic departments within the university or college should be encouraged to explore the ways in which the laboratory school may be of benefit to them. These departments would certainly be able to assist the school with educational resources and the staff with specialized advice within their subject area. The laboratory school has a responsibility to extend its influence outside the campus through interchanges of ideas with other laboratory schools, and by acting as a resource to public schools, not only by way of programmes, but by providing a consultative service.

Appropriate staffing. The kind of staff considered most appropriate to the laboratory school would depend upon what one conceives the appropriate role of the school to be, and upon the nature of the school's relationship to the college or university. Ohles (1967), for example, acknowledges that the laboratory school should be where research is undertaken, but places the responsibility for the initiation and design firmly with the college or university rather than the laboratory school staff.

Rather than deplore the fact that laboratory school staff are often not accorded status equal to that of members of faculty, Ohles believes that the laboratory school positions should be redefined so that what he sees as the 'myth of parity with the rest of the college' no longer persists. He believes that such a changed recognition would lead to more effective and productive results from the laboratory school.

Ohles would agree with Hunter, that the quality of staffing within the laboratory school is of paramount importance. An interesting suggestion with regard to some laboratory staff positions is made by Hunter who proposes that certain teachers from the public schools should be given the opportunity to join the laboratory school staff for a limited period of, say, one or two years. These teachers would, she contends, bring with them the flavour of the 'real world' and, on return to the public schools, would be able to assume leadership roles.

In the keeping with the experimental role of the laboratory school, there would often be student teachers on the staff to allow the investigation and evaluation of training programmes which may be intended for use elsewhere. In marked contrast to the position in many former laboratory schools, the student teachers would not be in the school for the purpose of the traditional teaching practice.

Heterogeneous pupil-intake. As has been already noted, a frequent criticism made of laboratory schools has been that of the atypical nature of the pupil intake and the consequent lack of generalizability of research findings to other school populations. The pupils in many laboratory schools have often come from the one socio-economic area and have included a high proportion of children belonging to academic staff of the university or college. Hunter claims that 'admittance procedures which guarantee heterogeneity and are impervious to political or economic pressures must be determined' (p. 16). She believes that it is essential that parents are made fully aware of the research orientation of the school and have the opportunity to send their children elsewhere if so desired. Parents should realize that the curriculum of the school at any point of time will differ from that of the normal school and that it would be only at the time of graduation that they could expect their child to have met usual school requirements.

Adequate facilities and budget. The unusual nature of the laboratory school programme necessitates a generous allocation of funds for personnel, facilities and space additional to the requirements of the normal school. Unless funds are forthcoming, in keeping with the importance of the school's unique function, and unless there is adequate flexibility in budgeting and facilities, the laboratory school will be unable to realize its potential.

Forthcoming co-operating school programmes

As has been noted, one of the most interesting developments in field-based teacher education programmes in recent years is that of the 'portal school'. According to Evans (1975), these are schools which 'volunteer for and are selected by teacher training institutions for high involvement and co-operation in the training process' (p. 46). The portal school is an expression of a trend towards what are seen as more realistic teacher education programmes in which colleges and schools co-operate in both coursework and field experience. It would be reasonable to expect that many co-operative programmes of the future will incorporate some of the characteristics of the portal school. Bush (1975) confirms this as a possibility in his vision of what he calls the 'Special School for Teacher Education' of the future.

A co-operating relationship of the future. The 'special school', as visualized by Bush, would be a school within the public system which voluntarily becomes a teacher education school, for a nominated period of about three to five years. The partners in the project would include the teacher education institution(s), the local school, the school system, members of the professions with professional association links at local, state and national levels, and representatives of state and federal government. Bush comments that 'each will have an authentic and vigorous voice in the enterprise'. The composition of the personnel undergoing training would be a novel feature of the school. It would include students just beginning teacher education courses, experienced teachers undergoing retraining perhaps in new areas of speciality, interested senior elementary or high school students wishing to work with younger children, and members of the community who seek qualifications to subsequently become part of teaching teams. Bush describes the staffing pattern and responsibilities thus:

> This school is saturated with personnel, up to double the regular staff. It includes, in addition to the regular staff: (a) A substantial group (5–20) of neophyte trainees from one or more neighboring institutions of higher education. They will spend substantial, though varying amounts of time, from half to full day, from one to four

semesters, and (b) a corps of regular faculty from neighboring teacher education institutions whose disciplinary and professional backgrounds will match the training needs of the neophyte and advanced trainees, and the designated problem areas of need in the school. They will be assigned for part or all of their collegiate load to the school site. They will participate in the life of the school as team members with regular school staff. In addition, they will offer seminars and classes in which (often simultaneously) both neophyte and advanced trainees will be enrolled. They will share with the regular staff the counseling and advisory responsibilities for neophytes. (p. 149)

A distinctive characteristic of the school is its 'problem-solving and inquiry orientation' and an emphasis upon 'research and development'. The school would, by virtue of the supplementary and varied staffing during its time as a special school for teacher education, enrich its educational climate with lasting effects. By teacher education institutions entering into a relationship such as that described, for a fixed term only with a particular school, it would be possible for the associated benefits to be spread widely over a period of time. Bush concludes:

> Teacher education thus moves in the next decade into a phase in which the entire school, in a natural setting rather than the individual trainee as at present, becomes the main unit for teacher education. (p. 149)

Developing future co-operative programmes. Conditions under which projected co-operative programmes may be successful are implied by a series of recommendations made by Hogle (1974) in relation to a field experience programme. Although some of these recommendations are specific to the kind of programme he is discussing, many of them will be recognized as appropriate guidelines for the development of a range of co-operative ventures between tertiary institutions and schools or other agencies. Hogle proposes the following:

—Though often difficult to predict and measure, it is imperative to ensure the educational value of off-campus experiences.

—A balance should be maintained between the attempt to serve large numbers of students and the effort to closely meet individual needs of a more select population.

—There is an ever-present challenge to maintain a meaningful correlation between classroom theory and off-campus practicum.

—Constant attention should be directed toward establishing and maintaining a mutual respect for the delicate and reciprocal balance between the training function and the service function.

—Utmost attention must be directed toward cultivating supportive faculty attitudes and commitment and toward providing adequate supervision.

—Crucial to the entire field-based operation is establishment and maintenance of a lasting and mutually constructive rapport between field site representatives and the institution of higher learning.

—There is a persistent need for periodic university-community exchanges and 'linkage' seminars.

—There should be full utilization of community personnel serving in reward-supported roles as adjunct professors.

—Reordering of priorities is necessary to provide adequate funds to meet projected institutional costs, particularly those related to transportation and staffing.

—As a crucial ingredient to any field-based endeavour, there must be a multi-faceted evaluation effort, constant review, and continual feedback from all involved participants.

—A consensus should be sought in arriving at statements of specific objectives, corresponding roles, and mutual expectations.

—There should exist an appreciation for the desirability of differential field sites, which should include both schools and community agencies.

—Tolerance and understanding should be exercised for such bureaucratic necessities as forms, procedure, contracts, schedules, records, etc.

—Continual effort should be made to establish and maintain a flexibility of operation in order to expand and improve, based on evaluative feedback.

—Educational efforts should be directed toward instilling in all parties involved a sense of responsibility and professionalism.

—There should exist a balance between those involved in fieldwork as volunteers because of their concerned interest and those who are part of the programme simply because it is required for a course or academic credit in their programme.

—Efforts should be continuously directed toward providing the feasibility of and striking a balance between meeting institutional demands for educationally valuable experiences and meeting societal needs for service.

—Safeguards should be established to guard against the most probably recurring problem areas: student cancellations, unmet expectations, altered needs, bureaucratic sluggishness, lack of punctuality, chronic absenteeism, and simple irresponsibility.

—Provisions must be made to provide and maintain an adequate student-field staff ratio.

—Procedures should be instituted so that students understand the twofold aspects of the programme; the one relatively circumscribed to provide certain learning experiences and job performance, the other flexible to afford an opportunity for initiative and imagination.

—Pains should be taken in matching the students' skills, attitudes, and knowledge with positions in which they can make the most meaningful contribution in their off-campus activities.

—Production and broad distribution of a brochure or guidebook which clearly identifies the roles, responsibilities, and expectations of all co-operative participants in the work-learning relationship is a necessity.

—Creation of a weekly or monthly newsletter to provide continuous and up-to-date exchange of current and future events of mutual interest and benefit to the university and community-at-large is highly desirable.

—To encourage and facilitate faculty and student participation, the development of a 'Catalogue of Offerings' which spells out the types of experiential learning opportunities that are available, along with the necessary prerequisite skills, actual responsibilities, and evaluation procedures that accompany each specific field experience is advisable.

—Finally, the challenge and promise of improved 'town-gown' relationships through well-run field experience programmes is ever present. University students can serve as a new and vital link in campus-community liaison efforts. (pp. 28–31)

Whatever form developments in teacher education programmes take, it would seem probable that there will be an increasing involvement of students in school contexts and of members of the teaching profession in the planning and implementation of co-operative ventures. The foregoing examples, discussion of problems, and guidelines may serve to widen the range of considerations and possibilities for institutions involved in the future planning of co-operative programmes. Perhaps equally informative might be the following accounts of how Australian teacher education programmes are co-operating with schools in the pursuit of a variety of goals.

SURVEY OF AUSTRALIAN CO-OPERATING SCHOOL ARRANGEMENTS

A survey was undertaken in October-November 1975 to explore special co-operating school arrangements which had recently been developed by Australian teacher education programmes. The survey instrument, consisting of a simple one-page check-list, was sent to the directors of all programmes. Mindful of the fact that these programmes had already been somewhat beseiged by questionnaires, including the substantial one from our innovations project, the instrument was deliberately small and required little open-ended response. The particular aims of this survey were to:

1. Discover the nature and extent of special relationships and arrangements which teacher education programmes have developed with one or a number of schools to facilitate activities beyond conventional practice teaching and microteaching schemes but not excluding them.
2. To find out whether the schools involved were primary or secondary institutions and whether they were located on- or off-campus.
3. To learn the names of the schools and their principals so that they could be communicated with directly if necessary.
4. To collect the data mentioned in 1, 2 and 3 above on the basis of which decisions could be made on selecting certain arrangements for case study.

The response to the questionnaire from the 68 institutions contacted was excellent. Fifty-six institutions (or 82 per cent) replied (see Table SAC.1). Of the replies, 39 (70 per cent) reported special arrangements with schools in addition to, or other than for the provision of practice teaching or microteaching

Table SAC.1 RESPONSE TO CO-OPERATING SCHOOL SURVEY

No. institutions sent questionnaire	68
No. institutions returned questionnaire	56
No. non-responding institutions	12
Response rate	82%

Table SAC.2 PROGRAMMES WITH SPECIAL CO-OPERATING SCHOOL ARRANGEMENTS

	No. responses	*% responses*
No. programmes reporting special arrangements (beyond practice teaching and microteaching)	39	70
No. programmes using schools for conventional microteaching and/or practice teaching only	17	30

(Table SAC.2). This quite large number of institutions apparently having special functions carried on in schools pleasantly surprised the investigators since such activities have been seldom mentioned either in Australian teacher education journals or at conferences.

Only eleven on-campus co-operating schools were reported (5 primary and 6 secondary). The word 'only' is used because, compared with the large number of on-campus schools in say the United States, this is a very small figure. However, even this is perhaps an unexpectedly high number for the Australian context.

In addition to this limited number of relationships with on-campus schools, most responding programmes (87 per cent) reported special links with at least one off-campus school. The number of off-campus schools co-operating with individual programmes varied from one to more than twenty. The most common number of on- and off-campus schools co-operating with any one programme was four (58 per cent of responses).

It was reported that the co-operating schools had a range of functions (Table SAC.3). Most of the schools provided for at least three of the twelve

Table SAC.3 FUNCTIONS OF SPECIAL CO-OPERATING SCHOOLS*

Function	No. responses	% responses
Providing practice teaching opportunities	35	90
Providing observational opportunities	30	77
Generating new ideas and approaches	22	56
Participating in methods/curriculum courses	21	54
Participating in workshop/seminars on teaching	21	54
Providing microteaching opportunities	21	54
Providing teaching opportunities for tertiary staff	19	49
Co-operating in research and development on teaching or curriculum	17	44
Co-operating in planning and evaluating new approaches to teacher preparation	17	44
Independently investigating problems of teaching and learning	14	36
Offering in-service education to teachers from other schools	12	31
Disseminating research findings, new approaches and new materials to other schools	10	23
Others:		
Involving student teachers in diagnostic and remedial work with children having learning difficulties	8	21
Involving student teachers in developing and/or trialling curriculum plans and materials and learning units	8	21
Providing the physical setting for tertiary courses on teaching and curriculum	7	18
Mutual institution-school consultation and discussion on educational problems, procedures, and materials	7	18
Sharing educational facilities, equipment and materials between institution and school	4	10

* All responses cited at least three functions.

designated functions on the questionnaire. A number of institutions (Salisbury CAE, Kelvin Grove CAE, Mt. Gravatt CAE, SCV Burwood, and Macquarie University), claimed that schools were co-operating with their programmes in all twelve functions. A follow-up of these claims, however, indicates that in most cases some of the functions were being carried out in a very minor, incidental way. In several other cases it seems the questionnaire was simply carelessly completed so that several functions were inadvertently checked. Salisbury CAE seems to be the only institution which through its two laboratory schools is managing to secure co-operation in most of the twelve functions listed, although a number of them are not yet as highly developed as that institution would wish.

The most common general functions of the special co-operating schools were the provision of practice teaching and observational opportunities for student teachers (cited by 90 per cent and 77 per cent of respondents respectively). In both these activities, as later case studies will reveal, there seems to be a strong movement away from conventional approaches. In practice teaching, students teach individual and small groups as well as whole classes. They come into schools on a continuous and sometimes incidental basis as well as for a block of time. Their work often focuses on specific competencies rather than on general procedures alone. They gradually become involved in a wide range of professional responsibilities. Co-operating-school staff play a special role in practice teaching supervision in several schemes. Sometimes they give 'neutral-party' counselling for students having teaching problems, and at other times they and their classes provide remedial practice teaching for students experiencing pronounced difficulties (e.g., University of Sydney). These practices are specially adapted to the needs of each student. In observational work there is less stress on the fully prepared formal 'model' lessons. Students observe children, specific teaching tasks, and a variety of strategies. They sometimes participate in planning and in implementing the teaching as it proceeds. Some observation informally involves only individual or small groups of student teachers rather than complete sections crammed into classrooms. On occasions the observations consist of pre-arranged viewing of specially prepared teaching; at other times they involve incidental viewing of regular teaching (e.g., Armidale CAE). In a small number of co-operating schools unobtrusive observations are facilitated by closed-circuit television relayed to school or college rooms and by special 'viewing' classrooms with one-way-vision screens (e.g., on-campus schools at Salisbury CAE and Brisbane KTC).

Practice teaching and observational work in certain co-operating schools were seen as specially valuable by some institutions since these schools were regarded as places which themselves generated new ideas and practices (56 per cent of responses) and did not simply take the word from the teacher education programme. These schools were thus committed to their own innovatory approaches and did not seem inhibited, as co-operating schools sometimes are, by the requirements of the teacher education institution.

One important new development in connection with co-operating schools is the reciprocal staffing arrangements whereby selected teachers participate in the education courses and the curriculum courses of the teacher education programme (54 per cent of responses for each type of course), and teacher education staff participate in the teaching of school pupils (49 per cent of responses), (e.g., Salisbury CAE). Sometimes teachers participated in the teacher education courses alongside the lecturer; at other times they were responsible for whole or part of the course or were occasional, visiting tutors. In some arrangements the course involvement of teachers was linked with their demonstration work in classrooms (e.g., University of Sydney). In 18 per cent of cases teacher participation in the teaching and curriculum courses was facilitated by the fact that the courses were conducted in school locations. Teacher educator involvement in teaching pupils was often accompanied by student observations and team teaching with the class teacher and students. Often, but not always associated with school-based teacher education projects, schemes of reciprocal staffing have much to commend them. Links between theory and practice are strongly forged. Courses, characterized by reality and relevance, tend to take on a new vitality. Teachers gain a greater sense of professional worth. Lecturers are seen to teach and this expands their credibility in the eyes of both students and teachers (e.g., SCV Hawthorn).

Co-operating schools are also fairly heavily engaged in facilitating micro-teaching programmes (54 per cent of responses). Sometimes they supply the rooms and the pupil groups, at other times their pupils are transported to the teacher education campus. In a number of microteaching programmes, co-operating schools provide special teaching booths and school staff advise students on the preparation of micro-lessons and give students feedback on their performance (e.g., Newcastle CAE). In several programmes school staff are involved in the initial discussions with students on videotaped model teaching episodes. In a few others they themselves actually provide the videotaped or 'live' teaching segments (e.g., Churchlands CAE).

Co-operative research and development work by teacher education and school staff was reported in 44 per cent of responses. A number of these research projects related to open education and several others related to children's learning generally and in the curriculum areas, especially social studies, music, English and mathematics. Most of the co-operative activity seemed to be of the developmental kind. There tended to be a lot of work in developing videotaped and other simulation material on teaching (e.g., SCV Burwood). Within some curriculum areas, and especially in social studies, there is also considerable effort in developing resource units for teachers and individualized learning materials for pupils. In addition to this collaborative activity, it was reported (36 per cent of responses) that some teachers were independently investigating problems of teaching and learning. In most cases this work was supported by funds from the Innovations Programme of the Schools Commission.

Schools were reported to be co-operating in planning and evaluating of new approaches to teacher preparation (44 per cent of responses). Generally this was connected with teacher involvement in the evaluation of pilot school-based teacher education programmes (e.g., Western Australian Secondary TC). More specifically, in a number of schools teachers are involved in providing feedback on new practice teaching plans, and in several programmes they are invited to comment on the adequacy of the course in terms of what students brought to practice teaching (e.g., Macquarie University). There was one collaborative project on the evaluation of a microteaching programme in terms of pupil attainment (e.g., Newcastle CAE), and another on the training of practice teaching supervisors in specific competencies (e.g., James Cook University).

The involvement of teachers in co-operating schools in research and development projects is a small but promising trend (e.g., University of Sydney). Teacher educators are beginning to realize that they have no monopoly on professional knowledge. The teacher-practitioner can provide fresh and invaluable insights into professional problems of all kinds. What is more, the teacher is in a ready position to *apply* the results of any research and development activity in which he is involved. It is to be hoped that collaborative work of this nature will expand and gain the support it deserves.

The provision of in-service education for other teachers was a function of a number of co-operating schools (31 per cent of responses). Generally this took the form of lectures, discussions, and observational work (e.g., Darling Downs IAE). In a few cases this work was co-operatively carried out with the staff of the teacher education programme. Linked with this was an effort to disseminate to other schools the results of research, development and innovation (reported by 23 per cent of respondents). Several schools communicated the results of their work in local education journals. In one case, a teacher education institution (Salisbury CAE) published a regular bulletin reporting college and co-operating school activities.

The 'other functions' section of the questionnaire revealed five interesting additional activities facilitated by special co-operating school arrangements. It was reported by 21 per cent of respondents that students under the guidance of tertiary staff and/or teachers had become involved in diagnostic and remedial teaching with children experiencing learning difficulties (e.g., Kelvin Grove CAE and Capricornia IAE). In some cases this work focused on a single area such as reading, but in other instances it encompassed all problem areas. Another 21 per cent of responses indicated that students, again with the guidance of lecturers and/or teachers, had become involved in developing and trying out programmes of work in curriculum areas, new curriculum materials and pupil learning units. Commercially developed approaches, such as *Man: A Course of Study* (MACOS) programmes, and the *Australian Science Education Project* (ASEP) materials, were also being trialled by students (e.g., Mackie CAE).

Co-operating arrangements also included mutual consultation and discussion between teachers and teacher education staff on educational problems, procedures and materials (18 per cent of responses). This activity was both incidental and formalized in nature. For instance, regular discussions were held on co-operating functions (e.g., practice teaching or observations), and lecturers were available to give advice to teachers on say, approaches to particular curriculum areas.

Sharing educational facilities, equipment and materials between teacher education institution and school was reported in 10 per cent of co-operative schemes. For example, teachers and pupils were given access to such institution facilities as library, swimming pool and oval, while student teachers were given access to school picture files, science equipment, and pupil reference books (e.g., Townsville CAE and Armidale Demonstration School).

Although the survey data reveal a large number and extensive range of teacher education activities being carried out with the co-operation of schools, it does not indicate the degree to which individual institutions have developed each of the listed school functions. Follow-up inquiries, which led to case studies of selected arrangements produced the strong impression that in many co-operative ventures the functions were mainly small scale, unsophisticated and informal in nature. This point needs to be emphasized because the above analysis tends to paint too glowing a picture. Having said this, one must add that it is nevertheless a very promising scene. New co-operating relationships with schools are being formed. Activities introduced in collaboration with the schools are recognized as valuable by all the parties concerned. In some situations, however, there seem to be at least two inhibiting factors to co-operative enterprises. On the one hand, a few teacher education staff hold such co-operative activities in low esteem. Some mistakenly see themselves as having a monopoly on professional knowledge and wisdom and regard school teachers as both academically and professionally naive with little to offer teacher education. Others feel threatened at the prospect of being challenged by the realities of schooling from which they have tried so hard to escape. On the other hand, some school teachers do not want their complacency to be disturbed by involvement in teacher education. Others object to increased responsibilities, no matter how small or how professionally beneficial to them, without payment. Fear of escalating financial commitments has, in turn, made teacher education institutions cautious in initiating or expanding co-operating programmes involving teachers.

CASE STUDIES OF AUSTRALIAN CO-OPERATING SCHOOL VENTURES

Following a procedure similar to that used in the innovations project (see Chapter 3), case studies were made of fourteen co-operating school arrangements throughout Australia. Again, the case study approach had two parts: (i) a descriptive statement from the person responsible for, or closely associated with the co-operating arrangement written, if possible, within an organizational framework suggested by the project, and (ii) a reflective commentary prepared by one of the project team based on data collected from interviews with representatives of various groups involved in the scheme, and from a study of the plan in operation and of material and facilities connected with it.

The co-operating plans of which case studies have been made have been selected on at least one of the following three bases: First, some were chosen because the questionnaire returns had indicated that the schools were providing a range of interesting functions. The application of this criterion raised queries concerning the interpretation of the questionnaire returns. When twenty co-operating arrangements were approached because of the claimed breadth of school functions, more than half admitted that their involvement in many of the checked activities was either not yet operationalized or so slight as to be insignificant. A second basis of selection for case study was the organizational and administrative machinery which characterized the co-operating relationships. Some case studies have been chosen to exemplify either simple unstructured, informal arrangements or more complex, carefully designed formal agreements. A third consideration that led to the selection of several schemes is their particular stage in a co-operating relationship. One scheme is in the process of initiation (i.e., North Sydney Demonstration School), several are quite well established (e.g., Madison Park Laboratory Primary School), and another seems likely to be terminated or, at least, attenuated (i.e., Armidale Demonstration School).

The case studies appear under the name(s) of the person(s) who provided the statement. The commentaries were compiled by the project members whose initials conclude them. The case studies are sequenced rather arbitrarily from simple, informal, single-function ventures to more complicated, formalized multi-function arrangements.

AN EXPLORATION OF THE CONCEPT OF ACTOR/TEACHER IN PRIMARY AND PRE-SCHOOL CONTEXTS

by Kelvin Grove College of Advanced Education and Oakleigh State Primary School

PAM HONEYWILL
Lecturer in Oral Communication and Drama

K. LEWIS
Principal of Oakleigh Primary School

Background and Context

The relationship between Oakleigh School and the college should be viewed as an embryonic one. It began in 1974, when Pam Honeywill (Drama Lecturer) approached the principal of the school to seek his co-operation for groups of actor/teachers teams to implement an exploratory programme with primary-age children. The actor/teacher role involves combining a number of concepts current in drama method, namely: *children's theatre*, which is primarily concerned with entertainment but relies on theatrical skills and techniques; *developmental drama*, which involves participation in experiences that foster social, emotional, intellectual or physical growth; and *drama as a method* of teaching curriculum content. The last idea involves taking particular curriculum units, for example, 'magnetism', and devising dramatic sketches to embody the principles involved.

The principal of the school received the request enthusiastically because he believed there should be greater co-operation with the college, and this could be 'one thin edge of the wedge'. The school itself was fortunate in having a large open hall which facilitated the involvement of students, without stretching the resources of the school. The co-operative relationship began in quite a low-key manner, therefore, but is showing signs of developing more substantial aspects, such as joint planning of experiences for children and the closer involvement of students with particular teachers. These developments are based on the co-operative attitude of the principal and the growing realization by college staff of the importance of practical experience for developing competent actor/teacher skills.

Aims and Principles of Operation

The aims of the relationship are not formally set out, and in fact have changed considerably each year. Initially the programme aimed at providing college students with an opportunity to explore the scope of the actor/teacher concept. The advantages of the programme for the school were secondary to this major goal. It appears, however, that as the idea of the actor/teacher has matured there has been an increasing concern to integrate the involvement of college students with the curriculum and goals of the school. The co-operative programme therefore is beginning to consider the mutual benefits that can be promoted and planning has proceeded recently on this basis.

The principles of the co-operative relationship are based on 'friendly' participation. Both the principal of the school and the college lecturer view the relationship existing between them as being on a person to person basis. The principal, too, is concerned to allow teachers freedom to participate or not, depending on their own preferences. The more recent proposals for co-operative planning, moreover, are viewed by school and college as of immediate benefit to the co-operating class teachers rather than as a research vehicle for the college.

The Plan and Its Implementation

College students are involved at the school one afternoon each week, when two teams of three students work with different classes in programmes of approximately one-half hour. The content and scope of the programmes are being jointly planned by the college students, the teachers and the drama lecturer from college. During 1974–5 the actor/teacher teams worked with all classes in the attached pre-school and the primary school. In 1976, however, the project will focus on repeated involvement of two or three classes with actor/teacher teams.

Problems and Effectiveness

The relationship has been effective in meeting the rather limited goals established. The continued involvement during 1976 suggests that the college and school are satisfied with the operation of the co-operative programme, although the principal of the school is concerned that it does not expand greatly. The informal agreement depends on goodwill from both sides, and while the personalities involved remain with the project the informal arrangement is envisaged as being entirely satisfactory.

Commentary

The relationship between Oakleigh Primary School and the Kelvin Grove College of Advanced Education is an example of the large number of informal arrangements between schools and tertiary institutions. It exemplifies the necessary reliance that teacher training programmes have on schools, not only to provide practice teaching experiences, but to co-operate in the planning, implementation and evaluation of the innovative approaches to curriculum and teacher training itself. The concept of an actor/teacher is an innovative one, which the drama lecturer initially trialled at Oakleigh School, simply to determine its worth and feasability. The success of the involvement, interestingly, did not mean that planning proceeded from the college alone. Rather the need was highlighted for co-operative planning between school and college with more reliance on teachers to suggest ideas and participate in evaluation.

The principal of the school occupies a central role in enabling the informal relationship to prosper. His own attitudes appear quite crucial: he maintains that teacher training needs to be much more closely associated with actual school situations, and commented that he saw the involvement of the drama section as a means of expanding such association.

The teachers' co-operation is also crucial in this situation because although they receive payment for the normal practice teaching period, their involvement with the actor/teacher teams is entirely voluntary. There is recognition on both sides that increased involvement would substantially change the attitude of teachers since much more of their time would need to be spent in co-operative planning and other activities. At the moment, however, the chance to be involved in an innovative programme, and their appreciation of the worthwhileness of the college's involvement has maintained the goodwill of the teachers at the school.

[P. R.]

SCHOOL ATTACHMENT IN 'MACOS'—ALEXANDER MACKIE COLLEGE OF ADVANCED EDUCATION AND GLENMORE ROAD PUBLIC SCHOOL

P. Brownie
Lecturer in Social Science

R. Whitaker
Class Teacher

Background and Context

Within the Teacher Development Programme at Alexander Mackie CAE, Dr Dawn Thew has introduced school-attachment workshops in specific curriculum areas. In semester 4, students spend one half-day in schools on one elected curriculum area, and in semester 5 one full-day a week in other chosen areas. The aim of the school-based workshops is to apply previously selected curriculum studies in classroom settings. Lecturers in nine curriculum areas establish objectives, and plan various workshops with teachers and students. Teachers lead the workshop activities and are free to adapt them to the needs of both pupils and students. For this work they are paid supervisory rates. College curriculum lecturers liaise with schools in an advisory capacity. Generally, any one curriculum workshop activity is in no more than two schools and lecturers spend an hour a week in each school. Each co-operating school has up to twelve students involved in workshops, three or four students attached to each class.

It was in the context of the school-attachment workshops that Brownie was able to incorporate the idea of college-school co-operation in the area of social studies, focusing on the initiation of a programme in *Man: A Course of Study* (MACOS).

The idea for school and college co-operation within the social studies area was conceived early in 1975 'over a beer' when authors were seeking a solution to a practical problem. As teachers we were each initiating a programme in *Man: A Course of Study*. The school lacked films, the college had a set, so co-operation seemed logical. The *quid pro quo* was that the school and the college would exchange ideas and report progress as their respective courses developed. Additionally, college students could visit the school to see and interact with pupils at 'the coal face'.

Dr Thew, Head of the Primary Programme at Mackie, and Mr Don Wallace, Principal at Glenmore Road, were enthusiastic supporters of the venture which was embodied in school attachment workshops but run as an essentially informal arrangement between friendly colleagues. Any costs (which were never great), were met by the staff. No insurmountable problems were encountered. Administrative difficulties of timing seemed to be our main concern which meant that it was hard to get to know individual classroom participants as well as we each would have liked.

Aims and Principles of Operation

While our aims were loosely defined, they were clearly registered in our own minds. These were to lift the level of our own experience in MACOS and to provide the opportunity for college students to observe and teach a MACOS class. The children, on the other hand were to be able to use certain college resources, facilities and staff. Students as individuals, small groups or sections were always made most welcome at the school which importantly was within a mile of the college.

The Plan and Its Implementation

Under the guidance of the class teacher, students worked with pupils in parallel learning situations often side by side. At other times students assumed a leadership role. They acted as discussion leaders on the ratio of say one to six or eight pupils. Visitations between campus and school, school and campus for the various sections of the course proved stimulating, as were joint visits to the zoo and gull beaches for animal-observation exercises. Through these varied contacts, students came to know certain pupils quite well.

Formalized functions then included students and pupils working together in the classroom on MACOS exercises; the leadership of groups by students; and students observing the class teacher working with his class. The reverse was also tried where teacher and class observed the lecturer working with his section. The children greatly enjoyed this reversal of roles. They also enjoyed an evening when their parents came to the school to learn about the project.

Contacts were made at least once a week during semester for the students, and at least twice a week for teacher-lecturer planning segments. The culmination of the association was a combined igloo-construction exercise followed by a highly ingenious winter sea ice festival.

Effectiveness

This does not seem to be a spectacular example of college-school co-operation but for all those involved it proved a highly stimulating and rewarding innovation. It facilitated the interaction of lecturer, teacher, student and pupil while engaged in the process of curriculum innovation. The exchange of ideas was mutually beneficial to all. It demonstrated how institutions could share resources, material and human, for the achievement of common purposes. Indeed, other schools, learning of the association, have sought similar schemes to be developed with them.

Commentary

The MACOS school-attachment workshop is a simple but important example of college-school co-operation for the improvement of an aspect of teacher preparation and of an area of the school curriculum. Opportunities for similar curriculum-innovation ventures are manifold.

Comments made on the school attachment programme, and on the MACOS workshops in particular, were uniformly positive. Lecturer, teacher, students and pupils all testified its value to them personally. For example, one pupil stated that it was interesting to have different people's ideas and perspectives in various tasks, that the opportunity for small group discussion under student leadership was stimulating, and that the resources the college or students provided made the work more worthwhile. Students and lecturers, however, agreed on three aspects of the school attachment scheme which could be improved: (i) They believed that school-attachment workshops should be directly linked with a college course running concurrently with it so that there would be greater opportunity to gather and refine relevant ideas and techniques. (ii) If feasible, teachers who participate in school attachment should be selected for their general teaching ability and their special competence in the workshop areas. (iii) Lecturers should have more time to work with both teacher and students during school attachment, not just to liaise but to co-operate in planning, teaching and evaluating. Similarly, teachers and students should have more time to discuss their work. Half-a-day for school attachment was seen as inadequate.

The provision of field work associated with particular curriculum studies is a growing practice in teacher education. If it seeks to involve lecturers, teachers, students and pupils in co-operative curriculum development, its full potential may perhaps be realized.

[C. T.]

CO-OPERATIVE PROGRAMME BETWEEN GABBINBAR STATE SCHOOL AND DARLING DOWNS INSTITUTE OF ADVANCED EDUCATION

B. Close
Senior Lecturer in Education

C. Crain

Principal, Gabbinbar State School

Background and Context

The relationship between Gabbinbar State School and the Darling Downs Institute developed informally, but included a number of formal aspects. The staff of the school and college met frequently because the school was used for practice teaching, and the college staff in many instances had children attending the school. The most important reason for the closeness of the relationship, however, was the attitude of the principal. He demonstrated an active interest in close co-operation between schools and the college, and he occupied the position of chairman of the in-school experience sub-committee of the Schools Advisory Board. The close contact that this position facilitated between the principal and college staff enabled mutual exchange of ideas to occur and the realization that the college and the Gabbinbar School endorsed similar approaches to education. The college staff found that Gabbinbar school offered students a supportive and worthwhile practical experience because the teaching staff adopted an accepting and professional attitude to the students, and the students were able to observe in practice many aspects of the courses provided by lecturers at the college. This realization led to an increasing co-operative relationship between the school and the college.

Aims and Principles of Operation

The aims of the close informal relationship are:

(i) To provide a supportive climate for students to begin their practical experience.

(ii) To provide practical examples of ideas and programmes suggested to students in lectures.

(iii) To provide the school staff with the resources available from the college, particularly in terms of ideas and innovative approaches.

The principles of operation focus on maintaining the channels of communication and reciprocation. Communication is regarded by college and school staff as crucial. The opportunity for open and frank discussions of problems and issues regarding college students, curriculum planning or innovations is highly regarded by both parties. The second principle, reciprocation, complements the first. The relationship has been maintained because it has been mutually beneficial. The school has been able to seek expert advice from college lecturers, who in turn have benefited from close contact with the day-to-day implementation of ideas and programmes. The role of the principal is vital in both instance. He occupies a formal position where communication channels are already open; and he can suggest through his contacts at that level ways in which college staff could actively support innovative programmes in his school.

The Plan and Its Implementation

The plan operates at a formal and an informal level. At the formal level the school provides opportunity for practice teaching experience. Informally this opportunity is extended by teachers, who offer students an invitation to work co-operatively with them in the classroom during periods after practice teaching. College staff also find that students experiencing difficulty with teaching are provided with a supportive environment and consequently use the school for remedial purposes.

In addition to practice teaching, the school provides a venue for lectures on topics closely related to its current policy. Lecturers on school organization, open education and classroom management have been held at the school with college and school staff participating. The close informal ties enables such lectures to be planned jointly without undue interference to the ongoing activities of the school.

Problems and Effectiveness

There appear to be few difficulties encountered in maintaining the close relationship between school and college. The relationship appears to thrive on the informal nature of the contacts. It could be improved by even greater mutual involvement, with more use of college personnel as consultants, and the participation of more school personnel in the teacher education programme.

Commentary

The relationship between Gabbinbar State School and the Darling Downs Institute of Advanced Education is an important example of a co-operating school arrangement. It exemplifies the mixture between formality and informality that appears necessary for co-operation to thrive. A number of school personnel stressed in their commentaries that the relationship was 'informal', a 'gentleman's agreement', and that they would not like a formal arrangement because 'it ties you down too much'. The stress on the informal nature of the relationship, however, must be viewed in the context of the central fundamental role of the principal in initiating and maintaining the relationship. The principal has formal contacts with the college through his position on the Board of Studies, the Schools Advisory Board and his chairmanship of the in-school experience sub-committee. Each of these are key positions, enabling him to monitor the problems and issues related to in-school experiences and facilitating contact with college staff on a regular basis.

Gabbinbar School appears vital to the teacher education programme, especially from the students' perspective. Their complaints about in-school experience focus on three areas: first, an unsupportive environment during practice teaching; a negligible opportunity to see theoretical ideas in practice; and lack of opportunity to observe a group of children over an extended period of time. Gabbinbar school has provided for supportive practice teaching experiences as well as exemplifying the approach to education adopted by college staff. In a limited way it has provided students with a chance to work over an extended period with one group of children. This has depended entirely on the student's initiative and relationship with the teacher.

The relationship highlights the need to base co-operative programmes on the principles of communication and reciprocation. School personnel in particular, are concerned that there be 'no coercion', and that the 'two-way dependence' remains the basis of the relationship. In practice this may mean more participation by college personnel in the ongoing activities of the school. While acknowledging this as a possible improvement, college staff suggest that demands on their time and heavy teaching loads, are severely limiting factors.

The problems of deployment of time and resources are the basic ones confronting college staff. They acknowledge the importance of an active involvement with the school but maintain it as an extra, over and above their normal teaching load at college. In order to enable a fuller involvement with the school it may be necessary to formally acknowledge a commitment to the school as a resource person, and either reduce other teaching commitments or appoint extra staff. From the school's angle the relationship is viewed positively as an 'informal one' that allows the school to decide policy and practice regardless of college attitudes. The maintenance of the school's autonomy need not be endangered by recognizing at a more formal level the role of the school in the teacher education programme. An important, and perhaps sufficient formalizing move, would be to acknowledge that the principal of the school should be appointed in joint consultation between the college and the State Department; so that the essential informality of the relationship could be maintained.

[P. R.]

CLAREMONT COLLEGE OF ADVANCED EDUCATION AND DALKEITH PRIMARY SCHOOL

W. March
Head of the Department of Professional Practice and Extension

Background and Context

The idea of co-operating schools developed out of a need for a school in close proximity to the college and also to relieve the pressure on the two campus schools which have been over-taxed in recent times and both of which are only staffed in a calibre similar to all other city schools. When the college decided on a mid-year intake for July each year another school was necessary for the development of the practicum.

Dalkeith Primary School, which is situated several miles from the college and provides for pupils from years 1 to 7, seemed a promising possibility. The principal, who has had more than twenty years' experience as a teacher and at least ten of these as a principal, was approached. The principal first sought the opinion of his staff before making a decision. Some staff members did not wish to become involved; it was a purely voluntary arrangement. One member of the writer's department was assigned the portfolio of arranging activities with this school. The mid-year intake consisted of forty-five students and there were very few initial costs. Accommodation at the school was rather limited to house the student teachers but they made do and most tutorial work was conducted outside or on a very large verandah which runs the full length of the school. Of the staff of fifteen teachers, four senior members offered to become wholly involved in the project and a number of others offered the use of their classes for various activities.

Aims and Principles of Operation

The aims were not documented as such. The co-operative arrangement was mainly for administrative convenience. They could probably be succinctly stated as: a desire to develop a close co-operative arrangement with a nearby school for our mutual advantage. Such co-operation should involve as many activities as possible.

The Plan and Its Implementation

The specific activities and procedures which were entered into with school personnel were as follows:

Microteaching

A class of children from the co-operating school is brought by bus to the college Micro-Centre. Those waiting for microteaching are gainfully employed with educational games until their turn comes around.

Macro-Microteaching

This activity is carried out on the Dalkeith school verandah and students teach a micro-lesson to half a class of children in a non-video situation. School personnel assist with lesson plans and supervise lessons together with college staff.

Teaching options

With regard to this activity, sometimes college students visit the school to teach a small group of children in subjects such as physical education and art. At other times the teaching option takes the form of curriculum-based micro-sessions in say mathematics and science in one of the college video studios.

Live teaching models

A group of college students spend one morning a week over at the school observing live modelling sessions given by both teachers from the school and by college lecturers. Both of these groups take part in the follow-up discussion after the demonstrations.

Block practices

Dalkeith school provides block practices in the same way that other associated schools do.

Unit practices

The school provides a very useful service to the college in this respect. Any students who are sick or unavoidably detained during block practices can be slotted into the school for one-day a week at short notice. Similarly, weak students can be slotted in for remedial teaching sessions.

In-service

As the college has made in-roads into the field of in-service this year, teachers from Dalkeith school are entitled to take part in our annual conference and also avail themselves of our short course non-credit offerings from 4.00–6.00 p.m. throughout third term. No special staffing arrangements were made for this co-operative effort. Members of the college department of Professional Practice all liaised with the school. No ancillary personnel were provided by the Education Department. The secretary of the department of Professional Practice helped facilitate a high degree of co-operation in all these activities.

Communication has been mainly *ad hoc* arrangements but formal channels have been employed through the principal to other staff. No special funding has been available for this project.

The Dalkeith school is of traditional design and the present building was built in the 1950s. No special accommodation or facilities are available.

Problems and Effectiveness

There are no special problems which have arisen in the co-operative arrangement. The programme has been considered sufficiently effective to maintain it in its present form.

Recommendations

Dalkeith is only one of a number of nearby schools with which the college has built up a close relationship. There are natural benefits to the school and the college when this is done effectively. It is intended that further co-operating relationships will be established with other schools, but in different areas of specialization.

Commentary

The establishing of a close relationship with a number of schools offers many potential advantages to a teacher education institution. This is particularly so, when, as in the case of Claremont, the campus schools are staffed no more favourably than other departmental schools. By including Dalkeith Primary School in its on-going programme, the college has succeeded in reducing pressure on the campus schools and in widening the range of observation and teaching opportunities open to its students.

Dalkeith Primary School is readily accessible to college students and is sufficiently close for pupils to be brought to the college when necessary, with minimum cost to the institution. Although proximity to the college is a contributing factor, it is the willingness of the principal and staff to involve the school in teacher education which has led to the success of the co-operative programme. The flexibility of the school is illustrated by its adjustment of daily activities to meet college requirements, often at short notice, its acceptance of students for remedial teaching, and the arrangement of block practice at other than normal times for students with particular needs.

Whereas the college gains in many ways from its association with the school, the benefits to the school are less apparent. Certainly, some pupils are able to take part in the reading clinic organized by the college, staff from the college are available as resource people if called upon, and college facilities are used from time to time by the school. It is interesting to note that, whereas a school less privileged than Dalkeith in staffing and facilities may wish to seek a close relationship with a college, the Dalkeith situation appears to be one where the association with the college is accepted by the school staff as a responsibility to the teaching profession, rather than sought as a means of enriching the school programme.

Although the staff generally are prepared to make their classes available for college activities, only a few teachers actually provide demonstration or modelling lessons. It may be not surprising that, with involvement of many school staff limited to that of supplying children for college activities, they may, from time to time, view the requirements of the college as disrupting, rather than contributing towards, their teaching programme. The pupils at Dalkeith, who are of above-average ability, react favourably to the college-related activities and are well able to adjust to varied experiences and teaching personnel. Although the parents of the pupils are aware that Dalkeith participates in the Claremont programme, they have not had cause to comment either favourably or unfavourably upon the association. The college students and staff value the opportunities that Dalkeith Primary School, along with several other co-operating schools, provides for relating theory to practice.

Although the objectives of the college-school programme have not been formally stated, a range of activities has evolved, providing opportunities for college students to interact with children, practise skills, and observe classes. Where a school is not specially staffed to cope with additional responsibilities there is a limit to the developments which are possible. It would be unrealistic to expect that the scope of the college-school programme at Dalkeith could be widened if the school staffing allocation remains at the present level.

The co-operative relationship had its origin in the need for the college to extend its programme to include more schools. As indicated, Dalkeith was a favourable choice because of its proximity to the college. As important a facilitating factor, however, was the long-standing friendship between the principal of the school and the head of the Department of Professional Practice, allowing the programme to develop in an atmosphere free from tensions and misunderstandings. The school was well suited to undertake additional tasks by virtue of its competent staff, able and enthusiastic pupils, and adequate facilities.

The area of consultation and communication is probably the most difficult in the development of a college-school programme. This is no less so in the Claremont-Dalkeith situation. Opportunities should be provided for the relevant college staff to meet with the teachers of the school to formulate and discuss objectives for the forthcoming year's programme. Ways should be explored whereby the school staff may come to feel more closely identified with the teacher preparation programme, but without the sacrifice of the time and energy they would wish to devote to their pupils. A further recommendation is that, if the advantages of the college-school relationships are to be viewed by the school staff as reciprocal, then ways in which the teachers and pupils can be expected to benefit from the association with the college should be further examined.

As mentioned in the case study, Dalkeith is one of a number of schools with which Claremont CAE has a special relationship. The concept of different kinds of college activities being undertaken in particular schools has much to commend it. It provides the opportunity to spread the load, and at the same time reduces the complexity of organization within any one school. It is the intention of Claremont to develop this policy further by focusing specific sections of its programme on additional individual schools.

The Claremont case study is particularly valuable to other teacher-education institutions in that it suggests many of the opportunities and challenges which may arise when an institution widens the range of schools with which it enjoys a special co-operating relationship.

[J. D.]

TOWNSVILLE COLLEGE OF ADVANCED EDUCATION AND SCHOOL CO-OPERATION IN TEACHING PRACTICE

JOHN D. ARMSTRONG
Vice-Principal

Background and Context

Students of the Townsville CAE do teaching practice in seventeen local state primary schools and three Catholic primary schools; students from Ayr, Cairns, and Mackay may attend practice schools in those centres (five schools at Cairns, two at Ayr, and five at Mackay).

In addition to these practice schools, students have access to a number of special schools (pre-school centres, kindergartens, opportunity schools, and various schools for the handicapped).

When the college opened in 1969, the teaching practice system was adopted from the existing metropolitan colleges. A Teaching Practice Committee was set up, with representatives from the college, the practice schools, and students. A basic rationale for a system of graduated practice teaching experiences was drawn up by the college's Education Department, and this has been refined and modified over the years. Inputs from supervising personnel, students and college staff have been instrumental in overcoming deficiencies and eliminating sources of friction.

The most persistent difficulty facing the college and the co-operating schools has been the need to keep demands on the schools within reasonable limits. Because of the relatively small number of suitably qualified and experienced supervisors (barely enough to take any one year group), students are at practice schools at various times for a total of up to twenty-one weeks per year.

Aims and Principles of Operation

The aims of the co-operating arrangement as formulated by the Teaching Practice Committee are:

(i)   to afford students the opportunity to observe children, teachers, classrooms, and schools as a framework for college education and curriculum studies;

(ii) to enable students to work with children, under supervision, in prepared teaching situations (this involves working with individual pupils, small groups, and whole classes in a developmental sequence of teaching experiences);

(iii) to enable students to analyse the teaching role and to acquire those skills needed for this role; and

(iv) to enable students to put into practice, under the guidance of experienced teachers, concepts, theories, and ideas presented in college courses.

The Plan and Its Implementation

Student activities at practice schools include (see Table T.1):

—observation of children, teaching behaviour, class organization and grouping, availability and use of resources, school administration, curriculum planning and implementation, evaluation procedures;

—lesson preparation and programme planning;

—a graduated sequence of teaching activities (individual pupils, small groups, whole class, continuous teaching programme, co-operative teaching programme);

—practice aimed at attaining teaching skills (use and operation of aids and equipment, lesson and unit planning);

—school policies, procedures, records, and returns, under the direction of the principal.

The role of the supervising teacher includes:

—providing opportunities for students to observe him/her teaching the class;

—providing students with the opportunity for varied teaching experiences;

—demonstrating particular teaching strategies and principles;

—giving guidance on, and supervising lesson preparation and presentation;

—advising on classroom management and organization;

—supervising and evaluating students' teaching performance;

—consulting with college personnel and reporting to the college on students' development as teachers;

—keeping students informed of his/her perceptions of their development as teachers.

The school principal is generally responsible for the co-ordination and supervision of the teaching practice programme; recommending members of staff as supervising teachers; conducting courses on school policies, procedures, records, and returns; organizing the programme of special lecturers, observations, and activities undertaken by students; observing and evaluating students and co-ordinating the school assessment of students.

College lecturers visit practising schools in order to consult informally with students and supervising teachers; liaise between college and schools; observe students teaching in their own curriculum areas; identify and report on weaknesses in teaching skills; supervise basic teaching skills programmes; act, where required, in a consultative role in the assessment of students' teaching.

In addition to the above, schools provide classes for the microteaching programme; curriculum lecturers and teachers plan and implement co-operative curriculum programmes; teachers with special skills or with special classes provide opportunities for observational visits by students; principals and teachers act as guest lecturers in college courses; school personnel have full access to the college's Library Resources Centre and other facilities.

Staffing arrangements

Supervising teachers are appointed by the college on the recommendation of the school principal.

Supervising teachers receive a supervising allowance (at present $20.50 per student per week); school administrative staff receive a co-ordinating allowance; specialist teachers (music teachers, teacher-librarians, and physical education teachers) receive a *pro rata* allowance for actual supervision duties.

Over the years, the practice schools have accepted increased responsibility for the implementation of the agreed teaching practice programme and for the assessment of students' teaching; college staff have increasingly adopted a consultative-advisory-liaising role.

Organization and administration

The nature of the teaching practice programme and the teaching practice calendar are determined by the Teaching Practice Committee. The composition of this committee is as follows:

—the Head of Department of Education Studies as Chairman;
—three members of the college staff appointed by the Director;
—three school principals elected by the local Principals Association;
—two supervising teachers elected by all supervisors;
—two students elected by the Students Union;
—the College Director and the Regional Director of Education as *ex officio* members.

Most formal communication occurs through the Teaching Practice Committee. College staff visit all schools in a consultative-liaising capacity.

The Head of Department of Education Studies is responsible for co-ordinating lecturers' visiting programmes and the allocation of students to schools. The teaching practice programme is funded out of normal college recurrent expenditure.

Buildings and facilities

There are no special buildings or facilities. Microteaching is conducted on-campus in studio-production areas of the Library Resources Centre.

Problems and Effectiveness

The chief recurring problem is one of communication; ensuring that supervising personnel are aware not only of the objectives of the teaching practice programme, but also of the orientation of college courses, especially in subject curriculum areas. Some progress has been made in overcoming this problem by holding in-service courses for teachers at the college. It is expected that the introduction of further in-service courses in 1977 (upgrading Diploma of Teaching and fourth-year B.Ed. programmes) will further diminish the problem of communication.

The programme in its present form offers students a carefully graduated sequence of teaching experiences under the supervision of experienced teachers. In the main, practice school personnel seem satisfied with their responsible role, although some express concern at the amount of time for which they have students.

One of the strengths of the arrangement is the commitment of school personnel to their role in the training of young teachers. After seven years of operation, the vast majority of supervisors have retained their enthusiasm for having students; most are highly supportive of their students.

The enrolment of supervising teachers in the college's part-time Dip. Teach. and B.Ed. courses will bring about a greater understanding on the part of practice school personnel of the orientation of the college's teacher education programme. Increasing participation by college staff in co-operative curriculum ventures in the schools will undoubtedly engender a closer relationship between education theory and classroom practice.

Table T.1 TEACHING PRACTICE—AN OVERVIEW

FIRST YEAR

SEMESTER 1–3 weeks

Week 1: Observation of children, classrooms, teaching behaviour.

Weeks 2 and 3: Students will act as teachers' aides as required. The supervisor will allot informal lessons with individual pupils and small groups as the student demonstrates readiness for them (approx. 5 hours/week of prepared teaching activities).

SEMESTER 2–3 weeks

1 hour/week: Informal whole class.

3 hours/week: Small groups.

Remainder: Act as teachers' aides as required.

(Note: First-year students do not study method subjects at college).

RECORDS REQUIRED

Teaching Log

Portfolio

PRINCIPALS' COURSES
1. School policies and procedures.
2. Principles of classroom teaching.

SECOND YEAR

SEMESTER 3–3 weeks
5 hours/week: Prepared lessons with the whole class.
5 hours/week: Prepared lessons with small groups.
Other work with individual pupils and small groups as required by the supervisor.
(Note: Students are taking only half the curriculum subjects at college at this stage).

SEMESTER 4–3 weeks
Weeks 1 and 2: As above.
Week 3: A continuous teaching programme.
(Note: All curriculum subjects have now been taken or are being taken at college at
this stage).

RECORDS REQUIRED
Teaching Log
Portfolio

PRINCIPALS' COURSES
1. School policies and procedures.
2. Curriculum principles; the C.C.P.

THIRD YEAR

SEMESTER 5–3 weeks
Approximately 2 hours/day class teaching plus work with individual pupils and small
groups as directed by the supervisor.
(Note: Students should be given the opportunity to plan and teach units in their advanced
curriculum study subject).
Preparation of a C.C.P. for implementation in the semester 6 practice.

SEMESTER 6–3 weeks
A continuous teaching programme to implement a C.C.P. prepared during the three
weeks of the first semester practice.

RECORDS REQUIRED
Teaching Log
Current Curriculum Programme

PRINCIPALS' COURSE
1. School records.
2. Administrative procedures and returns.

Commentary

A major advantage claimed for the co-operating relationships involved in the
Townsville CAE's teaching practice programme stems, it is believed, from the

large degree of responsibility offered school personnel for conducting the programme. The acceptance of this responsibility by supervising teachers tends to encourage greater commitment to the programme, greater involvement with students, and, more generally, an increased sense of professional worth. These things certainly seemed to be happening. Supervisors and principals were closely identified with the programme and with the progress of 'their' student 'colleagues'.

This major strength of the programme, ironically, is associated with its major weaknesses. First, student numbers make it difficult to find sufficient supervisors who are uniformly competent and enlightened. The lecturers, supervisors and students admitted that some supervisors were poor teachers and unsympathetic towards students. With such people having a primary role in the practice programme, their students had a 'bad trot'. Second, supervisors generally seemed unaware of the innovative approaches to teaching and learning advocated at college. They relied on information from their principals on what the college expected or on the outlines in the college handbook. Students remarked that the teaching demonstrated and ideas recommended by their supervisors often conflicted with ideas espoused by the college. While students appreciated the college's ideas they became 'two-faced' and taught as their supervisors proposed —after all, as one student put it, *they* 'were to judge our work by *their* standards'. Third, students complained that supervisors did not have a common framework for assessing their work. Evaluative procedures were very subjective. Supervisors admitted this, but said they tried to overcome it by within-school supervisors' meetings.

All groups were aware of these weaknesses. College staff recognized the need for training programmes for supervisors, for meetings with supervisors before and after practice, for greater lecturer involvement in the programmes and with schools generally. They realize that while the programme promoted the socialization of students into the school system, it did so with a strong tendency to conserve established ways. Measures were required to make the relationship with schools one which took into account both continuity *and* change in teaching. *Lecturers spoke strongly of the pressing need to expand the college's contacts with schools.* For example, it was suggested that college staff might co-operate with schools in curriculum advice and development; workshops on teaching and curriculum might be held in schools with both lecturers, teachers and students involved; guidance and remedial services to schools might be offered through on- or off-campus clinics; and an innovative campus school might be established for a variety of teacher-education experiences.

It should be acknowledged that at the college there are a number of trends in the above directions already. Some supervisors have been involved in a twelve week in-service course. In second year, pupils come to the campus to facilitate a microteaching programme. This is followed by whole-class teaching in schools with peer, lecturer and sometimes school-principal feedback. In an Advanced Curriculum course in third year, a group of students is building a programme in a school. A teacher librarian comes into college as a visiting lecturer, as do several school principals. The college library resources centre is available for teacher use and college facilities (such as its swimming pool) are used by school pupils.

An interesting point about the co-operating relationship between college and school for practice teaching is that the supervisors themselves, while they valued the responsibilities delegated to them, wanted more knowledge of college courses and more interaction with college staff. Some believed that more college staff involvement with schools would have a salutary influence on those people as well, a few of whom, it was feared, had lost contact with practice!

There are three other worthwhile aspects of the practice programme that warrant comment. One is the gradual build-up of student tasks and responsibilities throughout the three-year course. Students commented favourably on the sequencing of experiences. The second are the 'school policies, principles and procedures' lectures given during practice by principals. Students found them very realistic and helpful. The third is the development and implementation by students with teacher guidance of a 'Current Curriculum Programme' in the final block practices. This constitutes a valuable experience in extended planning which student teachers elsewhere all too often miss.

[C. T.]

THE PEDAGOGICS PROGRAMME

Faculty of Education
James Cook University

W. HAWKINS
Senior Lecturer in Education
(on behalf of the Pedagogics Committee)

Background and Context

In the final two years of the Bachelor of Education degree programme for prospective secondary teachers at James Cook University, students explore the nature and functioning of teaching and the school curriculum. They are introduced to the broad theoretical issues of curriculum development and examine curriculum and instruction related to their specialized teaching subjects. These curriculum studies seek to acquaint them with concepts and skills which will enable them to engage meaningfully in the Pedagogics Programme.

The Pedagogics Programme introduces the student to practical teaching by involving him in supervised school experience throughout the third and fourth years of the degree. In addition, professional seminars, centred on problems of teaching, are held regularly throughout each term.

Aims and Principles of Operation

The general aims of the Pedagogics Programme are:

(i) To gradually introduce the student teacher to his work in the classroom, then to expand and extend this introduction in a variety of classroom settings.

(ii) To create an awareness in the student teacher of his professional responsibilities, of the complex interpersonal relationships in school and of the overall structure of the curriculum.

Figure C.1 ADMINISTRATIVE RELATIONSHIPS IN THE PEDAGOGICS PROGRAMME

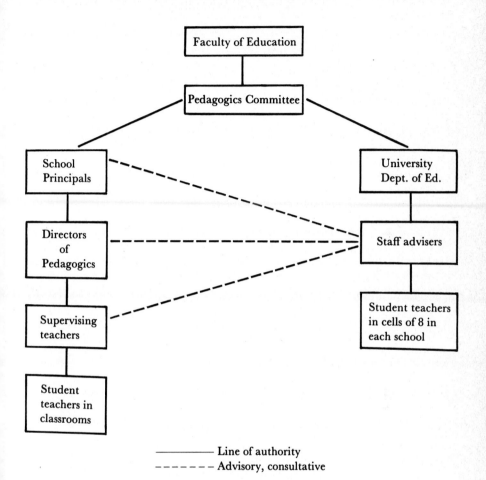

——————— Line of authority
– – – – – – Advisory, consultative

(iii) To develop the student teacher's understanding of, and his ability to relate to his pupils.

(iv) To develop the student teacher's competence in planning, teaching and evaluating his special teaching subjects.

The main principle of operation of the Pedagogics Programme is the *corporate responsibility* for planning, conducting and evaluating the programme shared by the participating schools and the university. The responsibility for the policy and administration of the programme is held by the Pedagogics Committee which consists of the principals of the schools, pedagogic directors, student representatives, and members of the Faculty of Education. (The detailed administrative relationships in the Pedagogics Programme are set out in Figure C.1). The central purpose of the establishment of this committee was to develop a genuine corporate concern and accountability between schools and university for the in-school component of the B.Ed. course.

At the school level greater responsibility is also given to the supervising teacher in planning and evaluating the student teacher's experiences.

The Plan and Its Implementation

In the third year of the B.Ed. degree the Pedagogics Programme (Pedagogics I) comprises a course of 200 hours of school experience plus professional seminars.

To provide the flexibility necessary for students to integrate their Pedagogics Programme with other university commitments, school experiences are planned under a private contract with the supervising teacher. Each student is expected to spend three-and-a-half hours each week in school, in addition to a full week in February, July, and September.

The year's work covers three areas: (i) the student teacher and the school, (ii) the student teacher and the pupil, and (iii) the student teacher and special teaching subjects. These define very broadly the programme for each of the three terms.

Evaluation of the student's teaching is provided by his supervisor; frequent television recording provides an additional basis for observation and analysis. These recorded sequences also give the student a basis for a longitudinal comparison of his teaching at different stages. This feedback is school-centred in the sense that the student, in consultation with his supervisor, plans, executes, and evaluates the sequence. Samples of the recorded sequences are used within the faculty's Guided Self-Analysis Programme outside the school setting.

The detailed aims and procedures for each term are as follows:

Term 1—The student teacher and the school

The aims of the term's work are:

(1) To give the student teacher a sense of

    (i)   his professional responsibilities, his privileges, his rights;

    (ii) his relations with other teachers, with pupils, with non-teaching staff, with school administrators;

    (iii) his authority for what he does, including what he teaches and why he teaches it;

    (iv) the overall structure of the courses in his teaching subjects;

    (v) broad school curriculum.

(2) To introduce the student teacher to the classroom.

PROCEDURES FOR TERM 1

(1) The term is introduced by a one-week introductory course to include:

    (i)   lectures from subject teachers on syllabuses and workbooks relevant to the students' curriculum areas;

    (ii) demonstrations and practice in the use of media;

    (iii) observation and discussion of teaching in a variety of subject areas at different grade levels;

    (iv) assignment to supervisors to whom the student will be attached for the remainder of the year.

(2) The student teacher engages in classroom activities under the guidance of his supervising teacher. He assists with small groups, individual tutorials, class discussions, remedial work, marking and testing, the preparation of teaching materials and the like.

(3) Students proceed from small and simple activities to larger and more complex ones at varying rates.

(4) The student teacher spends at least one day per term with the principal, the deputy-principal, and the senior mistress. During this time he observes and assists with the work they do.

(5) If the supervising teacher agrees, school experience may be restricted to one subject at one level in the school (e.g., English to Grades 11 and 12).

Term 2—The student teacher and the pupil

The programme in this term aims at developing the student teacher's relations with his pupils. He should become aware of particular aspects of his role as a teacher, especially those which relate to advising pupils, assessing their work, and recording information. Relations as adviser and reporter to parents are stressed.

PROCEDURES FOR TERM 2

(1) There is more teaching in term 2 than in term 1, but restricted in range and in size of groups. At the supervising teacher's discretion, the student teacher may began to take classes of all sizes during this term. Teaching practice may be restricted to one subject but should not be over more than two subjects.

(2) Teaching experience is extended to various school grades and to various levels of pupil performance in a grade. The student teacher should reach an awareness of the wide variation in pupil performance up and down, as well as across the school.

(3) Pupil interviews are conducted by the student teacher.

(4) If necessary, and at the discretion of the supervising teacher, the student teacher may be attached from time to time to a second teacher for special purposes.

(5) A continuous teaching period similar to that in first term is provided in the last week of term 2 vacation.

Term 3—The student teacher and his special teaching subjects

The programme in this term concentrates the attention of the student teacher upon the subjects he teaches. The work in this term also aims to extend and expand the experiences provided in terms 1 and 2. The student teacher learns: (i) some of the methods applied to teaching his subjects; (ii) his authority for teaching the particular subject matter; (iii) why and how he assesses the subject matter; and (iv) how to prepare work books for a subject.

PROCEDURES FOR TERM 3

(1) The student teacher participates in at least two subject areas over a wide range of work up and down the school.

(2) He accepts responsibility for at least two classes for as wide as possible an area of work.

(3) He takes classes of all sizes and performs all the work the supervising teacher would carry out with those classes.

In fourth year, students spend a further 200 hours in the Pedagogics II course which again includes school experience and professional seminars. The organizational patterns and procedures of this course are as follows:

There are two periods of block practice teaching for fourth-year students. The first block practice period is preceded by two weeks of one day per week visits to the school to arrange and organize such teaching. The second block practice is also preceded by a one day visit to the school, to be arranged at a time which is convenient to the supervising teacher during the students' vacation. Each block practice is of four weeks' duration.

In the week following the completion of the first block practice, students are asked to evaluate their programme and there are opportunities during this week for liaison between the school and the university division of Curriculum and Pedagogics. Where a student is considered satisfactory after the completion of the first block practice, he has the option of completing the second block practice outside Townsville. This must be done in consultation with the school.

School-centred video-feedback activities continue to provide the student teacher with opportunities for completing and refining his instructional skills. The year aims at rounding off the student as a professional teacher.

PROCEDURES FOR FOURTH YEAR

(1) The student teacher is introduced to the full range of classes and conditions for his specialist subjects.
(2) Audiovisual skills and skills of materials-preparation are reviewed.
(3) Observation in sections of the school, unfamiliar to the student is provided for.
(4) As students may be required to teach a third subject, some experience is provided for this. The third subject will be chosen in the light of the probability of the student being required to teach it.
(5) As a general principle, the student changes schools and supervisors at the commencement of the fourth year.

Assessment

The Teacher Competence Check List defines the major teaching competencies which the Pedagogics Programme aims to develop. This check list provides a focus for the student and supervising teacher as the student progressively attempts to master these competencies over the two-year period. The student is encouraged to use the check list as a guide in his efforts towards continual self-improvement. The teacher finds the check list helpful in post-lesson discussions with the student.

Assessment Checkpoints

THIRD YEAR

(i) At the end of term 2 and prior to the third block experience, the student is advised whether acceptable standards of development are being met. This takes the form of written comments in relation to the check list.
(ii) At the completion of the third-year programme each student is assessed as falling into one of two categories—'pass on' or 'stay'. The 'stay' category

provides for prescribed additional experience following the September block-practice period.

FOURTH YEAR

(i) At the end of the first block experience (July), students are advised whether acceptable standards of development are being met. This takes the form of written comments in relation to the check list.

(ii) At the completion of the fourth-year programme students will be classified as 'pass' or 'fail'.

Commentary

Fundamentally, the administrative arrangements of James Cook University's Pedagogics Programme seek to develop a strong *commitment* to the programme by the participating schools. This commitment is developed by *shared responsibility* between schools and university for planning, implementing and evaluating the programme. School principals and directors of pedagogics (deputy principals) are, in fact, in the majority on the Pedagogics Committee—the executive, policy-making body, which, among other things develops the general guidelines governing the programme. In addition, the supervising teachers are given a large measure of responsibility for planning and assessing students' in-school experience, though university staff endeavour to liaise with them as often as possible. Underpinning the ideas of school commitment to, and shared responsibility for school experience is an 'acceptance of the fact that the university does not have a corner of the market of knowledge about teacher education'— the profession itself can make a genuine contribution.

Interviews with principals, directors of pedagogics and supervising teachers seem to confirm the fact that a deep sense of commitment to the programme is being developed. They spoke of it as 'our programme' and of the students as 'our students'. Students were apparently fully integrated into the professional and social activities of schools and, after graduation, kept in touch with supervisors for advice. Generally the school personnel commended the university on its responsiveness to feedback from the schools and its recognition that the profession can contribute to teacher preparation. They thought that an 'admirable partnership' was being evolved. It was agreed that the small size of the undertaking was part of the reason for its success. It involved only eight schools in a limited region. In a larger operation, interest and involvement probably would not be so great, unless the scheme was broken down into small organizational units.

All directors of pedagogics and supervisors were committed to the general scope and sequence of the programme set out in the course guidelines. They praised particularly the gradual approach to introducing students to teaching. They enjoyed the autonomy the guidelines allowed them. On the other hand, the group of teachers interviewed were not uncritical of the programme and the degree course. Some would have liked membership on the Pedagogics Committee to enable them to become directly involved in general policy-making. A number of directors of pedagogics and supervisors held the opinion that students should gain some background to teaching during the first and second years of the degree to prevent them commencing practice teaching in the third year with little or no relevant understandings. They also felt that the curriculum and instruction courses in third year were insufficiently practical in nature to inject a realistic flow of ideas into the practicum. It is perhaps significant that the students who were interviewed also supported both these sets of comments.

Although this corporate scheme has much to commend it, there are two quite serious problems. The devolution of much of the responsibility for detailed planning and day-to-day supervision of practice teaching to the teacher supervisors means that the *quality of the supervision is critical*. Increasingly there is difficulty in selecting appropriate supervisors from the number available in each school. Even when suitable supervisors are chosen they often have meagre skill in the art of supervision and little knowledge of what is being advocated by the university. The university is mindful of this problem and has initiated a training programme for supervisors in teaching skills as a first step. Already supervisors have found this training course has provided them with useful specific background to pursue positively with students. Some supervisors and students admitted that previously there had been some conflict between the theory in the university's courses and the perceptions of teaching and advice given to students by supervisors. The supervisors, however, seemed anxious to have as much background and guidance as the university can provide. A second problem inherent in the programme is that once the university delegates such a large measure of the responsibility for the practical components of teacher education to the schools, *there is a danger that both university staff and students may come to regard practice teaching as a low-valued activity*. Some supervisors believed there was 'already too much distance between some university people and the schools themselves'. The students echoed this opinion and proposed that supervisors and lecturers should come together with students for both seminars on teaching and curriculum and for discussions on the aims, nature and problems of practice teaching.

In all, it seems that increased school responsibility for the practice of teaching has much to recommend it, especially if the responsibility is judiciously shared. It needs to be backed up, however, with the careful selection and training of supervising teachers and abundant, creative and continuing contacts with schools by the teaching staff.

[C. T.]

MICROTEACHING AND MACROTEACHING IN PRIMARY SCHOOLS CO-OPERATING WITH THE NEWCASTLE COLLEGE OF ADVANCED EDUCATION

T. J. Fullerton
Co-ordinator, First-Year School Experience Programme

Background and Context

The first-year school experience programme (Principles and Practices of Teaching I) was planned late in 1973 when secondary schools in the Newcastle area were unable to find sufficient places for first-year students for block practice.

Figure N.1 FLOW CHART OF FIRST YEAR SCHOOL EXPERIENCE PROGRAMME

1. *TEACHING SKILLS THEORY*
   Activities: Treatment of a particular teaching
   skills and preparation of lesson for microteaching.
   Location: NCAE

2. *TEACHING SKILLS MICRO-PRACTICE*
   Activities: Teaching of a planned lesson under
   video conditions.
   Location: New Lambton South School/Lambton School

3. *TEACHING SKILLS: THEORY (FEEDBACK)*
   Activities: Analysis of a microteaching tape and
   preparation of lesson for macroteaching.
   Location: NCAE

4. *TEACHING SKILLS: MACRO-PRACTICE*
   Activities: Teaching of a planned lesson to a
   full class of children
   Location: Waratah or Waratah West/
        Heaton or Wallsend School

Persons involved in the initial planning were T. J. Fullerton, L. M. Koder, R. S. Murray and T. J. Sheedy.

Since its introduction in March 1974, the programme has been continually modified and refined. These changes have been brought about by a series of meetings which sample student, teacher and lecturer opinion. Student opinion, which is surveyed both formally and informally, is first considered by education specialists who suggest modifications which reflect their own and student opinions. Further refinements are made when these suggestions are presented to curriculum specialists for their reactions. Copies of the modified programme are then sent to co-operating schools where it is considered by all participating teachers. Following this, a representative from each school (six teachers in all) meets with representatives from the college (five curriculum specialists and one education specialist) and make the final alterations to the programme.

The current programme features a sequence of four main student experiences (see Figure N.1) which involve college and school staff in a variety of responsibilities. Presently it caters for two hundred and eighty first-year primary student teachers who spend half-a-day each week either preparing for, or teaching, a lesson under microteaching or macroteaching conditions. There are two teachers involved in any one day for microteaching supervision with nine teachers involved with macroteaching supervision. In addition, there are seven to twelve curriculum specialists and four education specialists helping at the various locations.

The initial costs of the programme included payment to four supervising teachers each week (there was only microteaching in the original programme) and the $20,000 for the purchase of audiovisual equipment. Double portable classrooms were converted to microteaching booths for approximately $8,000 by the Education Department.

In general, the programme is conceived as the basis for a projected three-year (six semester) continuous school-based programme for primary and infants students which attempts to integrate and relate, in a practical manner, the curriculum and education courses that the students are concurrently undertaking.

Aims and Principles of Operation

The programme is seen as a comprehensive and integrated series of practical experiences designed to complement the academic studies undertaken by first-year students and, at the same time, to make a significant and meaningful contribution to the achievement of the overall objectives of the Diploma in Teaching Programme (Primary-Infant). The experiences, which are undertaken in school and non-school settings (mainly the former), concentrate on the practical work involved in the professional preparation of student teachers.

Specifically, the programme aims at providing opportunities for students:

(i)   to develop self awareness;
(ii) to be introduced to schools, teaching and professional responsibilities in a gradual and systematic fashion;
(iii) to observe, discuss and practise specific teaching skills in controlled situations;
(iv) to relate theory to practice in a more meaningful way;
(v)   to know and understand children in a variety of educational settings; and
(vi) to acquire appropriate professional attitudes and outlooks.

Particular emphasis is given to the integration of theory and practice as first year primary students concurrently pursue a course in Educational Psychology which examines many of the psychological principles practised in the programme (e.g., Gagne, Bruner, Skinner, etc.).

At the end of each semester students are expected to have developed a number of competencies. For example, to qualify for the extended period of practice teaching at the end of Semester One students will need to be able to:

—analyse the relationships of Gagne's learning types to content in each of the various primary curriculum study areas (English, Mathematics, Music, Physical Education and Social Science).
—write instructional objectives in the various primary curriculum study areas using performance based terminology and containing the various components specified by Gagne.
—differentiate between content and procedure in designing lessons.
—construct criterion exercises that are consistent with the planned instructional objectives for lessons.
—sequence the procedural steps of each lesson in terms of pupil and teacher behaviours.
—relate the procedural steps of the lesson to the appropriate instructional events specified by Gagne.

—differentiate between teacher and pupil performance in appraising teaching performance.

—reach seventy-five per cent criterion level in each of the tests relating to the theoretical knowledge of the treated teaching skills; namely, reinforcement, variability and questioning.

—show evidence of applying the teaching skills of reinforcement, variability and questioning in both microteaching and macroteaching situations.

—apply the Gagne teaching model in both microteaching and macroteaching situations.

—analyse the performance of teaching skills of peers and self under live and videotaped conditions.

—demonstrate competence in the use of the chalkboard.

—assemble the videotape recording equipment and videotape a peer teaching a lesson.

The Plan and Its Implementation

Two schools specialize in microteaching (New Lambton South and Lambton). Four other schools specialize in macroteaching (Heaton, Wallsend, Waratah and Waratah West). The programme is spread over two half-days with a different microteaching school and two different macroteaching schools being involved on each occasion.

On any one of the days allocated, four student sections (35 students) are each located at a different location. For microteaching, student-section groups are halved and two, one-and-a-half-hour teaching sessions are conducted. The first student group, on arriving at the microteaching school, assembles the videotape recording equipment and prepares the rooms for teaching. Students work in pairs with each member teaching consecutive and related twenty-minute lessons. While one student teaches, the other operates the videotape recording equipment. In all, eight or nine lessons are taught simultaneously, all of which are supervised by either the class teacher, curriculum specialist or education specialist. At the conclusion of the two lessons (40 minutes) time is allowed for self, peer and supervisor appraisal. Following this students assemble in another room where the supervising teacher conducts a general 'wash-up' session. While this is in progress, two students supervise the teacher's class doing previously set work and the education and curriculum specialists meet the other half of the student group to prepare for their microteaching experience.

For macroteaching, nine supervising teachers from two different schools are involved each day that the programme operates. Two student microteaching teams combine to form a macroteaching team of four which is attached permanently to one of the supervising teachers for this experience. Students are required to teach lessons in each of the first year curriculum study areas (English, mathematics, music, physical education and social science) during each visit to their assigned classes and, at the same time, apply the skills practised in the microteaching setting using an expository model of teaching. As well as making comments on the general teaching behaviour of his students, the supervising teacher rates each student along various dimensions of a classroom observation scale and ensures that non-teaching students analyze the teaching skill performance of their teaching peer. By the end of the semester, all students have taught in all first year curriculum study areas in either both microteaching and/or macroteaching settings practising three teaching skills.

Staffing arrangements

No special appointments were made for the operation of the programme other than a technical attendant who was appointed in 1976. Prior to 1976, lecturers were generally assigned to the programme regardless of interest. This year, however, the number of education lecturers involved was reduced from eight to four with each lecturer volunteering on the basis of interest. Curriculum specialists are automatically assigned to the programme if they happen to be lecturing to a first-year section.

Schools involved in the programme were nominated by the Education Department. Teachers from the various schools participate on a voluntary basis and are paid on the basis of a rate determined by the Public Service Board for practice teaching. (Schools were surveyed by the Education Department late in 1975 for teachers interested in supervising at the microteaching schools.)

Organization and administration

RESPECTIVE ROLES AND RESPONSIBILITIES OF GROUPS

(a) *Teacher Education staff*

EDUCATION SPECIALISTS:

(i) prepare students for the application and analysis of the teaching skills for both the microteaching and macroteaching sessions;

(ii) rate the instructional preparation (and evaluation) of students for micro-teaching and macroteaching on a five-point scale for instructional objectives, content, criterion exercises, procedure, instructional events and post-lesson evaluation and record each of these ratings on the back of each student's workbook;

(iii) supervise and rate on a five-point scale two or three students at each micro-teaching session and record the ratings on the back of each student's workbook;

(iv) maintain a full record of the performance of each student on the various activities involved in the programme;

(v) visit the schools when his students are involved in the macroteaching experience, survey all participating classes and attend to any immediate problems;

(vi) consult with supervising teachers and curriculum specialists in order to identify students who could be 'at risk' during the block practice teaching period.

CURRICULUM SPECIALISTS:

(i) liaise with participating teachers from the microteaching schools to organize the content that students will subsequently teach at the schools;

(ii) design a semester programme of instruction in their respective curriculum areas for lower and upper primary levels; (These programmes will be taught by students in the macroteaching experiences.)

(iii) prepare students, in terms of content, for both microteaching and macro-teaching sessions;

(iv) rate the instructional preparation of students for their microteaching session on a five-point scale for instructional objectives, content, criterion exercises, procedure and instructional events and record these ratings on the back of each student's workbook; (This responsibility is shared with the education specialist.)

(v) supervise and rate on a five-point scale two or three students at the micro-teaching session and record the ratings on the back of each student's work book;

(vi) supervise students teaching in his particular curriculum area at the macro-teaching experience. (Lessons are timetabled at each macroteaching school in such a way that each curriculum specialist can supervise a series of four or five lessons in his area without leaving the school.)

(b) *School staff*

MICROTEACHING SUPERVISORS:

(i) prepare a programme of work to be carried out by children during the microteaching evaluation session. Two students are supplied for supervision of the class for this period.

(ii) allocate children to the required number of groups and accompany them to the microteaching unit. As far as possible the same groups and rooms are maintained throughout the year.

(iii) supervise and rate on a five-point scale the microteaching experiences of two students. General comments relating to the skill under inspection, relevance of content, success of procedural steps, and effectiveness of evaluation are given to the students prior to meeting with the full group of students. The individual feedback session lasts about ten minutes.

(iv) meet with full group of students to answer questions regarding individual differences of the children on any teaching problems that arose during the session. The duration of this evaluation session is at the discretion of the supervising teacher.

In addition to the above responsibilities, it is hoped that supervising teachers familiarize themselves with Gagne's theory of learning and instruction so that the theory espoused at college can be made more meaningful at a practical level. The instructional events specified in Gagne's theory are of vital importance to lesson presentation.

MACROTEACHING SUPERVISORS:

(i) check student lesson notes to see that they have been approved by the college supervisor. Only approved lessons are taught. Lesson approval can be determined by checking the top right hand corner of each student's lesson notes.

(ii) teach programme lessons not taught by students. This situation occurs when students are either absent from the macroteaching experience or have failed to have their lesson notes approved. (It is not essential that these lessons be taught on the day allocated for macroteaching.)

(iii) check (✓) the Personal and Professional Section on the Student Record Sheet for each visit;

(iv) check (✓) the lesson taught on the Student Record Sheet. Each student should attempt a different lesson on each visit to the school.

(v) rate each student's teaching performance on the Classroom Observation

Scale and enter the ratings on the Student Record Sheet and the Instructional Implementation Section of the Teaching Skills Observation Record (Macroteaching) in the student's workbook. Eventually students will select the dimensions for rating but, initially, lessons are only rated along the following dimensions—Level of Attention, Teacher-Initiated Problem Solving, Teacher Presentation, Task Orientation, Clarity, and Enthusiasm.

(vi) ensure that non-teaching students observe and analyse the teaching skills of the student teaching. On the first visit there is only one skill for analysis; the second visit there are two; and the third visit three. The relevant skills to be practised and analysed by the various sections are listed below.

Sections

100, 101C, 101D, 101G		108, 101F, 101E, 101H
Visit One	Q	V
Visit Two	QV	VQ
Visit Three	QVR	VQR
Teaching Skills:	R—Reinforcement	
	V—Variability	
	Q—Questioning	

(vii) check that the teaching student enters the results of the skill analyses by his peers in the appropriate columns in the Teaching Skills Observation Record (Macroteaching) in his workbook;

(viii) comment on the Student Record Sheet when the student's performance is of a highly positive or a highly negative nature.

Each school and the teacher education institution has a co-ordinator who is responsible for the operation of the programme at the respective locations. At school level all co-ordinators are in a promotion's position. All communication is done by way of the various co-ordinators.

Buildings and facilities

All schools, which are situated within a nine kilometre radius from the college, were nominated by the Education Department. There are no special facilities at the macroteaching schools, but two double portable rooms have been converted to create eight 'mini' classrooms (approximately four metres square) at each of the microteaching schools. Each room is carpeted and furnished with chairs and trapezoidal desks and is equipped with a chalkboard and power points. Also, the division of rooms with canite walls improves the acoustics and enables students to attach charts and other appropriate aids to the walls to facilitate lesson presentation. The conversions were financed by the Education Department and were carried out after consultation with the college.

PROBLEMS

Problems encountered in the operation of the programme centred around three general areas. These included difficulties in communication at both college and school levels and inadequate technical support for the programme. Communication between schools and college has been greatly increased with the detailed specification of the various responsibilities of the co-operating teachers.

At the request of the schools, the college has assumed the responsibility of developing units of work in the five curriculum study areas, for which students are made accountable in their macroteaching experience. In addition, peer analysis of the teaching skills in the macroteaching situation, together with the use of a common classroom observation scale by supervising teachers, has clarified and improved the feedback aspects of the programme.

Communication between personnel involved at the college level has been improved to a large extent with participating lecturers becoming more familiar with all aspects of the programme. The introduction of particular teaching strategies (expository and discovery) to which all content and skills are related, has done much to establish common frames of reference for participants at all levels. At the same time, this change has conflicted with the ideas of some of the curriculum specialists who find it difficult to work with such constraints. This problem is related to the total course structure as certain curriculum specialists have only the one opportunity to meet primary students and part of this time is devoted to this programme.

Improved technical support was given to the programme in 1976 with the appointment of a technician to assist the programme whenever it is in operation. In addition, direct support to the programme has been provided by the college Library Resources Centre which checks to ensure that all students analyze their videotapes during the week following the microteaching session.

Effectiveness

Anecdotal evidence would suggest that the programme has had a positive influence on the teaching behaviour of students in their block practice teaching. Pupil performance has been used as a criterion for teacher effectiveness to compare the relative contributions of block practice teaching and microteaching (1974 programme) to the teaching effectiveness of students and it is intended to eventually compare these results with the 1976 programme. The effectiveness of the various programmes over the past three years is also being examined with respect to discrepancies between students' perceptions of ideal and actual experiences in school practice. The results from these empirical studies are still being processed.

Irrespective of how well planned any continuous programme is, much of its effectiveness is lost if it is not followed up in the block practice period. Schools tend to be uninformed of what college expectations of students are and there are persons at both college and school levels who see a definite distinction between college programmes and teaching practice. To improve this situation, an in-service programme is being conducted in 1976 to train teachers in supervisory techniques for first-year students.

The first-year programme is planned to extend into second and third years. Both programmes will be guided by the same principles as the first-year programme with theory being undertaken in education and curriculum courses being directly related to practice. In the pilot programme that is presently being conducted at second-year level, attention is also being given to the needs of probationary teachers which were expressed at a 1975 in-service conference. The planning for the pilot programme was designed by two college representatives, one representative from in-service and six school representatives.

REFERENCES

Fullerton, T. J. and L. M. Koder, 'Student teaching: an integrated approach', *South Pacific Journal of Teacher Education*, 1975, 3, 2, 42–9.

A paper on the 1975 programme was presented at the Perth National Conference on the Practicum in 1975.

Northern Rivers CAE and Newcastle CAE have co-operated to produce a coloured film on the 1975 programme.

The commercial materials employed in the courses are:

Turney, C. *et al.*, *Sydney Micro Skills Series 1 Handbook*, Sydney University Press, 1973.

Turney, C. *et al.*, *Sydney Micro Skills Series 2 Handbook*, Sydney University Press, 1975.

Examples of the locally developed materials used in the courses are:

Newcastle CAE, *Principles and Practices of Teaching I: Primary Macroteaching Student Records*, Newcastle 1976.

Newcastle CAE, *Principles and Practices of Teaching II: Primary Pilot Programme*, Newcastle 1976.

Newcastle CAE, *Principles and Practices of Teaching II: Primary Workbook*, Newcastle 1976.

Commentary

The fundamental concern of the first-year school experience programme at Newcastle CAE is the meaningful linking of educational theory and practice. This concern is pursued in four main ways: (i) Students are involved in a sequence of co-ordinated experiences, beginning at the college with the observation and analysis of a particular teaching behaviour modelled in an audiovisual programme. This is followed by the application of this teaching behaviour in a micro- practice lesson given by students in the specially equipped co-operating schools. These videotaped lessons are replayed, with supervisor feedback, at the college. Finally, students re-apply the teaching behaviour in a lesson given to a full class in other co-operating schools, with feedback provided by peers and supervisors. (ii) To provide common instructional frameworks for the application of the specific teaching skills, expository and discovery models of teaching are employed by students based on principles emerging from the Educational Psychology course which runs concurrently with the programme. (iii) Curriculum lecturers work with teachers in developing units of work in various subjects for student guidance in preparing macroteaching lessons. These set out a sequence of topics with learning outcomes, objectives, criterion exercises and prerequisite behaviours. (iv) The programme is supported by 'workbooks' for students, lecturers and teachers. These set out objectives, organizational arrangements, summaries of theory, instructions on the use of VTR equipment, guidelines for lesson planning, microteaching analysis, records, and macroteaching appraisal sheets. In addition, supervising teachers have a booklet to guide their evaluation of students' macroteaching performances. This is an elaborate system of materials providing useful information and guidance for all concerned.

The programme seems to have three main problems. First, it seeks to involve college staff from both curriculum studies and education studies in preparing students at college in relevant skills, strategies and content for microteaching and macroteaching and in supervising students' application of these things in micro- and macroteaching in schools. Some resistance has been exhibited by curriculum lecturers to becoming involved in contributing to a new course conceived by someone outside their area. This problem is being gradually overcome, and the co-operation of curriculum staff in devising sequentially arranged learning units for student guidance in macroteaching has been an interesting feature of the programme. A second problem has been the background of the supervising teachers. To provide accurate and consistent feedback to students they must have a common frame of reference and a thorough understanding both of the theoretical and practical elements of the skills and strategies advocated at college. This applies to the teachers supervising both the micro- and macroteaching *and* the block practice later in the year. Students remarked that teachers seemed to have little background understanding of the skills and procedures and sometimes were rather reluctant to discuss performances. The problem of teacher background has been tackled through a 'workbook' setting out various supervisor responsibilities and some of theory, and containing observational and recording devices; through informal liaison with college staff; and through a foreshadowed in-service course for supervising teachers. The third problem area relates to the availability of sufficient hardware, software and accommodation to conduct the programme. More audiovisual equipment is required, as is more space in the college to facilitate replays of videotaped student teaching. The availability of equipment in schools and student use of school software (e.g., stencils and transparencies) are also areas of concern.

Student reaction to the programme has been most favourable. They appreciated the contact with schools from the outset of their course. They liked the idea of concentrating on specific skills with small groups of children. They valued videotaped feedback on their performances, even though it was rather threatening at first. They liked working in groups with peers in discussing problems, observing, and making suggestions on teaching. They thought the idea of a sequence of experiences from microteaching through macroteaching to block practice teaching helped them be eased into teaching with minimal trauma.

The students did, however, have several negative comments to make. The uncertainties of not knowing children or equipment available at schools were worrying aspects of microteaching. Some of the content topics suggested for macroteaching were sometimes too broad for one lesson and unsuited to the pupils. More feedback from teachers, particularly positive information, was thought to be desirable. Curriculum lecturers sometimes provided inadequate background in their courses for macroteaching in particular subjects.

School staff participating in supervision of the programme commented favourably on their involvement in planning the microteaching content topics, on the confidence and positive attitudes to advice on the part of students, on the fact that college staff now seem to know what they are after in student teaching, on the thorough student preparation of weekly macro-lessons, and generally on the college's realization that teachers have something to offer the programme. The school staff had two main constructive comments: the need for more time to hold discussions with students about their macroteaching, and the need for 'supervisor education' so they could become '*au fait* with the ideas and techniques being preached at the college'.

In the development of this Newcastle programme co-operating schools play a vital role. Increasingly their staff have had an important part in planning and evaluating the work. Teacher supervisors are on the spot to help students and provide them with feedback comments. The mini-classrooms in several schools facilitate microteaching activities. The staffroom accommodation, the equipment and materials of the schools are generally placed at students' disposal. The programme has won growing support within schools and within the college. Plans are in hand to refine its operation in first year by linking it with block teaching practice and to extend the programme into second year and even third year.

[C. T.]

CHURCHLANDS COLLEGE OF ADVANCED EDUCATION AND CHURCHLANDS PRIMARY SCHOOL

D. K. O'Dwyer
Assistant Vice-Principal, Professional School, Churchlands CAE, in association with lecturers participating in the co-operative programme

Background and Context

Churchlands College opened with an intake of first-year students to the three year Diploma of Teaching (Primary) course in 1973. Adjacent to the campus a new open-area primary school, Churchlands, also opened, the original local school building having been incorporated within the college.

Aims and Principles of Operation

From the outset the college has adopted a policy of encouraging co-operation and involvement with schools in the professional programme both for core and elective studies. Each department and individual staff member has access to schools, teachers and pupils in developing their courses. A rather loose administrative rein, held by the head of the Teaching Practice Department, is intended to preserve the situation and ensure that no particular school is over-used. During the three years it has been open, the college has maintained a very valued relationship with the schools in the vicinity. A particularly close and mutually beneficial relationship has developed with Churchlands Primary, virtually an 'on-campus' school.

Apart from the customary arrangements associated with block teaching practice periods and demonstration lessons, there is no formalized arrangement, organization, administration, staff arrangement, use of buildings and facilities. What does exist is a very close, informal relationship.

The Plan and Its Implementation

No particular facet of this relationship can be singled out as a special co-operating arrangement. Nor can any generalization, other than that of college policy and the willingness of the school, be abstracted from the variety of interchange that occurs. The Art, Education, Junior Primary, Teaching Practice, Oral English and Drama, Physical Education and Science Departments of the college have all been involved with Churchlands Primary School. Activities range over normal teaching practice; microteaching; remedial teaching practice; demonstrations; observation of facilities; learning activities and pupils; college staff teaching in the school; school staff participating in aspects of the college programme, and involve a two-way flow of personnel, staff, students and pupils between the school and the college. It would appear that the appropriate course of action here is to set out a sample of activities undertaken in co-operation with Churchlands Primary School as reported by those directly concerned.

Education Department

Participating lecturers: Mr David Bambach and Mr Len King
  1972–4: Visits of Open Education elective groups to observe classrooms (physical arrangements, student-teacher interactions). Discussions with teachers on 'openness'.
  1974–5: Visits to Open Education elective classes by the school principal, Mr Barry Prosser, to talk on open education; its problems, possibilities and prospects.
  1975: The principal of the school served on discussion panels before first year Foundations of Education students. Topics included the Aims of Education-Translation Into School Policy, Teaching Problems, and School Regulations.

The school served as a practical base for students trying out a Language Expression learning centre.

Art Department

Participating lecturer: Mr Ray Montgomery
  During Term I, 1975, the writer taught a series of nine art lessons at the Churchlands Primary School. These were a further development of a series of similar lessons taken in 1974. Videotapes of the lessons were made for instructional use with students at Churchlands College. A personal approach was made to the school principal for permission to use his school. This was granted and he suggested that the author contact, individually, the teachers of the classes he wished to use. The college contracted to provide art media and drawing paper from college stocks.
  Each of the lessons involved approximately thirty children and was of 35–40 minutes duration. Lessons were timetabled for the first teaching period in the school's afternoon programme. This time coincided with the college lunch period—avoiding clashes with lecture responsibilities, also allowing time to arrange classroom furniture, organize art materials and prepare TV lighting and filming equipment. Prior to each lesson the writer discussed with the college TV producer, Mr D. Parmiter, and script assistant, Miss J. Overton, the format of each lesson and what material was required to produce a 10–15 minute videotape for general instructional use with college Expressive Arts and Skills Art core courses and/or Curriculum and Instructional Art Education electives.
  Three art lessons were taken with each class and they were designed to develop the children's creative responses in drawing from imaginative, memory and observational sources. In each of the observation drawings the class teachers participated as the children's model—apart from this they took no other formal part in the lessons.
  The results of the programme were quite satisfactory. The teaching-learning contacts made by the author with the children and teachers were good. College students and art staff reaction to the videotapes produced was sound. Future

college-school programmes may be developed along similar lines, varying the art media and techniques or the teaching methods and classroom procedures to be used.

Science Department

Participating lecturer: Dr Rhona Giles

A project developed following a discussion amongst Science Department staff indicating that three members, Dr Miles Nelson, Denis Goodrum and the writer were interested in incorporating some child teaching in the professional elective courses we were conducting during third term, 1975. The writer wished to provide the students taking these electives with some opportunity to apply child-centred activity methods to biological and nutritional areas in greater depth and continuity than is usually possible, and also to observe the degree of effectiveness of a variety of programmes.

Miles Nelson made arrangements with the principal for classes to be available to the Science Department at appropriate times. The writer contacted the teachers involved and they allocated children into groups of four or five to which each student was assigned. Students were given the option of working in pairs and combining two groups. Science Department facilities were used so there were no additional costs except perishable food products for the Nutritional Science electives which cost approximately $5.00 per week.

Students carried out a teaching programme for one hour per week during ten weeks for the Biological Science unit, and five weeks for Nutritional Science. They were encouraged to develop their own programmes and submit these for group discussion and suggestions prior to use. They were given support, advice, resource material, and time for preparation and making teaching aids concurrent with the teaching activities. Students were encouraged to use simple materials and equipment appropriate to primary science as much as possible and had the facilities to construct teaching aids. A wide range of library reference material and curriculum material was available for the many varied programmes carried out. We were appreciative of local background information supplied by officers of the Nature Advisory Service, Department of Education, and of resources supplied from the Dairy Laboratory, Department of Agriculture, which has been visited by the Nutritional Science group. Biological Science elective students were able to observe successful biological teaching projects in operation at the Southwell Primary School also.

The organization for both electives worked quite smoothly. Probably time was the most limiting factor for some enterprises as children became involved in what they were doing and were reluctant to stop. We received complete co-operation from the teachers, the only requests made by the school were to collect the children from their classrooms before the lessons and to return them on time for the following lessons.

Both associations are considered to have been worthwhile ventures and we would like to include child involvement in both electives again. However, the writer would also like to try out similar activities in classroom conditions to test the feasibility of the programme in the future.

Problems and Effectiveness

From these reports the general tenor of the relationship between Churchlands Primary School and the college can be appreciated. Comments on the effectiveness of aspects of the programme have been included in the above reports.

The college makes extensive use of Churchlands Primary School and deeply appreciates the co-operation of the principal and his staff. That the college in turn serves some needs of the school, its staff and pupils, may be implicit in their willing participation in the teacher education programme.

Recommendations

No major changes are envisaged. Possible developments in some areas are foreshadowed in the above reports from staff members who have been involved in the co-operative programme.

Commentary

A school on campus opens a range of possibilities for a teacher-education institution and, indeed, for the school itself. At Churchlands, observation and practical teaching experiences are facilitated for college students by their ready access to pupils from the campus school. The proximity of the college to the school has contributed towards the development of a close relationship and mutual understanding between college and school staff and has facilitated the arrangement of integrated activities.

The school considers its relationship to the college to be beneficial, both for the professional development of its teachers and the enriched curriculum offered its pupils. Teachers value the stimulating interaction with college staff and students which they feel causes them to reflect upon a range of possible teaching methods and educational issues, thus widening their perspectives. The college staff and students make a very positive contribution to the school curriculum in certain specialized areas, allowing the regular teachers to devote more attention to a narrower range of basic subjects.

The teachers at Churchlands Primary School have been given the opportunity to share in college-sponsored educational visits and some members of the school staff participate in lecture sessions, but to a limited extent. The ability of the school to draw upon college staff as resource people for in-service conferences conducted at the school is a further advantage of the relationship.

When it was first proposed that Churchlands Primary School would become closely associated with Churchlands College, the parents of the pupils were somewhat wary of the venture. As the programme has developed, however, the school's association with the college has been recognized, along with the quality of school staffing and the open architecture, as a positive attraction. These factors have contributed towards a high enrolment with consequent over-crowding. Student teachers appreciate the opportunities arising from the close association between the college and the school, but consider the children some-what challenging to work with. They attribute their difficulties to an 'over-exposure' of the Churchlands pupils to college activities.

The 'over-exposure' of Churchlands pupils may be more apparent than real. Possibly because of accommodation difficulties within the school, most activities involving college students and school pupils take place at the college. These occasions are sufficiently frequent for staff to claim that pupils in fact view the college as part of their 'natural environment'. It may be, however, that the frequent movement of pupils from one location to another has an unsettling effect which college students attribute to 'over-exposure'. Whatever the cause, the fact that college students perceive the Churchlands children as 'different' from those in other schools is worthy of attention. (An interesting observation made by school staff is that the Churchlands children, because of their constant interaction with college students, are far more perceptive of good teaching than are pupils in other schools and therefore present a greater threat to the student teacher.)

Lest it may be thought that the college makes excessive demands upon the school, mention should be made of the fact that the college programme, which initially involved the campus school more exclusively, has been modified to ensure that pupils will not be disadvantaged through college activities. Children are brought in from other schools for microteaching experiences.

As suggested in the accompanying report, the relationship between the college and the school is an informal one. Precise objectives do not appear to have been communicated or in fact formulated, although they are implicit within the programme. Through observation and practical experiences college students have varied and frequent opportunities to integrate theory with practice, what many would consider to be a major objective of a campus school.

In the development of a close relationship between a college of advanced education and a school it is important that each institution retains its identity. Churchlands Primary School staff value their autonomy and their contribution to the students in training would seem to be the richer because of this. In the early stages of a mutual programme effective communication is essential. As the programme develops and becomes established it is possible to take it for granted that all are aware of the primary aims of the enterprise. As staff changes occur in both institutions and as programmes change in emphasis, there is a need for periodic review, clarification of objectives and a re-establishment of procedures. The Churchlands staffs may consider it worthwhile to engage in such an activity. Joint seminars where teachers may be presented with an over-view of college aims and courses and in which common purposes may be explored could prove beneficial.

In terms of the present allocation of staff to the school, teacher involvement, time available, accommodation problems and the level of participation of pupils at Churchlands Primary School, it would seem that further developments will embrace other schools rather than the school on campus. There are, however, some activities for which a campus school is particularly well suited which it may seem appropriate to extend. Such an area is that of remedial teaching in which some work has taken place already at the Churchlands campus school.

Although it is to be expected that Churchlands College of Advanced Education will develop its programme to include a wider range of co-operating schools, the campus primary school can be expected to continue to play a central and effective role in the teacher education programme.

[J. D.]

EXAMPLES OF CO-OPERATION BETWEEN SCHOOLS AND CAPRICORNIA INSTITUTE OF ADVANCED EDUCATION

Dr I. Gasson
Chairman, School of Education

L. Larking
Senior Lecturer, School Experience Co-ordinator

Dr C. Caruso
Senior Lecturer, Remedial Education

The School of Education at the Capricornia Institute of Advanced Education maintains a good relationship with the schools and the Regional Education Office and a number of co-operative ventures have resulted.

An important feature of the co-operation which occurs is that ideas and initiatives for opportunities to co-operate do not all originate in the institute. For full co-operation to occur the climate of acceptance of ideas from both an institution and the schools must exist. An institution must not only request support for its own ideas of co-operation but must also implement some of the ideas which arise in the schools.

Three examples of co-operation outlined in this section exemplify this philosophy. The initiative for 'The Simulation Workshop for the Induction of Beginning Teachers' came from the Regional Education Office in Rockhampton; whereas the ideas for 'The First Year School Experience Programme' and 'The In-school Reading Programme' came from the institute.

The Simulation Workshop for the Induction of Beginning Teachers

The School of Education at the Capricornia Institute of Advanced Education and the Central Region Education Office in Rockhampton are co-operating in a three-day workshop to facilitate the induction of third-year students into the Queensland teaching service.

The material for the workshop involving simulation exercises for beginning teachers was prepared by Mr L. Roles, Regional Inspector for primary schools, with the help of a group of primary school principals in Rockhampton. After examining a draft proposal, Dr Gasson agreed to incorporate the workshop into the third year of the 1976 teacher education programme.

Specifically the workshop aims to simulate some of the problems faced by a new appointee from the date he receives his appointment, until a few days after he has started teaching.

The workshop will be staffed by sixteen principals and three inspectors from the Regional Education Office. In addition Dr Gasson and a lecturer from the institute's School of Education will observe and help as the need arises. Subsequently, Mr Roles and Dr Gasson will invite comments from both staff and students regarding the success of the venture, and ways in which its effectiveness can be determined when students are appointed to a school.

There will be sixty third-year students in the three-day workshop and it will be repeated later in the year for another sixty third-year students. The students will be divided into twelve groups of five with a principal or inspector as the leader of each group. The principals who have arranged a particular segment of the workshop will not have special groups during their segment, but will be free to direct it.

The workshop will commence with the provision and discussion of detailed information about a hypothetical primary class. The participants will be expected to draw upon the information in this scenario when responding to questions and tasks in the six topics examined during the workshop. The six topics will all include two main aspects: discussion in small groups and role play by individuals or groups.

The first of the six topics is *What Do I Do First?* Responses to this question for three different points in time will be requested: when the appointment is received; the week prior to the opening of the school; and during the first few days of teaching. The second topic is *Types of Timetables*. The students will be asked to discuss and prepare different types of timetables according to such criteria as age of children, teaching techniques, available resources and their own educational philosophy. The third topic is *Grouping*. Participants will be required to identify different ways of grouping children, and then to group children in several ways based on both the academic and interpersonal (sociogram) data provided. Fourthly, *Evaluation and Assessment* will be explored. Topics will include the nature, purpose and criteria of a good evaluation programme; types of evaluation, and methods of compiling records. In addition to discussion, participants will be asked to complete a report card from provided data and discuss it with a 'parent'. A fifth segment of the workshop will be devoted to the *Organization of a Reading Programme*. The students will base their responses to questions on pupil profiles, including provided reading ages. They will be asked to respond to a number of tasks in which they will have to prepare reading programmes for a variety of situations together with indications of how they would evaluate the results. The last segment will deal with the *Physical Arrangement of Rooms*. In this session students will become aware of the list of standard furniture available, and will discuss the various alternative room arrangements and the educational philosophies which they reflect. They will be required to make up several room arrangements with materials provided.

The site selected for the workshop is a school in Rockhampton, which has the facilities where groups can be far enough apart not to impinge on neighbouring groups but where overall direction can be given from a central point. This facility could have been provided at the institute, but it was felt that a school will add another element of realism to the simulation, and also the school has the materials and resources with which the student will come into close contact when he starts teaching. The economics of the workshop are such that no cost is charged to the institute.

The First-Year School Experience Programme

For the past two years the School Experience Programme of the Diploma of Teaching at CIAE has consisted of a number of one-day visits to schools for first-year students and a series of block teaching rounds later in the course. All the local state department of education schools have been involved in the programme and there have been sufficient teachers available for students to be placed with teachers on a one-to-one basis. Payment is made to both teachers and principals according to rates set down in the Queensland Industrial Agreement.

Paralleling the one-day per week visits to schools is a three-hour per week compulsory course for first-year students in the first semester entitled 'Looking in Classrooms'. The title of the course was taken from the set text of the same name (Good and Brophy, 1973). The course was planned by Mr L. Larking, who, with a team of five lecturers, saw the advantages of integrating the regular weekly visits of students to schools with a study of classroom instructional procedures and the analysis of classroom interaction. An aim of the course is to heighten the students' awareness of classroom procedures through having them observe classrooms at first-hand while at the same time building up their confidence and competence in interacting with small groups of children.

Each week at the institute a lecture focuses on some aspect of the instructional process. This lecture is presented to the total group of first-year students. The programme allows lectures to team teach if desired, and the fact that no lecturer is called to participate in a main lecture on more than four occasions means that each lecture is well prepared and student interest is high.

Teachers in schools each have a copy of the detailed course outline and therefore know the lecture topic for the week. They are thus in the position to demonstrate and discuss with students further detail concerning the focus for the week.

Students are trained in recording verbal interaction in the classroom, using either the Flanders System of Interaction Analysis (Flanders, 1970) or the Cerli Verbal Behaviour Classification System (Breningmeyer, 1970). These recording instruments provide students with a lens through which interaction in the classroom can be viewed, evaluated and discussed later in a tutorial. Time is also spent in this tutorial hour discussing the 'Teacher Competency Development System' booklets (Popham and Baker, 1973). This material including the accompanying tapes and filmstrips, form a competency-based section of the course.

A second tutorial hour is reserved for developing student-teacher competence in selected teaching skills. A survey among a sample of local teachers indicated that questioning was the teaching skill most needed by our students. This skill, along with the skills involved in lesson introductions, and small group discussions, form the basis for this part of the course.

In this second tutorial hour each group of fifteen students is divided into three groups of five, and in three small adjacent rooms using video equipment, opportunity is provided for students to practise the aforementioned skills in a peer group situation. Check lists are provided for the students so that during the replay of the videotape, practice is given in identifying the skills as they occur. Apart from discussion following the replay of a tape, no formal assessment of the student's performance is attempted.

Opportunity to practise teaching skills with children either individually or in small groups, is provided on each of the one-day visits to schools. One of the assignments requires the students to audiotape a series of question-discussion sessions made with a small group of children and do a written analysis of his teaching style. The written analysis of the question-discussion sessions is assessed from the standpoint of the student's ability to identify the teaching skills and evaluate features of the verbal interaction.

School principals co-operate in the programme of school visits by holding seminar sessions within the schools. At these meetings principals discuss with students detail concerning the organization of the school and other matters raised by the students.

Support for the course 'Looking in Classrooms', as indicated by the results of a survey among students, has been very high on the grounds of its relevance to teaching. Advantages of the course are that it introduces students early in their programme to the realities of classroom experience; it breaks down the complexity of the interaction and instructional process of the classroom by focusing each week on just one aspect of classroom procedure; it provides a 'safe' introduction for students to work with children individually and in small groups; it gives students ample time to prepare lesson material between each visit to schools; it allows students early in their course to assess whether they are suited to a career of teaching; and it allows institute staff to have an input and follow-up to the school visits.

The In-School Reading Programme

The idea for creating a reading course incorporating a practical component for pre-service teachers originated from Dr C. R. Caruso's post-graduate training in remedial education. It was apparent how valuable were the clinical classes, where one was given the opportunity to try out the theories and techniques learnt, on a clientele that presented a wide range of remedial and learning problems. The model is based on the way medical practitioners are trained: internship under the supervision of a qualified surgeon in the emergency ward.

It was hypothesized that if student teachers could handle the twenty per cent of children with the greatest reading difficulties, as well as associated problems such as discipline, poor self-image, slow learning and under-achieving, that they would be capable of teaching reading to an entire class.

It was further reasoned that these children could be taken out of the classroom for two hours a week, given individual tuition and supervised by members of the college and the school principal. Further, at the completion of the programme, the principal and the teachers could be given a case history of each child, what materials and techniques succeeded, as well as recommendations for further treatment. The availability of these case histories and recommendations to ensuing years' students, and teachers, could provide the basis for continuing tuition.

A close neighbourhood school with a capable principal and staff had to be found. In our area, Glenmore Primary School was selected as its principal, Mr Frank Cridland, had a reputation for innovation and the ability to 'sell' a programme to his staff and parents.

The reading course was divided into three parts: a lecture, a tutorial and a practical session in the school. The assignments were a collection of teacher made materials, a log-book of what the students did with their respective child, and a final case history of their child. The log-book was to be submitted by the individual student, but the materials and case history were to be a joint effort with the other student who was working with the child. This was to encourage team teaching and good record keeping that could be interpreted and implemented by others.

The first three to four weeks of the course were devoted to preparing the students in the A, B, C's of reading instruction and the tutorial sessions were devoted to making reading games, informal reading inventories, and learning how to gauge the reading levels, of books, comics, magazines, etc. During these initial weeks, plans were made with the principal regarding the times for the student visits. Arrangements were made to work with two groups of twenty-five children; one group on Mondays and Wednesdays, and the other on Tuesdays and Thursdays. Where possible, one group was from the infant classes and the other from the upper primary, to make for more homogeneous grouping and easier supervision. Thus it was possible to work with fifty children for two hours utilizing one hundred students.

In the subsequent weeks the content of the course was developed in the lectures, and the tutorials were devoted to preparing for, and discussing outcomes of, the practical sessions. During these practical sessions, the students had a log-book containing the day's lesson plan and their previous week's evaluation. In this way, the log-book could be easily referred to, a check made of the plan and a notation made about how well the lesson was proceeding. It was found to be quite easy for the lecturer to observe a group of twenty students with their respective children twice each during a one hour session, randomly picking a sample of five for a more detailed observation.

Some students had difficulty understanding how one to one tuition or small group teaching could prepare them for a whole class of pupils. They needed to be reassured that if a student has the ability to diagnose the reading problems of the children with greatest number of reading difficulties, then he could handle the reading problems of a whole class.

Teachers could be concerned about the students' methods, and what they are finding out about their pupils, particularly whether a child's failure is in any way a reflection on their teaching ability. This situation was avoided by openly discussing methods and results with the classroom teachers, encouraging them to observe, giving them the case histories, and emphasizing the belief that teaching is like firing a shot gun! No matter how good the aim (the teaching), even the best will still miss a few targets.

REFERENCES

Breningmeyer, E., 'Cerli Verbal Behaviour System' in Simon, A. and E. Boyer (eds), *Mirrors of Behaviour*, Vol. 8, Research for Better Schools, Philadelphia 1970.

Flanders, N. A., *Analyzing Teaching Behaviour*, Addison-Wesley, London 1970.

Good, T. L. and J. E. Brophy, *Looking in Classrooms*, Harper and Row, London 1973.

Popham, W. J. and E. L. Baker, *Teacher Competency Development System*, Prentice-Hall, New Jersey 1973.

Commentary

Each of the three examples of tertiary institution and school co-operation described by the staff of the Capricornia IAE has much to commend it. So too has the general rationale for co-operation—that is, that *each* body has a part to play both in initiating ideas, formulating plans and facilitating their implementation.

The idea of the simulation workshop for beginning teachers was initiated by the local school system, planned by school personnel and approved by the institute. Its implementation and evaluation will involve both school and institute staff, especially the former. The workshop will be based on a school and will use school resources.

The workshop organization is excellent. It will be incorporated in the third-year course for primary student teachers about to graduate. Sixty students will be involved in the three-day workshop. Simulation and workshop activities will be pursued in small groups of five students led by an inspector of school principal. The six topics chosen for consideration seem typically high priority ones with beginning teachers. There are two notable omissions, however, the problems of planning and programming, and of classroom management and discipline. Perhaps, too, provision could have been made to students to raise some of their own particular concerns.

The idea of school-college co-operation in teacher induction is an important one. This co-operative plan focuses on a pre-appointment set of experiences. It is to be hoped that the joint interest in helping the beginning teacher will not end here and that co-operative schemes will be devised to support and assist the teacher during the first year of his appointment.

Running parallel to the first-year school experience programme of the Capricornia IAE, Larking has introduced a course 'Looking in Classrooms'. The work in the three-hour-per-week course feeds directly into the one-day per week continuous school practice. The course includes (i) work on interaction analysis which students apply in their class observations, and (ii) analyses of selected teaching skills which students apply in videotaped peer microteaching on campus, and then re-apply with individual or small groups of children in their weekly school visits.

Students involved in Larking's course commented favourably on this early, sharply focused and non-threatening introduction to schools and teaching. More courses like 'Looking in Classrooms' having direct practical application, they believed, should be introduced. They were critical, however, of the American examples of teaching which were used as microteaching models— these seemed rehearsed and the accents were 'off-putting'. More generally, the students viewed unfavourably a number of aspects of their first-year teaching practice. For example, (i) supervising teachers ('associate teachers') seemed to know little about what students were learning at college, especially the micro-teaching skills. (ii) The one-day a week in schools gave students little opportunity to feel part of the school or form relationships with children and, where teachers followed rigid timetables, students tended to observe and teach the same thing each week. (iii) Students tended to teach as the teachers did, not as the institute advocated. One student said she even found herself 'even using the teacher's phrases'! Students thought this was inevitable because they had to satisfy their evaluators, because they were so inexperienced, and because they 'seldom saw their lecturers in schools, let alone saw them teach'.

The Capricornia co-operative relationship with schools for the school experience programme has given much responsibility to principals and teachers for students' work. This seems only a good thing where schools can help student teachers explore and refine the teacher education course learnings. Where it means conflict with, or denigration of such learnings, it is clearly a bad thing. Much more thought needs to be given by most Australian teacher education programmes to the development of common, enlightened frames of reference between teacher educators and co-operating teacher supervisors of practice teaching.

The in-school reading programme is representative of a number of similar developments in Australian teacher education programmes whereby, (i) the school provides field-work opportunities for students working with pupils on a specific curriculum area, and (ii) the college students and lecturers provide a service to the school by helping children with learning difficulties in these curriculum areas.

In the Capricornia scheme students, working in pairs, provide diagnostic and remedial reading instruction to individual pupils for two hours each week. This work is prepared for in college lectures and tutorials and is supervised in school locations by the lecturers and the school principal. Unfortunately teachers are not directly involved in implementing the programmes, apparently because of 'industrial reasons' (payment constraints). However, at the completion of the semesters' work, the students give the teachers a case history of each child, an outline of the materials and techniques they have used, and make recommendations for further treatment. During remedial reading sessions the class teacher is freed to work with other children.

Students interviewed generally had positive attitudes to the programme. They felt that the experience enabled them to learn to relate to individual children and provided them with competence in a basic and difficult area of instruction. The pupils reported being highly motivated by the new games and materials the students introduced, and they thought the individual teaching was helping their reading.

Field work experiences such as the Capricornia IAE in-school reading programme are an extremely valuable adjunct to college-based courses. Ideally, they are activities that should involve teachers co-operatively in all their phases. If teachers, or rather their professional organizations, demand payment for such mutually educative experiences for children, teachers and student teachers, then one has serious doubts about the ideals of 'professionalism' held by such organizations.

[C. T.]

ARMIDALE COLLEGE OF ADVANCED EDUCATION AND ARMIDALE DEMONSTRATION SCHOOL

Dr W. Newman
Director, Educational Services

Background and Context

A very close relationship has always existed between the Armidale Demonstration School and the Armidale College of Advanced Education, formerly Armidale Teachers College. Since the college was founded forty-eight years ago, the school, under one name or another, has been closely associated with it.

Until comparatively recent times, the chief contributions of the demonstration school to the working of the college were the provision of formal lesson demonstrations and block practice teaching opportunities. In 1973 a decision was made to offer all teachers in all Armidale schools the opportunity to take part in the college demonstration lesson programme. While some teachers in other schools accepted the offer and have provided some demonstration lessons for the college, most of such lessons are still provided by Armidale Demonstration School.

The 1973 decision to spread demonstration lessons around the Armidale schools was a result of new thinking in the college about professional experience and practice teaching programmes. At that time, it was decided, after discussion between the college and the schools, to introduce a 'continuous' practice teaching programme for all first year students. This decision had a number of implications for the schools concerned:

(i)   All schools would have regular weekly three-hour sessions when first year students would visit for observation, demonstration and practice.
(ii) Because of these regular visits, the former demonstration programme for first-year students was no longer required. It was, in effect, integrated into the continuous practice programme.
(iii) This meant that the overall number of formal demonstration lessons required by the college was significantly reduced while more informal observations were significantly increased.

The implementing of the continuous practice programme in 1974 marked a turning point in the relationship between the college and the demonstration school. Whereas the school had previously been predominantly concerned with demonstration lessons and block practice teaching, it now became concerned, along with the other schools, in regular weekly student visits. Because of these visits, the school was no longer able to make its previous very significant contribution to block practice. Second and third year student practice places in the Armidale area were greatly reduced because teachers involved in the continuous programme could not be expected to accept as well students for block practice.

As indicated above, however, the demonstration school still retained a major interest in providing formal demonstrations for second and third year students. In this respect, its contribution differed from that of the other schools in Armidale.

As a concomitant of the continuous practice programme, and because of the school's proximity to the college, it found itself increasingly involved in incidental observation visits in addition to the regular weekly visits, by students and lecturers. In many ways, therefore, as the 'demonstration' function of the school decreased, its 'observation' function increased.

When the college became an autonomous institution, late in 1974, it became responsible for the payment of annual allowances for teachers in demonstration schools, a cost previously borne by the NSW Department of Education. The college, in accepting this financial responsibility, was then in a position to decide whether or not it would pay these allowances, that is, whether or not it wished to retain the services of an officially designated 'demonstration' school.

Aims and Principles of the Plan

In an endeavour to consolidate and extend the changing function of the demonstration school, in 1975 the college formulated plans concerning the future relationship between it and co-operating schools. This was done in close consultation with the district inspector and the school principal. Then in July the following proposal was submitted to the NSW Department of Education:

In our considerations at the college, we have been guided by a number of specific needs:

(a) The need to provide students with opportunities to observe children in teaching situations which are as natural as possible.

(b) The need to reduce to an absolute minimum, the use of the "demonstration" type lesson given by a teacher before a massed audience.

(c) The need to have access to competent teachers who are prepared to have their lessons videotaped for college use.

(d) The need to provide students with the maximum opportunity to share ideas with established and successful teachers.

(e) The need to have access to a school organized on a basis compatible with the early childhood to sixth grade integration theme of the proposed B.Ed. degree of the college.

With these needs in mind, we have formulated the following proposal . . . :

1. That the term "demonstration" be dropped from the titles of the three schools in Armidale currently designated as such.

(a) That the existing relationship between the college and Martins Gully and Kelly's Plains schools continue unchanged except that in future they be known simply as Martins Gully Public School and Kelly's Plains Public School.

(b) That existing staffing arrangements and staff selection procedures for Martins Gully and Kelly's Plains schools continue.

(c) That the Armidale Demonstration School be known in future as the Armidale Public School.

(d) That the principal of the Armidale Public School, be as closely involved as possible in the staff selection procedures applied to his school.

(e) That teachers offered appointment at the Armidale Public School be appraised by way of a written statement prepared jointly by the college and the department, of the special nature and function of the school.

(f) That teachers be appointed to Armidale Public School only if they agree with and are prepared to accept the special functions of the school as outlined to them.

2. That the Armidale Public School be reorganized on such a basis that no distinction is drawn between infants department and primary department.

(a) That the school have a non-teaching deputy principal. The college sees such a position as essential for effective co-ordination of the activities envisaged as a result of the special function of the school and is prepared to meet the cost of the differential involved in the salary of a teaching and non-teaching deputy.

(b) That the school have a minimum of three deputy masters.

3. That the school be organized in such a way that maximum opportunity is provided for students to observe children in teaching situations which are as natural as possible.

(a) That formal group demonstration lessons be replaced by videotape lessons without observers. The college is prepared to install permanent videotaping facilities in rooms to make such videotaping possible.

(b) That rooms be set aside in the school building in which teachers, lecturers and students may work with a small group of pupils. The college is prepared to meet the cost of any structural alterations necessary to the building.

(c) That a direct computer link be established between the school and the college. The college is prepared to meet all costs of terminal installation and maintenance within the school.

(d) That a direct television cable link be established between the school and the college to enable each institution to observe activities being conducted in the other. The college is prepared to meet all costs involved.

(e) That the college supply the school with audiovisual equipment for permanent installation and the services of a full-time audiovisual technician to be based in the school.

4. That the school provide the college with maximum opportunities for students to interact with and observe pupils.

(a) That the school have special responsibility for the observation programme of first year B.Ed. students during Terms II and III of each year.

(b) That the school be involved in the continuous practice teaching programme set down for second year B.Ed. students in the first term of each year.

(c) That except in specially negotiated situations, the school should not be involved in block practice teaching.

5. That all other primary schools in Armidale be invited to take part in continuous practice teaching in term I of each year and block practice in terms II and III of each year.

(a) That, as a long term objective, observation facilities be provided by the college in schools other than Armidale Public School.

(b) That, subject to the approval of the principal concerned, any teacher in any Armidale school may take part in observation and videotaping programmes of the college if they wish to do so.

6. That the college meet the cost of "allowances" paid to teachers on the staff of Armidale Public School for their special assistance to the college. The amount of the "allowance" paid to each teacher would not be less than the existing annual "demonstration allowance".

The State Education Department's informal reaction to the proposal was the counter-suggestion that the college consider spreading the foreshadowed activities over a number of Armidale schools. These comments and increasing financial constraints within the college led to a revised proposal that the three demonstration schools in the region, including Armidale, revert to ordinary primary schools with *no* special appointments or salary allowances. These schools would be involved in the continuous and block teaching practice programmes, with the former Armidale Demonstration School being especially involved in the observation and professional-workshop programmes of the college.

No firm decision on the future of the Armidale Demonstration School has yet been reached. Discussions on the prospective status of the school are continuing between the education department and the college officers. Regardless of the outcome of these discussions, it is hoped, and anticipated, that the relationship between the demonstration school and the college will continue at least along present lines. Because of the location of the school, it is expected that it will always be in demand for observation visits. If the decision is made not to retain it as a 'demonstration' school with specialized staffing, it could well play a reduced part in providing formal demonstration lessons.

In summary, the relationship between Armidale CAE and the Armidale Demonstration School is in the process of change. In the past, it provided formal demonstration lessons and block practice sessions. At present, it provides observation and practice situations for the continuous practice programme, along with a reduced number of formal lessons. In the future, it could well move further away from a formal lesson function and further towards an observation function.

As an observation school, it is very well suited. A fall in pupil numbers over recent years has meant that a number of rooms are available for discussion sessions with teachers, pupils and college students. As it was originally designed to cope with a formal demonstration situation, its rooms are large and most appropriate for group observation visits. It has a good library and a large assembly hall.

Commentary

In most of the Australian states the role of the demonstration school is changing dramatically. Some demonstration schools have reverted to ordinary public schools, others continue to participate in teacher education on a much reduced scale, and a number have taken on substantially modified or new functions in co-operation with tertiary institutions.

The Armidale Demonstration School is an example of a demonstration school which, while it will probably revert to a 'public school' classification, will continue to play a part in teacher education. A number of factors have typically led to the demise of demonstration schools like Armidale. Among them are: (i) *The difficulty of recruiting suitable staff.* A growing number of teachers invited to work in demonstration schools because of their teaching ability, decline, despite extra salary allowances and fees, enhanced opportunities for promotion, the prestige of the position and the generally superior working conditions. They seem to shy-away from the work load and pressures presumably associated with such work. The consequence is that sometimes much less suitable people are accepted into demonstration-teacher ranks. Teacher education institutions currently comment on the poor quality of teaching or the traditional style of pedagogy and class organization exemplified by many demonstration school teachers. (ii) *The difficulty of communication, and sometimes conflict between the teacher education programme and the school.* Demonstration teachers sometimes complain that teacher educators do not convey clearly what they would like to see implemented. At other times they complain that lecturers request impossible or even unsound approaches, or methods which clash with the teachers' aims and procedures. Lecturers, on the other hand, complain that the teachers 'do not deliver the goods' and do not adequately follow suggestions. One of the reasons for this poor communication and/or conflict is the lack of time that both lecturers and teachers have for mutual consultation and planning. Indeed, in most crowded CAE timetables it has become impossible to block-off periods for demonstrations. Lecturers endeavour to fit them into their lecture hours. (iii) *Complaints from student teachers about the artificiality and uselessness of demonstrations.* Unfortunately many demonstrations are formal displays before an audience. Often students do not participate in either planning, executing or follow-up of the particular piece of teaching. The episode is not part of a sequenced programme. And, what is an unforgivable aspect, there is sometimes little or no relationship between the demonstration and the college courses. Students make these complaints particularly after they have experienced the comparatively mundane classroom life in practice teaching schools. Sometimes lecturers themselves display negative attitudes to the value of demonstrations and this inevitably rubs off on students. (iv) *Financial constraints within the teacher education programme.* As the teachers colleges have become autonomous institutions they have had to accept the responsibility for paying the special salary allowances to teacher-demonstrators. This has meant a re-examination of the value of demonstration schools. (v) *Movement to spread teacher education activities among as many schools as possible.* One suspects that within some state departments of education, senior officers have tended to react negatively against what they perceive as an *élitism* or exclusiveness in the specially staffed and equipped demonstration schools. The result has been the encouragement of teacher education programmes to distribute students' observational and practical experiences widely. Similarly, some teacher educators seem committed to the idea that all practical experiences should be in 'ordinary' schools with 'ordinary' teachers. (vi) *The increasing use of audiovisual techniques* to bring recorded teaching segments into the campus classroom is seen by many as more useful and less costly than the provision of 'live' observations. (vii) *Failure of teacher educators, teachers and administrators to explore fully the potentially valuable new roles in teacher education of the demonstration school.* The possibilities for tertiary institution-school collaboration are numerous and there are many co-operative plans which could produce mutual benefits to teachers and pupils, teacher educators and students.

Most of the above seven factors, with varying degrees of significance, seem to have contributed to the present situation in relation to the Armidale Demonstration School. For example, several lecturers who were interviewed made comments on the fact that some teachers were apparently not specially selected and were non-innovative, and that they had been disappointed with the way in which their suggestions for demonstrations had been translated into practice. On the other hand, several other lecturers, particularly in the field of physical education, remarked on the value and excellence of the demonstrations for their students. Most college staff complained of the difficulty of finding time in their programme to thoroughly consult with teachers and simply to timetable the viewing of demonstrations. Student-teacher reactions to demonstrations seem varied. All spoke of the potential value of observational work, particularly in the first year. Some thought that formal demonstrations were artificial and an extensive programme of such experiences would be 'a drag'. School staff admitted that demonstrations were rather unpopular with some students, but the full blame for this would not be accepted by the school. Sometimes teachers were inadequately briefed on what they were to do. Occasionally lecturers did not turn up at lessons. This 'low-valuing' of demonstration activity rubbed-off on some students who ceased to attend. Poor student attendance in turn tended to disillusion teachers who had gone to considerable trouble to prepare lessons.

Ironically, the college lecturers who were interviewed all subscribed strongly to the importance and value of modelling behaviour in learning to become a teacher. They admitted that a specially staffed demonstration school could provide 'live' and 'recorded' instances of such behaviour. They acknowledged too that by the dispersal of first-year observational work among all schools in the district as part of the continuous practice programme, some students were being exposed to mediocre teaching and that the 'perpetuation of the established ways' could well be promoted. Several lecturers emphasized the need for increased 'dialogue' between the college and the school leading to the realization that there are ways through which both institutions can assist and learn from each other in educational pursuits. It appears that a number of staff would like to see a special co-operating relationship with the demonstration school established.

They saw merit in the apparently shelved proposal. Other lecturers would go further and incorporate such arrangements as collaborative research, reciprocal staffing for courses and practical work, and shared use of accommodation and resources. One lecturer had developed a proposal for the conjoint establishment of a Primary Curriculum Laboratory at the school. This facility would be staffed by school and college personnel and would become a resource of print and non-print materials for use of teachers, college staff and students. The school's principal spoke of its willingness to explore new co-operating relationships with the college beyond and including demonstration work.

The future of the Armidale Demonstration School is clouded. Perhaps this case study has revealed positive attitudes in both college and school towards the establishment of new, improved and closer relationships. It would seem a pity if the possibilities of fuller co-operation between two institutions, in such ideal physical proximity, were lost because of relatively small financial constraints or the lack of enthusiasm of administrative officers.

[C. T.]

THE ROLE OF BALLAM PARK TECHNICAL SCHOOL AS A CO-OPERATING SCHOOL WITH THE STATE COLLEGE OF VICTORIA AT HAWTHORN

K. SMITH
Senior Lecturer, Curriculum Studies

Background and Context

Although Ballam Park Technical School (hereafter BPTS) is closely associated with the school experience element of a number of teacher education institutions, this paper refers only to its role as a co-operating school with the SCV Hawthorn. This college operates an intern system in which student teachers undertake either a one or two year 'end-on' course while simultaneously teaching for two days each week in a Victorian technical school.

During 1975 BPTS co-operated with the SCV Hawthorn in two different programmes, viz.;

(i) Nine student teachers undertook their teaching practice experience for two days each week at the school. They were teaching in the following subject areas: carpentry and joinery, fitting and machining, automotive practices, maths and science, fashion design, English and social studies (humanities). Each student teacher had both a school and a college supervisor and the school's teaching practice co-ordinator assumed the major responsibility for the programmes of all student teachers in the school. In matters relating to teaching practice the co-ordinator communicated directly with the Head of School at SCV Hawthorn. All school supervisors were paid an allowance of $175.73 per half year by the college.

(ii) Fourteen student teachers in the humanities area were involved in the BPTS programme every Wednesday for four hours. This involvement was in addition to their normal two days per week teaching practice commitment in their own schools. It was in fact two-thirds of their Diploma of Education method programme.

The remainder of this paper is devoted to a description of this school-based method programme.

Over the past few years both students and lecturers in the humanities method area at SCV Hawthorn have expressed dissatisfaction with the course. Students complained of irrelevance and a general failure to meet the survival needs of beginning teachers. Lecturers were unhappy that despite their best efforts student teachers were being socialized into the prevailing narrow paradigms of teaching in their practice schools. Numerous research studies (McAulay, 1960; Price, 1961; Harrison, 1968) indicated the influence of school supervisors on the teaching behaviours of their students while college lecturers appeared to fail to maintain any lasting effect once students began full-time teaching. Furthermore, the work of Albert Yee (1968) at the University of Texas indicated the need for a re-examination of teaching practice arrangements. He examined interpersonal relationships in the triad of student teacher, school supervisor and college supervisor and concluded:

> The student-teaching triad appears to seek greater dyadic balance at the cost of decreased triad cohesiveness. Balance is found in dyadic coalitions, especially between the leaders; and negative dyads between leaders and the student teachers. The student teaching triad seems to degenerate and become less of a viable group as time passes. (Yee, 1968, p. 106)

It was clear that new approaches were necessary. How were college method lecturers, 'ivory towered' and remote from children, to exert any lasting influence on the attitudes and teaching behaviours of their students? Recent researches by Sigall and Helmreich (1969), McGinnies (1973) and by Cooper *et al.* (1974) all pointed to the importance of source and communicator credibility in both the extent and direction of attitude change. It was decided to field-test these findings in the area of teacher education by attempting to increase the credibility, visibility and accessibility of method lecturers. This meant moving our method programmes from the college to selected schools where lecturers could work *simultaneously* as teachers of children and lecturers of student teachers.

BPTS was selected by Smith as his school-base because:

(i) Its expressed and practised educational aims are similar to his own.
(ii) The school's innovative programme in open and core studies provide a unique opportunity for student teachers to gain experience in both open and self-contained classrooms.
(iii) The administration and staff of this comparatively new school are operating a total staff approach to the problems of an evolving philosophy and organization. The subsequent flexibility of approach provides an excellent setting for student teachers to observe the complex operations and growth of a new school.

Aims of the Programme

The major aims of the programme include:

(i) To bring student teachers into contact with two to three children in a supportive rather than judgemental situation.

(ii) To provide opportunities for student teachers to develop a personal teaching style based on guided experience, in a variety of teaching strategies.

(iii) To assist student teachers to develop skills in the area of curriculum development, implementation and evaluation.

(iv) To encourage student teachers to see their subject as part of the total school curriculum by regular observation and participation in unfamiliar subject areas.

(v) To improve communication between the school and college.

(vi) To provide the college lecturer with continuing experience as a secondary teacher.

(vii) To encourage a team approach to the task of teacher education involving student teachers, college lecturers and interested members of staff.

(viii) To help student teachers develop personal and appropriate responses to highly specific problems of illiteracy, innumeracy, etc.

The Plan and Its Implementation

A typical Wednesday at BPTS was spent as follows:

9.00–10.00 a.m. The college lecturer was available to the student teachers for individual consultation with regard to problems in their own schools. When no such consultation was necessary the group worked in the school's remedial centre.

10.20–11.20 a.m. Student teachers contracted into one of the following options or a negotiated alternative:

(a) Team teaching in the open classroom in co-operation with the school staff.

(b) Observation of teachers representing a wide cross-section of teaching styles and subject areas.

(c) Participation (as a secondary student) in a normal class (e.g., three student teachers undertook metalwork on a regular basis and were able to closely examine both teacher and students over an extended period).

(d) Student-teacher 'group chat'—a chance to swap ideas and experiences with other members of the group.

11.25 a.m.–12.25 p.m. This was the key activity. The college lecturer assumed the major responsibility for the teaching of a Form I co-ed group of thirty-two. Each student teacher took the responsibility of 'teaching' two to three pupils. Whole-of-class lessons, group activities, excursions, etc. were conducted.

1.30–3.00 p.m. The total college group met in the school's conference room to discuss the morning's activities, plan future sessions, and relate recent practice to relevant theory.

Problems and Effectiveness

This school-based method programme has been evaluated by an independent evaluator and, despite the claim that it has been 'clearly successful' in most of its objectives, some significant alterations are planned for 1976. It is intended to increase the time of the college lecturer in the school so that his functions may extend beyond the homogeneous method group. He could become the on-the-spot college representative and hopefully reduce the induction anxieties of beginning teachers. Secondly, it is planned to involve the college lecturer, student teachers, staff and children of the school in a combined project designed to develop social science materials for use in the open area. To support this combined pre-service, in-service project a grant of $950 has been made available by the National Committee for the Social Sciences. It will be the responsibility of the college lecturer to establish and maintain the necessary liaison between the college and co-operating school so that this project may develop.

This pilot study at BPTS in 1975 appears to offer some real hope that a genuine, equal partnership between a teacher education institution and co-operating school can emerge. If teacher educators seriously intend their programmes to exert a lasting influence on the attitudes and teaching behaviours of their students, then approaches such as school-based teacher education might well be considered.

> The minimal goal for each graduate of the undergraduate training program must be the student's belief in his ability to cope with the classroom. Unless this is accomplished before the completion of (initial) teacher training, there is not much evidence to support the hope that the teacher will develop into the best teacher he can become, since the present school situation seems oriented toward teacher survival rather than teacher growth. (Aspy, 1969, p. 308)

REFERENCES

Aspy, D. N., 'Maslow and Teachers in Training', *The Journal of Teacher Education*, 1969, 20, 3, 303–8.

Cooper, J., J. M. Darley and J. E. Henderson, 'On the Effectiveness of Deviant and Conventional-appearing Communicators', *Journal of Personality and Social Psychology*, 1974, 29, 6.

Harrison, A., 'Teacher Education Objectives—A Lack of Congruence', *The Journal of Teacher Education*, 1968, 19, 3.

McAulay, J. D., 'How Much Influence has a Co-operating Teacher?' *The Journal of Teacher Education*, 1960, 11.

McGinnies, E., 'Initial Attitude, Source Credibility, and Involvement as Factors in Persuasion', *Journal of Experimental Social Psychology*, 1973, 9.

Price, R. D., 'The Influence of Supervising Teachers', *The Journal of Teacher Education*, 1961, 12.

Sigall, H. and R. Helmreich, 'Opinion Changes as a Function of Stress and Communicator Credibility', *Journal of Experimental Social Psychology*, 1969, 5.

Yee, A. H., 'Interpersonal Relationships in the Student-Teaching Triad', *The Journal of Teacher Education*, 1968, 19, 1, 95–112.

Commentary

What specific benefits did the particular co-operation with this school give the field-testing of the new course? Perhaps foremost, the school provided a context for teacher education which was open to influence by the teacher educator and sensitive to the needs of student teachers. It was not a negative or hostile context but one in which, consequent on staff acceptance of the school's full role teacher education, there was a high level of goodwill for the developing programme. The positive relationship also meant that students were offered a large degree of choice in observing many different teachers, even in non-humanities subjects, in 'natural' classroom conditions over extended periods of time.

The importance of the positive school context to this teacher education programme ought not to be underestimated. For these educators, such a context is far more than just a more pleasant place for students to learn. The contention is that without such a context, and the very close communication between lecturer, teachers and students for which it is a necessary condition, it is likely that students' most important problems in teaching may remain unexamined. That is to say, a less positive context is also one in which there is minimal communication between all three groups and in which as a consequence minimal student development takes place. It is maintained that only where each person is readily accessible to each other person is relatively full and therefore 'realistic' communication possible.

Another particular benefit of using this secondary technical school was that for the humanities students, there were many opportunities to talk with and observe trade teachers. On several occasions student teachers became pupils in practical classes to increase their understanding of this area of the curriculum. More extensive contact with the whole school staff, perhaps resulting from the fuller part the school is playing in teacher education, appears to have made this opportunity possible.

A range of alternative curricula and organizational plans are being investigated at the school. There are therefore many opportunities for students to observe and contrast these arrangements in a naturalistic setting as they attempt to construct their personal teaching approaches. This situation did not, of course, result from Ballam Park's role as a co-operating school but was a reason for its selection for this role by the teacher educator.

Having the opportunity to work extensively in a large state secondary school afforded students with very radical personal beliefs an opportunity to assess the work situation in which they would be involved as state-employed teachers. Though the process of assessment was difficult for all of those affected, it does seem preferable for it to be undertaken with as much information available as possible to students, rather than later when full teaching responsibility has been accepted. Such an assessment would be much more limited in schools under more usual practice teaching conditions.

The formal relationship which exists between the two institutions does not differ from that between the college and any other school to which students are sent for practice teaching. The special relationship has arisen through informal contact and discussion between the individual college lecturer, the principal and the staff. The contact began with the college lecturer's supervisory visits to the school and the relationship has been enhanced by the chance placement of several of the lecturer's former students at the school.

Central to the development of the current relationship is clearly a high level of congruence in the educational views of the lecturer and principal. The lecturer has confidence in the general pattern of educational practice in the school and especially in the innovatory policy of the principal. On the other hand, the principal is deeply committed to the teacher education course design being tried. The point is worth stressing because in discussions with other method lecturers not reported in this book, the issue of congruence between the views of the teacher educators involved at a school and the principal emerged many times as the single most important factor influencing the success of the co-operative arrangement. The importance of this factor appears to lie both in the principal's efforts to develop practices in his school to which the teacher educator is also committed, and in the principal and executive staff's willingness to carry out thoroughly the additional administrative tasks imposed by the school's teacher education role.

Both the teacher educator and school principal in this case spoke strongly in favour of the informal nature of the co-operative relationship, because they considered an effective relationship was usually a function of the personalities involved, because an informal relationship meant that the 'natural' quality of the school was safeguarded and because the relationship could be readily terminated if the policy of either institution changed substantially.

The advantages of an informal relationship, however, need to be considered alongside the issue of the central importance of quality of the principal and the desirability of sustaining a relationship with a school over a long period to ensure that some members of the school staff have experience in teacher education. No formal relationship at all might mean that only short-term projects can be developed and that the development of teacher education programmes will be retarded by the continual need to establish new relationships with schools. It should be remembered that the lecturer and principal established their working relationship at Ballam Park over a number of years: it is unlikely that a school could be used for special teacher education purposes under a minimum of one year's discussion and familiarization.

A useful compromise arrangement might be to give the staff of tertiary institutions the right to participate in the appointment of executive staff to co-operating schools as a means of ensuring continuity of a positive working relationship. This is a minimal level of interference, which is very similar to tertiary institution personnel searching for principals and schools in which they can effectively work. It has the potential advantage of stabilizing the relationship, thus providing a school in which there will always be some teachers who have been inducted into a fuller teacher education role. It would also ensure that principals accepting appointment to such a school would expect to carry the additional administrative burden imposed by the school's teacher education work.

Such a minimal formal relationship might also help to overcome, in part, the isolation of a highly fertile innovation from the mainstream of discussion and planning in both tertiary institution and state education department. A formal acknowledgement of the additional role of the school may make what is happening there more visible to key decision-makers. Both educators interviewed in this case study mentioned the lack of effective communication with decision-makers and the consequent dearth of very basic resources for the programme.

It would be a great pity if the relationship so far built were to be attenuated or terminated by the inevitable process of staff change.

[G. W.]

THE CO-OPERATING SCHOOL AS A BASE FOR A COURSE IN PRIMARY TEACHER EDUCATION

University of Sydney and North Sydney Demonstration School

G. WILLIAMS

Assistant Lecturer in Education and project co-ordinator

Background and Context

In 1975 the University of Sydney and the NSW Department of Education entered into a formal agreement concerning the university's involvement with North Sydney Demonstration School as a special co-operating school. The envisaged functions of the co-operating programme have already been discussed elsewhere in this book (see p. 137). In brief, the proposed functions range from the provision of observational and microteaching opportunities for student teachers, through reciprocal staffing arrangements, to co-operative research and development on teaching, learning and curriculum. Under the agreement co-operative schemes were to be supervised by an advisory committee comprising representatives of parents and teachers and of the school executive, state department and university. One of the first projects approved by this committee for implementation was the pilot school-based programme for final-year Bachelor of Education primary students. The initiation of the project is the subject of the following account.

What kind of experience in schools in the final part of a student's course is most likely to assist him to successfully take up a full professional role in his first years of teaching? There is good reason to doubt that, for many students, this objective is adequately met by intermittent experience in schools (irrespective of the distribution of time) while the students are *primarily* based in a tertiary institution. The difficulties faced by beginning teachers are numerous. Perhaps among the most prominent are a lack of awareness of the major institutional constraints within which they are working, an inability to manage learning programmes for young children effectively and continuously over an extended period of time, and an uncertain grasp of curricula procedures and materials suggested in lectures.

These and other difficulties may result in part from practice teaching being seen as pseudo-teaching by many students, however carefully the experience is planned and implemented. It is seen as pseudo-teaching because it is intermittent, because many of the most important long-term classroom management decisions have been made before the student begins and because there is a tendency for the student to view 'lessons' as relatively discreet from each other and somewhat inconsequential for pupils' learning.

Is, therefore, a co-operating school a better place than a tertiary institution in which to be based during the final stages of a teacher-education course so that a full teaching role can be progressively taken up? This case study is a preliminary report of a pilot study of a school-based primary teacher education course conducted at North Sydney Demonstration School by the Department of Education in the University of Sydney during 1976.

Aims of Principles of Operation

Space permits only some of the aims of this course to be mentioned, rather than all of them to be discussed. Broadly speaking, however, we aimed to provide an environment in which students could make a sustained, long-term contribution to the education of children. It was also to be a context in which students could assimilate ideas about curriculum materials and methods from people actually using the ideas, and then themselves experiment with the use of these ideas almost immediately. We further hoped to make some contribution to the continuing education of the staff of the co-operating school.

The Plan and Its Implementation

Six students, from those entering the final year of the four-year Bachelor of Education course, were invited to participate. Invitations were not issued to randomly selected students: no honours students were included in the group, and an attempt was made to include students with a variety of attitudes to the course and profession, and different levels of accomplishment in practice teaching during 1975. By the end of their third year the students had completed two years of work in the Faculty of Arts and one year of professional work, including training in basic teaching skills, practice teaching and seminar-workshops in four curriculum areas.

A full-time member of the 1975 university staff agreed to work part-time at the school during 1976 to co-ordinate the pilot course. Arrangements were also made to employ an independent evaluator (from another university) to assess the project.

Prior to commencing work in the course, all members of the group were known to each other. Four meetings were held during the last two months of 1975 to discuss the structure of the 1976 course. Four of the six students, together with the part-time co-ordinator, visited schools in Adelaide, Geelong and Melbourne for two weeks in February. This experience appeared to be highly valuable as a means of increasing each individual's understanding of other people in the group and the nature of their task during the coming year. Its impact will be more fully discussed in a subsequent report.

During the latter part of 1975, the proposed course was extensively discussed with and modified by the school principal, the infants' mistress and staff of the co-operating school.

Students in the pilot course spent three days per week at the co-operating school during the whole academic year to complete the requirements for the university's Year IV professional courses in primary education, and attended the university on one day per week for work with the university-based group, in a special course.[1] The major part of the three days at the school was spent in teaching, both individually and co-operatively with class teachers. Students worked with whole-class groups, with small, intensive groups, and over a full term with an individual child in need of special assistance. As well as teaching in various ways within a class, students participated in extra-class club, sporting and lunch-time activities.[2] A heavy emphasis was placed on *co-operative* planning

---

[1] This course is designed to facilitate the students' specialization in a relevant area of professional practice.

[2] The project co-ordinator also worked with a particular teacher and class for one-and-a-half hours per day.

for teaching so that the students would participate in the making of as many important decisions as possible, and would learn to share responsibility for a group of pupils.

A seminar was held on each of the three days. Each week, one seminar was offered by a teacher, one by a student and one by the project co-ordinator, who also attended all other seminars. Seminars were open to members of the school staff, and on some occasions they incorporated the school staff meeting. Topics of seminars were decided on each term through extensive discussion of perceived needs by all members of the group. A programme of seminars was subsequently drawn up by the school principal and project co-ordinator. This programme was referred to the student group for final acceptance.

Teachers conducting seminars were observed in their classrooms, usually during the morning preceding the seminar conducted by that teacher in the afternoon. Teachers were paid the agreed NSW rate for having students work with their classes ($2.67 per day at the time of writing) and the university's part-time staff rate for conducting seminars ($15.79 per hour). The total cost of the pilot course (excluding the independent evaluator's fees) was approximately $5,000. This figure represents a rather higher cost per student than many teacher education institutions currently spend on in-school experience programmes, but we do not believe this is an insurmountable difficulty. For example, a transfer of funds from savings in the 'method' lecture area would partially cover the additional cost.

Students in the pilot course spent a little more than half the time in seminars compared with students in the established course, and more than twice the number of days in teaching. The demand on student time was therefore much more heavy in the pilot course.

A specific example may help to elucidate the structure of the seminar programme and its relationship with the students' teaching. One topic studied extensively during the first term was the teaching of reading in the infants and junior primary school. (More work on the teaching of reading was also undertaken later in the year.) During first term, seminars were given by teachers on the procedures *they were then using* for pre-reading activities, the teaching of phonics, the development of comprehension abilities, and for implementing and using the 'Breakthrough to Literacy' programme. In each case, teachers were observed using these procedures prior to their seminars. Student seminars were concerned with a discussion of the theoretical rationale for 'Breakthrough to Literacy', the relationship between comprehension abilities and language experience approaches, 'ita' and 'Words-in-Colour' schemes, and materials available to teachers for early diagnosis of perceptual difficulty. As part of their preparation for seminars, students consulted teachers and university staff members, as well as the project co-ordinator. (It should be noted that the 'ita' and 'Words-in-Colour' schemes were not in use at the school. Seminars were not restricted to *only* those curricula materials used in the school.) Seminars led by the project co-ordinator were concerned with the use of children's literature in early reading programmes, and with further discussion of theoretical issues raised in teacher- and student-led seminars.

All students were expected to devote a considerable amount of time to teaching reading, and to use ideas and modify ideas suggested in seminars. In some cases, students worked for the full term with a small group in the class requiring remedial help; one student, impressed by the stress on meaningful materials in the 'Breakthrough to Literacy' programme, adapted this scheme for use with a twelve year old non-reader. The project co-ordinator worked with a senior class in developing picture and early reading books for kindergarten classes. These materials were examined in seminars and later utilized by two of the students in their own classes. At the request of another two students, the project co-ordinator led discussions of children's books with children from a student's class to illustrate questioning techniques. In these and many other ways ideas put forward in seminars were employed by all members of the group.

Problems and Effectiveness

No detailed evaluative comment is as yet available but up to the time of writing the students, the school principal and members of staff who had worked with students commented very favourably on the course and the observed developments in the students' teaching. A future publication will provide a fuller account of the project, and evaluative comments from the independent evaluator and others involved in the pilot course.

Some modification of the structure of the course was carried out during the year. The original plan to hold all seminars after school was modified after only three weeks of the first term because it was found that this arrangement left too little time for co-operative planning by teachers and students. On two afternoons seminars were held during school time, but this change meant that there were fewer opportunities for teachers to participate in seminars, other than as seminar leaders. Students also requested an informal lunch-time meeting on one day each week to discuss individual problems (and successes!). This additional meeting proved to be a highly valuable forum of ideas.

Some minor difficulties in communication with some teachers were experienced, chiefly because the teachers still had an expectation that students would come with an armoury of methods and materials, rather than that ideas would be learned and developed *during* the term. This resulted in some premature evaluation of the quality of students' work by staff and criticism of excessively 'soft' supervision within one department of the school. A series of consultations with staff was held and a discussion paper written to reargue the rationale of the course.

An anticipated difficulty was that the resources of the staff might prove inadequate to meet the needs of the students for methods *and* their theoretical background. This was not the case, partly because the teachers thoroughly prepared material for seminars and were able to supply extensive reading lists to which students resorted after initial seminar presentations. Further, the school's previous role as a demonstration school within the state department meant that more highly qualified staff than would normally be found in randomly selected schools were available.

Recommendations

Clearly, a discussion of the implications of this project should await the report of the independent evaluator. Some general ideas, gleaned from work during the first two terms, are offered below.

Contact between the teacher educator and the school staff at least twelve months before commencement of a similar course would be essential, to establish a positive climate for communication and to familiarize the teacher educator with the resources of the staff. In particular, there should be a high level of congruence between the educational theory and practice of the teacher educator and the school principal.

Early discussion of the structure of the course should be held with both student teachers and school staff, so that the assumptions made about the course and the work load entailed by it are clearly understood. Preliminary discussion of this kind also permits the teacher educator to make a more informed judgement about the placement of students with co-operating teachers.

Obviously central to the structure of the course is that the teacher educator should be teaching regularly in at least one classroom. Intermittent contact with many groups has not been found to be nearly so valuable for the course as regular contact with at least one group of children.

Commentary

Since this project was only ten weeks old when its co-ordinator was invited to develop his case study statement, and because the project was undergoing formative evaluation by an independent evaluator, it was decided that the research team would not attempt to gather data for an evaluative commentary. A detailed report on the pilot study will be available early in 1977.

[C. T.]

WORKING WITH SCHOOLS

Macquarie University

K. J. Eltis
Senior Lecturer in Education and Co-ordinator,
School Experience Programme

Background and Context

Care in the arrangement, ordering and structuring of practical experiences is more important than the amount of time spent on them.[1]

A university which involves itself heavily in teacher education, as Macquarie University does, is in a unique position. Those responsible for the development of the programme of teacher education, and for its implementation, can draw directly on what is seen as a necessarily broad range of sources:

—on what is happening in the school situation (the so-called 'real' world);
—on theory and speculation put forward by leaders in the field of teacher education;
—on research reports having direct relevance to the programme's own problems and concerns.

And indeed, they can initiate worthwhile action-research as was done in 1972 at Macquarie [2] into microteaching. Such research can lead to a balanced review of practices being followed in the implementation of the programme and informed recommendations for change can be put forward.

Aims and Principles of Operation

What should result is a programme, which will be of great value to students in that it represents an effective blend of theory and practice. Such has always been the aim at Macquarie and while the blend may have been varied over the years—especially as a result of advice fed to us by our master teachers, students and staff—we have actively pursued the goal originally outlined in the First Report of the Vice-Chancellor:

> A new University has the obligation and the opportunity to consider the distinctive strengths that it will develop and the areas in which it will train professional people *at the highest level*. Macquarie decided in 1967 that the training of the graduate teacher would be a major interest and decided to think the whole matter through afresh. As a result a pattern of teacher education is now going into effect which departs in significant ways from that common in Australian universities. *It aims at bringing education as professional activity into a close productive association with academic learning. There will be an interweaving of academic learning and professional training and practice. The hope is to train scholar teachers rather than educational technicians.*[3]

To realize that aim of producing a 'scholar teacher' we have always acknowledged the co-operative role that all involved in the programme must play:

> A three-fold partnership, involving the scholar in his particular discipline or subject area, the educationalist endowed with knowledge of educational theory, and the teacher skilled in the practical applications in the classroom, all fostering the development of the scholar teacher has become the core of the Macquarie concept of teacher education. [4]

The Plan and Its Implementation

For the Macquarie student, contact with the 'teacher skilled in the practical applications in the classroom' begins, in a limited way, in his third year and culminates in a full programme in his fourth and final year when he undertakes a programme of visits to a school during each week of term and additionally for some 'block' sessions of teaching. The basic idea behind the B.A. Dip.Ed. programme is that the course of teacher training should run concurrent with the student's academic programme. By the time students enrol for the first of their professional courses (i.e. courses given by lecturers in the teacher education programme and directed specifically at curriculum and teaching in schools), they have normally completed a first year course designed to introduce them to the study of education, plus, as a minimum, one further course from the School of Education containing a large component of educational psychology. As well, most students have completed two years of academic study in their proposed teaching areas or in those areas where they intend to complete a 'major'. In the third and fourth years of their programme students continue their academic programme and begin the first of the professional courses.

During third year, students do a basic course called *Curriculum and Instruction in the Infants'/Primary School* or *Curriculum and Instruction in the Secondary School*, depending on their specialization. Students at this stage do not go to schools on a regular basis for practice teaching. A review of earlier practices was carried out in 1972 and when the results of a microteaching experiment were published in 1972 it was felt that it was possible to reduce the amount of time students needed to spend in schools. Earlier it had been the practice to have third year students work under the guidance of a master teacher for half-a-day per week throughout the university term. Currently students are given background information about schools in their context, and about the aims of education and curriculum developments. In addition a large component is given over to the development of basic teaching skills.

In the course *Curriculum and Instruction in the Infants'/Primary School* each workshop group of students is attached to one of eleven co-operating schools. Students, accompanied by the group's lecturer, spend four hours per week in their co-operating school for a little less than half the total number of days available within the course.

In the early part of the year students are chiefly involved in interviewing individual children and observing the modelling of teaching skills by selected teachers within the school. Students discuss and select curriculum content appropriate to the needs, interests and abilities of the children within the class and present this to small groups of children. Students are encouraged to team teach or observe each other while teaching small groups of children, to allow them to exchange ideas on one another's progress.

Secondary students, in the course *Curriculum and Instruction in the Secondary School*, have direct contact with schools in three ways. In first term, as part of their work on the secondary school in context, students form groups and visit one of the sixty or so 'target' schools which are invited to participate. They interview the principal, key personnel, pupils, and some parents, to discuss the school's aims, function and organization, and the expectations held by these various people. They also visit a social agency connected with the school to broaden their understanding of the role of the school in the community. At the same time students are grouped into workshops according to their teaching areas to study curriculum development and to investigate teaching approaches and skills. They are introduced to various teaching skills and strategies by viewing model films before participating in microteaching practice sessions firstly at the university with fellow students and then with pupils in selected high schools, called 'co-operating schools'. There are thirteen such schools in this programme. Finally, all students participate in a Teacher Aide Programme whereby they are attached to a supervising teacher in a school. They make up to six visits to their school during the year following their microteaching experience. The aim of this programme is to help students gain an appreciation of the complexities of school life and classroom encounters without overwhelming them while they are still developing teaching skills through their microteaching programme. Care is taken to ensure that the three schools visited by the student in this year are all different.

The changes in the programme which were introduced from 1973 have resulted in greater control over the kinds of experiences the student should have to prepare him for teaching in a classroom in his final year. It has been possible to direct students' attention more precisely to specific skills to be developed and thereby develop a greater degree of professional competence before the student faces all of the complexities of the total classroom situation.

In the fourth year of his programme each student enrols in a curriculum course (e.g., English or Science in the Secondary School, or Curriculum and Instruction in the Infants'/Primary School II) and, as well, regularly attends a school as part of a programme called School Experience. The lecturer he has in his curriculum programme will also supervise his work in the schools thus ensuring a link between curriculum courses and the teaching component. While at his school the student works under the guidance of a master teacher in a kind of apprentice situation. The visiting pattern for the year is worked out to the mutual convenience of the student and the master teacher, keeping the advice in Figure M.1 in mind.

Figure M.1

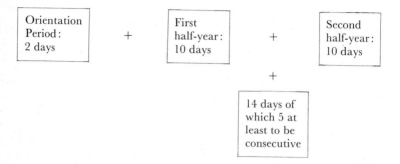

In the Macquarie programme we have never looked on the practice teaching component as some kind of initiation rite. We have always stressed the supportive role of both the master teacher and the lecturing staff and have discouraged any approach designed to give the student some kind of rude awakening by having him thrown into a class either to sink or swim on his first day of school.

> In the Macquarie pattern it is proposed that the student's experience of school life, of the conditions of the classroom, should be steady, continuous and consolidated. The influence upon the student of the teacher with whom he will be associated will likewise be expected to work steadily throughout his training. [5]

> We have departed from the method of block practice teaching and have developed a program of continuing experience in the schools over a long period. The student is assigned to a Master Teacher selected by the University. It was our hope that a true discipleship would develop between the student and the teacher that would show some of the best features of the discipleship that develops between a young doctor in training and a distinguished practitioner. We hoped, too, that a mutual respect between student and practitioner and a productive interaction between theory and practice would develop. [6]

From these two comments it should be obvious that the master teacher is viewed as a key figure in the programme. In recent years we have tried to produce a more effective 'three-fold partnership' by beginning the year with a meeting of all students, master teachers and lecturing staff so that all parties involved come together at the university to discuss the aims of the programme and ways of realizing them. As students select their schools during February at the normal university enrolment period, this meeting can take place on the Tuesday before lectures begin. After this Orientation Workshop students make two visits to their schools to complete a two-day orientation programme before classes begin at the university. To facilitate communication and assist the master teacher in his work with his students, a handbook called *The School Experience Program: A Guide for Students and Master Teachers*, is produced annually and is given to all participating in the programme, including the principals of those schools accepting Macquarie students. This guide is prepared with master teacher and student help and the advice contained in it reflects their experience and mature consideration.

After the initial Orientation Workshop the master teacher attends the university on five further occasions for a School Experience Seminar conducted in teaching subject discipline areas. Planning of these seminars is usually carried out by a planning committee consisting of master teachers and supervising lecturers, and often includes students. We seek to conduct a truly professional programme of seminars where all participate and contribute fully—students, master teachers and lecturing staff. Experience has clearly shown us, and others who work in and have researched the field, that there is a need for a common frame of reference when talking about teaching behaviour and effective teaching. As practitioners, we have our own mini-models of teaching, our own ways of describing classroom events, which derive from our own training and experience. And the students have their own view of teaching, too, quite apart from any additional complications which can arise if a student and his master teacher do not share the same values at a more general level. The purpose of these school experience seminars is to foster discussion about what it is we are looking for in the developing teacher so that we can take a step towards achieving our goal of training 'professional people at the highest level' and avoid the situation so aptly summarized by Morrison and McIntyre:

> It is not surprising that supervisors should differ so much in their criteria of a "good teacher". Having no evidence on what sort of people are good teachers, and little on what sort of teaching is good teaching, each must rely on his own opinions. These opinions must reflect largely what each supervisor believes has been effective in his own teaching; and since each has a different personality, has different teaching experiences and, for lack of authoritative guidance, has formulated his conclusions from these experiences in his own way, it would be surprising if opinions did not differ radically. [7]

Through discussion of student teaching and progress, attention is focused on particular aspects of teaching and teacher-student supervising, as, for instance:

—what makes an effective teacher;
—observing teaching;
—providing feedback on teaching;
—studying different teaching styles;
—student teacher and teacher expectations;
—developing specific teaching skills and implementing them;
—approaching discipline and classroom management problems.

We seek to promote a greater understanding of the student's dilemma as he proceeds to build up his own confidence, skills and philosophy as a teacher. Master teacher comments over the years when we have carried out extensive evaluations of the School Experience Programme indicate that seminars are a 'learning experience in themselves', and that they are 'rewarding in renewing enthusiasm and developing discussion'.[8] Not only does much that is useful flow from discussions of various issues, such as those cited above, but an understanding is developed of the paucity of knowledge in these fields and the resultant difficulty in training teachers is far better appreciated by all involved. Master teachers and students are surprised as they come to realize in the course of the discussions that Dunkin and Biddle appear to be right when they say:

What do we really know about teaching? Young people who are about to become teachers are anxious to acquire the substantive knowledge of their chosen field; those who are already teachers would like to improve their skills; and teacher educators would like to supply both with knowledge that has been verified through rigorous research. Unfortunately, most of these persons will be disappointed in their search for knowledge. Most of the questions they will ask have yet to be studied at all, and much of the research on teaching conducted so far does not provide adequate answers. [9]

We are currently trying in our seminar programme, with master teacher assistance, to tackle some aspects of the model of teaching used by Dunkin and Biddle in their review of research into teaching.[10] We are also developing a set of activities and/or lessons in each subject area which it is felt students should complete during the year. When and how these are to be carried out in the classroom will be decided by individual master teachers working with students. Coupled with this set of activities we hope to define more precisely the stages by which a student's teaching sequence might be expected to develop. In this way, not only will we be helping with lesson types and activities, but we will be moving towards a more balanced programme of skill development which, in turn, will be related to the student's abilities and to his microteaching training in his third year programme. Thus we will have a better idea of what we are looking for at each stage of a student teacher's progress and the student will have a better idea of how he is being evaluated.

Obviously the School Experience Programme is a vital part in the process of developing a scholar teacher who will later fulfil the role of an interactive and innovative professional. While the School Experience Programme which presents the student with the opportunity for regular classroom teaching occurs only in the final year of the B.A., Dip.Ed. programme, it is certainly at the centre of the student's professional courses. And students view it as the most valued part of their training, as responses to our evaluations have shown.[11]

That our hope of 'co-operative involvement' has been achieved, at least in part, is evidenced by responses by master teachers in our evaluation. Our desire to have master teachers committed to the programme and ready to be constructive in suggesting ways of varying it has been fulfilled. Such a spirit of co-operative involvement is essential for the success of any teacher education programme. Nothing can have more detrimental effects on student progress than that situation where distrust exists between teachers in the schools and those responsible for the training programme 'back at the institution', who are 'away from the real world'. It is to the ultimate advantage of students in the programme that teacher educators explore as many avenues as possible to gain maximum involvement by teachers in the field and to encourage them to express their views about courses, approaches followed, and difficulties associated with supervising students in schools.

It is certain that 'care in the arrangement, ordering and structuring of practical experiences is more important than the amount of time spent on them'. However, it is just as certain that, if the practical components of the student's programme do not help him to integrate what he has been doing at a more theoretical level, then the whole programme will have failed badly.

REFERENCES

1. *Third Report of the Vice Chancellor*, Macquarie University, 1973, p. 5.
2. See Levis, D. S., *An Investigation of the Effects of Practice and Feedback Variations on*

Secondary Student Teachers' Performance in Selected Questioning Skills and Attitudes within Controlled Teaching Settings, unpublished Ph.D. dissertation, Macquarie University, 1974.

3. *First Report of the Vice Chancellor*, Macquarie University, 1969, p. 24.
4. *The School Experience Program: A Guide for Students and Master Teachers*, Macquarie University, 1976, p. 2.
5. *First Report of the Vice Chancellor*, Macquarie University, 1969, p. 42.
6. *Second Report of the Vice Chancellor*, Macquarie University, 1972, p. 9.
7. Morrison, A. and D. McIntyre, *Teachers and Teaching*, Penguin Books, 1969, p. 52.
8. Eltis, K. J., *Report on the School Experience Program, 1974*, mimeographed paper, Macquarie University, 1974.
9. Dunkin, M. J. and Biddle, B. J., *The Study of Teaching*, Holt, Rinehart, New York 1974, p. 11.
10. Ibid., p. 38.
11. Eltis, K. J., *Report on the School Experience Program, 1974*, and *Report on the School Experience Program, 1975*, mimeographed papers, Macquarie University, 1974 and 1975.

Commentary

Schools participate in the Macquarie programme in two substantially different ways. The more general use is of selected members of staff of approximately sixty schools, who are employed as co-operating teachers in the already widely publicized Macquarie practice teaching pattern. Macquarie's emphasis is on the contribution of the *individual* master teacher rather than on the use of the whole school for teacher education purposes. From interviews with students and master teachers, it is clear that staff of some of the sixty schools who are not master teachers refuse *any* participation in even informal teacher education activities because they are not employed as master teachers.

Eleven primary schools and thirteen secondary schools are used in more specific ways in the third year programme. In primary schools students observe selected teachers using specific teaching skills, may teach small groups of pupils for short periods of time, and may have subsequent discussion of this experience with their lecturers. Each lecturer has contact with the same student group for the year, and each group returns to the same school for the year. Close contact is therefore established in many cases between individual lecturers and the staff of the schools to which they regularly go. In the secondary programme, schools supply facilities for microteaching and for the initiation of students to the organization of the school. A liaison officer is appointed from the school staff to assist in organizing this programme, but there is otherwise only very short-term school staff involvement.

A distinctive feature of both forms of using schools is the extent of long-term student contact with only a few schools during his training. The assumption is that this arrangement allows a student to penetrate a school much more thoroughly than short-term visits to several schools. In this way he is made aware of the real situation he can expect in the school of his first appointment. This advantage is modified, however, by a diminution of the number of classroom and school arrangements seen by each student during the third and fourth year programmes. Students who participated in our interview spoke strongly of the need for opportunities to make an assessment of a greater variety of educational practices, as well as to retain the advantages of the long-term contact with schools. The students also tended to feel that after one term they had learned most of what a master teacher had to offer and thought there would be advantage in working with more than one teacher in fourth year.

Over the whole time the Macquarie programme has been operating, there has been regular consultation with master teachers to review the programme's design. This extensive, careful consultation is rare and has clearly been of great benefit both to the structure of the programme and to relationships with master teachers. The latter spoke warmly of the satisfaction they felt at the ideas being taken seriously, and at seeing the course structure changed accordingly.

There is, nevertheless, a rate of change of between a-half and two-thirds of master teachers each year. The main reason offered by the staff for this high rate is that the teachers represent a select group who rapidly become eligible for promotion and move in order to accept new, more responsible positions. Some attenuation because of teachers' poor support for the programme has occurred but was seen to be a minor factor. Evidence that the morale of master teachers is generally high, and that the rate of change is a product of system-wide factors, was found in the very high rate of seminar attendance, which averages over 90 per cent.

Despite the obviously high level of goodwill between teachers and teacher educators, and the care exercised in the training of master teachers through seminar discussions, students reported a high level of variation in the quality of guidance offered at the classroom level. Whilst speaking of the rich experience available to the students with whom a high level of consultation was maintained, the students interviewed also pointed out the severe disadvantage of having to work for a full year with one teacher where this consultation was *not* available. The disadvantage is the more severe since so much learning of classroom techniques is required during the fourth year of the course.

Under the present course structure, students do not make contact with children in schools until third year. In the secondary programme this is, even then, limited short-term contact through microteaching and the school orientation programme. The number of days spent in the in-school experience programme was stated by the university staff to be the lowest of any tertiary institution in Australia. Students interviewed believed more extensive, earlier contact with children would be an advantage. It is anticipated that future infants/primary students will work with individual children attending the on-campus school for special education. This seems to be a significant move away from restricting all in-school training experience to the 'real' environment towards using specially developed facilities for particular training purposes.

The notion of maintaining 'reality' in in-school experience programmes through minimal intervention in the staffing and conduct of schools used for practice teaching is one which was very commonly expressed in interviews conducted for this study. The view finds much of its basis in the strong reaction to the atypicality of former demonstration schools and the educational programmes they maintained. However, it would certainly be useful to have more evidence on the value of having schools available to play a variety of *training* rather than *performance* roles, as Macquarie apparently intends to do, at least within the infants/primary programme.

[G. W.]

SALISBURY COLLEGE OF ADVANCED EDUCATION AND MADISON PARK LABORATORY PRIMARY AND JUNIOR PRIMARY SCHOOLS

R. A. STONE, Principal of the Primary School, in association with
Miss P. COSH, Principal of the Junior Primary School

Background and Context

R. A. Stone was appointed to Madison Park (a school of some 1,000 primary and junior primary children) in 1972 and renewed acquaintance with Bob Coggins, Director of the nearby Salisbury College of Advanced Education. He outlined the Salisbury policy of teacher education. The college had accepted the fact that demonstration schools could no longer cope with the volume of student teachers and had decided to base the Salisbury teacher education programme on the use of normal primary and secondary schools. However, this programme would also require a special relationship with on-campus laboratory schools which would involve:

(i)   Provision of special and corrective classroom experiences for students with revealed teaching deficiency.
(ii) Situational facilities for staff, senior students and the teachers to undertake research particularly into new methods of classroom organization or new classroom techniques.
(iii) Facilities for lecturers in general and specific methods courses to illustrate for students the application of specific procedures and techniques in a classroom and for students to apply these with small groups of children.
(iv) The use of experienced teachers to give occasional lectures in the college courses on education.

There was already an on-campus secondary school but no primary or junior primary. We were close to Salisbury College—would we accept the role? Stone had been a principal throughout the surge of innovations in South Australian schools from the mid-60's and had seen school staffs, increasingly diluted in experience by rapid promotion, study leave, consultant roles and a flood of youthful entrants, try to cope with such increasingly complex situations. It seemed to him that the profession itself must take a heavier responsibility for influencing pre-service training and this was an opportunity to exert such influence.

During 1972 we geared for this role. The lecturer-in-charge of student teaching practice (Ben Hartshorne) was in old friend and colleague. Together we explored a variety of activities such as remedial teaching situations, small group practical sessions after tutorials, videotaping of teaching techniques, some microteaching, lectures by teachers, conducted visits to classrooms, etc. At the end of 1972 it was evident that the most important factor was to recruit staff interested in this work and able to maintain a school programme while working with the college. The Education Department called for volunteers for such work and the response was excellent.

At the beginning of 1973 the whole Madison Park primary staff of twenty-two teachers met with Salisbury personnel at a residential conference to shape the programme for the coming years.

Aims and Principles of Operation

The aims which emerged could be summarized as:

(i) Integration of theory and practice in professional courses.
(ii) Provision of special teaching opportunities, including microteaching, for students.
(iii) Facilitation of college staff involvement in classroom teaching.
(iv) Opportunities for educational research by college staff in conjunction with school staff and sometimes graduate-diploma students.
(v) Opportunities for remedial teaching for students with difficulties.

The Plan and Its Implementation

We deliberately organized our school to promote the above aims. Madison Park School is made up of clusters of buildings both conventional and open plan. We turned each cluster into a mini-school housing about 120 children from Year 3 to Year 7. Each mini-school could operate as a unit within the broad framework of school policy and each was expected to present different examples of teacher co-operation, grouping of children and so on. The result was a rich diversity of climate, organization and techniques available for use by the Salisbury professional courses. We built in flexible staffing arrangements to release special teacher talents, and as a result our expressive arts programme in physical education, music, drama and so on became a feature. We added such innovations as year group curriculum planning sessions, after school recreation teams, a country camp school, etc., until we felt we had a school with a suitable degree of balance, versatility and excellence of performance to carry out the above aims with Salisbury College of Advanced Education.

Specific activities which have occurred during the four-year relationship could be broadly grouped into three main areas:

The first area is where the children are used in small groups or large groups by Salisbury personnel—either students or lecturers. This requires of our teaching staff a flexible organization, patience, the ability to make good the breaks in the learning programme and acceptance of the responsibility to assure parents that this is being done. For example, Drama department students set up drama experiences with small groups of children. This involved all of the drama pupils and twelve of our Year 7 pupils over a period of some weeks. Children's literature students worked through a series of literature workshop experiences with most of our twenty-two classes over a period of weeks. Music students and their lecturers explored various music experiences with groups of our pupils. Mrs J. Folauhola, for example, voluntarily works each Wednesday evening with our instrumental group of violins, violas and cellos.

The second area is where the classroom teacher is directly involved with the student teacher. For example, we usually have about thirty students in the practice teaching blocks. We have students who have had some teaching deficiency revealed in another school come to us over extended periods for extra help and possible remediation.

Our teachers arrange Open Days where a particular subject field is emphasized. Usually 150 students visit on these days and are given check-lists to assist their observation of the displays, lessons and activities prepared by the teachers. These sessions, which are held regularly, are mandatory for the student teachers.

We have classes of our children and teachers resident in the college observation classroom for a week at a time. A closed circuit TV monitor showing activities of a class is positioned in the college foyer which also has displays of the children's work. Students may also observe the continuous classroom activity through the viewing-screen. Lecturers take student groups into the viewing room to observe particular techniques, and remote-control cameras tape lessons which may involve the class teacher or a college lecturer working with the pupils. A library of such tapes is being built-up for future use. The children consider this a real adventure and thoroughly enjoy the novelty of their surroundings, the gymnasium, the art and music rooms and, of course, the college pool. Parents are invited to the viewing room and are invariably fascinated by this uninterrupted study of their children. Of course this puts great pressure on the teacher so we all try to take some lessons during the week to give the classroom teacher a break. In addition to this, our demonstration teachers are always prepared to give the traditional demonstration lesson on request.

During 1975 the microteaching procedures were altered. Each of seventy student teachers attended the school for four sessions of microteaching where on each occasion a fifteen-minute segment of the student's lesson was videotaped and the playback discussed by the co-operating teacher and student. Checklists of the student's performance were sent back to the college for review.

The school holds an annual two-day conference for exit students about to take up appointment. The programme includes practical aspects of establishment relationships, routine and organization, and the general induction of the beginning teacher into the profession. The teachers have developed a 'resource pack for the beginning teacher' for these conferences. This year 150 Salisbury exit teachers attended the conference at the school—those students in fact with whom we have had a close association for the past three years.

The third area is where school personnel are directly involved with college lecturers. Examples of this involvement include

—research projects carried out by teachers and lecturers,
—combined teaching projects where a lecturer has become part of a classroom team, and
—tutorials and lectures in which members of the school staff have participated at the college.

There has been an extensive use of videotaping and other audiovisual material to demonstrate various organizations and techniques, both for use at the college and for illustration at in-service conferences. One such example was the making of a videotape of a reading programme within an open space unit. When the videotape was shown at the college the teachers concerned were present and spoke to the students both at the lecture and tutorial sessions on their reading programme. A full day was required to make this fifteen-minute videotape. Many other such tapes on mathematics, social studies, and so on have been made during the past four years.

Staffing Arrangements

In 1973 a group of teachers volunteered for this work so that in 1972–3 the programme received no salary loadings, fees, etc., from any source. In 1974 the schools was declared a demonstration school and at that time the existing staff plus inward transfers became demonstration assistants. In 1975 demonstration schools were disestablished in South Australia, but while demonstration teachers remained at Madison Park they would retain their $531 per annum loading. Many of these experienced, upward-mobile teachers are being promoted and there is no special policy for attracting replacements for this work. There are no appointments of senior staff or ancillary personnel special to this work. The Salisbury College has not been required to pay any salary, lecture fees, money for videotaping or for any other of the activities mentioned above.

Organization and Administration

The initiation of the programme four years ago was relatively easy because of the friendships of the people most vitally concerned. It has been necessary to ensure that such informal relationships do not result in casual organization. In recent years our deputy principals and the Salisbury lecturer/teacher, Joe Tyney, have been responsible for arranging specific details after formal planning has been conducted early in the year between senior staff and the Salisbury Teaching Studies Department. Whatever we do is subject to teacher discussion at staff meetings.

Buildings and Facilities

There are no special facilities at Madison Park and our classrooms and staff room are shared by all. Perhaps our relationship with the college is enhanced by our often being overcrowded and physically it is impossible not to make contacts. It would be ideal to have a special discussion room to hold about 150 students.

Problems and Effectiveness

The staff enjoy the stimulation of this work, but innovations in their school programme have also attracted large numbers of visitors so that pressures on teachers are great and our days are often too full. Communication and public relations are factors requiring constant attention between such partners as a primary school which is a fairly compact single-purpose institution and a large and complex tertiary institution. We really have very few problems, apart from that of maintaining sufficient experienced staff.

The personal and professional links between Madison Park and Salisbury have created what must be an unusual relationship between a primary school and a college of advanced education. In the 'hurly-burly' of this relationship, the emerging knowledge and feedback we hope will prove of increasing value for the practical training of student teachers at the Salisbury CAE.

Recommendations

The provision of supernumerary staffing either from the department, the college, or both, would add the necessary flexibility, ease pressure on staff, allow a greater use of our resources, and ensure adequate communication.

The original relationship consisted more in the primary school setting up situations in response to the needs of the college. In recent years there has been an equal penetration of the college by the primary school in both resources and influence. We would hope that the future will see a well-planned balance of both types of activity in the interests of future teachers.

Commentary*

The relationship between Salisbury College of Advanced Education and Madison Park Primary School is clearly very different from that existing between the college and other schools. The concept of a laboratory campus school was firmly established when the college was planned, and it is clear that, pending the construction of a campus school, many of the original ideas for the campus school were implemented in the college-Madison Park programme. There is, however, no evidence in the current programme to suggest that the special relationship of the school was intended to be of a temporary nature. When a campus school finally eventuates, it seems probable that the present close association of the college with Madison Park Primary School will be maintained.

Clearly, the choice of school was fortunate in that it had an imaginative and enterprising principal and was close to the college. The recognition by the South Australian Education Department of the school's potential function resulted in a staffing policy which placed the college-primary school enterprise on a sure footing. As detailed in the above statement, the school principal played an active part in consciously shaping the school structure and programme to meet the school's new role.

The close association between the college and the school has been stimulating to lecturers, teachers and the college students who observe or take part in the school programme. The co-operative planning, of which the initial residential conference is an example, has resulted in a joint awareness in college and school staff of a wide range of purposes embracing both institutions. The teachers accept, and indeed welcome, the additional teacher education responsibilities. The college lecturers take particular interest in this school, with some, as in the area of music, contributing to the school programme over and above the needs of their own particular college course.

Indirect benefits accrue from having a competent school staff interested in teacher education and interacting with college lecturers. The Education Department recognizes Madison Park to be a stimulating institution and directs a steady stream of visitors and teachers to the school for observation and discussion purposes. Although the school staff readily acknowledge benefits deriving from their close association with the college, the Madison Park Primary School has a stature independent of the college, as witnessed by the in-service conferences it organizes for teachers in the service and those about to enter teaching. The school values its autonomy and exercises it both in its independent programmes and in its willingness to be outspoken in what it may see as deficiencies in the college programme.

The college students benefit from continuous opportunities for visitation, either in relation to specific courses, or individual projects, or to follow up particular interests. The school staff are well-respected by college students for their professional outlook, keen interest and effectiveness in the classroom. Indeed, some students wonder whether Madison Park is atypical of schools generally, and likely to give them an unrealistic expectation of the school of their first appointment.

With such a comprehensive programme operating at Madison Park the

* In this commentary, for purposes of clarity, the two schools have been treated as one since both have a similar relationship with the college.

teachers have more demands on their time than is usual in other schools. A strong case could be put for supplementary staffing. An aspect which causes the principal some concern is that of finance. As much of the school's energy is devoted to extended programmes involving the college, limited time can be given to fund-raising activities through which many schools derive additional facilities. Although the college makes facilities such as swimming pool, auditorium and equipment available to the school, it may be that means of additional funding should be explored.

As mentioned, teachers, lecturers and student teachers find the relationship between the two institutions stimulating and productive. The pupils accept as normal the observation and participation activities of visitors, whether from overseas, the Education Department, or the college. The pupils appear to be aware of the special role of the school and welcome interaction with student teachers to whom they are generally most supportive. The interest of parents in the college-school relationship is encouraged, an example of which is the visit of parents to the college on occasions when their child's class is having lessons at the college in the observation classroom.

The objectives of the programme are being met to varying degrees. The relationship of theory to practice is clearly illustrated on a continuing basis. The teachers work in close association with the relevant methods lecturers and on occasions participate in lecture sessions at the college and at the school. Remedial programmes for students who have experienced difficulties in teaching practice have generally been effective. The total amount of research that has been undertaken at the laboratory school does not reflect an emphasis on this kind of activity.

The facilitating factors of sound staffing and proximity to the college have been referred to with respect to the co-operative programme. Initial uncertainties regarding the appropriate roles of the college and the school were dispelled during the first year of the association, assisted by informal discussion and joint conferences. Problems which remain are those of the need for additional staffing and the lack of sufficient accommodation for school-based lectures and discussions with college students.

As seems to be the case in all college-school programmes, there is need for the maintenance of continuous communication. This is closely related to the staffing situation both at the school and the college. The college has a lecturer appointed as a 'lecturer teacher' whose special function is to facilitate the co-operative programme. Although recognizing the problems of the availability of time, it would seem likely to be beneficial if more college staff were to avail themselves of the opportunities to establish a link with the school on 'open mornings' and other occasions.

The Salisbury CAE-Madison Park Primary School relationship has several features which may well be worth consideration by other institutions intending to enter into a co-operative programme. Probably that which comes through most forcefully in this study is that of the selection of school staff who are predisposed towards an enriched teacher role that includes teacher education. Such a policy engenders a confidence and respect within the college for the co-operating school as an effective institution in its own right. As a result, the school does not become regarded as the lesser partner. The consultation with school representatives in the formulation of college courses and the seeking of continuous feedback from the teachers of the school helps to ensure that the school is regarded as, and recognizes itself to be, a valued participant in the programme.

As was suggested earlier, the matter of financial commitment of one institution to the other is a matter for early consideration. At the time that the Madison Park-college programme was initiated both institutions were within the South Australian Education Department. Where the institutions are financed by different funding bodies, a more formal agreement regarding finance would seem appropriate.

The extensive and varied nature of the programme would suggest that the college will need to develop a close relationship with one or two other co-operating schools if Madison Park is not more generously staffed in the future. It would be unlikely that the college would seek to duplicate the present function of Madison Park, but may consider the advantages of focusing upon certain subject areas, for example, the creative arts, in other schools. In considering this possibility the college should be mindful that if a relationship of such quality as that held with Madison Park is to be established it will require sustained communication and a willingness and ability to contribute to the school programme.

[J. D.]

5   CONCLUSION

This conclusion is intentionally brief. The diversity of ideas and practices mentioned in previous chapters are the essence of this book. Many of the ideas and practices are new and challenging and, it is hoped, have already spoken for themselves. In this concluding statement we wish to provide summarized answers to a limited number of key questions chosen from the many asked when we visited teacher education institutions either to conduct the survey or to carry out case studies. These questions seem an appropriate means of pulling together the main threads of the book. As far as possible the answers given are based on our investigations, but, as will be seen, they also draw upon our personal experience and predispositions. Most of the answers relate directly to the Australian educational context.

Do Australian teacher education programmes have a discernible policy on educational innovation?

While there is a great deal of minor, isolated and sometimes superficial innovatory activity going on in Australian teacher education programmes, the overall impression is that institutions have given no real thought and formed no strong commitment to questions of educational change. Some programmes give lip-service in their statements of objectives to such ideas as exemplifying innovative approaches and producing innovative teachers, but there is little concerted attempt to follow such ideas through.

As pointed out in the introduction to this volume, teacher education has a vital part to play in both reflecting and stimulating change. On the one hand it must change in response to changes in the nature and purposes of schooling and, on the other hand, it must promote the continuing development of the school system. Teacher education can promote changes in schools in two main ways: (i) through the new ideas and approaches it introduces to prospective teachers; and (ii) through the attitudes towards, understandings of, and skills in the *process* of innovation developed in students by experience in innovative schools and in an innovative training programme.

But teacher education must be committed to change for another fundamental reason. Teacher educators must be constantly seeking new ways of improving their own teaching and the learning of their students. Unfortunately, however, relatively few teacher educators seem to be examining either the short- or long-term effects of their work on students and, in the light of this, to be systematically introducing improved ways of teaching and learning. Some worthwhile changes have been made, but many have been piecemeal or limited in their application.

If, as some authorities suggest, 'teacher education must be rooted in a commitment to educational change' (Joyce and Weil, 1972, p. 6), then Australian programmes will need to engage in serious deliberation concerning much of their present purposes and processes and to undertake quite substantial reforms.

408

Currently what are the main innovative concerns in teacher education overseas and in Australia?

The main lines of innovation within teacher education programmes of western countries are strikingly similar. Programme structures are being modified to achieve greater integration between theoretical and practical components and between specific courses. More co-ordination between programmes of teacher education is enabling students destined to teach in various levels of schooling to undertake at least part of their preparation together. Students are being provided with wider choice between elective courses and even alternative programmes according to their needs and interests. Much greater importance is being attached to providing practical experiences on-campus, in schools and in the community in connection with all professional course components. Associated with this and the need to integrate theory and practice, programmes are forming new and closer relationships with schools. Largely to make programmes more relevant to the needs of teachers, schools and society new courses have been introduced. Foremost among these are courses on human relations, remedial and special education, urban education, ethnic and minority groups, media and communication, and open education. Much attention is being given, especially in education courses, to analyzing the work of the teacher into teaching competencies and to making these the focus of the programme.

Methodological changes are being adopted both to improve student learning and to exemplify the nature of the teaching being advocated for use in schools. Methods stress greater involvement of students and their personal and interpersonal development. Generally, much more emphasis is being given to small group discussion and inquiry, individualized learning and independent study. Team teaching of course units by staff from the same or adjacent disciplines is common. Also being introduced is the teaming of students, teachers and/or tertiary staff in school or campus contexts. The particular techniques of simulation and microteaching are quickly becoming accepted procedures. Educational materials and technology of various kinds are having a strong impact and elaborate resources centres are being established to facilitate their use. Assessment procedures are changing. More use is being made of continuous assessment employing a variety of techniques. The provision of feedback to students on their progress towards specified goals is becoming a feature. Follow-up work often grows out of assessment. Importance is being attached to student self-assessment and, to a limited extent, to peer appraisal. Many programmes are endeavouring to make assessment procedures as non-threatening and non-competitive as possible.

What important aspects of Australian teacher education seem to merit a greater amount of innovatory activity?

Although innovations in Australian teacher education seem to touch upon all those areas regarded by authorities as important lines of development, there are a number of quite fundamental areas is need of much further exploration. Foremost among these are: (i) the analysis of the projected roles of the teacher into basic skills and understandings and the development of courses, techniques and materials to promote their acquisition by students; (ii) the development of programmes which recognize the individual personal and professional needs and interests of students, and which use course structures and methodologies to facilitate student learning; (iii) the exemplification in teacher education of the teaching and learning strategies and technologies being advocated for use in the schools; (iv) the purposeful integration of educational theory and research with various practical experiences on- and off-campus; (v) the imaginative exploration of relationships with schools for the mutual benefit of all concerned—students, teachers, lecturers and pupils; (vi) the examination of the most appropriate ways of facilitating the students' smooth transition to full teaching responsibility and of providing them, as teachers, with motivation and opportunity to continue and deepen their professional education; and (vii) more generally, the penetrating consideration of the short- and long-term goals of teacher education in terms of continuity and change in education and society, and the design of complete model programmes to serve these goals.

What are the main benefits to be derived from the new co-operating relationships teacher education programmes are forming with schools?

Teacher education may derive a number of important advantages from the formation of close co-operating relationships with schools. Some of the most significant of these advantages seem to be—(i) Special co-operating schools can provide a setting where students can observe and participate in innovative approaches to education—a setting where new ideas are generated and tested. As far as possible the school's curriculum should reflect the ideas advocated in the teacher education programme so that students might gain practical experience with these ideas under the supervision of effective teachers sharing the same frame of reference as that held by the teacher educators. (ii) Under co-operating school arrangements school and teacher education staff might collaborate in pertinent research and development on teaching and curriculum, in co-operative and reciprocal teaching within the school and teacher education programme, in jointly conducting in-service courses, in planning and evaluating the school and teacher education programmes, in sharing of ideas on varied educational issues, and in disseminating to other institutions the results of the co-operative effort.

Schools can offer much to teacher education, and teacher education can offer much to schools. By entering into a genuine partnership under which ideas, staff expertise and material resources are mutually shared, teachers, lecturers, students and school pupils might all profit greatly.

What factors appear basic to the development of new co-operating relationships with schools?

The development of close and productive relationships between teacher education institutions and schools requires much care and effort. Experience overseas with laboratory and portal schools has indicated that the following factors seem to be basic to such relationships. Initially, the objectives of the college-school co-operation should be collaboratively formulated and communicated to all concerned, including parents and educational authorities. The respective role expectations of college and school staff should be made explicit. Once objectives have been agreed upon, a flexible off-campus programme should be progressively developed, evaluated and refined. Teachers and lecturers must both be involved in this process. Similarly teachers might participate in the design and appraisal of on-campus courses. Ideally, too, both on- and off-campus programmes might be reciprocally and co-operatively staffed by school and college personnel. It is vital that the staff of the respective institutions respect and value the contribution which each can make to teacher education and to schooling.

The operation of the off-campus programme must be carefully monitored to ensure that demands on the school are not excessive and that the children's learning is not adversely effected. Formal and informal channels of communication between staff must be abundant. Resources of college and school should be shared for the benefit of all. While co-operation and sharing will be the keynote of the operation, the autonomy of each institution must be carefully preserved.

Several other conditions related to the co-operating school itself should optimize such relations. The school should be as physically close to college as possible. School staff should be specially selected for the quality of their ideas, their competence and for their interest in teacher education. If possible, the college should play a part in their selection. The pupil population should not be atypical of the general run of schools. Finally, it is essential that the co-operative programme be appropriately funded to cover staff allowances and the provision of necessary materials and facilities.

What are the main weaknesses of innovation strategies being followed by Australian teacher educators?

The main weaknesses in strategies of innovation seem to lie within the processes of initiating ideas, planning, evaluating and disseminating.

From the outset programme leaders need to create a context which encourages staff at all levels to initiate ideas on educational improvement. Ideas for change need to be sought and valued, not just imposed or promoted by senior staff. Once an idea has been accepted as worth pursuing, an attempt should be made to involve in planning its implementation as many representatives of those people to be directly affected by the plan as is feasible. Planning demands careful deliberation and this requires time, which too often is not made flexibly available to planners. Unfortunately, too, much planning is narrowly conceived and pursued in isolation from related aspects of a teacher education programme. During planning, objectives need to be carefully and comprehensively specified and thought given to the articulation of the plans with the other components of the programme. Opposition to many innovations has been experienced because of inadequate communication. As plans evolve and are implemented, a concerted attempt must be made to inform all staff and interested parties outside the programme (e.g. co-operating teachers and the Education Department) about what is envisaged or operating. Financial constraints are, of course, relevant in any planning; yet it does seem in the Australian context that much planning is too much restricted in its boldness by monetary considerations. Clearly research and development funds outside and within institutions need to be substantially increased.

Evaluation is the most neglected and poorly handled aspect of innovatory activity. Many teacher educators seem suspicious of, even threatened by the idea of evaluation, and/or uninformed on its procedures. Some seem to think of evaluation only in terms of 'before and after' research design. Few seem to realize that evaluation can be most profitably used as the innovation is being implemented to guide its formative improvement. Very few teacher educators seem acquainted with recent literature on the functions and varied techniques of evaluation as they relate to educational innovation (e.g. Parlett and Hamilton, 1972).

The dissemination of information about innovation in teacher education both in Australia and overseas is also inadequate. Often information on what is taking place in an innovation does not go beyond the personnel directly involved in the activity. Other people in the parent institution, let alone those in other institutions, seldom hear about what has been achieved. Considerable thought needs to be given to the improvement of both formal and informal channels of communication within and between institutions.

What steps might be taken to promote worthwhile innovative improvements in Australian teacher education programmes?

There is no simple answer to this question. But one point is clear. If the quality of teacher education is of pivotal importance in an educational system, then steps undertaken to ensure its continuous improvement must be regarded as top priority. Among the measures that might be adopted to promote the improvement of Australian teacher education programmes, the following seem the most promising.

Probably the first step is for teacher education institutions to develop policies for the progressive evaluation and renovation of their work in terms of existing and changed objectives. Such policies might apply to all aspects of the teacher education process—organization and administration, course content and methodology, and so on. Policies of review and revision must, of course, maintain a reasonable balance between continuity and change to avoid unsettling discontinuities and even confusion. It is, however, one thing to devise a policy and another thing to create the conditions to make it effective. Staff will need encouragement to innovate. At the local level this means, among other things, time for staff to participate as fully as possible in innovatory activity and money and resources to support the activity and publish its results.

One way that teacher education institutions might organizationally display a commitment to educational change is by the establishment on campus of small centres for research and development and the improvement of teaching and learning. In these centres teacher educators might jointly pursue projects directly related to the improvement of a programme; consult with experts on innovation design, management and evaluation; and undergo training related to new approaches to teacher education and strategies for their implementation.

Too many innovative Australian teacher educators have been working in isolation. There is a strong need for greatly increased professional interchange between staff at all levels both within and between institutions. This could be achieved through such measures as the exchange of printed materials on new developments, brief and prolonged visitations, reciprocal staffing arrangements, cross-institution projects on common problems involving staff collaboration, and the organization of regional workshops and conferences on particular aspects of change in teacher education. Similar conferences and workshops might be also held at state or national level. Beyond this there is need for a central clearing house to collate and disseminate information bi-annually or annually on innovation in progress and completed both in Australia and overseas.

The education of teacher educators has been seen by many as a critical issue in the improvement of teacher education (Bush, 1968). There is a need in Australia for universities to develop a greater variety of post-graduate courses more directly related to the professional activities of teacher educators. Such courses should provide opportunity for the penetrating study of (i) the research and theory, content and processes related to advances in teacher education overseas and in Australia; (ii) the role of teacher education in reflecting and promoting change in school and society; and (iii) the strategies for initiating, managing and evaluating innovation in teacher education. The courses might also involve teacher educators in the pursuit of research and development projects related to their professional interests and the innovative needs of their particular institutions. Similar courses for both beginning lecturers and co-operating teachers might be offered by the colleges of advanced education themselves. Some might lead to a post-graduate degree or diploma while others might be little more than informal, non-award in-house workshops.

Finally, it is evident that existing grants for research and development in Australian teacher education are insufficient. Many teacher educators are keen to innovate but financial constraints seriously discourage them. If increased funds are made available however, they should go hand in hand with staff training programmes and/or consultancy services to ensure that the teacher educators make the most of their innovatory activity. While there is a strong need to support specific, sharply focused intra-institution projects, there is equally a need to encourage, perhaps through commissioning, inter-institution teams to work on broader problems of common interest.

Teacher education has made great strides over the past decade or so. Today there is wide interest in its improvement. Its prospects are bright, but much will depend on the concern of governments and the initiative of teacher educators. One can only hope for government concern which will foster such initiative and for initiative which will foster concern.

REFERENCES

Introduction

Centre for Educational Research and Innovation (CERI), *Case Studies in Educational Innovation: IV. Strategies for Innovation in Education*, OECD, Paris 1973.

Cohen, S. W. *et al.*, *Teacher Education, 1973–1975*, Report of the Special Committee on Teacher Education, Australian Commission on Advanced Education, Canberra 1973.

Ryan, K. (ed.), *Teacher Education*, The Seventy-fourth Yearbook of the National Society for the Study of Education, University of Chicago Press, 1975.

Chapter 1

MINOR INNOVATORY TRENDS

Asian Institute for Teacher Educators, *Basic Experiences—Direct and Indirect—for Integrating Theory and Practice in Teacher Education*, University of the Philippines, 1972.

Asian Institute for Teacher Educators, *Integration and Modernization of Teacher Education Curriculum*, University of the Philippines, 1972.

Atkin, J. M. and J. J. Raths, 'Changing Patterns of Teacher Education' in *New Patterns of Teacher Education and Tasks*: Country Experience—United States, OECD, Paris 1974.

Bentley, R., *New Directions in Teacher Education in Canada: Alternative Programme at the University of British Columbia*, Paper presented to the SPATE Conference, Brisbane July 1976.

Buck, B. A. *et al.*, *Interdisciplinary Teacher Education in Early Childhood*, Mankato State College, 1973.

Clark, R. J. and D. J. Kingsbury, 'Simultaneous Alternative Teacher Preparation Programs', *Phi Delta Kappan*, March 1973, 477–80.

Eggleston, S. J., 'United Kingdom: Innovative Trends to Teacher Training and Retraining' in *New Patterns of Teacher Education and Tasks*: Country Experience—Belgium, France, United Kingdom, OECD, Paris 1974.

Marklund, S. and B. Gran, 'Research and Innovation in Teacher Education' in *New Patterns of Teacher Education and Tasks*: Country Experience—Sweden, OECD, Paris 1974.

Renshaw, P., 'The Objectives and Structure of the College Curriculum' in Tibble, J. W. (ed.), *The Future of Teacher Education*, Routledge and Kegan Paul, London 1971.

Renshaw, P., 'A Flexible Curriculum for Teacher Education' in Lomax, D. E. (ed.), *The Education of Teachers in Britain*, Wiley, London 1973.

Report of the Minister's Committee on the Training of Elementary School Teachers, Ontario Department of Education, 1966.

Smith, B. O. *et al.*, *Teachers for the Real World*, American Association of Colleges for Teacher Education, 1969.

Warwick, D. (ed.), *New Directions in the Professional Training of Teachers*, University of Lancaster, 1974.

Wilkit 1, *The Four Cons of Teaching*, 1974.

COMPETENCY-BASED TEACHER EDUCATION

Atkin, J. M. and J. J. Raths, 'Changing Patterns of Teacher Education' in *New Patterns of Teacher Education and Tasks:* Country Experience—United States, OECD, Paris 1974.

Broudy, H. S., *A Critique of Performance-based Teacher Education*, American Association of Colleges for Teacher Education, 1972.

Conant, J. B., *The Education of American Teachers*, McGraw-Hill, New York 1963.

Cooper, J. M., W. A. Weber and C. E. Johnson, *A Systems Approach to Program Design*, McCutchan, Berkeley 1973.

Dodl, N. R., *The Florida Catalog of Teacher Competencies*, Florida Department of Education, 1973.

Elam, S., *Performance-based Teacher Education: What is the State of the Art?* American Association of Colleges for Teacher Education, 1971.

Gage, N. L. and P. H. Winne, 'Performance-based Teacher Education' in Ryan, K. (ed.), *Teacher Education*, The Seventy-fourth Yearbook of the National Society for the Study of Education, University of Chicago Press, 1975.

Heath, R. W. and M. A. Nielson, *The Myth of Performance-based Teacher Education*, Paper presented at the Annual Meeting of the American Educational Research Association, New Orleans 1973.

Holt, J., *How Children Fail*, Pitman, New York 1964.

Houston, W. R., *Strategies and Resources for Developing a Competency-based Teacher Education Program*, New York State Education Department, 1972.

Houston, W. R., *Resources for Performance-based Education*, University of the State of New York, 1973a.

Houston, W. R., *Resources for Competency-based Education: Supplement A*, University of the State of New York, 1973b.

Houston, W. R. and R. B. Howsam, *Competency-based Teacher Education—Progress, Problems and Prospects*, Science Research Associates, 1972.

Howsam, R. B., 'Performance-based Instruction', *Today's Education*, April 1972, 61, 33–40.

Koerner, J. D., *The Miseducation of American Teachers*, Penguin Books, Baltimore 1963.

Kohl, H., *36 Children*, New American Library, 1967.

Rosner, B. and P. Kay, 'Will the Promise of C/PBTE be Fulfilled?' *Phi Delta Kappan*, January 1974, 290–5.

Rosner, B. *et al.*, *The Power of Competency-based Teacher Education*, Allyn and Bacon, Boston 1972.

Ryan, K. (ed.), *Teacher Education*, The Seventy-fourth Yearbook of the National Society for the Study of Education, University of Chicago Press, 1975.

Schmieder, A. A., *Competency-based Teacher Education: The State of the Scene*, American Association of Colleges for Teacher Education, 1973.

Turner, R. L. (ed.), *A General Catalog of Teaching Skills*, Multi-State Consortium on Performance-based Teacher Education, 1973.

Wilson, A. P. and W. W. Curtis, 'The States Mandate Performance-based Teacher Education', *Phi Delta Kappan*, October 1973, 76–7.

HUMANISTIC TEACHER EDUCATION

Battaglini, D., M. Pirkl and O. Horner, 'Developing a Humanistic Competency-based Curriculum for Pre-Service Elementary Science Teachers—Two Years Experience', *Science Education*, 1975, 59 (3), 357–72.

Blume, R. A., 'Humanizing Teacher Education', *Phi Delta Kappan*, March 1971, 52, 411–15.

Bown, O. and H. G. Richek, 'Teachers-to-be: Extroversion/Introversion Self-perceptions', *Elementary School Journal*, 1969, 70 (3), 164–70.

Buchanan, M. M., 'Preparing Teachers to be Persons', *Phi Delta Kappan*, 1971, 52 (10), 614–17.

Busby, W. A., D. Avila, R. Blume, A. W. Combs, and L. Oberlin, *An Experiment in Teacher Education Utilizing the "Self-as-Instrument" Concept*, Manuscript, University of Florida, Gainesville 1970.

Cohen, S. and R. Hersh, 'Behaviourism and Humanism: A Synthesis for Teacher Education', *Journal of Teacher Education*, 1972, 23 (2), 172–6.

Combs, A. W., 'The Personal Approach to Good Teaching', *Educational Leadership*, 1964, 21, 369–77, 399.

Combs, A. W., *The Professional Education of Teachers: A Perceptual View of Teacher Preparation*, Allyn and Bacon, Boston 1965.

Combs, A. W. and D. W. Soper, 'The Helping Relationship as Described by "Good" and "Poor" Teachers', *Journal of Teacher Education*, 1963, 14, 64–7.

Combs, A. W. *et al.*, *Florida Studies in the Helping Professions*, University of Florida Social Science Monograph No. 37, University of Florida Press, Gainesville 1969.

Combs, A. W., D. L. Avila and W. W. Purkey, *Helping Relationships: Basic Concepts for the Helping Professions*, Allyn and Bacon, Boston 1971.

Dinkmeyer, D., 'The C-Group: Focus on Self as Instrument', *Phi Delta Kappan*, 1971, 52 (10), 617–19.

Durcharme, E. R. and R. J. Nash, 'Humanizing Teacher Education for the Last Quarter of the Twentieth Century', *Journal of Teacher Education*, 1975, 26 (3), 222–8.

Fuller, F. F., 'A Conceptual Framework for a Personalized Teacher Education Program', *Theory into Practice*, 1974, 13 (2), 112–22.

Halamandaris, P. C. and A. J. Loughton, 'Empathy-competence: A Search for New Direction in Canadian Teacher Education', *Educational Technology*, 1972, 12 (11), 20–2.

Iannone, R. V. and J. L. Carline, 'A Humanistic Approach to Teacher Education', *Journal of Teacher Education*, 1971, 22 (4), 429–33.

Lickona, T., in 'Excellence in Teacher Education', *Today's Education*, September-October 1973, 90–1.

Loper, H. and A. W. Combs, 'The Helping Relationship as seen by Teachers and Therapists', *Journal of Consulting Psychology*, 1962, 26, 288.

Menges, R. J. and W. C. McGaghie, 'Personalized Instruction in Educational Psychology', *Development and Experiment in College Teaching*, Report No. 10, C.I.C. Panel on Research and Development of Instructional Resources, 1974.

Patterson, C. H., *Humanistic Education*, Prentice-Hall, Englewood Cliffs, N. J. 1973.

Petersen, V., R. Calvin and J. Yutzy, 'Human Relations Training, Contracting and Field Experiences: An Integrative Approach to Teaching Educational Foundations', *Peabody Journal of Education*, July 1975, 52, 267–72.

Rogers, C. R., 'Significant Learning in Therapy and in Education', *Educational Leadership*, 1959, 16, 232–42.

Rogers, C. R., 'The Characteristics of a Helping Relationship', *Harvard Educational Review*, 1962, 32, 416–30.

Taylor, B. L., P. A. Doyle and J. A. Link, 'A More Humane Teacher Education', *Educational Leadership*, 1971, 28, 668–70.

Usher, R. H., *The Relationship of Perceptions of Self, Others and the Helping Task to Certain Measures of College Faculty Effectiveness*, unpublished doctoral dissertation, University of Florida, 1966.

Wass, H. and A. W. Combs, *A Follow-up Study of On-the-Job Behaviour of Elementary Teachers Trained in an Innovative and a Traditional Program of Teacher Preparation*, Final Report, U.S. Department of Health, Education and Welfare, Project No. 2-D-028, Office of Education Region 4, February 1973.

Wass, H., R. A. Blume, A. W. Combs and W. D. Hedges, *Humanistic Teacher Education: An Experiment in Systematic Curriculum Innovation*, Shields, Fort Collins 1974.

RENOVATION OF PRACTICE TEACHING

Abrell, R. L., 'The Humanistic Supervision Enhances Growth and Improves Instruction', *Educational Leadership*, 1974, 32 (3), 212–16.

Andrews, L. O., 'Trends and Issues in Student Teaching in the Secondary School', *High School Journal*, 1967, 50 (6), 309–15.

Asian Institute for Teacher Education, *Basic Experiences—Direct and Indirect—for Integrating Theory and Practice in Teacher Education*, Final Report of Third Sub-Regional Workshop on Teacher Education, Kabul 1972. Unesco sponsored, University of Philippines, Quezon 1972.

Aubertine, H. E., 'Use of Micro-teaching in Training Supervising Teachers', *High School Journal*, 1967, 51, 99–106.

Barnett, D. C., 'The Emergence of New Concepts for Teacher Education Field Experience', *Interchange*, 1975, 6 (1), 44–8.

Barnett, D. C. and M. Aldous, 'Ten Principles Underlying a Teacher Education Program for Native People', *The Northian*, 1973, 9 (3), 36–8.

Beckett, J. W., 'The Role of Supervising Teacher in Secondary Education', unpublished doctoral dissertation, Cornell University, 1968, *Dissertation Abstracts*, 1969, 29, 43–5.

Belt, W. D., *Microteaching Observed and Critiqued by a Group of Trainees*, Paper presented at Annual Meeting of the American Educational Research Association, 1967.

Blomgren, G. and E. M. Juergenson, 'Work Experience for Teachers', *The Agricultural Education Magazine*, 1972, 45 (4), 84–5.

Bloom, J. M. and R. C. Senger, 'Exploring an Autotelic Approach to Preparing Supervisors', *Contemporary Education*, 1971, 43, 272–5.

Blumberg, A. and P. Cusick, 'Supervisor-Teacher Interaction: An Analysis of Verbal Behaviour', *Education*, 1970, 91 (2), 126–34.

Blume, R. A., 'Humanizing Teacher Education', *Phi Delta Kappan*, 1971, 52, 411–15.

Board of Teacher Education, N.S.W., Statement on the Practical Experience Component of Teacher Education Courses, April 1976.

Borg, W. R., 'Moving Towards a Breakthrough in Teacher Education', *Education*, 1975, 95 (4), 302–23.

Britts, M., 'Symposium on Student Teaching', *Instructor*, August 1969, 106–7.

Browning, R. W., *A Study of Job Satisfactions and Dissatisfactions of Co-operating Teachers in the Secondary Schools of Topeka*, unpublished doctoral dissertation, University of Kansas, 1968.

Burge, E. W., *The Relationship of Certain Personality Attributes to the Verbal Behaviour of Selected Students in the Secondary School Classroom*, unpublished doctoral dissertation, North Texas State University, Ann Arbor, Michigan, University Microfilms, 1967, No. 67–8079.

Buttery, T. J. and D. A. Michalak, 'The Teaching Clinic: A Peer Supervision Process', *Education*, 1975, 95 (3), 263–9.

Caspari, I. E. and S. J. Eggleston, 'A New Approach to Supervision of Teaching Practice', *Education for Teaching*, 1965, 68.

Chambers, G., 'Relating Theory to Practice in Student Teaching', *Peabody Journal of Education*, 1969, 47, 137–40.

Clark, J. M. 'Supervision of Teaching Practice', *Education for Teaching*, 1967, 70.

Clothier, G. and E. Kingsley, *Enriching Student Teaching Relationships*, Midwest Educational Training and Research Organization, Shawnee Mission, Kansas 1973.

Cope, E., *School Experience in Teacher Education*, University of Bristol, 1971.

Copeland, W. D., *The Effect of Laboratory Training in Specific Teaching Skills on the Classroom Performance of Student Teachers*, unpublished doctoral dissertation, Notre Dame, Indiana 1973.

Cooper, J. O., *The Congruence of Theoretical Orientation and Behaviour in the Individual Supervising Conference*, unpublished doctoral dissertation, Cornell University, 1964.

Cornett, J. D., *A Survey of Research Relative to Supervision of Student Teachers at the Secondary Level*, unpublished doctoral dissertation, University of Arkansas, 1966.

Coulter, F., *Perceptions of Classroom Behaviour by Supervisors and Student Teachers*, Paper presented at the National Conference on Teacher Education on the Practicum, Mt Lawley, Perth 1975.

Cruickshank, D. R., *Teaching Problems Laboratory*, Science Research Associates, Chicago 1967.

Cullinan, T., *Interlude Programs in U.S. Undergraduate Education*, Report 1, Interlude Research Program, Menlo Park, California 1969.

Dean's Committee on a Native Teacher Training Program *A Proposal for a Native Indian Teacher Education Program*, Report, University of British Columbia, 1974.

Deines, J., 'The Winnipeg Center Project: Teacher Education for Inner-city People', *Interchange*, 1973, 4, 106–10.

Deiseach, D., 'Some Custom-tailoring Needed', *Education Canada*, June 1974, 4–9.

De Long, G., "Towards More Meaningful Teacher Preparation', *Journal of Teacher Education*, 1971, 22 (1), 15–17.

Dembo, M. H. and N. Hickerson, 'An Integrated Approach to Foundation Courses in Teacher Education', *Education*, 1971, 92 (1), 96–100.

Detwiler, T. P., 'Student Teaching. Is Dismal the Right Word?', *Today's Education*, 1971, 60 (4), 70.

Du Vall, C. R. and J. A. Yutzey, 'A Program to Train Skilled Supervisors of Student Teachers', *Supervisors Quarterly*, 1971, 6, 24–7.

Eaker, R. E., 'A Clinical Approach to Classroom Observation: An American View', *Trends in Education*, July 1974, 43–5.

Eberly, D. J., *An Agenda for Off-Campus Learning Experiences*, Report No. 2, Interlude Research Program, Menlo Park, California 1969.

Eggleston, S. J., 'Innovative Trends to Teacher Training and Retraining', *New Patterns of Teacher Education and Tasks:* Country Experience—Belgium, France, United Kingdom, OECD, Paris 1974.

Ehman, L., *A Comparison of Three Sources of Classroom Data: Teachers, Students and Systematic Observations*, Paper presented at the American Educational Research Association Conference, 1970.

Elliott, R. J., *Changes in Openness of Student Teachers as a Function of Openness of Supervising and Co-operating Teachers*, unpublished doctoral dissertation, University of Alabama, 1964.

Emmer, E. T., *Classroom Observation Scales: A Manual*, Research and Development Centre for Teacher Education, University of Taxas, Austin 1970.

Engel, B., 'Teachers in Training Take a Turn as Aides', *Education Canada*, 1975, 15 (2), 22–5.

Erickson, J. E., 'On the Development of School Supervisory Personnel: A Case in Point', *Journal of Teacher Education*, 1969, 20, 66–9.

Esposito, J. P., G. E. Smith and H. J. Brubach, 'A Delineation of the Supervisory Role', *Education*, 1975, 96 (1), 63–7.

Evans, A., 'College and School Relationships' in Hewitt, S. (ed.), *The Training of Teachers: A Factual Survey*, University of London Press, 1971.

Evans, L. M., 'Towards Field-Centred Teacher Education: Trends in the U.S.A.', *Education for Teaching*, 1975, 96, 43–50.

Ezer, M. and R. Lambert, 'Residency in Supervision: A Unique Role for Laboratory Schools', *Peabody Journal of Education*, 1966, 44, 155–9.

Garner, A. E., 'The Co-operating Teacher and Human Relations', *Education*, 1971, 92 (2), 99–106.

Gewinner, M. N., *A Study of the Results of the Interaction of Student Teachers with their Supervising Teachers During the Student Teaching Period*, unpublished doctoral dissertation, Mississippi State University, 1968.

Goldhammer, R., *Clinical Supervision*, Holt, Rinehart and Winston, New York 1969.

Goodkind, T. B., *An Evaluation of the Effectiveness of the Micro-Teaching Technique in the Training of Elementary School Teachers*, Paper presented at Annual Meeting of the American Educational Research Association, 1968.

Griffiths, A. and A. H. Moore, 'Schools and Teaching Practice', *Education for Teaching*, 1967, 74, 33–9.

Hale, J. R. and R. A. Spanjer, *Systematic and Objective Analysis of Instruction*, Commercial-Educational Instruction Services, Portland, Oregon 1972.

Harp, M. W., 'Early Field Experiences—A Maturing Force', *Elementary School Journal*, 1974, 74 (6), 367–74.

Harwood, F. and H. B. Miller, 'The Intern Teaching Program in the Urban School: Impact on Instructional Improvement', *Journal of Teacher Education*, 1972, 23 (4), 427–30.

Hilsinger, R. and B. Schantz, *Reallocating Teacher Education Resources in the Temple-Philadelphia Portal Schools*, College of Education, Temple University, roneo, 1973.

H.M.S.O., *Plowden Report: Children and Their Teachers, The Training of Primary School Teachers*, 1967.

Hilliard, P. and C. L. Durrance, 'Guiding Student Teaching Experiences', *Association for Student Teaching Bulletin*, 1968, 1, 10–11.

Hogle, H. I., 'Teacher Education and Experimental Learning', *Viewpoints*, 1974, 50 (5), 23–48.

Howsam, R. B. and W. R. Houston, *Competency-based Teacher Education—Progress, Problems and Prospects*, Science Research Associates, Chicago 1974.

Hoy, W., 'The Influence of Experience on the Beginning Teacher', *School Review*, 1968, 76, 312–23.

Huber, J. and B. Ward, 'Pre-service Confidence Through Microteaching', *Education*, 1969, 90, 65–8.

Hussell, I. and A. Smithers, 'Changes in the Educational Opinions of Student Teachers Associated with College Experience and School Practice', *Research in Education*, 1974, 11.

Iannaccone, L., 'Student Teaching: A Transitional Stage in the Making of a Teacher', *Theory into Practice*, 1963, 2, 73–80.

Ishler, R. E., 'An Experimental Study Using Withall's Social-EmotionalClimate Index to Determine the Effectiveness of Feedback as a Means of Changing Student Teachers' Verbal Behaviour', *The Journal of Educational Research*, 1967, 61, 121–3.

Jacobs, E. B., *Personal and Instructional Variables as Related to Changes in Educational Attitudes of Prospective Elementary School Teachers During Two Phases of the Teachers Education Program*, unpublished doctoral dissertation, Northern Illinois University, 1967.

Johnson, E. G., 'Improving the Student Teaching Experience', *Improving College and University Teaching*, 1970, 18, 167.

Jordan, A. C., 'Improving Student Teacher Evaluation', *Peabody Journal of Education*, 1967, 45, 139–42.

Julian, C. M., *Effect of Pre-student Teaching Laboratory Experiences on Attitudes of Prospective Elementary Teachers*, East Texas State University, 1973.

Kahn, P., 'The Student Teacher Also Serves', *Peabody Journal of Education*, 1971, 48, 177–9.

Keach, E. T., *Elementary School Student Teaching: A Casebook*, John Wiley and Sons, New York 1966.

Kersh, B. Y., *Classroom Simulation: Further Studies on Dimension of Realism*, Final Report, Oregon, State System of Higher Education, 1965.

Knight, D. and J. Wayne, 'The School and the University: Co-operative Roles in Student Teaching', *Elementary School Journal*, 1970, 70 (6), 317–20.

Knowlson, H., 'The School-based Tutor', *Trends in Education*, 1973, 31, 3–9.

Koontz, D. E. and K. H. Maddox, 'Student Teaching at Job Corps Centres: Fostering Alternatives in Teacher Education', *Journal of Teacher Education*, 1972, 23 (4), 431–4.

Languis, M. L., 'Elementary School Science—Mathematics Teaching Laboratory', *Development and Experiment in College Teaching*, CIC Panel on Research and Development of Instructional Resources, Report No. 4, Spring 1968.

Lantz, D. L., 'The Relationship of University Supervisors' and Supervising Teachers' Ratings to Observed Student Teachers' Behaviour', *American Educational Research Journal*, 1967, 4, 279–88.

Lee, J. D., 'The Practical Training of Teachers: A Survey of Techniques', *West African Journal of Education*, 1973, 17 (2), 195–206.

Lett, W. R., *Some Difficulties in Role Adoption for the Beginning Teacher*, Paper presented at the ANZAAS Conference, Port Moresby 1970.

Lewis, I., 'The Reform of Teaching Practice', in Warwick, D. (ed.), *New Directions in the Professional Training of Teachers*, University of Lancaster, 1974.

Lewis, I., 'Teacher Training: Professional or Peripheral?', *Education for Teaching*, 1975, 96, 35–42.

Logan, D., 'The Student Teacher' in Calthrop, K. and G. Owens (eds), *Teachers for Tomorrow. Diverse and Radical Views About Teacher Education*, Heinemann, London 1971.

Lomax, D. (ed.), *The Education of Teachers in Britain*, John Wiley and Sons, London 1973.

Lowther, M. A., 'Most and Least Helpful Activities of Supervising Teachers', *Clearing House*, 1968, 43, 40–3.

McDonald, M. B., *An Analysis of Secondary Student Teachers' Effectiveness as Perceived by Self, Pupils and Supervising Teachers*, unpublished doctoral dissertation, Western Michigan University, 1971. Abstract, *Dissertation Abstracts International*, 1971, 32.

McFarlane, H. S., *Intelligent Teachers*, Routledge and Kegan Paul, London 1973.

MacGraw, F. M., *The Use of 35mm Time-Lapse Photography as a Feedback and Observation Instrument in Teacher Education*, unpublished doctoral dissertation, Stanford University, University Microfilms, Ann Arbor, Michigan 1966.

McKean, R. C. and H. H. Mills, *The Supervisor*, Center for Applied Research in Education, Washington 1964.

McNeil, J. D., *Towards Accountable Teachers*, Holt, Rinehart and Winston, New York 1971.

Matthews, C. C., *The Classroom Verbal Behavior of Selected Secondary School Science Student Teachers and Their Co-operating Classroom Teachers*, unpublished doctoral dissertation, Cornell University, Ann Arbor, Michigan, University Microfilms, 1967, No. 67–1394.

Mayfield, J. R., *An Evaluation of Certain Aspects of the Laboratory Experiences Program of the School of Education, Auburn University*, unpublished doctoral dissertation, Auburn University, 1973.

Medley, D. M., 'The Language of Teacher Behavior: Communicating the Results of Structured Observations to Teachers', *Journal of Teacher Education*, 1971, 22, 165–7.

Milanovich, A. 'Wanted: More Good Supervising Teachers', *Elementary School Journal*, 1966, 67, 22–7.

Miller, H., *An Analysis of the Organisation and Administration of Secondary Student Teaching Practices in the Seven State Colleges and Universities of Kentucky*, unpublished doctoral dissertation, 1970.

Morgan, L. J., *A Comparison of the Evaluation Given and the Better Grade Recommended for Selected Secondary Student Teachers by Their College Supervisors, Their Co-operating Teachers, Their Pupils and Themselves*, unpublished doctoral dissertation, St Louis University, 1971. Abstract, *Dissertation Abstracts International*, 1972, 32, 4471.

Muuss, R. E., 'Differential Effects of Studying Versus Teaching on Teachers' Attitudes', *Journal of Educational Research*, 1969, 63, 185–9.

Myers, C., C. Watts, J. White and J. M. Yonts, 'Co-operative Teacher Education Programs: Old Acquaintances Create New Partnerships', *Peabody Journal of Education*, 1971, 49, 12–19.

Nelson, M. A., 'Co-operating Teacher Training', *Journal of Teacher Education*, 1972, 23, 367–70.

Ogletree, J. R. *et al.*, 'Preparing Educational Supervisors', *Educational Leadership*, 1962, 20, 163–6.

Osmon, R. V., *Associative Factors in Changes of Student Teachers' Attitudes During Student Teaching*, unpublished doctoral dissertation, Indiana University, 1959.

Parker, J. L. and R. J. Withycombe, 'Mediation in An Alternative Teacher Training Program', *Phi Delta Kappan*, March 1973, 483–5.

Petrusich, M. M., 'Some Thoughts on Teacher Education', *Journal of Teacher Education*, 1969, 20 (1), 49–50.

Poole, C. and E. Gaudry, 'Some Effects of Teaching Practice', *Australian Journal of Education*, 1974, 18 (3), 255–63.

Portal Schools, Council of Great City Schools, Portal Schools, Steering Committee in Co-operation with the Teachers Corps, Washington, 1972, OEC-0-71-3354 (916).

Price, W. J., 'The Student Teacher as Indented Servant', *Journal of Teacher Education*, 1972, 23 (3), 352–4.

Rexinger, L., 'Enriching Laboratory Experiences', *Educational Leadership*, 1969, 26, 389–93.

Rowlands, E., 'Modifying Classroom Behaviour of Trainee-Teachers with a Walkie-Talkie', *Australian Journal of Education*, 1968, 12, 244–51.

Seperson, M. and B. R. Joyce, 'Teaching Styles of Student Teachers as Related to Those of Their Co-operating Teachers', *Educational Leadership Research Supplement*, November 1973, 146–51.

Shaftel, F. R. and C. Shaftel, *Role-playing for Social Values*, Prentice-Hall, Englewood Cliffs, New Jersey 1967.

Silberman, C. E., 'Even Student Teaching is Dismal', *Today's Education*, 1971, 60 (1), 22–5.

Smith, C. L. and E. L. Sagan, 'A Taxonomy for Planning Field Experiences', *Peabody Journal of Education*, January 1975, 89–96.

Sorensen, G. and R. Halpert, 'Stress in Student Teaching', *California Journal of Educational Research*, 1968, 19, 28–33.

Stanton, H. E., 'The Diagnostic Rating of Teaching Performance Scale', *Australian Journal of Education*, 1971, 15, 95–103.

Stanton, H. E., 'Pupil Generated Feedback in the Education of Teachers', *Education News*, 1972, 13 (11), 16–20.

Thew, D. M., *The Nature of the Practicum in Teacher Education*, unpublished paper, Alexander Mackie CAE, 1976.

Tibble, J. W., *The Future of Teacher Education*, Routledge and Kegan Paul, London 1971.

Trimmer, R., 'Tell Us More Student Teacher', *Journal of Teacher Education*, 1961, 21, 229–31.

Tuckman, B. W. and W. F. Oliver, 'Effectiveness of Feedback to Teachers as a Function of Source', *Journal of Educational Psychology*, 1968, 59, 297–301.

Turney, C. and D. A. Thew, 'Twenty Basic Practicum Issues' in *Innovation in In-school Experience in Australian Teacher Education*, presented at the Perth Conference on the Practicum in Teacher Education, August 1975.

Twelker, P. A., *Simulation Materials*, Oregon State System of Higher Education, 1968.

Underhill, R. G., *The Relation of Elementary Student Teacher Empathy (Affective Sensitivity), Change in Supervising Teacher Empathy and Student Teaching Success*, unpublished doctoral dissertation, Michigan State University, 1969.

Walberg, H. J., S. Metzner, R. M. Todd and P. M. Henry 'Effects of Tutoring and Practice Teaching on Self-Concept and Attitudes in Education Students', *Journal of Teacher Education*, 1968, 19, 283–91.

Wass, H., R. A. Blume, A. W. Combs and W. D. Hedges, *Humanistic Teacher Education: An Experiment in Systematic Curriculum Innovation*, Shields, Fort Collins 1974.

Weinstock, H. R. and C. M. Peccolo, 'Do Students' Ideas and Attitudes Survive Practice Teaching?', *Elementary School Journal*, 1970, 70 (4), 210–18.

Winn, W., 'Videotaping Teaching Practice: Strengths and Weaknesses', *Audiovisual Instruction*, 1974, 19 (1), 18–20.

Yee, A. H., 'Interpersonal Relationships in the Student-Teaching Triad', *The Journal of Teacher Education*, 1968, 19, 95–112.

Yee, A. H., 'Do Co-operating Teachers Influence the Attitudes of Student Teachers?', *Journal of Educational Psychology*, 1969, 60, 327–32.

Young, D. B., *Effective Supervisory Conferences: Strategies for Modifying Teacher Behaviour*, paper presented to Annual Conference of ASCD, Chicago 1969.

NEW METHODS, MATERIALS AND TECHNOLOGY

Allen, D. W. and R. J. Clark Jr., 'Microteaching: Its Rationale', *The High School Journal*, 1967, 51, 75–9.

Allen, D. W. and A. W. Eve, 'Microteaching', *Theory into Practice*, 1968, 7 (5), 185–7.

Altman, B. E., 'Micro Team Teaching with Student Teachers', *Instructor*, October 1969, 2, 88–9.

Asian Institute for Teacher Educators, *Integration and Modernization of Teacher Education Curriculum*, University of the Philippines, 1972.

Barnard, J. D., 'The Lecture-Demonstration *vs* the Problem-Solving Method of Teaching in a College Science Course', *Science Education*, 1942, 26, 121–32.

Basic Guidelines for Media and Technology in Teacher Education. Association for Educational Communications and Technology, Washington 1971.

Beach, L. R., *Learning and Student Interaction in Small Self-directed College Groups*, U.S. Department of Health, Education and Welfare, 1970.

Berliner, D. C., *Microteaching and the Technical Skills Approach to Teacher Training*, Stanford Center for Research and Development in Teaching, 1969.

Bishop, A. J. and R. C. Whitfield, *Situations in Teaching*, McGraw-Hill, London 1972.

Boardman, R., 'The Theory and Practice of Educational Simulation', *Educational Research*, June 1969, 11 (3), 179–84.

Borg, W. R. and D. R. Stone, *Protocol Materials as a Tool for Changing Teacher Behaviour*, Utah State University, 1974.

Borg, W. R. and C. Stowitschek, *Utah State University Protocol Project: Final Report, 1971–2*, U.S. Department of Health, Education and Welfare, 1972.

Borg, W. R. *et al.*, *The Minicourse: A Microteaching Approach to Teacher Education*, Macmillan Educational Series, 1970.

Casey, J. E. and B. E. Weaver, 'An Evaluation of Lecture Method and Small Group Method of Teaching in Terms of Knowledge of Content, Teacher Attitude and Social Status', *Journal of the Colorado-Wyoming Academy of Science*, 1956, 4, 54.

Clark, C. M. *et al.*, *Teacher Self-Improvement Through Teacher Training Products: An Experimental Course*, Stanford Center for Research and Development in Teaching, 1974.

Computers and the School: Final Report, Scottish Education Department, Edinburgh 1972.

Cruickshank, D. R., *Inner-City Simulation Laboratory*, SRA, Chicago 1969.

Cruickshank, D. R., 'Teacher Education Looks at Simulation: A Review of Selected Uses and Research Results' in Tansey, P. J. (ed.), *Educational Aspects of Simulation*, McGraw-Hill, 1971, 185–203.

Cruickshank, D. R., 'Notions of Simulation and Games: A Preliminary Inquiry', *Educational Technology*, 1972a, 12, 17–19.

Cruickshank, D. R., 'The Developing Notion of Protocol Materials', *Journal of Teacher Education*, 1972b, 23 (3), 281–5.

Cruickshank, D. R. and F. Broadbent, 'Investigation to Determine Effects of Simulation Training on Student Teacher Behaviour', *Educational Technology*, 1969, 9 (10), 50–4.

Cruickshank, D. R. *et al.*, *Teaching Problems Laboratory*, SRA, Chicago 1967.

Duthie, J. H., *Department of Education: Resources Centre*, roneo, University of Stirling, March 1973a.

Duthie, J. H., *Operation of Microteaching Suite*, roneo, University of Stirling, March 1973b.

Eggleston, S. J., 'United Kingdom: Innovative Trends to Teacher Training and Retraining' in *New Patterns of Teacher Education and Tasks: Country Experience—Belgium, France, United Kingdom*, OECD, Paris 1974.

Eglash, A., 'A Group Discussion Method of Teaching Psychology', *Journal of Educational Psychology*, 1954, 45, 257–67.

Elliott, P. N., 'Characteristics and Relationships of Various Criteria of College and University Teaching', *Purdue University Studies of Higher Education*, 1950, 70, 5–61.

Foxall, A. and T. Evans, 'Closed-Circuit Television in Training for Teachers in Further Educational Institutions', *Programmed Learning and Educational Technology*, May 1973, 10 (3), 170–80.

Garten, T. R. and J. A. Hudson, 'A Strategy in the Use of Videotape to Evaluate Recognition of Component Teaching Skills', *Audiovisual Instruction*, May 1974, 19 (5), 24–5.

Guetzkow, H. (ed.), *Simulation in International Relations: Development for Research and Teaching*, Prentice-Hall, New Jersey 1963.

Hall, K. A. *et al.*, 'A Triumph for CAI', *Phi Delta Kappan*, September 1974, 70–2.

Hilliard, F. H. (ed.), *Teaching the Teachers: Trends in Teacher Education*, Allen and Unwin, London 1971.

Hirschman, C. S., *An Investigation of the Small Group Discussion Classroom Method on Criteria of Understanding, Pleasantness, and Self-Confidence Induced*, unpublished master's thesis, University of Pittsburgh, 1952.

Hughes, P. W. and R. D. Traill, 'Simulation Methods in Teacher Education', *The Australian Journal of Education*, June 1975, 19 (2), 113–26.

Hunter, E., *Encounter in the Classroom*, Holt, Rinehart and Winston, New York 1972.

Husband, R. W., 'A Statistical Comparison of the Efficacy of Large Lecture *vs* Small Recitation Sections upon Achievement in General Psychology', *Journal of Psychology*, 1951, 31, 297–300.

Johnson, J. A. *et al.*, 'Videotape Recording in Teacher Education', *Educational Technology*, May 1969, 9 (5), 48–53.

Languis, M. L. *et al.*, 'Teaming: Innovation in Teacher Education', *Educational Leadership*, 1968, 26 (8), 806–10.

Lomax, D. E. (ed.), *The Education of Teachers in Britain*, Wiley, London 1973.

McLeish, J., *The Lecture Method*, Cambridge Institute of Education Monograph, 1968.

Page, J. L. and T. W. Peterman, 'Module Teamwork in Teacher Education', *Audiovisual Instruction*, February 1974, 19 (2), 72–3.

Perrott, E., 'Microteaching' in Warwick, D. (ed.), *New Directions in the Professional Training of Teachers*, University of Lancaster, 1974.

Reed, K., 'The Role of Videotape Recordings in the Training of Teachers', *International Journal of Instructional Media*, 1975–6, 3 (2), 117–24.

Report of the Minister's Committee on the Training of Elementary School Teachers, Ontario Department of Education, 1966.

Ruja, H., 'Outcomes of Lecture and Discussion Procedures in Three College Courses', *Journal of Experimental Education*, 1954, 22, 385–94.

Semmel, M. I., 'Toward the Development of a Computer-Assisted Teacher Training System (CATTS)', *International Review of Education*, 1972, 18 (5), 561–8.

Short, M. and M. Rosum (eds), *Microteaching: A Technique for Training Teachers to Teach Elementary Children*, Illinois State University, 1972.

Smith, B. O. *et al.*, *Teachers for the Real World*, American Association of Colleges for Teacher Education, 1969.

Sorber, E. R., 'Individualization of Instruction for Teacher Corpsmen', *Educational Technology*, August 1969, 9 (8), 31–5.

Sterns, H. N., 'Team Teaching in Teacher Education Programs', *Journal of Teacher Education*, 1972, 23 (3), 318–22.

Stewart, J. W. and J. Shank, 'Student-Teacher Contracting: A Vehicle for Individualizing Instruction', *Audiovisual Instruction*, January 1973, 18 (1), 31–4.

Tansey, P. J. (ed.), *Educational Aspects of Simulation*, McGraw-Hill, London 1971.

Tansey, P. J. and D. Unwin, *Simulation and Gaming in Education*, Methuen, London 1969.

Telfer, R. and J. Rees, *Teacher Tactics: A Critical Incident Approach to Problems Involving Teachers*, Symes, Sydney 1975.

Thomas, L. A. and R. M. Jones, 'Teacher-Centered In-Service—The Development of a CCTV Model', *Audiovisual Instruction*, January 1974, 19 (1), 23–5.

Tom, A. R., 'In Search of Training Materials for Supervising Teachers', *Peabody Journal of Education*, January 1975, 52 (2), 84– 8.

Turney, C. *et al.*, *Microteaching: Research, Theory and Practice*, Sydney University Press, 1973.

Twelker, P., *Some Reflections on the Innovation of Simulation and Gaming*, a paper presented at the First Annual Conference, the Society for Academic Gaming and Simulation in

Education and Training, Berkshire College of Education, Reading 1970.

Ward, B. E., *A Survey of Microteaching in NCATE—Accredited Secondary Education Programs*, Stanford Center for Research and Development in Teaching, 1970.

Winn, W., 'Videotaping Teaching Practice: Strengths and Weaknesses', *Audiovisual Instruction*, January 1974, 19 (1), 18–20.

RENEWAL OF IN-SERVICE EDUCATION

Australian Commission on Advanced Education, *Teacher Education 1973–75*, Australian Government Publishing Service, Canberra 1973.

Baum, D. C. and T. G. Chastian, 'Training Packages: An Innovative Approach for Increasing IMC/RMC Potential for In-Service Training in Special Education', *Educational Technology*, 1972, 12 (9), 46–9.

Bolam, R. and K. Baker, *The Teacher Induction Pilot Schemes—The National Evaluators' Report*, mimeographed, University of Bristol, 1975.

Brimm, J. L. and D. J. Tollett, 'How Do Teachers Feel About In-Service Education?', *Educational Leadership*, 1974, 31 (6), 521–5.

East, M. A., 'Political Scientists and Teacher Education: An In-Service Program in International Affairs', *High School Journal*, 1972, 55, 357–70.

Evans, E. D., *Transition to Teaching*, Holt, Rinehart and Winston, New York 1976.

James, Lord, Chairman, *Teacher Education and Training*, Her Majesty's Stationary Office, London 1972.

Jecks, D. A. (ed.), *Influences in Australian Education*, Carrolls, Perth 1974.

Lee, M., 'The Role of the Colleges of Education in the In-Service Education of Teachers', *Education for Teaching*, Spring 1975, 96, 3–11.

Liverpool Education Committee, *Pilot Scheme for the Induction of New Teachers, Report No. 1—Organisation*, Liverpool 1975.

Liverpool Education Committee, *Pilot Scheme for the Induction of New Teachers, Report No. 2—Appointment of Teacher-Tutors*, Liverpool 1975.

Liverpool Education Committee, *Pilot Scheme for the Induction of New Teachers, Report No. 3—Teacher-Tutor Briefings*, Liverpool 1975.

Liverpool Education Committee, *Pilot Scheme for the Induction of New Teachers, Report No. 4—Release of New Teachers from Teaching Duties for Induction Program*, Liverpool 1975.

Liverpool Education Committee, *Pilot Scheme for the Induction of New Teachers, Report No. 5—Induction Year Programme*, Liverpool 1975.

Liverpool Education Committee, *Pilot Scheme for the Induction of New Teachers, Report No. 6—Staffing Implications*, Liverpool 1975.

Mason, T. and F. Rohde, 'In-Service Education in White Bear Lake', *Theory into Practice*, 1972, 11 (4), 236–8.

Mayer, V. J., J. F. Disinger and A. L. White, 'Evaluation of An In-Service Program for Earth Science Teachers', *Science Education*, 1975, 59 (2), 145–54.

Merwin, W. C., 'Competency-Based Modules for In-service Education', *Educational Leadership*, 1974, 31 (4), 329–32.

Mullins, J. W., 'Regional In-Service Programs in Texas', *Theory into Practice*, 1972, 11 (4), 232–5.

Muskopf, A. and J. Moss, 'Open Education—An In-Service Model', *Elementary School Journal*, 1972, 73 (3), 117–24.

O'Hare, R. M., *In-Service Education*, Education Department, Adelaide 1971.

Organisation for Economic Co-operation and Development, *Initial and Continuing Training of Teachers—New Trends and Concepts*, mimeographed, OECD, Paris 1974.

Organisation for Economic Co-operation and Development, *New Patterns of Teacher Education and Tasks*, OECD, Paris 1974.

Organisation for Economic Co-operation and Development, *New Patterns of Teacher Education and Tasks—Belgium, France, United Kingdom*, OECD, Paris 1974.

Organisation for Economic Co-operation and Development, *New Patterns of Teacher Education and Tasks—United States*, OECD, Paris 1974.

Poliakoff, L., 'Teacher Centers: An Outline of Current Information', *Journal of Teacher Education*, 1972, 23 (3), 389–97.

Richardson, J. A. and J. Bowen (eds), *The Preparation of Teachers in Australia*, Cheshire, Melbourne 1967.

Rust, V. D., 'Teachers' Centres in England', *Elementary School Journal*, 1973, 73 (4), 182–92.

Ryan, K. (ed.), *Teacher Education*, National Society for the Study of Education, University of Chicago Press, Chicago 1975.

Stinson, R. H., 'The Western Ontario Field Center', *Theory into Practice*, 1972, 11 (4), 267–72.

Tibble, J. W. (ed.), *The Future of Teacher Education*, Routledge and Kegan Paul, London 1971.

Tillis, C. R. and D. E. Lattart, 'Teachers Teaching Teachers—In-Service Training in Environmental Education', *Journal of Teacher Education*, 1974, 25 (2), 160–2.

University of Exeter, Institute of Education, *Regional Committee for In-Service Education Longer Courses*, Exeter 1972.

University of Liverpool, *Liverpool Pilot Induction Scheme: Evaluation Report 12*, Liverpool 1975.

Walton, J., *Resources Organisation on an Area Basis*, mimeographed, 1974.

Walton, J., 'Teachers' Centres: Their Role and Function', *Forum*, 1972, 15 (1), 15–17.

Watkins, R. *et al.*, *In-Service Training: Structure and Content*, Ward Lock Educational, Birkenhead 1973.

Whitmore, J. R., J. L. Crist and R. W. Marx, *An Experimental In-Service Teacher Education Program for Distressed Elementary Schools*, Stanford Center for Research and Development in Teaching, Stanford 1974.

Chapter 4

Ashmore, H. L., 'An Evaluation of State-Supported Campus Laboratory Schools in Selected Southeastern Schools', *Educational Administration and Supervision*, 1951, 37, 80–97.

Bettleheim, B., 'Toward a New School', *Elementary School Journal*, 1958, 59, 61–7.

Blair, L. C. *et al.*, *The Purposes, Functions and Uniqueness of the College-Controlled Laboratory School*, Bulletin of the Association for Student Teaching No. 9, Loch Haven, Pennsylvania 1958.

Brown, W. B., M. Naslund, and N. Dederick, 'Los Angeles City Schools—Partner in Teacher Education', *Journal of Teacher Education*, 1961, 12 (1), 60–5.

Bryan, R. C., 'The Vital Role of the Campus School', *Journal of Teacher Education*, 1961, 12, 275–81.

Bucklen, H. E., 'The Campus School—What are its Functions?', *Journal of Teacher Education*, 1952, 3, 201–3.

Bush, R. N., 'Teacher Education for the Future: Focus upon an Entire School', *Journal of Teacher Education*, 1975, 26 (2), 148–9.

Campeau, P., *University Elementary Schools*, UCLA, roneo, 1972.

Capie, W., 'A Modular Methods Course in Conjunction with Portal Schools', *Science Education*, 1973, 57, 71–5.

Cappa, D., 'College-Controlled Laboratory Schools', *Improving College and University Teaching*, 1972, 20 (2), 110–11.

Chittenden, M. D., 'The Oswego Normal and Training School', *Educational Administration and Supervision*, 1925, 11, 325–32.

Dawson, M. A., 'Current Practices in Participation', *Educational Administration and Supervision*, 1937, 294–306.

Deputy, E. C. and R. Reed, 'How Do Training-School Pupils Succeed in the Junior High School?', *Educational Administration and Supervision*, 1933, 19, 607–12.

Dillon, B., 'Innovation and Collaboration—A Public School Educator Speaks', *Journal of Teacher Education*, 1974, 25, 256–7.

Eulie, J. and F. Gray, 'University-School Cooperation: A Case-Study', *Educational Leadership*, 1973, 30, 416–19.

Evans, L. M., 'Towards Field-Centred Teacher Education: Trends in the U.S.A.', *Education for Teaching*, 1975, 96, 43–50.

Ezer, M. and R. Lambert, 'The Residency in Supervision: A Unique Role for Laboratory Schools', *Peabody Journal of Education*, 1966, 44, 155–9.

Findlay, J. J., 'The Study of Curricula and Method', *Demonstration School Record*, 1908, 1, 30–41.

Fremdling, E.,' 'Teacher Education at the University Elementary School, UCLA', *ULCA Educator*, 1974, 16 (2), 21–2.

Fristoe, D., 'Early Beginnings of Laboratory Schools', *Educational Administration and Supervision*, 1942, 28, 219–32.

Gaskill, A. R. and A. A. Carlson, 'Is the Campus Laboratory School Obsolescent?', *School and Society*, March 1958.

Gilland, T. M., 'The Contribution of a Campus Elementary School to a Program of Teacher Education', *Educational Administration and Supervision*, 1933, 19, 481–95.

Goodlad, J. I., 'The Reconstruction of Teacher Education', *Teachers College Record*, 1970, 71 (1), 61–72.

Harwood, F. and B. Miller, 'The Intern Teaching Program in the Urban School, Impact on Instructional Improvement', *Journal of Teacher Education*, 1970, 23, 427–30.

Hayes, D. T. and E. W. Campbell, 'Real Education: Students and Staff Plan Democratic Learning Experiences in a Summer Demonstration School', *Educational Administration and Supervision*, 1948, 34, 1–24.

Hilsinger, R. and B. Shantz, *Reallocating Teacher Education Resources in the Temple-Philadelphia Portal Schools*, College of Education, Temple University, roneo, 1973.

Hogle, H. I., 'Teacher Education and Experiential Learning', *Viewpoints*, 1974, 50 (5), 23–47.

Hunter, M., 'Expanding Roles of Laboratory Schools', *Phi Delta Kappan*, 1970, 52, 14–19.

Hunter, M., 'UES at UCLA: Why is a Laboratory School', *Instructor*, June-July 1971, reprint.

Hunter, M., *A Decade at the University Elementary School*, UCLA, roneo, 1974.

Jamison, O. G. *et al.*, 'A Community Program in the Laboratory School of a State Teachers' College', *Progressive Education*, 1940, 17, 327–35.

Kachur, D. S., 'What's Negotiable? A Look at Student Teaching Programmes', *NASSP Bulletin*, 1973, 57 (377), 41–6.

Kachur, D. S. and D. C. Lang, 'Negotiating Clinical Experiences: Do the College and Universities Want In?', *Journal of Teacher Education*, 1975, 26 (3), 202–5.

King, A. R. Jr., *Current Program Plan: Curriculum Research and Development Group — Education Development, Budget Period 1973–1975*, University of Hawaii, 1973.

Knight, D. A. and J. I. Wayne, 'School and the University: Cooperative Roles in Student Teaching', *Elementary School Journal*, 1970, 70 (6), 317–20.

Lamb, L., *Planning Closed Circuit Television Systems for Laboratory Schools for Colleges of Education*, unpublished doctoral dissertation, University of Missouri, 1961.

Lamb, P. M. 'The Laboratory School: An Historical Perspective', *Journal of Educational Research*, 1962, 56 (2), 107–9.

Land, E., *The Nature and Quality of Pre-Student Teaching Laboratory Experiences in Campus Elementary Laboratory Schools Affiliated with State Colleges and Universities*, unpublished doctoral dissertation, University of Virginia, 1969.

Lang, D. C., 'Current Theory and Practice in Connection with the Function of the Campus Laboratory School', *Educational Administration and Supervision*, 1959, 45, 36–43.

Larsen, A. H., *Administrative Control of State Teachers College Campus Secondary Schools*, unpublished doctoral dissertation, University of Wisconsin, 1939.

Larsen, A. H., 'Functions of the Secondary Training-School in Teacher Education', *Educational Administration and Supervision*, 1942, 28, 65–8.

Lomax, D. E. (ed.), *The Education of Teachers in Britain*, Wiley, London 1973.

Ludeman, W. W., 'Do Pupils Lose Under Practice Teachers?', *Educational Administration and Supervision*, 1929, 14, 101–4.

McAulay, J. D., 'How Much Influence Has a Co-operating Teacher?', *Journal of Teacher Education*, 1960, 11 (1), 79–83.

McGeoch, D. and P. Quim, 'Clinical Experiences in a Teacher Education Center', *Journal of Teacher Education*, 1975, 26 (2), 176–9.

McNabb, D., 'An Analysis of Financial Support Patterns, Staff Relationships and Problems which led to the Closing of Laboratory Schools at Public-Supported Teacher Education Institutions Between 1964 and 1972', *ERIC*, 1973, 26322.

Maddox, K. and J. Flaherty, 'Appalachia Develops Unique Approach to Teacher Education', *Journal of Teacher Education*, 1971, 22, 185–8.

Mayhew, K. C. and A. C. Edwards, *The Dewey School*, Appleton-Century, New York 1939.

Mead, A. R., 'Advantages and Disadvantages of Campus and "Off-Campus" Laboratory Schools', *Educational Administration and Supervision*, 1930, 16, 196–207.

Mead, A. R., 'Why Doesn't the Training School Make Better Progress?', *Educational Administration and Supervision*, 1939, 25, 71–3.

Mead, A. R., 'The Model School Concept vs. the Laboratory Experience in Solving Problems', *Educational Administration and Supervision*, 1950, 36, 433–5.

Monroe, G. and H. Talmage, 'Cooperative Programme in Urban Teacher Education', *Journal of Teacher Education*, 1970, 21, 469–77.

Morin, G. 'An Evaluation of the Pre-Service Laboratory Experience', *ERIC*, 1974, 11634.

Mosley, P. A., 'Teacher Preparation: A Shared Responsibility', *Educational Leadership*, 1973, 30, 408–11.

Myers, C. B. *et al.*, 'Cooperative Teacher Education: Old Acquaintances Create New Partnerships', *Peabody Journal of Education*, 1971, 49, 12–19.

Nelson, M., 'Cooperating Teacher Training', *Journal of Teacher Education*, 1972, 23 (3), 367–70.

Ohles, J. F., 'The Laboratory School', *Education Digest*, 1962, 27, 27–9.

Ohles, J. F., 'Is the Laboratory School Worth Saving?', *Education Digest*, 1967, 33, 43–5.

Olma, B., 'Report on a Cooperative Student Teacher Program: A Pilot Study', *Journal of Experimental Education*, 1973, 41 (4), 88–96.

Palm, R. R., 'Laboratory Schools as Leaders in Curriculum Development', *School and Society*, 1941a, 53, 644–7.

Palm, R. R., 'Curriculum Experimentation in Laboratory Schools of State Teachers' Colleges', *Educational Administration and Supervision*, 1941b, 27, 629–32.

Petrie, R. G., *SODIA: A New Model Elementary Teacher Training Program*, Department of Elementary Education, Utah State University, roneo, 1973.

Poliakoff, L., 'The Finances of School-College Cooperation in Teacher Education', *Journal of Teacher Education*, 1971, 22, 359–65.

Price, R. 'The Influence of Supervising Teachers', *Journal of Teacher Education*, 1961, 12 (4), 471–5.

Reports of the Minister of Education, Government Printer, South Australia, 1969, 1971.

Riechard, D., 'A Method that Can Make a Difference', *Journal of Teacher Education*, 1974, 25, 163–5.

Rock, W. and A. Virgilo, 'Major Breakthrough in Teacher Education Achieved', *Journal of Teacher Education*, 1971, 22, 274–6.

Rogers, D., 'The Role of the Campus School in the Child Development Program', *Educational Administration and Supervision*, April 1952, 38, 229–34.

Ruchkin, J., 'Cooperative Myths and Realities', *Educational Leadership*, 1973a, 30 (7), 659–63.

Ruchkin, J., 'Teacher Centres: How Does One School-College Collaboration Work?', *Journal of Teacher Education*, 1973b, 25, 170–4.

Russell, J. E., 'The Speyer School', *Teachers College Record*, 1902, 3, 1–5.

Ryan, K. (ed.), *Teacher Education*, The Seventy-fourth Yearbook of the National Society for the Study of Education, University of Chicago Press, 1975.

Rzepka, L., 'The Campus School: Its Search for Identity', *Journal of Teacher Education*, 1962, 13, 24–9.

Sale, L., *An Analysis of the Functions of Campus Elementary Laboratory Schools Affiliated with State Colleges and Universities*, unpublished doctoral dissertation, Indiana University, 1967.

Schwartz, H., 'When University and Schools Relate', *Educational Leadership*, 1973, 30, 397–400.

Seperson, M. and B. Joyce, 'Teaching Styles of Student Teachers as Related to Those of Their Cooperating Teachers', *Educational Leadership*, 1973, 31 (2), 146–51.

Shadick, R., 'The Interrelationships of the Role of a Laboratory School', *Journal of Teacher Education*, 1966, 17, 198–204.

Shuff, M. and R. V. Shuff, 'Designed for Excellence: A Programme for Laboratory Experiences', *Journal of Teacher Education*, 1972, 23, 215–9.

Shultz, A. J., 'Report of the Principal of the Teachers' College', *Report of the Minister of Education*, Government Printer, South Australia, Adelaide 1929.

Strebel, R. F., 'The Scholastic Status of Pupils Taught by Student Teachers', *Educational Administration and Supervision*, 1932, 18, 99–103.

Taggart, G. L., *SODIA: A New Model Elementary Teacher Education Program*, Entry for the 1973–4 Distinguished Achievement Awards Program, Utah State University, 1974.

Thayer, G., 'The Teacher Education Laboratory and Developments in Teacher Education', *UCLA Educator*, 1974, 16, 24–7.

Thomas, G. G., 'Role of the Laboratory School in Introducing Educational Practices', *Educational Leadership*, April 1956, 13, 407–11.

Tyler, R. W., 'The Work of the Summer Demonstration Schools', *Elementary School Journal*, 1940, 41, 6–7.

Walsh, H. M., 'Let's Move the Methods Course Off-Campus', *Journal of Teacher Education*, 1970, 21 (3), 347–51.

West, F. and T. Gadsden, 'A Major Role for Laboratory Schools', *Educational Leadership*, 1973, 30, 412–15.

White, N. D., *The Status and Potential of College Laboratory Schools*, unpublished doctoral dissertation, George Peabody College for Teachers, 1964.

Willis, D. E., 'An Experiment in Cooperative Enquiry. The Portland, Oregon, T.T.T.', *Journal of Teacher Education*, 1975, 26 (3), 214–17.

Yearbook of the American Association of Teachers Colleges, 1926.

Chapter 5

Bush, R. N., *New Directions for Research and Development in Teacher Education*, Stanford Center for Research and Development in Teaching, 1968.

Joyce, B. and M. Weil, *Perspectives for Reform in Teacher Education*, Prentice-Hall, Englewood Cliffs, New Jersey 1972.

Partlett M. and D. Hamilton, *Evaluation as Illumination: A New Approach to the Study of Innovatory Programs*, Centre for Research in the Educational Sciences, University of Edinburgh, 1972.

Appendix 1

SURVEY OF INNOVATION IN AUSTRALIAN TEACHER EDUCATION

Name of Institution	Response to request for innovative titles	No. of innovations cited in initial response	No. of questionnaires returned	Information only supplied	Case studies undertaken (not included in questionnaire nos.)	TOTAL
A.C.T.						
Canberra CAE	✓	8	7	0	3	10
NEW SOUTH WALES						
Alexander Mackie CAE	✓	18	9	2	1	12
Armidale CAE	✓	5	1	0	1	2
Australian College of Phys. Educ.	✓	6	6	1		7
Catholic College of Education	✓	0	0	0		0
Catholic TC	✓	1	1	0		1
Good Samaritan TC	—	0	0	0		0
Goulburn CAE	✓	17	5	1		6
The Guild TC	—	0	0	0		0
Kuring-gai CAE	✓	27	19	0		19
Macquarie Univ.	✓	20	14	1	2	17
Milperra CAE	✓			1		1
Mitchell CAE	✓	11	6	1		7
Mount St. Mary College	✓	4	3	0		3
Nepean CAE	✓	13	7	0		7
Newcastle CAE	✓	24	17	1	1	19
NSW State Conservatorium of Music	✓	0	0	0		0
Northern Rivers CAE	✓	0	0	0		0
Nursery School TC	✓	8	7	0		7
Riverina CAE	✓	5	3	0		3
Sydney Kindergarten TC	✓	7	3	0		3
Sydney TC	✓	0	0	0		0

Name of Institution	Response to request for innovative titles	No. of innovations cited in initial response	No. of questionnaires returned	Information only supplied	Case studies undertaken (not included in question-naire nos.)	TOTAL
University of Newcastle	✓	4	1	0		1
University of New England	✓	7	0	1		1
University of NSW	—	0	0	0		0
University of Sydney	✓	5	3	1		4
Wollongong Inst. of Education	✓	15	6	0		6
Wollongong Univ.	✓	2	0	0		0
QUEENSLAND						
Brisbane Kinder-garten TC	—	0	0	0		0
Capricornia Inst. of Adv. Educ.	✓	3	0	0		0
Catherine McAuley TC	—	0	0	0		0
Darling Downs Inst. of Adv. Educ.	✓	5	1	0		1
James Cook Univ. of Nth. Queensland	✓	1	1	0	1	2
Kelvin Grove CAE	✓	41	15	4	2	21
Mt. Gravatt CAE	✓	19	11	0		11
North Brisbane CAE	✓	12	7	0		7
Queensland Conser-vatorium of Music	✓	6	2	0		2
Townsville CAE	✓	12	7	0		7
University of Queensland	✓	3	2	0	1	3
Xavier TC	✓	2	1	0		1
SOUTH AUSTRALIA						
Adelaide CAE	✓	5	5	0		5
Flinders Univ. of South Australia	✓	10	8	1	1	10
Kingston CAE	—	0	0	0		0
Murray Park CAE	✓	9	2	0		2
Salisbury CAE	✓	10	4	4	1	9
Sturt CAE	✓	13	2	4	1	7
Torrens CAE	✓	3	4	0		4
University of Adelaide	—	0	0	0		0
TASMANIA						
Tasmanian CAE (Northern campus)	✓	1	1	0		1
Tasmanian CAE	✓	20	3	1		4
University of Tasmania	✓	1	1	0		1

Name of Institution	Response to request for innovative titles	No. of innovations cited in initial response	No. of questionnaires returned	Information only supplied	Case studies undertaken (not included in questionnaire nos.)	TOTAL
VICTORIA						
Aquinas College	✓	5	1	0		1
Gippsland Inst. of Technology	✓	1	0	1		1
La Trobe Univ.	✓	1	1	0		1
Mercy College	✓	8	4	0		4
Monash University	✓	8	1	1		2
State College of Vic. at Ballarat	✓	5	3	0		3
SCV at Bendigo	✓	41	13	0		13
SCV at Burwood	✓	9	5	0		5
SCV at Coburg	✓	8	5	1		6
SCV at Frankston	✓	9	8	0		8
SCV at Geelong	✓	5	1	0		1
SCV at Hawthorn	✓	9	7	0	1	8
SCV Inst. of Catholic Educ. Christ College	✓	13	1	0		1
SCV Inst. of Early Childhood Devt.	✓	9	5	2		7
SCV at Melbourne	✓	23	11	2		13
SCV at Rusden	✓	20	10	1	1	12
SCV at Toorak	✓	13	5	0		5
University of Melbourne	✓	1	0	0	1	1
WESTERN AUSTRALIA						
Churchlands CAE	✓	2	1	0	1	2
Claremont TC	✓	73	36	0		36
Graylands TC	✓	5	1	0		1
Mt. Lawley CAE	✓	18	8	1		9
Murdoch Univ.	✓	4	0	0	1	1
University of Western Australia	✓	4	0	0		0
WA Educ. Dept.	✓	1	0	0	1	1
WA Inst. of Tech.	✓	6	1	0		1
WA Secondary TC	✓	2	1	0	1	2
					TOTAL	22	379

Appendix 2

COMPENDIUM OF INNOVATIONS IN AUSTRALIAN TEACHER EDUCATION

INNOVATOR/S	TITLE OF INNOVATION	DESCRIPTION
A. AUSTRALIAN CAPITAL TERRITORY		
1. Canberra CAE		
G. Burkhardt & S. Richardson	Curriculum Resources Centre	The development of a resource of curriculum materials and facilities for such activities as display, materials preparation, independent study and research, and audiovisual presentations.
D. Driscoll & P. Fensham	Australian Science Education Project	The involvement of science educators in the development of a range of curriculum units suitable for the professional education of pre-service teachers of science.
P. Hughes	Inter-disciplinary Courses	Team-taught courses in the interrelated areas of Education and Curriculum based on the contributory disciplines of philosophy, psychology, sociology and history.
P. Hughes & R. Traill	Early Offers Scheme	Entry for students on the basis of school recommendations.
D. Kendall	An Inter-disciplinary Approach to the Creative Arts in Primary Schools	Inter-disciplinary study within the creative arts with emphasis on the development of suitable language and perceptual skills, and the emergence of a self-directed learner.
D. Kendall	Interpersonal Skill Training for Teachers	An interpersonal skill training programme based on the theories of Louis Raths, concerning the emotional and thinking needs of children.
D. Kendall	Early Childhood Creative Arts: Organic Teaching	Programme involves the development of the student-teacher as a creative person and also as one capable of facilitating the development of children through the creative arts.
N. Russell	Innovation in Education	The course is aimed at developing skills in analyzing innovation in education (M.Ed. students) primarily through case studies.

INNOVATOR/S	TITLE OF INNOVATION	DESCRIPTION
R. Traill	Mature-Age Entry	Enables mature-age students from varying backgrounds the opportunity to enter a tertiary education programme.
R. Traill	Simulation Process	The use of a simulation programme in the development of teaching skills.
B. NEW SOUTH WALES		
1. Alexander Mackie CAE		
A. Anderson	School-Based Workshop on Science Teaching	Trainee teachers work with small primary groups in total school situation.
H. Brissenden	Music-Integrated Approach and Team Teaching	Music Education Study Programme involving integration of subject areas and team teaching.
R. Conners & W. Barry	Integrated Programme	Open-education experience for student teachers in the primary programme.
B. Fone	Drama Course—Improvization and Sensitivity Experience	Combination of encounter-group methods, drama skills, and their application to the classroom situation.
B. Fulton *et al.*	Art Method Course	School- and community-based activities that allow for a significant degree of student choice.
J. Schell	Assessment of Physical Fitness	Physical Fitness assessment of students over 12–14 week period.
D. Thew	Tutorial System for Tutorial Advising	Students in primary education programme are allocated in small groups to a tutor who provides advice on academic, administrative and personal issues and problems.
D. Thew	Residential Conferences	Programme involves residential experience in workshop/field activities for pre-service students.
D. Thew	Primary Education Programme	Programme of teacher development allowing for maximum elective units.
D. Thew	Teacher Development Programme	A course in the Diploma of Teaching which combines situational teaching, microteaching, practice teaching, school observation, and school attachment, residential conferences, and excursions, and is designed to develop professional skills, strategies and understandings.

INNOVATOR/S	TITLE OF INNOVATION	DESCRIPTION
D. Thew	School Attachment	School-based teaching workshops involving half- or one-day per week and related to specific curriculum areas.
G. Tyndall & M. Symonds	Admission and Selection of Applicants in Art	Preliminary enrolment of students on schools' recommendation.
2. Armidale CAE		
Y. Mackay	Computer-Feedback Techniques	Programme involves detailed feedback messages from the teaching environment to the student teacher.
W. Newman	Continuous Practice Teaching	First-year students are attached to classes in small groups for three hours a week to undertake sequenced observational and teaching experiences linked with college courses.
3. Australian College of Physical Education		
J. Butt	Practice Teaching on Weekly Basis	Students have regular weekly contact with a group of children.
J. Butt	Practice Teaching—Block of Four Weeks	Final experience, before graduation, in residential situation.
J. Butt	Education—Core Course in Physical Education	Study of the theories of teaching with an emphasis on seminar/workshop methods.
J. Butt	National and State Coaches as Visiting Lecturers	Programme involves the presentation of modern and advanced thinking in sports coaching.
J. Butt *et al.*	Personal Physical Fitness Appraisal	Students elect to be tested at the end of each term.
J. Butt	Practice Teaching Assessment by Profile	Method of assessing students during practice teaching sessions.
4. Catholic TC		
J. Martin	Use of Student Teacher to Implement Precision Teaching Techniques for Reading Remediation	Introduction of precision teaching methods to local schools.
5. Goulburn CAE		
R. Kay	Use of Interaction Analysis and Microteaching	Research into the effects of training in interaction analysis and microteaching on the practice teaching performance of trainee teachers.

INNOVATOR/S	TITLE OF INNOVATION	DESCRIPTION
W. Laird	Models Construction	All students make a model or teaching aid for use in mathematics teaching.
K. Laws & T. Kruger	Sciences Curriculum	Integration at theoretical and practical levels of social and natural science curriculum study.
J. McNeill	Professional Skills Renewal Programme	Residential in-service courses based on audiovisual programmes on specific teaching skills.
R. Shane	Use of ETV Van during Practice Teaching	Van equipped for VTR work travels around schools with two lecturers and one technician filming students on practice.
B. Wells	Shadow Geometry and Reflections	Geometric concepts are presented by means of a discovery programme.
6. Kuring-gai CAE M. Barnacoat & R. Polglase	Ceramics and Man	Team teaching of the various aspects of ceramics.
A. Bergund	English I—Curriculum	Curriculum programme with emphasis on student attitudes rather than content.
E. Best & G. Turnbull	Study of Motor Performance	Students observe the behaviour of children in respect to guide questions.
G. Browne	Factors Affecting Students at Practice Teaching	Research involving large college sample, on factors stated by students that significantly affect their practice teaching.
K. Dewes, G. Kennedy & R. Stafford	Processes of Science	Introductory unit for preparing primary school teachers, based on processes.
J. Driscoll & A. Blewitt	Asian Studies	Pilot course comprising an inter-disciplinary study of Asian civilizations.
A. Edmonds & W. Ticehurst	Laboratory Techniques	Unit in special skills required by science teachers for application in laboratory settings.
N. Gash	Race Relations—Australia and Papua New Guinea	Pilot course for an inter-disciplinary study of race relations in Australia and New Guinea.
R. Holland	Media Studies	Film production and appreciation, college newspaper production, and individual projects.

INNOVATOR/S	TITLE OF INNOVATION	DESCRIPTION
R. Holland	Assessment in English	Progressive assessment through assignments, exercises, practical work, tutorial and seminar participation.
J. Keith	Science Method for Graduate-Dip.Ed. Course	Programme has large practical element with emphasis on the techniques of science teaching.
J. Keith	Pollution Studies	Programme seeks to provide experiences which will allow informed discussion of the problems of environmental pollution and its control.
J. Keith	Environmental Science	Programme consists of scientific studies as a basis for informed judgements on environmental matters.
L. Lodge	Children's Writing	Study of the process of writing and its application in schools.
J. McFarlane	Introduction to Teaching	Integration of method lectures, demonstrations and practice teaching in an inter-disciplinary approach.
R. Smith & J. Gledhill	Teaching Controversial Issues	Training in classroom group processes by active involvement in small-group discussion situations.
M. Trask	B.Ed. in Teacher Librarianship	Proposed four-year integrated programme incorporating General Studies, Education Studies, Curriculum Studies, Library and Information Studies, Education and Library Practice.
M. Trask	Graduate Diploma in Teacher Librarianship	Proposed one-year programme for potential teacher/librarians following degree and graduate-diploma in education.
G. Turnbull	Physical Education Lecturing	Student involvement is encouraged by questions prior to lectures, which are later illustrated in a practical context.
7. Macquarie University		
B. Baldie	Competency-Based Programme in Language Arts	The design, trialling and evaluation of a number of competency-based modules in primary language arts.
H. Barnes	Primary Social Science	The design, trialling and evaluation of competency-based modules relating to the teaching of the social sciences at primary level.

INNOVATOR/S	TITLE OF INNOVATION	DESCRIPTION
W. Butts	Microteaching: Models for the Science Student	Provides a sequence of microteaching models in which teaching skills are gradually built up from oral presentation through to the presentation of a practical lesson.
W. Butts	Science Laboratory Skills Development Programme	Students work alone or in pairs on self-instructional modules.
W. Butts	Competency-based Programme in Secondary Science	Extended workshop sessions where students develop certain specific skills relevant to teaching.
W. Butts	Integration of School Experience and Microteaching—Science	Programme allows for students to observe classroom teaching and engage in microteaching during the same visit.
W. Butts	Minicourses for Secondary Science Students	Students present an approach to the teaching of one aspect of senior secondary school science to their peers in two-hour sessions.
D. Cohen	Curriculum Individualization in Curriculum Studies	Programme to increase curriculum relevance of curriculum studies for participating students.
J. Conroy	Competency-based Programme in Infants/Primary Teacher Education	Competency-based programme with emphasis on school experience, curriculum and teaching skills.
K. Eltis	School Experience Programme—'Pilot Study'	Pilot study to examine the effects of various 'mixes' of student teaching and microteaching across the two years of the Teacher Education Programme.
G. Finlayson	Adjusting to Teaching Courses for Probational Secondary Teachers	Short residential courses for first-year-out secondary teachers providing support and cross-disciplinary professional studies.
N. Hall & M. Sim	Development of Helping and Communication Skills for School Librarians	Attempts to identify and assist students to develop appropriate basic skills for school librarianship.
N. Hall & M. Sim	Specific Tasks for Teacher Librarians	Attempts to identify and classify specific tasks performed by teacher librarians and to design materials and develop evaluative techniques related to them.

INNOVATOR/S	TITLE OF INNOVATION	DESCRIPTION
D. Levis *et al.*	The Design and Evaluation of Competency-based Modules for Pre-service and In-service Teacher Education	A research and development project concerned with the effects on student and pupil learning of self-instructional modules on specific teaching behaviours.
G. Nucifora	Competence through Experience	A competency-based programme to study the child, the curriculum and instruction relating to primary education.
D. Phillips *et al.*	Optional Units—Secondary History	Programme provides students with optional units of study which they can select according to interests, abilities and needs.
J. Walsh	Primary Science	Workshops and construction of modules concerned with developing science concepts and skills relevant to primary teaching.
8. Milperra CAE D. Crawley & M. Koder	In-school Experience Programme	Programme for developing specific skills, knowledge and attitudes through seminars, microteaching, demonstrations and full-class teaching.
9. Mitchell CAE C. Billington	A Laboratory Approach to Mathematics	Students work through a set of workshop cards on various topics.
J. Hague	Use of Space, Time and Teachers	Programme develops students' awareness of use of space, time and personnel in primary context.
E. Mahon	Kodaly Music	Concentrated programme of practical work in local-school kindergartens.
D. Taylor	Individualized Instruction at Tertiary Level	Students assessed on a profile similar to SRA laboratory in Small Schools Course and Foundations of Education.
D. Taylor	Consolidated Block Practice	One full semester of teaching practice with short in-college period between change of schools.
D. Taylor	Community-aid Programme	Students undertake work in community organizations and schools as part of their practical field work.
D. Taylor	Local Field Work	Two students per class on directed practical work for one hour per week in Stage III.

INNOVATOR/S	TITLE OF INNOVATION	DESCRIPTION
10. Mount St. Mary College		
P. Butler	Internship	Programme of teacher training that allows for student evaluation and participation in curriculum decisions.
D. Stewart	Sandwich Course	Students are given full responsibility for a class over a two-year period, after one year at Mt. St. Mary and two years at university. They then return to university for the remainder of their course.
D. Stewart	Pre-university Course in Teacher Education	Students taking the four year B.A. Dip.Ed. course do year one at Mt. St. Mary. They have weekly teaching under the direction of the college.
11. Nepean CAE		
G. Dunn	Modified English Grammar and English Expression	Modified traditional English grammar course based upon the development of teacher-competence in certain areas of written expression.
A. Roberts	Graded, Group Teaching	Isolation of certain aspects of teaching so that each is manageable and suitably graded for first-year students in practice teaching.
A. Roberts	Drama Special Studies	Presentation of children's play in an outdoor setting where children follow the actors from place to place.
A. Roberts	Developing Teacher Presence	Application of Stanislavsky's workshop theatre approach to the development of teacher presence.
M. Smith	Human Relations Course	Small groups of students in primarily discussion situation gain insight into human relationships and the concept of self-hood.
L. Trist	Primary Science	Programme to assist primary teachers in using pupil-centred, open-ended discovery-type methods in the teaching of science.
L. Trist	Field Studies	Programme provides integration of primary science curriculum studies with field activities.
12. Newcastle CAE		
J. Bennett	Special Education Courses & Special Education Clinic	Multi-disciplinary courses linked with the building of a Special Education Clinic and Teaching Centre.

INNOVATOR/S	TITLE OF INNOVATION	DESCRIPTION
R. Coulton & S. Murray	Mathematics Education	Additional in-school practical teaching experience in mathematics in a teach-reteach cycle.
E. Crago	Open Group in Primary Education	Open approach to teacher education based on individual reading assignments together with weekly school experience and discussion groups.
R. Flanagan	Effect of Use of Programmable Calculator in College Experimental Physics	Programme seeks to examine the effect of the use of a programmable calculator on student attitude to physics.
T. Fullerton	First-Year Primary School Experience	Observation, discussion and practice of specific teaching skills in controlled situations, thereby relating theory to practice in a more meaningful way.
J. Gill	Social Science—Resources and Teaching Strategies	Development of teaching materials for third and fourth grade classes in social science using small group and microteaching strategies.
E. Goggin	Teaching of Nutrition in Primary Schools	In-training and in-service courses to enable teachers to encourage and inform children about nutritional matters.
R. Haywood	Effects of Three Different Marking Procedures on Creative Writing	Examination of three varying methods of marking to find the most productive.
R. Haywood	Busing Migrant Children to NCAE for Microteaching, Demonstrations and TV Recordings	Trainee teachers see competent TEFL teachers handling a withdrawal group of migrants.
J. Miles	Evaluation of the Open Teaching Procedure at Newcastle CAE	Empirical assessment of outcomes of 'Crago schemes' using personality, I-E and Crowne and Marlowe Scales.
B. Morrison	Use of Litho Slides in Speech Training	Project involves the preparation of colour slides and audiotaped sound track material designed to help partially hearing children learn the basic speech sounds.
W. Newling	Teaching in a Different Community	Students lived in Riverina homes and taught at Griffith school.
J. Rees	Teaching Problems Course	An elective course for third year primary and secondary students based on a consideration of simulated teacher-pupil, teacher-teacher, teacher-administrator and teacher-community problems.

INNOVATOR/S	TITLE OF INNOVATION	DESCRIPTION
T. Sheedy	Research Analysis of Models of Teaching and Their Use in Science Teacher Education	Preparation of audiovisual material of teachers using models in schools, also written descriptions and methods of analysis.
L. Smith	Religion and Society	Depth study of one world religion, the significance of religion in society and aspects of the sociology of religion.
R. Telfer	Country Community Practice Teaching	Final year students appointed in two's to the northwestern schools for a period of three weeks.
R. Telfer	Use of In-Baskets in Educational Administration Courses	School administrators in training are given background data to play the role of principal when provided with a series of memos, letters, etc. in his office in-basket. They have to indicate probable procedure, reasons for, and rate according to urgency.
J. Thorpe	Improvement in Reading Competencies	Improvement in reading competence and associated skills by the use of specially recorded stories to be used in conjunction with a set of readers designed to present a graded use of vocabulary.
R. Wilson	Variation in Approach to Teaching and Evaluating	Approach to Education II varied each term, the variety of methods allowing for a fairer basis for assessment.
13. Nursery School TC		
D. Bridges	Teacher Education in Music	Integrated improvisation in singing with instruments and movement.
A. Fountain	Community Involvement	Provision of opportunities for students to work directly with parent groups in the community.
A. Fountain	Continuous Practice	Students practice teach one day per week throughout their course.
L. Huntsman	Practice-Based Field Work in Human Development	Continuous practice to facilitate the relationships between education and psychological theory.
G. Lewis	Selection Procedures	The intake of students are selected by 'suitability' tests and an interview.
J. Simons	Tutorial Teaching	The majority of teaching is conducted in tutorial groups of 14–18 students.
J. Simons	Teaching Practice Programme	Continuous practice placement for each student featuring 'cross-age' tutoring and co-operative student curriculum development.

INNOVATOR/S	TITLE OF INNOVATION	DESCRIPTION
14. Riverina CAE		
F. Ebbech	Pre-school Course	An integrated approach under child development which takes the place of separate subjects in professional studies.
D. Hill	Science Curriculum	Development of materials analyzing the role of science as a facilitator of cognitive development.
J. Pinson	Practice Teaching	Introduction to practice teaching for first year students involving small groups of children, microteaching, etc.
15. Sydney Kindergarten TC		
B. Cooke	Music as Creative Art	The teaching of music experimentation with a 'sound and silence' approach.
P. Morgan	Micro and Mini Teaching	The use of more individualized and specific teaching situations in addition to usual teaching practice.
H. Newton	Use of Video Equipment	Development of teaching-technique films, child development films on specific topics and teaching/learning experiences, at the pre-school level.
16. University of Newcastle		
R. Collis	Trainee Teacher Involvement with Children's Level of Cognitive Development	Short course in Piagetian-oriented psychology, followed by the gathering of children's responses in a particular subject matter area and relating it to original Piagetian orientation.
17. University of New England		
J. Irvine	School-Based Testing Practicum and Case-Study Approach to Learning Problems	School-based programme involving students in the case-study approach to children with learning difficulties.
18. University of Sydney		
N. Hatton	Micro Skills Pilot Scheme	Microteaching as part of an on-going programme in teacher development.
N. Hatton	In-school Experience	Students are in contact with pupils and staff in a particular school, over an extended period.
J. Rothery & R. Arnold	Small Groups Practice Teaching Programme	Students commence practice by working with small groups of pupils.

INNOVATOR/S	TITLE OF INNOVATION	DESCRIPTION
C. Turney *et al.*	Teaching Skills Development Project	The development of research-based courses on basic teaching behaviours (mediated by audiovisual programmes and handbooks) for use in pre- and in-service teacher education.
19. Wollongong IAE		
N. Aylward	An Approach to In-school Experience	Students prepare a lesson in pairs acting as a team; lesson is then videotaped with subsequent group discussion and evaluation.
A. Bell	Plastics in the Primary School—A New Craft Form	Experiments in identifying and using waste plastics as material for primary school crafts.
A. Chapple & F. Osborne	Curriculum Studies 'C' Craft	New approach to craft with a group of third year students emphasizing attitudes rather than skills.
M. Harris	Science Method	Integrated method, subject matter courses to prepare for use of 1975 secondary syllabus.
K. McLellan	Aid to Remedial Readers	Task force approach by students to remedial reading situation in the schools.
W. Winser	Field Work Programme	Lesson involvement for first year students giving clinical and observational experience.
C. QUEENSLAND **1. Darling Downs IAE**		
R. Browne & R. Skilton	Practice Teaching: An Analysis of Present Policies and Desirable Future Directions	Initial exploratory study of ten Queensland teacher education programmes—evaluation of policy and practice and possible alternatives.
2. James Cook University		
W. Hawkins	The Effects of Supervisors on the Performance of Student Teachers	Testing the general hypothesis that technical skill performance in student teachers will be enhanced when supervising teachers are trained in the same skills.
W. Hawkins	School Experience: A University-School Partnership Model	The students' in-school experience programme in the final two years of the secondary B.Ed. degree is planned and administered by a joint committee of school and university staff, and within the schools, supervising teachers have responsibility for planning and evaluating the students' work.

INNOVATOR/S	TITLE OF INNOVATION	DESCRIPTION
3. Kelvin Grove CAE		
R. Adie	Problem Solving Approach to Psychological Issues	Students in small groups identify problems encountered in practical teaching and other experience using Miles' problem-solving cycle as the main model.
R. Adie	Interpersonal Communication & Relationships Course	A course within the in-service programme for secondary school resource teachers designed to develop skills in relating effectively to colleagues and students.
J. Ashton	Music—200	Development of aural, literacy and appreciation skills through programmed theory instruction.
G. Bruce	Film Appreciation	Development of a basis for criticizing films primarily through film-making.
G. Bruce	Recent Trends in Australian Literature and Film	First-hand experience of contemporary Australian film and literature (commercial and experimental).
P. Feeney	Graduate Diploma in Outdoor Education	Enables students to initiate outdoor education activities in a wide range of disciplines.
D. Fogarty	Teaching Awareness Programme	Integration of microteaching and simulation to develop awareness by the student of himself as a teacher and of criteria of teaching skills.
E. Hall & G. Jones	Practicum in Primary Mathematics	Students develop mathematical aids, activities, games and puzzles suitable for a laboratory approach to primary mathematics and learn to take responsibility for providing diagnostic and remediation activities for a child experiencing difficulties.
R. Hardingham	Bachelor of Education	Full-time, part-time courses for three year trained teachers with at least one year of teaching experience, involving general professional studies.
G. Jones	Mathematics in a Laboratory Setting	Proposed project aims to provide learning experiences in mathematics content and curricula for prospective primary teachers in a laboratory setting.
S. McFarlane	Oral Communication of Literature	Enjoyment and appreciation of literature through oral communication.

INNOVATOR/S	TITLE OF INNOVATION	DESCRIPTION
N. McIntyre	Graduate Diploma in Outdoor Education	Management and co-ordination of outdoor resources and facilities for use in education—introduced through a field study centre.
M. Mannison	Variables of the Open Classroom	Ways of modifying conventional classrooms and of organizing open classrooms.
M. Mannison	Use of Media	Students learn from each other through the presentation of experiences in form of film, videotape, etc.
M. Mannison	Active Involvement in Tutorials and Seminar Groups	Various techniques to insure participation and interest of students—emphasis on personal interaction.
M. Mannison	Teacher Education and Environmental Psychology	Field-based learning experiences of observing behaviour changes following modification of the school environment.
J. Marsh	Science and the Environment	Introduction to environmental sciences with emphasis on practical and field work.
F. Matthews	How We Can Learn About Clothes	Integrates all elements of clothing: psychological, sociological aspects, pattern making etc. and attempts to investigate and evaluate suitable learning activities for secondary school programmes (pre- and in-service students).
B. O'Connor	Preparing Resource Teachers for Secondary Schools	An in-service Graduate Diploma course designed to provide teachers in secondary schools trained to assist with pupils having special learning problems.
B. Scriven	Courses for Provisionally-Registered Teachers	Eight semester unit part-time and external studies courses of sufficient breadth and depth to enable practising teachers to qualify for registration.
B. Scriven	Upgrading Course for Qualified Teachers —leading to the Diploma of Teaching	Provides teachers with a course of study of sufficient breadth, depth and interest to satisfy requirements for a diploma while taking into consideration their practical experience.
B. Scriven	Eight-week Updating Course for Secondary Teachers	Intensive professional refresher courses half-professional and half-subject centred.

INNOVATOR/S	TITLE OF INNOVATION	DESCRIPTION
D. Young	Workshop Approach to English Curriculum Studies	An attempt to bridge the gap between theory and practice through student planning and evaluation etc. in the learning of their new roles as secondary school teachers.
4. Mount Gravatt CAE		
T. Cronk	Work Experience in the Education of Commerce Teachers	The introduction of a work observation programme into curriculum courses in commerce and economics, during teacher training.
N. Hart	Communication Centre and Child Clinical Sessions	The juxtaposition of a language laboratory, psychology laboratory and audiometric testing facilities and a language development research unit for the study of language communication.
N. Hart	Language Research Project	Analysis of oral language of children $4\frac{1}{2}$ to $6\frac{1}{2}$ years and production of reading programme and reading materials based on this analysis.
N. Hart	Special Education—Seven Areas	The commonalities across the education of the normal and across various areas of handicap are exploited in an interweaving of seven courses.
I. McKinley	Music for General Education	A general course using the 'Kodaly-style' approach to class music teaching.
C. McRobbie	Seminar for Laboratory Assistants	Week-long seminar for laboratory assistants of secondary schools, with practical emphasis.
C. McRobbie	In-service Science Course for Primary School Teachers	Course involves the development of a variety of approaches to primary science with emphasis on practical work.
G. Roberts & R. Cullen	Development of Science	Elective programme for science students aimed at providing a bridge between the sciences and the humanities.
Social Studies Department	A Multiphase Programme in Social Studies Curriculum for Teacher Education	An integrated programme for the practical teaching of social studies through a workshop situation involving student self-constructed items.
K. Tronc	A Pilot Project in the Development and Evaluation of Videotaped Simulation Materials	Simulation materials for use in pre-service courses of general teaching and in-service courses of educational administration.

INNOVATOR/S	TITLE OF INNOVATION	DESCRIPTION
K. Tronc	Graduate Diploma in School Administration	Two year part-time course for teacher administrators with considerable use of simulation techniques.
5. North Brisbane CAE		
N. Beer	Fundamental Skills in Teaching	Students use of audiotapes to check their level of performance, so that individual rates of progress in acquisition of skills may be allowed for.
J. Cook	Home Visits with Aboriginal Families (Selective Activity in Ed. 319 — Aborigines, A Minority Group in Education)	This option within the course involves tutoring an aboriginal child and the mutual self-discovery of getting to know an aboriginal family on familiar terms, through weekly visits.
V. Carvor	Ethnic Dance Course	An attempt to integrate aspects of social studies, music and dance in a socio-cultural study of the cultural contributions made by migrant groups in Australian society, with particular reference to dance.
M. Fogarty	An Approach to Courses Dealing with Modern Developments in Primary Education	Course involves methods and forms of organization, e.g., team-teaching and an open education approach.
I. Ginns	Individualized Science Instruction for First Year Trainee Teachers	Creation and development of positive student attitudes to teaching of science, conservation, etc. through individual and group instruction.
O. McMahon	Early Childhood Education	Education of young children as an integrated unit providing continuity rather than being divided into pre-school and infant education (students have combined lectures and separate practice).
G. Streets	New Approach to Practice Teaching Organization	Organization that ensures greater provision for college staff to exercise an advisory function for student teachers during practice teaching.
6. Queensland Conservatorium of Music		
J. Gilfedder	Total Culture of the Age — Approach to the History of Music and the Arts	Study of parallel manifestations in the History of Human Culture.
A. Lane	Writing Techniques Part IV	A synthesis of practical, theoretical and historical strands with a new approach incorporating student-created material.
7. Townsville CAE		
P. Bamford	Psychology of Interpersonal Behaviour	Introduction of structured human relations experiences designed to promote group interaction and self-awareness.

INNOVATOR/S	TITLE OF INNOVATION	DESCRIPTION
P. Brown & I. Putt	Open Book Assessment	To provide a situation in which application of knowledge rather than recall can be assessed.
H. Crowther	Environmental Studies	Development of awareness and understanding of environmental studies in a student oriented, individualized programme incorporating field investigations.
S. Elms	The Preparation and Use of Audiovisual Instructional Media as Lecture Material in Physical Education	Enables analysis of techniques etc., without time spent travelling to venues, and greater flexibility.
M. Gallagher & P. Marland	Use of Simulation Techniques	Students develop a repertoire of instructional strategies primarily through simulation activities in small groups.
J. King	Computer Education	Appreciation of history and function of electronic computers and their social/educational application.
J. La Trobe & Iles	Open Access Education	Enables students to understand assumptions underlying open education and to clarify their conceptions of the teacher/pupil role primarily through an examination of various practices.
8. University of Queensland		
B. Cox	Workshop Practicals (for Dip.Ed. geography students)	Variety of co-ordinated student activities as an alternative to lecture-type information-giving.
N. Holland	Curriculum Theory (Masters' level)	Post-graduate Education degree that seeks primarily to clarify the nature of the phenomena 'curriculum'.
R. Smith *et al.*	School-Based Course	A mainly school-based course in secondary teacher preparation for a group of students pursuing the Diploma in Education.
9. Xavier TC		
L. Larkin	Continuous Practicum	Practice teaching one morning per week throughout the year allowing opportunity for more thorough college assessment and student self-assessment.
D. SOUTH AUSTRALIA **1. Adelaide CAE**		
D. Dent	Towards Independent Media Education	Programme to individualize student media experiences by specifying sequences of tasks and providing feedback and follow-up.

INNOVATOR/S	TITLE OF INNOVATION	DESCRIPTION
W. Ey	Teaching Experience	Students spend half a day per week, generally in the same school, working in the area of physical education.
W. Ey	Physical Education Laboratory School	Children are transported to the college for practical sessions with the students which are preceded and followed by staff consultation.
I. Mitchell	B.A.E. Project—Upgrading External Studies Facilities	Development of alternate media approaches together with greater liaison through country visits and residential seminars.
R. Swain	Flexible Teaching-Learning Areas	Provision of areas that can be used for lectures, tutorials, seminars and informal experiences as a step towards corporate identity and co-operative learning.
2. Flinders University		
D. Briggs	Programme for M.Ed. and Dip.Ed. Administration	Proposed programme based on andragogical principles of individual selection of work closely related to the work situation.
G. Copper	Special Education Programme	Programme for the preparation of teachers of exceptional children.
D. Grundy & K. Simpson	Alternative Dip. Ed.	Discussions and pilot studies are under way to consider alternative pathways to the Dip.Ed.
B. Hyams	Participant Schools	Programme involves a two-month block of teaching practice and the involvement of senior school administrators in the University Department of Education.
K. McConnochie	Aboriginal Education	Students involved in the programme undertake extensive field work in isolated areas.
K. McConnochie	Assessment Procedures	Contract between student and lecturer for work and grades in course on race relations.
R. Paddick	B.Ed.—Physical Education	Programme has general approach with a focus on the student's physical activity and curriculum development.
G. Teasdale	Dip.Ed. (Primary)	Normal Dip.Ed. programme with a primary option.
G. Teasdale	Bachelor of Education Internship Programme	Students in final year of the primary B.Ed. degree are employed full-time in schools with help from 'teaching advisers' and involvement in seminars and conferences.

INNOVATOR/S	TITLE OF INNOVATION	DESCRIPTION
3. Murray Park CAE		
F. Golding	Campus Classes	A two teacher open unit is taught by staff from nearby state school with input from college staff. Students observe and assist in programme.
F. Golding	Teacher-Tutor Scheme	Use of teachers in circuit schools as tutors in curriculum studies and in-school experience programmes.
4. Salisbury CAE		
P. Drew & J. Tyney	Microteaching	Microteaching used to develop skills, identify remedial students and give the teacher self-confidence.
D. Homer	Electives in T.E.P.	Wide variety of course choices available to students in the teacher education programme.
D. Homer	Lecturer-Teacher Programme	Lecturers given the opportunity to work in a school as part of their overall work, and school staff involved in college programme as tutor-teachers.
D. Paul	Graduate Diploma in Teaching	Course designed to provide opportunity for an extension of work beyond the ordinary diploma.
D. Paul	Training All Levels Together	Semester-system programme that allows students to develop the necessary specialist interest areas whilst all participating in the basic course structure.
D. Paul & E. Otto	Curriculum Evaluation—A Pilot Study	Pilot study as first stage of a long-term investigation into the effectiveness of the teacher education programme at Salisbury CAE.
J. Pearman & J. Dunn	Teacher-Tutor Appointments to an On-Campus Laboratory School	Teachers, with reduced teaching load, participate in college methods courses, provide observational opportunities on their lessons, assist students in practice teaching preparation, and provide remedial post-practice teaching experiences for students.
R. Schultz	Assessment Procedures	Students choose one of three assessment options.
J. Tyney	Primary Laboratory School	Provision of special professional experiences on- and off-campus for students through co-operation with nearby school.

INNOVATOR/S	TITLE OF INNOVATION	DESCRIPTION
5. Sturt CAE P. Gunning	Issues in Teaching Course	A Course which follows students' final block practice and which seeks to flexibly meet their professional needs emerging from experience in schools.
J. Palmer	Field Experience Programme	Students undertake nine weeks of field experience in schools during which specific activities are undertaken in an attempt to achieve clear and stated objectives.
E. Sandercock	Science Programme	Pre-service science education programme for primary and secondary teachers with emphasis on ways of learning science.
E. Sandercock	Logical Thinking in First-Year Students	Investigation utilizing Piaget's scheme of evaluation of the ability to think logically.
B. Young	Teacher Education Assessment	Questionnaire to assess student practice and reaction to course.
B. Young	Revised Field Experience Programme	Research project involving a comparative analysis of several programmes focusing specifically on the effectiveness of school experiences in pre-service education.
B. Young	Critical Appraisal of Technique	Thesis on critical appraisal of the Delphi Technique as an educational research instrument.
6. Torrens CAE A. Morley	Art Education in Tertiary Open Space Teaching	Programme provides open space learning situations for tertiary students to sample open-space teaching.
M. Resek	Alberton Project (formerly Queenstown Project)	Project provides for involvement of students in community affairs.
M. Watson	Entry Requirements	Students are admitted to courses through the use of criteria other than examination and test results.
N. Whittingham	Semi-Specialist Physical Education	Course for primary students with special consideration given to the integration of physical education into the total learning situation.

INNOVATOR/S	TITLE OF INNOVATION	DESCRIPTION
E. TASMANIA		
1. Tasmania CAE, Mt. Nelson		
R. Kerrison	Curriculum Studies	Programme focuses attention on curriculum studies and allows for free choice, self-planning and self-pacing on behalf of the students.
E. McKay	Field Trip to Malaysia and Singapore	Field trip for students who have taken courses in S. E. Asian history and curriculum studies in the social sciences.
V. Walsh *et al.*	Child Study Centre/Latch-Key Children	Programme to provide interesting and purposeful activities for latch-key children in the North Hobart area.
B. Yaxley	Development of a Panel of Educational Associates	School appointed members of staff who liaise with the Division of Teacher Education on educational matters.
2. Tasmania CAE, Northern Campus		
M. Croft	Four Year Specialized Course in English, Speech and Drama	Programme aims to provide specialist teachers of English, Speech and Drama for high schools.
3. University of Tasmania		
R. Selby-Smith	Four Year B.Ed. Degree	Four-year concurrent course designed for those intending to teach at any level.
F. VICTORIA		
1. Aquinas College—Institute of Catholic Education		
G. Ferrall	Theatre in Education Group	Trainee teachers devise work to perform for children and conduct and develop drama workshops for children 8–10 years.
2. SCV Ballarat		
P. Coman	Employment of Associate Staff	Full-time practising teachers are employed to assist with the teacher education programme.
B. Fitzgerald	An Analysis of Entry and Exit Profiles & Characteristics of Student Teachers	A battery of entry and exit personality, attitude and aptitude tests complemented with progressive college performance data.
B. Fitzgerald	Community Internship Experience in Non-educational Situations.	All student teachers spend one semester attached as interns to personnel in a variety of non-education positions.

INNOVATOR/S	TITLE OF INNOVATION	DESCRIPTION
3. SCV Bendigo		
J. Brasier	Migrant Education	Unit for third year students involving visiting speakers and field work in special schools.
P. Cannon	Student-Centred Learning—Contemporary Education Issues	Student-centred discussion sessions at home of lecturer concerned.
F. Courtis	Specific Teaching Task—Art Education	Students involved in sequential teaching with groups of children.
K. Endersby	Visual Awareness through Simple Photography	Simple photography procedures, applicable to primary situation, used to develop students' visual awareness and external design concepts.
J. Higgs	Introduction to Archaeology	Students introduced to archaeology and archaeological method through fieldwork and lectures given by a current expert in the field.
W. Lomas	Language & Language Arts	Child's acquisition and development of language and application to literacy.
B. Reed	Ethnomusicology—Indonesia	Study of all aspects of the life and culture of Indonesia including the playing and singing of authentic Indonesian music and songs.
B. Reed	Driver Education Elective	Course in driver education with car supplied by General Motors.
R. Silverback	Field Work—Aboriginal, S.E. Asian and Australian studies.	Observation, residence and research in the geographic area of study.
R. Silverback	Language Studies—Aboriginal and Indonesian	Courses in Pitzantzatora and Bahasa Indonesia to enable students to have a working knowledge of the culture they are studying.
A. Watson	Insight into Aboriginality	Lecture programme for students and the general community by aborigines from a wide diversity of aboriginal situation, throughout Australia.
H. Wheeler	Language Acquisition	Field research project in language acquisition and/or development related to primary school or pre-school children.
F. York	Materials of Contemporary Music	Approaches contemporary music on a fully practical basis.

INNOVATOR/S	TITLE OF INNOVATION	DESCRIPTION
4. SCV Burwood		
M. Cameron	Learning Difficulties Clinic	Provision of diagnostic and remedial services for children and adults within the local community, source material for schools, and experience for trainee teachers.
J. Dueroth	Orientation Programme in Special Education	Three-week introductory programme in problems and issues in special education.
R. Jeans	Audiovisual Programme in Sign Language Instruction	Videotape programmed instruction in sign language of the deaf.
D. Power	Student Selection Project	Continuing research into empirically verifiable predictions of teaching and academic success of student teachers in special education.
J. Towler	Liaison Officers	Co-ordination of teaching experience programmes involving school liaison, evaluation and remediation programmes.
5. SCV Christ College		
B. Daffey	Mathematics Achievement and Attitudes	Short-term experiment to compare two treatment methods for cognitive factors and to investigate associated affective matters.
6. SCV Coburg		
R. Fitzgerald	Use of VTR as an Assessment Tool	Extensive use of VTR as a coaching and correcting tool for students in Health and Physical Education programmes.
L. Greagg	Investigation into Occupational Choice and Attitudes of Older Students	Investigation of occupational background of older students, their reasons for choosing college courses, their specific problems and their attitudes to their college experience.
P. Griffin	Utilization of Community Resources	Identification and utilization of resources outside the school boundaries.
J. Izard & E. Palmer	Materials for a Course in Curriculum Planning	Provision of teaching materials with associated evaluation items for intending teachers.
N. Schleiger	Mathematics Programme for Teachers	Development of topic booklets to enable some students to proceed at their own rates.

INNOVATOR/S	TITLE OF INNOVATION	DESCRIPTION
7. SCV Frankston R. Bilsborough	Aural Discrimination Programme	Students are encouraged to explore and experience all aspects of sound and the relationship of such sound in the present-day musical world of the child in developing music concepts and discrimination.
T. Jones	Approach to the Appreciation Music	Extension of students' range of listening experience, increase in awareness of elements of music, and provision of a core of technical language.
T. Jones	Group Instrumental Programme	Group piano teaching of five-year-olds.
T. Jones	Group Music—Piano	Use of an electronic piano laboratory to determine appropriate teaching structures for various ability levels.
T. Jones	Group Instrumental Teaching—Guitar	Various strategies being used to determine an appropriate method of group guitar instruction for college and primary students.
J. Lacy	'Man: A Course of Study'	Trainee teachers are given a practical approach to a Grade V Social Studies course being introduced in Victorian schools.
D. Stamp	'MACOS'	The planning and teaching of primary social studies units with reference to MACOS (Man: A Course of Study).
I. Walker	Integrated child Development Field Studies	Attempt to link child development theory with practical experiences in the classroom.
8. SCV Geelong C. Henry	Conversion Course	Conversion course from trained Primary Teacher's Certificate to Diploma.
9. Gippsland IAE J. Lawry	Trends in Teacher Education	
10. SCV Hawthorn P. Aver	School-based Programme at Ferntree Gully	Programme offered support and assistance to trainee teachers at Ferntree Gully Technical School and developed cross-method discussions with teachers from all disciplines.

INNOVATOR/S	TITLE OF INNOVATION	DESCRIPTION
M. Cigler	Technical English Reading Programmes	Reading programmes designed for apprentices of different trades and those likely to enter trades.
M. Cigler	Australian History in Multi-Cultural Education	An investigation of the contribution of non-British ethnic groups to the development of Australia.
J. Crawley, J. Stebbins, et al.	Integrated Studies Programme	Open-education type of course in which students largely determine the directions and content of the course, with an emphasis on cross-disciplinary approaches.
D. Enshaw	Drama in the Classroom	Students undertake teaching practice with college lecturer, based in schools.
N. Morris	Communication and Learning	Research project in human communication and implications for this in the learning process.
B. Phipps	School-based Teacher Education Programmes	A series of school-based projects conducted by methods lecturers in the one-year Diploma of Education programme.
S. Strong	Role of Teachers in Victorian Technical Education	Opinions of teachers collected to define their roles as a basis for evaluation and change of teacher education courses.
11. IECD R. Boreham	Migrant Education	Programme attempts to examine the implications of a culturally diverse society, the nature of prejudice and new teaching strategies and appropriate curriculum design for the changing nature of society.
N. Dougan	Toddler Group	Toddler group is conducted on campus for two days per week for observation purposes.
M. Foote	Parent/Teacher Relationships	Programme devised to recognize the importance of co-operation between teachers and parents in the educational process of the young child.
P. Martin	Field Experiences in Teacher Education	Provision of a comprehensive set of field experiences covering three years for students undertaking the Diploma of Teaching.
J. Rogers	Creative Writing and Writing for Children	Encouragement of students to write imaginatively and to utilize and synthesize their knowledge of children and literature.

INNOVATOR/S	TITLE OF INNOVATION	DESCRIPTION
V. Volk	In-service Course	Provision of a variety of in-service courses for pre-school teachers.
M. Yule	Conversion Course	Provision of a conversion course for country pre-school teachers to be offered in the country rather than on campus.
12. La Trobe University		
S. Oates	Task-Approach to Diploma of Education	Programme presents a problem approach with method and theory questions associated with school practice.
13. SCV Melbourne		
R. Biddington	Four-Year Degree for All Teachers	A 'point-system' teachers preparation programme with allowance for specialization and an emphasis on student responsibility.
J. Clark	Self-Paced Learning	Keller Plan course for third year students in Electromagnetism and Relativity.
G. Eley	Use of Keller's P.S.I. System in an Introductory Educational Psychology Course	Course content broken into small units which must be mastered before proceeding.
F. Hindley *et al.*	Graduate Dip.Ed.	Students and staff offered choice of six alternative programmes which may vary in pattern of school experience, underlying philosophies and amount of pre-determined structure.
J. Mitchell & M. Goode	Video Cassette Retrieval of Information	Programmes are recorded on colour video cassette from off air programmes and own productions.
K. Pigdon	Social Science 'A'	Unstructured programme based on the community (i.e. analysis of social institutions) with content determined by the needs and interests of the group.
G. Poynter	School-Based Units on Social Sciences	Programme involves total integration of theory with school practice in social science.
K. Runciman	Ascertainment of Entrance Skills of Teachers Undertaking P. G. Training Course in Special Education	Programme undertaken in order to provide levels of offering at the beginning of course in special education.
J. Ryan	Lectures/Seminars in Chemistry Education	Programme links academic and education studies and allows for presentation of papers on topics in chemistry.

INNOVATOR/S	TITLE OF INNOVATION	DESCRIPTION
B. Scott	Outdoor Education Centre—Noojee	Centre utilized for outdoor education activities and studies as well as informal socializing.
G. Scott	Environmental Science Course	Four-year concurrent programme involving the disciplines of biology, geography, physical science, sociology, economics, and politics.
A. Stutterd	Geography in Education	Programme attempts to integrate other tertiary studies in geography and is an introduction to teaching geography in the schools.
14. Mercy College T. Finkel & B. Cigler	Identifying Early Primary School Children with Basic Skill Weaknesses	Identifying of early primary school children with perceptual or perceptual-motor skills.
J. Hassall	Cultural Mathematics	Programme with emphasis on the nature of mathematics and its uses in contemporary society and in history.
B. Scott	Toy Science—A Unit of First Year Science	Development of science concepts and skills through directed, structured investigation of the characteristics of types of toys.
15. Monash University R. Gunstone	Camps and Environmental Education	Programme allows for inter-disciplinary field trips and student social interaction.
J. Theobald	Dip.Ed. Programme	Student involvement in the planning and direction of the programme.
16. SCV Rusden J. Atkinson	Concurrent Teacher Education Programme	Programme provides units of education studies and teaching practice in the third and fourth year of course.
E. Byrt	Core and Elective Programme in Education	Programme has nine units, six core and three elective, thus allowing students to follow their special interests in education for one-third of the course.
D. Clift	Physical Science	Programme is environmentally centred and is suitable for students with no previous background in physics or chemistry.
G. Duke	Environmental Studies in Schools	Programme's main emphasis is conservation with an inter-disciplinary approach.

INNOVATOR/S	TITLE OF INNOVATION	DESCRIPTION
G. Duke	Four-Year Undergraduate Programme in Environmental Studies	Inter-disciplinary programme with an emphasis on man's relationship with the environment.
M. Gill	Practice Teaching	Programme allows for greater involvement of school staff and school-based seminars for students undertaking practice teaching.
M. Gill	The First Year of Teaching: An In-service Course for Teachers	A ten-week, first-term evening seminar/lecture/workshop course for a small group of secondary teachers based largely on their expressed needs.
A. Holden	Teacher Preparation for Secretarial Studies	Programme involves an audio-steno laboratory approach.
O. Mackenzie	Integrated Social Science	Programme provides integrative treatment of history, geography, politics, economics and sociology.
F. Milne	School Practice	Programme provides for practice teaching in the schools two days per week, throughout the year.
H. Overberg	Migrant Studies	Programme provides a sociological view of the problems of multi-culturalism.
17. SCV Toorak		
M. Edwards	Migrant Teachers Retraining Course	Programme with intensive English segment enabling teachers from non-English-speaking countries to gain relevant qualifications to teach in Australia.
M. Edwards	Intensive English for Migrant Student Teachers	The retraining of teachers and students from non-English-speaking countries, involving six months intensive English followed by one year of teacher training.
A. Millar	Diploma of Educational Technology	A one-year full-time course for teachers with five years' experience to train as school media specialists.
A. Ridsdale & P. Henry	The Migrant Child in the Classroom	Programme incorporates sociology and anthropology in order to consider the whole migrant child not just his language problems.
M. Ryan, K. Johnson & T. Noble	Learning Network	Programme provides students with access to a number of different institutions, organizations and children in a variety of settings.

INNOVATOR/S	TITLE OF INNOVATION	DESCRIPTION
18. University of Melbourne		
G. Dow	Course B: School-based Teacher Education	A group of students in the secondary Diploma in Education undertake all their theoretical and practical work in schools with the co-operation of lectures and teachers.
G. WESTERN AUSTRALIA		
1. Churchlands CAE		
D. Bambach	Integrated Programme in Education and Psychology	Course integrates learning theory, personality theory, curriculum studies, measurement and evaluation.
D. O'Dwyer	Co-ordinated Methods Programme	An inter-disciplinary, team-taught course in Curriculum and Instruction, Educational Studies and practice teaching, focusing on teaching and learning strategies in the various school subjects.
2. Claremont TC		
C. Coroneos	The Epic	Course covers all the well-known epics of the world starting from Homer and going as far as the epic-novel of the present-day.
C. Coroneos	Introductory French	Course starts from scratch and goes as far as sub-tertiary level including language and cultural background.
C. Coroneos	Introductory Indonesian	Course starts from scratch and goes as far as sub-tertiary level including language and cultural background.
M. Cullen	The Application of the Taxonomy of Educational Objectives to Teaching and Evaluation in the Primary School	Given the general aims and an outline of a syllabus topic, the student formulates specific objectives, stated in behavioural terms, covering the areas of knowledge, understanding, skills and attitudes.
I. Eastwood	Linguistics and the Teaching of English as a Second Language	Teaching techniques involved in modern second language instruction for migrant and aboriginal children.
S. Gallagher	The Acquisition & Development of Language & Language Socialization and Education	Programme provides a scientific background and approach to the study of language.
G. Gibbs	Theatre III and Children's Theatre	Comparative approach to theatre utilizing workshops, movement, mime, etc.

INNOVATOR/S	TITLE OF INNOVATION	DESCRIPTION
G. Gibbs	Graduate Diploma in Drama in Education	Course has fifty per cent practical content working with children on a continuous basis.
G. Gibbs	In-service Drama in Education and Conversion Course	In-service course incorporating the latest ideas in workshops and reading in drama and education.
G. Gibbs	Staff Development—Lecturer Extension	Staff gain practical experience in film, TV and theatre to enrich and develop their expertise.
G. Gibbs & B. Perich	Speech and Drama	Courses encompassing children's theatre, oral communication, film and television and drama in education with an emphasis on the role of drama as a general teaching method.
W. Grono	Oral Interpretation of Poetry	Students read poetry to an audience in such a way as to communicate as much of the poem's meaning as is possible in one reading.
I. Hooker & R. Haselhurst	Multi-Aspect Assessment in Courses of Education	Course assessment based on tutorial papers and participation, objective tests and weekly worksheets.
S. de la Hunty	Mathematics 111 and 112	Electives that allow entry into tertiary academic mathematics with or without tertiary entrance qualifications.
S. de la Hunty	Basic Statistics and Computer	Course involves computer familiarization and most commonly used techniques in statistics, for understanding educational literature and classroom application.
S. de la Hunty	Computer 211	Course in basic computer programming.
P. Julian	Drama in Education	Comparison of modern techniques in educational drama in practical demonstrations with extensive use of VTR equipment.
I. Lonnie	Microteaching	VTR microteaching unit oriented to pre-practice teaching strategies and post-practice remediation.
T. McGowan	Tape-based Lectures	Research material is gathered on tapes followed by group discussion and interpretation.
T. McGowan	History III WA Facts and Fallacies	Study of social, economic and political history of WA through primary source material.

INNOVATOR/S	TITLE OF INNOVATION	DESCRIPTION
M. McKercher	Associate Diploma in Health Education	Two-year course for health workers, medical officers and para-medical team workers.
M. McKercher	Unisex Games Instruction	Men and women students complete courses in male and female type sports to equip them to take all games when teaching.
M. McKercher	Student Self-Rating	Students in physical education major assess their peers in the elective group.
M. McKercher	Programmed Instruction in Biomechanics	Work book course in biomechanics where students complete and submit college prepared booklets.
M. McKercher	Micro Instruction in Organization and Administration in Physical Education	Students utilize a variety of methodological approaches with small groups, in an area of physical education.
M. McKercher	Programmed Instruction in Recreation	Programmed instruction in courses on badminton, table tennis, golf and squash.
M. McKercher	Personal Development	Programme allows for student-staff interaction in mutual interest courses (e.g., chess, wine tasting, etc.).
P. McMillan	Environmental Biology	Series of units to develop awareness of the biotic environment and the impact of man on that environment.
N. Madigan & J. Calcutt	Creative Stitchery	Assimilation of formal needlework into basic art courses.
W. March	Interstate Exchange Practice	Interstate (WA and Queensland) exchange visit of students on practical teaching assignments.
I. Napper	Effect of Attitude on Science Teaching	Pilot study with teachers in in-service courses to determine the effect of children's attitudes on their science learning.
I. Napper	In-service Course in Science Education	Course for teachers to introduce them to discovery methods in the classroom.
I. Napper	Use of ASEP materials in a Background Course in Science Content	Programme uses ASEP units to compensate for differences in the students' science background.

INNOVATOR/S	TITLE OF INNOVATION	DESCRIPTION
I. Napper	Use of Discovery Strategies for Science Concept Development	Project to show how primary children can learn science concepts through discovery methods.
S. Tilinger	Australia in Conflict	Programme looks at Australian history as a series of conflicts, with emphasis on the use of source material.
S. Tilinger	Innovation in Economics Course	Programme seeks to integrate theory and practice and show the relevance of economics to current issues.
3. Graylands TC		
D. Ibbotson	Teaching of Aboriginal Children	Three-month 'internship' for students in northwestern and Kimberley schools.
4. Mount Lawley CAE		
B. Buchanan	Resource Room Facility	Establishment of a resource room facility at Coolbinia Primary School.
B. Hird	Individualized Reading in Primary School	Experiment using pre- and post-test situation where primary school students select own reading material and teachers use this material to develop reading skills.
B. Hird	Flexible Timetabling—Primary Language Arts	Block timetabling for language arts, involving student choice of session times. Final year trainees experiment with concept during their long-term practice.
A. Jones	Open Teaching Laboratories	Attempt to provide students with relevant classroom experience in an 'open' climate.
I. Malcolm	Modern Language Teacher Education Programme	Programme to prepare primary teachers in the teaching of French, Italian and Indonesian.
J. Sherwood	Graduate Diploma in Aboriginal Education	Course for qualified teachers integrating studies in anthropology, linguistics and Aboriginal education, together with a supervised research project.
J. Sherwood	Aboriginal Studies	A comprehensive major study within the Diploma of Teaching Programme to prepare primary trainees to teach Aboriginal children and Aboriginal culture.

INNOVATOR/S	TITLE OF INNOVATION	DESCRIPTION
E. Thomas	The Kinesthetic/Synergetic Environment	Comprehensive study of sensory stimulus and response through a multi-media environment, using activities which exploit the potential of current image and sound projection technology, interfaced with recent art activity concepts and group interaction situations.
A. True	Graduate Diploma in Music Education	Proposed one-year course for practising primary teachers to equip them to become resource personnel in music education.
5. WA Institute of Technology		
W. Neal	Theory and Practice of Teaching	Part of teacher education programme that allows the student to develop his own style and strategies with video/audio feedback facilities.
6. WA Secondary TC		
J. Ashley	Sight Singing—Tonal Memory Trainer	Construction and evaluation of an electronic device designed to facilitate the learning of sight singing by music education students.
L. Vlahov	Nedlands Action Project	Innovative, school-based programme for post-graduate diploma in education students in secondary education.
7. WA Education Department		
P. Deschamp & E. Styles	Seminars for Newly-Graduated Teachers	A course for first-year-out primary and secondary teachers conducted in small groups and based on the teachers' professional needs.

INDEX